THE OMBUDSMAN IN THE MODERN STATE

The ombudsman institution is a global phenomenon. It is a critical part of the public law frameworks of modern liberal democracies. This is the first edited collection to examine the place of the ombudsman in the modern state. It brings together key international scholars to discuss current and future challenges for the ombudsman institution and the systems of government within which they operate.

The book is international in scope with authors heralding from most continents – Canada, the Netherlands, the United Kingdom, Australia, New Zealand, Hong Kong, Germany and Austria. This global analysis is both in-depth and expansive in its coverage of the operation of ombudsmen across civil and common law legal systems.

The book has two key themes:

- the enduring question of the location and operation of the ombudsman institution within public law systems in a changing state, and
- the challenges faced by the institution in contemporary governance.

This collection adds to the public law scholarship by addressing a common problem faced by all avenues of public law review – the evolving nature of modern public administration.

The Ombudsman in the Modern State

Edited by
Matthew Groves
and
Anita Stuhmcke

• HART •
OXFORD • LONDON • NEW YORK • NEW DELHI • SYDNEY

HART PUBLISHING
Bloomsbury Publishing Plc
Kemp House, Chawley Park, Cumnor Hill, Oxford, OX2 9PH, UK
1385 Broadway, New York, NY 10018, USA
29 Earlsfort Terrace, Dublin 2, Ireland

First published in Great Britain 2022

A catalogue record for this book is available from the British Library.

Library of Congress Cataloging-in-Publication data

Names: Groves, Matthew, editor. | Stuhmcke, Anita, editor.

Title: The Ombudsman in the modern state / edited by Matthew Groves and Anita Stuhmcke.

Description: Oxford ; New York : Hart, 2022. | Includes bibliographical references and index.

Identifiers: LCCN 2021062203 (print) | LCCN 2021062204 (ebook) | ISBN 9781509943241 (hardback) | ISBN 9781509943289 (paperback) | ISBN 9781509943265 (pdf) | ISBN 9781509943258 (Epub)

Subjects: LCSH: Ombudspersons.

Classification: LCC K3416 .O43 2022 (print) | LCC K3416 (ebook) | DDC 342/.0667—dc23/eng/20220204

LC record available at https://lccn.loc.gov/2021062203

LC ebook record available at https://lccn.loc.gov/2021062204

ISBN: HB: 978-1-50994-324-1
ePDF: 978-1-50994-326-5
ePub: 978-1-50994-325-8

Typeset by Compuscript Ltd, Shannon

FOREWORD

The ombudsman office in its modern European form is generally traced back to the creation of the Swedish Parliamentary Ombudsman in 1809, although the institution may in fact be much older and its origins may not be Swedish or even European; clear parallels are found in early medieval times in Asia and the Islamic world. This is hardly remarkable. Governments come in all shapes and sizes, but as Anita Stuhmcke and Matthew Groves, editors of this valuable collection of papers, point out, one feature of government recurs: mistakes. Mistakes generate complaints, which demand some sort of response from all but the most authoritarian of governments; thus complaints generate some sort of machinery for complaints-handling, often an ombudsman figure or body. There are very few states where there is no ombudsman or ombudsman-like machinery and many states have more than one public ombudsman. And ombudsmen are not, of course, confined to the public sector. The idea was quickly adopted throughout the private sector, where complaints-handling is today a recognised function of consumer service departments. In chapter eight of this volume, John McMillan, whose experience of public sector complaint-handling is unrivalled, turns his attention to industry ombudsmen, asking what the public ombudsmen can learn from their increasingly sophisticated systems and methods.

Until recently, however, ombudsman literature did not keep up with the galloping worldwide spread of the institution (The International Ombudsman Association, formed in 2005, today claims over 1000 members, while the International Ombudsman Institute, established in 1978, represents more than 200 independent ombudsman institutions from more than 100 countries). There were, of course, pioneers, in the UK notably Patrick Birkinshaw, Roy Gregory, Philip Giddings and Mary Seniveratne,[1] but ombudsmanship was in practice woefully neglected both as a research topic and in teaching, where judicial review ruled virtually unchallenged. In the last decade, this has begun to change, and there is now a *Research Handbook on Ombudsman* which is transnational and interdisciplinary in its coverage.[2]

This volume, a worthy addition to the growing literature, follows the tradition of interdisciplinarity and transnationality; ombudsmen are an apt subject for

[1] P Birkinshaw, *Grievances, Remedies and the State* (1985); R Gregory and P Giddings, *Righting Wrongs: The Ombudsman in Six Continents* (2000); M Seniveviratne, *Ombudsmen, Public Services and Administrative Justice* (2002).

[2] M Hertogh and R Kirkham (eds), *Research Handbook on the Ombudsman* (Edward Elgar, 2018).

comparative law. There are accounts of ombudsmen and ombudsman-machinery in several jurisdictions. There is a nice blend of theory with empirical studies from authors working in several disciplines. There is renewed discussion of topics that have been the subject of perennial debate, casting new light on the appropriate relationship of ombudsmen with courts and suggesting reasons for their lack of mandatory remedies. Much new ground is also covered.

Over the years, a wide variety of roles has been suggested for the ombudsman. Ann Abraham, a recent UK Parliamentary Commissioner, suggests a constitutional role.[3] Nick O'Brien believes the ombudsman should act as an independent 'demosprudential agent of active democratic citizenship' (chapter 14). This, however, is to situate the ombudsman at a high constitutional level. A more mundane function is envisaged by Naomi Creutzfeldt, who situates ombudsmen on the ground floor level of the administrative justice system. Drawing a comparison with tribunals, she nonetheless concludes that the two systems fail to promote a shared identity or, indeed, to interact in any meaningful way.

In line with the focus on complaints-handling in contemporary public administration, the Westminster Parliament emphasised the need for an effective and inclusive complaints-handling service.[4] This has pushed ombudsmen in two diametrically opposed directions. In Scotland, the provision of an ombudsman unit tasked with advising administration on the effectiveness of their complaints-handling systems has led on to a regulatory role, pointing perhaps to the ombudsman as regulator. Ombudsman services have also experimented with less formal investigatory methods and greater transparency – the introduction of direct contact with users, telephone interviews, mediation, early resolution and other methods associated with fashionable proportionate dispute resolution. The use of technology to help meet growing user expectations is described in chapter 10 by Rob Behrens, the UK Parliamentary Ombudsman, and an experiment with 'consultation days' by the Austrian Ombudsman Board (*Volksanwaltschaft*) is the subject of a multi-disciplinary case study in chapter 13.

Perhaps the greatest challenge currently faced by administrative law is digitalisation. Reliance on digital technology in judicial systems and public services is progressing fast – many would say too fast – presenting many challenges. These find a place in several contributions, which attempt to predict the likely impact of transition to a digital process and a consequential digitalised environment on both administrators and users of public services.

From Parliamentary Commissioner to 'guardian of good public administration', from small claims court to key component of our system of administrative justice, from public advocate to adjudicator, the ombudsman has come a long

[3] A Abraham, 'The Ombudsman as Part of the UK Constitution: A Contested Role' [2008] *Parliamentary Affairs* 206.

[4] PASC, *When Citizens Complain* (2007–08, HC 409); PASC, *More Complaints Please!* (2013–14, HC 229).

way from the sweeper up of small claims and complaints that courts would not handle.[5] As time and technology bring further changes, there are doubtless many more ombudsman functions to be tried.

Carol Harlow
Emeritus Professor
London School of Economics

[5] JUSTICE, *The Citizen and the Administration* (1961).

CONTENTS

ABOUT THE CONTRIBUTORS

Rob Behrens has been Parliamentary and Health Service Ombudsman in the UK since 2017. Previously he was Complaints Commissioner to the Bar Standards Board in England and Wales, and Higher Education Ombudsman in England and Wales. Having begun as an academic, Rob joined the Cabinet Office in 1988. He was sent as a UK Civil Servant to work with the liberation movements in South Africa to assist in creating a post-apartheid civil service. Subsequently, Rob worked in 26 countries' transition, before being appointed a senior civil servant and becoming Secretary to the Committee on Standards in Public Life. Rob is a Visiting Professor at UCL, and was appointed CBE in the Queen's New Year Hours List in 2016. He is an elected member of the World Board of the International Ombudsman Institute.

Naomi Creutzfeldt is a Professor of Socio Legal Studies at the University of Westminster. She teaches public law, civil and commercial dispute resolution, artificial intelligence and algorithmic dispute resolution and socio-legal research methods. Her interests in ADR, as pathways of informal dispute resolution, have a broader scope, addressing questions of access to justice, vulnerability and consumer protection. She is the author of *Ombudsmen and ADR* (Palgrave McMillan, 2018).

Julia Dahlvik earned her PhD in Sociology in 2014 at the University of Vienna, Austria, and currently works at the University of Applied Sciences FH Campus Vienna. Her recent research focuses on law and society, organisations and public administration. She is a founding member and co-speaker of the Law & Society section of the Austrian Sociological Association and was the local coordinator of the Research Committee on Sociology of Law at the Third ISA Forum 2016. Julia has edited and published numerous books and articles. Her latest research project was a mixed-methods study on the Austrian Ombudsman Board.

Chris Gill is a Lecturer in Public Law at the University of Glasgow. His research interests include administrative justice (with a particular focus on ombudsman and complaint systems), access to justice, and alternative dispute resolution. Chris's current projects include research on access to justice for people in vulnerable circumstance, legislative reform of the ombudsman in the UK, the role of parliamentarians in grievance resolution, and the relationship between administrative justice institutions and bureaucracies. Chris sits on the Administrative Justice Council's Academic Panel, the Public Law Project's Academic Panel, and the Ombudsman Association's Validation Committee.

Matthew Groves is the Alfred Deakin Professor of Law, in the Law School of Deakin University Australia. Matthew has published many authored and edited books, including Aronson, Groves and Weeks, *Judicial Review of Administrative Action and Government Liability* (7th edn, Thomson Reuters, 2022), which is Australia's leading administrative law text, and Creyke, Groves, McMillan and Smyth, *Control of Government Action: Text, Cases and Commentary* (6th edn, LexisNexis, 2022), which is the leading Australian student work in administrative law. Matthew is also a fellow of the Australian Academy of Law and the General Editor of the *Australian Journal of Administrative Law*.

Marc Hertogh is Full Professor of Socio-Legal Studies at the University of Groningen, the Netherlands. His research focuses on law and governance, with a special interest in administrative justice and legal consciousness. His books include: The Oxford Handbook of Administrative Justice (Oxford University Press, 2021) (with Richard Kirkham, Robert Thomas and Joe Tomlinson); *Nobody's Law: Legal Consciousness and Legal Alienation in Everyday Life* (Palgrave Macmillan, 2018); Research Handbook on the Ombudsman (Edward Elgar Publishing, 2018) (with Richard Kirkham); and *Judicial Review and Bureaucratic Impact* (Cambridge University Press, 2004) (with Simon Halliday).

Carolyn Hirst is an independent researcher in her own business (Hirstworks), where she also works as a mediator, investigator, complaints reviewer and coach. She has served as a Deputy Scottish Public Services Ombudsman and as the interim Principal Ombudsman at Ombudsman Services. Carolyn is an Honorary Research Fellow at Queen Margaret University, where she previously worked as a part-time Lecturer in Ombudsman and Complaint Handling Practice. Her current Board positions include Non-executive Director of NHS Lothian and Board Member of the Parliamentary and Health Service Ombudsman.

Richard Kirkham is a senior lecturer in the Law Faculty of Sheffield University. Richard's research focuses on administrative justice, with a particular interest in the ombudsman sector and judicial review. He has written widely on the ombudsman, including Buck, Kirkham and Thompson, *The Ombudsman Enterprise and Administrative Justice* (Ashgate Publishing, 2011), and was the joint editor (with Marc Hertogh) of *Research Handbook on the Ombudsman* (Edward Elgar, 2018) and (with Chris Gill) *A Manifesto for Ombudsman Reform* (Palgrave MacMillan, 2020). He currently sits on the Standards Board of the Furniture and Home Improvement Ombudsman and is a member of the Ombudsman Association's Validation Committee. Richard has also authored several reviews of ombudsman schemes, including the Local Government Ombudsman in England, the Gibraltar Public Services Ombudsman and the Parliamentary Ombudsman, and has written a report on accountability in the sector for the Nuffield Foundation, 'The Ombudsman, Accountability and the Courts'.

Martina Kollegger has a Bachelor's Degree in Sociology and is currently finishing her BA in English and American Studies at the University of Vienna. She worked as a project assistant for a research project on the Austrian Ombudsman Board at the University of Applied Sciences FH Campus Vienna.

Maaike de Langen is the former Head of Strategy and Policy of the National Ombudsman of the Netherlands, where she worked from 2009 to 2017. She is currently Program Lead of Justice for All with the Pathfinders for Peaceful, Just and Inclusive Societies at New York University's Center on International Cooperation.

Gavin McBurnie is an Honorary Research Fellow at Queen Margaret University. Gavin started out as a medical practitioner before entering health service management in both Scotland and England. He spent seven years at the UK's Parliamentary and Health Service Ombudsman in various director roles. As well as his MB ChB, he has an MBA and an LLM. He was awarded a PhD for his research, which examined the approaches used by health ombudsmen in their system improvement role and how bodies respond to these differing approaches.

John McMillan is an Emeritus Professor at the Australian National University, where he taught administrative and constitutional law from 1983 to 2003. He is a co-author of *Control of Government Action: Text, Cases and Commentary* (5th edn, LexisNexis, 2019). John has held the statutory positions of Commonwealth Ombudsman (2003–10), Integrity Commissioner (Acting) for the Australian Commission for Law Enforcement Integrity (2007), Australian Information Commissioner (2010–15), NSW Ombudsman (Acting) (2015–17), member of the Australian Copyright Tribunal (2015–18) and member of the Administrative Review Council (2003–14).

Nick O'Brien has held senior positions at the Legal Services Ombudsman, Disability Rights Commission and the UK Parliamentary Ombudsman, and has been a Specialist Adviser to the House of Commons Public Administration Select Committee. He is currently a judge in the Mental Health Review Tribunal. He has co-authored two books: with Mary Seneviratne, Ombudsmen at the Crossroads (Palgrave Macmillan, 2017), and with Margaret Doyle, Reimagining Administrative Justice (Palgrave Macmillan, 2019). He is the winner of the Bernard Crick Prize 2019 awarded by the Political Quarterly.

Ron Paterson is Emeritus Professor of Law at the University of Auckland. He has served in a range of Ombudsman-like roles, including as New Zealand Health and Disability Commissioner (2000–10), Chair of the Banking Ombudsman Scheme (2010–2013) and Parliamentary Ombudsman (2013–16).

Axel Pohn-Weidinger earned his doctoral degree from the University of Paris 8 in 2014. He was a postdoctoral researcher at the École des Hautes Études en Sciences Sociales in Paris from 2014 to 2016 and then worked as a lecturer at the University of Göttingen (Germany) from 2016 to 2019. In 2019, he was appointed as an associate professor at the Department of Sociology of the University of Strasbourg in 2019. Axel's research interests centre on the sociology of the welfare state, the sociology of law, the sociology of work and the ethnography of literacy. He currently works on ombuds institutions from a comparative sociological perspective.

Linda C Reif is Associate Dean (Graduate Studies) and CN Professor of International Trade at the Faculty of Law, University of Alberta. She has published extensively on national human rights institutions, ombuds institutions, independent children's rights institutions and other international law topics. Her works include *Ombuds Institutions, Good Governance and the International Human Rights System* (2nd rev edn, Brill/Nijhoff, 2020), co-authorship of *International Law: Chiefly as Interpreted and Applied in Canada* (9th edn, Emond, 2019) and numerous law review articles and book chapters, including in the *Harvard Human Rights Journal* and *Human Rights Law Review*. Professor Reif has provided editing, consulting and academic services to organisations such as the Commonwealth Secretariat, International Ombudsman Institute (IOI) and Academic Council on the UN System. She was Editor of Publications of the IOI (1989–2009), including *The International Ombudsman Yearbook* (Martinus Nijhoff). She served as Director of Legal Services, Office of the Alberta Ombudsman (1991).

Anita Stuhmcke is a Professor and Dean of the Law Faculty at the University of Technology Sydney, Australia. Anita is widely acknowledged as one of Australia's leading scholars on ombudsman issues and as a leading international scholar in the field. She has a particular research interest in the ways in which law operates as a continuum of effectiveness, and this has led her to interrogate the operation of the ombudsman institution as an instrument of democratic accountability in terms of the citizen, industry, the consumer, government agencies and the wider legal system. Anita is widely cited – both nationally and internationally – having published many journal articles and book chapters, written policy submissions which have impacted the development of law and policy, performed consultancy work for both Australian and New Zealand ombudsmen. and acted as an expert witness in *Telecommunications Industry Ombudsman Ltd v Commissioner of State Revenue (Vic)* [2017] VSC 286.

Stephen Thomson is a Senior Lecturer at ANU College of Law, The Australian National University. He is a Legal Adviser to the Ombudsman of Hong Kong, a member of the Constitutional Affairs and Human Rights Committee of the Law Society of Hong Kong, and an examiner on the Overseas Lawyers Qualification Examination. His work includes *Administrative Law in Hong Kong* (Cambridge University Press, 2018), *The Nobile Officium* (Avizandum/Edinburgh University Press, 2015) and articles in a range of leading journals, including the *Oxford Journal of Legal Studies, Public Law* and *Melbourne University Law Review*. Stephen's report on the reform of civil procedure in Scotland was included by the Scottish Civil Justice Council in its proposal for legislative reform. He received his PhD from the University of Edinburgh, and was a Herbert Smith Freehills Visitor at the University of Cambridge.

Greg Weeks is a professor in the ANU College of Law at the Australian National University. He has published widely on his research interests, which are primarily related to judicial review, state liability and remedies against public authorities. He is the author of *Soft Law and Public Authorities: Remedies and Reform* (Hart Publishing, 2016) and a co-author of *Government Liability: Principles and Remedies* (LexisNexis, 2019) and *Judicial Review of Administrative Action and Government Liability* (7th edn, Thomson Reuters, 2022), Australia's leading administrative law text. With Matthew Groves, he was the editor of two collections of essays: *Legitimate Expectations in the Common Law World* (Hart Publishing, 2016) and *Administrative Redress Inside and Outside the Courts: Essays in Honour of Robyn Creyke and John McMillan* (Federation Press, 2019). Greg is the General Editor of the *Australian Journal of Administrative Law*.

Chris Wheeler has long worked in public sector administration, including an appointment as Deputy Ombudsman of New South Wales. For this and other public sector work, Chris was awarded the Australian Public Service Medal (PSM). He is currently Commissioner (part time) on the Greyhound Welfare and Integrity Commission of New South Wales, a solicitor, a consultant on complaint and whistleblower management and Specialist Advisor, Ethical Conduct with the Centium Group.

Jane Williams is a Senior Lecturer in Dispute Resolution at Queen Margaret University in the Consumer Dispute Resolution Centre. Her current research focuses on consumer experiences of complaint handling in the context of consumer alternative dispute resolution, vulnerable consumers, the impact of being complained about and fairness in complaint handling. She was a former manager in Trading Standards and is a member of the Chartered Trading Standards Institute. She has extensive experience of running short courses for regulators, ombudsman organisations and complaint handlers working in both the public and private sectors. Until recently, Jane was a consumer representative on the Scottish Civil Justice Council and a member of their Access to Justice Committee.

1

The Evolution and Future of the Ombuds

MATTHEW GROVES AND ANITA STUHMCKE

The very title of this book – *The Ombudsman in the Modern State* – presumes that the ombuds institution will continue to exist, but in so doing it must continue to evolve. That is because we proceed on the assumption that government and its individual elements will continue to develop relentlessly. This book examines one part of government that is as dynamic as it is static – dealing with complaints about bad government. As much as government evolves, one constant feature of government remains: mistakes. The form of those mistakes might change, so the error previously made by a person standing behind a counter might now be made through an automated decision-making process, but their substantive nature remains eerily familiar. Public agencies and their staff make decisions or devise policies that are unfair or wrong, or perhaps explain or implement their decisions in a clumsy manner. The people affected by those decisions and policies have a grievance and want to be heard, preferably by an office independent of the agency or official that caused the problem. Ombuds[1] assume a central role in meeting that need.

Introduced in its modern form as the Justitieombudsmannen in 1809 in civil law in Sweden, the first common law ombuds was established in 1962 in New Zealand. That transition of the institution from a civil law to a common law system of government provoked debate about what precisely the institution should do.[2] Although ombuds are now a well settled aspect of modern government,

[1] As discussed below, we use the term 'ombuds' throughout our chapter. The reader will find differing terminology used for the ombudsman institution by authors throughout this book. As editors, we have explicitly not prescribed any particular term, rather choosing to support individual authors to apply in their preference.

[2] C Harlow, 'Ombudsmen in Search of a Role' (1978) 41 *MLR* 446, 452–53, who argued that the role had not settled upon a distinctive or clear role in its first ten years of operation in Britain. Harlow thought that the key role of ombuds should be to identify maladministration, suggest how it could be improved and negotiate the required changes. This conception meant that complaints from individuals might be important, but were perhaps most useful as a means to identify maladministration.

debate about the proper mission of the institution continues.[3] This book does not seek to answer that debate, only to continue it. Drawing on authors from across the globe, from common law and civil law countries, the challenge set for the authors contributing to this collection is the interrogation of this evolution. This task is challenging. There are several core tensions which make this so, including the impact of artificial intelligence (AI) on both the agencies investigated by ombuds and the ombuds' own processes, the enduring nature of many issues facing ombuds, such as the impact that the apparently low political priority of ombuds offices has on the institution itself.

I. International but Still a Mystery

The ombuds institution is truly global, yet continues to defy generic definition.[4] Today's international ombuds institution is integral to the public law frameworks of modern liberal democracies. This is due both to the sheer volume of complaints that ombuds receive and to their unique jurisdiction and powers. Globally, in the modern state, the 'ombudsman concept' refers to this distinctive approach to the institutions receipt, handling and resolution of a citizen's complaint and its capacity to take in wider problems of maladministration. To some extent, ombuds are defined by what they are not.[5] Ombuds are institutionally separate from the departments and other arms of government they investigate, yet they are a public sector agency. Ombuds are not courts and do not conduct reviews according to the same doctrinal precision of the courts.[6] Nor do they make and remake decisions, which is typically the hallmark of tribunals. Unlike courts and tribunals,

[3] A search over one database (HeinOnline) for the term 'Ombudsman' and 'future' threw up 30,134 results. While no doubt most are tangential, some notable results with future as the focus include N O'Brien, 'What Future for the Ombudsman?' (2015) 86 *Political Quarterly* 72; A Abraham, 'The Future in International Perspective: the Ombudsman as Agent of Rights, Justice and Democracy' (2008) 61 *Parliamentary Affairs* 681.

[4] The global standing of the institution was confirmed by a resolution of the UN General Assembly, 'The Role of the Ombudsman and Mediator Institutions in the Promotion and Protection of Human Rights, Good Governance and the Rule of Law' (A/RES/75/186, adopted 16 December 2020). That resolution encouraged governments to protect or honour many attributes of their ombuds, but it did not offer or adopt a definition of the institution.

[5] A parallel can be drawn here with Dworkin's famous description of discretion as the hole within a doughnut. Discretion, according to that metaphor, was a relative concept that was defined by the absence of restriction in the surrounding structure of power: R Dworkin, *Taking Rights Seriously* (Harvard University Press, 1977) 31. Ombuds occupy a similar position in public law frameworks because they exercise functions and offer solutions that are typically not available through other parts of the framework.

[6] The different standard is not necessarily bad. The current state Ombudsman of Victoria hinted so when declaring that her 'personal favourite' reason she is able to investigate is that a decision or action is 'just plain wrong': D Glass, 'Common Sense and Clean Hands' (2019) 43 *Melbourne University Law Review* 369, 373.

ombuds have no enforcement power.[7] Ombuds instead undertake free, fast and non-binding review of individual decisions or wider governmental practices, and are guided in this work by standards quite distinct from those used by courts and tribunals.

Stephen Thomson's chapter in this collection questions whether that limit should continue. He suggests that ombuds could be granted limited powers of enforcement which would not, if crafted and managed carefully, undermine the conceptual foundation of ombuds. This suggestion is arguably an extension of the small but noticeable number of judicial review cases where courts have entertained claims about the scope of ombuds' powers or the lawfulness of their processes.[8] The grant of modest enforcement powers represents an equally modest strike back on the part of ombuds, which suggests that the potential competition between courts and ombuds Thomson is anxious to avoid has already started. Any suggestion to invest ombuds with remedial or enforcement powers stands against all of history. This remedial limitation is not simply part of the shared Scandinavian *Grundnorm* of the institution. It is often what distinguishes ombuds from other complaint mechanisms and is widely thought a part of its secret for success. Here, the institution breaks the chain of authoritative decision-making and does so by not interfering, at least in a formal or direct legal sense, with the administrative process.

As ombuds disavow the formal, technical and often adversarial approach of courts,[9] the institution lends itself more easily to comparative work across both civil and common law jurisdictions than either courts or tribunals. Comparative scholarship about the courts is generally thought difficult, though not impossible, by reason of the different methodologies of the civil and common law worlds.[10] That problem has never troubled the ombuds because it remains the only public law innovation that has been embraced in the common law world without any real attempt to hide its European origins.[11] The avoidance of judicial methodologies

[7] One contributor to this book has previously argued that this aspect of ombuds is widely accepted, except perhaps by complainants: R Kirkham, 'Explaining the Lack of Enforcement Power Possessed by the Ombudsman' (2008) 30 *Journal of Social Welfare and Family Law* 253.

[8] A recent empirical study suggests that the impact of legal actions involving ombuds means that courts may have a useful but limited role in influencing the interpretation and development of the actions of ombuds: A Stuhmcke, 'Ombudsman Litigation: The Relationship between the Australian Ombudsman and the Courts' in G Weeks and M Groves (eds), *Administrative Redress In and Out of the Courts* (Federation Press, 2019).

[9] Though relations between ombuds and an agency can become quite adversarial.

[10] See, eg J Boughey, 'Administrative Law: The Next Frontier for Comparative Law' (2013) 62 *International & Comparative Law Quarterly* 55, who notes that comparative scholars long shied away from public law, and administrative law in particular, because of the complexity of national schemes of administrative decision-making and review.

[11] This is all the more remarkable because of the exceptional hostility toward European public law innovations displayed by the influential public law scholar AV Dicey, who not only derided the principles of European public law, but also flatly rejected suggestions that they could find a way into common law jurisdictions. Recent scholarship has argued that Dicey's view of European public law was an evolving one, with more subtlety than first thought: MD Walters, 'Public Law and Ordinary Legal Method: Revisiting Dicey's Approach to "Droit Administratif"' (2016) 66 *University of Toronto Law Journal* 53.

and their associated procedural morass means that comparative analysis of ombuds is not muddied by the problems which arise in comparative analysis of courts and their often vastly different constitutional settings and localised quirks of procedure.[12]

The chapter of Greg Weeks attempts to identify one of the bright lines needed to understand the shared focus of the ombuds institution. He makes clear that maladministration is the focal point for the institution but that there are other key aspects of the institution, notably the wide remedial discretion, the lack of final determinative powers and the morality of its determinations, which in combination distinguish ombuds from the traditional work of courts and tribunals. Weeks argues that courts and tribunals are largely unsuccessful in doing what an ombuds does – examine maladministration in its widest sense. Individual ombuds can adopt quite different philosophies and processes for their office, but they are all founded upon a 'legal and policy architecture' that is 'substantially common worldwide'.[13] That universal foundation eases the path for comparative scholarship. The different constitutional and operational settings of ombuds, but with a shared history and function, is a theme which echoes throughout this collection. Ron Patterson's chapter on the New Zealand Parliamentary Ombudsman, the first common law ombuds in the world, is an excellent example of the importance of jurisdiction and operational context for ombuds. Patterson's chapter explores the New Zealand Health and Disability Commissioner and its 'oversight' by the New Zealand Parliamentary Ombudsman. In doing so, the chapter explores age-old themes shared by the institution across the globe: access to services; transparency of services; and ensuring fairness of decision-makers. Similarly, Chris Wheeler's chapter focuses on the jurisdiction and operation of one of the seven Australian ombuds, the NSW Ombudsman, and in doing so draws out challenges which face ombuds in the modern state around the world. Wheeler identifies and interrogates five major challenges for the future for ombuds. Some are ongoing and some are new: independence, resourcing, proliferation, technology and adaptability. Wheeler's chapter singles out the enormous changes brought about by the technological changes over the past 20 years which have made and will continue to make seismic changes to the environment in which ombuds operate. Wheeler observes that the increasing use of automation to make discretionary decisions has created a significant challenge for ombuds, which will be a growing problem over time.

[12] That is not to say that ombuds do not develop their own norms and procedures. There is clearly a growing use of managerial approaches by ombuds: C Gill, T Mullen and N Vivian, 'The Managerial Ombudsman' (2020) 83 *MLR* 797. While views may differ about the value of that approach, the adoption of this or any other approach by ombuds will inevitably be obscure to the public.

[13] B Yeom, 'The Legality of Walking Away from Public Service Ombudsman Reports: The United Kingdom Experience' (2017) 43 *Monash University Law Review* 386, 418.

II. The Impact of AI on an Institution Founded on the Value of the Human Touch

As Wheeler's chapter identifies, technology is a significant and ongoing globally shared external pressure brought to bear upon the office of the ombuds in the modern state. This topic is further taken up by Creutzfeldt in chapter seven, who reflects upon technology, ombuds and legal consciousness. Her chapter pushes debate into wider notions of justice and how digitalisation meets citizen demands. Creutzfeldt's chapter examines a wider dilemma now facing public law – how do systems of administration accommodate AI and technological developments?[14] The issue becomes all the more pressing for ombuds, who are likely to become increasingly occupied by complaints from people who felt they were not accommodated by a process. Time-honoured complaints about 'faceless bureaucrats' will assume a literal quality in the age of digital government. The problem will come into sharp focus as ombuds simultaneously consider complaints about decisions with an increasingly machine-led component while they seek to adopt similar systems to manage complaints.[15] The problem also has a sharper edge for ombuds when account is taken of the dignitarian element of administrative law, which acknowledges the inherent value of treating those affected by the exercise of official power with respect.[16] The solutions suggested by Lord Sales seemed designed to locate a suitable place for the courts in settling these problems. Sales proposed a combination of ex ante and ex post scrutiny of significant use of AI in government. The ex ante stage could involve notice and consultation, to enable feedback and advance knowledge about significant new schemes or algorithmic processes.[17] The ex post mechanisms occurring after AI-driven changes had commenced operation could include ways to filter those complaints requiring more attention, with perhaps judicial oversight reserved for the small number of cases that raised systemic issues.[18] Sales is especially concerned to identify a suitable site for the work of the courts, though his combination of preliminary scrutiny and test cases implicitly leaves open a role for ombuds in his acknowledgement that simple, informal review will always

[14] Harlow and Rawlings see the impact of the digital age upon the delivery of public services as one of the key challenges now facing public law: C Harlow and R Rawlings, 'Proceduralism and Automation: Challenges to the Values of Administrative Law' in E Fisher, J King and A Young (eds), *The Foundations and Future of Public Law* (Oxford University Press, 2021).

[15] Lord Sales has cautioned that privatised, then automated, government threatens in the longer term to move people 'from citizen to consumer and then on to serf': Lord Sales, 'Algorithms, Artificial Intelligence and the Law' (2020) 25 *Judicial Review* 46, 52.

[16] See, eg *Osborn v Parole Board* [2014] AC 1115, 1149 [68] (Lord Reed); *Hossain v Minister for Immigration and Border Protection* (2018) 264 CLR 123, 147–48 [72] (Edelman J); *Minister for Immigration and Border Protection v Stretton* (2016) 237 FCR 1, 5 [9] (Allsop CJ).

[17] Sales' proposal for advance consultation sits comfortably within existing English consultation requirements that govern some public sector decisions: *R (Moseley) v London Borough of Haringey* [2014] 1 WLR 3947.

[18] Sales (n 15) 55–56.

be required.[19] It is, however, revealing that Sales suggests the creation of a new 'expert algorithm commission' as an oversight body but does not once consider deployment of ombuds.

III. Age-Old Problems in the Midst of an AI Revolution

The recent explosion in the number of official inquiries and academic scholarship on the impact of technology on public administration has the potential to obscure the point that technology draws into focus problems that many affected by public agencies have long experienced. Many people who are adversely affected by official decisions struggle to access and understand the processes which affect them. A loose parallel can be drawn with a person who in recent decades might have struggled to apply for a pension or other public benefit because they were not very literate, could not afford a bus fare to visit a government office or perhaps did not have easy access to a telephone. These different examples of access to, and understanding of, decision-making and complaint processes are not too different from the struggles many now face when attempting to lodge online forms or understand the automated processes often used to determine them. Those of us who struggle to grasp the nature of computer coding probably fail to realise that the lengthy paper forms used by agencies may have been just as indecipherable to many as coding.[20] When characterised this way, another constant feature of government is apparent – the relative vulnerability of many who interact with or complain about government.

Indeed, the existence of a possibility to complain does not translate into equal opportunity to do so. Not all social groups access the institution in the same proportion. Complaints made to government ombuds are rarely made from people who are socially disadvantaged.[21] They are made by people who are from older, middle-class backgrounds rather than from the lower-class, young or minority groups.[22] International research has confirmed that the general profile of the user

[19] This approach echoes that of Hildebrandt, who calls for 'legal protection by design' so that protective legal principles are embedded within autonomous systems and their discrete elements such as algorithms. The challenge Hildebrandt identifies is 'the task of articulating compatibility with a legal norm into an architecture, protocol, standard, hardware configuration, operating system, App or grid': M Hildebrandt, *Smart Technologies and the End(s) of Law: Novel Entanglements of Law and Technology* (Edward Elgar, 2015) 218.

[20] Coding is only one of many forms of automation or technological assistance used by public agencies and individual officials, all of which involve different levels of human involvement: M Zalnieriute, L Bennett Moses and G Williams, 'Automation of Government Decision-Making' (2019) 82 *MLR* 425, 432–35.

[21] B Hubeau, 'The Profile of Complainants: How to Overcome the "Matthew Effect"?' in M Hertogh and R Kirkham (eds), *Research Handbook on Ombudsman* (Edward Elgar, 2018).

[22] S Van Roosbroek and S Van de Walle, 'The Relationship between Ombudsman, Government and Citizens: A Survey Analysis' (2008) 24 *Negotiation Journal* 287 (this finding was based upon a survey of 626 complainants in Belgium).

of ombuds services is 'a man or a woman in middle age with a higher education and a reasonable income and enough bureaucractical competencies'.[23] Thus, more powerful members of society are able to take better advantage of the ombuds institution, which is designed to support all members of society regardless of race, class, gender or age. The autonomous liberal individual is not necessarily in a position to bring a complaint to an ombuds.

This age-old problem of vulnerability is examined by Linda Reif in her chapter about the rights of older people. Reif examines how ombuds face similar challenges across both different jurisdictions and different types of ombuds institutions – most notably, classic-based and human rights-based ombuds. Urging a higher priority be placed upon the rights and needs of seniors by ombuds institutions, Rief's contribution is a reminder of how ombuds preserve and protect the rights of vulnerable individuals. In chapter eight, Nick O'Brien further focuses upon disability rights to take up the challenge of conceptualising the role of the institution with respect to rights more broadly. Using disability rights, O'Brien offers a means to reconceptualise how ombuds may promote and protect equality as an aspect of good administration for all citizens.[24] Here, O'Brien transcends vulnerability as being a legalistic and individual rights-based construct. O'Brien argues that the classic ombuds institution needs to be reimagined to emphasise renewed concern for communitarian perspectives, ethical principles and institutional networks. If those steps are taken by ombuds themselves, the dynamics of control over the institution naturally shifts towards ombuds rather than governments or legislatures. O'Brien urges a 'demosprudential' framework to capture this notion of the rights protection function that the ombuds has long had. His argument is to conceive of rights not in a legal sense, but in one where the priority of principles, community and network rules over individualism and over boundary-observing but isolated accountability. In so doing, we are alerted to the limitations of the ombuds as a redress mechanism, given that the state, as the institution which creates institutions that perpetuate individual inequality, may be equally poorly placed to improve institutional remedies for collective vulnerability.

However, the powers and responsibilities of an ombuds, together with the national, state and localised environment within which an office operates, necessitates difference. For example, some government ombuds are also human rights ombuds, others include private industries within their jurisdiction and still

[23] Such as that undertaken in 2002 by N Van Zutphen, who reviewed the research in the USA, Germany, Spain, the Netherlands, the UK and Belgium: N Van Zutphen, 'Profiel van de verzoekers van de ombudsdiensten 1975–2000: Een literatuurstudie' in R Anderson and B Hubeaeu (eds), *De ombudsman in België na een decennium: Een zoektocht naar de meerwaarde van de ombudsfunctie in de samenleving* (Die Keure, 2002). See also T Buck, R Kirkham and B Thompson, *The Ombudsman Enterprise and Administrative Justice* (Ashgate, 2011).

[24] A more general argument for this approach is made in L Sossin, 'Designing Administrative Justice' (2017) 34 *Windsor Yearbook of Access of Justice* 74. Sossin argues that a 'human centred design perspective', by which the formation and reform of tribunals is guided by the perspective of users of a service rather than its operators, is inevitably more likely to foster administrative justice. The argument can apply well beyond Sossin's focus on tribunals.

others sit with the branch of the legislature rather than the executive – yet all are identified as ombuds. Perhaps of even more interest are the global gaps. Some jurisdictions, such as the USA and Germany ('ombudspersonen'), have adopted an ad hoc model or an inconsistent state-based model, or have adopted variations of the ombuds – either institutional or industry ombuds. For example, while early proposals for a federal ombuds were suggested in the USA,[25] that jurisdiction has found favour in an organisational model of the institution, or where public sector ombuds exist within the USA they are found at a state and municipal level and are less numerous than in other equivalent modern liberal democracies.[26] Put simply, the ombuds has not spread through the tiers of American government nearly so much as it has in other Western countries.[27]

IV. Official Neglect and its Accidental Value

The second issue is the historic absence of scholarly attention paid to the institution, which makes our task harder. Ombuds can be rightly described as neglected, at least in terms of public law scholarship, for the simple reason that they do not attract the same level of attention as courts, tribunals and parliaments. Ombuds are arguably as neglected by parliaments as they are by scholars. This book takes no position on legislative neglect because we remain unsure whether it is a bad thing. This suggestion places us at odds with the position two contributors to this book recently took elsewhere. In their *Manifesto for Ombudsman Reform*,[28] Richard Kirkham and Chris Gill make a detailed case for thorough reform of the UK ombuds that places legislative reform at the heart of change. That suggestion is an understandable response to official reform proposals, which have stalled since a draft bill was published in 2016.[29] The number of critics who rounded on the draft bill suggest that these delays may have inadvertently helped the ombuds to make reforms that might be regretted.[30] Kirkham and Gill proceed on

[25] In 1969 the American Bar Association proposed a federal ombuds: V Hartke, 'Ombudsman: Mediator between the Citizen and His Government' (1973–74) 10 *California Western Law Review* 325, 351.

[26] The first state ombuds in America was established in Hawaii in 1967, but very few other jurisdictions have followed suit.

[27] The influential administrative law scholar KC Davis was an early enthusiast for adoption of the institution in the USA: KC Davis, 'Ombudsmen in America: Officers to Criticize Administrative Action' (1961) 109 *University of Pennsylvania Law Review* 1057. He thought that '[A]merican ingenuity can adapt this basic idea to our institutions and can develop it further': 1076.

[28] R Kirkham and C Gill (eds), *A Manifesto for Ombudsman Reform* (Routledge, 2020).

[29] This date relates to the Public Services Ombudsman Bill of 2016, which, in turn, can be traced to the report: Law Commission for England and Wales, *Public Services Ombudsman* (Law Com No 329, HC 1136).

[30] See N Obrien, *No End of Searching: A Comment on the Draft Public Service Ombudsman Bill 2016* (2017) https://ukaji.org/2017/02/02/no-end-of-searching-a-comment-on-the-draft-public-service-ombudsman-bill-2016/; R Kirkham and B Thompson, *An Initial Commentary on the Draft Public Services Ombuds Bill* (2016) https://ukaji.org/2016/12/20/an-initial-commentary-on-the-draft-public-services-ombuds-bill/.

the assumption that a government might cast aside self interest, adopt common sense and draft a more effective legislative foundation for reform. The behaviour of modern governments suggests such admirable assumptions will run aground on political realism.[31] A delay that will have reached six years with the publication of this book suggests that the UK draft bill died somewhere between Brexit and COVID, with perhaps the same chances of life that attend some of the many promises made by the advocates of Brexit.

That political cynicism is one reason this book does not advocate for a detailed programme of legislative reform. The book instead examines what is, and also what could, happen by reason of legislative neglect. What ombuds can and indeed must do is refashion their processes as best they can. This suggestion is not a timid one. When courts refashion principles, we laud their innovation. In common law jurisdictions, we also regard this as a key responsibility of the judicial branch of government – to revise and innovate, sometime in large leaps, as circumstances demand. Nick O'Brien's support of the demosprudential approach is an overt expression of the approach that many ombuds adopt, perhaps sometimes without realising it.[32]

In what may be described as a slow burn, scholarly books[33] devoted solely to the ombuds institution have been only recently increasing,[34] with contributions now expanding to reflect the curious position of the institution as both political and legal – and so often crossing disciplines and methodologies. In this collection, we see this mixture of methodological approaches. The chapter by Julia Dahlvik, Axel Pohn-Weidinger and Martina Kollegger is an excellent example of how socio-legal ombuds research is increasingly being undertaken to usefully address gaps and inform an international audience about the public encounter between citizens and ombudspersons. This chapter provides insights into the operation of the Austrian ombuds built on a multi-method approach. It combines multiple methodological

[31] A problem made more difficult because of the extent to which ombuds can advocate for change which affects their own offices: D Johns and H Staper, *The Future of Ombudship in Canada* (2020) www.ombudsman.ab.ca/the-future-of-ombudship-in-canada/.

[32] This aspect of ombuds work can be transposed to the framework of E Manzini, *Design, When Everybody Designs – An Introduction to Design for Social Innovation* (Rachel Coad tr, MIT Press, 2015). Manzini divides social innovation between diffuse and expert design. The former is done by the public in general, while the latter is done by those experts whose work sparks or supports important social change. The place of ombuds is obvious.

[33] There is a plethora of material produced by ombuds themselves, as well as by the International Ombudsman Institute. See, eg Gabriele Kucsko-Stadlmayer, *European Ombudsman Institutions. A Comparative Law Study on the Diverse Implementation of an Idea* (Springer, 2008); *European Ombudsman Institutions and Their Legal Basis* (Springer, 2008); Ursula Kriebaum and Gabriele Kucsko-Stadlmayer, *Asian Ombudsman Institutions* (Verlag Osterreich, 2016); V Ayeni, L Reif and H Thomas, *Strengthening Ombudsman and Human Rights Institutions in Commonwealth Small and Island States* (Chameleon Press, 2000). See also important historical journal contributions such as the *International Ombudsman Yearbook*.

[34] Beginning with Larry Hill's treatise *The Model Ombudsman* (Princeton University Press, 1976). There was a long wait until M Seneviratne, *Ombudsman* (Butterworths LexisNexis, 2002). There has now been a positive flurry of texts: T Buck, R Kirkham and B Thompson, *The Ombudsman Enterprise and Administrative Justice* (Routledge, 2011); Hertogh and Kirkham (n 21).

perspectives, including qualitative and quantitative approaches, and the authors conclude with the plea that comparative approaches that include public ombuds institutions in different national contexts will provide useful insights to promote theory building in this field. Indeed, the genesis of this book is part of this growth in both interdisciplinarity methodologies and critical focus upon ombuds. It is the next step in the larger project which began in Hertogh and Kirkham's edited collection, *Research Handbook on Ombudsman*.[35] This collection continues that tradition of producing a collection that is transnational in focus yet jurisdictionally specific. Both collections highlight the curious nature of the ombuds as sitting between disciplines and between state structures – not part of the judiciary and trying to maintain an independence from the bodies that fund them – the executive and the legislature. Kirkham's chapter in this collection takes a deep dive into this issue and exposes shifts in the regulation of the ombuds sector in the UK. Kirkham begins from the premise that the position of the ombuds as an accountability institution is contestable. This gives space to highlight how the sector has defied, or perhaps transcended, government regulation. In this mapping as to how the modern ombuds sector is currently regulated, Kirkham observes a shift towards decentred regulation whereby regulation has been passed on from government to professional ombuds networks themselves. Kirkham articulates how the ombuds sector in the UK is now 'supervised' by the judiciary but has mainly developed its own self-regulatory initiatives. As Kirkham's chapter shows, this book extends the views of Hertogh and Kirkham. The collection reinforces points such as the need for further and diverse ombuds research and further probes the question of how the institution continues to make itself essential in the modern state.

However, this collection is more than an extension. The book steps off from previous works – it notes that the nature and function of an ombuds are, of course, influenced by the stakeholders and adversaries within the administrative system, while investigating the growth of forces that may have little to do with the localised jurisdiction of the ombuds in question. The focus on the modern state exposes the future of the ombuds as being increasingly dependent upon emerging external forces. How the institution will navigate change brought about by the global pandemic, climate change, movements such as Black Lives Matter and Me Too, neoliberalism, a global understanding of rights, advances in applications of global social media influencers and companies, as well as the advances of AI is ongoing. All place increased emphasis upon the necessity of scholarly interrogation as to whether the institution remains fit for purpose.

This observation highlights a final tension. Here, we acknowledge that the problems of bureaucracy and the deficit of power between the governed and the governors that the institution seeks to address are age old. Concerns about both the reach of bureaucratic power and its inscrutable nature may have become

[35] Hertogh and Kirkham (n 21).

prominent in recent decades, but they have a much longer lineage.[36] While the omnipotent reach of government may be begrudgingly accepted by the realists among us, one of the counter responses of modern society has been the growing expectation that official action should include a level of administrative justice.[37] This is justice of the modern kind – not the technical kind offered by the courts, which is laden with as many complex procedures as it is expensive lawyers who understand them. It is instead a functional regime of accountability and oversight, which operates to ensure that the rights and interests of individuals are properly safeguarded in government decision-making.[38]

This role of the ombuds in the modern state has not shifted.[39] In promoting administrative justice, fairness and a citizen-centric administrative service delivery, the ombuds are continuing what is now over 200 years of tradition. However, both problematic and unresolved systemic issues remain in the ombuds world. Independence of the institution, resources and its constitutional place in government are perennial points of discussion.[40] Indeed, the most fundamental parameters of the operation of the ombuds are still an enigma. As Bradley observes 'one important issue with which an analysis of the ombuds system must deal is precisely the issue of whether an individual derives and kind of subjective "right" to the maintenance of fair and efficient standards of administration'.[41]

[36] A well-known British example is the so-called 'Donoughmore Report', the full title of which was *Report of the British Committee on "Ministers" Powers* (Cmd 4060, 1932). That report was sparked by the searing criticisms of ministerial and bureaucratic power in Lord Hewart, *The New Despotism* (Ernst Benn, 1929). The concerns of the Donoughmore Report were echoed in America: JM Gaus, 'The Report of the British Committee on Minister's Power' (1932) 26 *American Political Science Review* 1142.

[37] We neither offer nor presume a precise definition of administrative justice. That may seem odd, but we are conscious of the recent cautions of a pioneer of the concept: M Adler, 'Models of Administrative Justice' in J Tomlinson, R Thomas, M Hertogh and R Kirkham (eds), *The Oxford Handbook of Administrative Justice* (Oxford University Press, 2021). Adler argues that every model of administrative justice invariably reflects whatever its author seeks to vindicate. The same surely applies to any definition of the concept.

[38] This simple definition reflects what Creyke has described as the 'minimum meaning' of administrative justice: R Creyke, 'Administrative Justice in Australia' in M Adler (ed), *Administrative Justice in Context* (Hart Publishing, 2010) 271, 274.

[39] Though we note that the introduction of ombuds offices itself marked a shift in modern governance. A former Chief Justice of New South Wales argued that ombuds and other innovations in public accountability, such as freedom of information legislation and statutory rights to reasons for decisions, introduced a notion of 'administrative responsibility'. This responsibility created a level of direct contact and accountability between decision-makers and the people affected by bureaucratic decisions: JJ Spigelman, 'Foundations of Administrative Law: Towards General Principles of Administrative Law' (1998) 58 *Australian Journal of Public Administration* 3, 7.

[40] Such issues are embodied in Art 1 of the so-called 'Venice Principles': [Council of Europe] European Commission for Democracy, *Principles on the Protection and Promotion of the Ombudsman Institution* (CDL-AD (2019) 005). Although the Venice Principles involve a level of compromise, in the form of generality of principles so that they may be applicable across different legal and political systems, they provide a more complete framework than earlier such documents: L Glušac, 'A Critical Appraisal of the Venice Principles on the Protection and Promotion of the Ombudsman: An Equivalent to the Paris Principles?' (2021) 21 *Human Rights Law Review* 22.

[41] AW Bradley, 'Role of Ombudsman in Relations to Citizen's Rights' (1980) 39 *CLJ* 304, 306.

The notions of rights, responsibilities and indeed the accountability of ombuds themselves remain issues of debate for scholars and practitioners alike.

These perennial issues are each important, but they also point to wider questions about the identity and place of the ombuds institution in the modern world. Here, an entrenched issue for the operation of the ombuds in the modern state is the use of the title 'ombudsman' and the connection of the title to the individual office holder. This issue has a duality. At its simplest, it is a debate as to the gendered nature of the title itself.[42] Bondy and Doyle have explained that the use of the title 'ombudsman' has sexist connotations.[43] Hence many would regard the form used in the title of this book – Ombudsman – as somewhat inaccurate, or at least outdated. We agree that the changing nature of the state and the plethora of alternative titles used to name ombuds institutions make the gendered description of the institution at best awkward and at worst backward, but the longstanding 'brand recognition' of that title is undeniable. While not perfect, ombuds is a useful shorthand or umbrella term to capture all institutions in jurisdictions where the ombudsman title is not controlled or restricted.[44] Perhaps more complex is that the title raises a further issue, the merging of the institution with the individual who bears the title 'ombudsman'. The person who bears the title becomes the office. In the modern state, we have seen recent examples where the individual office holder has been killed or persecuted for their role.[45] These tragedies expose the identity and place of the institution in the modern state as being more than a complaint investigator, or even an administrative system fixer. The extreme price paid by these individuals who have held the title of an ombuds exposes the strength of the institution in democratic, and less than democratic, states. Within the global rise of nationalist populism, this loss of life and personal cost evidences the fact that the public benefit delivered by an ombuds may be one which is not always aligned with the policy direction or political desires of ruling parties or other powerful forces.

The identity and place of the ombuds in the modern state necessarily involves a wide grouping of stakeholders, customers and clients outside of the ombuds

[42] The use of the term 'simple' is not intended to detract from the importance of the issue.

[43] V Bondy and M Doyle, 'What's in a Name? A Discussion Paper on Ombudsman Terminology' in Hertogh and Kirkham (n 21) 485.

[44] In South Australia, the internal use of the title by a government agency is prohibited: Ombudsman Act 1972 (SA), s 32; Ombudsman Act 1975 (NZ), s 28A(1). Since 1991, in New Zealand it has been necessary to have a statutory appointment or the permission of the Chief Ombudsman before the title is used; this has been given to two industry ombuds in New Zealand.

[45] Chronox Manek, the Chief Ombudsman of Papua New Guinea, survived an assassination attempt when he was shot in the arm in 2009: 'PNG's Anti-Corruption Boss Left for Dead' *Sydney Morning Herald* (14 December 2009). Silvestre de la Toba Camacho, the Mexican Human Rights Ombudsman, was killed in a shooting (with his son) in 2017: https://hrdmemorial.org/ru/mexico-human-rights-ombudsman-shot-dead-in-baja-california/. One of the latest instances of government persecution is that of the Polish Ombudsman, Adam Bodnar, and the ongoing rule of law crisis over the new ombuds' appointment: P Dam, 'Poland's Top Watchdog Removed at Government's Behest' (Human Rights Watch, 15 April 2021) www.hrw.org/news/2021/04/15/polands-top-watchdog-removed-governments-behest.

institution and government. A number of contributions in this collection challenge us with this point. Gavin McBurnie approaches this by creating a new conceptual model to explain how bodies respond to the outputs of ombuds. Using the response of healthcare organisations and healthcare professionals to the Scottish Public Service Ombudsman, McBurnie suggests that the ability of an ombuds to contribute to system improvement is determined by the motivational postures adopted by persons within bodies in jurisdiction in response to the ombuds output. McBurnie's chapter usefully suggests that the response of the organisation means that some ombuds investigation reports may create significant change while other investigation reports create little change. Chris Gill, Carolyn Hirst and Jane Williams also address the negative impact of complaints upon complaint system actors. They interrogate the usefulness of therapeutic jurisprudence and its application to complaint systems as a means to designing roles of public services ombuds to support more therapeutic approaches. Their chapter centres the issue of ombuds as role models, noting that, as architects of governance, the ombuds are not simply authorities that can issue statutory/non-statutory guidance and monitor its compliance, but that they play a key role as therapeutic actors in designing, encouraging and modelling an ethic of care for the well-being of everyone affected by complaint systems. Examining the role of ombuds in the context of UK public services, the chapter centres what is important across ombuds globally – the fact that ongoing relationships are at the heart of many citizen–state interactions. The chapter explores the implications of ombuds' influence on redress and the opportunity the institution has to bring about more positive change in complaint systems and public administration in order to address the systemic and widespread problems of first-tier complaint handling.

V. Deciding the Structural Place or Institutional Function of Ombuds

We noted earlier that the ombuds is perhaps the only public law institution that has been adopted widely throughout the common law world. This adoption has not been accompanied with the development of any overarching theoretical conception of the constitutional place of the institution.[46] The chapters in this collection do not identify an obvious constitutional home for the ombuds, but instead focus on the significance of the role of the ombuds in the modern state, wherever it might be. Questions about location and function cannot be easily unpicked. Such questions continue to arise, however, because ombuds do not fall

[46] Sporadic litigation in common law jurisdictions has enabled the judiciary to partially fill that theoretical gap by adopting a soft-touch form of supervisory oversight: R Kirkham and A Stuhmcke, 'The Common Law Theory and Practice of the Ombudsman/Judiciary Relationship' (2020) 49 *Common Law World Review* 56.

easily within traditional conceptions of the separation of powers.[47] They exercise review functions, but are nothing like the courts. Ombuds arguably operate within the executive arm of government, but are granted a level of independence – unlike other elements of the executive. The chapters in the first part of this book examine those questions surrounding the work of ombuds, to explain the work of the institution, its relationship with the executive and the courts, and why the relatively narrow remedial powers of ombuds may in fact be a benefit rather than a limitation. The second key theme of this book is the challenges faced by ombuds in contemporary governance. Ombuds may not fit comfortably within the executive or judicial arms of government, but they are subject to many of the same challenges faced by them. How can long-standing rights of review adapt to changes in modern governance, such as outsourcing or the rise of digital decision-making in government agencies? The chapters in the second part of the book examine such individual issues to draw attention to the wider question posed to ombuds by changes in modern governance – should the ombuds adapt and, if so, how?

Theoretical debates about the most appropriate constitutional location of ombuds were labelled as a 'first-world problem' long before that refined insult was popularised. Gregory categorised public sector ombuds by reference to economic development rather than constitutional structure. He noted that the early adopters of the institution, including the Scandinavian countries, New Zealand and Australia, were prosperous nations in which democracy and the rule of law did not face any truly serious threats. Governance in these countries was sufficiently stable that a key function of the ombuds was to protect against the perils of big government. In those states yet to become stable democracies, where basic norms of democracy or the rule of law may still come under serious threat, ombuds protect against bad government.[48] The chapters in this collection are drawn from authors in jurisdictions where the problem is big, rather than bad, government,[49] but that focus is not intended to discount the important issues faced by ombuds in countries where the struggle with bad government remains at the forefront.

The distinction between big/bad government has arguably become less relevant during the COVID-19 pandemic, when this collection was written. Rob Behrens

[47] In our own jurisdiction of Australia, this debate has led some to argue that there is (or should be) a fourth 'integrity arm' of government. This fourth arm also includes anti-corruption bodies and the agencies responsible for privacy and freedom of information. The fourth arm notion can be traced to B Ackerman, 'The New Separation of Powers' (2000) 113 *Harvard Law Review* 633. See also A Abraham, 'The Ombudsman as Part of the UK Constitution: A Contested Role?' (2008) 61 *Parliamentary Affairs* 206. One member of the High Court of Australia has responded to the concept by a chapter with a revealing title: S Gageler, 'Three is Plenty' in G Weeks and M Groves (eds), *Administrative Redress In and Out of the Courts* (Federation Press, 2019).

[48] R Gregory, 'The Value and Functions of the Ombudsman: An International Perspective' in R Anderson and B Hubeaeu (eds), *De ombudsman in België na een decennium: Een zoektocht naar de meerwaarde van de ombudsfunctie in de samenleving* (Die Keure, 2002).

[49] An author who was to cover these issues, using South Africa as a case study, was unfortunately forced to withdraw from our project.

captures this moment in time in chapter ten, observing that 'no colleague in the International Ombudsman Institute, or anywhere else either, anticipated the COVID-19 pandemic or its profound impact on ombuds operations, both through the crisis and afterwards'. Behrens is currently the UK Parliamentary and Health Service Ombudsman (PHSO), and his most recent published study, entitled 'The Art of the Ombudsman: Leadership through International Crisis',[50] together with the 2020–2021 Annual Report of the PHSO,[51] maps and analyses the impact of the pandemic – marking it as a critical and ongoing external force upon the development and efficacy of ombuds globally.[52] In an insightful chapter which applies the lessons of a lived experience, Behrens takes us on a journey of humility and strength – individual attributes of the chapter author as well as an impression of what has impact and efficacy for any individual seeking to perform the role of an ombuds.

The external forces do not have to be so sudden or so obvious. Hertogh's chapter reminds us of a long-standing issue for the office of an ombuds – the examination of specific issues and complaints which contain wider social, economic and environmental problems. This chapter provides a meta-example of the classical government ombuds dilemma of when to draw away from individual complaints to consider a wider public policy issue. Yet, while a long-standing dilemma, Hertogh's mention of counter-democracy plugs into the need for the ombuds to fill the legitimacy gap that has arisen. We can also connect Hertogh's chapter to a point made by Harlow and Rawlings, who talk about the increasing use by UK ombuds of the 'big inquiry' about problems of really wide impact. Harlow and Rawlings say that this greater use of the 'big inquiry' has changed the role of ombuds but has not yet gone too far (a point they do not define). Hertogh's paper is not so much about a 'big inquiry' as about a 'big issue'.

A further example of the institution adapting to a changed modern state is that of the proliferation of industry ombuds, explored in the chapter by John McMillan. Focusing on the differences between government and industry ombuds, McMillan turns to what public ombuds may learn from their industry counterparts. The answer to this question provides a key component to access to justice across different ombuds systems. Just as the government ombuds is embedded amongst state institutions and it follows that there is a level of pretence

[50] Rob Behrens, 'The Art of the Ombudsman: Leadership through International Crisis' (6 April 2021) www.ombudsman.org.uk/publications/art-ombudsman-leadership-through-international-crisis. This study is based on responses from 53 ombuds schemes in 37 different countries, which comprises 24% of International Ombudsman Institute members.

[51] The Ombudsman's Annual Report and Accounts 2020–2021.

[52] See the Victorian Ombudsman report into the confinement of people within a set of public housing blocks: www.ombudsman.vic.gov.au/our-impact/investigation-reports/investigation-into-the-detention-and-treatment-of-public-housing-residents-arising-from-a-covid-19-hard-lockdown-in-july-2020/. The government of the day flatly rejected the findings of this report, though it is notable that a subsequent period of isolation imposed on one of those same public housing blocks appeared to adopt many of the Ombudsman's suggestions: M Simons, 'As COVID Returns to Flemington's Public Housing Estate, the Response is Markedly Different' *The Age* (7 August 2021).

in the attempt to cleanly separate the state institution from the state (or, indeed, from other state institutions), that pretence also applies to industry ombuds. Here, McMillan finds similarity rather than difference – perhaps again showing how the shared attributes of the institution traverse difference. This issue of ombuds protection raises an issue dealt with by Maaike de Langen in her chapter, which focuses on protections available for government ombuds. De Langen reminds us of the role of the ombuds at both a global and a local level. In a chapter that begins with the Venice Principles, a statement of the United Nations which recognises the importance of the ombuds as an integral part of a democratic system, de Langen addresses the newly introduced global protections offered to ombuds and to citizens who wish to access justice through the institution. Just as McMillan questions the original creation of industry ombuds, de Langen's chapter brushes against the fact that state creation of an ombuds office does not automatically lead us to conclude that it is effective in ensuring good administration. Ombuds may be established by a government with the best of intentions, such as when a state is making the transition to a democratic government or is consolidating its democratic structure, or when established democracies wish to fine-tune their institutions.[53] However, ombuds can also be established by governments which want to give the appearance of taking steps to improve complaint-handling processes and administrative justice, while the reality is that there is little material change after the institution begins operations. The degree of success an ombuds will have in building good governance necessarily depends on a number of legal, political, financial and social factors affecting the institution. De Langen explores the response of the ombuds from the Netherlands as an example to highlight this ombuds conundrum – that access to review of government decisions may well be dependent upon the ombuds' style as much as its substance. Indeed, it may be that style of dispute resolution overcomes structural impediments to the ability of the ombuds to provide access to justice, including an uneven distribution of wealth, power and opportunity, and the normative legal and political framework within which the institution operates.

VI. Conclusion

Our tentative conclusion is an unsurprising one. The ombuds institution clearly has a future, but the precise nature of that future is not entirely clear. That uncertainty is due in part to the ongoing impact of the global COVID-19 pandemic, which has shaken many assumptions about governance but has also exposed as many strengths in global systems of accountability as it has fault lines. The scale

[53] LC Reif, 'Building Democratic Institutions: The Role of National Human Rights Institutions in Good Governance and Human Rights Protection' (2000) 13 *Harvard Human Rights Journal* 23, 23.

and scope of the pandemic exposes how ombuds are embedded in relationships of institutional dependency and is subject to political and structural inequalities. During the chaos of COVID-19, ombuds have continued to hold governments to account by 'considering that health and safety measures are reaching all of its citizens, and particularly its vulnerable citizens, in the most timely, effective and just way'.[54] COVID-19 may be a new and unwelcome part of society, but the work of ombuds to investigate and advise upon government action and inaction is not. It follows that the issue which confronts a collection such as this – or, perhaps more accurately, the challenge to be laid down for future collections – is how to future-proof the place of the ombuds in the modern state. The socio-political origins of the ombuds institution, predicated upon the weakness of the individual citizen, has not changed. Indeed, access to justice and effective resolution of individual citizen complaints is essential to a healthy democracy. Government must be held accountable. In this space, there is a need for ombuds review of citizen complaints about poor or rude service through to serious maladministration. There remains a future ongoing need for an independent institution to interrogate administrative decision-making – an institution which is free and quick.

Yet, as observed throughout this collection, the external environment is subject to rapid change. Technology and other forces external to government continue to evolve – often in unforeseen and unpredictable ways. Yet, there is a constant. Most obviously, the state determines the statutory basis for government and industry ombuds, as well as resourcing. Thus, conferral and withdrawal of jurisdiction as well as financing the office for its programmes and functions will be determined by economic and political differentials between institutions. The ombuds institution is both in a position of competing for resources and jurisdiction as well as attempting to hold such institutions accountable for good decision-making. Ultimately, the danger is to the independence of the ombuds, in that any dependency may compromise the pursuit of its institutional aims. This danger is also one of perception,[55] the threat being that the ombuds may be seen to serve the underlying administration of the state rather than serving administrative justice. It is from this perspective that we lay down the challenge to future ombuds scholarship – to continue to interrogate and reinforce the positioning of the institution as one which centres citizen complaints and attains administrative justice for the individual. The question of whether and how this can be done is one we look forward to participating in as a future focus of research and debate.

[54] C Field, 'The Ombudsman's Role during and post COVID-19 Pandemic' (speech, Bangkok, 2 April 2021) 2, www.ombudsman.wa.gov.au/Publications/Documents/speeches/Ombudsman-Thailand-21st-Anniversary-Speech-Chris-Field-2-April-2021.pdf.

[55] A Stuhmcke, 'The Commonwealth Ombudsman: Still Fit for Purpose?' (AUSPUBLAW, 2021) https://auspublaw.org/2021/09/the-commonwealth-ombudsman-still-fit-for-purpose/.

PART 1

The Place of the Ombudsman in Modern Governance

2

Maladministration: The Particular Jurisdiction of the Ombudsman

GREG WEEKS*

I. Introduction

The office of the ombudsman is much misunderstood. Is it better viewed as part of the executive or the judiciary? Is it a fragile institution, unprotected with security of tenure? Is it a 'toothless tiger'? The one constant in the face of such inquiries is that ombudsmen don't seem to care, or at least carry on with great effectiveness as though they don't. I would argue in any case that such queries are beside the point[1] and that the one thing that must be understood about the ombudsman is that it is an office with a particular purpose. The ombudsman has evolved to address maladministration, much like the echidna has evolved precisely so that it might raid anthills with its unique snout. Both ombudsman and echidna may safely claim that they are perfectly adapted to do what each of them does. Such a contention about maladministration requires that I start with a brief nod to history.

The institution of ombudsman already had a long history in Sweden[2] when it first appeared in New Zealand[3] and Great Britain[4] in the 1960s. It subsequently

* I owe a debt of thanks to two exceedingly generous colleagues, both former Commonwealth Ombudsmen: Dennis Pearce, for his invaluable advice as I prepared this chapter; and John McMillan, for sharing his experiences as an ombudsman with me over several years. My wife Rachael kindly explained evolution and the role of the echidna within it. All errors are my own.

[1] In fact, I have had my say on this point and won't repeat myself unless it is necessary; see G Weeks, 'Attacks on Integrity Offices: A Separation of Powers Riddle' in G Weeks and M Groves (eds), *Administrative Redress In and Out of the Courts: Essays in Honour of Robin Creyke and John McMillan* (Federation Press, 2019) 25.

[2] The Swedish Parliamentary Ombudsman, or 'Riksdagens Ombudsman', was created in 1809: A Stuhmcke, 'The Evolution of the Classical Ombudsman: A View from the Antipodes' (2012) 2 *International Journal of Public Law and Policy* 83, 83.

[3] Parliamentary Commissioner (Ombudsman) Act 1962 (NZ).

[4] Parliamentary Commissioner Act 1967 (UK). Writing a few years after the creation of the Parliamentary Commissioner for Administration (PCA) in Great Britain, Benjafield and Whitmore observed that the New Zealand iteration of this office enjoyed a greater 'breadth [and] depth of power' than its British successor: DG Benjafield and H Whitmore, *Principles of Australian Administrative Law*, 4th edn (Law Book Co, 1971) 158.

flourished in Australia during the 1970s to the extent that, within 12 years, every Australian jurisdiction had created an ombudsman's office.[5] The security of the ombudsman concept has also been more or less assured since not long after that time and it now sits comfortably amongst other 'administrative law' institutions,[6] complementing Australia's highly developed system of tribunals and its judiciary.[7] However, although they are frequently at least complementary, the functions and concerns of ombudsmen are not identical to other administrative law bodies. The jurisdictions of courts and tribunals are conceived on different lines to that of ombudsmen, not least because (as we are perennially reminded) ombudsmen lack determinative powers of the sort possessed and wielded by those bodies.[8] The tendency to dismiss ombudsmen[9] as 'toothless tigers'[10] is inapt at least because it suggests that ombudsmen necessarily operate within an adversarial system. To the contrary, it cannot be denied that ombudsmen's success derives from their effective exercise of *influence* rather than merely from wielding *power*. They have long since learned to use a lack of 'teeth' to their advantage.[11]

Of course, it is the constitutional position of the Commonwealth Ombudsman in particular which prevents that office from exercising a determinative function.[12] This does not alter the fact that the Commonwealth Ombudsman's office has made significant tactical use of its influence and that its use of that influence has been highly effective. One of the reasons for this is that ombudsmen

[5] For the legislative details of this rapid development, see J Boughey, E Rock and G Weeks, *Government Liability: Principles and Remedies* (LexisNexis Australia, 2019) 237–38.

[6] Gleeson CJ pointed out extra-curially that institutions, including the Administrative Appeals Tribunal and the Commonwealth Ombudsman, and statutory schemes, including the Administrative Decisions (Judicial Review) Act 1977 (Cth) and the Freedom of Information Act 1982 (Cth), were 'never intended to stand alone', but to form an entire legislative scheme 'that reflects a certain set of values concerning public administration': Chief Justice AM Gleeson, 'Outcome, Process and the Rule of Law' (speech delivered at the Administrative Appeals Tribunal 30th Anniversary, Canberra, 2 August 2006).

[7] See L Pearson, 'The Vision Splendid: Australian Tribunals in the 21st Century' in AJ Connolly and D Stewart (eds), *Public Law in the Age of Statutes: Essays in Honour of Dennis Pearce* (Federation Press, 2015) 161.

[8] The Victorian Ombudsman made the point that while she 'can't enforce [her] recommendations … [she] could, and would, monitor them', including by making them a matter of public record where appropriate: D Glass, 'Common Sense and Clean Hands: An Ombudsman's View of Justice' (2019) 43 *Melbourne University Law Review* 369, 377.

[9] Harlow and Rawlings noted the rejection of an analogous attempt to give the UK Press Complaints Commission more 'bite' on the basis that allowing that watchdog body to impose fines would undermine its work as a dispute resolution service: C Harlow and R Rawlings, *Law and Administration*, 3rd edn (Cambridge University Press, 2009) 469. It is possible that the word 'watchdog' was apt to mislead.

[10] Creyke and McMillan have noted – and refuted – this characterisation across several editions of their case book; see now R Creyke et al, *Control of Government Action: Text, Cases and Commentary*, 5th edn (LexisNexis, 2019) 244.

[11] See G Weeks, *Soft Law and Public Authorities: Remedies and Reform* (Hart Publishing, 2016) 238.

[12] While the constitutional oddity of the Commonwealth Ombudsman has been noted frequently, Basten JA has stated more generally that the role of ombudsman in state (and, we may assume, territory) systems 'does not fit happily within a governmental structure notionally divided into a tripartite separation of powers': *Kaldas v Barbour* (2017) 326 FLR 122, 198 [312].

are not restricted to examining legal errors – much less jurisdictional errors, the touchstone of judicial review in Australia[13] – but can examine maladministration in that term's broadest sense. This is a vital point of distinction because it follows that an ombudsman is not restricted to negative examinations of excesses of power or suboptimal exercises of discretion but can take active steps to seek to improve administrative processes. In this respect, ombudsmen stand alone within the scheme of administrative law bodies and contribute an essential function to modern administrative law, especially within the set of government bodies said to have an integrity role.[14]

This chapter will examine the specific jurisdiction of the ombudsman and the consequences of its capacity to look at, and remedy, maladministration in a comprehensive way.

II. Jurisdiction to Address Maladministration

Because maladministration extends beyond mere illegality to more generally framed allegations of injustice, it typically falls within the broader remedial remit granted to ombudsmen but not within those of courts and tribunals. Dennis Pearce conducted a review of Australian ombudsman legislation which revealed that, while not identical, the respective statutes are generally similar and state that ombudsmen are empowered to investigate certain types of complaint:[15]

- action which is a matter of administration;
- unreasonable failure to act; and
- recommendations made to ministers.

In its Swedish genesis, the ombudsman was said not to 'take up complaints about the way in which a civil servant has exercised his discretion unless it appears that the discretion has been so abused as not to amount to an exercise of discretion at all'.[16] This description of the jurisdiction of the Swedish ombudsman bears strong

[13] This remains true notwithstanding some persuasive criticisms of the High Court's approach, particularly over the last 25 years; see L Burton Crawford and J Boughey, 'The Centrality of Jurisdictional Error: Rationale and Consequences' (2019) 30 *Public Law Review* 18.

[14] I do not propose to comment on the so-called integrity branch other than to say that its utility and very existence are points on which highly respected minds differ; see, eg J McMillan, 'Re-thinking the Separation of Powers' (2010) 38 *Federal Law Review* 423; *cf* S Gageler, 'Three is Plenty' in Weeks and Groves (n 1) 12.

[15] D Pearce, 'The Jurisdiction of Australian Government Ombudsmen' in M Groves (ed), *Law and Government in Australia: Essays in Honour of Enid Campbell* (2005) 110, 111–14.

[16] H Bland, H Whitmore and PH Bailey, *Interim Report of the Committee on Administrative Discretions* (1973) Parliamentary Paper No 53 of 1973 (*Bland Committee Interim Report*) 8 [32], citing: KJ Keith, 'The Ombudsman and "Wrong" Decisions' (1971) 4 *New Zealand Universities Law Review* 361. See also KC Wheare, *Maladministration and its Remedies* (Stevens and Sons, 1973) 120.

similarities to Latham CJ's reasoning as to the basis on which a statutory decision-maker's opinion can be challenged under judicial review,[17] with the key difference being that an ombudsman's conclusion on this point would not need to represent a legal consequence in order for him or her to proceed. The English Parliamentary Commissioner for Administration (PCA) stood apart from this aspect of the first ombudsmen because its statute was understood to focus 'on maladministration in relation to a decision, not on the discretionary power conferred by statute'.[18]

The term 'maladministration' does not appear in the Ombudsman Act 1976 (Cth),[19] nor does it appear in any of the state or territory statutes,[20] bar one. The Victorian Act includes as one of its objectives that it is 'to provide for the identification, investigation, exposure and prevention of maladministration',[21] although maladministration is not defined at any point within the legislation. That is also true of the UK legislation,[22] although it alludes to meanings of maladministration at a couple of points. In section 12, headed 'Interpretation', the Parliamentary Commissioner Act 1967 (UK) uses maladministration to identify a lack of jurisdiction in declaring that: 'nothing in this Act authorises or requires the Commissioner

[17] *R v Connell; ex parte Hetton Bellbird Collieries Ltd* (1944) 69 CLR 407, 432. His Honour's judgment preceded by some years the similar reasoning of Lord Greene MR in *Associated Provincial Picture Houses Ltd v Wednesbury Corporation* [1948] 1 KB 223.

[18] *Bland Committee Interim Report* (n 16) 9 [37]. The Committee members commented that a very broad jurisdiction to review decisions 'would be a perfect example of power without responsibility and of giving power to someone who carried no responsibility for the making of policy to judge the desirability of that policy'. Policy is not within an ombudsman's remit: P Craig, *Administrative Law*, 8th edn (Sweet and Maxwell, 2016) 214. Many ombudsmen nonetheless take pains to avoid the policy behind a flawed administrative process because there is no need to address it; 'a decision so bad that the ombudsman might regard it as maladministrative on [the basis that it was an unmeritorious public policy decision] will ordinarily have been arrived at precisely because of a series of fundamental administrative failings': T Buck, R Kirkham and B Thompson, *The Ombudsman Enterprise and Administrative Justice* (Ashgate, 2011) 112.

[19] The report of the Committee which led to the creation of the Commonwealth Ombudsman twice referred to 'maladministration or irregularities in administration' as being within the scope of that office: H Bland, H Whitmore and PH Bailey, *Final Report of the Committee on Administrative Discretions* (1973) Parliamentary Paper No 316 of 1973 (*Bland Committee Final Report*) 59–60 [11] and [18]. A third reference was made to 'maladministration and proper process': ibid 70 [72]. By contrast, the website of the Australian and New Zealand Ombudsman Association (ANZOA), which represents Australian and New Zealand ombudsmen, does not mention maladministration at all in its explanation of the role of ombudsmen; see ANZOA, 'Ombudsman: A Particular Model of Alternative Dispute Resolution' <www.anzoa.com.au/about-ombudsmen.html>.

[20] Parliamentary Commissioner Act 1971 (WA); Ombudsman Act 1972 (SA); Ombudsman Act 1974 (NSW); Ombudsman Act 1978 (Tas); Ombudsman Act 1989 (ACT); Ombudsman Act 2001 (Qld); Ombudsman Act 2009 (NT). This is also true in New Zealand; see Parliamentary Commissioner (Ombudsman) Act 1962 (NZ) and Ombudsmen Act 1975 (NZ). In its original form, the NSW Act referred to the Ombudsman's capacity to investigate and report on conduct of a public authority which was 'wrong', defined at s 5(2) in terms similar to grounds of judicial review. That nomenclature has since been played down and the section repealed, although the Act currently has a similar list at s 26(1); see also Ombudsman Act 1976 (Cth), s 15(1)(a)(v).

[21] Ombudsman Act 1973 (Vic), s 2A(b).

[22] Parliamentary Commissioner Act 1967 (UK); *cf Bland Committee Interim Report* (n 16) 9 [38].

to question the merits of *a decision taken without maladministration* by a government department or other authority in the exercise of a discretion vested in that department or authority' (emphasis added).[23]

Maladministration is also used to point to jurisdiction in a positive sense. The PCA may, inter alia, investigate action, to which the legislation applies, taken by or on behalf of a government department or authority:

> being action taken in the exercise of administrative functions of that department or authority, in any case where a written complaint is duly made to a member of the House of Commons by a member of the public who *claims to have sustained injustice in consequence of maladministration* in connection with the action so taken … (emphasis added)[24]

The UK legislation also recognises that one of the perils of maladministration is that it is often based on an irremediable injustice. Hence, the PCA 'may, if he thinks fit, lay before each House of Parliament a special report upon the case' following the investigation described in section 5, if:

> it appears to the [PCA] that injustice has been caused to the person aggrieved in consequence of maladministration and that the injustice has not been, or will not be, remedied …[25]

In the UK at least, it seems to be established that, while the PCA's jurisdiction does not in general extend to matters of a judicial or legislative nature, including the content of rules, it is highly flexible.[26] Specifically, it has broad powers to investigate the exercise of statutory orders, 'allowing an investigation of maladministration in the administrative process leading to the actual making of the order'.[27] This focus is essentially replicated in the 'action' that Australian ombudsmen are empowered by statute to investigate. For example, the Commonwealth Ombudsman can investigate a 'matter of administration' either in response to a complaint or on his or her own motion.[28] That jurisdiction is then limited on a similar basis to that of the PCA.

III. What Is Maladministration?

The provision in section 5 of the UK's Parliamentary Commissioner Act 1967 extracted above points to a partial definition of maladministration: in summary, it is conduct capable of causing injustice and is possibly systemic in that it

[23] Parliamentary Commissioner Act 1967 (UK), s 12(3).
[24] Parliamentary Commissioner Act 1967 (UK), s 5(1).
[25] Parliamentary Commissioner Act 1967 (UK), s 10(3).
[26] Buck et al (n 18) 110–12.
[27] Craig (n 18) 212 [8-019].
[28] Ombudsman Act 1976 (Cth), s 5(1); *cf* Parliamentary Commissioner Act 1967 (UK), s 5(1).

might foreseeably continue if left unremedied.[29] That definition is incomplete.[30] For example, Harlow and Rawlings noted the prevalence of what they called 'mundane maladministration', including 'widespread delays, poor communication and inaccurate information to clients, badly trained staff, and failures of communication with other agencies'.[31] Whether any of these issues causes 'injustice' (as opposed to mere inconvenience) to an aggrieved individual in a particular case is not a point capable of being generalised. They are, however, clearly of great importance and central to the function of the ombudsman in dealing with structural issues around governance. To describe such issues as 'mundane' is not to diminish their importance; it merely employs the standard definition of such matters as being 'everyday, dull [or] routine'.[32]

Such a description of maladministration is often accurate, since it will frequently be the case that injustice is caused by inattention rather than malice, or by poor governance rather than corrupt conduct. This point was made evident in the 2017–18 Annual Report of the Commonwealth Ombudsman, which noted that, of the instances of disclosable conduct prior to an investigation being undertaken, 'the most identified types … are broad-based, such as breach of a law or maladministration, which can capture a large range of actions'.[33] This appears to define maladministration as occupying one of two broad types of conduct leading to injustice, the other being breach of one or more laws. The conclusion that an agency or department has engaged in maladministration requires only that its internal processes are in some way flawed, a conclusion falling short of illegality.

It is interesting, however, that what amounts to maladministration is by no means clear cut.[34] For example, the Commonwealth Ombudsman issued a fact sheet in 2008 which catalogued 16 different categories of administrative deficiency. That fact sheet has since been withdrawn from the Ombudsman's website, on which a more recent fact sheet reduces the forms of administrative deficiency to three categories.[35] It is probable that this step was taken because

[29] See, eg the allegations of members of the Administrative Appeals Tribunal that that body was 'in crisis' due 'in substantial part to maladministration by the government': M Seccombe, 'Political Stacking Leaves Appeals Tribunal in Chaos' *The Saturday Paper* (24–30 November 2018). Such allegations may simultaneously be correct and yet disclose no 'wrongdoing' of the sort remediable in judicial proceedings. They may prove nothing more than that government decisions seldom please everyone.

[30] A fact indicated by the choice to extend the jurisdiction of several UK ombudsman schemes to investigate alleged 'failures of service'; see Buck et al (n 18) 108–12.

[31] Harlow and Rawlings (n 9) 78.

[32] See the definition of 'mundane' in L Brown (ed), *The New Shorter Oxford English Dictionary*, 4th edn (Oxford University Press, 1993).

[33] Commonwealth Ombudsman, *Annual Report 2017–18* (2018) 64.

[34] For example, as in *Edwards v Chesterfield Royal Hospital NHS Foundation Trust* [2012] 2 AC 22, the overlay of a complex legislative scheme might complicate an otherwise straightforward allegation of maladministration.

[35] Covering 'actions that are: unlawful, unreasonable, unjust, oppressive, improperly discriminatory or otherwise wrong; not explained properly by an agency; [or] based on a law or policy that was unreasonable, unjust, oppressive or improperly discriminatory': Commonwealth Ombudsman, *Ombudsman Investigations* www.ombudsman.gov.au/__data/assets/pdf_file/0030/35598/Ombudsman-Investigations.pdf.

the original, finely calibrated set of ways to describe administrative deficiencies in fact created a greater workload for the Ombudsman in dealing with agencies dissatisfied with *how* their actions were described as deficient,[36] without creating a greater understanding on the part of those agencies about the nature of their deficient actions.

In some ways, defining maladministration is reminiscent of the standard legislative provision which requires tribunals to operate in a way which is 'fair, just, economical, informal and quick'.[37] That formula is not expected (nor is it always possible) to be applied in the literal terms of the statute,[38] and the High Court has warned that, while it might be exhortatory or aspirational, it does not bind a tribunal to each of the several named outcomes.[39] One of the reasons for this is that the requirements of 'justice', say, might not allow the tribunal to apply the fullest measure of 'economy'; and what is 'fair' might not coincide in a particular case with what is 'informal' or 'quick'. Similarly, while maladministration might be illustrated in many cases by delay, speed might also be inconsistent with good administration in some cases, for example, by causing a decision-maker to fail in some respect, such as: to test an administrative project, procedures or technology adequately; to take the time to ensure that new staff are properly trained; or to focus on the quality of the service provided rather than only the number of clients served.[40] Speed, just as easily as delay, might indicate the presence of maladministration. It follows that the kinds of error or failure that lead to maladministration are not so easily pinned down that they can be captured in a definitive list.

This could easily be the reason why ombudsmen's legislation is apt to mention maladministration seldom or not at all – it has a greater flexibility when there is a general consensus as to its meaning that is not subject to the precision of judicial examination (for example, during the course of litigation[41]) by being defined in specific terms. It is certainly not the case that the term 'maladministration' was unknown when Australian ombudsman legislation was drafted. In

This fact sheet also states that most complaints are resolved without the need to decide whether there has been an administrative deficiency at all. Where that is not the case, there is precedent for a finding of maladministration to be judicially reviewable where it contains one or more legal errors; see *Walters v Drummond* [2019] QSC 290, [261].

[36] Anecdotal evidence from former ombudsmen indicates that it is valuable to retain some flexibility in how maladministration is described, since an agency might be more apt to accept, for example, a finding that it has been 'unreasonable' rather than that it has acted 'contrary to law'.

[37] See, eg *Administrative Appeals Tribunal Act 1975* (Cth), s 2A(b).

[38] Boughey et al (n 5) 174.

[39] See *Minister for Immigration and Citizenship v Li* (2013) 249 CLR 332, 358 [51] (Hayne, Kiefel and Bell JJ); 372 [96] (Gageler J).

[40] Harlow and Rawlings (n 9) 78, citing the report of the Parliamentary Commissioner for Administration, *Investigation of Complaints against the Child Support Agency* (1994/95, HC 135) iii.

[41] While ombudsmen are sometimes parties to litigation, it has been argued that this is 'when they are at their least effective, since they are in the realm of law rather than maladministration': Boughey et al (n 5) 260. Aronson expressed this point by stating that 'silk at 15 paces is not meant to be the way ombudsmen operate': M Aronson, 'Ombudsmen and Crime Busters: Ships Passing in the Night' in Weeks and Groves (n 1) 178, 181.

its Interim Report, the Bland Committee traced a central concern with maladministration back to the earliest examples of the ombudsman as an institution.[42] This is no coincidence, since the ombudsman is not concerned primarily with law but with justice and for this reason stands apart from other administrative law bodies.[43] Maladministration is a concept that goes to justice rather than law;[44] hence, law speaks to what *may* be done and maladministration to what *ought* to be done.[45] Further to this point, there is persuasive authority in Australia that courts' judicial review functions *may not*, for constitutional reasons, be exercised 'for the purpose of enabling the judicial branch of government to impose upon the executive branch its ideas of good administration'.[46] Ombudsmen look at maladministration not only because it is important but also because others cannot. Consequently, any guidelines to good administration published by ombudsmen tend to be 'intimately linked with a finding of maladministration'.[47]

In a speech given in 2019,[48] Deborah Glass, the Victorian Ombudsman, distinguished her powers to deal with maladministration (defined as 'usually something short of outright corruption but still wrong') from her complaint-handling role. She identified cases involving maladministration as involving 'people acting on their temptation to do things the easy way or for ulterior motives – many who try to justify their actions by claiming the rules don't really apply to them'.[49] This category of misuse of power – which is narrower than I have framed the concept of maladministration above – need not necessarily come to the attention of ombudsmen *other than* by the office's complaint-handling function.[50] What is important is that ombudsmen have the authority to investigate conduct by public officers that falls short of ideal practice. There is no need for such conduct

[42] *Bland Committee Interim Report* (n 16) 8 [32].

[43] Enderby J accepted a series of propositions about the ombudsman in *Ainsworth v The Ombudsman* (1988) 17 NSWLR 276, 283. These included that it 'is a unique institution' which 'does not deal directly or in any legal way with legal rights'. See the text accompanying n 6 above.

[44] There are isolated instances of courts referring to maladministration outside the context of considering the jurisdiction of ombudsmen; see, eg *Goodwin Street Developments Pty Ltd v DSD Builders Pty Ltd* (2018) 98 NSWLR 712, 723 (Basten JA, considering the standard by which bad faith might be proved).

[45] See Glass (n 8) 383, citing E Burke, 'On Conciliation with America' in WJ Bryan and FW Halsey (eds), *The World's Famous Orations: Ireland 1775–1902* (Funk & Wagnalls, 1906) vol 6, 3, 31. I have slightly amended the words of both authors the better to make my point.

[46] *Re Minister for Immigration and Multicultural Affairs; ex parte Lam* (2003) 214 CLR 1, 12 [32] (Gleeson CJ).

[47] Craig (n 18) 213. See, eg the guides provided by Commonwealth Ombudsman: www.ombudsman.gov.au/better-practice-guides.

[48] Glass (n 8) 377.

[49] ibid 378.

[50] This is true of the particular example given by Glass, involving misuse of public funds by senior managers of certain ski resorts; see Victorian Ombudsman, *Investigation into Allegations of Improper Conduct by Officers at the Mount Buller and Mount Stirling Resort Management Board* (20 March 2017) Parliamentary Paper No 280. The Ombudsman's jurisdiction would no less have been engaged if a complaint had been made about the managers' conduct.

to be corrupt, otherwise criminal or even in breach of specific legislation to fall within the ombudsman's jurisdiction. Such conduct can properly be described as maladministration.

Glass's distinction between the complaints-handling and maladministration functions of an ombudsman's office does not necessarily align the latter with the systemic or 'integrity' functions of ombudsmen.[51] She identified

> the core principle that taxpayers' money should not be used for personal gain – whatever the excuse. And part of [an ombudsman's] role is to look at the cleanliness of the hands – and fingernails – of those who take from the public purse.[52]

I suggest that this is a general standard of good administration[53] rather than one which falls within the specific statutory remit of ombudsmen.[54] Indeed, ombudsmen are specifically forbidden to investigate potential maladministration committed by a range of entities.[55] Looking at the misuse of government funds is not solely within the remit of the relevant ombudsman, especially since it will frequently amount to corrupt or even criminal behaviour in any case. Other integrity bodies – like the Auditor General and standing anti-corruption commissions – have specialised roles within this space. As Glass's example demonstrates, however, using public money for personal gain will frequently be a form of maladministration with which an ombudsman is particularly capable of dealing.

Some other observations that might assist to define maladministration follow. First, it has been contended that 'nobody can define maladministration in plain terms',[56] a conclusion which emerges clearly from the discussion above. Maladministration is a term whose content lies in the eye of the beholder, with the result that what is 'mundane' to some might be of vital importance to others. Likewise, an alleged breach of the standards of 'good administration' might be partly or wholly excused by the circumstances in which it was made, such as whether there were other considerations which the decision-maker needed (or elected) to take into account. The term 'maladministration' alone tells us nothing of the context in such examples. It is a conclusory term, a 'label … reached after applying other tests'.[57] While this does not necessarily indicate

[51] See, eg A Stuhmcke, 'Ombudsmen and Integrity Review' in L Pearson, C Harlow and M Taggart (eds), *Administrative Law in a Changing State: Essays in Honour of Mark Aronson* (Hart Publishing, 2008) 349.

[52] Glass (n 8) 378.

[53] *cf* n 21 above. There are distinct equitable overtones to the expectation that persons entrusted with the control of public monies should have 'clean hands', although the equitable discretion to withhold remedies from an applicant without 'clean hands' obviously has significant differences. Comparisons between public law and equity are frequently made, but seldom point to direct connections rather than general influences; see Boughey et al (n 5) 374–77.

[54] See, eg Ombudsman Act 1976 (Cth), s 5(1).

[55] See, eg Ombudsman Act 1976 (Cth), s 5(2).

[56] Wheare (n 16) 6, citing evidence given by Sir Edmund Compton, Britain's first PCA, before a Parliamentary Committee.

[57] M Aronson, M Groves and G Weeks, *Judicial Review of Administrative Action and Government Liability*, 6th edn (Thomson Reuters, 2017) 20 [1.110]. The authors note by analogy that 'negligence' states a conclusion but is not itself a test for whether that conclusion is made out.

that the term is either wholly unhelpful or even in disfavour,[58] it does presuppose that it should be understood in the context of the entirety of a public entity's capacity to exercise power.

Secondly, notwithstanding the first point, Sir Kenneth Wheare asserted that most people think that they could recognise an example of maladministration if they saw it.[59] Others have shown similar confidence in their capacity to be able to recognise what they have not yet seen,[60] but that should not disguise the fact that there is more than mere subjective reaction to identifying maladministration. It also indicates why ombudsmen are uniquely equipped to determine whether and to what extent maladministration has occurred and what the appropriate response to that fact should be. Weighing factors in that way is not something for which courts or even tribunals are best suited.

Thirdly, the meaning of 'maladministration' must depend heavily on the meaning of 'administration'.[61] Where both meanings depend extensively on opinion, either might be justified. However, the type of 'administration' over which Australian ombudsmen have oversight is usually defined with some precision by the relevant ombudsman's governing statute.[62] It is not maladministration in the relevant sense if it falls outside the statutory remit of the ombudsman. The ombudsman does have a particular jurisdiction, denied to courts,[63] to determine 'whether particular administrative practices are prudent or efficient'[64] or otherwise amount to 'good' administration. Those that don't meet this standard might amount to maladministration; they might on the other hand simply amount to something less than best practice. The ombudsman's dependence on using persuasion (rather than the kinds of remedies

[58] Jurisdictional error is a conclusory term whose status as the basis of Australian judicial review is not impeded by that fact. The distinction between statutory provisions which were 'mandatory' as opposed to those which were merely 'directory' was also disapproved in *Project Blue Sky v Australian Broadcast Authority* (1998) 194 CLR 355, 374 (Brennan CJ), 390 (McHugh, Gummow, Kirby and Hayne JJ). These terms are nonetheless 'still useful'; see Aronson et al (n 57) [1.50].

[59] Wheare (n 16) 6.

[60] See, eg *Jacobellis v Ohio*, 378 US 184, 197 (1964) (Stewart J); *Cadogan Estates Ltd v Morris* [1998] EWCA Civ 1671, [17] (Stuart-Smith LJ).

[61] Wheare (n 16) 6.

[62] This is also true of a body such as the English Revenue Adjudicator, which deals essentially with questions of maladministration but exercises determinative powers under contract; see Harlow and Rawlings (n 9) 458–59. The same is true of industry ombudsmen in Australia.

[63] To say that such a jurisdiction has been 'denied' to courts does not adequately indicate that they show no desire to exercise it. Gleeson CJ stated that the High Court's constitutional judicial review jurisdiction does not permit it to impose its 'ideas of good administration' on the executive branch: *Lam* (n 46) 12 [32]. This observation extends to the jurisdiction of state and territory courts and can be read as carrying the implication that, even possessing the jurisdiction to bind other entities with a statutory or executive power to form their own ideas on the topic as to the meaning of 'good administration', it would not make doing so a good idea.

[64] *Minister for Immigration and Multicultural Affairs v Bhardwaj* (2002) 209 CLR 597, 645 [150] (Hayne J). His Honour went on to say that 'there would be little dispute that characteristics of prudence and efficiency are relevant to good administrative practice'.

commonly imposed by court orders) and proceeding through the exercise of 'soft' varieties of power means that the institution is uniquely placed to encourage better practices in executive bodies without having to find that existing inadequate practices amount to maladministration. Such encouragement has proved extremely effective,[65] whereas the capacity to make findings has occasionally been somewhat fraught.[66]

Once maladministration has been identified, it remains to be determined what the ombudsman is able to do about it. After all, complainants to the ombudsman always want a remedy. The very fact that ombudsmen 'have no power to *order* remedies because they lack the constitutional capacity to make binding declarations of right' causes their focus to be 'much more practical than that of a court exercising a judicial review function or even that of a merits review tribunal'.[67]

The following section considers remedies for maladministration.

IV. Remedies for Maladministration

The jurisdiction to issue certain remedies is an important consideration, where it is relevant. However, it is a concept which attaches most frequently to judicially issued relief. Ombudsmen, by contrast, have a jurisdiction to 'investigate action … that relates to a matter of administration' or to assume certain functions under a statutory scheme,[68] but have no power at all to make determinative orders or issue remedies in the manner of a court or tribunal. This is no deficiency in the ombudsman model; to the contrary, it is a point of significant strength for the institution. Not for nothing did Sir Kenneth Wheare comment as long ago as 1973 that 'perhaps the most striking feature in the search for more effective remedies for maladministration … has been the discovery of the Ombudsman'.[69]

It is still worth starting any consideration of remedies by considering judicial remedies, which do not generally respond to maladministration unless it also amounts to a breach of the law. Even then, much depends on the nature of the alleged breach and the action said to arise thereby; to paraphrase Jordan CJ, there

[65] Weeks (n 11) 245.

[66] See *Chairperson, Aboriginal and Torres Strait Islander Commission v Commonwealth Ombudsman* (1995) 63 FCR 163, in which Einfeld J distinguished the capacity to make 'findings' (which lay without the Ombudsman's jurisdiction) and 'opinions' (which the Ombudsman had the power to make). This was one of only a few cases which has purported to guide ombudsmen in the exercise of their statutory powers and it was not entirely helpful; one former Commonwealth Ombudsman described Einfeld J's distinction between findings and opinions as 'debatable and impractical': McMillan (n 14) 427.

[67] Weeks (n 11) 244.

[68] See, eg Ombudsman Act 1976 (Cth), s 5(1), (2) and (3).

[69] Wheare (n 16) 141.

are breaches and breaches[70] whose 'criteria of discrimination between [them] are not determinable in advance'.[71]

For example, an attempt to obtain a private law damages remedy by classifying maladministration as misfeasance in public office has been mooted on several occasions[72] but generally this ignores the fact that claims in tort for misfeasance are very hard to establish.[73] To consider one case, there was no doubt that the plaintiffs in *Mengel* had been victims of maladministration: their cattle were quarantined by government stock inspectors and their movement restricted for months in the mistaken belief that the cattle were diseased.[74] The purpose of the stock inspectors' acts was to be understood within the context of an Australia-wide campaign to eliminate tuberculosis and brucellosis in cattle but the existence of that campaign alone did nothing to make their acts valid. When the quarantine and related restriction was lifted, the plaintiffs had lost a considerable sum of money by not being allowed to sell their cattle at the optimal time. The plaintiffs suffered significant loss as a result of this maladministration.

The *Mengel* plaintiffs were nonetheless unsuccessful in a claim for misfeasance in public office,[75] substantially because that tort requires that the defendants (who must be public officers) have acted with malice targeted at the plaintiffs with the intention of deliberately inflicting harm upon them.[76] The judiciary, over many years and in several countries, has deliberately placed stringent limits on the application of this tort. Their purpose in doing so – in part, to prevent every mistake by a public officer being addressed as a claim for an award of damages in tort – is understandable but could not be further from the purpose informing the notion of maladministration. The former is precise, forbidding and legalistic to a greater degree than almost any other publicly oriented doctrine. Maladministration, on the other hand, is an essentially practical concept designed to identify poor practice in the public sphere and allow a body without powers limited to determination of legal issues (generally, an ombudsman) to remedy it promptly wherever possible. The tort of misfeasance in public office is the wrong tool with which to redress maladministration.

[70] His Honour's reference to 'mistakes and mistakes' was to make the point that not every error of law is jurisdictional (to use the modern parlance): *Ex parte Hebburn Ltd; Re Kearsley Shire Council* (1947) 47 SR (NSW) 416, 420. The elegance of his expression has since been judicially co-opted to other circumstances; see, eg *Harris v Digital Pulse Pty Ltd* (2003) 56 NSWLR 298, 323 [122] (Mason P).

[71] *Holt v Cox* (1997) 23 ACSR 590 (Mason P).

[72] Particularly in the wake of *Northern Territory v Mengel* (1995) 185 CLR 307.

[73] See Aronson et al (n 57) [19.640].

[74] They were certainly mistaken, but the significance of whether the order authorising quarantine of the cattle was invalid or unlawful necessitated deeper analysis in the High Court: *Mengel* (n 72) 363 (Deane J); *cf Northern Territory v Mengel* (1994) 83 LGERA 371, 419 (Priestley J).

[75] Mark Aronson is the most prolific modern author on this tort; specifically to *Mengel*, see M Aronson, 'Misfeasance in Public Office: A Very Peculiar Tort' (2011) 35 *Melbourne University Law Review* 1, 4; M Aronson, 'Misfeasance in Public Office: Some Unfinished Business' (2016) 132 *LQR* 426, 432; Aronson et al (n 57) [19.6].

[76] The facts of *Mengel* stopped a long way short of establishing malice. Even cases featuring much more severe official misbehaviour have failed to result in a finding of misfeasance in public office; see, eg *Sanders v Snell* (1998) 196 CLR 329.

There have, however, been other attempts to fashion a remedy to address losses caused by maladministration.

A. Attempts to Broaden the Remedial Response to Maladministration

(i) Legislative

Australia has adopted a relatively stable approach to the question whether maladministration can be remediable through a judicial order for compensation: unless the decision or conduct in question gives rise to liability in judicial proceedings, the courts do not consider it their role to remedy maladministration.[77] Furthermore, it is generally accepted that if we were to yield to the temptation to increase the range of judicial remedies, such as by remedying maladministration with damages, that step must only be taken after accepting that it would undeniably alter the existing judicial review remedies.[78] Maladministration is also not a ground for judicial review in the UK – 'the question is only "has the public body acted unlawfully?"'.[79] The position in the UK is therefore essentially the same as that in Australia but has settled in that place by way of a more fraught process.

In 2003, a leading English barrister described the availability of 'reparation' for maladministration as 'law's final frontier',[80] thereby speaking truer than he might have known. The UK Law Commission was then on the verge of a comprehensive analysis of monetary remedies in public law,[81] followed by one on administrative redress generally.[82] The latter report was flawed,[83] but that is to be expected of a process undertaken to provide a watertight solution to such an

[77] Note, by contrast, the long-standing support by senior English judges for the notion that for every wrong there must be a (judicial) remedy: *X (Minors) v Bedfordshire County Council* [1995] 2 AC 633, 663 (Lord Bingham); *Abbott v Sullivan* [1952] 1 All ER 226, 231 (Lord Denning). With respect, the reality has proved far more complex than their Lordships' intuitive sense of justice allowed; see E Rock and G Weeks, 'Monetary Awards for Public Law Wrongs: Australia's Resistant Legal Landscape' (2018) 41 *University of New South Wales Law Journal* 1159, 1167.

[78] See *New South Wales v Paige* (2002) 60 NSWLR 371, 404 (Spigelman CJ).

[79] *R (Grimsby Institute) v Chief Executive of Skills Funding* [2010] EWHC 2134 (Admin), [101].

[80] M Fordham QC, 'Reparation for Maladministration: Public Law's Final Frontier' [2003] 8 *Judicial Review* 104. He now sits as Justice Fordham in the Queen's Bench Division of the High Court of England and Wales.

[81] Law Commission, 'Monetary Remedies in Public Law: A Discussion Paper' (2004).

[82] A consultation paper in 2008 was followed by a report: Law Commission, *Administrative Redress: Public Bodies and the Citizen* (Law Com No 322, 2010).

[83] For example, submissions to the Law Commission's consultation paper rightly took issue with the limitation of liability to circumstances in which the claimant's loss was caused by an administrative decision involving 'serious fault' and for acts which were 'truly public', two question-begging concepts. See Law Commission, 'Administrative Redress: Public Bodies and the Citizen – Analysis of Consultation Responses' (2010) [2.96]–[2.106].

intractable problem. Those flaws alone were insufficient to justify the description of the Law Commission's work as a 'débâcle' by Sedley LJ in his lengthy judicial obituary for it in 2011.[84] Rather, his Lordship correctly identified the government as having been the party which sent the Law Commission's proposed scheme 'to the sea-bed',[85] using its status as the 'key stakeholder'[86] to express its firm, complete and intractable opposition to the solutions proposed to the issue of obtaining redress in the face of administrative maladministration.[87] Even if this had been a brilliant set of proposals, the opposition of government would have made it unworkable. The Law Commission understood this and published a much more limited report instead.[88]

(ii) Judicial

One notoriously ill-starred attempt to extend damages liability to decisions and conduct of public officers was made judicially by the High Court of Australia in *Beaudesert*.[89] In that case, a unanimous bench of Taylor, Menzies and Owen JJ purported to apply tortious liability to ultra vires decisions and conduct (but not to all maladministration as we now define it). The 'Beaudesert tort' thus created provided

> that, independently of trespass, negligence or nuisance but by an action for damages upon the case, a person who suffers harm or loss as the inevitable consequence of the unlawful, intentional and positive acts of another is entitled to recover damages from that other.[90]

The majority in *Mengel* noted that the statement of principle in *Beaudesert* left it inherently ambiguous whether 'unlawful' referred to 'an act forbidden by law or, simply, an unauthorised act in the sense of an act that is *ultra vires* and void'.[91] It concluded that the preferable view was that the High Court in *Beaudesert* had intended to refer to an act *forbidden* by law, rather than one which was merely *invalid*. Accordingly, it did 'not extend to all unlawful acts and that, at least in that regard, it is in need of further definition'.[92]

[84] *Mohammed v Home Office* [2011] 1 WLR 2862, 2869–71; see especially at [23].
[85] *Mohammed v Home Office* [2011] 1 WLR 2862, 2870.
[86] Law Commission, *Administrative Redress: Public Bodies and the Citizen* (n 82) 1 [1.3].
[87] 'This opposition was expressed both in the formal response and in discussions at both ministerial and official level. Government's formal response was a single document agreed across Government. This is extremely unusual, if not unique, in recent times': ibid.
[88] Law Commission, *Public Services Ombudsmen* (Law Com No 329, 2011).
[89] *Beaudesert Shire Council v Smith* (1966) 120 CLR 145.
[90] ibid 156. Their Honours went on to say that 'It may be that a wider proposition could be justified, but the proposition we have stated covers this case'. However, it soon became clear that few were prepared to entertain even their 'narrower' proposition.
[91] *Mengel* (n 72) 336 (Mason CJ, Dawson, Toohey, Gaudron & McHugh JJ). See also M Aronson and H Whitmore, *Public Torts and Contracts* (Law Book Co, 1982) 132–33; G Dworkin and A Harari, 'The *Beaudesert* Decision – Raising the Ghost of the Action upon the Case (Part II)' (1967) 40 *Australian Law Journal* 347, 347.
[92] *Mengel* (n 72) 343.

This it did not get, since the High Court's consideration of this point came in the process of abolishing the 'embryonic' but innominate Beaudesert tort.[93] The Privy Council (guided by Lord Diplock) had by this time already moved swiftly from viewing *Beaudesert* with concern[94] to rejecting it completely.[95] It seems that the Judicial Committee, which in 1982 still heard some Australian appeals, was in no doubt at all about the meaning of 'unlawful' as used in *Beaudesert*.[96] In fact, while it had in general 'been accorded an icy reception' by the academy,[97] *Beaudesert* was never 'beloved of the judiciary' either.[98] Mason J said, fewer than seven years after the decision in *Beaudesert*, that:

> It seems to me that for the plaintiff to succeed in his special action on the case he must show something more than a mere breach of the statute and consequential damage; he must show something over and above what would ground liability for breach of statutory duty if the action were available. As I see the case, he has not succeeded in showing that the act was tortious (and not merely a contravention of the statute), that its inevitable consequence was to cause damage to the plaintiff, or that there was an intention to cause harm to the plaintiff.[99]

Menzies J, who was part of the High Court which handed down *Beaudesert*, joined in approval of Mason J's judgment on appeal 'without criticism or comment'.[100] Although it was not until more than 20 years later that *Mengel* finally did away with *Beaudesert*, it is clear that the writing was on the wall for its eventual demise almost immediately.

This point is reinforced by the fact that, notwithstanding the breadth of its expression, the Beaudesert tort had not been applied before the decision of the Northern Territory Supreme Court in *Mengel*[101] and there is no record of a plaintiff ever having succeeded on this basis.[102] Save for a brief explanation by the High Court,[103] the principle has not been mentioned in an Australian judgment

[93] ibid 343.
[94] *Dunlop v Woollahra Municipal Council* [1982] AC 158, 170–71.
[95] *Lonrho Ltd v Shell Petroleum Co Ltd [No 2]* [1982] AC 173.
[96] GP Barton, 'Damages in Administrative Law' in M Taggart (ed), *Judicial Review of Administrative Action in the 1980s: Problems and Prospects* (Cambridge University Press, 1986) 123, 133.
[97] ibid 132. See, eg G Dworkin and A Harari, 'The *Beaudesert* Decision – Raising the Ghost of the Action upon the Case (Part I)' (1967) 40 *Australian Law Journal* 296; G Dworkin and A Harari, 'The *Beaudesert* Decision – Raising the Ghost of the Action upon the Case (Part II)' (1967) 40 *Australian Law Journal* 347. These articles were 'influential in generating such mistrust of the [*Beaudesert*] decision as to bring into serious question the very existence of the new cause of action': M Aronson and H Whitmore, *Public Torts and Contracts* (1982) 132 (footnote omitted). Phegan cited Dworkin and Harari in support of his statement that the *Beaudesert* principle was 'suspect from its inception': CS Phegan, 'Damages for Improper Exercise of Statutory Powers' (1980) 9 *Sydney Law Review* 93, 119.
[98] C Harlow, *Compensation and Government Torts* (1982) 67.
[99] *Kitano v The Commonwealth* (1973) 129 CLR 151, 174–75.
[100] Barton, 'Damages in Administrative Law' (n 96) 132.
[101] *Northern Territory v Mengel* (1994) 83 LGERA 371. See K Mason, 'The Rule of Law' in PD Finn (ed), *Essays on Law and Government, Volume 1: Principles and Values* (1995) 114, 133–34; *cf Shooter v Commissioner of Irrigation and Water Supply* (1972) 39 QCLLR 11.
[102] Aronson and Whitmore (n 97) 132.
[103] *Sanders v Snell* (1998) 196 CLR 329, 343–44.

since *Mengel*. Instead, it is considered to have been no more than a 'temporary diversion'.[104]

The *Beaudesert* misadventure is one that the courts are reluctant to revisit, with the consequence that, if liability in tort is to be the basis on which loss caused by maladministration is compensated, such liability would need to be legislatively created,[105] although one assumes the appetite for such an approach must also be limited. Any adoption of a principle under which tort liability is connected directly to the validity of decision-making will indicate a fundamental change of direction not only for Australia but for countries with a similar legal heritage, including Canada, New Zealand and the UK, where 'illegality is not a form of "fault"'.[106] Neither *Beaudesert* nor a possible legislative remedy would solve the fundamental problem that courts are not well placed to address issues of poor administration occasioning loss. They tend – understandably, perhaps – to fixate on issues like validity, which are not the point of maladministration.

Rather, it is a broad conception of government accountability that might ground a judicial damages remedy,[107] if anything does. Before that can happen, there are fundamental and justified concerns that must be addressed (or 'nettles' that must be grasped).[108] Some of these

> are pragmatic in nature (for example, claims that there might be overkill and impacts on public resourcing), while others are based in principle (for example, claims that public law damages would produce incoherence in the law and interfere with the separation of powers).[109]

An aversion to providing judicial remedies for maladministration has its origins deep within the DNA of our common law system. Imperfect attempts at reform risk suffering the fate of the Beaudesert tort or the Law Commission's inquiry into administrative redress. If reform comes to the judicial handling of maladministration, it will come slowly.

[104] *Perre v Apand Pty Ltd* (1999) 198 CLR 180, 306 (Hayne J).

[105] Lords Bingham and Carswell each referred specifically to the fact that it is preferable for a legislative solution to fundamental legal issues to be introduced through legislation, informed by a law reform body like the Law Commission, rather than in a judgment on an isolated legal question: *Watkins v Secretary of State for the Home Department* [2006] 2 AC 395, 409 and 425.

[106] PW Hogg, PJ Monahan and WK Wright, *Liability of the Crown* (Carswell, 4th edn, 2011) 206, fn 268. The authors noted that 'liability founded upon illegality is thought of as a species of strict liability'. In *Takaro v Rowling* [1978] 2 NZLR 314, 324, Woodhouse J cited Professor Davis as saying that 'Invalidity is not the test of fault and it should not be the test of liability': KC Davis, *Administrative Law Treatise*, 1st edn (West Publishing Co, 1958) 487. This 'succinct' statement (in Woodhouse J's expression) of the law as it stood in the USA in 1958 and since now looks a little simplistic but remains orthodox. See also Aronson and Whitmore (n 97) 59.

[107] See P Cane, 'Damages in Public Law' (1999) 9 *Otago Law Review* 489, 516.

[108] Fordham (n 80) 108. See also n 74 above.

[109] Rock and Weeks (n 77) 1160.

V. Non-judicial Remedies for Maladministration

There is one highly effective mechanism for receiving a compensatory payment without exploring questions of legal liability. 'Public' ombudsmen 'have the function of reviewing government maladministration without the capacity to provide relief directly to individuals so affected'.[110] While they lack the capacity to provide remedies through the exercise of determinative powers, they have the capacity to recommend relief. If that sounds somewhat underpowered by comparison to the remedial functions available to courts, there are a few points to consider. The first is that ombudsmen are not limited to recommending relief of the sort that lies within judicial competence, a conclusion which seems obvious once it is remembered that ombudsmen have a particular remit to investigate maladministration and that that concept has a broader coverage than illegality, the usual basis for the application of judicial remedies.[111]

The second point about ombudsmen is that they do not generally *want* determinative powers anyway, particularly given the suspicion that 'the exercise of those powers would result in ombudsmen defending numerous judicial review applications at significant cost to their time and budgets'.[112] A more cogent reason is that ombudsmen are masters of persuasion, a status that depends to a significant extent on the fact that they do not usually find themselves as parties to litigation against the government. When an ombudsman asks a government body to do something, history shows that they are likely to get what they want. It is doubtful that ombudsmen would be even a fraction as successful if all they had to use was a power to make binding determinations.

The third point is that the absence of *legal* liability or enforceable *rights* does not indicate the lack of a *moral* claim against government. This, after all, is frequently the point of maladministration: that the government may not have broken any laws but nonetheless bears responsibility for the harm suffered by an individual (for example, because it used its power in a manner that was not available to a private entity in the same position).

To tie these points together, let us consider a leading example of how ombudsmen can be effective in obtaining pecuniary remedies for maladministration: the judicious use of discretionary payment schemes.[113] In particular, it is appropriate to the topic of this chapter to consider a non-statutory scheme for *Compensation*

[110] Weeks (n 1) 25, 32. This point sets them apart from their 'private' or industry namesakes.
[111] Weeks (n 11) 250.
[112] Weeks (n 1) 32.
[113] There are many such schemes, discussed in detail in Boughey et al (n 5) 297–307 (Commonwealth schemes), 313–21 (state and territory schemes) and 321–26 (subject specific schemes). See S Lim, N Ng and G Weeks, 'Government Schemes for Extra-judicial Compensation: An Assessment' (2020) 100 *AIAL Forum* 79.

for Detriment caused by Defective Administration[114] (better known as the CDDA Scheme), administered by the Commonwealth Department of Finance.

The CDDA Guide sets out a few basic propositions for the availability of the scheme: it is a remedial option of last resort (meaning that an applicant must have exhausted all other options available to him or her);[115] claims are decided within individual departments by the minister or another expressly authorised official;[116] the discretion to make a payment is limited to circumstances when 'a person or organisation has suffered detriment as a result of the entity's defective administration [and] … there is no legal requirement to make a payment';[117] and a compensation payment depends on the decision-maker subjectively forming the 'opinion that an official of the entity, acting, or purporting to act, in the course of duty, has directly caused a claimant to suffer detriment, or, conversely, prevented the claimant from avoiding detriment'.[118]

The discretion inherent in the process described above is thrown into relief by the limited options for judicial review of the decision reached. Decisions under the CDDA Scheme are subject to (the usual limited application of) judicial review under section 75(v) of the Australian Constitution and section 39B of the Judiciary Act 1903 (Cth) but not under the Administrative Decisions (Judicial Review) Act 1977 because they are not made 'under an enactment'.[119] However, the Commonwealth Ombudsman is able to review complaints about decisions made in response to CDDA claims[120] and, given the deep connection between that office and the CDDA Scheme, is the right body to do so.

For years since it was first created,[121] the CDDA Scheme was essentially a secret. The fact that it was a secret known to the Commonwealth Ombudsman reinforced the overwhelming likelihood that a successful claimant would need to be backed by that office: for one thing, they would not otherwise know that the Scheme existed and for another, the Ombudsman's recommendation was at one stage more or less

[114] Commonwealth Department of Finance, *Resource Management Guide No 409: Scheme for Compensation for Detriment caused by Defective Administration* (2017) www.finance.gov.au/publications/resource-management-guides/scheme-compensation-detriment-caused-defective-administration-rmg-409 (hereafter CDDA Guide). The scheme's operation is supported by s 61 of the *Constitution*.

[115] CDDA Guide, [20]–[21].

[116] ibid [2] and [7]. The Department of Finance decides claims under the Public Governance, Performance and Accountability Act 2013 (Cth).

[117] CDDA Guide (n 114) [1].

[118] ibid [17].

[119] Administrative Decisions (Judicial Review) Act 1977 (Cth), s 3 (definitions of 'decision to which this Act applies' and 'enactment'); CDDA Guide (n 114) [92]; *Smith v Oakenfull* (2004) 134 FCR 413, 418 (Dowsett J).

[120] CDDA Guide (n 114) [4], [28], [91]–[92].

[121] The CDDA Scheme was originally established by the Commonwealth Department of Finance *Estimates Memorandum* vol 1995/4 (1995) and was subject to further revised iterations in finance circulars in 2001, 2006, 2009 and 2014 prior to its current version.

a *sine qua non* for receiving a payment.[122] Even now, although the Ombudsman cannot compel an agency to make a payment under the CDDA Scheme or reconsider its refusal to do so, when the office makes submissions recommending a CDDA payment, its involvement is hugely influential. Its involvement is not technically 'sufficient', but it remains undeniably significant if for no other reason than that the Commonwealth Ombudsman has an unchallenged level of influence over payments of compensation for losses caused by maladministration.

VI. Conclusion

Maladministration is in many ways a nebulous term, but it is rendered easier to understand by looking at what opposes it. Just as dark can to some extent be defined as the absence of light and, closer to the theme of this chapter, the merits of a decision can be defined as whatever remains after judicial review's remedial capacities have been exhausted, so too can we look at maladministration as the greatest single point of focus for ombudsmen. Addressing maladministration is what ombudsmen do. This chapter has gone further and suggested that judicial and legislative attempts to respond to maladministration lead to either disappointment or disaster – it is simply not a good fit for courts to look at issues of morality (rather than legality) or what amounts to good government. Such a jurisdiction is uniquely suited to the ombudsman.

[122] 'The terms of the [CDDA Scheme] formerly recognised [prior to 2014] that, where the Ombudsman had recommended that a compensation payment be made, that alone was a "sufficient basis for payment" by the agency': G Weeks, *Soft Law and Public Authorities: Remedies and Reform* (Hart Publishing, 2016) 253.

3

The Enforceability of Ombudsman Remedies and Competition with Judicial Review

STEPHEN THOMSON*

I. Introduction

Ombudsmen are a valuable component of the various means available for expressing grievances about public administration and securing administrative justice, complementing other channels such as judicial review, administrative tribunals, inquiries, internal resolution, complaints mechanisms and alternative dispute resolution (ADR). The specific advantage of ombudsmen, particularly when contrasted with more formal resolution processes, is their ability to provide a comparatively accessible, affordable (often free) and expeditious means of expressing grievances against public bodies. In addition, their focus on maladministration means that their purview extends beyond important but limited considerations of legality to those of good (or bad) administrative practice and service delivery. Far less constrained than courts by the separation of powers and legality/merits considerations, ombudsmen can not only provide a less formal channel for dispute settlement that is not purely remedy-driven, but also extend beyond a 'fire-fighting' role to one of 'fire-watching', 'fire-prevention' or even proactive 'fire-lighting'.[1]

Nevertheless, complainants may still choose the ombudsman over other forms of redress with the sole or principal objective of seeking the award of a remedy or corrective outcome. Other channels for obtaining remedies might be avoided for a variety of reasons: they may be too expensive, time-consuming

* I am grateful to the editors and co-contributors for valuable feedback and suggestions on a draft of this chapter. I would also like to thank Frankie Wong for research assistance. All views expressed and any errors are my own. The work in this chapter was partially supported by a grant from City University of Hong Kong (Project No 7200606).

[1] See C Harlow and R Rawlings, *Law and Administration* (Cambridge University Press, 2009) 528–69; A Abraham, 'Making Sense of the Muddle: The Ombudsman and Administrative Justice, 2002–2011' (2012) 34 *Journal of Social Welfare and Family Law* 91.

or difficult to understand; applicable time limits for using other channels might have expired; or other, perhaps insurmountable, barriers may be faced, such as evidentiary or standing rules. Although ombudsmen have a role to play not only in remedial work, such as in 'getting it right' in the first place by providing knowledge and advice to public authorities on good administration,[2] it is on the remedial aspect of ombudswork that this chapter focuses. Ombudsmen clearly perform a different function from courts conducting judicial review, but ombudsmen, courts and other forms of redress sit on a spectrum, with some features in common and overlapping characteristics. There is no categorical or definitional reason why ombudsmen should not be able to award remedies: ombudsmen may be celebrated for their 'beyond legality' or 'beyond remedies' approach, yet some complainants seek remedies via ombudsmen and many complainants might not have complained to ombudsmen in the first place had they not anticipated the possibility of a remedy or corrective outcome.[3] This includes the award of remedies in situations of unlawful conduct by public authorities, for ombudsmen are not prohibited from considering issues of legality when scrutinising public administration. Indeed, in some cases, the maladministration will be primarily or exclusively unlawful in nature.

The question of whether ombudsmen should be capable of awarding binding remedies has long been discussed in ombudsman scholarship. Richard Kirkham noted that it was 'generally agreed upon by the ombudsmen themselves, public authorities and academics … that creating … enforcement powers would be detrimental to the overall ombudsman scheme', but that the 'one constituency that would be most likely to differ in their conclusion would be complainants'.[4] Public authorities might, for example, be 'more likely to employ lawyers in their dealings with the ombudsman … less cooperative in the provision of information, and much less likely to admit areas of fault and explore with the ombudsman alternative solutions'.[5] These are valid points and important considerations. However, this chapter focuses on a narrower but no less relevant question that has received comparatively little attention, namely the potential for overlap and competition between remedies awarded by ombudsmen and remedies awarded via judicial review. This comprises a more legal-systemic viewpoint on the specific ways in which ombudsmen and judicial review remedies might interface, interact and compete.

[2] T Buck, R Kirkham and B Thompson, *The Ombudsman Enterprise and Administrative Justice* (Routledge, 2016) 91.

[3] See G Weeks, *Soft Law and Public Authorities: Remedies and Reform* (Hart Publishing, 2016) 248–51.

[4] R Kirkham, 'Explaining the Lack of Enforcement Power Possessed by the Ombudsman' (2008) 30 *Journal of Social Welfare and Family Law* 253, 253. Greg Weeks has also stated in this volume that 'ombudsmen … do not generally *want* determinative powers anyway': G Weeks, 'Maladministration: The Particular Jurisdiction of the Ombudsman' ch 2 in this volume.

[5] Kirkham (n 4) 260.

The chapter begins with a brief survey of the enforceability of ombudsman remedies, primarily in the UK. It shall be seen that very few ombudsmen have the power to award enforceable remedies, and those that do typically require courts as a medium for enforcement, diminishing the remedial 'power' of the ombudsmen in question. The rationale for declining to invest ombudsmen with remedial power is considered next, as the widespread absence of an enforceable remedial framework reinforces an apparent lack of appetite for a 'hard-edged' model of ombudswork. The chapter then discusses the permissibility of overlap or competition between ombudsman remedies and remedies made available by judicial review. Finally, three models are set out which could be used to functionally differentiate or avoid overlap or competition between ombudsman remedies and judicial review remedies if ombudsmen were to be invested with more enforceable remedial power, namely sequential distinctiveness, jurisdictional distinctiveness and remedial distinctiveness.

It should be noted at the outset that this chapter is not a call for the investment of directly enforceable remedial power in ombudsmen. Rather, the chapter is an offering of new perspectives that may be used to further consider how remedial aspects of ombudswork and judicial review might interface and interrelate. This may be of particular interest to policymakers and stakeholders involved in institutional design. It envisages (though does not necessarily advocate) a potential refashioning of the ombudsman institution rather than a reworking of the courts and the judicial function – in other words, a 'remedialisation' of ombudswork rather than a 'de-remedialisation' of judicial work. Indeed, this author has argued for the maintenance of categorical and functional distinction between courts and ombudsmen, and that 'ombudsmen are not, and should not be, courts of law'.[6] In addition, the chapter is not directly concerned with the distinct issue of ombudsmen and their findings and determinations being themselves subject to judicial review, which has been addressed elsewhere.[7]

II. A Brief Survey of the Enforceability of Ombudsman Remedies

Ombudsmen rarely have the power to award directly enforceable remedies. There are some limited exceptions, particularly in Africa. The Supreme Court of South Africa held that the Public Protector was entitled to take remedial action

[6] S Thomson, 'Ombudsmen as Courts' (2022) 42 *OJLS* (forthcoming) (advance article available at DOI: https://doi.org/10.1093/ojls/gqaa056).

[7] See, eg J Varuhas, 'Governmental Rejections of Ombudsman Findings: What Role for the Courts?' (2009) 72 *MLR* 102; P Birkinshaw, 'Grievances, Remedies and the State – Revisited and Re-appraised' in M Adler (ed), *Administrative Justice in Context* (Hart Publishing, 2010) 361–63; R Kirkham, 'Implementing the Recommendations of an Ombudsman … Again' (2011) 33 *Journal of Social Welfare and Family Law* L 71; and Buck et al (n 2) ch 6.

in her own right,[8] while in Zambia the Public Protector is given a statutory power to enforce its own recommendations.[9] Recommendations of the Kenyan Commission on Administrative Justice were recently held by the Court of Appeal of Kenya to have the force of law.[10] Yet some of the African ombudsmen are said to have moved 'far away … from the original concept of the institution',[11] and are the exception rather than the rule.

Elsewhere, it is the rule rather than the exception that prevails: ombudsmen typically have no powers to directly enforce their own determinations and recommendations. The blueprint of remedial ombudswork is the production of a report by the ombudsman following a private and comparatively informal process of investigation. Typically, that report is then sent to the body complained of and/or put in the public domain, potentially including recommendations on the award of remedies or a specified outcome in or beyond the instant case. It will usually then be for the body complained of to decide whether or not to award any remedies in line with the ombudsman's recommendations. There are some examples of ombudsmen whose findings have been judicially held to be effectively (but not actually) binding, as in *R v Local Commissioner for Administration, ex p Eastleigh BC*[12] and *R (Bradley) v Secretary of State for Work and Pensions*.[13] However, the effect of these cases is sometimes overstated; the former considered the specific interpretation of an authority's duties under the Local Government Act 1974[14] and the latter an extension of that interpretation to the Parliamentary Commissioner Act 1967.[15] Failure by investigated authorities to implement ombudsman recommendations can, of course, be tested for lawfulness on the standard grounds of judicial review,[16] such as for breach of a legitimate expectation, failure to take into account a relevant consideration or unreasonableness. However, these cases do not extend to a more general principle, such as that ombudsman findings are actually binding and directly enforceable in and of themselves, nor do they encompass recommendations.

[8] *The South African Broadcasting Corporation Ltd v Democratic Alliance*, Case No 393/2015, 8 October 2015, para 53.

[9] The Public Protector Act 2016 (No 15 of 2016) (Zambia), s 19.

[10] *Commission on Administrative Justice v Kenya Vision 2030 Delivery Board*, Civil Appeal No 141 of 2015 (judgment dated 27 September 2019).

[11] VO Ayeni, 'Fifty Years of the Ombudsman in Africa' in M Hertogh and R Kirkham (eds), *Research Handbook on the Ombudsman* (Edward Elgar, 2018) 228.

[12] [1988] QB 855.

[13] [2007] EWHC 242 (Admin), [2007] Pens LR 87 [58].

[14] *R v Local Commissioner for Administration, ex p Eastleigh BC* [1988] QB 855, 867, citing the Local Government Act 1974, ss 30–31.

[15] *R (Bradley) v Secretary of State for Work and Pensions* [2007] EWHC 242 (Admin), [2007] Pens LR 87 [51] and [58]. See further Varuhas (n 7); B Yeom, 'The Legality of Walking Away from Public Service Ombudsman Reports: The United Kingdom's Experience' (2017) 43 *Monash University Law Review* 386.

[16] Kirkham (n 7) 77.

Perhaps the ombudsmen that come closest in the common law world (but certainly in the UK) to being able to award directly enforceable remedies are the Pensions Ombudsman (PO) and the Financial Ombudsman Service (FOS). It should be noted at the outset that these are private sector ombudsmen rather than public sector (and therefore archetypal) ombudsmen.[17] While public sector ombudsmen receive complaints against public bodies or bodies delivering public services, private sector ombudsmen receive complaints (often, but not exclusively, from consumers) against private sector entities such as banks, pensions providers and legal services providers. The PO is unusually 'judicial' in character, and objected vigorously in a factsheet[18] and an unrelated dispute[19] to the characterisation of its determinations by the Chancery Division as not being 'an order of a competent court' for the purposes of the equitable right of recoupment because the PO is not a court.[20] It is clear that the PO is not a court of law, however much it might insist otherwise.[21]

However, of specific relevance to the current discussion is that the PO's power to issue 'final and binding' determinations relates more to the issues of res judicata and issue estoppel and less to remedial finality and enforceability. The PO can essentially award remedies, but this is challengeable in the courts both by way of appeal[22] and by judicial review. Moreover, the PO has no power to enforce its own remedies. Although it is provided that PO determinations or directions shall be enforceable in the county court (in England and Wales) or by the sheriff (in Scotland), as if they were a judgment or order thereof,[23] and that where (in England and Wales) the PO directs the payment of money or the taking or refraining from taking of any step, the County Court Rules 1981 concerning the enforcement of judgments and the payment of judgment debts shall apply to the direction as if it were a county court judgment or order,[24] the PO is still dependent on a court of law for the enforceability of its determinations. PO remedies are therefore not enforceable in the manner of court judgments and do not directly compete in that regard with judicial remedies.[25]

The FOS, meanwhile, is only capable of making final and binding determinations (and thus 'awarding remedies') if the complainant notifies the FOS that he

[17] See also R Kirkham and A Stuhmcke, 'The Common Law Theory and Practice of the Ombudsman/Judiciary Relationship' (2020) 49 *Common Law World Review* 56, 60.

[18] The Pensions Ombudsman, 'Recoupment in Overpayment Cases: The Pensions Ombudsman is a "Competent Court"' (April 2019) www.pensions-ombudsman.org.uk/sites/default/files/publication/files/Recoupment-in-Overpayment-case-.pdf.

[19] PO-16856 (*Dr E*) (25 October 2018).

[20] *Burgess v BIC UK Ltd* [2018] EWHC 785 (Ch), para 168.

[21] Thomson (n 6).

[22] Pension Schemes Act 1993, s 151(4).

[23] Pension Schemes Act 1993, s 151(5).

[24] County Court (Pensions Ombudsman) (Enforcement of Directions and Determinations) Rules 1993, SI 1993/1978.

[25] The PO and the FOS, and their relationship with courts and remedies, are discussed in detail in Thomson (n 6).

accepts the determination,[26] which reduces the analogy with judicial remedies, which do not depend on party consent. Separately, the Secretary of State may make an order by way of statutory instrument authorising a housing ombudsman under an approved scheme to apply to a court or tribunal for an order that a determination made by the ombudsman may be enforced as if it were an order of a court,[27] and any determination or direction of the Ombudsman for the Board of the Pension Protection Fund is enforceable in a county court as if it were a judgment or order of that court (in England and Wales), or as an extract registered decree arbitral bearing a warrant for execution issued by a sheriff court (in Scotland).[28] However, in each case, the enforceability of the remedy is to a greater or lesser extent reliant on enforcement by a court of law – in other words, by a categorically distinct institution – and accordingly such 'remedies' are capable of clear differentiation from judicial remedies.

Of the UK public sector ombudsmen, the Northern Ireland Public Services Ombudsman (NIPSO) comes closest to the power to award enforceable remedies. An aggrieved person whom the NIPSO has reported to have sustained an injustice may apply to the county court for damages and/or an order directing the listed authority[29] to take or refrain from taking a particular action.[30] It is expressly provided that disobedience to that order by the authority or any member or officer of the authority may be treated as contempt of court to which Article 55 of the County Courts (Northern Ireland) Order 1980 applies.[31] It is further provided that where there is a finding by the NIPSO of systemic maladministration in a listed authority or where systemic injustice has been sustained as a result of the exercise of professional judgement, the Attorney General for Northern Ireland may, at the request of the NIPSO, apply to the High Court for injunction, declaration or other relief.[32] When the court is deciding whether there has been systemic maladministration or systemic injustice, it may take into account not only the matters investigated by the NIPSO, but also any other matters which appear to the court to be relevant.[33]

There does not appear to have been any litigation to date in which the court has made such a determination,[34] but this raises an interesting area of overlap between the function of the ombudsman and the function of the court. The proper forum for investigating complaints by persons aggrieved against listed

[26] Financial Services and Markets Act 2000, s 228(5).
[27] Housing Act 1996, sch 2, para 7D.
[28] Pensions Act 2004, s 217(2).
[29] Listed authorities are enumerated in sch 3 to the Act and cover a range of bodies, including local government, education, policing, arts, health, housing and charitable bodies. The Office of the First Minister and the Deputy First Minister may by order amend sch 3 by adding or omitting an authority or altering its description: Public Services Ombudsman Act (Northern Ireland) 2016, s 12(2).
[30] Public Services Ombudsman Act (Northern Ireland) 2016, ss 52–53.
[31] Public Services Ombudsman Act (Northern Ireland) 2016, s 53(5).
[32] Public Services Ombudsman Act (Northern Ireland) 2016, ss 54–55.
[33] Public Services Ombudsman Act (Northern Ireland) 2016, s 55(4).
[34] See also Buck (n 2) fn 75.

authorities is the NIPSO,[35] and the reporting procedure is fairly standard for ombudsmen, including the sending of the investigation report to the aggrieved person and the investigated listed authority,[36] the power to publish an investigation report in the public interest[37] and, where an injustice sustained by an aggrieved person has not been, or will not be, remedied or adequately remedied, the power to lay an investigation report before the legislature (in this case, the Northern Ireland Assembly).[38] The NIPSO does not have a directly enforceable power per se in relation to its investigation reports, yet an aggrieved person has a statutory power, on the back of the NIPSO's investigation report, to obtain damages or injunctive remedies, thus giving the court the power to decide whether and to what extent the NIPSO's findings should have legal consequences. Furthermore, the Attorney General for Northern Ireland may, at the request of the NIPSO, apply to the court for injunction, declaration or other relief in cases of systemic maladministration or systemic injustice, but the court has an express statutory power to consider any relevant materials above and beyond the matters investigated by the NIPSO.

The findings of the NIPSO may therefore serve as the basis for the award of judicial remedies, whether in favour of the aggrieved person or against the listed authority, but is there any overlap in the remedies offered by the NIPSO and the courts? Strictly speaking, the answer would be negative, considering that the NIPSO has no directly enforceable power per se in relation to its investigation reports. Yet the possibility exists for a finding or recommendation of the NIPSO to be fully or partly implemented or acted upon by a listed authority, only for this to be followed by one or more judicial remedies in relation to the same finding or recommendation. The overall structure appears to be one that is graduated, beginning with a 'soft' approach at the NIPSO stage, before hardening into a more 'legal' approach at the judicial stage. It should, however, be noted that the vesting of these indirect enforcement powers was specific to the politically sensitive context in Northern Ireland,[39] thus the NIPSO might not serve as an appropriate comparator for ombudsmen in other jurisdictions.

III. The Rationale for Declining to Invest Ombudsmen with Enforceable Remedial Power

In an administrative law context, different avenues of redress tend not to afford the same remedies. However, this is not always the case. For example, an

[35] Public Services Ombudsman Act (Northern Ireland) 2016, s 5.
[36] Public Services Ombudsman Act (Northern Ireland) 2016, s 43.
[37] Public Services Ombudsman Act (Northern Ireland) 2016, s 44.
[38] Public Services Ombudsman Act (Northern Ireland) 2016, s 46.
[39] See R Kirkham, 'Explaining the Lack of Enforcement Power Possessed by the Ombudsman' (2008) 30 *Journal of Social Welfare and Family Law* 253, 259.

administrative tribunal may have a statutory power to direct a decision-maker to retake a decision,[40] while a court has the power to direct a decision-maker to retake a decision using an injunctive or mandatory remedy. This does not necessarily lead to an unacceptable competition between administrative tribunals and courts as avenues of redress, as there is an established legal protocol on the sequencing of redress: in this case, a person is typically required to use a statutory appeal mechanism (including to an administrative tribunal) prior to attempting judicial review.[41] Thus, even though there is remedial overlap between an administrative tribunal and judicial review in this example, they are not directly competing avenues of redress inasmuch as the aggrieved person does not enjoy a general choice between the two avenues of redress: ordinarily, he or she must utilise the administrative tribunal before judicial review can be contemplated.[42] Furthermore – though this will vary with the statutory power of the individual tribunal – the administrative tribunal will often have no power to enforce its own remedy, meaning that the courts become the default avenue of last resort for enforcement, regardless of the remedial avenue initially selected.

It has sometimes been suggested that ombudsman remedies should be enforceable rather than merely advisory, typically as a response to the perception that ombudsmen are 'toothless tigers'[43] or 'ombudsmice'.[44] Disadvantages to making ombudsman remedies enforceable include the potential for a significant 'legalisation' or 'lawyerisation' of the ombudsman process and institution, and its dealings with both complainants and investigated public authorities. The latter may and probably would adopt a more defensive and less cooperative stance in relation to the ombudsman, being less likely to admit fault or to explore alternative means of resolution.[45] The investigation process would likely have to be formalised, with hearings, formal submissions, disclosures and opportunities for rebuttal and cross-examination more likely to feature and be accompanied by significant time, cost and resource implications, including the possibility of having to allow legal representation. The principle of open justice may require that ombudsman processes are opened up to public view and made sufficiently transparent.[46] This may undermine and even frustrate some of the advantages of the ombudsman as a distinct channel for expressing grievances, including accessibility, informality, relative speed and inexpensiveness (or even being free to complainants). If the ombudsman process begins to assume the costs, time and complexity of litigation, its specific value as an institution will become less clear and its

[40] In some cases, administrative tribunals have the power to make a new decision.

[41] *R v Inland Revenue Commissioners, ex p Preston* [1985] AC 835 (HL), 852.

[42] *R v Chief Constable of the Merseyside Police, ex p Calveley* [1986] QB 424; *R v Secretary of State for the Home Department, ex p Swati* [1986] 1 WLR 477, 485C–D.

[43] A. Stuhmcke, 'The Ombudsman' in M Groves (ed), *Modern Administrative Law in Australia: Concepts and Context* (Cambridge University Press, 2014) 335.

[44] WB Gwyn, 'The British PCA: "Ombudsman or Ombudsmouse?"' (1973) 35 *Journal of Politics* 45.

[45] Kirkham (n 39) 260.

[46] *Kennedy v Charity Commission* [2014] UKSC 20, [2015] AC 455.

offering less attractive to potential complainants. It has also been argued that investing ombudsmen with determinative powers may be counterproductive.[47]

Moreover, aspects of existing ombudsman powers and processes may have to be modified or even removed if ombudsmen were given the power to award remedies. For example, some ombudsmen have the power to initiate their own investigations, without being in receipt of a complaint in relation to the subject matter of the proposed investigation.[48] In this regard, it would

> have to be considered whether it is appropriate for the Ombudsman to have the power to conduct direct investigations, as potential complainants could be prejudiced by the conduct of a direct investigation, noting that a remedy could have resulted had the investigation been initiated by submission of a complaint. Conversely, if potential complainants could rely on a direct investigation to support the award of a remedy, the Ombudsman would have to tread very carefully before launching a direct investigation, as this could open the floodgates and instigate a tide of claims against an organisation.[49]

Other unexpected consequences may arise: if the ombudsman has the power to award remedies, thus introducing a quasi-judicial element to the ombudsman's work, can the ombudsman continue (as is the case for many ombudsmen) to be appointed by the executive[50] or the legislative[51] branch? Would the ombudsman effectively be implanted in the judicial branch?[52] Must not an ombudsman with any quasi-judicial function be given some of the appointment, tenure and independence protections enjoyed by judges? And might not the obligations of ombudsmen be vastly altered – can an inquisitorial mode of proceeding continue to be justified if the ombudsman can award remedies? Could ombudsmen continue to have the close and cooperative relationship with public authorities that they often

[47] M. Groves, 'Ombudsmen's Jurisdiction in Prisons' (2002) 28 *Monash University Law Review* 181, 202.

[48] Though own-motion investigations are sometimes launched after the receipt of a number of similar, individual complaints, indicating a wider systemic problem which the ombudsman then seeks to investigate.

[49] S Thomson, *Administrative Law in Hong Kong* (Cambridge University Press, 2018) 329.

[50] For example, the Local Government and Social Care Ombudsman is appointed by Her Majesty on the recommendation of the Secretary of State (Local Government Act 1974, s 23(4)) and the Housing Ombudsman is appointed by the Secretary of State (Housing Ombudsman Scheme, r 59).

[51] For example, the Parliamentary Commissioner for Administration and the Health Service Commissioner (who are the same individual) are appointed by Her Majesty by Letters Patent upon approval by the House of Commons (House of Commons, Public Administration Select Committee, *Pre-appointment hearing for the post of Parliamentary and Health Service Ombudsman* (HC 2010–12, 1220-I) 16) and the Scottish Public Services Ombudsman is appointed by Her Majesty on the nomination of the Scottish Parliament (Scottish Public Services Ombudsman Act 2002, s 1(1)).

[52] It has been argued that the 'outcomes or remedies applicants are seeking through an Ombudsman are political rather than judicial': Yeom (n 15) 417. However, Richard Kirkham and Anita Stuhmcke set out four models of constitutional integration for the ombudsman, namely the small-claims court model, the political model, the supervisory model and the integrity model, which could point to a range of remedial conceptualisations of the ombudsman: Kirkham and Stuhmcke (n 17) 61–62. The 'primary role' of the ombudsman has still been described as one of adjudication: Kirkham and Stuhmcke (n 17) 59.

enjoy without facing a charge of partiality? Similarly, could a continued role for the ombudsman as a quasi-advocate for complainants be justified? Should appeal mechanisms be set up to allow aggrieved parties to challenge the ombudsman's award of (or refusal to award) remedies?[53]

The investment in ombudsmen of a power to award remedies would be potentially transformative, raising many and varied complexities. In order to preserve the utility of the ombudsman as a distinct institution, these issues would have to be navigated very carefully before proceeding with such a reform. Nevertheless, if there was support for a reform of this nature, questions would arise as to the relationship between remedies made available by the ombudsman and remedies made available by judicial review.[54] How should they be distinguished? Would this result in a functional sharing of jurisdiction, or a competition between their respective powers and jurisdictions? How could the potential for duplication of workload be minimised or removed? How would the unique utility of each process and/or institution be protected?

IV. Permissibility of Overlap or Competition between Ombudsman Remedies and Judicial Review Remedies

If ombudsmen were capable of offering remedies that were equivalent to remedies available in judicial review, would this really be intolerable or undesirable? The potential for forum shopping already exists in relation to judicial remedies. For example, it was considered that judicial review proceedings could more easily be brought in England than in Scotland in relation to a UK matter that could competently be challenged in either jurisdiction, on the basis of comparatively more liberal rules on standing in England.[55] However, forum shopping on a jurisdictional basis raises different issues from forum shopping on an institutional basis within a single jurisdiction. If ombudsmen and courts offered effectively equivalent remedies, the ombudsman may be preferable for a wide variety of reasons, such as being cheaper (and typically free of charge[56]); being more user-friendly and easier to understand; not requiring the instruction of legal representatives; being less confrontational, less stressful and less risky (from the perspective of losing in court and potentially being subject to an order for costs); typically allowing more

[53] Kirkham and Stuhmcke (n 17) 63.

[54] This proceeds on the assumption that courts and judicial review are not substantially reformed so as to make their work more ombuds-like.

[55] See S Thomson, 'The Influence of English Judicial Review on Scots Judicial Review' in S Jhaveri and M Ramsden (eds), *Judicial Review of Administrative Action Across the Common Law World: Origins and Adaptation* (Cambridge University Press, 2021) 81.

[56] It is now provided in the Venice Principles that any individual or legal person shall have the right to free, unhindered and free-of-charge access to the ombudsman, and to file a complaint: European Commission for Democracy Through Law (Venice Commission), *Principles on the Protection and Promotion of the Ombudsman Institution ('The Venice Principles')*, adopted on 15–16 March 2019.

privacy for the complainant; having longer time limits within which to lodge a complaint; having lower evidentiary requirements and no formal proof thresholds; and potentially (but not necessarily) being quicker.

Trevor Buck, Richard Kirkham and Brian Thompson were of the view that the ombudsman's lack of enforcement powers 'rarely leads to any disadvantage for the complainant, as for most ombudsman schemes virtually all recommendations are implemented'.[57] It is true that the ombudsman's investigation process may well have to be lengthened and formalised should it be made able to offer remedies equivalent to those awarded in a judicial process, and the investigation process may have to incorporate quasi-judicial elements, such as by holding hearings and providing opportunities for legal representation. These would likely bring concomitant time and resource costs, including the potential for reduced access to justice. However, this depends, inter alia, on what remedies the ombudsman is able to offer. If a court was empowered to award 'softer' remedies, such as forcing a public authority to issue an apology, and this remedial power was shared with an ombudsman, the ombudsman investigation process need not incur much, if any, lengthening or formalisation.

Nevertheless, if ombudsmen and courts offered effectively equivalent remedies, the courts might retain advantages over the ombudsman as the preferred avenue of redress. The courts may be said to have less discretion than the ombudsman over whether to accept the complaint at the outset (subject to the requirements of a leave or permission stage in judicial review).[58] Courts also have universal jurisdiction over justiciable subject matter, whereas ombudsman jurisdiction tends to be restricted to specific spheres or lists of bodies. Courts offer a definitive statement of the law and the creation and application of precedents. There is less scope for delay or prevarication on the part of a public authority in litigation than in response to an ombudsman complaint. There is also less scope in litigation than in an ombudsman complaint for the remedy made available by a public authority to differ considerably from the remedy recommended or ordered.[59] The courts might also be seen as a more hard-nosed and aggressive form of challenge, which might be viewed by some aggrieved persons as preferable from the perspective of hoping to push the public authority into settling or resolving the matter out of fear of losing in court, or for reputational reasons; the ombudsman, by contrast, might be viewed as a softer option of which the public authority is not really afraid. Yet there will be aggrieved persons who do not favour a confrontational approach and prefer to use the ombudsman over litigation specifically for that reason.

The idea of proportionate dispute resolution (PDR)[60] also calls into question whether ombudsmen should have enforceable remedies. A substantial number

[57] Buck et al (n 2) 110. This does not, however, tell us how ambitious or otherwise those recommendations are. If most recommendations are fairly unambitious or uncontentious, they are more likely to be accepted and implemented by the relevant public authorities.

[58] In England, see Civil Procedure Rules (CPR), r 54.4.

[59] Buck et al (n 2) 110.

[60] See M Adler, 'The Idea of Proportionality in Dispute Resolution' (2008) 30 *Journal of Social Welfare and Family Law* 309.

(but by no means all) of the complaints submitted to ombudsmen, even those that lead to successful outcomes, relate to what might be considered comparatively minor matters relative to those featured in litigation. That is not at all to downplay the importance or consequential nature of those matters to individual complainants, nor the role that the ombudsman has to play more broadly in the administrative justice system. It is simply to point out that many ombudsman complaints would likely be struck out by a court for raising issues or grievances considered too minor or academic to proceed to a full trial.[61] The ability of ombudsmen to award enforceable remedies in relation to such issues, considering the likely imperative for an increase in formality and procedural rigour in the ombudsman process that such an innovation would require, may lead to a substantial number of cases in which the resources consumed are disproportionate to the nature and gravity of the complaint. Ombudsmen may therefore need to turn away such cases at a preliminary stage. The investment in ombudsmen of the power to award enforceable remedies might therefore be incompatible with the principle of PDR, at least in some cases. Yet this will be shaped by the remedies on offer and the extent to which the investigation process is lengthened and formalised.

V. Functional Differentiation between Ombudsman Remedies and Judicial Review Remedies

Moving beyond the more generic disadvantages of investing ombudsmen with the power to award enforceable remedies, what additional challenges might be faced in the overlap and competition between ombudsman remedies and judicial review remedies? At present, ombudsmen are often statutorily restrained from investigating matters that could or should have been brought by way of court or tribunal proceedings. For example, the Parliamentary Commissioner Act 1967 provides that:

> (2) Except as hereinafter provided, the Commissioner shall not conduct an investigation under this Act in respect of any of the following matters, that is to say –
>
> (a) any action in respect of which the person aggrieved has or had a right of appeal, reference or review to or before a tribunal constituted by or under any enactment or by virtue of Her Majesty's prerogative;
>
> (b) any action in respect of which the person aggrieved has or had a remedy by way of proceedings in any court of law:

[61] It must nevertheless be acknowledged, as noted by Neil Duxbury, that the decisions of public bodies can be susceptible to judicial review 'even when they affect hardly anyone': N Duxbury, 'The Outer Limits of English Judicial Review' [2017] *PL* 235, 240.

> Provided that the Commissioner may conduct an investigation notwithstanding that the person aggrieved has or had such a right or remedy if satisfied that in the particular circumstances it is not reasonable to expect him to resort or have resorted to it.[62]

Similarly, the more recent Public Services Ombudsman (Wales) Act 2019 provides that:

> (1) The Ombudsman may not investigate a matter under section 3 if the person aggrieved has or had –
>
> (a) a right of appeal, reference or review to or before a tribunal constituted under an enactment or by virtue of Her Majesty's prerogative,
>
> (b) a right of appeal to a Minister of the Crown, the Welsh Ministers, the First Minister for Wales or the Counsel General to the Welsh Government, or
>
> (c) a remedy by way of proceedings in a court of law.
>
> (2) But subsection (1) does not apply if the Ombudsman is satisfied that, in the particular circumstances, it is not reasonable to expect the person to resort, or to have resorted, to the right or remedy.[63]

Noting that courts typically expect persons to utilise rights of appeal, including to tribunals, before attempting judicial review, this envisages the following prioritisation of remedial channels: (i) appeal mechanisms, (ii) court proceedings, (iii) ombudsmen. In this sense, ombudsmen are the least prioritised as they are envisaged by the legislative framework as the most residual in nature.[64] This order or sequencing of remedial channels could easily enough be changed by legislative reform, though it may be noted that such a prioritisation would not necessarily have to be changed should ombudsman remedies be made enforceable in a manner whereby they might overlap or compete with remedies made available by judicial review. Indeed, remedial overlap or competition may be affected by rules on remedial prioritisation, but overlap and competition can remain whether or not remedial channels are prioritised in this manner. It is therefore possible to invest ombudsmen with the power to award enforceable remedies, but to retain a distinctiveness in the ombudsman institution by requiring complainants to first utilise appeal mechanisms (where available), then court proceedings (where appropriate), before contemplating bringing their grievance to the ombudsman. Remedial overlap or equivalence does not require a collapsing of rules on remedial prioritisation or sequencing.

Nevertheless, one of the main questions will be the extent to which the ombudsman offers something distinctive as a remedial mechanism where it is capable of awarding remedies that potentially overlap or compete with remedies made available by judicial review. There are various ways in which that distinctiveness could manifest, though each raises its own questions and issues. The three models of

[62] Parliamentary Commissioner Act 1967, s 5.

[63] Public Services Ombudsman (Wales) Act 2019, s 13.

[64] Though ombudsmen might be considered a form of alternative dispute resolution (ADR) that should be attempted before litigation: see n 66.

distinctiveness proposed in this chapter are sequential distinctiveness, jurisdictional distinctiveness and remedial distinctiveness.

A. Sequential Distinctiveness: Primary Claims and Residual Claims

One possibility is for the ombudsman to serve as a channel for residual claims that were not successfully vindicated through either an appeal mechanism or court proceedings. This could be due to a multitude of different reasons, including a failure to comply with or inability to meet time limits;[65] an inability to satisfy evidentiary burdens and proof thresholds; an inability to fulfil standing criteria; and cost barriers, including a failure to secure legal aid. In these circumstances, a complainant could quite legitimately come before the ombudsman (as at present) and seek remedies, though clearly the ombudsman could not be so attractive – such as being significantly faster, cheaper or more accessible, while offering similar remedies to those made available by judicial review – that an applicant can effectively elect to 'skip' appeal mechanisms and court proceedings and complain in the first instance to the ombudsman. Rules on remedial prioritisation or sequencing could play an important role here in ensuring the ombudsman does not become the remedial avenue of first resort.

Another reason for failure to successfully vindicate a claim using either an appeal mechanism or court proceedings is failure on the merits. However, this raises difficult issues relating to res judicata. In particular, if a claim failed on its merits before a court, it would be difficult for an ombudsman to be able to investigate the complaint with the potential to award remedies without confounding the nature of the ombudsman's work and the rules on res judicata. An ombudsman could not feasibly be invested with the actual or effective power to question or reopen judicial findings and determinations. It would also be a matter of great sensitivity were an ombudsman to be given the power to investigate a claim that had been the subject of court proceedings by accepting all of the court's findings and determinations and then using the subsequent investigation to delve into matters that were not ventilated in the court proceedings or which add to matters that were ventilated. This approach could well give rise to additional material that could call into question the correctness of the court's decision and would carry substantial risks for the sanctity of judicial proceedings.

[65] For example, it is provided by s 6(3) of the Parliamentary Commissioner Act 1967 that 'A complaint shall not be entertained under this Act unless it is made to a member of the House of Commons not later than twelve months from the day on which the person aggrieved first had notice of the matters alleged in the complaint' (though this may be extended, as provided for in the section); in contrast, an applicant for judicial review must file their claim form 'promptly and in any event not later than 3 months after the grounds to make the claim first arose' (CPR 54.5(1)). A person may therefore be out of time to apply for judicial review but within time to complain to the ombudsman.

The investment in ombudsmen of a power to award enforceable remedies would therefore likely be most sustainable by preserving rules on remedial prioritisation or sequencing, and perhaps having a general bar on ombudsmen investigating claims that failed on their merits in a court (unless the matters raised before the ombudsman are sufficiently distinct from the matters raised in court). If the rules on remedial prioritisation or sequencing were relaxed, or the ombudsman was empowered to award remedies in relation to cases that failed on their merits in court proceedings, ombudsmen could not feasibly be invested with the power to award enforceable remedies without the risk of causing substantial harm to the operation of existing institutions or a wholesale refashioning of the nature of the ombudsman's work and process.

It is conceivable that ombudsmen deal not with residual claims that could have been but were not successfully vindicated in the courts, but with primary claims that have for good reason not been taken to the courts. In other words, rather than court proceedings being prioritised over ombudsman complaints, ombudsman complaints could be prioritised over court proceedings, thus rendering courts the remedial channel for dealing with residual claims. This is in principle not as radical as it first appears, as courts already deal to a greater or lesser extent with residual claims that could have or should have been vindicated through appeal mechanisms, including via administrative tribunals. While it may make little sense to prioritise ombudsman complaints over court proceedings where ombudsmen cannot award remedies, it could make more sense where ombudsmen were empowered to award remedies. Ombudsmen could be viewed as a form of ADR that courts generally expect applicants to have attempted before resorting to judicial review – indeed, there is already a practice direction to that effect.[66] In fact, the rendering of ombudsman complaints as the primary rather than residual form of claim may encounter fewer procedural and jurisdictional difficulties than if ombudsman complaints deal with residual claims that could have or should have been vindicated through court proceedings, including diminished risks for res judicata and the sanctity of judicial proceedings.

B. Jurisdictional Distinctiveness: Lawful Maladministration versus Unlawful Maladministration

A possible way of making ombudsman remedies enforceable while avoiding or minimising overlap or competition with judicial remedies is to segregate instances of lawful maladministration from unlawful maladministration.

[66] Para 8 of the Practice Direction on Pre-Action Conduct and Protocols states that 'Litigation should be a last resort' and that 'the parties should consider whether negotiation or some other form of ADR might enable them to settle their dispute without commencing proceedings', before including 'Ombudsmen schemes' among the forms of ADR enumerated in para 10 thereof.

Maladministration is not and should not be technically defined, lest specific instances of bad administrative practice should occur that do not fall within an existing formulaic definition.[67] A broad array of examples of maladministration have been given. The 'Crossman catalogue' referred to bias, neglect, inattention, delay, incompetence, inaptitude, perversity, turpitude and arbitrariness.[68] The Annual Report for 1993 issued by the UK Parliamentary Commissioner for Administration gave a number of other examples of maladministration:[69]

- Rudeness (though this is a matter of degree)
- Unwillingness to treat the complainant as a person with rights
- Refusal to answer reasonable questions
- Neglecting to inform a complainant on request of his or her rights or entitlements
- Knowingly giving advice which is misleading or inadequate
- Ignoring valid advice or overruling considerations which would produce an uncomfortable result for the overruler
- Offering no redress or manifestly disproportionate redress
- Showing bias, whether because of colour, sex or any other grounds
- Omissions to notify those who thereby lose a right of appeal
- Refusal to inform adequately of the right to appeal
- Faulty procedures
- Failure by management to monitor compliance with adequate procedures
- Cavalier disregard of guidance which is intended to be followed in the interest of equitable treatment to those who use a service
- Partiality
- Failure to mitigate the effects of rigid adherence to the letter of the law where that produces manifestly inequitable treatment.

Additional examples might include:[70]

- Inconsistency
- Dishonesty
- Failure to assign one or more specific members of staff to an enquirer/person subject to a decision throughout the life cycle of the enquiry/decision-making process
- Failure to be capable of contact through more than one channel of communication (post, telephone, email, instant messaging service, etc)

[67] See Weeks (n 4).
[68] HC Deb 18 October 1966, vol 734, col 51.
[69] Parliamentary Commissioner for Administration, *Annual Report for 1993* (HC 290, 1993–94).
[70] Thomson (n 49) 322.

- Long waiting times in telephone queues
- Unreasonably expensive cost to contact organisation by telephone
- Burying contact information in difficult-to-access areas of a website
- Broken links, out-of-date information and other inadequacies on the organisation's website
- Failure to comply with published targets, including targets relating to response times and the time within which a decision shall be made
- Use of inappropriately technical or specialist language in communications
- Routinely responding with standard form responses rather than directly engaging with the substance of enquiries
- Adoption of unreasonable policies (whether or not unreasonable in the *Wednesbury* sense)
- Lack of proportionality
- Inflexibility beyond that required to meet legal obligations
- Obstinacy or unhelpfulness.

These examples of maladministration cover a broad array of administrative behaviour but, importantly, they include both lawful and unlawful conduct. Maladministration is necessarily broader than unlawful conduct,[71] though many instances of unlawful conduct would also comprise maladministration. Lawful maladministration – for example, inefficiency, failure to answer customer queries or poor staff attitude – could not be litigated as, of course, judicial review is bound to fail if no unlawfulness is established or even alleged. Meanwhile, unlawful maladministration – for example, bias, fettering of discretion or breach of a legitimate expectation – could be litigated by reason of their unlawfulness. The ombudsman, which typically has jurisdiction over both lawful and unlawful instances of maladministration,[72] could therefore be invested with the power to award enforceable remedies in cases of lawful maladministration, but not in cases of unlawful maladministration, to avoid competing with or duplicating the work of the courts. In this way, the remedial work of ombudsmen and courts could be distinguished without creating an area of direct remedial overlap.

However, this could raise more questions than it answers and cause more problems than it solves. First, how are lawful maladministration and unlawful maladministration to be segregated? A case might involve maladministration of which one aspect is putatively lawful and another aspect is putatively unlawful, yet they might not be easily or feasibly separated. This may lead to significant uncertainty about how, or even if, the issues can be separated and dealt with by two different remedial channels. If a complainant sought remedies in relation to both

[71] Yeom (n 15) 391.

[72] P Cane, *Administrative Tribunals and Adjudication* (Hart Publishing, 2009) 257.

the lawful and unlawful aspects of maladministration, it would seem necessary to pursue the lawful aspect via the ombudsman and the unlawful aspect via court proceedings. Yet parallel proceedings of this kind could generate extensive procedural and jurisdictional complexities that may register as a significant cost in any cost–benefit analysis of a reform of this nature.

Second, several examples of maladministration can be either lawful or unlawful, such as bias. The establishment of unlawful bias in an application for judicial review would require that the standard of proof is discharged on the strength of the evidence presented in the case. However, if the standard of proof is not discharged and unlawful bias is not established, that does not necessarily mean that putatively lawful bias does not remain as an element of maladministration in the case. Similarly, a claim for *Wednesbury* unreasonableness (with its high thresholds) may be unsuccessful in an application for judicial review, but that does not mean that there is no unreasonable conduct on the part of the public authority that cannot yet be addressed through the ombudsman. The ombudsman is, as a matter of general principle, not expected to satisfy the same high thresholds as are required in an application for judicial review, not least because there are rarely strict rules of evidence in place in ombuds processes. While the ombudsman could therefore investigate for (lawful) maladministration rather than unlawfulness in the alleged bias, in order to protect institutional and jurisdictional integrity it would have to be careful not to encounter some of the difficulties already raised, particularly in relation to res judicata and the sanctity of judicial proceedings. The same applies to unreasonableness and any other example of maladministration that straddles the legality/illegality divide.

Third, who would be responsible for separating the lawful and unlawful aspects of maladministration in a given case? Would this require that a person first applies for judicial review, so that the 'lawful' aspects of maladministration are left as residual issues at the conclusion of the litigation that can then be referred to the ombudsman? To what extent would the court's findings in the judicial review application thereafter have an impact on the ombudsman's investigation? It would seem jurisdictionally inappropriate for the ombudsman to be given the power to decide on whether an instance of maladministration is lawful or unlawful – after all, ombudsmen tend not to be part of the judicial branch[73] – yet it would largely defeat the purpose of resorting to an ombudsman if a person first had to obtain a court's opinion on the boundaries of legality in relation to an individual case. It is possible that a person could be permitted, subject to rules on delay and time limits, to seek a remedy from the ombudsman in relation to the lawful aspects of maladministration, and then to seek a remedy from the courts in relation to the unlawful aspects of maladministration. The ombudsman's findings could even be used as evidence in the court proceedings. However, this would still require a

[73] In some jurisdictions, the vesting of judicial power outside the judicial branch is considered unlawful and/or unconstitutional.

line to be drawn between the lawful and unlawful aspects of maladministration in the individual case, and still encounter difficulties about who is to draw that line and how it is to be drawn. Similar problems would be encountered were unlawful maladministration to be removed from the ombudsman's jurisdiction so that it only had oversight of lawful maladministration. It would therefore appear that the segregation of lawful from unlawful maladministration would not prove a realistic means of segregating the remedial work of ombudsmen from that of courts.

C. Remedial Distinctiveness

A further option to avoid or minimise any overlap between ombudsman remedies and judicial review remedies is simply to invest ombudsmen with remedies that are not substantively equivalent to remedies made available by judicial review. This comprises two aspects. First, it should be ensured that ombudsmen are not given the power to award remedies that are available through judicial review, such as injunctive and declaratory remedies. Second, ombudsmen should be empowered to award remedies that are not available through judicial review, such as the power to compel an apology of an investigated body,[74] require the payment of a distinct category of compensation (perhaps one that is not based on damages),[75] require the payment of a fine to the local or central state treasury, certify that a body's act, omission, conduct, process, policy or practice is an instance of maladministration (though which makes no comment on the lawfulness thereof), require reconsideration or review of a policy or practice, or publicly censure an authority.[76] In this way, the complainant can select the appropriate institution before which to pursue his or her complaint based inter alia on the desired remedy or remedies – an extension of the existing differentiation between ombudsman and court processes as available channels for expressing grievances against public bodies.

There may be some complexities in using this model for differentiating ombudsman and court functions, but they do not appear to be as difficult or objectionable as in some of the other models for functional differentiation. For example, if a complainant obtains the remedy of a compelled apology from the ombudsman, sufficient controls may need to be put in place to ensure that this does not

[74] This may vary depending on any apologies legislation in place in a given jurisdiction.

[75] This would not be entirely new to all ombudsmen: see the Housing Act 1996, sch 2, para 7(2)(a).

[76] The Taiwanese ombudsman, the Control Yuan, has the power to impeach or censure public officials: S Thomson, 'The Public Sector Ombudsman in Greater China: Four "Chinese" Models of Administrative Supervision' (2017) 39 *University of Pennsylvania Journal of International Law* 435, 472–74. Censure could, however, extend to a public authority as a whole. The UK's Housing Ombudsman Scheme (approved under s 51 of, and sch 2 to, the Housing Act 1996) is an example of an existing censure mechanism: Housing Ombudsman Scheme, paras 47–48. A different example is the Public Service Ombudsman for Wales's power to declare on its website that a listed authority's complaint-handling procedure does not comply with the Ombudsman's model complaint-handling procedure: Public Services Ombudsman (Wales) Act 2019, s 39.

equate to an admission of legal fault that could thereafter be actioned in a court of law. Controls of this nature are to varying degrees already contained in apologies legislation.[77] Similarly, if a complainant obtains the remedy of payment of compensation from the ombudsman, rules may have to be in place to prevent a form of double recovery whereby the complainant can profit by obtaining compensation from the ombudsman and damages or some other payment via the courts. Yet this could be addressed with relative ease by the enactment of recovery rules, such as in rules of court and/or the prevailing ombudsman legislation. An aggrieved person would therefore be able to select whether to complain to the ombudsman or to apply for judicial review (or such other legal mechanism available to enforce public law remedies[78]) based on the desired remedy or remedies. This would allow ombudsmen to enjoy more directly enforceable, 'hard' powers, while reducing or eliminating the potential for direct competition with the courts. Rules on remedial prioritisation or sequencing may also have a role to play in facilitating or strengthening this form of functional distinctiveness.

VI. Conclusion

The ombudsman is regarded as a valuable component of the administrative justice toolkit, not least due to its 'beyond legality' and 'beyond remedies' approach. However, many complainants may elect to pursue an ombudsman complaint with the sole or principal objective of obtaining a remedy or corrective outcome. There is already remedial overlap between other institutions, such as between courts and administrative tribunals, and there is no categorical or definitional reason why ombudsmen should not also be able to award remedies. Nevertheless, the broad trend has been one of declining to invest ombudsmen with the power to award directly enforceable remedies, doubtless strongly influenced by the desire to maintain institutional distinctiveness and to avoid the formalisation and associated costs that would likely eventuate in ombudsman proceedings were such a reform to be implemented.

If, however, it was decided that ombudsmen should be invested with the power to award remedies, the relationship between ombudsman remedies and remedies made available by judicial review would have to be carefully navigated and established. Overlap or competition between ombudsman and judicial review remedies are not of themselves intolerable, but they cannot be permitted to the extent that

[77] Compensation Act 2006, s 2; Apologies (Scotland) Act 2016, s 1. See also Northern Ireland Ombudsman, 'Guidance on Issuing an Apology' (March 2011) https://nipso.org.uk/site/wp-content/uploads/2016/02/2dfa3d4d-2b55-4bcb-8670-bd99f76eba4e.pdf.

[78] Such as an injunction under s 30 of the Senior Courts Act 1981 restraining a person from acting in any office in which they are not entitled to act (CPR, r 54.2(d)) or an order for specific performance of a statutory duty in Scotland (Court of Session Act 1988, s 45(b); Rules of the Court of Session 1994, r 58.2).

they undermine or frustrate the specific value of the ombudsman as an institution, nor unduly interfere with or undermine the judicial process and the sanctity of judicial proceedings.

This chapter has suggested three non-exclusive ways of maintaining functional distinctiveness between ombudsmen and courts as remedial avenues should ombudsmen be invested with the power to award directly enforceable remedies. Sequential distinctiveness, differentiating primary and residual claims, may be used in isolation, or in combination with other means, to establish the order in which remedial avenues should be attempted. The establishment of the ombudsman as the primary channel and the courts as the residual channel may encounter fewer difficulties than the reverse, and is to some extent already reflective of the relationship between court and administrative tribunal proceedings. Second, jurisdictional distinctiveness could be maintained between the two remedial channels, in particular by segregating lawful maladministration and unlawful maladministration, but this approach may generate more complexities and conundrums than it solves, not least as considerations of maladministration are necessarily broader than considerations of legality. Third, a model of remedial distinctiveness may be adopted whereby courts and ombudsmen are each empowered to award remedies not available via the other institution. This may involve investing ombudsmen with the power to award new remedies, such as compelled apologies, payments of compensation and censure. This model could be combined with a form of sequential distinctiveness to optimise effectiveness and balance.

There does not appear to be a general appetite (except, perhaps, among complainants) for investing ombudsmen with the power to award directly enforceable remedies, but with private sector ombudsmen being given greater such powers, the question of remedies will linger on in relation to public sector ombudsmen. In consideration of that question, and in devising workable solutions that maintain institutional integrity and effectiveness, the specific interface and relationship between ombudsman remedies and judicial review remedies must be carefully established. The complexities are not insurmountable, and some forms of differentiation – such as sequential or remedial differentiation – appear to generate fewer difficulties. For some, however, it might be as much a matter of principle as one of practice that ombudsmen should not have the power to award remedies, even if a path through the procedural complexities can be identified.

4

Understanding the Response from Health Organisations to Health Ombudsman Investigations – A New Conceptual Model

GAVIN McBURNIE

I. Introduction

My research into the Scottish Public Service Ombudsman (SPSO) indicates that the contribution of the SPSO to system improvement remains more aspirational than real. The response of healthcare organisations and healthcare professionals (hereafter bodies in jurisdiction) to the decisions and recommendations of complaints investigated by the SPSO is dependent upon the assessment, by bodies in jurisdiction, of the validity of the SPSO investigation report. Bodies in jurisdiction review the SPSO's complaint investigation reports and decide with how much of the investigation report they agree. This influences their subsequent motivation to implement the associated recommendations and creates a large degree of variability in the effectiveness of health ombudsman recommendations, with some recommendations potentially delivering significant change while other recommendations result in little change. What influences the response from bodies in jurisdiction is the nature of their relationship with the SPSO and the model of administrative control utilised by the SPSO.

II. Background

In the developed world, the modern state has seen a significantly increased role for the state in public administration and the provision of services. In parallel to this development has been the development of bodies, such as tribunals and ombudsman, which have the express purpose of overseeing public administrative bodies.[1] The growth of ombudsman has been a worldwide phenomenon and there has been a parallel development of ombudsman associations, both globally (eg the International Ombudsman Institute) and regionally (eg the Ombudsman Association, the Australia and New Zealand Ombudsman Association and the Caribbean Ombudsman Association). These bodies encourage collective learning and the sharing of best practice. It is suggested that the result of this is that, although ombudsman are local organisations, there are many similarities to be found across ombudsman schemes internationally as ombudsman offices learn from each other.

Ombudsman were originally conceived of as complaint resolution bodies with a primary focus on the resolution of individual complaints: when the Australian government was considering the establishment of the Commonwealth Ombudsman, it asked itself whether the putative role of the new ombudsman office was to 'swat flies or to hunt lions', before concluding that it was the former.[2] Over time, the role has developed. The former Australian Commonwealth Ombudsman Colin Neave declared that the idea of the ombudsman as being simply a complaint handler was a 'very old-fashioned notion', stating that ombudsman contributed towards system improvement.[3] The former Parliamentary and Health Service Ombudsman Ann Abraham claimed that there was an 'ombudsman dividend', where the ombudsman office is able to utilise its investigations, reports and guidance to contribute to system improvement.[4] In recent years, the claim that an important role for ombudsman is to contribute to system improvement has been made by academics,[5] with this move from complaint handler to contributor to system improvement described, by Harlow and Rawlings, as a move from 'fire-fighting' to 'fire-watching'.[6] Research on the contribution of ombudsman to system improvement is limited,[7] with Gill stating that the available evidence demonstrates

[1] A Gamble and R Thomas, 'The Changing Context of Governance: Implications for Administration and Justice' in M Adler (ed), *Administrative Justice in Context* (Hart Publishing, 2010).

[2] R Snell, 'Australian Ombudsman: A Continual Work in Progress' in M Groves and HP Lee (eds), *Australian Administrative Law: Fundamentals, Principles and Doctrines* (Cambridge University Press, 2007).

[3] C Neave, 'Exploring the Role of the Commonwealth Ombudsman in Relation to Parliament' (Senate Occasional Lecture, Canberra, November 2014).

[4] A Abraham, 'Making Sense of the Muddle: The Ombudsman and Administrative Justice, 2002–2011' (2012) 34 *Journal of Social Welfare and Family Law* 91.

[5] See, eg A Stuhmcke, '"Each for Themselves" or "One for All"? The Changing Emphasis of the Commonwealth Ombudsman' (2010) 38 *Federal Law Review* 143; C Gill, 'Right First Time: The Role of Ombudsman in Influencing Administrative Decision-Making' (2011) 33 *Journal of Social Welfare and Family Law* 181; J Healy and M Walton, 'Health Ombudsmen in Polycentric Regulatory Fields: England, New Zealand and Australia' (2016) 75 *Australian Journal of Public Administration* 492.

[6] C Harlow and R Rawlings, *Law and Administration*, 3rd edn (Cambridge University Press, 2009) 537–42.

[7] See, eg M Hertogh, 'Why the Ombudsman Does Not Promote Public Trust in Government: Lessons from the Low Countries' (2013) 35 *Journal of Social Welfare and Family Law* 245; M Siemiatycki, A Noack, J Kane, M Yvan Valade, F Crean, Al Lim and G Cook, 'The Impact of Ombudsman Investigations on Public Administration: A Case Study and an Evaluation Guide' (Office of the Toronto Ombudsman, 2015); A Stuhmcke, 'Evaluating the Effectiveness of an Ombudsman: A Riddle, Wrapped

a 'mixed picture of the influence that the ombudsman may have in this area'.[8] This may be because, as Carney et al argue, attempting to deliver both individual complaint handling and system improvement is problematic 'both conceptually and in the overall governance system'.[9]

III. Health Ombudsman

Health ombudsman are a relatively rare form of ombudsman institution. They are ombudsman schemes that have oversight of complaints about some or all of the delivery of healthcare within a country or territory, normally as the second-tier body for health complaints. It is usual for health ombudsman to have, either as a statutory responsibility or as a strategic objective, the purpose of contributing to the improvement of the overall healthcare system.

Within the UK, the Parliamentary and Health Service Ombudsman and the three public service ombudsman for the UK's devolved administrations (Scotland, Wales and Northern Ireland) all have responsibility for publicly provided healthcare, as does the ombudsman for the British overseas territory of Gibraltar. South Africa established a stand-alone health ombudsman scheme in 2016 which has responsibility for complaints about both privately and publicly delivered healthcare. In New Zealand there exists the New Zealand Health and Disability Commission, whilst in Australia each state or territory will have a health complaints entity either as a stand-alone organisation or as an element within a broader complaints commission office. In New Zealand and Australia, the second-tier complaint bodies are able to consider complaints about both publicly and privately provided healthcare. Some of these offices will have responsibility for unregulated healthcare provision (such as Queensland) or be able to take disciplinary action against healthcare professionals (such as New Zealand, New South Wales and Queensland).

The impetus behind the establishment of health ombudsman was found in low levels of public satisfaction with complaint handling by hospitals and healthcare professionals, limited alternative means of securing redress, less difficult alternatives to medical negligence claims and a desire for greater accountability from health organisations and healthcare professionals.[10]

in a Mystery Inside an Enigma' (International Ombudsman Institute Biennial Conference, Wellington, November 2012); Gill (n 5).

[8] Gill (n 5).

[9] T Carney, M Walton, M Chiarella and P Kelly, 'Health Complaints and Practitioner Regulation: Justice, Protection or Prevention?' (2017) 26 *Griffith Law Review* 65, 82.

[10] For Australia, see F Beaupart, T Carney, M Chiarella, C Satchell, M Walton, B Bennett and P Kelly, 'Regulating Healthcare Complaints: A Literature Review' (2014) 27 *International Journal of Health Care Quality Assurance* 505; J Smith-Merry, M Walton, J Healy and C Hobbs, 'Responses by Hospital Complaints Managers to Recommendations for Systemic Reforms by Health Complaints Commissions' (2017) 41 *Australian Health Review* 527. For the UK, see R Gregory and P Giddings, *The Ombudsman, the Citizen and Parliament* (Politico Publishing, 2002).

IV. Chapter Outline

The following section provides information concerning the research methodology adopted in the research. The chapter then outlines a novel conceptual model, produced as part of my research, detailing the differing elements within its construction, which are drawn from existing academic research and the theoretical construct of institutional logics. It considers these different elements and their relationships. Finally, the chapter applies this conceptual model to a worked example involving the responses from three Scottish health boards which participated in the research into the investigation of health complaints by the SPSO. Where the views of participants are included within the worked example, the participant is identified by a computer-based random female name generator.

V. Research Methodology

My research was an international qualitative case study using a critical realism research paradigm. The underpinning research hypothesis was that health ombudsman make a significant contribution to the improvement of the healthcare system as a result of its activities and relationships with bodies in jurisdiction. The SPSO was one of the ombudsman that participated in the research, from which seven participants were interviewed. These were drawn from staff across the SPSO – both hierarchically and functionally. For this research, the relevant bodies in jurisdiction were Scottish health boards.[11] Interviews were conducted with a total of 22 health board employees drawn from the three health boards that agreed to participate. The health board participants were drawn from three principal staff groups: director level staff, nursing staff and complaint management/corporate functions staff.

In addition to the interviews, the data considered in the research included a review of publicly available documents, principally obtained from the bodies' websites.

My research also involved the Office of the Health Ombudsman Queensland, and the outcome of my research, together with the results of international research drawn from the Netherlands, Australia and the UK, which contributed to the development of the underlying conceptual model, suggests that the model is applicable to other jurisdictions both administratively and geographically, due to the normative approach adopted by the institution across jurisdictions, although further research is required to test this suggestion.

[11] Health boards are state-run organisations responsible for the delivery of publicly provided healthcare within a specific geographical area. There are 14 geographical health boards in Scotland responsible for hospital, primary community and mental health services.

VI. The SPSO

The SPSO was founded on a statutory basis – the Scottish Public Services Ombudsman Act 2002. The Scottish Public Services Ombudsman is not only the ombudsman for health complaints, but, as the name suggests, is the ombudsman for complaints about all public services in Scotland.[12] The statute does not confer upon the SPSO the power to conduct systemic investigations. The Public Services Reform (Scotland) Act 2010 requires the SPSO both to publish a set of complaint-handling principles and model complaint-handling procedures with which bodies in jurisdiction must comply. The vision of the SPSO is to 'contribute actively and positively to Scotland's development and delivery of first-class public services: putting people and learning at the heart of what we do by being innovative and world-leading in our approach to complaints, reviews and standards'.[13]

The SPSO post holder has corporation sole status. A corporation sole is a specific individual who embodies an official position which is a separate legal identity and can only be established via statute. While an ombudsman will, necessarily, employ staff to enable her to discharge her responsibilities, the ombudsman is responsible for all decisions made in her name. Consequently, the ombudsman has total authority and is formally answerable only to parliament. This is of relevance to this research as, at the time of the interviews with health board participants, the current Ombudsman had not long assumed her role, yet health board participants had already identified a change in approach from the SPSO, with the new approach being described as more cooperative and less aggressive.

Table 1 Total complaints received and outcomes of health complaints received and considered by the SPSO – 2017/18–2019/20[14]

	2017/18	**2018/19**	**2019/20**
Total number of complaints received	4125	4188	4332
Number of health complaints	1403	1331	1562
Health complaints closed after investigation	440	454	391
Number of health complaints upheld/partly upheld	126	260	213
Number of health complaints not upheld	172	182	173

[12] C Hirst, 'Mapping the Bodies involved in Health Redress in the United Kingdom' (UKAJI, 2018) https://ukaji.org/2018/03/29/mapping-the-bodies-involved-in-health-redress-in-the-united-kingdom/.

[13] Scottish Public Services Ombudsman, 'SPSO Business Plan 2019–2020', 2 www.spso.org.uk/sites/spso/files/communications_material/business_information/BusinessPlan/2019-20%20BusinessPlan.pdf.

[14] Scottish Public Services Ombudsman, 'Statistics, 2019' www.spso.org.uk/statistics. Numbers do not add up exactly due to a small number of other reasons for case closure, such as withdrawn by complainant.

VII. Building the Conceptual Model

In this section, a novel conceptual model is detailed, drawing on previously published international research. The subsequent section of the chapter provides a worked example of this model in action, complete with examples and comments from participants from both the SPSO and health boards.

Health ombudsman will have, either as a strategic objective or as a statutory requirement, an intention to contribute to improvement of the system over which they have oversight. In relation to individual complaints, an ombudsman will issue, to a body under its jurisdiction (in this case, a health board), a report detailing the result of its investigation together with its associated recommendations, which are intended to prompt a response from the body concerned to correct identified failings. The ombudsman's objective is that the report will lead to the body changing some aspect of its activities resulting in system improvement. For example, the SPSO may recommend to a health board that certain staff receive training in a particular procedure. If the health board accepts the recommendation and the staff receive that training, the intention is that these newly trained staff will conduct that procedure more appropriately and thus improve the service provided. This basic proposition is shown diagrammatically in Figure 1.

Figure 1 Basic diagram demonstrating how ombudsman contribute to system improvement

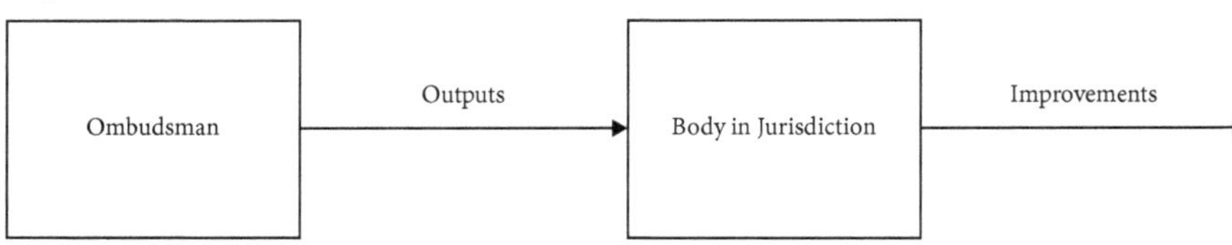

Stuhmcke identified two types of output from ombudsman: those which are direct and measurable and those which are indirect and immeasurable.[15] Stuhmcke also identified thick and thin changes resulting from ombudsman outputs. Thick changes are policy changes while thin changes are procedural changes. These can be incorporated into the basic model as illustrated in Figure 2.

Figure 2 Revised diagram incorporating the work of Stuhmcke

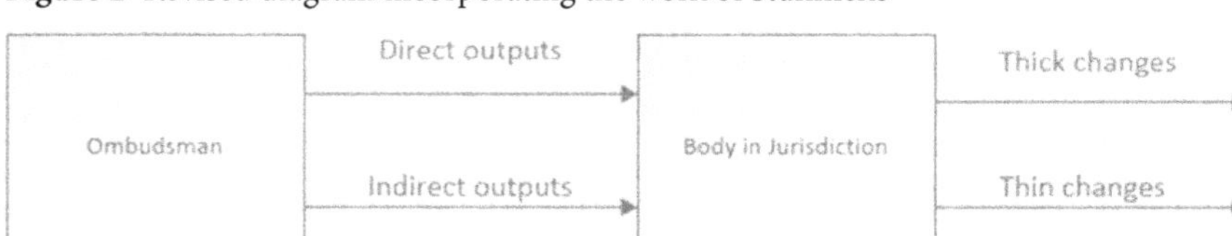

[15] A Stuhmcke, 'Evaluating Ombudsman: A Case Study in Developing a Quantitative Methodology to Measure the Performance of the Ombudsman' in International Ombudsman Institute and L Reif (eds), *The International Ombudsman Yearbook*, vol 10 (MNP/Brill, 2006).

This revised model can then be refined through consideration of Hertogh's two models of administrative control, which are cooperative and coercive control respectively.[16] Hertogh compared the impact of both ombudsman and courts, and found that the impact of courts in the Netherlands arose through their powers of coercion, while, for the Netherlands National Ombudsman, Hertogh found that the ombudsman's impact arose from their cooperative approach with bodies in jurisdiction.[17] Hertogh concluded that the degree of impact achieved by either courts or ombudsman relates to their style of administrative control. Hertogh further concluded that the cooperative approach adopted by the Netherlands ombudsman led to better communication, with better understood and accepted decisions, and suggested that it was likely that the ombudsman had more policy impact than courts.[18] It is worth noting that Hertogh has also stated that the Netherlands ombudsman may, on occasion, utilise a coercive approach dependent upon the body and the issue concerned.[19] This suggests that both approaches to administrative control can coexist within an organisation, although, in practice, one will become the dominant approach.

Hertogh suggests that administrative decision-making in response to the decision of an ombudsman comprises three consecutive stages, with each stage associated with an important question that needs to be answered by the body. The first phase, referred to as the information phase, requires the body to ask itself what the decision and the associated recommendations from the ombudsman are; the second phase, the transformation phase, requires the body to ask itself what the decision means for it; while in the third stage, the processing phase, the body asks itself what it should do with the decision.[20]

Hertogh argued that for each of these three implementations stages there is a corresponding barrier to change: firstly, the decisions and recommendations made by the ombudsman may lack sufficient clarity; secondly, a significant gap may exist between the ombudsman's decision and the extant values and policies of the body concerned; and thirdly, the body concerned may exhibit defensive behaviours. The relationship between Hertogh's stages and barriers is shown diagrammatically in Figure 3.

Hertogh suggests that the impact of an ombudsman is 'determined by the degree to which their decisions result in (some of) these three barriers'.[21] Hertogh's model can now be integrated into the proposed new model, as indicated in Figure 4.

[16] M Hertogh, 'Coercion, Cooperation and Control: Understanding the Policy Impact of Administrative Courts and Ombudsman in the Netherlands' (2001) 23 *Law and Policy* 47.

[17] ibid.

[18] ibid 63.

[19] M Hertogh, personal communication (Zoom seminar 'Ombuds in the Modern State', December 2020).

[20] Hertogh (n 16) 58.

[21] ibid 59.

Figure 3 Relationship between implementation stages and associated barriers

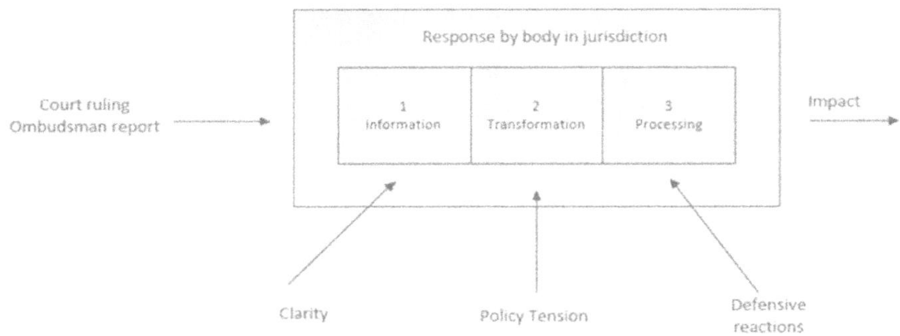

Figure 4 Revised model incorporating Hertogh's model of administrative control

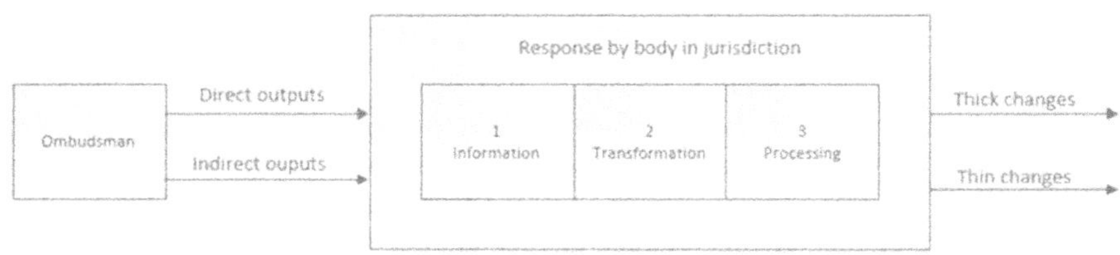

As Hertogh's model suggests, organisations must decide how to respond when subject to the decisions and recommendations from an external controller such as a court or ombudsman. Braithwaite, Professor of the Regulatory Institutions Network at the Australian National University in Canberra, suggests that the responses from organisations to their oversight bodies will be strongly influenced by the motivational postures adopted by individuals within these organisations.[22]

Braithwaite describes the responses from organisations to the outputs of oversight bodies as 'motivational postures' and suggests that these motivational postures provide an important insight into the organisation's attitude to its oversight body and its willingness to accept this body's rules and processes.[23] Braithwaite defines five motivational postures, which are: commitment, which indicates a willingness to accept the authority and recommendations of the external controller; capitulation, which indicates acceptance of the authority's conditions as a means of avoiding trouble and having a quiet life; disengagement, which indicates that the body views the authority of its oversight body as irrelevant; game playing, which indicates that the body will try to appear as if it is accepting of the controller's authority while actively trying to circumvent that authority; and resistance, which indicates opposition to the controller's

[22] V Braithwaite, 'Defiance and Motivational Postures' in D Weisburd and G Bruinsma (eds), *Encyclopedia of Criminology and Criminal Justice* (Springer Science and Business Media, 2014).

[23] ibid 915.

authority. Individuals and organisations are able to adopt more than one motivational posture, with the result that several motivational postures can coexist. If oversight bodies understand the motivational postures adopted by people and organisations, then they are better able to engender cooperation from the bodies concerned, thus improving their own effectiveness.[24]

In Australia, Smith-Merry et al found that the concept of motivational postures was applicable to the responses by hospital complaint managers to the findings and recommendations made by their second-tier health complaint entity.[25] Smith-Merry et al further found that respondents, echoing Hertogh's model of cooperative control, indicated that recommendations were more likely to be implemented if there had been discussion of the proposed recommendations prior to their finalisation.[26]

It is suggested that the motivational postures adopted by individuals and organisations will impact upon the transformation and processing stages in Hertogh's model. That is, the motivational posture that is adopted will affect how individuals and organisations interpret what the decision will mean for them, how the recommendations relate to the goals and policies of the body, and how best the body should respond. Braithwaite's suggestion of motivational postures is added to the model as indicated in Figure 5.

Figure 5 Revised diagram incorporating the work of Braithwaite

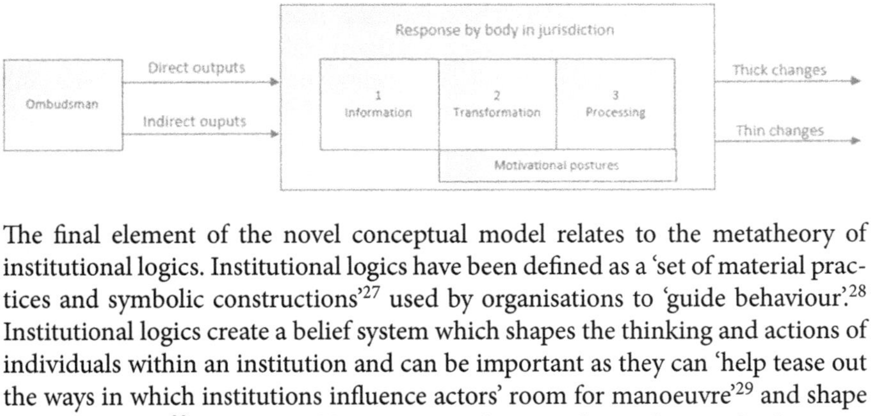

The final element of the novel conceptual model relates to the metatheory of institutional logics. Institutional logics have been defined as a 'set of material practices and symbolic constructions'[27] used by organisations to 'guide behaviour'.[28] Institutional logics create a belief system which shapes the thinking and actions of individuals within an institution and can be important as they can 'help tease out the ways in which institutions influence actors' room for manoeuvre'[29] and shape their reasoning.[30] Institutional logics act as a framework to influence the decisions

[24] ibid 918.
[25] Smith-Merry et al (n 10).
[26] ibid 531–32.
[27] R Friedland and RR Alford, 'Bringing Society Back In: Symbols, Practices, and Institutional Contradictions' in WW Powell and PJ DiMaggio (eds), *The New Institutionalism in Organisational Analysis* (University of Chicago Press, 1991).
[28] A Dodds and N Kodate, 'Accountability, Organisational Learning and Risks to Patient Safety in England: Conflict or Compromise?' (2011) 13 *Health, Risk and Society* 327, 329.
[29] ibid 329.
[30] PH Thornton, W Ocasio and M Lounsbury, *The Institutional Logics Perspective: A New Approach to Culture, Structure, and Process* (Oxford University Press, 2012).

and behaviours of organisations and organisational actors. Each institutional logic demonstrates 'unique organizing principles, practices and symbols that influence individual and organizational behaviour'.[31]

Within individual institutions, differing institutional logics are likely to coexist and compete for dominance.[32] The dominant institutional logic will guide how individuals respond to a given situation as the individual will be embedded within a broader cultural structure that will both enable and constrain the individual's agency.[33] While organisations may hold within themselves competing institutional logics, there tends to be consistency in institutional logics among organisations working in the same area of activity. Where this occurs, this is known as an institutional field, which has 'collectively agreed upon rules, norms and practices to which their members adhere'.[34]

The area of healthcare is such an institutional field. Healthcare was long subject to the institutional logic of professional judgement and self-regulation, but its dominance has been significantly reduced due to many high-profile medical scandals. Consequently, in the area of the quality of healthcare and patient safety, two new alternative logics arose: an accountability logic and a learning logic.[35] Health organisations will demonstrate a complex mix of all three logics, with all three competing for dominance and exhibited at different times.

The accountability logic focuses on assigning responsibility and is founded upon the belief that healthcare clinicians should be held answerable for their actions and be able to defend their actions by comparing their practice with that of their colleagues. It is thus centred upon notions of individual responsibility. Meanwhile, the learning logic places an emphasis on organisational learning and stresses the importance of learning from a review of current practice and warning flags such as complaints and patient safety incidents. With this logic, healthcare organisations and professionals should use phenomena such as patient safety incidents and complaints as opportunities to learn. The learning logic is predicated upon the basis that if health professionals routinely reflected upon their performance, with the intention of identifying areas of practice which could be improved, and appropriate learning is then undertaken, then the quality of healthcare would be enhanced. However, Dodds and Kodate claim that the learning and accountability logics are in conflict and that there is a lack of agreement over which of these two logics should dominate in the healthcare improvement arena.[36]

As with any other organisation, the offices of health ombudsman will have their own institutional logics and, again, one of these logics will become the dominant logic. Health ombudsman, as part of the healthcare regulatory network,

[31] ibid 2.38.

[32] Dodds and Kodate (n 28) 329; Thornton et al (n 30).

[33] ibid.

[34] JM Purdy and B Gray, 'Conflicting Logics. Mechanisms of Diffusion, and Multilevel Dynamics in Emerging Institutional Fields' (2009) 52 *Academy of Management Journal* 355, 357.

[35] ibid.

[36] Dodds and Kodate (n 28).

demonstrate both the accountability and learning logics, which reflect their dual roles in the regulation of healthcare: firstly, complaint arbitration, in which they utilise the accountability logic, and secondly, their contribution to system improvement, in which they utilise the learning logic. Dodds and Kodate's proposition that the accountability and learning logics are in conflict for dominance will also be true for health ombudsman, and the dominant logic within an ombudsman will influence the relationship between the ombudsman and a body in jurisdiction. The metatheory of institutional logics is incorporated into the conceptual model as indicated in Figure 6.

Figure 6 Revised model highlighting the possible institutional logics dominant within health ombudsman

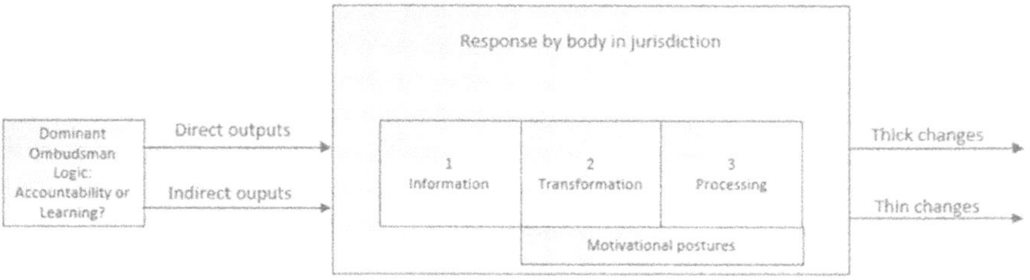

Synthesising the academic research together with the theory of institutional logics has enabled the author to create this new conceptual model to explain how bodies respond to the outputs of their ombudsman. This model suggests that the ability of an ombudsman to contribute to system improvement is determined by the motivational postures adopted by persons within bodies in jurisdiction in response to the ombudsman output. These motivational postures then mediate the transformation and processing phases of the body's response to the ombudsman, as well as the barriers to implementation (policy tension and defensive behaviours) integral to Hertogh's model of administrative control. The result of this will be a number of changes which can be categorised as thick or thin dependent upon whether they are policy or procedural changes. As examples, policy changes may relate to the construction and implementation of local clinical guidelines while 'procedural changes' may relate to training or communication.

The motivational posture adopted by staff within a body in jurisdiction will be strongly influenced by the nature of the relationship that exists between the ombudsman and that body. The nature of this relationship will be based upon the administrative model of control adopted by the ombudsman, being either the coercive or cooperative model of control and which will, in turn, be strongly influenced by the dominant institutional logic that exists within the ombudsman office. An accountability logic will result in a different model of control and relationship between ombudsman and body in jurisdiction, and thus the motivational posture that is likely to be adopted by the body, compared to that which may be adopted where the dominant logic within the ombudsman is a learning logic. This relationship is shown diagrammatically in Figure 7.

Figure 7 Relationship between the differing elements in the conceptual model

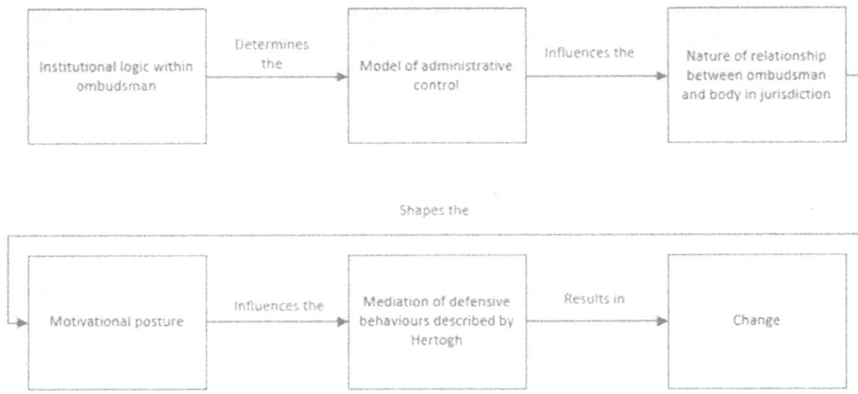

Earlier in this chapter there was the suggestion that, although ombudsman are independent organisations, their sharing of learning and best practice means that there are many similarities to be found between the schemes. As will be discussed below, the changing approaches to recommendations being made by ombudsman offices in differing countries but which are similar in intent and general approach suggests that this model can apply internationally.

VIII. Applying the New Conceptual Model

In the previous section, the elements of a new conceptual model were detailed and their interrelationship highlighted. In this section, the model is considered further by way of its applicability to a worked real-life example using the output of my research. For the purposes of this chapter, the focus is on the SPSO's individual complaint-handling activity.

Perhaps counter-intuitively, the discussion follows the reverse of the model outlined in Figure 7. As stated earlier, the underpinning research paradigm used in this research was that of critical realism. Put simply, a critical realist will conduct case-study research to observe a phenomenon under investigation with a view to understanding the mechanisms that generate the observations made. This can be conducted on an iterative basis to identify more deep-lying mechanisms. The overall intention is to develop a theory or model which best explains the observations that have been made.

The discussion, therefore, begins by considering the dominant motivational postures that are adopted by staff within health boards towards the SPSO, which will determine how they respond to SPSO investigation reports. These motivational postures are the most easily observable response from health boards towards the SPSO. However, such postures do not arise de novo; rather, they are generated. In this model, it is proposed that the mechanism that generates the observed motivational postures is the nature of the relationship that exists between the SPSO and health boards. Thus, Hertogh's models of administrative control and their effect on the nature of the relationship between the SPSO and health boards are considered. Again, the model of administrative control utilised by the SPSO does not arise de novo but is also generated, and it is suggested that the mechanism that generates the model of administrative control adopted by the SPSO is the SPSO's underlying dominant institutional logic. The discussion continues, therefore, with a reflection on the institutional logics that influence how the SPSO conducts its complaint work.

IX. The First Element of the Model: Motivational Postures

The motivational postures adopted by health board staff will mediate their response to investigation reports produced by the SPSO. They will influence how health board staff determine what the decision means for them and how much they should comply with the recommendations.

Two dominant motivational postures were voiced by participants from health boards: commitment and capitulation. There was also a degree of disengagement that was voiced by participants from the Scottish health boards in respect of their attitude towards the SPSO, but this was smaller in scale in comparison to the motivational postures of commitment and capitulation. However, as will be noted below, although participants voiced little actual disengagement, in the research, it was identified, from the responses of participants, that disengagement may be more widespread within clinical staff in health boards.

Typical views supportive of a motivational posture of commitment were the need to take the ombudsman seriously and reflect upon what they have said (Trish), the fact that an independent investigation has been undertaken by the ombudsman which supported the SPSO's opinion (Fiona) and a thorough investigation had taken place highlighting a failure that needed to be addressed (Justine). Jessica noted that an upheld complaint, while a shock and upsetting for some staff, was important for the health board as it enabled it to learn, a view shared by Trish, who described receiving an upheld report as 'sore' but also an important source of learning. Meg viewed investigation reports as 'gifts'. Several participants saw the ombudsman's role as important, being an external reviewer (Phoebe), in driving improvement (Tess) and as an organisation from which to learn (Trish). The view was, perhaps, best summed up by Jackie, who said that the most important objective was 'to make the patient, the complainant, whoever it may be, feel better and feel that we've properly listened to the recommendations and are acting upon them'.

The second dominant motivational posture described was that of capitulation. Here, health board participants felt that they were obligated to comply with the ombudsman for fear of sanction. 'We don't see it as an opportunity, we see it as a threat' (Vicky) and 'we're saying, "we don't think that recommendation is right", but we have been told by our bosses you just have to accept it' (Darcie). Yvonne stated 'we're sitting in the camp of defensiveness. We're doing it because we think we're going to get into trouble, and therefore, the commitment is lacking.' 'I think it was always seen as they [the SPSO] were there to put a sanction, so the minute you hear the Ombudsman you think "Ugh"' (Isobel). This sanction appeared to relate to reputational risk for the health board: 'We have to deliver on the recommendations. And, if we don't, they [the SPSO] don't close the case, and they write to our Chief Executive, and that comes back to reputational issues' (Jackie); 'We probably risk assess it [the SPSO report]. What's going to have the biggest impact for us, because you don't want to end up on the front page of the Daily Record'[37] (Jill); and 'I guess the thing is, there's a pretty clear message around these kind of … there's that whole bit around reputational risk' (Tess). This feeling of fear led to some interesting characterisations of the SPSO: 'everyone says, "the Ombudsman". It's like the grim reaper' (Darcie); 'It's like Big Brother watching you a wee bit' (Trish); and 'It's keeping the wolf away from the door' (Eleanor).

A third motivational posture, that of disengagement, was identified, but to a lesser degree in terms of specific responses from participants. There were comments such as 'the SPSO? Who? I don't really care what they [say], you know' (Vicky) or 'other things we think, "Really?" It's almost making recommendations for the sake of it rather than genuinely understanding what happens in the system' (Donna). This sense of disengagement may be more widespread than participants suggested, as two issues were raised repeatedly by participants: firstly, where health board staff disagreed with the SPSO's clinical advice, they were not able to discuss this advice, leaving health board staff frustrated and unheard; and secondly, health board staff did not believe that SPSO staff always understood the complexities and nuances of the delivery of modern healthcare. The consequence of these issues is that clinicians and managers may not be convinced by either the investigation decision or the subsequent recommendations, and this creates problems for implementation: if the clinicians do not agree with a report, 'how do we deliver the action plan for improvement?' (Meg). The risk is that clinicians, and perhaps some managers too, become disengaged from the process. As it is clinicians who are responsible for developing and implementing clinical guidelines, if they become disengaged from the process then there is a risk that changes that are made will be cosmetic, engineered to demonstrate apparent compliance with the recommendations rather than prompted by commitment.

In these situations, the sense of the researcher is that the motivation that compels compliance is capitulation. Participants were clear that they did not want to be on the wrong side of the SPSO and, while the SPSO has no direct powers

[37] The *Daily Record* is the largest circulation daily newspaper in Scotland.

over health boards and clinicians, the threat of adverse publicity and possible professional sanctions from referrals to regulators is enough to secure apparent compliance. Complying through a fear of sanctions of whatever type rather than through a sense of commitment is, however, liable to result in informational learning, with the minimum possible actions undertaken to appear compliant.

It also appears that the motivational posture that is demonstrated is not absolute, either for health boards as an entity or for individuals within health boards. As suggested by the literature, staff in health boards may hold differing motivational postures. This indicates that the motivational posture adopted by a person or body can be contextual, specific to the immediate situation and personal, so different people may adopt differing motivational postures when faced with the same situation. Different individuals within health boards may adopt differing motivational postures when faced with the same report dependent upon the view that they hold of that report. The implication is that any change that arises as a result of a decision will be dependent upon the specifics of its production, and this may vary from case to case. Individuals within the health board will review the SPSO investigation report and recommendation(s) and decide with how much they agree. If the findings of the investigation and associated recommendations are accepted, then commitment to implementation of the recommendations is likely to be greater. If the SPSO findings and recommendations are not really accepted by health boards, a motivational posture of capitulation will probably be adopted and there will be reduced commitment to implementation. Thus, the dominant motivational posture exhibited by individuals will vary dependent upon the result and implications of individual reports and recommendations. Some ombudsman investigations may deliver significant change while others deliver only limited change.

X. The Second Element of the Model: Model of Administrative Control

This variable impact, noted above, is important as it is likely that the SPSO's ability to contribute to improvement of the healthcare system is less than it would intend, and is due, in large part, to the nature of the relationship that exists between it and the health boards. The interviews with participants indicate that this is principally due to the way that the SPSO conducts its investigations – many comments from participants suggested that SPSO investigations were procedurally unfair, in that health boards were often voiceless during the investigation and unable to state their case. This was particularly frustrating where there was a difference of clinical judgement, where the complaint was described as 'feel[ing] like it goes into the ether' (Eleanor). This was felt to be unsatisfactory by health board participants, who noted that 'These people are just doing a job the same as us, so why can't we phone up and question them?' (Emma). Importantly, Phoebe noted that better communication would aid both the SPSO and the health boards: 'I think the more communication probably the better for both ways. For the ombudsman to understand more, but also for the teams here to actually be able to recollect some things in a different way and view things differently' (Phoebe).

As a result of the way that the SPSO conducts its investigations, health board participants view the model of administrative control as coercive rather than cooperative. Many participants commented on the lack of a cooperative approach adopted by the SPSO: 'I think their view would be [that] it [the SPSO] is collaborative but from a services point of view I would say it's pretty remote' (Fiona); 'there's not an engagement and dialogue with us around that in any shape or form' (Meg); 'they tell us. And it's not a communication, it's not collaborative' (Jackie); 'I'm not sure the relationship between the SPSO and the health board is collaborative enough. They are very separate' (Yvonne); and 'they're not very approachable really, they're sort of in their ivory tower almost' (Jessica).

This feeling that the SPSO is distant and not cooperative is due largely to the lack of interaction between the SPSO and the health boards during an investigation. Participants reported that communication between the SPSO and health boards was sparse and mainly conducted through email: 'it feels like an administrative process … I think it's bureaucratic' (Rhoda); 'it seems to be just black and white. You take everything from what's written' (Darcie); and 'but that's what I see as missing because they're there and we're here and only the twain shall meet in writing' (Donna).

Similar to the findings in Australia and the Netherlands,[38] participants from the health boards were keen to have conversations around the issues contained within the complaint under investigation by the SPSO but felt frustrated that these conversations could not occur. The problem for the SPSO is that, due to the lack of interactions between it and the health boards, the only means by which the latter are able to judge the SPSO investigation is the report. Where health boards are not persuaded by the report, they will be less committed to fully comply with the associated recommendations. As Meg stated, 'So, there are occasions where they proceed to print things that our clinicians don't agree with. Which gives us a challenge back from the board then, how do we deliver the action plan for improvement?'

Even when health boards were able to comment, at the draft stage of the investigation report or after the issuance of a decision letter, participants felt that they could not challenge the SPSO or that doing so was of little value as it was unlikely to lead to change. There was a feeling among many participants that it was inappropriate to challenge the ombudsman: 'I was always made to feel as if you shouldn't question anything they ask you' (Emma); 'I think it's almost a given that your starting point is that you don't challenge the ombudsman (Tess); 'I don't think they like being challenged' (Vicky); and 'I get the sense they're [the SPSO

[38] See Smith-Merry et al (n 10); Hertogh (n 16).

are] quite directive and not really open to a challenge'. This last view was supported by Rhoda, who stated that 'we challenged once and the Ombudsman came back and chastised us for challenging it … It felt quite punitive'. Many participants questioned the utility of challenging the ombudsman: 'Generally speaking, in my experience, the ombudsman very, very, very, very rarely amends the report unless it's factual accuracy' (Phoebe) and 'I don't know that there's been anything that they've [the health board has] ever challenged … that actually the Ombudsman's said "Okay I agree with you. That actually we'll change that"' (Emma).

This was particularly the case when there were disagreements about the clinical advice. Firstly, there was concern about the clinical advice received by the SPSO and its role in determining the outcome of the complaint. It was not uncommon for clinicians within a health board to have a differing clinical view from that of the clinical advisor employed by the SPSO. Many participants picked up on the fact that there can be several legitimate yet differing clinical judgements: 'there are lots of experts in the field [that] may have a different view' (Fiona); 'sometimes there's no right or wrong answer' (Emma); and 'they (the clinical advisor] are one person, they're not sense testing with others' (Meg). Relationships between clinicians and the SPSO 'become quite tense' (Deirdre).

Where health boards tried to challenge the clinical advice received by the SPSO, it was felt by participants to be pointless: 'We have challenged it [the clinical advice], and we've been told, this is the clinical advisor for the panel, and this is the outcome, so, therefore, there you go' (Rhoda) and 'You've not got much grounds if you've got, "I disagree with your clinical advisor". They'll [the SPSO] go "tough"' (Jackie). This occurs even where a health board responds to the SPSO citing clinical guidelines which it believes support their clinician and his or her actions, but feels that they 'did not get anywhere' (Isobel).

One participant provided an interesting example where her health board obtained two independent reviews of their clinician's actions, one of which was obtained from a clinician completely independent from their health board. Both independent reviews were supportive of the health board's clinician, but the SPSO was unmoved: 'we didn't really get anywhere' (Isobel) as the SPSO relied on their original, sole piece of clinical advice. This places the health board in a difficult position. It, and the clinician involved, will certainly be sceptical, at best, about whether they have made an error, and this will impact upon the motivational posture that they will adopt in response to the investigation report. A motivational posture of capitulation by the health board to avoid adverse reputational risk will probably be adopted, while the clinician may become disengaged from making any change. What is clear is that there will be a lack of real commitment to implement any associated recommendation.

To compound matters for health board staff, participants in the study claimed that the SPSO lacked transparency, not only with regard to the identity of the clinical advisor, but also with regard to their expertise in the area about which the clinical advisor was providing advice. Clinicians and health boards were in the position of having to accept clinical judgements with which they did not agree, without being able to assess whether the clinical advisor had the experience or status to provide such advice. This concern was exacerbated when the SPSO's clinical advisor was critical of clinicians who were recognised as clinical leaders in the area concerned (Donna) but where it was unclear about the experience and status of the clinician providing the advice. Finally, it was reported that the SPSO would not allow health boards to discuss the clinical issues involved with the clinical advisor to aid better understanding by both parties about why the clinician took the actions that they did, or why the advisor provided the advice that they had submitted (Fiona, Eleanor, Jessica and Jackie). The result was to leave clinicians feeling unheard and 'undervalued' (Isobel).

The consequence of this lack of cooperation between the SPSO and health boards was the development of negative views about the SPSO from health board participants: 'I think they're more dictatorial' (Jackie); 'they almost seem to be in a place where they're untouchable' (Jessica); 'it actually feels quite aggressive … it feels really persecutory at times' (Rhoda); and 'very much a kind of stick approach as opposed to engagement, working collaboratively' (Fiona). This belief that the SPSO is distant, uncooperative and potentially aggressive, combined with a need for health boards to be seen to comply with the SPSO for fear of adverse publicity or the laying of reports before the Scottish Parliament, engenders a view from health board participants that there was little that appeared to be cooperative about the relationship between the SPSO and health boards, but, rather, a coercive relationship predicated upon the authority of the SPSO where the obligations on health boards to comply are explicit. This suggests that different ombudsman institutions may adopt differing models of administrative control and that it would be wrong to assume that only the cooperative model of administrative control applies to ombudsman.

A second issue raised by participants was their concern about whether the SPSO understood the complexities and context of delivering healthcare which may affect both decisions and recommendations. Jessica was concerned, as

> we've had some [reports] where medical staff have been really quite troubled about some of the things that have been said, because at the end of the day, we're a district hospital and maybe the advisor – I don't know where they came from.

Meanwhile, Trish was equally troubled: 'you think, "You're just not getting that. We don't have whatever it is you say is on tap, as you say, because we're not a tertiary hospital, full of lots of different specialities"'. Donna expressed concern about the SPSO's 'lack of general understanding about how the system works these days', while Isobel suggested that implementing recommendations across a health board area may be difficult due to differing local circumstances, 'so, I think that some of the complexities of what we have to deal with is[*sic*] quite difficult'. In fact, Isobel was even blunter, describing some recommendations as 'wild stuff', to which she thought 'Okay. Right. Move on'.

These are examples of the frustrations expressed by staff within district hospitals who felt that the advice provided to the SPSO did not make sufficient recognition of the realities in providing healthcare in a Scottish district hospital. They expressed concern that the clinical advisor had an unrealistic understanding of what was deliverable within such a setting.

This highlights the challenge that exists for lay ombudsman offices considering health complaints, particularly those of a clinical nature. The focus of the complaint may concern a very specific clinical issue where there may be no absolute right or wrong, so relies on clinical judgement and requires the input of an external clinical advisor. Recommendations need to take account of the structure and context of local healthcare delivery, which can vary widely between health organisations. There will be the temptation for the SPSO to over rely on their clinical advisor – which, for many health board participants, appears to be the situation that exists.

At the time of the interviews with SPSO participants, the SPSO had relatively recently introduced a new approach to making recommendations, with this drive for change coming from within the SPSO:

> I think it came out of a concern from CRs[39] a couple of years ago that we were making the same recommendation to the same body about the same thing and that, that didn't seem to be being particularly effective ... Before, we kind of sat there, at our desks, and tried to think what has gone wrong and what can fix it (Ellie).

In the revised approach, it was

> really up to the organisation to work out how they achieve that [the appropriate response to the upheld failing] ... so, we are putting the onus back on the organisation and saying, you, we have noticed some mistakes but it is still your system, so you take ownership of it and fix it, and tell us how you fixed it (Ellie).

The rationale behind this change in approach by the SPSO was that

> we [the SPSO] may not always be best placed to make a recommendation that is appropriate because we might not know fully the extent of the organisation's structures and resources and so on. So, we might make a recommendation that we think is quite an appropriate and straightforward recommendation and, but it may have quite an impact on the organisation (Mary).

This suggests that the SPSO is trying to adopt a more cooperative approach with health boards in the formulation of recommendations, moving from an approach where it (the SPSO) details the recommendation to an approach which provides for a greater role in the determination of an appropriate recommendation.

In some ways, this appears similar to the many 'roads to Rome approach' used by the Netherlands ombudsman. Hertogh, in his research into the Netherlands ombudsman and two agencies in its jurisdiction – the Netherlands tax authority and the student finance agency – found that staff from the Netherlands ombudsman also adopted a collaborative approach and had regular communications with bodies in jurisdiction about the investigation and recommendations, as well as

[39] CRs are complaint investigators – the SPSO calls them case reviewers.

regular interactions outside formal investigations.[40] Hertogh found that the bodies may make alternative suggestions to the ombudsman about proposed recommendations and cited one respondent as saying that 'there are many roads that lead to Rome' and that the discussions with the ombudsman allowed the body to 'select the road that is most efficient'.[41] Hertogh suggests that what was most effective about discussions between the ombudsman and bodies in jurisdiction was that such discussions could enable the ombudsman to overcome the potential blocks to implementation that he had identified in his research. Hertogh suggests that a facilitative, collaborative approach used by ombudsman may allow the body to implement the recommendations in ways that are consistent with their reality, thus improving compliance and delivering greater improvement.[42]

In their research on the motivational postures adopted by hospital complaint managers to their Australian health complaint oversight bodies, Smith-Merry et al found that complaint managers would also welcome a collaborative approach between ombudsman and health organisations with more discussion and negotiation as they felt that this would enable the production of more feasible recommendations and realistic timescales.[43]

Finally, as noted above, my research also included the Office of the Health Ombudsman Queensland (OHOQ), and it is interesting to note that in its systemic investigation activities, OHOQ too was adopting a more interactive, cooperative approach with health organisations to develop meaningful recommendations. Whether this is a move from ombudsman internationally to work more collaboratively with bodies in jurisdiction or just a coincidence from a small sample is uncertain, but worthy of further research.

Although the SPSO is attempting to develop a more cooperative approach with bodies in jurisdiction, currently the coercive approach is the dominant approach and this has consequences for the SPSO in relation to Hertogh's barriers to change within bodies in jurisdiction, namely those of clarity of recommendation, policy tension and defensive behaviours.

XI. Clarity of Recommendations

The first potential barrier described by Hertogh was that proposed recommendations needed to be clear.[44] It was evident from the results that many participants did not always find recommendations to be clear in their intent, with over a quarter of participants, without prompting, describing SPSO recommendations as 'woolly'.

[40] Hertogh (n 16).

[41] ibid 57.

[42] ibid 63–64. Hertogh contrasts the coercive approach of the Dutch administrative courts with the 'cooperative control' of Dutch ombudsmen that is based upon communication and negotiation.

[43] Smith-Merry et al (n 10).

[44] Hertogh (n 16).

Other issues raised include: 'some of them [recommendations] will be very, very generic. And the generic ones are the ones that are harder for us' (Isobel); 'some of these things you think, well we've sent them the policy, so what's wrong with the policy? … If we've to review, what is it in the policy that you think needs reviewed? That's not clear. It just maybe says, "Policy should be reviewed?"' (Jill); and 'you'd love to see them in the boardroom to say "What do you mean by that? Explain what you actually want us to do", because again in black and white, I can read that and think I don't know how I can deliver that … ?' (Darcie).

This lack of clarity in the reports and recommendations can be a challenge for participants: 'it's very difficult to know, sometimes, what she's expecting of us. It would be good to have a clearer picture of what he or she feels we should be doing differently' (Jill). A lack of clarity from the SPSO about what is intended will clearly make it more difficult for health boards to deliver the intended changes.

XII. Policy Tension

The acceptability of an ombudsman decision is determined by the difference between a decision and the existing organisational programme and the level of commitment to that programme by the body, so that the greater the change, the less likely it will be implemented. This is Hertogh's policy tension.[45]

Concerns were raised from participants about the achievability of the recommendations proposed by the SPSO. Concerns were about issues ranging from failures by the SPSO to understand the implications of the recommendations in terms of the necessary work to see the recommendation implemented, which was memorably described as 'industries around the SPSO' (Darcie), to the deliverability of the recommendations through a failure to understand the complexity of the modern healthcare system or the importance of the local context, 'a health service is a health service is a health service. It is to a certain degree but local context is important' (Meg), allied to an unwillingness to listen to the service (Donna). In addition, as previously discussed, in many cases health professionals will be unconvinced by the clinical advice used by the SPSO and its subsequent decision. When this occurs, there will lesser acceptance of the need for change and commitment to make change. Organisations may implement changes for 'symbolic' rather than 'instrumental' purposes, that is, without making significant operational changes.[46] Making symbolic changes is the result of organisations seeking to maintain legitimacy in the eyes of their oversight body while, in practice, making as little change as possible.[47]

[45] ibid.

[46] CA Heimer, 'Competing Institutions: Law, Medicine and Family in Neonatal Intensive Care' (1999) 33 *Law and Society Review* 17.

[47] ibid.

These concerns reflect the policy tensions that can arise where health boards and people within them assess the implications to the health board arising from a recommendation made by the SPSO. The greater the gap between the recommendation and the existing organisational approach, the less likely the recommendation will be fully implemented. As participants clearly thought that, on occasion, recommendations were unrealistic and not rooted in everyday reality, it is clear that policy tensions will inevitably arise.

XIII. Defensive Behaviours

It is well known that clinicians do not always respond positively when they are personally the subject of a complaint,[48] with many doctors exhibiting negative attitudes.[49] Such attitudes are likely to be enhanced by a focus on errors,[50] and focusing on errors is exactly what the SPSO does. For a fuller discussion of this subject, see the chapter in this book by Gill et al. In its investigation reports, the SPSO uses the language of adjudication, such as phrases like 'upheld' and 'not upheld', and also uses words such as 'failings' and 'unreasonable' – language which reinforces the idea of error.

One factor that may worsen the experience for clinicians who receive a complaint and which may encourage defensive behaviours is the complaints process that is utilised. Nash et al claim that doctors wanted the complaints process to be transparent and to be overseen by competent staff.[51] Bourne et al found that what was particularly stressful for doctors were the uncertain duration of the investigation, poor communication between clinician and complaint handler and the unpredictability of the complaints process and procedures, with many viewing the complaints process as biased in favour of the complainant.[52] As a result, doctors 'felt neglected and betrayed by complaints procedures'.[53] This reinforces

[48] S Zengin, B Al, E Yavuz, G Kursunkoseler, R Guzel, M Sabak and C Yildirm, 'Analysis of Complaints Lodged by Patients Attending a University Hospital: A 4-Year Analysis' (2014) 22 *Journal of Forensic and Legal Medicine* 121.

[49] See W Cunningham, 'New Zealand Doctors' Attitudes towards the Complaints and Disciplinary Process' (2004) 117 *New Zealand Medical Journal* 1198; D Douglas and RD Harrison, 'Turning Around Patient Complaints in a Regional Hospital' (1996) 19 *Australian Health Review* 126; TH Gallagher and W Levinson, 'Physicians with Multiple Patient Complaints: Ending Our Silence' (2013) 22 *BMJ Quality and Safety* 521.

[50] D Gray and S Williams, 'From Blaming to Learning: Re-framing Organisational Learning from Adverse Events' (2011) 18 *The Learning Organisation* 438.

[51] L Nash, C Tennant and M Walton, 'The Psychological Impact of Complaints and Negligence Suits on Doctors' (2004) 12 *Australasian Psychiatry* 278.

[52] T Bourne, J Vanderhaegen, R Vranken, L Wynants, B De Cock, M Peters, D Timmerman, B Van Calster, M Jalmbrant and C Van Audenhove, 'Doctors' Experiences and Their Perception of the Most Stressful Aspects of Complaints Processes in the UK: An Analysis of Qualitative Survey Data' (2016) 6(7) *BMJ Open* doi:10.1136/bmjopen-2016-011711.

[53] ibid 2.

the negative response from doctors, and it is here that the SPSO performs badly. The SPSO does not set out in advance how long an investigation may take, and its performance standard is to complete 85 per cent of investigations in 12 months.[54] During an investigation, there is, generally, little in the way of communication between the SPSO and the health board, so the health board is unaware of exactly what is happening during the investigation and is frustrated, as previously noted, at not being able to discuss the clinical aspects of the case.

Defensive behaviours from clinicians and other staff were seen to be a potential problem by participants: 'we can all be quite defensive when we're responding to complaints' (Eleanor); 'I have witnessed other folk … getting quite defensive and feeling that some of the recommendations or commentary is personal' (Deirdre); and 'nobody wants their care criticised at all, which is very difficult' (Isobel). As several participants reported, the result of all these factors for many clinicians is defensive behaviours. The presence of defensive behaviours by clinicians may result in attempts to block or distort information[55] and reduced efforts to learn from complaints.[56] Thus, attempts by the SPSO to improve the delivery of healthcare may be compromised.

The triad of obstacles identified by Hertogh[57] is, therefore, exhibited: the purpose behind recommendations may be unclear, a significant policy tension may arise between what is proposed and what the health board considers deliverable, and clinicians and managers may demonstrate defensive behaviours. Any of these obstacles would be a significant block, but it is possible that all three will exist for any given SPSO report. If it is only the fear of sanction that may arise from non-compliance that drives action, it would be realistic to expect that the response from health boards will be diminished and that they may deliver little more than the minimum change.

XIV. The Third Element of the Conceptual Model: Institutional Logics

The model of administrative control within the SPSO is shaped by the dominant institutional logic held within it. The SPSO has a dominant coercive model of administrative control and this is shaped by a dominant accountability institutional logic.

[54] SPSO, 'Performance Indicators' (2020) www.spso.org.uk/performance-indicators.

[55] C Argyris, *Overcoming Organisational Defences – Facilitating Organizational Learning* (Allyn & Bacon, 1990).

[56] C Homburg and A Furst, 'See No Evil, Hear No Evil, Speak No Evil: A Study of Defensive Organisational Behaviour towards Customer Complaints' (2007) 35 *Journal of the Academy of Marketing Science* 523.

[57] ibid.

Thus, the third element within this new model is that of the metatheory of institutional logics, which acts as a framework that influences the decisions and actions of individuals and organisations. In the field of healthcare quality and regulation there exist two dominant institutional logics, the accountability and learning logics. Identifying the dominant institutional logic within the SPSO is challenging as the SPSO attempts to utilise both types. The accountability logic is used by the SPSO in the investigation and adjudication of complaints. The language of published investigation reports and decision summaries is full of words indicative of a dominant accountability logic: there is a focus on error, complaints are upheld or not upheld, clinicians 'should' have done something they had not done and professionals and organisations have failed or acted unreasonably. In fact, a review of summary investigation reports finds repeated use of the term 'unreasonable'. It appears that clinicians have not been wrong or made an error; they have been unreasonable or acted unreasonably.

At the same time, the SPSO has revised its approach to recommendations, where it is increasingly attempting to use a learning logic. The intention of this revised approach is to provide organisations with the ability to identify their own 'road to Rome', which is more indicative of a learning logic as it may encourage organisations to reflect on identified problems and develop credible solutions. However, this new approach to recommendations is more prescriptive than suggested by some of the SPSO participants in this research. While health boards are instructed in broad terms about what they should do to achieve a specified outcome, the evidence required by the SPSO to confirm compliance with recommendations acts as a constraint. Health boards may be told what they have to do, what would be acceptable documents to confirm compliance and by when the recommendations must be completed. In practice, recommendations turn out to be more prescriptive than might have been suggested by some of the SPSO participants in this research, which suggests a more dominant accountability type logic than a learning logic. These two institutional logics make for uneasy bedfellows and, inevitably, one of these logics will become the dominant logic. This dominant logic will affect the nature of the relationship between the SPSO and the health boards. The dominant institutional logic within the SPSO is that of accountability, with its principal focus on the adjudication of complaint investigations using normative standards, the reasonableness of clinicians, error and prescriptive recommendations.

It has been claimed that ombudsman exert a diagonal form of accountability with bodies in jurisdiction.[58] Diagonal forms of accountability combine elements from both vertical accountability, where a formal power relationship

[58] W Frees, W Van Acker and G Bouckaert, 'The Role of Feedback, Accountability and Learning in Organizational Change and Innovation: A Theoretical Framework' (2015) LIPSE Project Working Paper No 5 https://limo.libis.be/primo-explore/fulldisplay?docid=LIRIAS1867056&context=L&vid=Lirias&search_scope=Lirias&tab=default_tab&lang=en_US&fromSitemap=1.

exists between parties, and horizontal accountability, where there is no formal power relationship but where accountability is offered voluntarily. However, as the dominant institutional logic of the SPSO is the accountability logic, the form of accountability between the SPSO and health boards is more vertical than diagonal. As this accountability institutional logic determines the attitudes and behaviours of staff within the SPSO, it will significantly influence the form of administrative control that is adopted by the SPSO and the nature of its relationship with health boards.

XV. Conclusion

The SPSO relies principally upon its use of recommendations arising from upheld complaints to contribute to system improvement. The responses from health professionals to these recommendations are dependent upon their opinion about the validity of the individual decision and recommendations. That is, while, within health boards, there will be dominant motivational postures, the response from health professionals is, to a large degree, complaint dependent. Where health professionals agree with the investigation report, there will be a greater commitment to implementing the associated recommendations. Staff within health boards effectively triage SPSO investigation reports and make their own decision about the validity of the report. This decision by health boards guides their response and creates a large degree of potential variability in their response, with some investigation reports creating significant change while others creating little change. This explains the equivocal findings from previous academic research, as noted by Gill.[59]

A new conceptual model was presented to explain how health organisations respond to SPSO investigation reports. Key to implementing change were the motivational postures adopted by individuals and health organisations, which, in turn, were created by the nature of the relationship that exists between the health ombudsman and health bodies. The nature of this relationship was strongly influenced by the dominant institutional logic adopted by the health ombudsman. Two dominant motivational postures were identified for the SPSO, those of commitment and capitulation, where the motivational posture of capitulation was more prevalent due to a relationship between the SPSO and the health boards that was more coercive than cooperative in nature, this relationship being influenced by a dominant accountability logic within the SPSO.

The issue for the SPSO to consider is what it wants to be – a body holding healthcare organisations and clinicians to account or one that works with healthcare organisations and professionals to facilitate learning from complaints which

[59] Gill (n 5).

lead to system improvements. Currently the SPSO is trying to attempt both. But, as Dodds and Kodate note, in relation to the attempts by the National Health Service in England to utilise both approaches in regard to the patient safety agenda, the result is that 'two differing logics are being promulgated as policy, and applied in practice, to the same organisational field simultaneously, with no escape for those who work in the service, and little official recognition of the conflicts between these alternative policies'. They conclude that this approach is harmful to patients.[60] Purdy and Gray, in their research on institutional logics in the area of alternative dispute resolution in the USA, identified some organisations that attempted to combine institutional logics of accountability and learning, but found that ultimately one logic dominated.[61] This is in keeping with other claims about institutional logics: that, although multiple institutional logics may coexist within an organisation, one will always end up becoming the dominant institutional logic within an organisation. As Carney et al state, balancing a focus on system improvement with individual complains resolution is problematic 'both conceptually and in the overall governance system'.[62] The SPSO has to decide which institutional logic it wishes to be dominant within its organisation.

Both forms of institutional logic – accountability logic and learning logic – are legitimate choices for the SPSO. If it chooses to focus on adjudication and the holding of healthcare organisations and professionals to account, then there is a need for it to review its operations to maximise procedural fairness in the process to enhance its legitimacy with bodies in jurisdiction, including improving the transparency of its investigations and providing health boards with a voice during the investigation. If the SPSO chooses to focus on maximising learning, then there is a need for it to change the way it interacts with bodies in jurisdiction and conduct its investigations. While participants from health boards indicated that they would be very happy to work with the SPSO on maximising learning, so too may patients. Carney et al note that health complainants are often very interested in the impact of their complaint on the quality of services,[63] while both Friele et al and Bismark et al found that, for complainants, service improvement is a common objective to be obtained through complaining.[64] However, attempting to utilise both institutional logics is likely to frustrate the less dominant approach, in this case the contribution by the SPSO to system improvement.

[60] Dodds and Kodate (n 28) 341.

[61] JM Purdy and B Gray, 'Conflicting Logics. Mechanisms of Diffusion, and Multilevel Dynamics in Emerging Institutional Fields' (2009) 52 *Academy of Management Journal* 355.

[62] Carney et al (n 9) 82.

[63] ibid.

[64] RD Friele, S Kruikemeier, JDJ Jany, JM Rafemakers and R Coppen, 'Comparing the Outcome of Two Different Procedures to Handle Complaints from a Patient's Perspective' (2013) 20 *Journal of Forensic and Legal Medicine* 290; MM Bismark, MJ Spittal, AJ Gogos, RL Gruen and DM Studdert, 'Remedies Sought and Obtained in Healthcare Complaints' (2011) 20 *BMJ Quality and Safety* 806.

5

The Role of Ombuds Institutes in Providing Equal Access to Justice for All

MAAIKE DE LANGEN

I. Introduction

The United Nations' 2030 Agenda sets 17 ambitious sustainable development goals (SDGs). In this global agenda, SDG16 established access to justice for all as a universal goal for the first time.[1] The adoption of this goal has sparked a shift in the understanding and operationalisation of access to justice. An emerging global movement now argues that justice is central to socio-economic development and that people should be at the centre of justice.[2] This is called people-centred justice.

In this chapter, I discuss the relevance of people-centred justice for the ombuds function.[3] Based on a case study of reforms implemented by the National Ombudsman of the Netherlands, I will compare the ombuds methods developed in the Netherlands to the principles of people-centred justice put forward in the context of SDG16. I will show how the ombuds institute of the Netherlands, in a move which predated the introduction of the SDG16, transitioned away from semi-adjudicative methods to a people-centred approach *avant la lettre*.

[1] The full text of SDG16 is to 'promote peaceful and inclusive societies for sustainable development, provide access to justice for all and build effective, accountable and inclusive institutions at all levels': https://sdgs.un.org/goals/goal16. Although the SDGs were adopted in 2015, they reflect and build upon decades of earlier work by the UN and its many governmental and non-governmental partners.

[2] Task Force on Justice, 'Justice for All – Final Report' (Center on International Cooperation, 2019) www.justice.sdg16.plus/report.

[3] In this chapter, I use the terms ombuds or ombuds institute, which are considered gender neutral, where I write about the institute in general. Where I refer to the National Ombudsman of the Netherlands, I follow the official, constitutional designation as 'ombudsman'. For more on the gendered nature of the term ombudsman, see V Bondy and M Doyle, 'What's in a Name? A Discussion Paper in Ombuds Terminology' in M Hertogh and R Kirkham (eds), *Research Handbook on the Ombudsman* (Edward Elgar Publishing, 2018).

Ombuds institutes have long been seen as quasi-judicial institutions, with both their operations and understanding of their role mirroring those of courts or tribunals. The global movement for people-centred justice, sparked by the adoption of SDG16, provides a new justification for ombuds institutes to turn away from this quasi-judicial approach. As I will show, SDG16 offers an opportunity for ombuds institutes to embrace their unique role as providers of people-centred justice services in the modern state.

I conclude that ombuds institutes should seize this opportunity to strengthen their own effectiveness and relevance, and change the understanding of their role, their vision and their operations to align with the principles of people-centred justice. At the global level, ombuds institutes and the International Ombudsman Institute (IOI) should articulate and leverage the contribution of ombuds institutes to the SDGs and attain recognition for their vital role in the social justice landscape in their countries.

II. The 2030 Agenda and the Goal to Provide Access to Justice for All

The 2030 Agenda

In 2015, world leaders gathered at the United Nations to adopt the 2030 Agenda. This is not a binding agreement, but a global plan of action meant to underpin national strategies and collaborative partnerships for the achievement of a set of universal goals.[4] These global goals were agreed after an extensive process of multilateral negotiation, with input from a global consultation process which involved more than 1 million people and gathered priorities to help build a collective vision of 'the world we want'.[5] The goals cover a range of social, economic and environmental objectives, and include topics such as poverty and hunger, education, healthcare, gender equality, water and sanitation, sustainable energy, employment, reducing inequality, combating climate change, and protecting the oceans and ecosystems.[6] They provide a platform for people, organisations and countries to align their actions and collaborate more effectively to achieve shared ambitions.

SDG16 on Peaceful, Just and Inclusive Societies

Goal 16 is to 'promote peaceful and inclusive societies for sustainable development, provide access to justice for all and build effective, accountable and inclusive

[4] UN General Assembly Resolution A/RES/70/1, https://sdgs.un.org/2030agenda.

[5] United Nations Development Group, 'A Million Voices: The World We Want, A Sustainable Future with Dignity for All' (2013) https://unsdg.un.org/sites/default/files/The-World-we-Want.pdf.

[6] For a description of the 17 Sustainable Development Goals, see https://sdgs.un.org/goals.

institutions at all levels'.[7] It includes nine targets covering a range of topics related to violence reduction, the combating of illicit financial flows and organised crime, the reduction of corruption and bribery, the need for access to information and participatory decision-making, and the provision of legal identity for all.

The inclusion of access to justice in a universal agenda for economic and social development recognises the fact that justice systems are fundamental to the achievement of the other goals. As many have said in discussions at and around the United Nations, 'Justice is a thread that runs through all 17 Sustainable Development Goals'.[8]

The importance of peace, justice and inclusion seems a natural progression as part of a broader agenda for societies across the world, especially as these concepts are foundational in the ability to achieve the other goals. Yet, the inclusion of a universal goal on peace, justice and inclusion in the 2030 agenda was hard fought. Once SDG16 was adopted, a number of the countries that supported it came together at a global level to work together as the Pathfinders for Peaceful, Just and Inclusive Societies.[9] The group developed a roadmap for the achievement of SDG16 in which they defined three so-called 'grand challenges'.[10] The first grand challenge that countries chose to collaborate on was the provision of equal access to justice for all.

The Task Force on Justice

In order to devise a strategy for the achievement of the goal of providing justice for all by 2030, the Pathfinders set up an international Task Force on Justice.[11] Chaired by ministers from the Netherlands, Argentina and Sierra Leone and the Elders,[12] the Task Force was composed of a group of experts from different countries and sectors. Its goal was to set a policy and learning agenda, while raising ambition and increasing political will.

The work of the Task Force on Justice was organised around four main questions:[13] How many people currently lack access to justice and what does this justice gap look like? What is the case for action and investment in equal access to

[7] https://sdgs.un.org/goals/goal16.

[8] Task Force on Justice (n 2).

[9] D Steven, 'History and Prospects, the Pathfinders for Peaceful, Just and Inclusive Societies' (April 2018) https://cic.nyu.edu/sites/default/files/pathfinders_history_and_prospects_23apr18.pdf. The website of the Pathfinders for Peaceful, Just and Inclusive Societies is at www.sdg16.plus/.

[10] Pathfinders for Peaceful, Just and Inclusive Societies, 'The Roadmap for Peaceful, Just and Inclusive Societies – A Call to Action to Change our World' (Center on International Cooperation, 2019) www.sdg16.plus/roadmap.

[11] The website of the Task Force on Justice is at www.justice.sdg16.plus/.

[12] An independent group of global leaders working together for peace, justice and human rights. The group was founded by Nelson Mandela in 2007. See https://theelders.org/.

[13] For the terms of reference of the Task Force on Justice, see www.justice.sdg16.plus/task-force-on-justice.

justice for all? What strategies, tools and approaches will increase access to justice? And lastly, what commitments should national and local actors make to closing the justice gap and how can international cooperation support access to justice at the national level?

A two-year process of policy research followed. This was highly collaborative.[14] A wide range of organisations contributed research and evidence, facilitated meetings and working groups, and compiled reports as inputs to the overall work of the Task Force.[15] The end result was the *Justice for All* report, which brought together data and evidence on these overarching questions, as well as a wide range of underlying issues and questions.[16]

III. A New Understanding of Access to Justice

From this work emerged a new understanding of access to justice, presented in the *Justice for All* report.[17] To begin with, the report takes a broad understanding of the word 'justice' and does not focus on access to justice systems as we currently know them: the judges, courts and institutions. It argues that 'we live in a world where justice systems only deliver justice for the few', and estimates that 5.1 billion people do not have meaningful access to justice. This is the global justice gap.

Rather than focusing on 'buildings, processes and institutions', the *Justice for All* report emphasises the need to put justice at the heart of development.[18] As a consequence, the report shifts focus to what justice systems should be providing: the foundations for a society in which people are able to stand up for their rights, resolve disputes peacefully, address structural injustices, have a fair chance in the economy and can participate freely in public life. This new approach understands access to justice as the ability of people to resolve and prevent their justice problems, and to use justice as a platform to participate in their economies and societies.[19] It combines a pragmatic approach, aimed at problem-solving in individual cases with a direct impact on people's lives, with the understanding that a focus on people's problems will shine a light on practical bottlenecks and structural injustices in society, and provide an empirical basis to raise and address systemic problems that impact people's lives.

An empirical approach is also applied to understand people's justice journeys from problem to solution.[20] The report focuses on the need to improve the quality

[14] M de Langen and K Gerlach, 'Forging the International Movement for Achieving Justice for All' (Center on International Cooperation, 2020) https://papers.ssrn.com/sol3/papers.cfm?abstract_id=3870816.

[15] All related reports and publications are available at www.justice.sdg16.plus/report.

[16] Task Force on Justice (n 2).

[17] ibid.

[18] ibid.

[19] ibid.

[20] ibid.

of justice journeys through the empowerment of people and communities, the provision of people-centred justice services and the achievement of fair outcomes. The report goes on to identify the ways in which justice works for the prevention of violence and conflict, and it identifies the levers for change that policy-makers can use to reform their justice system: data, innovation, smarter investments and diverse partnerships. This new understanding of access to justice has become known as 'people-centred justice'.

In February 2019, the Hague Declaration on Equal Access to Justice for All by 2030 was endorsed by 22 governments.[21] This declaration included five principles of people-centred justice, which have since been endorsed in other multilateral declarations and action plans.[22] Most recently, these principles were reiterated and endorsed in a joint letter to the UN Secretary General.[23]

The principles of people-centred justice are: to put people and their legal needs at the centre of justice systems; to solve justice problems; to improve the quality of justice journeys; to use justice for prevention; and to enable people to access services and opportunities. These principles flow from and are underpinned by the *Justice for All* report.[24] I will return to these principles after the case study.

IV. The Ombuds Institute and People-Centred Justice

The notion of people-centred justice as described above is a natural fit with the work and techniques of ombuds institutes. Three central characteristics that have long been the hallmark of ombuds institutes are well aligned with people-centred justice:

- The free and easy access for citizens, with no fees or charges and a general absence of formal or procedural requirements to submit a complaint or grievance to the ombudsman.
- The application of flexible approaches to resolving the problem at hand, using fact-finding, mediation, public reporting and other methods to respond to grievances and address injustices.

[21] The Declaration on Equal Access to Justice for All by 2030 was adopted at the Ministerial Roundtable on Access to Justice, hosted by HE Sigrid Kaag, Minister for Foreign Trade and International Cooperation of the Netherlands, in the Peace Palace in The Hague on 7 February 2019. The declaration was endorsed by: the Ministers of Justice or their deputies or the Attorney Generals of Afghanistan, Argentina, Canada, Ethiopia, Gambia, Guinea, Indonesia, Libya, the Netherlands, Niger, Palestinian Territories, Rwanda, Sierra Leone, Timor-Leste, Tunisia, Uganda, and Ukraine and the Ministers of International Cooperation or their deputies from Finland, Luxembourg, the Netherlands, Switzerland and the UK. The text is available at https://bf889554-6857-4cfe-8d55-8770007b8841.filesusr.com/ugd/90b3d6_9357f6ca843f452db89b671b1675524e.pdf.

[22] Buenos Aires Declaration and G7+ Action Plan.

[23] Joint Letter to the UN Secretary-General of 14 April 2021, 'Reimagining Social Contracts: A Call to Put People at the Center of Justice' www.justice.sdg16.plus/ministerial.

[24] Task Force on Justice (n 2).

- The interaction between individual cases and structural improvements, which takes shape, for example, in periodic reports to the legislative branch, as well as own-motion investigations with recommendations to the executive branch.

Beyond this alignment at the level of the ombuds technique, however, lies a fundamental question about the identity of the ombuds institute, which has been answered in different ways by both office holders and academics in different contexts. The question, simply put, is: Is the ombuds a special form of administrative court or tribunal, or is it something of a different nature?

One direction of development of ombuds institutes has been to mimic courts: they are often staffed by lawyers, and they apply legal methods and procedures. Interactions are preferably in written form, and the focus is on establishing facts and deciding the case in an essentially adversarial model. In both the UK and Australia, an 'imposition of judicial values on the ombudsman sector' caused by the supervisory role of the judiciary in those jurisdictions has pushed ombuds institutes in this direction.[25] The other direction chosen by ombuds institutes is that they are fundamentally different from courts, and not just because they cannot take legally binding decisions. Both academics and office holders have emphasised profound differences in role, function, powers, purpose and methods, even though there is no clear vocabulary to express this 'otherness'; this non-court nature of ombuds institutes.[26]

Nick O'Brien distinguishes these two distinct ways of framing and understanding the role of the ombuds and labels them legal liberalism or 'individualistic legalism' on the one hand and legal pragmatism or 'deliberative problem-solving' on the other.[27] The first, legal liberalism or individualistic legalism, has had as an underlying philosophy to bring the ombuds institute 'ever closer to the quasi-judicial adjudicative model of responding to grievance'.[28] The 'modest proposal' that O'Brien makes in his chapter is that ombuds institutes 'must boldly break out of the constraints imposed by individualistic legalism'.[29] He goes on to write:

> Instead of positioning itself as an institution whose relentless evolution drives it toward emulation of the judicial process, or indeed towards an 'alternative' form of 'dispute resolution' which is merely a mirror image of that process, it must re-imagine itself as a form of social ordering based on its own distinctive technique and seek a theoretical context in which that technique can flourish, without an apology to other forms of social ordering such as adjudication and mediation.[30]

[25] R Kirkham and A Stuhmcke, 'The Common Law Theory and Practice of the Ombudsman/Judiciary Relationship' (2020) 49 *Common Law World Review* 56.

[26] The issue here is not simply the non-judicial nature of ombuds, but equally the concepts that ombuds administer, which do not necessarily have any equivalence with traditional legal concepts. The analysis of maladministration by Greg Weeks in ch 2 of this book explains how that concept is central to the work of ombuds but is a difficult one for courts to grasp.

[27] N O'Brien, 'Ombudsmen and Public Authorities: A Modest Proposal' in Hertogh and Kirkham (n 3).

[28] ibid 43.

[29] ibid 45.

[30] ibid.

It is true that, depending on their legislative framework, most ombuds institutes have a high degree of flexibility in how they fulfil their mandate. Office holders have discretion as to which direction they wish to develop the institute – to be more like courts, claiming space among the more conventional players in the administrative justice landscape, or to emphasise the differences from regular court procedures and make optimal use of their unique added value.[31]

I argue in this chapter that the sustainable development goals and the concept of people-centred justice that has emerged as the new understanding of access to justice provide a theoretical context as well as a normative imperative for ombuds institutes to choose this second, non-court-like direction of problem-solving and to understand and articulate their role in these terms. When ombudsman embrace their role as non-court providers of people-centred justice services, they will strengthen their contribution to the provision of equal access to justice for all.

V. Case Study of the Netherlands Ombuds Institute

In this case study, I describe the approaches and strategies developed by the National Ombudsman of the Netherlands between 2006 and 2016, drawing from my own experience working in the institute for the majority of those years. The case study reflects on both the vision for the ombuds institute that was developed and the implementation of those ideas in practice. As will become clear, this conceptualisation and these approaches and strategies amounted to a clear push of the institute in the second direction described above: away from its quasi-judicial identity and methods towards a problem-solving, non-court-like role, as an actor that mediates the relationship between citizens and their authorities.[32]

A New Vision for the Work of the Ombudsman

Shortly after his appointment as National Ombudsman of the Netherlands in 2005, Alex Brenninkmeijer started to lay out a new vision for understanding interactions between people and the authorities.[33] This vision played out in the assessment of public sector organisations, as well as in the development of recommendations for improving public services. Three central concepts underpinned this vision of the ombudsman.

[31] This possibility is central to the arguments of Nick O'Brien, in ch 14 of this volume.

[32] During this period, similarly innovative practices were attempted in other parts of the Dutch legal system. An example is the novel and proactive procedures adopted by judges in the Dutch Administrative Court, which were designed to help parties understand how the court sought to treat them fairly. See A Verburg and B Schueler, 'Procedural Justice in Dutch Administrative Court Proceedings' (2014) 10 *Utrecht Law Review* 56.

[33] An early articulation of this vision was expressed in the Van Slingelandtlezing Lecture given by Alex Brenninkmeijer in November 2006. A version of the lecture was published as: A Brenninkmeijer, 'Eerlijk bestuur: Over rechtmatigheid en behoorlijkheid' (2007) 16 *Bestuurskunde* 58.

(i) Lifeworld versus System World

The first central concept is that many complaints that are submitted to the ombudsman can be traced back to tensions between the lifeworld (the reality of citizens) and the system world (the context in which bureaucracies and civil servants operate).[34] Based on the work of Jurgen Habermas, amongst others, this distinction is a useful model to analyse where things go wrong between people and the authorities. To give an example, for a government system, accuracy and legality are highly prioritised. It is important to calculate the amount of social security someone is entitled to correctly, even if that means the transfer of funds has to be delayed by three months. For a person facing financial difficulties, who is on the brink of eviction and needs the money to pay rent and avoid debts, the timing of the payment is much more important than that the amount is right to the last penny.

The clash between the lifeworld and the system world is evident from a significant number of complaints that reach the ombudsman which convey incredulity or desperation about how the system operates and the indifference that civil servants display at the impacts on people's lives. The writings of Franz Kafka powerfully convey the alienation that people experience when systems impose their unemotional logic on people's lives.[35] This understanding is important in empathising with the complainant and re-establishing communication with the authorities.[36]

(ii) Interfaces

Modern societies are complex and require large-scale operations for the efficient processing of benefits, taxation and decision-making. Having a bureaucracy that operates as a system, and with the logic of the system world, is therefore inevitable. But the complexity of the systems often impacts the ability of people to access the public services that they are entitled to. To better understand the complaints and deal with the grievances appropriately, it is useful to focus on the touchpoints between people's lives and the bureaucracy, which can be characterised as interfaces. The relationship between citizens and the public authorities passes through such interfaces: phone calls that are not returned; forms that are difficult to fill out; police officers that are unruffled in the face of exceptional circumstances; and websites that force people to choose between categories where none apply.

[34] AF Brenninkmeijer, 'Eerlijk bestuur: Over rechtmatigheid en behoorlijkheid' (2007) 16 *Bestuurskunde* 58; National Ombudsman, *Regel is regel, is niet genoeg*, Annual Report 2006. Parliamentary reference: Verslag van de Nationale ombudsman over 2006, Kamerstukken II 2006/07, 30 990, 2.

[35] A Brenninkmeijer, 'Kafka als icoon' (2010) 3 *Christen Democratische Verkenningen* 58.

[36] This argument seems to underpin the analysis of J Williams, C Gill and C Hirst, 'Towards Therapeutic Complaints Resolution', ch 12 of this volume.

The authorities carry responsibility for shaping these interfaces in such a way that they are relevant to people's lives and underpin a positive interaction with the authorities. Any relationship can encounter conflict, so understanding conflicts and processes of escalation and de-escalation are critical to designing effective interfaces.[37] They also need to take account of the differences between people in terms of their abilities and needs and then design the interfaces from that perspective, not that of the bureaucracy, allowing it to respond flexibly depending on the people and the situation.

(iii) Law versus Proper Conduct

A third central notion is that 'the law[] is not enough'.[38] Clearly, public sector organisations should respect the law and adhere to the principle of legality. But the National Ombudsman emphasised that following procedures is insufficient. To evaluate complaints, the Ombudsman uses the notion of proper conduct, a set of norms for the relationship between citizen and the authorities.[39] The requirements of proper conduct are the normative framework that indicates what citizens can reasonably expect from public sector organisations. For example, when someone has to wait seven months for a response to a simple request to his or her municipality, it may not be against the law, but the Ombudsman sees it as a violation of the requirement of expeditious service.

Relationship between Citizen and State

These different elements of the vision led to a changing understanding of the relationship between citizen and the state.[40] Moving away from an overly rationalised and often vertical or top-down interaction between people and the authorities, the National Ombudsman proposed a horizontal understanding of this relationship and a recognition of both its rational and emotional components.

This also impacted how the Ombudsman chose to mediate the relationship between citizens and the authorities. Its horizontal understanding of the relationship with citizens, the importance of interfaces and the holistic and flexible approach focused on problem-solving was important to how the ombuds institute carried out its own functions.

[37] National Ombudsman, *Voorbij het conflict*, Annual Report 2009. Parliamentary reference: Verslag van de Nationale ombudsman over 2009, Kamerstukken II 2009/10, 32322, 2.

[38] In Dutch: *Regel is regel, is niet genoeg*, which was the title and the central concept presented by the National Ombudsman in his Annual Report 2006 (n 33).

[39] Guidelines on proper conduct, published by the National Ombudsman of the Netherlands in English in May 2015, www.nationaleombudsman.nl/folders-en-brochures/guidelines-on-proper-conduct.

[40] National Ombudsman, *Burgerschap verzilverd*, Annual Report 2007. Parliamentary reference: Verslag van de Nationale ombudsman over 2007, Kamerstukken II 2007/08, 31 363, 2.

Implementation: Innovating Complaint Handling

The ombuds institute is not only a complaint handling and oversight mechanism for public sector organisations, it is also a bureaucracy and therefore a system in and of itself. In order to 'practise what it preached', the institute overhauled its way of dealing with complaints by applying these central concepts to its own practice. In the period 2006–16, the ombuds institute innovated all aspects of complaint handling and its interactions with citizens. While much was written about the vision, little has been published about the implementation in practice.[41] Some of the central initiatives are briefly described here.

(i) The Intervention Method

The first was the establishment and development of the intervention method as a way to handle complaints. The default procedure assumed by the Dutch Administrative Law Act is that the National Ombudsman investigates a complaint and publishes a report.[42] The reality has always been that only a small number of all complaints lodged by citizens result in a written, public report by the ombuds institute. In practice, many complaints are better addressed by resolving the actual problem and, where necessary, addressing underlying issues. This is called the intervention method. Evaluations showed that citizens were more satisfied in cases where their problem was resolved than in those where they received a written report from the Ombudsman. Someone waiting for a tax return is more interested in receiving funds in the bank than in a long investigation culminating in a statement that indeed they should receive the reimbursements, while still not having the actual money. Someone who has a violent encounter with the police might prefer a personal conversation with the police officer in question about what had happened and why, including an apology where appropriate, over a written report, even if that formally establishes that the action was wrong.

The intervention method entails investigation, often in the form of communicating with both the complainant and the relevant civil servants to find out where the problem occurred, what is behind it and what needs to be done to resolve it; then, depending on the specifics of the case, getting the authorities to take corrective action, to explain and apologise, to take part in a mediation or to remedy the problem in some other way.

[41] The exception to this is G Bekman, 'Change Programme: National Ombudsman of the Netherlands' www.nationaleombudsman.nl/uploads/change_programme_national_ombudsman_of_the_netherlands_dublin_version.pdf.

[42] M de Langen, 'Investigative Powers of the Ombudsman: A Brief Description of the Legal Context of Own Initiative Investigations by the National Ombudsman of the Netherlands' (21 September 2017) SSRN: https://ssrn.com/abstract=3048042.

(ii) Direct Approach

Building on the expansion of the use of the intervention method, the second major innovation was what was called the direct approach or immediate response (in Dutch: *direct aanpakken*). This changed the service delivery to citizens and hence the basic workflow in the organisation. In the previous situation, citizens would call the front office, who evaluated the admissibility of the complaint through a series of questions. If the Ombudsman could deal with the complaint, citizens had to submit the complaint in writing. The written complaint then entered the normal workflow of being received, recorded and distributed to an investigator, who would look into it and contact the citizen a few weeks later.

With the direct approach, the front office still performed an initial screening, but then transferred the call so that the citizen would be in direct contact with the investigator during their initial phone call. This resulted in much quicker service:

> [W]ithout any knowledge of the problem the investigator now explores together with the complainant what the problem is. This allows for a very open and inquisitive approach that leads to a more problem-solving outcome. If the case is solved in this way, no files have to be made nor have there any letters to be written.[43]

This change clearly redefined the interaction between the ombuds institute and citizens, who now only have to call and explain their issue. There is no need to write letters detailing complaints. This facilitates access for all people, not least the significant number of people who are functionally illiterate: 18 per cent of the adult population in the Netherlands.[44] Additionally, when investigators communicate by phone the interaction is immediate, and if the complainant does not understand what they are saying, they will be prompted to explain themselves in plain language. This results in better service delivery.

An added benefit was that many simple cases were resolved with less burden on the organisation, so there were significant efficiency gains. The institute went on to develop quality criteria for phone interactions, including that each call had to be answered within 20 seconds and a complainant could not be transferred more than once, only from the front office to the investigator.[45] Such guidelines were based on data about customer experience from the private sector.

(iii) Communication, Mediation and Listening Skills

To be successful in this much more direct communication, staff received extensive training to develop the appropriate communication, mediation and listening skills. In the phone calls, they needed to combine multiple functions. On the one

[43] Bekman (n 41).

[44] Aanpak van laaggeletterdheid, *Rapport Algemene Rekenkamer* (Report of the Court of Auditors of the Netherlands, 2016) www.rekenkamer.nl/publicaties/rapporten/2016/04/20/aanpak-van-laaggeletterdheid.

[45] Bekman (n 41).

hand, they needed to ensure that people were taken seriously and felt heard, while on the other they also needed to understand the issue at hand, collect the relevant information, make a legal diagnosis, understand the context, any related issues or underlying conflicts, and identify the best next step.

People tied up in alienating procedures can be extremely frustrated, so managing emotions and de-escalating conflict were important skills to possess. In more serious cases, the complaint could be a way to express mourning over loss, for example of the complainant's health, a job or a family member. Staff were therefore trained to recognise stages of mourning and common expressions of grief, learning the necessary communication skills to address such emotions effectively. The direct exchanges enabled staff to identify underlying problems and hence provide a better service to the people that contacted the institute. Here, too, better service went hand-in-hand with efficiency gains.

A relatively high percentage of people that lodge a complaint have a mental health issue, which complicates communication. The institute analysed the different types of difficult behaviour that people displayed and developed appropriate responses for staff.[46] The goal was to empower all staff with the communication and listening skills to respond effectively in such situations. In extreme situations, one staff member who was specialised in this work was available to provide support to staff or take over.

Conclusion

In conclusion, the National Ombudsman of the Netherlands developed a new vision and, in parallel, transformed its complaint handling. This new vision was also the basis of a significant development and strengthening of the Ombudsman's own-motion investigations, described elsewhere.[47] These changes meant a decisive shift away from a quasi-judicial understanding of the role of the ombuds institute and an embracing of the unique possibilities that the ombuds institute has to resolve people's justice problems with authority. A review of the institute conducted in 2010 demonstrated that citizens greatly appreciated the institute's way of working: on average, they gave their experience with the Ombudsman the extremely high rating of 8.2 on a 10-point scale.[48] The final assessment of the Ombudsman by participants in the review process was almost unanimously

[46] 'The story behind the complaint', published in Dutch as Nationale Ombudsman, 'Het Verhaal achter de Klacht, Effectief omgaan met lastig klaaggedrag; een praktische handreiking' (2008) www.nationaleombudsman.nl/uploads/hetverhaalachterdeklacht.pdf.

[47] M de Langen, E Govers, R van Zutphen, 'Effectiveness and Independence of the Ombudsman's Own-Motion Investigations: A Practitioner's Perspective from the Netherlands' in Hertogh and Kirkham (n 3).

[48] 'Reflectie op de Nationale ombudsman' www.verwey-jonker.nl/publicatie/reflectie-op-de-nationale-ombudsman/.

positive and they deemed the Ombudsman indispensable in a social democracy. The review concluded that with its new vision and methods, the institute amplifies people's voices and forces the authorities to continuously improve.[49]

VI. An Early Experience in People-Centred Justice?

Let us now return to the notion of people-centred justice, to compare the way that the National Ombudsman of the Netherlands innovated its complaint handling in the period from 2006 to 2016, as described in the case study, to the five principles of people-centred justice included in the Hague Declaration of 2019.

First Principle: Put People at the Centre

The first notion of putting people and their justice needs at the centre was operationalised in several ways in the change process of the National Ombudsman. By making the process more personal, staff could better respond to the needs that people expressed and adapt their communication style and level of abstraction to the abilities of the person they were talking to. In addition, the organisation was restructured so that the teams were organised around the problems people faced, not around the systems and structures of the public sector.[50]

Second Principle: Solve Justice Problems

The process has a strong focus on helping people solve the problem at hand and not on a procedural, formalistic or normative response to complaints. In order to make its interventions successful, the organisation worked with a network of contact persons that could contribute to identifying bottlenecks and finding solutions. Lastly, the skills that the staff used to understand what people complained about helped to actually get to the core of the problem, including underlying issues, rather than just respond to a much more limited definition of the complaint that used to be formulated in written complaints.

Principles of people-centred justice

Put people and their justice needs at the centre of justice systems

Solve justice problems

Improve the quality of justice journeys

Use justice for prevention

Provide people with the means to access services and opportunities

Hague Declaration on Equal Access to Justice for All by 2030

[49] ibid.
[50] Bekman (n 41).

Third Principle: Improve Justice Journeys

Improving justice journeys, according to the people-centred approach to justice, requires investment in three stages: empowering people, providing people-centred services and delivering fair outcomes. From the outset, the objective of the National Ombudsman was to make the experience that people had when they contacted the Ombudsman markedly different from their interactions with other public organisations. Many of the people that contacted the Ombudsman were empowered with the information they needed for a next step or a better understanding of the issue they were dealing with. The service delivery was made more people-centred throughout, using insights and evidence from other sectors, including around hospitality and research about people's experience with call centres.

In terms of fair outcomes, when people were asked for feedback about their interaction with the ombuds institute, questions were included that focused specifically on people's assessment of the outcome and their experience with the process. This topic was heavily debated internally, since many complaint handlers assumed that people were happy when they got their way, or 'won', and unhappy when they 'lost'. Evidence from the social sciences is quite strong that people separate their evaluation of the outcome from their experience.[51] These insights around procedural justice were shared internally and discussed on many occasions, and were confirmed by the feedback collected from complainants.

Fourth Principle: Use Justice for Prevention

In terms of using justice for prevention, there were two ways in which this was practised in the work of the National Ombudsman. Firstly, as mentioned above, the general understanding of the staff about conflict theory, the escalation ladder and de-escalation techniques was increased. This translated into much more effective and efficient communications, which prevented many complaints procedures from becoming protracted and draining affairs, which benefited both staff and citizens. Another dimension of prevention is the way in which the Ombudsman used the information from individual cases to develop structural recommendations to public authorities to improve their policies, procedures and operations. Own motion investigations were used to dig deeper into issues that emerged repeatedly in the complaint handling.[52]

[51] AT Marseille, BWN Waard, A Tollenaar, P Laskewitz and C Boxum, *De praktijk van de Nieuwe zaaksbehandeling in het bestuursrecht* (Ministerie van Binnenlandse Zaken en Koninkrijksrelaties, Project Prettig Contact met de Overheid, 2015) https://prettigcontactmetdeoverheid.nl/sites/default/files/documenten/BZK%20NZB%20Rapport%20pdf.pdf.

[52] de Langen et al (n 47).

Fifth Principle: Provide People with Means to Access Services and Opportunities

The final principle of people-centred justice relates to providing people with means to access services and opportunities. The Ombudsman provides accessible justice services that can help people break through the legal, administrative and practical barriers they face to obtain documents, access public services and receive the benefits and protections they are entitled to.

Conclusion

Based on the above case study, it is clear that the experience of the National Ombudsman of the Netherlands significantly aligns with the five principles of people-centred justice. As such, it is a relevant experience for the implementation of people-centred justice *avant la lettre*.

In light of this analysis, I conclude that the emerging paradigm of people-centred justice can be useful for ombuds institutes to better articulate their role and contribution as distinct from that of courts and tribunals. The global movement for people-centred justice can provide both a theoretical framework and an authorising environment for ombuds institutes that make this same choice to move away from a quasi-judicial, adversarial role and embrace the identity of problem-solving and people-centred justice service providers in the modern state.

VII. Positioning Ombuds Institutes at the Global Level

At the international level, it seems there are two somewhat different lines of engagement for ombuds institutes. On the one hand, there is the global cooperation of National Human Rights Institutes in the context of GANHRI, the Global Alliance of National Human Rights Institutions.[53] GANHRI decides on applications for the coveted A-status accreditation for national human rights institutes with the UN's Human Rights Council and is affiliated with the Office of the High Commissioner for Human Rights. They can be considered the guardians of the 'Paris Principles'. Ombuds institutes in some cases are the national human rights institute and can apply for A-status if they meet the criteria.

The second line of engagement is through the International Ombudsman Institute, as well as the Council of Europe's Venice Commission, which established its own 'Venice Principles' on the protection and promotion of the ombuds

[53] The GANHRI website is at www.ohchr.org/EN/Countries/NHRI/Pages/About-GANHRI.aspx.

institution.[54] A recent development out of this circuit is the adoption of a UN General Assembly resolution on the role of ombudsman and mediator institutions in the promotion and protection of human rights, good governance and the rule of law.[55] The resolution seems to be adopted after intense lobbying and was hailed by the IOI as 'the culmination of the International Ombudsman Institute's work to develop a closer relationship with the UN'.[56] Remarkably, this resolution seems to mostly be aimed at claiming position for ombuds institutes in relation to discussions about the rule of law and human rights. Through the resolution, the Venice Principles, which were adopted in the context of the Council of Europe, have effectively been endorsed as the new global standard for ombudsman. A surprising omission, certainly from the perspective of building a closer relationship with the UN, is that the resolution makes no mention of the UN's 2030 Agenda or of the Sustainable Development Goals.

At the global level, the choice between quasi-judicial approaches and problem-solving non-court-like approaches repeats itself in some ways. To date, the focus at the global level has been primarily on the contribution of ombuds and mediator institutes to the promotion of human rights, good governance and the rule of law. This aligns with the role of ombuds institutes as quasi-judicial bodies and a more legalistic approach. Interestingly, this comes at a time when the human rights world is recognising that its legalism has significantly limited its impacts.[57] Rather than presenting themselves as a watered-down versions of national human rights institutes, ombuds institutes should communicate the critical role they can fulfil to build peaceful, just and inclusive societies and demonstrate the powerful contributions they can make to providing equal access to justice for all. As is clear from the analysis presented in this chapter, ombuds institutes are uniquely placed to contribute to the achievement of the SDGs.

As at the national level, they can use this to differentiate themselves from other human rights institutions and claim recognition for their unique role in the social justice landscape in their countries. They can propose a more practical and realistic agenda for realising rights and providing people with real opportunities.

At the global level, ombuds institutes and the IOI should articulate and leverage the contribution that ombuds institutes can make to the achievement of the

[54] European Commission for Democracy through Law (Venice Commission), Opinion 897/2017 containing the Venice Principles on the protection and the promotion of the ombudsman institution, www.venice.coe.int/webforms/documents/default.aspx?pdffile=CDL-AD(2019)005-e.

[55] 'The Role of Ombudsman and Mediator Institutions in the Promotion and Protection of Human Rights, Good Governance and the Rule of Law': UN General Assembly Resolution, adopted 16 December 2020 (UN Resolution A/RES/75/168) https://undocs.org/en/A/RES/75/186.

[56] 'United Nations Recognises Importance of Independent Ombudsman', press release 18 December 2021, www.theioi.org/ioi-news/current-news/united-nations-recognises-importance-of-independent-ombudsman.

[57] J Fraser, 'Challenging State-Centricity and Legalism: Promoting the Role of Social Institutions in the Domestic Implementation of International Human Rights Law' (2019) 23 *International Journal of Human Rights* 974.

UN's 2030 Agenda. The IOI could take this forward by working with the United Nations to include this in the next report from the Secretary-General, which member states have requested be submitted in 2022.

In a recent development, the IOI adopted the Dublin Declaration on 25 May 2021 at its General Assembly during the 2021 World Conference. This declaration acknowledges that 'Ombudsman institutions play an important role in the implementation of the United Nations' 2030 Agenda on Sustainable Development, especially Sustainable Development Goal (SDG) N° 16 on access to justice for all and strong, effective, and accountable institutions at all levels', and underlines the contribution ombuds institutes make.[58]

VIII. Ombuds Institutes and Their Contribution to the SDGs

Many different types of organisations, from universities and businesses to municipalities and civil society organisations, are aligning their work with the UN's 2030 Agenda. Ombuds institutes are well placed to contribute to the achievement of the SDGs in several ways. The following is a direct adaptation of the points raised in an article that this author published in mid-May 2021, in which I identified the contributions that ombuds institutes can make.[59]

Closing the Justice Gap

The most direct contribution that ombuds institutes make is to the achievement of goal 16 and target 16.3 to 'provide equal access to justice for all'. Research done for the Task Force on Justice estimated that globally 5.1 billion people do not have meaningful access to justice and 1.5 billion people have unresolved justice problems.[60] Analysis of survey data from more than 100 countries has shown that getting access to public services is among the most common problems that people face.[61] Globally, 19 per cent of the people that have a justice problem have a problem related to accessing public services.[62]

[58] The Dublin Declaration was adopted at the General Assembly of the IOI during its 12th IOI World Conference on 'Giving Voice to the Voiceless' www.theioi.org/ioi-news/current-news/general-assembly-adopts-by-laws-reform-and-dublin-declaration.

[59] M de Langen, 'Eight Ways Ombuds Institutes Can Contribute to the SDGs' (IISD SDG Knowledge hub, 19 May 2021) https://sdg.iisd.org/commentary/guest-articles/eight-ways-ombuds-institutes-can-contribute-to-the-sdgs/.

[60] Task Force on Justice (n 2); World Justice Project, 'Measuring the Justice Gap: A People-Centered Assessment of Unmet Justice Needs Around the World' (World Justice Project, 2019) https://worldjusticeproject.org/our-work/research-and-data/access-justice/measuring-justice-gap.

[61] World Justice Project (n 60).

[62] ibid.

Resolving people's problems in accessing public services is at the heart of the work that ombuds institutes perform around the world, enhancing access to public services with free, simple, accessible and informal complaint handling. If ombuds institutes do what they do and do it well, then the access to justice they provide is their most direct contribution to the SDGs. Through their work, they can help resolve justice problems related to access to public services and contribute to closing the justice gap.

Supporting and Promoting the Shift to People-Centred Justice

Beyond their own direct role, ombuds institutes can contribute to the shift to people-centred justice in the justice sector as a whole. Their work can inspire innovations in the broader justice sector – supporting and promoting the shift to people-centred justice as the most effective way to provide equal access to justice for all. Ombuds institutes are typically much less restricted by procedural requirements than other justice actors, with legislation leaving their modus operandi largely open. Instead of mimicking court procedures, they can steer their institute in the direction of problem-solving and the delivery of people-centred justice services, as we have seen. They are therefore well placed to innovate their services and discover what works best to resolve people's justice problems.

These experiences can contribute to improving the quality of justice journeys and collecting data and evidence to develop a better understanding of how best to resolve justice problems that people face. As such, they can help set a broader agenda for change for the justice sector, where civil, criminal and administrative courts and tribunals can learn from and perhaps mimic the operations of the ombuds institute. They can enable this by sharing their innovations, experiences and insights to support a stronger problem-solving approach. Given the more natural 'iterative' techniques that ombuds use, they can also be an example for how to strengthen the links between the individual cases that they resolve and the structural improvements that are necessary to prevent justice issues from occurring in the first place.[63] Learning from individual cases to address structural problems can be enhanced by more systematic collection of data about complaints and the publication of this data in an open format.[64] Where they have the mandate to handle complaints about key formal justice institutions, such as the police or courts, ombuds institutes can make recommendations on how to improve their service delivery based on a people-centred approach to justice, in line with SDG16.

[63] de Langen (n 59).

[64] One of the commitments in the National Action Plan for Open Government of the Netherlands seeks to create data standards that promote learning from individual complaints to make structural improvements. See: www.opengovpartnership.org/members/netherlands/commitments/NL0051/.

Contributions to the SDGs More Broadly

The broader contributions ombuds institutes can make to the achievement of the SDGs are plenty:

1. Access to justice is a prerequisite for the achievement of the other SDGs and in particular the promise to leave no one behind.[65] This notion of 'leaving no one behind' implies that public investments should be targeted to those who need them most. Ombuds institutes can identify the particular groups needing public services and ensure their access.
2. In addition, it is crucial to empower those that are at risk of being left behind, and enable women, youth, minority groups, people with disabilities and others to stand up for their rights. There is a particular role here for ombuds institutes with a specific focus group, such as children, veterans or prisoners.
3. There is a natural tendency for ombuds institutes to concentrate on procedural norms, since they need to be independent of political parties and neutral in their actions and assessments. However, since the SDGs have been adopted as universal goals, they can be used to include a more substantive assessment of complaints, providing material norms to assess complaints against, in addition to the mostly procedural requirements of proper conduct. This enables a broader evaluation of public conduct and contributes to fair outcomes.
4. In the same vein, ombuds institutes can use the sustainable development goals as a framework to decide and prioritise topics for their own-motion investigation as well as their strategic agenda. Such normative work and recommendations to the executive branch influence the behaviour of public authorities and has the potential to better align it to the achievement of the SDGs.
5. The 2030 Agenda includes a framework of SDG targets and indicators, and countries can report their progress through the voluntary review process.[66] They do this by submitting a Voluntary National Report (VNR) to the United Nations. Neither the substance nor the methodology, or the frequency of submitting a VNR, is prescribed, as the whole process has been set up as voluntary. Yet nearly all UN member states have submitted reports, and the quality of VNRs is increasing over time. Ombuds institutes can provide data and evidence as input to the national VNR process, in particular when it comes to SDG16.[67]
6. Looking at the wide range of topics covered by the 2030 Agenda, ombuds institutes can implement actions inspired by SDGs in their own management

[65] Task Force on Justice (n 2).

[66] More information on Voluntary National Reviews is available at the sustainable Development Knowledge Platform at https://sustainabledevelopment.un.org/vnrs/.

[67] National Human Rights Institutions engaging with the Sustainable Development Goals (SDGs), published by GANHRI in June 2017, https://ganhri.org/wp-content/uploads/2019/12/GANHRI_NHRIs-engaging-with-the-SDGs_UpdatedVersion.pdf.

practices. For example, they could evaluate energy use in their offices (SDG 7) or adopt sustainable procurement processes (SDG 12). In terms of gender equality (SDG 5), they can ensure equal pay for equal work for their staff and equal opportunities for leadership at all levels of the organisation.

7. Modelled on the VNRs, many different types of organisations have reviewed their own contributions to the achievement of the SDGs. In 2018, New York was the first city to publish a Voluntary Local Review.[68] Recent years have seen many more Voluntary Local Reviews emerge, as well as Voluntary University Reviews.[69] Ombuds institutes could follow suit by publishing a Voluntary Ombuds Review, outlining their contributions along the dimensions discussed in this article.

There are undoubtedly other connections that ombuds institutes can make to the United Nations institutionally and to the goals that the UN has set in its 2030 Agenda. A consistent investment by ombuds institutes at the national level along these lines will enable the IOI to articulate and leverage this contribution at the global level.

IX. The Ombuds Institute and Its Unique Role in the Modern State

As I write this in 2021, our world is reeling from the coronavirus pandemic. Its public health and economic impacts have had immediate and hard-hitting consequences across the globe. The socio-political impacts are visible already and will play out over many years as people question and rethink the role of the state, their trust in government and how to better rebuild.[70] Fundamental questions about our societies and the role of the state have emerged. The pandemic has put a spotlight on the inequalities between and within countries. Sparked by the death of George Floyd, the Black Lives Matter protests spread not just throughout the USA, but across the globe, calling attention to the structural racism and fundamental injustices that exist in countries everywhere. State institutions will need to respond to these increasing demands for justice and equality. They will also have to be held accountable for the public health emergency measures and their enforcement, including excesses and abuses that may have occurred. And the state will need to

[68] www.sdgnederland.nl/nieuws/new-york-eerste-stad-ter-wereld-die-zich-aan-sdgs-gaat-meten/.

[69] https://sdg.iisd.org/news/first-voluntary-university-and-state-level-reviews-demonstrate-us-engines-of-sdg-action/.

[70] A series of briefings on Justice in a Pandemic, co-authored by a large group of international experts, were published in 2020 and 2021 to discuss Justice for All and the Public Health Emergency, Justice for All and the Economic Crisis, and Justice for All and the Social Contract in Peril, respectively. All can be found at www.justice.sdg16.plus/justice-in-a-pandemic.

answer for the effective use of resources to fight the pandemic and the fairness of the distribution of relief measures.

With the relation between citizens and the state under pressure and at a time of growing mistrust against authorities writ large, ombuds institutes have an important role to play in terms of both accountability and social justice. With a keen eye for individual instances of injustice or maladministration, they can resolve legitimate grievances and identify larger patterns of dysfunction. They can be focal points of 'organised distrust',[71] and as such can contribute to stability and progress.

It is in this space that ombuds institutes can and should assert their role beyond that of quasi-judicial institutions and take their position as a core part of the social justice landscape.[72] Although responding to individual grievances remains a foundational task, their role is much larger than that. Through their work, they contribute to elemental fairness and equality in society. By channelling societal discontent, they can ensure that this contributes to reforms and increased effectiveness of institutions, as opposed to unrest, rising tensions and instability in society. That can and should be the role of the ombuds institute in the modern state: to contribute to more effective and fair state institutions, to a more benevolent relationship between citizens and the state and to trust between people, communities and the state. By embracing and developing people-centred approaches, ombuds institutes can contribute to social justice and sustainable development.

[71] This term is taken from P Rosanvallon, *Counter-Democracy, Politics in an Age of Distrust* (Cambridge University Press, 2008). Rosanvallon argues that the almost inevitable inability of elected officials to keep many (or most) of their promises has created a space for 'indirect forms of democracy': 274. He suggests that citizens hold their elected representatives to account through forms of oversight, prevention (of misconduct) and judgement (through independent agencies). Ombuds clearly have an important role within this analysis.

[72] O'Brien (n 27).

PART 2

The Challenge of Modern Governance to Ombudsmen

6

Bringing the Ombudsman Role and Powers into the Twenty-first Century

CHRIS WHEELER

I. Introduction – What is the Future of Ombudsman as a Worldwide Institution?

Most ombudsman around the world have faced, are facing and are likely to face significant challenges. Depending on a range of jurisdiction specific circumstances, I argue the likely major challenges for the future generally relate to five factors: independence, resourcing, proliferation, technology and adaptability.

First, independence. When established internationally, ombudsman had different degrees of independence and over time many have had to mount strong cases to increase their perceived and actual levels of independence from the government of the day. While actual and perceived independence, and associated impartiality, are essential for the credibility of ombudsman, there are some very serious downsides.

The second factor relates to resourcing. The resourcing of ombudsman is a common issue for most ombudsman around the world, and most likely one of increasing importance the longer each has been established. The government of the day in many jurisdictions, and certainly in most Australian jurisdictions, have a largely unfettered discretion as to the funding provided to the ombudsman. Governments have an inbuilt conflict of interests in relation to the funding of bodies over which they have little or no direct control that can cause them embarrassment. One of the most effective indirect controls governments have over ombudsman is their ability to limit the nature and scale of the ombudsman's operations by restricting funding.

Proliferation is the third factor. Particularly over the last two decades, it is not uncommon to see a proliferation in many jurisdictions of bodies performing integrity and governance-related functions. There are a range of possible explanations for such proliferation, including ad hoc reactions to scandals or other crises, powerful individuals in government looking to their legacy of achievements while in office,[1] reluctance by governments to give greater powers or jurisdiction to existing bodies that are seen as potential threats over which they have little direct control and the influence of powerful sectional interests demanding that specialist stand-alone bodies be created to address their concerns or protect the interests of those they represent.

Technology is the fourth factor. The massive changes brought about by the technological changes over the past 20 years have and will continue to make seismic changes to the environment in which ombudsman operate. Technology has already revolutionised the operating systems and equipment used by ombudsman, drastically improving their efficiency. The uptake of technology across organisations within ombudsman jurisdiction opens up possibilities for further efficiencies and increased effectiveness through direct access to the intranets, internal case management systems and databases of such organisations. The increasing use of automation to make discretionary decisions has created a significant challenge for ombudsman, which will be a growing problem over time.

Adaptability is the fifth factor. Over the past 40 years or so, the environment in which ombudsman operate has changed radically. As much as they have been able within the constraints of their legislation, many ombudsman have significantly changed the ways in which they perform their roles in attempts to adapt to these changing circumstances.

II. What is an Australian Parliamentary Ombudsman?

I have based my analysis of what I see as the five contemporary challenges facing ombudsman into the future on the experiences of the Australian parliamentary ombudsman. The focus on that particular jurisdiction is not intended to suggest that there is anything unique about the ombudsman model that has been adopted in Australia, or that the Australian experience will necessarily translate to other jurisdictions. The next two sections of this chapter give some context to those ombudsman.

There are nine Australian parliamentary ombudsman – one in each State and Territory.[2] Each was established under legislation passed by each jurisdiction's

[1] Examples are referred to in C Wheeler, 'Review of Administrative Conduct and Decisions in NSW since 1974 – an Ad Hoc and Incremental Approach to Radical Change' (2012) 71 *AIAL Forum* 34, 34.

[2] Ombudsman Act 1976 (Cth); Parliamentary Commissioner Act 1971 (WA); Ombudsman Act 1972 (SA); Ombudsman Act 1973 (Vic); Parliamentary Commissioner Act 1974, now replaced by the Ombudsman Act 2001 (Qld); Ombudsman Act 1974 (NSW); Ombudsman Act 1978 (Tas); Ombudsman (Northern Territory) Act 1978 (NT) now replaced by the Ombudsman Act 2009 (NT); Ombudsman Act 1989 (ACT).

legislative branch of government as a way to review citizen concerns about the exercise of discretionary powers by the executive branch of government.[3] The recognition of the need for such a body reflected a widespread recognition that the traditional forms of accountability, such as ministerial responsibility and the ability of individual parliamentarians to pursue complaints from their constituents about the actions of government, had ceased to be effective. The original legislation establishing ombudsman in various Australian jurisdictions back in the 1970s established organisations that had many common features. Over time, however, the legislated jurisdictions and modes of operation of each ombudsman have diverged significantly.[4] The different models of ombudsman that can be found in the nine Australian jurisdictions could be thought of as an experiment exploring different ways to address common issues.[5] The significant differences that have developed over time in the jurisdictions, functions, powers and approaches of these ombudsman may well be of interest to other ombudsman around the world that are or could in future be facing similar challenges.

Today, while most Australian government ombudsman share the same title and all perform a largely similar function in relation to public administration, there is little else they now have in common in terms of their enabling legislation, the nature and scope of their jurisdictions and their modes of operation. While the jurisdictions of some ombudsman are still primarily focused on complaints relating to public administration, the breadth of the jurisdictions of others can be particularly extensive.[6] The extent to which ombudsman offices are resourced differs significantly, for example some ombudsman are 'relatively' well resourced to perform

[3] The Australian ombudsman office is often traced to the Commonwealth Administrative Review Committee, Parliament of Australia, Kerr Committee Report (1971), yet the State of Western Australia was the first Australian jurisdiction to establish an Ombudsman, with the Parliamentary Commissioner Act 1971, proclaimed on 12 May 1972.

[4] The differences within public sector ombudsman must be distinguished from the different types of ombudsman. The latter are usefully divided by Harlow and Rawlings into the three categories of: public service ombudsman, meaning all such offices established by legislation and given a remit to consider the actions of government and official agencies; statutory ombudsman, which are those public sector ombudsman given an oversight role in a specific sector, such as a legal services ombudsman; private ombudsman, which are typically not supported by statute but instead operate by agreement of some sort and provide oversight of a private sector activity: C Harlow and R Rawlings, *Law and Administration*, 4th edn (Cambridge University Press, 2021) 565–66. The ombudsman of Australia all fall within Harlow and Rawlings's first category, but are still very different.

[5] This phenomenon is quite common in Australia, with the various jurisdictions often adopting different approaches to address similar issues relevant to government accountability, such as anti-corruption bodies, whistleblowing schemes and legislation enabling public access to official information and privacy. In all of these instances, the scheme created to govern the relevant issue can vary greatly between the different Australian jurisdictions. Such differences could be explained by and described as local solutions to local problems.

[6] For example, apart from the 'traditional' ombudsman function relating to public administration, the jurisdiction of the Tasmanian Ombudsman includes right to information (freedom of information), personal information protection, public interest disclosures (whistleblowing), health complaints, custodial inspections, prison and mental health official visitors and energy industry.

the various functions within their jurisdictions, whereas others face significant difficulties even meeting their minimum statutory obligations.[7] Another resource-related issue is that some Australian ombudsman (notably those in Victoria and South Australia) are subject to direction by anti-corruption agencies to undertake investigations referred to them, and most ombudsman can have complaints referred to them by their legislatures which they are obliged to investigate.[8]

Other differences between ombudsman are that while some hold regular hearings where witnesses can be required to attend and give evidence on oath, others do not; and some ombudsman make numerous special reports to their relevant parliament, while others do so selectively. A common feature of Australian ombudsman is that they are obliged to conduct their investigations in private, so there are no public hearings.[9] Another important feature is that ombudsman can only be dismissed from office with the agreement of the legislature (other than in circumstances such as convictions for serious offences, physical or mental incapacity, incompetence, misconduct, bankruptcy, or the like).

Some ombudsman offices vary from what might be considered to be the norm in other ways. For example, four ombudsman statutes contain a specific provision which confirms that the office is not subject to official direction from governments or their ministers.[10] But an ombudsman can be influenced in other ways. At least three ombudsman have a specific provision in their enabling legislation providing for oversight by a standing committee of the legislature and/or an inspector appointed by the executive government for that purpose.[11] None of these, or any other, provisions enable a parliamentary committee to direct an ombudsman to investigate or refrain from investigating an issue. It follows that the extent of these

[7] To take a somewhat extreme example in the Australian context, the Tasmanian Ombudsman has over 130 separate statutory functions under 17 different Acts of Parliament, many of which are quite complex to understand and time consuming to implement. Up until at least mid-2020, the Ombudsman was expected to perform these functions with less than 20 staff.

[8] For example, the power of the Victorian Parliament to refer any matter to the Victorian Ombudsman for investigation and report: Ombudsman Act 1973 (Vic), s 16; the power of the Victorian Independent Broad-based Anti-corruption Commission to refer a matter to the Victorian Ombudsman and require information as to the actions taken on the referral: Independent Broad-based Anti-corruption Commission Act 2011 (Vic), ss 73, 78; the power of the South Australian Parliament to require investigation of a matter by the Ombudsman: Ombudsman Act 1972 (SA), s 14; the obligations on the South Australian Ombudsman to deal with matters referred by the Independent Commission Against Corruption: Ombudsman Act 1972) (SA), s 14B; and the power of the Western Australian Parliament to require investigation of a matter by the Parliamentary Commissioner for Administrative Investigations: Parliamentary Commissioner Act 1971 (WA), s 15.

[9] In Australia, this distinguishes ombudsman from anti-corruption agencies that can hold their hearings in public (either at their sole discretion or in certain circumstances). This issue has proved to be a significant sticking point with proposals in recent years to establish a Federal anti-corruption body.

[10] Constitution Act 1975 (Vic), s 94E (6), Ombudsman Act 2001 (Qld), s 13; Ombudsman Act 2009 (NT), s 12; and Ombudsman Act 1989 (ACT), s 4B. It could be argued that this is implied in the enabling legislation of the other ombudsman, given their terms of appointment and the limited circumstances in which they can be removed from office.

[11] Ombudsman Act 1973 (Vic), ss 26G–I; Ombudsman Act 1974 (NSW), ss 31A–J; Ombudsman Act 2001 (Qld), s 89.

parliamentary powers is to enable ombudsman to appear before the hearings of a parliamentary committee, in accordance with normal parliamentary practice in Australia. The parliamentary committees that oversee or somehow monitor ombudsman are typically comprised of members of the government and opposition of the day, and operate in a bipartisan manner. These aspects of parliamentary committees place them at a 'middle distance' from ombudsman, in the sense that their role does not enable them to direct or interfere with the work of an ombudsman, which thus maintains the independence of the office.[12] At the same time, however, these committees can create a level of knowledge and commitment within parliamentarians that fosters the institutional support required for the implementation of the recommendation of ombudsman.[13]

One novel exception is section 16(1) of the Ombudsman Act 1973 (Vic), which enables either chamber of the Victorian Parliament to 'refer to the Ombudsman for investigation and report any matter' which the chambers 'considers should be investigated'. The Victorian Ombudsman is obliged to investigate any references made under this unique power.[14] When the power was exercised for the first and only time, the resulting litigation confirmed the unremarkable point that a power to refer 'any matter' for investigation meant exactly that.[15] The circumstances of that case illustrate the difficulties when politicians are able to direct the work of ombudsman. The upper chamber of the Victorian Parliament, which was not controlled by the government, requested the ombudsman investigate claims that the government party had unlawfully deployed administrative staff to assist its members during the previous election. The subsequent report found that many of these claims were substantiated,[16] but the government essentially ignored the report. It is notable, however, that many of the problems revealed by the ombudsman's report were quietly addressed beforehand.[17]

[12] Though no Australian parliament has gone so far as the New Zealand approach, which divides parliamentary oversight of the ombudsman between three committees for the differing issues of budgetary, strategic and oversight. This fragmentation of oversight makes parliamentary dictation all but impossible: L Ferguson, 'Parliament's Watchdogs – New Zealand's Officers of Parliament' (2010) 25 *Parliamentary Affairs* 133.

[13] This role of parliamentary committees reflects arguments that ombudsman require a careful balance between independence from executive governments and a level of institutional support. See R Kirkham and A Stuhmcke, 'The Common Law Theory and Practice of the Ombudsman/Judiciary Relationship' (2020) 49 *Common Law World Review* 56.

[14] The power can be exercised by either the Legislative Assembly or the Legislative Council, which are respectively the lower and upper houses of the Victorian Parliament, or a joint parliamentary committee of both houses. The Ombudsman Act 1973 (Vic), ss 26G–I; Ombudsman Act 1974 (NSW), ss 31A–J; Ombudsman Act 2001 (Qld), s 89. See also n 8.

[15] *Attorney-General (Vic) v Glass* (2016) 51 VR 381.

[16] Victorian Ombudsman, *Investigation of a Matter Referred from the Legislative Council on 25 November 2015* (2018) https://assets.ombudsman.vic.gov.au/assets/Reports/Parliamentary-Reports/1-PDF-Report-Files/Investigation-of-a-matter-referred-from-the-Legislative-Council-on-25-November-2015.pdf?mtime=20191220100042.

[17] ibid 163–67. The Victorian Ombudsman suggested that further reforms were required: 168–72.

The differences between ombudsman highlighted above are likely to impact on the capacity of each to address some or all of the challenges outlined at the start of this chapter.

III. Introduction of Ombudsman into Australian Public Administration

In a 2012 paper, I noted that:

> The history of the development of the functions and powers of the Ombudsman mirrors the changes that occurred in the same period in the overall administrative review framework in NSW. These changes have been ad hoc and incremental, generally in response to: scandals; Royal Commissions or inquiries by Parliamentary Committees; amendments to legislation introduced by the Opposition, independents or minority party MPs holding the balance of power during Parliamentary debates on Bills; or initiatives that can be traced directly to the personal views, philosophies or enthusiasms of a Minister for Justice, an Attorney General and a Premier. An alternative title for this part of the paper could be 'More By Good Luck Than Good Planning'.[18]

The experience in a number of Australian jurisdictions has been that the concept of an ombudsman did not have strong support across government. As the Tasmanian academic Rick Snell noted:

> The Ombudsman has toiled long and hard in a hostile environment where it has been treated as an interloper by the courts, as an alien by agencies, has been unfamiliar to lawyers and has been largely abandoned by its natural protector and ally (Parliament).[19]

In that paper, Rick Snell went on to describe submissions made to a 1991 Senate Committee Review into the Commonwealth Ombudsman in the following terms: 'The tenor and tone of many of the agencies' submissions to the 1991 Senate Review highlighted that even after 15 years on the scene, the Ombudsman, toothless or otherwise, was still regarded as an intruder.'[20]

The initial negative reaction to the establishment of the ombudsman persisted for many years, waxing and waning with both the electoral cycle and the length of time that a particular party was in government (the longer a government was in office, the more negative the attitude of that government was likely to be).[21]

[18] Wheeler (n 1) 34.

[19] R Snell, 'Towards an Understanding of a Constitutional Misfit: Four Snapshots of the Ombudsman Enigma' in C Finn (ed), *Sunrise or Sunset? Administrative Law in the New Millennium* (AIAL, 2000) 204.

[20] ibid 194.

[21] Wheeler (n 1) 40.

In the mid 1980s, the then Saskatchewan Ombudsman, David Tickell, listed a number of what he referred to as 'realities' about the relationship between the ombudsman and the government of the day, including:

> Governments … tend to view even constructive criticism as 'political' criticism … Governments dearly hope that the Ombudsman will keep his issues internal to government systems and not make them the subject of public discussion and debate. In Saskatchewan, governments will oppose structural moves to firm up the Ombudsman's accountability to the legislature and to reduce his dependence on the executive branch. This occurs, I assume, because the executive branch fears some loss of control over the Ombudsman's activities … Unless an Ombudsman operates on the premise that a satisfied government overrides his other responsibilities, his working relationship with government will never be entirely harmonious. Where a government is displeased, an Ombudsman can anticipate paying some kind of price for its displeasure …[22]

From personal experience as the Deputy NSW Ombudsman from 1994 to 2019, it was clear in the 1980s and early 1990s that the attitude of the public sector generally to the NSW Ombudsman was a mixture of dismissive and wary. This was an unknown entity whose role was either not understood or seen as an unnecessary or worrying intrusion into the closed and secretive world of the public sector. It was not entirely unexpected that ministers and senior public officials would be concerned about what were seen at the time as the exceptional powers of the Ombudsman, largely equivalent to the powers of a Royal Commission, that could be exercised at will by a public official who was not subject to ministerial control.[23]

The negative attitude also manifested itself in the way public sector agencies generally, and public sector lawyers in particular, interpreted ombudsman legislation. In NSW, the ability of the Ombudsman to perform the statutory functions of office was hampered by the adoption by the then Crown Solicitor, agency in-house lawyers and public sector agencies generally of a very narrow interpretation of the jurisdiction and powers of the Ombudsman under the Ombudsman Act 1974 (NSW).[24] This approach continued for 20 years, until the decision of

[22] Saskatchewan Ombudsman, *Annual Report 1984–85*.

[23] Royal commissions have a particular role in modern Australian society. They are established under letters patent and typically given extraordinary powers. The modern practice of royal commissions in Australia has seen them deployed to review scandals of particular notoriety, leading them to be described as 'the highest form of public inquiry': J Beqiraj, S Garahan and K Shuttleworth, *Ombudsman Schemes and Effective Access to Justice: A Study of International Practices and Trends* (International Bar Association, 2018) 23. Royal commissions are essentially regarded as the 'nuclear option' in Australian public life, which means that the grant to ombudsman of the powers equivalent to a royal commission struck fear and confusion into many public officials.

[24] Various cases where such an approach was argued include: *Boyd v The Ombudsman* [1981] 2 NSWLR 308; *Moroney v The Ombudsman* [1982] 2 NSWLR 591; *The Ombudsman v Moroney* [1983] 1 NSWLR 317; *Commissioner of Police v Deputy Ombudsman* (unreported, NSW Supreme Court, 9 September 1990); *Botany Council v The Ombudsman* [1995] NSWSC 38; *Botany Council v The Ombudsman* (1995) 37 NSWLR 357; *'K' v NSW Ombudsman & Anor* [2000] NSWSC 771; *Ombudsman v Koopman* (2003) 58 NSWLR 182.

Botany Council v The Ombudsman in the NSW Court of Appeal.[25] Kirby P, with whom Sheller and Powell JJA agreed, held that the powers of the Ombudsman were 'beneficial provisions designed in the public interest for the important object of improving public administration and increasing its accountability', and for this reason should not be read down.[26] This case had a significant impact on how the Ombudsman's jurisdiction was viewed by the then Crown Solicitor and across the public sector generally. The negative attitude to ombudsman was also manifest in the general attitudes of ministers to ombudsman reports. In the 1980s and early 1990s, the standard response was for ministers to defend their agencies or officials and attack the credibility of the ombudsman's report or decry the interference of the Ombudsman in the running of the agency or function.[27]

Today, ombudsman are generally seen as an integral part of the public administration landscape in each Australian jurisdiction. This is partly due to the ongoing efforts of ombudsman over the years to demonstrate that they add value and are focused primarily on appropriately addressing individual citizen concerns and improving public administration generally. It is also partly because ombudsman have been in place in most Australian jurisdictions for over 40 years, so the vast majority of public officials today have grown up with ombudsman being a fact of life.

IV. Meeting the Challenges Faced by Ombudsman

A. Achieving and Maintaining Independence

The Australian ombudsman were given different degrees of independence when first established, and over time a number had to mount strong cases to increase their perceived and actual levels of independence from the government of the day.

[25] *Botany Council v The Ombudsman* (1995) 37 NSWLR 357. The Canadian Supreme Court adopted a similarly broad interpretation of ombudsman legislation 11 years earlier in *British Columbia Development Corporation v Friedman (Ombudsman)* [1984] 2 SCR 447. In the *Botany* case, a local council challenged the jurisdiction of the NSW Ombudsman to act on his own motion under the Ombudsman Act 1974 (NSW) to investigate the council's refusal to amend personal records under the then Freedom of Information Act. The Ombudsman argued that the 'privative clause' contained in s 35A of the Ombudsman Act 1974 (NSW), which limits the jurisdiction of courts to review the conduct of a person or body, precluded the action being brought. At that time, the general attitude of the courts to privative clauses was to read them so narrowly that they effectively served little purpose (an issue since resolved in the Ombudsman's favour by the NSW Court of Appeal in *Kaldas v Barbour* (2017) 350 ALR 292). In the *Botany* case, the Court was reluctant to consider whether the private clause in that Act would be effective to prevent such an action and, with the consent of the Ombudsman, decided to consider the merits of the case. This was said to be on the basis that if the case had no merit, there would then be no need to consider whether the privative clause prevented the Court from considering the merits of the case.

[26] (1995) 37 NSWLR 357, 368. In *Attorney-General (Vic) v Glass* (2016) 51 VR 381, the literal approach taken to the scope of powers to refer issues for investigation by the Victorian Ombudsman resulted in an equally expansive reading of the ombudsman's powers.

[27] Examples are referred to in the NSW Ombudsman, *Annual Report 1985–86*, 5–9, 30–32.

For example, the 'level of independence of the NSW Ombudsman was a significant issue for many years, and a regular topic discussed in most *Annual Reports* until the mid-1990s'.[28] The degree to which ombudsman are independent of government, or direction by other agencies as to how they exercise their discretionary powers, has been a significant issue over the years.

Initially, the debate focused on whether ombudsman should be seen as part of the executive branch of government or the legislative branch. As I noted in a 2012 article,[29] ombudsman are now generally seen by the executive and the judiciary[30] to be officers of the Parliament/legislature.[31] This view is reinforced by the fact that ombudsman can only be removed from office by the jurisdiction's governor upon the address of the Parliament/legislature (and in NSW the Joint Parliamentary Committee on the Office of the Ombudsman and the Law Enforcement Conduct Commission has a veto power over the appointment of the Ombudsman).[32] More recently, there has been some discussion about whether there should be a recognition of a fourth branch of government, an integrity branch.[33] While there has been some support for such a concept, the prevailing (but not universal) view in Australasia is that ombudsman are either formally identified as, or should be seen to be, officers of each jurisdiction's Parliament/legislature. As noted earlier, three of the nine Australian jurisdictions have formalised in legislation that their ombudsman is an officer of the Parliament; those jurisdictions plus one other have also specifically legislated that the ombudsman is not subject to direction. The terms of the legislation establishing the other Australian ombudsman clearly imply that they have independent discretion in the exercise of their statutory powers. The key ongoing issue for ombudsman is ensuring that the public perceives that the office

[28] Wheeler (n 1) 38.

[29] Wheeler (n 1).

[30] See, eg the comment by Enderby J in *Ainsworth v The Ombudsman* (1988) 17 NSWLR 276, 283 that 'An Ombudsman is a creature of Parliament'. Whealy J similarly commented in *K v NSW Ombudsman and Anor* [2000] NSWSC 771, [25] that the 'Ombudsman is an independent officer of the New South Wales Parliament'. The then Premier of New South Wales appeared to endorse such sentiments when he stated 'It would be clearly undesirable if the Ombudsman were accountable to me as Premier or to the Executive Government' [New South Wales Parliament] Legislative Assembly, *Hansard*, 24 May 1990.

[31] Nick O'Brien in ch 14 of this book emphasises the unique nature and differentiation of ombudsman from the judiciary.

[32] Ombudsman Act 1974 (NSW), s 6A.

[33] The existing branches being the legislative, judicial and executive branches. Suggestions of a fourth 'integrity' branch of government have met with a mixed response in Australian law. The notion can be traced to the influential article B Ackerman, 'The New Separation of Powers' (2000) 113 *Harvard Law Review* 633. The concept has received a mixed reception in Australia. See, eg JJ Spigelman, 'The Integrity Branch of Government' (2004) 78 *Australian Law Journal* 724 (a Chief Justice of New South Wales arguing in support of the concept); W Martin, 'Forewarned and Four-Armed: Administrative Law Values and the Fourth Arm of Government' (2014) 88 *Australian Law Journal* 106 (a Chief Justice of Western Australian doubting the value of recognising a new, distinct integrity branch of government); S Gageler, 'Three is Plenty' in G Weeks and M Groves (eds), *Administrative Redress In and Out of the Courts* (Federation Press, 2019) (a current member of the High Court of Australia arguing that Australian constitutional arrangements cannot and should not recognise any fourth arm of government).

acts impartially, which requires that each office is perceived to be independent of the government of the day.[34]

Where ombudsman have been successful in maintaining their actual and perceived independence, they are likely to have many 'stakeholders' but few, if any, vocal supporters or protectors (either individuals or organisations). Unlike corruption/integrity, transparency/access to information and privacy issues, and the bodies that perform those roles for example, with few notable exceptions it has only been in relatively recent years that ombudsman have been the subject of much academic interest.[35] Given the nature of their role to review the conduct and decisions of public officials and agencies, if they are performing those roles diligently, the likelihood of strong support from within executive government can be expected to be low. Over 30 years ago, the then Saskatchewan Ombudsman, David Tickell, highlighted this issue:

> To some extent, it may be inevitable that an Ombudsman who works up to his mandate will have something other than a smooth working relationship with the executive branch of government … Sooner or later there is a tendency to shoot the messenger when governments don't like the message …[36]

Probably the best ombudsman can expect in such circumstances is wary neutrality. The most likely sources of support for ombudsman are any committee of the legislature that has an oversight role in relation to the ombudsman, journalists who have a particular interest in public administration and opposition parties or politicians (although attempts to enlist the support of opposition politicians can be fraught).[37]

B. Resourcing

(i) The Current Position

The work of an ombudsman does not win votes for governments and often gives ammunition to the opposition. The work does not improve the reputations or

[34] See here the observations of Rob Behrens in ch 10 of this book on the importance of independence for public trust in an ombudsman scheme.

[35] One recent example of international academic scholarship is M Hertoch and R Kirkham, *Research Handbook on Ombudsman* (Edward Elgar, 2018). See also the discussion in the Introduction to this book.

[36] Saskatchewan Ombudsman, *Annual Report 1984–85*.

[37] In 2011, the then Commonwealth Ombudsman resigned after a little more than a year into his seven-year term of office after it was discovered that he provided questions to a senator, to be put during a Senate Committee estimates hearing. The content of the questions related to the lack of funding of the Commonwealth Ombudsman's Office and the ability of that Office to oversee immigration detention centres. His resignation was in response to a political backlash based on a perception he had entered the political fray by essentially colluding with a member of one political party giving evidence to Parliament. When the Ombudsman resigned, the then Special Minister for State stated that the Ombudsman's Office was 'a critical part of our system of government accountability and it needs to maintain the highest standards of independence, impartiality and integrity': P Osborne, 'Ombudsman Quits Over Greens Script' *Sydney Morning Herald* (20 October 2011).

career prospects of senior public officials and is often the source of criticism and sometimes career-limiting embarrassment. The work of ombudsman is also a source of inconvenient extra work for both governments and senior public officials, who have little control over what an ombudsman looks at, how they do it or the outcome. What little control governments have is through funding. Given human nature, it can be expected that governments will be reluctant to fund a body that is likely to cause them problems more than absolutely necessary (eg to avoid serious embarrassment).[38]

For much of the history of ombudsman in Australia, governments and senior bureaucrats have not recognised the significant public interest associated with the roles they perform. While the initial antipathy towards the introduction of ombudsman has waned over time, the resourcing of ombudsman has been an issue for each office since establishment. The government of the day in each jurisdiction (other than recently in Victoria) has had unfettered discretion as to the funding provided to the ombudsman. In Australia, this problem is not confined to ombudsman.[39] Researchers in other jurisdictions have voiced concern about the vulnerability of ombudsman to the uncertainties that can arise from the discretionary nature of executive funding decisions. The terminology adopted by Kirkham and Gill in their guiding principles for reform to ombudsman is revealing. Those authors suggest that a comprehensive reform agenda should allocate responsibility for oversight the ombudsman to a parliamentary committee, whose brief should include the appointment and funding of the office. The reference of Kirkham and Gill to 'funding (ie sponsorship)' usefully draws attention to the need for a champion of sorts for the ombudsman.[40] A champion could operate to counter, or at least minimise, the obvious contradiction faced by every executive government when settling the budget of an ombudsman office – why should a government provide proper funding to an agency whose work typically uses that funding to embarrass that same government?

Ombudsman have not been seen by governments as 'demand driven', ie budgets are not increased in line with increasing complaints. Budgets are increased each year generally in line with inflation, and a number of jurisdictions then apply an annual efficiency dividend, thereby reducing the budget.[41] In NSW, the Ombudsman has recently informed the Parliamentary Accountability Committee of the NSW Legislative Council (discussed in detail below) that, starting in the 2018–19 year from a base budget of $A29.5 million, the office is required to meet budget savings over the following 10 years that would total $10 million.

[38] This assumption would explain why the NSW Ombudsman seemed to have far more success obtaining extra funds in its child protection-related jurisdiction than its public administration jurisdiction.

[39] A Gray, 'Withholding Government Funding – A Branch of Freedom of Political Communication' (2013) 38 *Alternative Law Journal* 214. That article traces the growing habit of Australian governments to restrict or remove funding from community organisations that are advocates for change on politically sensitive issues.

[40] R Kirkham and C Gill, 'Five Principles for a New Public Services Ombudsman' in R Kirkham and C Gill (eds), *A Manifesto for Ombudsman Reform* (Routledge, 2020) 13, 34.

[41] Looking at the NSW Ombudsman, for example, other than in relatively recent years, when there have been some increases in funding in response to increased complaints, extra funding was only ever obtained when the Ombudsman was given a new statutory jurisdiction.

(ii) Indications of a Possible Change in Approach

There are indications of change to the funding of ombudsman in the modern state. An example of this are the recent changes in Victoria which have given a Victorian Parliamentary Committee power to review and make recommendations as to funding of integrity bodies in that jurisdiction. Another is the two reviews into the funding of integrity agencies currently underway in NSW.

The first of these two reviews is being undertaken by the Public Accountability Committee of the NSW Legislative Council (the PAC), which handed down its First Report in March 2020.[42] This review examined the funding processes and outcomes of the four key integrity institutions in New South Wales: the NSW Electoral Commission, the Independent Commission Against Corruption, the Law Enforcement Conduct Commission and the NSW Ombudsman.[43] The PAC also examined the funding of the Parliament.

The chair of the PAC expressed the following view in the foreword to the report:

> These institutions perform a vital role in maintaining the health of our democracy, by fighting corruption, ensuring fair elections, preventing abuses of government power and holding the government to account. To perform their functions each institution requires a high degree of independence from the government of the day and adequate resourcing. However, funding for these critical institutions is currently decided by the government of the day, largely behind closed doors. Despite their unique position each of these bodies follows a budget process that is substantially the same as the process for determining the funding for normal government departments. After years of reduced funding none of these integrity institutions have the resources they need to perform all of their statutory and constitutional functions.[44]

As was noted in the report, evidence given to the PAC by oversight bodies had highlighted that 'funding shortfalls can have disproportionate effects on small agencies as such agencies are often established to fulfil a specific function which limits their capacity to reprioritise or trim discretionary functions'.[45]

In evidence given to the PAC, the NSW Ombudsman argued that

> a budget process which makes an oversight body dependent on executive agencies and ministers may result in the body being unduly mindful of its financial dependency when exercising its functions and create an impulse towards a more cautious approach when taking public action that could be seen as critical of, or cause embarrassment to, government.[46]

The Ombudsman also argued that a dependency on the government for sufficient funding can give rise to a public perception that control over the purse strings

[42] NSW Legislative Council, Parliamentary Accountability Committee, *Budget Process for Independent Oversight Bodies and the NSW Parliament* (First Report, 2020) nsw.gov.au.

[43] The PAC referred to these integrity bodies as 'the bedrock of government accountability in New South Wales', ibid 34.

[44] ibid viii–ix.

[45] ibid 23–24.

[46] ibid 27.

gives the government leverage or an indirect influence over the oversight body, suggesting that this would be 'problematic as public confidence in the system of public sector oversight depends on the public accepting that the integrity agencies are indeed independent of government'.[47]

The PAC pointed out in its report that after years of reduced funding, none of the integrity institutions have the resources they need to perform their functions.[48] The PAC noted that other jurisdictions have established budget processes that provide much greater transparency and accountability. Examples referred to were the approach in Victoria, where budgets for the key integrity bodies are developed in consultation with the relevant parliamentary oversight committee, and the approach in New Zealand, where a parliamentary committee recommends budgets for the three statutory bodies classified as 'Officers of Parliament', one of which is the Ombudsman.[49]

The PAC made a number of recommendations, three of which are relevant to the NSW Ombudsman:[50]

1. That the parliamentary oversight committee for the Ombudsman review the annual budget submission and make recommendations as to funding priorities.
2. That the annual budget for the Ombudsman includes a set contingency fund to address unbudgeted financial demands, and a mechanism to access such funds.
3. That the Ombudsman be allocated its annual funding directly through the appropriation legislation, rather than the funding being allocated to the relevant minister, and the Ombudsman is not subject to reductions in funding during the financial year.

The second review into the funding of integrity agencies is being undertaken by the NSW Auditor-General, who made a Special Report to Parliament on 20 October 2020 entitled *The Effectiveness of the Financial Arrangements and Management Practices in Four Integrity Agencies*. In this review, the Auditor-General examined the funding processes and outcomes of the: NSW Electoral Commission, Independent Commission Against Corruption, Law Enforcement Conduct Commission and the NSW Ombudsman.

In the executive summary to the report, the Auditor-General expressed the following conclusions:

- The current approach to determining annual funding for the integrity agencies presents threats to their independent status. The approach is consistent with the legislative and constitutional framework for financial management in New South Wales, but it does not sufficiently recognise that the roles and functions

[47] ibid 28.
[48] ibid 34.
[49] ibid 33.
[50] ibid 36–37.

of the integrity agencies that are the focus of this audit are different to other departments and agencies.

- Aspects of the financial management mechanisms used to administer funding for the integrity agencies create tensions with their independent status. These mechanisms include the means of applying efficiency dividends, budget savings and reform measures, the provision of additional funding from DPC to the integrity agencies, and requests for the integrity agencies to report to DPC on their activities and outcomes.[51]

In summary, the Auditor-General found that the role of the government of the day in deciding annual funding for the integrity agencies threatens their independence. Referring to the common practice of governments to reduce the funding of many agencies by a fixed percentage each year, a practice referred to as 'efficiency dividends', the Auditor-General argued that the legality of actions taken by government to restrict the access of the integrity agencies to funds appropriated by the Parliament is contestable. As in the PAC report, a key issue highlighted in the Auditor-General's report was that some comparable jurisdictions have given their Parliaments a more direct involvement in the funding of integrity agencies.[52] In relation specifically to the NSW Ombudsman, key findings included: 'that the process for determining the annual appropriation funding for the Ombudsman does not fully recognise its independence and the Ombudsman's priorities are not directly linked to government priorities'.[53]

In this regard, the Auditor-General noted that:

> decisions about [Ombudsman's] appropriation funding are made with reference to the priorities and commitments of the government of the day … However, [the Ombudsman's] work is less likely to align with government priorities compared to projects and programs run by government departments and agencies.[54]

Conducted independently of each other, both reviews reached certain common findings and made similar recommendations. In summary, these were:

- actual and perceived independence from the government of the day is fundamentally important for the effectiveness of integrity bodies;
- there is a fundamental conflict of interests (or possibly duties) in the current arrangements for the funding of integrity bodies;
- there has been systemic long-term underfunding of integrity bodies; and
- the answer is for greater parliamentary oversight of and involvement in decisions about the funding of integrity bodies to ensure appropriate transparency and accountability of the funding process.

[51] NSW Audit Office, *The Effectiveness of the Financial Arrangements and Management Practices in Four Integrity Agencies* (Special Report, 20 October 2020) 4.
[52] ibid 7.
[53] ibid 33.
[54] ibid 33.

These findings are neither revolutionary nor unexpected. It is almost universally accepted that to be effective ombudsman must be, and must be perceived to be, impartial, which requires that they are and are perceived to be independent of the government of the day. Given that parliamentary ombudsman have jurisdiction over many aspects of executive government, governments clearly have a conflict of interests (or duties) in relation to the funding of a body that has the power to investigate the conduct of public sector bodies and officials (where the only non-statutory limitation on the exercise of such powers is the level of funding available to do so). This conflict, and its impact on the actual and perceived independence of an ombudsman, is exacerbated where such decisions are made behind closed doors. Given the widespread acceptance that ombudsman are officers of the Parliament, the most obvious way to achieve greater transparency and accountability is to increase the oversight role of the Parliament. In the absence of significant changes to the model, funding issues are almost entirely outside the control of ombudsman, although they can make submissions seeking further funding.

C. Proliferation

There has been, and will likely continue to be, a proliferation of integrity-related bodies in most Australian jurisdictions over time, for example anti-corruption, police complaints, prisons, human rights, anti-discrimination, access to information, privacy, whistleblowing, industry and other integrity, oversight, misconduct and/or complaint handling roles. Many ombudsman have seen their jurisdictions increase over time, and there have also been cycles of aggregation and disaggregation of integrity-related functions and bodies in some jurisdictions, notably NSW.

Proliferation of integrity bodies creates a range of issues. For example: multiple simultaneous uncoordinated investigations into the same or closely related issues; failures to ensure that all aspects of a problem are addressed in circumstances where aspects are in the jurisdictions of different integrity bodies;[55] bodies with overlapping jurisdictions failing to adopt consistent approaches for dealing with similar situations; and matters falling between the cracks where aspects of jurisdiction overlap. Lack of coordination can arise due to legal impediments to sharing any or specific types of information, or a reluctance to coordinate by bodies overprotective of their jurisdictions. A phenomenon that appears to be gaining traction in certain Australian jurisdictions, which has the potential to exacerbate the problems created by overlapping jurisdictions, is for anti-corruption bodies to be given expanded jurisdictions over 'non-corrupt' maladministration.[56] This can

[55] For example, where there are separate information/privacy-type commissioners and an ombudsman, where those commissioners do not have jurisdiction to address issues of possible maladministration identified in the relevant information/privacy related documents.

[56] Examples include the South Australian Independent Commission Against Corruption (ICAC), the Victorian Independent Broad-based Anti-corruption Commission, the NSW Law Enforcement Conduct Commission (which oversees police conduct), the Queensland Crime and Conduct

also create operational problems, given the fundamental differences in the focus, methodologies, skill sets and cultures best suited to addressing serious corrupt conduct and maladministration.[57]

Proliferation can also lead to public confusion as to which body is the most appropriate one to deal with a particular problem. Another proliferation issue is the costs involved in duplication of back office/corporate functions – or, looked at another way, a failure to take advantage of potential economies of scale. As noted earlier, the problem for ombudsman is that the reasons why separate integrity agencies are established are commonly because of a range of factors outside their control, such as: lobbying by groups with a vested interest who want an integrity body dedicated to or focused on their issue or the interests of the group they represent; attempts by the government of the day to be seen as taking significant action to address a current contentious issue; or attempts by the government of the day to create bodies they hope will be less likely to vigorously pursue the issues within the body's jurisdiction.

While proliferation is an issue almost entirely outside the control of ombudsman, they are in a position to put forward arguments countering calls for further proliferation. This could be by submissions to government, arguments put forward in annual or special reports to Parliament or those arising out of questioning at hearings held by any parliamentary oversight committee or commission of inquiry. How each ombudsman might go about doing this will depend a lot on the personality of that ombudsman and the relationship between the ombudsman and the government of the day.

D. Technology

There are at least two major challenges and two important opportunities for ombudsman created by the growth in the use of technology by organisations within their jurisdiction to automate processes and decisions.[58]

(i) Challenges

The first challenge relates to inappropriate use of technology. The constant demands from governments for increased efficiency and effectiveness is driving many agencies to automate as much decision-making as they are able. While many processes are easily (although often expensively) amenable to automation, as noted earlier,

Commission (another police oversight body) and the Western Australian Corruption and Crime Commission (which also had a wide jurisdiction that includes police conduct).

[57] Appendix A to Wheeler (n 1) 64–65.

[58] See ch 7 of this book by Naomi Creutzfeldt for an in-depth analysis of the impact of digitalisation on ombudsman.

attempts to automate 'discretionary'[59] decision-making are fraught with pitfalls. It is one thing to automate a step-by-step process where the questions are clear cut and available information is conclusive as to each step. It is entirely another where, for example:

- there will or may well be gaps in the required information;
- information must be interpreted based on a technical or other professional assessment;
- decisions are required to be based on a certain degree of 'satisfaction' about whether a certain state of affairs does or does not exist; or
- an assessment is required based on a nebulous 'public interest' assessment.

There has been guidance available to Australian government agencies on best practice in automated administrative decision-making since 2004, when the Australian Administrative Review Council (ARC) published a report entitled *Automated Assistance in Administrative Decision-Making*.[60] On the issue of discretionary decision-making, the ARC made an important distinction in the report between administrative decisions for which the decision-maker is required to exercise discretion and those for which no discretion is exercisable once the facts are established. In the latter case, the Council concludes that full automation of the decision-making process is appropriate. Where discretion is exercisable, however, the Council considers that the process should not be fully automated; in these circumstances, expert systems are best used as decision-making tools.

The ARC Report set out 27 best-practice principles for automated assistance in administrative decision-making. These principles distinguished between systems that make decisions and systems that help a decision-maker make a decision, noting that such systems would generally only be suitable for decisions involving non-discretionary elements. In this regard, the report argued that 'expert systems' should not automate the exercise of 'discretion'.

[59] The meaning of 'discretion' was considered by the Australian High Court in *Coal and Allied Operations Pty Ltd v Australian Industrial Relations Commission* (2000) 203 CLR 194, 204–05 [19], where a majority of the Court explained that a discretion: 'In general terms, it refers to a decision-making process in which "no one [consideration] and no combination of [considerations] is necessarily determinative of the result". Rather, the decision-maker is allowed some latitude as to the choice of the decision to be made. The latitude may be considerable as, for example, where the relevant considerations are confined only by the subject-matter and object of the legislation which confers the discretion. On the other hand, it may be quite narrow where, for example, the decision-maker is required to make a particular decision if he or she forms a particular opinion or value judgment.' The legal parameters of discretionary or evaluative judgments were further explained by the High Court in *Minister for Immigration and Citizenship v Li* (2013) 249 CLR 332. The *Li* case essentially signalled a closer level of scrutiny under the judicial review ground of unreasonableness, which narrowed the freedom bureaucratic officials have when exercising discretionary powers.

[60] Administrative Review Council, *Automated Assistance in Administrative Decision-Making 2004* (Report No 46, 2004) www.ag.gov.au/legal-system/publications/report-46-automated-assistance-administrative-decision-making-2004.

Building on this ARC Report, an *Automated Decision-Making Better Practice Guide* was developed by a cross-agency working group in 2007.[61] Despite the existence of this guidance, in July 2016 the Commonwealth Department of Human Services[62] launched an online debt recovery tool which automated much of its investigation and debt-raising process. This tool dramatically improved the efficiency of the system, speeding up the investigation and assessment process from 20,000 per year manually to 20,000 per week automated. Arising out of numerous complaints, the implementation of this tool was investigated by the Australian Commonwealth Ombudsman, resulting in a report in April 2017.[63] The problems identified with the tool in that report and subsequent inquiries received wide media attention over several years, eventually resulting in the government having to refund over $700m and to pay over $100m in compensation. This case highlighted the perils of introducing automated decision-making without proper consideration of appropriate 'transparency, usability and fairness'.[64]

Another example was the automation of fine debt recovery by the then NSW state agency charged with recovering such debts owed to the NSW state government. This agency had the power to issue a 'garnishee order' to a bank requiring the bank to deduct money from an individual's account and transfer it to the agency.[65] On receipt of a garnishee order, if a bank had an account in the name of the person nominated in the order that contains funds, it withdrew all available funds up to the amount set out in the order without notice or explanation to the account holder, even if that removed all funds from the account.[66]

The case studies in the NSW Ombudsman Annual Reports from 2012–13 to 2015–16 demonstrated how, where this occurred, it often had very serious

[61] This initial Better Practice Guide was updated by the Commonwealth Ombudsman, the Office of the Australian Information Commissioner and the Attorney-General's Department in 2019. The federal ombudsman recently published an update guide to automated decision-making: Commonwealth Ombudsman, *Automated Decision-Making Better Practice Guide* (2019) www.ombudsman.gov.au/__data/assets/pdf_file/0019/112276/Better-Practice-Complaint-Handling-Guide.pdf. The preface to that guide explains that it 'reflects the emergence of human-centred design as the accepted standard of better practice in service design, and opportunities to improve complaint handling presented by new technology, data analysis and behavioural insights'.

[62] A department that was part of the working group which developed the 2007 Better Practice Guide.

[63] Commonwealth Ombudsman, 'Centrelink's Automated Debt Raising and Recovery System: A Report about the Department of Human Services' (Report No 2 of 2017), available at www.ombudsman.gov.au/__data/assets/pdf_file/0022/43528/Report-Centrelinks-automated-debt-raising-and-recovery-system-April-2017.pdf. Aspects of this complex and large-scale disaster of public administration are explained in J Townsend, 'Better Decisions? Robodebt and the Failings of Merits Review' in J Boughey and K Miller (eds), *The Automated State – Implications, Challenges and Opportunities for Public Law* (Federation Press, 2021).

[64] Commonwealth Ombudsman, 'Lessons Learnt about Digital Transformation and Public Administration: Centrelink's Online Compliance Intervention' (Working Paper, 2017), available at www.ombudsman.gov.au/__data/assets/pdf_file/0024/48813/AIAL-OCI-Speech-and-Paper.pdf.

[65] After this chapter was written, the NSW Ombudsman made a Special Report to the NSW Parliament that addressed this issue: *The New Machinery of Government: Using Machine Technology in Administrative Decision-Making* (29 November 2021), available at www.ombo.nsw.gov.au/__data/assets/pdf_file/0005/123629/The-new-machinery-of-government-special-report_Front-section.pdf.

[66] NSW Ombudsman, *Annual Report 2013–14*, 68.

consequences for the persons concerned, who were often welfare recipients, including inability to buy food or medicine for themselves and their families until they received their next welfare payment, failure to pay rent, which could result in homelessness, etc. It was also noted in those reports that the people who were the subject of garnishee orders were not given any notice that the funds would be withdrawn or that they had been withdrawn, so they would have had no idea where the funds had gone. If they were able to contact the bank and find out that the agency had taken the funds, prior to the Ombudsman's involvement there was no information on the agency website to inform them that they could seek a refund of $100.[67]

In 2012–13, garnishee orders issued by the agency to recover fine debts increased from 7000 a month to 24,000 per month.[68] In its 2014–15 Annual Report, the NSW Ombudsman noted that complaints 'about garnishee orders issued by the [agency] has increased substantially this year, probably because the [agency] was issuing more orders'.[69] Year by year, the numbers of orders increased almost exponentially to many tens of thousands a month.[70] In its 2015–16 Annual Report, the Ombudsman identified a crucial issue being 'the importance of agency staff taking the time to ensure they understand a person's circumstances before making a decision that will negatively affect them'.[71] The Ombudsman went on: 'Given the impact [agency] enforcement may have on individuals, [agency] staff have a particular responsibility to balance the competing public interests of collecting fine debt and preventing vulnerable people being further distressed or made destitute and/or homeless'.[72]

The two examples referred to above highlight the second major technological challenge for ombudsman arising out of the automation of processes and decision-making. This is the difficulties it creates for ombudsman to identify such problems and assess whether those processes and decisions were fair, reasonable and lawful in the circumstances. The two examples demonstrate that it took some years for the full implications of these attempts at automation to be fully recognised and addressed. In the meantime, many vulnerable people suffered significantly. Leaving aside whether an ombudsman is likely to have the expertise and equipment to analyse the algorithms used to make such decisions, there could well be commercial-in-confidence/copyright issues restricting their access to the software. Even if they had the expertise and access, the staffing resources required to assess each complaint about such decisions will be significant.

[67] ibid.

[68] In a submission made by the agency to the NSW Parliament's Legislative Assembly, Legal Affairs Committee's 2014 'Review of Debt Recovery in NSW Wales'.

[69] NSW Ombudsman, *Annual Report 2014–15*, 66.

[70] The number of garnishee orders issued by Revenue NSW increased over time – from 6,905 in the 2010–11 financial year to more than 1.6 million in 2018–19: www.ombo.nsw.gov.au/__data/assets/pdf_file/0015/123630/The-new-machinery-of-government-special-report_Annexure-A.pdf.

[71] NSW Ombudsman, *Annual Report 2015–16*, 67.

[72] ibid 68.

A third challenge relates to accessibility. This is an issue for ombudsman because an increasing number of complainants are experiencing vulnerability for a range of reasons, possibly up to 50 per cent at any point in time. Examples of factors that can give rise to vulnerability include age, disability or reduced physical abilities, mental and/or physical health, particular circumstances such as family/ domestic violence and/or financial issues, literacy and/or language issues, and/or cultural or indigenous backgrounds. It can be expected that a number of those people will seek assistance to address issues they are experiencing in their dealing with public sector agencies or private sector bodies performing roles contracted out by the public sector. This will require ombudsman to modify their traditional modes of communication and operation.

It is also an issue for ombudsman as the almost universal take up of technological innovation and the use of social media have revolutionised communications. This has resulted in many sectors of society now predominantly using methods of communication that do not involve the traditional ways ombudsman have received complaints, ie letters, faxes, emails or even telephone calls. Options to address such accessibility issues are largely within the control of ombudsman.

(ii) Opportunities

On the plus side, technology has created some significant opportunities for ombudsman. Three major changes over the past 10–20 years in particular have opened up major efficiencies in the way Australian ombudsman perform their roles. The first is the adoption of the 'Whole of Government' concept, which has led to amalgamations of numerous agencies into 'mega' departments. The second is the general recognition that ombudsman are an integral part of government (although, as mentioned earlier, there is still debate whether ombudsman should be seen as part of the legislative or the executive branch of government). The third is the major technological changes that have taken place, which have had a huge impact on how government agencies operate. Taken together with the general recognition that ombudsman are an integral part of government, this appears to have led to a much greater level of voluntary cooperation with ombudsman across Australian jurisdictions.

(a) Direct Access to Agency Intranets

The IT revolution has enabled some ombudsman to obtain direct access to agency intranets, and in some cases agency case management systems or IT systems generally, often voluntarily or on occasion through statutory amendments. For example, most of the major agencies within the jurisdiction of the NSW Ombudsman have each voluntarily given that office direct access to their intranets. Those organisations did this because they could see the benefits for them in Ombudsman staff being able to directly access the information they needed to be able to address issues raised in complaints, without having to take up the time of agency staff to find such information and supply it to them. The Ombudsman benefited because frontline staff handling calls from the public or assessing complaints were able to obtain up-to-date information about agency policies, procedures, guidelines, activities, etc without having to go through the process of contacting relevant persons in agencies, explaining what they were after and why, and then waiting for those people to find the relevant information and get back to them.

(b) Direct Access to Relevant Agency Case Management Systems and/or Databases

The technological changes over recent decades have enabled agencies to move from paper-based records to electronic records that can be remotely accessed. Ombudsman Acts were drafted at a time when getting access to an agency's records normally required taking physical custody of the relevant files, often for extended periods of time. If operational imperatives required taking immediate custody of files, the agency would be deprived of its records for whatever period was deemed necessary by the Ombudsman. Even where agencies were required to produce records by a certain date, copying equipment was such that making copies of copious documents was seldom a realistic option.

With the advent of electronic records and the Internet, two or more parties can have real-time access to the same records. If a matter is within the jurisdiction of the ombudsman, and the ombudsman has appropriate IT security in place, there is no good reason why the authorised officers of the ombudsman should not be able to have direct access to relevant agency records for an appropriate purpose. This would, of course, be subject to direct access only being available to information the ombudsman could otherwise lawfully require the organisation to provide, and both the relevant agency and the ombudsman being able to audit such accesses to make sure they were for an appropriate purpose.

The ability to directly access agency databases has been in place for the NSW Ombudsman for many years in relation to several major agencies, some based on statutory requirements and others based on voluntary memoranda of understanding.

E. Adaptability

(i) Changing the Context in which Ombudsman Operate

The roles/functions and powers in parliamentary-type ombudsman legislation are, of course, drafted in the public sector, public administration and technological context that applied at the time. The operating environment of Australian ombudsman has changed radically since they were created in the 1970s, in ways never contemplated by those who drafted the initial legislation. However, over the same period, most Ombudsman Acts (or equivalent) have only been the subject of ad hoc incremental amendments. As highlighted in Appendix B, over the past

40 years there have been massive changes to the context in which Australian ombudsman perform their roles/functions.

(ii) Changes Made by Ombudsman to Address the Changes in their Operating Environments

Over the past 40 years, ombudsman in Australian jurisdictions have, to varying degrees, made changes to how they operate to address the changing circumstances in their operating environments. While offices differ, key changes have included moving away from formal investigations involving powers of compulsion and formal reports with findings about conduct to more preliminary inquiries focusing on informally identifying and resolving problems. This has included a greater emphasis on facilitating the resolution of disputes through mediation/conciliation. Another change has been a refocus from the substantive issues raised in individual complaints to a more proactive approach where the focus is on identifying and addressing systemic issues identified in complaints. This was described by Rick Snell as a move away from a 'complaint-focused incident-based approach to problem solving' to a more 'institution-focused and performance-based approach'.[73] Two related changes have been: a refocus from the substantive issues raised in complaints to an operational focus on how those substantive issues were or are being dealt with by the organisation concerned; and a greater emphasis on the provision of training and guidance to organisations within jurisdiction on effective complaint handling.[74]

In some jurisdictions, this has included greater use of 'own-motion' investigation powers to focus on systemic issues and/or audits of complaint-handling systems. Of course, whether and if so how extensive and how often such approaches are used by an ombudsman depends to a significant degree on the resourcing of that ombudsman.

A positive effect of these changes has been a change in the attitude of many public officials and organisations from a perception of ombudsman as a threat, opponent or nuisance to them being seen in a more positive light. From various media reports and ombudsman annual reports, it appears that governments across Australia are realising that ombudsman see their role as trying to assist the public sector to do a better job, not to just criticise with 20/20 hindsight. Another reason for the change in attitude may well be that many public officials have grown up in the era where ombudsman were a fact of life and not some novel and unwelcome intrusion into their work activities. Ombudsman have been able to make most of these changes either within their existing discretionary powers, through minor amendments to their Acts (eg preliminary inquiry powers and authorisations to facilitate the mediation of disputes), or by voluntary agreements with agencies.

[73] Snell (n 19).
[74] Such a provision is common in public interest disclosure and ombudsman legislation.

(iii) Changes Made by Some Governments that Have Assisted Ombudsman to Adapt to Changes in Their Operating Environments

(a) Keep Under Scrutiny Powers

Another mechanism that facilitates a proactive and preventative approach by an ombudsman is what is commonly referred to as a 'keep under scrutiny' power. These are powers for an ombudsman to keep under scrutiny the policies, procedures and practices of agencies that apply to certain functions they perform, for example the management and handling of complaints and the management of public interest disclosures. This was an integral part of all of the various jurisdictions given to the NSW Ombudsman since the late 1990s[75] and is now a common oversight mechanism included in legislation in many Australian jurisdictions.[76]

(b) Referral of Matters for Action and Report Back

As previously mentioned, when Ombudsman Acts were introduced in the 1970s, the agencies within their jurisdictions had little or no complaint-handling or investigation skills. Over time, the capacity of most agencies to handle complaints has greatly improved. Larger public-facing agencies generally have dedicated staff who are trained and/or experienced in complaint handling and conducting at least the more straightforward administrative investigations, and smaller agencies have access to comprehensive guidance to assist them. A mechanism that has therefore become common in oversight legislation over the years is a power to refer appropriate matters back to the agency concerned to be dealt with as directed by the oversight body, with progress reports being made on request and final reports

[75] Ombudsman Act 1974 (NSW), s 25Q (re systems for preventing and for handling and responding to disability reportable incidents), Ombudsman Act 1974 (NSW), s 25L (re the monitoring and assessment of the implementation of Aboriginal Programs), Public Interest Disclosures Act 1994 (NSW), ss 6B(1)(e), (f) and 6C (re the Ombudsman monitoring and auditing the exercise of functions under and compliance with the Act), Children's Guardian Act 2019 (NSW), ss 54–55 (re child protection related reportable conduct scheme, previously in s25B of the Ombudsman Act 1974 (NSW)) and Law Enforcement Conduct Commission Act 2016 (NSW), ss 27(1)(d) and 32(1) (formerly in a 'keep under scrutiny' function of the Ombudsman under the Police Act 1990 (NSW)).

[76] In Tasmania: Public Interest Disclosures Act 2002 (Tas), ss 8–10 (re reviewing the procedures of public bodies governing public interest disclosures) and Mental Health Act 2013 (Tas), s 156 (making reports on the extent to which the objects of the Act and the mental health service delivery principles are being met). In Victoria: Ombudsman Act 1973 (Vic), sa 13AA(1)(a) and 13D (re reviewing the complaint-handling practices and procedures of an authority, on its own motion or in response to a complaint) and Public Interest Disclosures Act 2012 (Vic), s 60 (re review of procedures in place for managing PIDs, at any time). In Queensland: Ombudsman Act 2001 (Qld), s 12(c), (d) (re considering the administrative practices of agencies generally and making recommendations or providing advice or training) and Public Interest Disclosures Act 2020 (Qld), s 59 (re the Ombudsman monitoring the management of public interest disclosures, including monitoring compliance with the Act and reviewing the way public service agencies deal with public interest disclosures). In South Australia: Ombudsman Act 1972 (SA), s 14A (re the conduct of administrative audits).

when the matter has been completed.[77] This approach benefits an ombudsman because monitoring or oversighting an inquiry or investigation being undertaken by an agency is generally less resource intensive than actually conducting the inquiry or investigation. The approach benefits agencies because in my experience most would prefer to conduct an inquiry or investigation than have this done by an external oversight/accountability agency.

V. Conclusions

There are a number of challenges that ombudsman have faced, are facing and/or are likely to face in the future. Some are matters that the ombudsman have an ability to directly address, while others are matters that require the intervention (or inaction) of governments. Of the six challenges for ombudsman referred to in this chapter, independence, resourcing and proliferation are the ones that will have the most impact on their future. Unfortunately, they are also the ones over which ombudsman have the least actual or potential control.

In my view, ombudsman are only likely to continue to exist as a widespread institution in anything like their current form if they are able to continually demonstrate they remain relevant by being competent at their roles, adding value and being perceived to be credible. Effectively spreading this message will in practice be something ombudsman will need to do themselves. However, historically it does not appear to me that effectively 'selling' their value has generally been a high priority for ombudsman. While I am only aware of one Ombudsman Act (or equivalent) anywhere in the world that has ever been repealed in an attempt to remove the ombudsman function,[78] it is possible for a government to retain the function but neuter the ombudsman. This could be achieved through funding cuts, by removing administrative functions or bodies from the ombudsman's jurisdiction, at least in theory, or by appointing ombudsman who are known to be incompetent or risk averse, or who would be concerned that their future career in that jurisdiction would either be damaged or advanced, depending on how the role was performed.

[77] For example, the Public Interest Disclosure Act 2002 (Tas), ss 38, 41, 42, 57, 69 and 76; Public Interest Disclosure Act 1994 (NSW), s 6B; formerly Ombudsman Act 1974 (NSW), s 26E, now Children's Guardian Act 2019 (NSW), s 43; Ombudsman Act 1974 (NSW), s 25U (re disability related matters); and various pieces of legislation establishing anti-corruption agencies.

[78] Vanuatu in 1998. See ER Hill, 'The Vanuatu Ombudsman' in A Jowitt and T Newton Cain (eds), *The Passage of Change – Law, Society and Governance in the Pacific* (ANU E Press, 2010) www.jstor.org/stable/j.ctt24h3jd.

Appendix A: Distinction between Corruption Fighting and Complaint Handling

There are good reasons for establishing corruption-fighting bodies in each jurisdiction to complement the work of the jurisdiction's ombudsman. While adequate to deal with maladministration, the traditional powers and approaches of ombudsman are not well suited to fighting serious systemic corruption. In designing mechanisms to deal with issues relating to administrative conduct and decisions on the one hand and corrupt conduct on the other, it is important to recognise that there are a large number of significant differences between complaint handling and corruption fighting. These can be summarised as follows:

Complaint handling	Corruption fighting
Focus	
Public sector officials and agencies	Public sector officials and public sector agencies (e.g in relation to corruption prevention)
	Private individuals
Subject matter	
Administrative conduct and decisions	Corrupt conduct
Improving public administration	Exposing and dealing with corrupt conduct
Dealing with complaints from the public	Preventing corrupt conduct
Customer service issues	
Exposing misconduct	
Relevance of intention	
Intention not required for unreasonable conduct or 'maladministration'	Intention required for corrupt conduct (which would include actual or constructive knowledge that the conduct was wrong and conduct arising out of clear moral failings)
Sources of information	
Complaints (primarily)	Intelligence (in theory from various sources including complaints)

(continued)

(Continued)

Complaint handling	Corruption fighting
Communication with complainants and people/organisations the subject of complaint/investigation	
Regular communication with complainants Complainants have certain legal rights to be informed of action taken Relative openness (ie communication with people the subject of investigation, the relevant agency and complainants, as and where appropriate)	Complaints are primarily a source of information. Ongoing contact with complainants unlikely Complainants, persons the subject of investigation and relevant agencies generally have no right to information (other than whistleblowers) Strict secrecy
Investigative approach	
Generally relatively open investigation techniques and procedures are as informal as possible Hearings in private using an inquisitorial approach	Generally more covert investigation techniques and formal hearing procedures Hearings can be in public using both adversarial and inquisitorial approaches
Volumes of work	
Large numbers of mainly small-scale investigations Large-scale complaint management activities, including communicating with complainants and relevant agencies	Small numbers of large-scale investigations
Procedural fairness	
Must inform the subjects of an investigation at the commencement of an investigation Obliged to inform people of proposed adverse comment and provide an opportunity to respond	Need not inform the subjects of an investigation until the investigation is largely completed
Outcome where allegation sustained	
Rectification Management action to address problems/improve systems Changes to policies or the law, or other resolution options	Prosecution, disciplinary action or dismissal At times, organisational changes are recommended Management action to address problems/improve systems
Resource implications	
Relatively inexpensive	Resource intensive

The differences between complaint handling and corruption fighting are likely to give rise to conflict between the two roles if both are performed by the same agency or if either agency is subject to the control and direction of the other. As a matter of principle, the avoidance of such conflict makes separation of the roles of fundamental importance. Additionally, as a practical matter, if the two roles were combined in one organisation it is likely that complaint handling (reactive, demand-driven/complaint-driven and high volume) will be given priority in resource allocation over corruption fighting (more proactive, discretionary, intelligence-based and low volume).

Appendix B: Some of the Key Changes in the Operating Environments of Australian Ombudsman since the 1970s/1980s

Context in the 1970s/1980s	Context in 2020s
No policies, procedures, practices to guide organisations to manage or handle complaints or administrative-type investigations	Comprehensive policies, procedures, practices to guide organisations to manage or handle complaints and administrative-type investigations
Most public sector entities[79] did not have any dedicated complaint-handling staff, and most complaints were dealt with by staff who drafted responses and saw their role as uncritically defending the organisation and minister	Most larger public-facing public sector entities have dedicated complaint-handling staff who generally understand that their role is to impartially assess and deal with complaints, and not to uncritically defend their organisation or minister
Staff of public sector entities who were directed to handle complaints or conduct investigations had no training in those roles	Dedicated complaint-handling and investigatory staff of public sector entities are likely to have received training in those roles, or such skills can be accessed from the private sector
Records were paper based	Records are largely electronic
Official communications were by paper-based letter, minute, file note or the like	Official communications are now commonly electronic, eg by email, virtual, telephone
There were no computers (other than rudimentary word processors, calculators, etc), intranets or Internet	All public sector entities have computers, IT systems, intranets and access to the Internet

(continued)

[79] Other than organisations such as the police, correctional agencies and certain statutory positions.

(Continued)

Context in the 1970s/1980s	Context in 2020s
There were numerous public sector departments, each focused largely on a particular role and reporting directly to a single minister	In most jurisdictions there is now a relatively small number of mega departments, each with multiple roles and often reporting to more than one minister
Most public works and services were funded and undertaken/provided directly by public sector entities	Most public works and services are funded by government but undertaken by non-public sector entities under contract or other arrangements
The jurisdiction of ombudsman was limited to public sector entities	The jurisdictions of several ombudsman have been expanded to include a range of non-public sector entities[80]
The concept of 'customer service' was not recognised as applicable to the work of the public sector	'Customer service' and customer satisfaction are now concepts seen as vitally important for the good working and reputation of the public sector and government as a whole
The idea that the public had any right to access information held by the public sector had gained no traction in any Australian jurisdiction	It is now recognised in legislation that the public have certain rights to access information held by the public sector, particularly information relating to them
The extremely rare whistleblower was regarded as a disloyal 'rat in the ranks' or 'dobber' who needed to be hunted down and weeded out	All Australian jurisdictions now have whistleblower protection/public interest disclosure legislation, and it is now recognised that disclosure of wrongdoing by staff is one of the best ways to identify such conduct
The only independent integrity-related agencies in each Australian jurisdiction were the Auditor-General and the ombudsman	In most Australian jurisdictions there are numerous independent (or semi-independent) entities that perform integrity-related roles

[80] In particular, the NSW Ombudsman and WA Ombudsman.

7

Ombuds and Tribunals in a Digital Era: Framing a Digital Legal Consciousness

NAOMI CREUTZFELDT[1]

I. Introduction

In this chapter, I discuss the move to using technology for dispute resolution as a feature of the modern state. I choose the administrative justice system as a site of the modern state in which this shift is taking place. The administrative justice system is made up of complaint schemes, ombuds,[2] tribunals and administrative courts.[3] It is concerned with the laws surrounding decision-making and dispute resolution of public bodies. In many countries, it deals with more cases than the criminal or private civil justice systems.[4] Yet, it remains an under-researched justice space. In this chapter, I study two sets of institutions of the administrative justice system: ombuds and tribunals. These institutions operate in parallel, although they have significant overlapping remits.[5] My main focus is on how ombuds and tribunals can work better together and what impact digitalisation can have on this process.[6]

[1] I am grateful to Joe Tomlinson and Ian Loader for helpful comments on an earlier draft of this chapter. Thanks also to the editors for suggestions on how to improve the structure and message of the chapter; it is so much better for it.

[2] Terminology: ombudsman singular and ombuds for the plural.

[3] M Harris and M Partington, *Administrative Justice in the 21th Century* (Hart Publishing, 1999).

[4] S Nason, A Sherlock, H Taylor and H Pritchard, 'Public Administration and Justice in Wales: Social Housing and Homelessness' (March 2020) http://adminjustice.bangor.ac.uk/Admin-Justice-Wales-Housing-Summary-FINAL-2020.pdf; R Thomas and J Tomlinson, 'Mapping Current Issues in Administrative Justice: Austerity and the "More Bureaucratic Rationality" Approach' (2017) 39 *Journal of Social Welfare and Family Law* 380.

[5] AW Bradley, 'The Role of the Ombudsman in Relation to the Protection of Citizens' Rights' (1980) 39 *CLJ* 304, www.jstor.org/stable/4506281; www.judiciary.uk/wp-content/uploads/JCO/Documents/Tribunals/tribunals_spring_2008.pdf.

[6] The original plan for this chapter was to evaluate the pilots that started in late 2019 and early 2020 between two sets of ombuds/tribunals in the UK (discussed later in this chapter). Part of this evaluation was intended to be an empirical analysis of in-depth interviews and surveys of those who administer procedures and of those who use them. The project came to a standstill due to the COVID-19 pandemic.

This discussion is embedded in the justice environment of the modern state, a new shared space of ombuds/tribunals and the digitalisation of justice.

In this chapter, I bring together institutions that do not typically interact with each other to discuss the merits of such interaction, as well as to propose an analytical framework through which to understand and evaluate the unstoppable move towards the digitalisation of procedures. To achieve this, the rest of the chapter is divided into three sections: section II discusses digitalisation of justice in the modern state and provides a case study of the UK digital reform programme; section III provides an overview of ombuds and tribunals, and introduces a case study of a unique partnership effort in the UK; and section IV introduces a theoretical lens through which to understand and evaluate people's and institutions' shift into a digital justice space, that of digital legal consciousness.

II. Digitalisation of Justice

The justice system is overstretched, constantly being expected to perform beyond its capacity and hence operating with delays, high costs, not providing access to justice for all and, as some argue, with outdated procedures.[7] This reality has led to a strongly endorsed shift from slow and tired paper-based, face-to-face procedures to a time- and cost-saving digital turn. Digitalisation of justice has slowly evolved in different shapes in justice systems around the world as a feature of the modern state.[8] These aspects of change must be considered against larger principles of justice, such as access to justice, vulnerability, open justice and the rule of law.

Digitalisation has forced justice systems to think about how to update and modernise their systems and procedures to deliver justice. To digitalise systems does not always mean to translate them from offline to online one to one. There are considerations about external service providers (platforms, secure systems, data collection, management and storage) as well as how best to share platforms, share innovation and benefit from open source and e-filing systems. The opportunities to build a shared network and system are manifold and need to be considered carefully, ethically and with an eye to the future. Therefore, one of the goals of introducing online dispute resolution (ODR) to the court system, for example, is to 'not only bring technology into the courts, but to leverage technology to improve the court process and use court modernization as an opportunity to re-evaluate underlying court processes and systems'.[9]

[7] R Sandefur, 'What We Know and Need to Know about the Legal Needs of the Public' (2015–16) 67 South Carolina Law Review 443; H Genn, *What People Do and Think about Going to Law* (Hart Publishing, 1999); P Pleasance, N Balmer and R Sandefur, *Paths to Justice: A Past, Present and Future Roadmap* (Nuffield Foundation, 2013) www.nuffieldfoundation.org/sites/default/files/files/PTJ%20 Roadmap%20NUFFIELD%20Published.pdf.

[8] J Tomlinson, 'Justice in the Digital State' (2019) http://library.oapen.org/bitstream/id/26ae919 3-09ca-4c98-b28b-664e709d5ccd/9781447340331.pdf; https://remotecourts.org.

[9] World Justice Forum, 'Realizing Justice for All' (April 2019) https://worldjusticeproject.org/sites/default/files/documents/2019-07-15%20Working%20Sessions%20Summaries%20FINAL_noalgorithms.pdf.

While *going digital* brings with it many advantages, the design needs to incorporate (and guarantee access to) those users who are vulnerable and for whom it is already a challenge to access the *offline* justice system. I describe elsewhere[10] the danger of digitalisation forcing us into a two-tier justice system: one for those who can navigate the online process and one for those who cannot. This needs to be avoided to protect access to justice for all via the court and tribunal system as well as the ombuds.

There are several levels of the *digital justice revolution*. One of them, which is very basic, is the digitalisation of case files. Its aim is to be freed of the tremendous paper load and to exchange files easily, and safely, between the parties. It saves time and money. This is happening in many places around the world. The next step is to create a system to manage the cases. In Pakistan, for example, an online case management system was introduced in the high courts in Islamabad and Lahore in 2017.[11]

Another path to digitalisation is the idea of the pop-up court. To counterbalance the wave of court closures in the UK due to austerity, a new model of court – the 'pop up court'[12] – was recommended by JUSTICE in 2016 that reconceptualises court and tribunal rooms as 'justice spaces'. This space would help forge a more digitally focused approach. 'Flexible justice spaces should be accommodated within a court and tribunal estate made up of a number of responsive and flexible parts.'[13]

The next level of digitalisation in the justice system is to move the offline, face-to-face process online.[14] This involves more fundamental changes to existing justice systems and is accomplished in different ways. The two approaches discussed here are to either create a specific law regulating a digital process (to design the law around user tools), and to then design the technology for the procedure and execute it in specific areas, or to translate existing law and its accompanying procedures into an online space. The latter, however, is creating considerable concerns about access to justice. A significant obstacle here is that people are used to the court/tribunal being a physical place and process with familiar rituals.[15] Tribunals and

[10] N Creutzfeldt, *Ombudsmen and ADR* (Palgrave, 2018).

[11] In 2019, the courts in Islamabad and Karachi were connected through video links (e-court system) to hear cases and make the courts more efficient and the judicial system more responsive. Global Village Space, 'Digital Justice: Historical Day for Pakistan's SC' (May 2019) www.globalvillagespace.com/digital-justice-historical-day-for-pakistans-sc/.

[12] O Bowcott, 'Pop-up Courts Needed to Help Create More Flexible Justice System – Report' *The Guardian* (London, 18 May 2016) www.theguardian.com/law/2016/may/18/pop-up-courts- needed-help-create-more-flexible-justice-system-thinktank-justice; JUSTICE, 'What Is a Court?' (2016) https://justice.org.uk/wp-content/uploads/2016/05/JUSTICE-What-is-a-Court-Report-2016.pdf.

[13] Parliament UK, 'Courts and Tribunal Reforms' (2019) https://publications.parliament.uk/pa/cm201919/cmselect/cmjust/190/19003.htm; www.nao.org.uk/other/hm-courts-tribunals-estate-visualisation/.

[14] Examples of the online courts of 21 countries are gathered at https://remotecourts.org.

[15] L Mulcahy and E Rowden, *The Democratic Courthouse: A Modern History of Design, Due Process and Dignity* (Routledge 2019).

courts, unlike tech companies that sell goods online (eBay,[16] Amazon, Alibaba[17]) and provide an ODR system for their customers, have to establish an online credibility. Put differently, for companies operating in the digital space only, it makes sense to use the same platform to resolve complaints. It is more complicated for traditional justice systems to move online.

There are success stories around the world of certain parts of national justice systems going digital. For example, British Columbia (Canada) launched its first ever online civil tribunal in 2017.[18] The system deals with small-value property and land disputes involving sums of up to $25,000, and includes party-to-party negotiations, facilitation and ultimately an adjudicator who can make a ruling with the same force as a court. I will make two observations about this court: first, the people who use it are typically not at risk or vulnerable (although some might be); and second, a new law was made to create an ODR process especially because of this. In the UK, for example, the process is happening the other way around – existing laws and procedures are being translated into the digital space.[19] This is causing acute problems for users, especially those who are vulnerable.

In the Netherlands, divorce and neighbourhood disputes went online through the *Rechtwijzer 2.0* platform.[20] 'The Legal Aid Board in the Netherlands developed *Rechtwijzer* to improve access to justice and legal information. Its primary goal is to encourage self-reliance by improving control over the conflict process and understanding of one's own and the other party's positions and motivations in the conflict. It is designed to assist conflict parties in solving legal conflicts on their own where possible, and finding the right kind of help where needed. A report evaluating the site[21] found that its users liked it, with results suggesting that *Rechtwijzer* has a positive short-term effect on self-efficacy beliefs, related to the conflict process. Similar to the Canadian example, this is a specialist area of disputes which lends itself to an online platform, and was designed for it.

In the UK,[22] a success story in the digital turn is the traffic penalty tribunal. The process is efficient, paperless and very timely, with some cases being resolved within hours.[23] Appeals and evidence are submitted and managed online. Parties can comment on the evidence submitted and there is a messaging system that

[16] S Hattotuwa, 'Conversation with Colin Rule, Director of Online Dispute Resolution for eBay and PayPal, ICT for peacebuilding' (21 September 2006) https://ict4peace.wordpress.com/2006/09/21/conversation-with-colin-rule-director-of-online-dispute-resolution-for-ebay- and-paypal/.

[17] Alibaba Presentation Notes, International Conference on Online Dispute Resolution (Beijing, China, 19–20 September 2016) www.alibaba.com/showroom/dispute-resolution.html.

[18] https://civilresolutionbc.ca.

[19] There was a bill to create a new framework – but it fell during Brexit instability.

[20] HIIL, 'Rechtwijzer 2.0: Technology that Puts Justice in Your Hands' www.legaltechdesign.com/2014/01/rechtwijzer-2-0-interactive-platform-to-justice/.

[21] https://core.ac.uk/download/pdf/31154843.pdf.

[22] Civil Litigation Tribunal, www.civilresolutionbc.ca/; Lord Justice Briggs, *Civil Courts Structure Review: Annual Report* (Judiciary England & Wales, 2016), www.judiciary.gov.uk/wp-content/uploads/2016/11/lcj-report-2016-final- web.pdf.

[23] www.trafficpenaltytribunal.gov.uk/publications/annual-reports/.

allows adjudicators to adopt an inquisitorial approach. People who are not able to go online are able to file a complaint through the traditional paper-based route and receive telephone assistance. As a result of this online tribunal, the cost for local authorities has gone down. The time spent on each case and its processing cost have both reduced enormously. The system also allows both local authorities and the tribunal to review its decisions and to learn from them.

These examples of online justice systems that work well have the shared feature that they cover a specific area of disputes that arguably lend themselves to an online procedure. There are various considerations when moving a process online. The move to online systems is challenging our traditional understanding of a court and what access to justice means. Digital justice, as Rabinovich-Einy and Katch[24] argue, holds enormous potential for increasing access to justice. Equally, these opportunities that ODR creates can also frustrate access and give rise to digital injustice.[25] Some fundamental questions about procedural justice have arisen, for example, because

> as digital technology became part of the design of certain dispute resolution processes, the question of what constitutes procedural justice arose, with elements such as speed of the process becoming more central than other features traditionally associated with procedural justice and disputant expectations.[26]

Having said that, often big data can do exactly this, monitoring the quality of process and outcome, uncovering biases and problems in the algorithms, and enabling dispute prevention. The introduction of digital justice has to be accompanied by an agenda to safeguard the rule of law, access to justice and open justice.

A. The Immediate Challenges to Digitalisation in Courts and Tribunals

Challenges that accompany a digitalisation agenda are discussed in this section. The digitalisation I am referring to here is the technology that is used to allow people to access a dispute resolution procedure through: an online portal; video hearings; ODR and algorithms; or other specialised digital platforms. In the examples below, I refer to justice systems that are traditionally paper based and face-to-face, but are now taking a digital turn. Here, I identify three immediate challenges to the digitalisation agenda: (i) where professionals meet technology; (ii) loss of legitimacy; and (iii) access to justice: users/non-users of the system.

[24] O Rabinovich-Einy and E Katch, 'Access to Digital Justice: Fair and Efficient Processes for the Modern Age' (2017) https://cardozojcr.com/wp-content/uploads/2017/05/CAC307_crop.pdf; E Katch and O Rabinovich-Einy, *Digital Justice* (Oxford University Press, 2017).

[25] ibid 648.

[26] C Rule, 'Quantifying the Economic Benefits of Effective Redress: Large E-Commerce Data Sets and the Cost–Benefit Case for Investing in Dispute Resolution' (2012) 34 *University of Arkansas at Little Rock Law Review* 767.

(i) Professionals Meet Technology

One challenge to digitalisation is the attitudes of the professionals administering it. Those who use and execute the system, especially at the top, are used to a certain etiquette of authority and process. Senior judges are now faced with people who design and maintain the technology teaching and telling them how to operate in a new digital justice space. This leaves those (typically in charge) with not enough technological know-how in vulnerable positions. They have to rethink and reclaim their authority in a new online space. This new dependence on systems designers and technology significantly changes traditional representations of justice. How might this impact on a court's legitimacy?

(ii) Losing Legitimacy?

What role does the tradition in the procedure of a court process have in relation to its legitimacy? Does the courthouse symbolise the authority of the community over the individual and lend legitimacy to the process? Rowden[27] explored these questions in relation to remote courthouses and the use of video links. The physical place of a courtroom and trial holds a special meaning.[28] The place of the trial has always been marked out as special.[29] A video link provides physical separation between participants within a trial and increases access for those who are physically remote from the court.[30] Rowden's empirical data showed that 'videolinked encounters make obtaining both a sense of the court space, and one's place within it, very difficult to achieve. Her data showed the symbolic importance of the court as an expression of shared values.'[31] In the court setting, which is filled with rituals and expectations, 'the legal profession performs specific social, economic, psychological and linguistic practices in the courtroom'.[32] Rowden concludes that current video links ignore the importance of rules and behaviour that a physical courtroom provides. This might have an impact on the delivery and acceptance of justice, thus leading to a loss of legitimacy.

The shift from a physical space (of a court) to a newly created digital one forces us to rethink the legitimacy not only of space but also of communication.[33]

[27] E Rowden, 'Distributed Courts and Legitimacy: What Do We Lose When We Lose the Courthouse?' (2015) 14 *Law Culture and the Humanities* 263.

[28] J Jaconelli, *Open Justice: A Critique of the Public Trial* (Oxford University Press, 2002).

[29] L Mulcahy, *Legal Architecture: Justice, Due Process, and the Place of Law* (Routledge, 2011) 17.

[30] E Rowden, 'Remote Participation and the Distributed Court: An Approach to Court Architecture in the Age of Video-Mediated Communications' (PhD thesis, University of Melbourne 2011) 67, https://minerva-access.unimelb.edu.au/handle/11343/36755.

[31] ibid 276.

[32] ibid 277.

[33] Example from China: 'Giving Online Hearings as Sense of Ritual: Across China: Internet Court Handles Cases Despite Coronavirus Epidemic' (China.org, March 2019) www.china.org.cn/china/Off_the_Wire/2020-03/10/content_75796760.htm.

A report by JUSTICE[34] showed that video conferencing has practical difficulties for vulnerable appellants. There is evidence that witnesses are perceived as less trustworthy when using video links as opposed to appearing in person.[35] A further study conducted on virtual mock trials showed that technology is not yet up to a standard where the principles of justice can be confidently upheld,[36] thus making those who can access the system vulnerable in ways they might not have been if presenting in person. Open justice is maintained through audio recordings of trials that are available; notes of hearings; and accredited media access.[37]

Hynes et al[38] found in their review of face-to-face hearings as opposed to video links that there is an uneasiness about the pace of change towards the abandonment of physical hearings. The concept of video hearings was tested in a study in the UK in 2018, to evaluate user experience of the HM Courts & Tribunals Service (HMCTS) video hearings pilot for party-to-state hearings where all parties participate remotely.[39] Two of the recommendations/findings of this small-scale self-selected study were:

> Many users were unable to take part in a video hearing due to the limitation of this first iteration of the technical product, which required a specific browser and hardware specifications, among other criteria. As the technical product improves to allow for a wider range of users, further testing should examine the wider user experience.
>
> Future developments need to include a strategy for addressing user vulnerabilities in video hearings or to identify a minimum standard of resilience that one needs to meet in order to participate in a video hearing instead of an in-person hearing. Other key areas for improvement include a strategy for the sharing of documents electronically, how to ensure open justice and streamlining protocols for judges.

In short, it turned out that the technology was not ready to provide a good experience for both sides and the system is not set up for vulnerable users. This pilot also included a detailed briefing of the few self-selected participants that guided them through the process that was in place just for the pilot but is not planned to be available for the real roll-out. How will this online system provide access to all parties, especially those who are vulnerable?

[34] JUSTICE, 'Understanding Courts' (2019) https://justice.org.uk/our-work/understanding-courts/.

[35] SG. Goodman, A Tobey, JM Batterman-Faunce, H Orcutt, S Thomas, C Shapiro and T Sachsenmaier, 'Face-to-Face Confrontation: Effects of Closed-Circuit Technology on Children's Eyewitness Testimony and Jurors' Decisions' (1998) 22 *Law and Human Behavior* 165.

[36] L Mulcahy, E Rowden and W Tweeder, 'Exploring the Case of Virtual Jury Trials during the COVID-19 Crisis' (2020) https://justice.org.uk/wp-content/uploads/2020/04/Mulcahy-Rowden-Virtual-trials-final.pdf.

[37] ibid 31.

[38] J Hynes, N Gill and Tomlinson J, 'In Defence of the Hearing? Emerging Geographies of Publicness, Materiality, Access and Communication in Court Hearings' [2020] *Geography Compass* https://onlinelibrary.wiley.com/doi/pdf/10.1111/gec3.12499.

[39] M Rossner and M McCurdy, 'Implementing Video Hearings (Party to State): A Process Evaluation' (2018) http://eprints.lse.ac.uk/90960/1/Rossner_Implementing-video-hearings_Author.pdf.

(iii) Access to Justice – Users and Non-users

One of the great challenges of the digitalisation of justice is to find a way to include minorities, disempowered groups and other vulnerable people.[40] The shift to digitalisation can be an opportunity, if executed and evaluated properly, to enhance access to justice.

> The move to online courts is an incredible opportunity to create a justice system that works well for everyone, whether they are an individual in crisis who has never been to court before, or a large organisation which regularly brings claims. We need to ensure that digital processes are designed and monitored in line with recognised access to justice principles. We also need to be able to measure how different groups fare under the online processes, compared with paper-based, or face-to-face systems.[41]

The shift to digital justice can only be a success for all if all can access and use it. There are, however, significant teething problems with online processes. For the time being, there is no equal access to online justice; it is work in progress.

A recent report on the ability of people to access the digital justice system in the UK found that:

> In order to ensure access to justice and fairness for those who are, for whatever reason, unable to interact with an online justice system, barriers preventing access to digital assistance must be overcome. Whilst digital technology will, for many, be advantageous and make accessing services easier, and over time, many will become more digitally able, there will nonetheless, remain those who are digitally challenged and digitally excluded. The new system must work for all users and reform must not leave behind those unable to access and participate in a digital justice system.[42]

The report highlights the need to think about digital literacy and how to help people who are digitally illiterate and thus excluded from accessing online justice. An integrated service providing adequate legal advice and support for those who are most vulnerable needs to be created. 'Technology has the capacity to enhance, empower and automate, but it also has the potential to exclude vulnerable members of society.'[43] This raises more questions, especially around access to

[40] DR Hensler, 'Our Courts, Ourselves: How the Alternative Dispute Resolution Movement is Re-Shaping Our Legal System' (2003) 108 *Penn State Law Review* 165, 170; JR Sternlight, 'ADR Is Here: Preliminary Reflections on Where It Fits in a System of Justice' (2003) 3 *Nevada Law Review* 274; N Byrom, 'Digital Justice: HMCTS Data Strategy and Delivering Access to Justice' (2019) https://research.thelegaleducationfoundation.org/wp-content/uploads/2019/09/Digital-Justice-Exec-Summary-FINAL.pdf; Creutzfeldt, *Ombudsmen and ADR* (n 9).

[41] Digital Justice, 'HMCTS Data Strategy and Delivering Access to Justice' www.disabilityrightsuk.org/news/2019/october/ensuring-access-justice-vulnerable-people-will-be-heart-governments-court-and; https://research.thelegaleducationfoundation.org/wp-content/uploads/2019/09/Digital-Justice-Exec-Summary-FINAL.pdf.

[42] D Sechi, 'Digitisation and Accessing Justice in the Community' (2020) https://ajc-justice.co.uk/wp-content/uploads/2020/04/Digitisation.pdf.

[43] Fabian Policy Report, 'The Right to Justice – The Final Report of the Bach Commission' (September 2017)18 https://fabians.org.uk/wp-content/uploads/2017/09/Bach-Commission_Right-to-Justice-Report-WEB-2.pdf.

justice: should technology be expected to improve access to justice? Further, as outlined above, there are different types of technology used in different settings, all confusingly referred to as *digitalisation*. There needs to be a clear distinction between which set-up is aimed at which institution, being mindful of its users, processes and outcomes.

In sum, technology provides both opportunities that need to be harnessed and challenges that need to be overcome. A system can develop and grow through collecting data to improve the process and outcome as well as including users' views to design a more responsive and user-friendly system. Such a system can then measure user satisfaction and trust. A recent example of a major modernisation and digital reform programme can be found in the UK. Where tradition meets change, the question about access to justice needs to be at the forefront of the reform. Is technology enhancing access to justice or not?

B. Current UK Developments and Reform programme

In 2016, the Ministry of Justice (MoJ) published its plans in *Transforming Our Justice System*.[44]

> The reforms outlined here will achieve that by combining our respected traditions with the enabling power of technology. The vision is to modernise and upgrade our justice system so that it works even better for everyone, from judges and legal professionals, to witnesses, litigants and the vulnerable victims of crime. When they have to engage with the system, we want everyone to have available to them the finest justice system in the world.
>
> We have the will and now the means to achieve this. The Government is committed to investing more than £700 million to modernise courts and tribunals, and over £270 million more in the criminal justice system.[45]

This substantial reform process aims to make justice accessible and proportionate by: offering different ways of resolving disputes; stripping out unnecessary procedure and costs; communicating with users so they know what to expect and do; allowing the judiciary to focus on matters of law; and using physical hearings only where necessary.[46] This reform process, operated by the MoJ and HMCTS, is one of the largest ever attempted. The move from overstretched and tired offline

[44] Ministry of Justice, *Transforming Our Justice System* (2016) https://assets.publishing.service.gov.uk/government/uploads/system/uploads/attachment_data/file/553261/joint-vision-statement.pdf.

[45] ibid 3.

[46] R Thomas and J Tomlinson, 'Current Issues in Administrative Justice: Examining Administrative Review, Better Initial Decisions, and Tribunal Reform' (2016) www.researchgate.net/profile/Robert_Thomas38/publication/311452870_Current_issues_in_administrative_justice_Examining_administrative_review_better_initial_decisions_and_tribunal_reform/links/58470fcc08aeda6968227a08/Current-issues-in-administrative-justice-Examining-administrative-review-better-initial-decisions-and-tribunal-reform.pdf.

systems to ODR is aimed at enabling users to interact more flexibly with the court and tribunal systems.[47]

It is essential, as mentioned above, that the reforms are measured according to an understanding of access to justice based on four minimum standards: access to the formal legal system; access to an effective hearing; access to a decision according to substantive law; and access to a remedy.[48] The government response to some concerns in a public consultation about vulnerable users was: 'tribunals deal with some of the most vulnerable people in society and we are committed to ensuring our services are accessible to all users and that no one is left behind'.[49] One also has to think about how to evaluate the new system in a way that will enable its constant updating and fine-tuning,[50] based on functionality and user experience.

As the legal profession meets technology, we have to be mindful of this relationship and how to best manage it. Tomlinson advocates that control of institutional design questions should not be yielded to those who possess technological expertise.[51] He warns of hidden methods and politics when deploying digital systems to institutions.[52] This raises an interesting point about those who conduct online procedures needing to work closely with tech experts in designing online spaces. As Tomlinson puts it: 'Technology is best conceived as a new material that has been discovered, which is to be added to the existing materials used in building systems.'[53]

Understanding technology as a new model through which to administer justice becomes a challenge if we consider traditional expectations of how to resolve a dispute.[54] Before returning the focus to the ombuds' and tribunals' efforts of

[47] ibid.

[48] D Bindman, 'Court Reforms Must Measure Impact on Vulnerable Litigants' (12 March 2019) www.legalfutures.co.uk/latest-news/court-reforms-must-measure- impact-on-vulnerable-litigants; https://assets.publishing.service.gov.uk/government/uploads/system/uploads/attachment_data/file/835778/DigitalJusticeFINAL.PDF.

[49] Ministry of Justice, *Transforming Our Justice System: Assisted Digital Strategy, Automatic Online Conviction and Statutory Standard Penalty, and Panel Composition in Tribunals* (2017) 23 https://consult.justice.gov.uk/digital-communications/transforming-our-justice-system-assisted-digital/results/transforming-our-justice-system-government-response.pdf.

[50] N Byrom, 'Digital Justice: HMCTS Data Strategy and Delivering Access to Justice Report and Recommendations' (2019) https://research.thelegaleducationfoundation.org/wp-content/uploads/2019/09/DigitalJusticeFINAL.pdf. The LEF advocated for the adoption of this definition to evaluate digital court systems. For each dimension of access to justice (formal legal system, effective hearing, fair decisions and legal remedies), there are data that should be collected as part of the evaluation framework. This includes collecting survey data on attitudes to the legal system, geo-demographic data on court users, data on types of claims initiated, data on perceptions of procedural justice, data on engagement with legal support, management information data as proxy for engagement, data on types of cases reaching judicial determination, research on judicial attitudes and behaviour on decision-making, and data on enforcement rates and time to enforcement.

[51] Tomlinson (n 7) 16.

[52] D Mulligan and K Bamberger, 'Saving Governance by Design' (2018) 106(3) *California Law Review*.

[53] Tomlinson (n 7) 16.

[54] L Mulcahy, *The Democratic Courthouse: A Modern History of Design, Due Process and Dignity* (Routledge, 2019).

partnership, current events have to enter into the discussion. While digitalisation was being implemented and tested furiously in the UK, and ombuds and tribunals were being creative about working together, the COVID-19 pandemic hit. This unique situation has accelerated digitalisation into the next phase and is likely to have a profound impact on the partnership, as well as on the digitalisation process. The following example also shows the risks and drawbacks of technology in the modern state.

C. COVID-19 as the Catalyst to Digitalisation

In early 2020, as the COVID-19 pandemic slowly emerged into our consciousness and then into our neighbourhoods, emergency measures were announced to transfer responsibility of large parts of the private sector to the public realm,[55] alongside exceptional powers[56] given to the executive to manage the situation (Coronavirus Act 2020[57]).[58] At this moment of intense alert, physical distancing and the country coming to a halt, people were forced into the digital space to pursue their everyday.[59] This forced jump into the digital realm clearly demonstrated that we are not suitably prepared for it. It is showing us the risks and drawbacks of technology in the modern state.[60] It makes us all feel like users, but even those who are relatively well prepared have encountered problems with technology. However, it also shows a hierarchy of access: those people who are able to act and function online have a clear advantage over those who are already challenged by online access and who are, arguably, hit the hardest by the pandemic. They are confronted with a new digital space that is difficult to access. This makes access to justice unequal in the new digital setting, which is very worrying. The current tenor in the UK is that digitalisation works for certain settings and certain cases, but not for others (mainly the low-value and low-risk ones).[61]

[55] HM Treasury, 'The Chancellor Rishi Sunak Provides an Updated Statement on Coronavirus (20 March 2020) www.gov.uk/government/speeches/the-chancellor-rishi-sunak-provides-an-updated-statement-on-coronavirus.

[56] E Mountbatten-O'Malley, 'The Emperor Has no Clothes: A Sober Analysis of the Government Response to Covid-19 (UKAJI, 2020) https://ukaji.org/2020/04/28/the-emperor-has-no-clothes-a-sober-analysis-of-the-government-response-to-covid-19/.

[57] www.legislation.gov.uk/ukpga/2020/7/contents/enacted.

[58] L Marsons, 'Covid 19 and the UK Administrative State' (adminlawblogorg, 31 March 2020) https://adminlawblog.org/2020/03/31/lee-marsons-covid-19-and-the-uk-administrative-state/; J King, 'The Lockdown is Lawful' (UK Constitutional Law Blog, 1 April 2020) https://ukconstitutionallaw.org/2020/04/01/jeff-king-the-lockdown-is-lawful/; J King, 'The Lockdown is Lawful: Part II' (UK Constitutional Law Blog, 2 April 2020) https://ukconstitutionallaw.org/2020/04/02/jeff-king-the-lockdown-is-lawful-part-ii/.

[59] Examples from around the world of how courts deal with being forced online by the pandemic, as well as existing online courts, can be found at https://remotecourts.org.

[60] J Rozenberg, 'Can remote Courts Truly Deliver Jsutice?' (*Law Gazette*, 18 May 2020) www.lawgazette.co.uk/commentary-and-opinion/can-remote-courts-truly-deliver-justice/5104279.article.

[61] J Tomlinson, J Hynes, J Maxwell and E Marshall, 'Judicial Review during the COIVD 19 Pandemic (Part II) (adminlawblog, 28 May 2020) https://adminlawblog.org/2020/05/28/joe-tomlinson-jo-hynes-jack-maxwell-and-emma-marshall-judicial-review-during-the-covid-19-pandemic-part-ii/.

The current pandemic has radically interfered not only with the way that courts function, but also with the way that ombuds and tribunals function. The Local Government and Social Care Ombudsman (LGSCO) has stopped all case work activity that demands information from or action by local authorities and care providers so that they can provide frontline services.[62] The Parliamentary and Health Service Ombudsman similarly decided not to place extra burdens on the health service during the pandemic. As of 26 March 2021, they are not accepting any new health complaints or progressing existing ones.[63] This means that existing cases will be backlogged and new cases will pile up. A similar problem has arisen with tribunals.

The tribunals have put in place emergency legislation to enable remote hearings and video conferences, and those tribunals that were piloting digital procedures have gone live. The Senior President of Tribunals (SPT) issued pilot practice directions to the tribunals to deal with the situation:

> During the Covid-19 pandemic, it may be necessary for tribunals to adjust their ways of working to limit the spread of the virus and manage their workloads appropriately. I have therefore decided to issue this Practice Direction on a pilot basis for a period of three months, although it may be reviewed within that period should it become inappropriate or unnecessary.[64]

The SPT has enabled judges to work remotely and hold hearings with parties and panels all operating remotely. Recordings of all proceedings will be made, so the decision-making is accessible. All non-urgent work is paused. Once the pandemic has passed, the system will be faced with an enormous backlog of cases and new cases. This is an example of a social experiment with digitalisation where there is no choice but to travel the path. Going back to the importance of making a digital system accessible for all, especially for the more vulnerable, it remains crucial to analyse how this exposure to digitalisation has worked, and why or why not. It is hoped that enough data can be collected to evaluate and learn from this extraordinary time in history.

To conclude, we are left with many questions about technology and its promises. How safe and easy is it to use? Who controls the use of technology, and what are appropriate benchmarks for this control? I will next discuss an example of the intersection between ombuds and tribunals, and the scope for technology to enhance access to justice in the modern state.

III. Ombuds and Tribunals

In this section, I first outline what ombuds and tribunals do and why the intersection between them matters, especially in the light of access to justice, digitalisation

[62] www.lgo.org.uk/announcement.

[63] www.ombudsman.org.uk/coronavirus-update.

[64] www.judiciary.uk/wp-content/uploads/2020/03/Mental-Health-Pilot-Practice-Direction-for-publication.pdf.

and the use of technology. As seen in the previous section, technology is supposed to provide a bridge to ideally benefit the institutions and the public. This assumes that institutions in the modern state that are run effectively serve the citizens. This is, however, not the case.[65] The system does not serve those who are vulnerable; rather, technology enhances the gap between vulnerable and able users.[66] The case study of the UK below illustrates this.

A. Ombuds

In 1809, the Swedish constitution created the office of the ombuds. The ombuds model was initially introduced as an administrative oversight body and has since developed and grown beyond these responsibilities. The model spread to other Nordic countries, making its way to New Zealand in 1962, before spreading throughout the world.[67] The ombuds filled a void in national legal systems, offering a combination of redress and justice where there was a lack of respect for human rights. The ombuds model, part of a system to resolve people's complaints, is shaped by the national, social and political context. The ombuds was imported to the national system to strengthen the existing legal order.[68] In other countries, the ombuds formed part of the expansion of the administrative sector.[69] Generally speaking, an ombuds aims to restore public confidence in administration.[70] The ability of the ombuds model to operate comfortably in a range of different legal systems, and perform the different roles and functions that it has been used to deliver, is part of the success of the institution.[71]

Ombuds throughout the world have the function to protect the individual (from the state) where there is an imbalance of power:

> In most countries around the world parliamentary control bodies are established, which monitor and implement the rule of law, the fight against corruption and good public administration. Although the specific role of the Ombudsman institution may vary, the holder of this office is legitimized by parliament – either through direct elections or through appointment by the head of state or government by or after consultation with parliament.

[65] L Tickle, 'Interview with Lisa Harker: Remote Family Courts Hearings Are Not Just or Humane' *The Guardian* (London, 2 June 2020) www.theguardian.com/society/2020/jun/02/lisa-harker-family-court-hearings-justice-failed-coronavirus-crisis; M Hertogh, *Nobody's Law: Legal Consciousness and Legal Alienation in Everyday Life* (Palgrave, 2018).

[66] SE Rogers, 'Bridging the 21st Century Digital Divide' (2016) 60 *TechTrends* 197, https://doi.org/10.1007/s11528-016-0057-0.

[67] L Reif, *The Ombudsman, Good Governance and the International Human Rights System* (Springer, 2013).

[68] T Buck, K Richard and B Thompson, *The Ombudsman Enterprise and Administrative Justice* (Ashgate, 2011) 10.

[69] K Heede, *European Ombudsman: Redress and Control at Union Level* (Kluwer Law International, 2000).

[70] Creutzfeldt, *Ombudsmen and ADR* (n 9) 37.

[71] G Kucsko-Stadlmayer, 'The Spread of the Ombudsman Idea in Europe' (International Ombudsman Institute Paper, 2009) www.theioi.org/downloads/34chi/Stockholm%20Conference_25.%20Back%20to%20the%20Roots_Gabriele%20Kucsko%20Stadlmayer.pdf.

> The role of Ombudsman institutions is to protect the people against violation of rights, abuse of powers, unfair decisions and maladministration. They play an increasingly important role in improving public administration while making the government's actions more open and its administration more accountable to the public.[72]

Ombuds have different powers and different remits throughout the world.[73] They were established to deal with grievances where no remedy was available in court because the matter was not justiciable as no legal right was infringed.[74] Ombuds typically look at the lack of fairness on the part of the government administration.[75] Some argue that ombuds have become a valuable model of dispute resolution as they are free to use for people, cost is kept down (there is no need for legal representation) and they operate flexible procedures.[76] Ombuds not only deal with grievances about public services, but also seek to improve the way in which that service operates. Ideally, ombuds feed back the complaints data they collect to help the service provider prevent the same issues from happening again. In a more ambitious scope, ombuds working together with government agencies and feeding back their complaint data can assist systemic learning and improve the system for all.

Usually, ombuds are committed to a set of values that guide their standards, conduct and ethics. Compared to the formal system of dispute resolution (courts), the ombuds model promises procedures that are speedy, cost effective and less formal. These promises are kept, among other things, by providing a different process to that of a court procedure. Decisions are taken by ombuds on the basis of what is fair and reasonable (reference annual report). Contact with an ombudsman typically does not take place face-to-face but over the phone, email or, in some cases, via post. The main channel for information and communication is digital.

Ombuds cover different types of disputes and have varied jurisdictions and powers.[77] These variations are reflected in the processes they offer. The ombuds model, due to its tremendous potential to process a high proportion of unmet legal needs for certain types of problems, draws its strength from its variety of contextual and conceptual adaptations.[78]

[72] International Ombudsman Institute, www.theioi.org/the-i-o-i.

[73] L Reif, *The Ombudsman, Good Governance, and the International Human Rights System* (Martinus Nijhoff, 2004); M Seneviratne, *Ombudsmen: Public Services and Administrative Justice* (Butterworths LexisNexis, 2002); Buck et al (n 66); N Creutzfeldt, 'What Do We Expect of Ombudsmen? Narratives of Everyday Engagements with the Informal Justice System' (2016) 12 *International Journal of Law in Context* 432; Creutzfeldt, *Ombudsmen and ADR* (n 9).

[74] Seneviratne (n 72).

[75] LC Reif, *The Ombudsman, Good Governance, and the International Human Rights System* (Martinus Nijhoff, 2004) 3.

[76] C Harlow, 'Ombudsmen in Search of a Role' (1978) 41 *MLR* 446; Creutzfeldt, *Ombudsmen and ADR* (n 9); Seneviratne (n 72).

[77] Creutzfeldt, *Ombudsmen and ADR* (n 9).

[78] S Carl, 'Toward a Definition and Taxonomy of Public Sector Ombudsmen' (2012) 55 *Canadian Public Administration* 203.

B. Tribunals

In 1923, Pillsbury described administrative tribunals in the USA as part of the system that blurs the strict separation of powers in the three branches of government, which has proven to be too rigid. Administrative tribunals therefore provide a quasi-legal solution.

> In exercising such quasi-judicial functions, these bodies pass upon and determine controversies arising under the laws which they administer, frequently using judicial machinery and judicial forms of trial.[79]
>
> The last twenty years have seen a marked increase in such administrative courts, notably with respect to public utility, trade, workmen's compensation and labour boards or commissions. These boards have been created in response to a public demand for increased efficiency of government and to meet special needs, and are in the main satisfactorily accomplishing the objects for which they were created.[80]

Tribunals develop over time, aligned to their jurisdiction and national context. In the UK, in the nineteenth century, tribunals emerged as multifunctional administrative entities operating in areas such as railways regulation and tax which, among other things, resolved disputes.[81] As Thomas outlines,

> the advent of the modern tribunal system can be traced back to the National Insurance Act 1911, which introduced unemployment insurance. The Act bypassed the ordinary courts by requiring that appeals against decisions of insurance officers be brought to a court of referees. In doing so, the Act introduced the concept of a local, non-legal tribunal that specialised in a particular area of administration.[82]

In a similar fashion as described in the USA above, tribunals in the UK developed into a hybrid space of being neither fully administrative not judicial.[83] (A quasi-judicial nature was placed upon the process a tribunal offers.)

During the 2000s, tribunals turned from being alternatives to the courts into a type of specialist court through the Tribunals, Courts and Enforcement Act 2007.[84] However, after a strong growth in tribunals in the 2000s, austerity brought a halt to this trajectory.[85] Lengthy procedures now cost more money and time.

[79] W Pillsbury, 'Administrative Tribunals' (1923) 36 *Harvard Law Review* 405, 406.

[80] ibid 407.

[81] C Stebbings, *Legal Foundations of Tribunals in Nineteenth Century England* (Cambridge University Press, 2006).

[82] R Thomas, 'Current Developments in UK Tribunals: Challenges for Administrative Justice' (19 April 2016) SSRN: https://ssrn.com/abstract=2766982; http://dx.doi.org/10.2139/ssrn.2766982.

[83] G Drewry, 'The Judicialisation of "Administrative" Tribunals in the UK: From Hewart to Leggatt' (2009) 28 *Transylvanian Review of Administrative Sciences* 45.

[84] Thomas (n 81).

[85] M Adler, 'The Rise and Fall of Administrative Justice – A Cautionary Tale' (2012) 8 *Socio-Legal Review* 28; R Kirkham, 'The Ombudsman, Tribunals and Administrative Justice Section: A 2020 Vision for the Ombudsman Sector (2016) 38 *Journal of Social Welfare and Family Law* 103.

Tribunals, being stuck between politics and law, are faced with growing challenges in the administrative justice system:

> [A]dministrative justice is not a single system in its own right, but a jumble of many disparate systems that exist on both vertical policy lines (eg tax, housing, education) and horizontal functional lines (eg tribunals, ombudsmen, and the courts). The highly fragmented nature of the 'system' and the strong influence of government normally produces ad hoc, sector-specific changes as opposed to system-wide reforms.[86]

Tribunals are not supposed to correct bad initial decision-making. However, collecting appeals outcomes can help to improve decision-making: getting it right means adapting from experience and changing procedures to guide future decisions (similar to the ombuds sharing their complaints data with local authorities to improve their work). This poses a real challenge for large-scale organisations – one that requires 'management, commitment, and careful preparation'.[87]

In summary, ombuds and tribunals inhabit a similar quasi-judicial space, existing in tension between politics, government, law and public scrutiny in the modern state. Although they inhabit the administrative justice space, they coexist in it, rather than assisting and learning from each other. Ombuds and tribunals have different processes and procedures for dealing with cases, but there are overlaps in their jurisdictions (see below). This is an overlooked space to improve the system. In the rest of this chapter, I start to explore the possibilities of harnessing these overlaps using the example of the ombuds/tribunals partnership pilots currently underway in the UK. This leads to the larger questions of digitalisation of justice and how to design and evaluate it.

C. Ombuds/Tribunals Partnership Pilots in England

Ombuds and tribunals in the UK operate in their own spaces in the administrative justice system with an overlap in their jurisdictions, but this is mainly unknown by the public. A recent initiative aims to address this by facilitating a few select pilot projects of familiarisation with ombudsmen and tribunals. It is a unique initiative, not originally thought of as part of the large modernisation and reform programme the UK is undertaking. Her Majesty's Courts and Tribunals Service is undergoing an ambitious reform programme, launched in September 2016.[88] The programme 'aims to bring new technology and modern ways of working to the way justice is administered'. One billion pounds is being invested to reform the courts and tribunals system. The aim is to build this modern system around the public who use it.

Here, I consider how the emerging ombuds/tribunals partnership pilots can benefit from the willingness to modernise, the drive to digitalisation and access

[86] Thomas (n 81) x.

[87] Administrative Justice and Tribunals Council (AJTC), *Putting It Right – A Strategic Approach to Resolving Administrative Disputes* (2012) http://ajtc.justice.gov.uk/docs/AJTC_Right_first_time_web(7).pdf.

[88] www.gov.uk/guidance/the-hmcts-reform-programme.

to justice as part of the modern state. As institutions that function alongside each other in the justice system, there are opportunities for ombuds and tribunals to join up processes to allow people access to a clearer path to redress.

In a lecture given by the SPT, Sir Ernest Ryder, at the Ombudsman Association Annual Conference in 2019,[89] a reform programme was charted to advocate a more user-friendly shared delivery of administrative justice.[90] He proposed a bold manifesto for change between ombuds and tribunals.[91]

(1) The ability of administrative courts and tribunals to refer matters that are prima facie maladministration to an ombudsman who can consider them using their own initiative powers. Courts used to do that in family law – they referred poor practice to the then social service inspectorates who reported back to the judge about it or published their own conclusions.
(2) A corresponding power in an ombudsman to refer to the Administrative Appeals Chamber of the Upper Tribunal – which is a United Kingdom Superior Court of Record – any issues they believe require guidance by judicial review determination or individual redress beyond their powers. The power to issue binding guidance should not be underestimated.
(3) A programme of interoperability – and what do I mean by that – judges able to work as ombuds and vice-versa – not just collaboration and co-operation but career paths and that includes for our case workers and case officers. One of our case officers has become a judge and others will follow. They have materially identical skills and abilities frameworks in both our services.
(4) A strong and single voice for change rooted in what our users want. They can and should be asked what do they want their justice space to be like.

Some concrete aspects of these proposals are joint training and liaison between ombuds and tribunals judges, and the intention to 'learn to communicate and engage better with the public in the ways our international colleagues do'.[92] A platform through which change is driven in the UK is the Administrative Justice Council (AJC).[93] It was established in 2018 as the successor body of the Administrative Justice Forum, which was abolished in 2017.[94] The AJC is the only body with oversight of the whole of the administrative justice system in the UK, advising government, including the devolved governments, and the judiciary on the development of that system. The AJC has different panels (pro bono, academic, advice sector) that work together as working groups on pressing issues. One of these issues is the ombuds/tribunals familiarisation pilot.

[89] Sir Ernest Ryder, Senior President of Tribunals and Chair of the Administrative Justice Council, speech at the Ombudsman Association's Conference, 'Driving Improvements: Collaboration and Peer Learning', Belfast, 21 May 2019, www.ombudsmanassociation.org/news/speech-sir-ernest-ryder-oa-conference-21-may-2019.

[90] R Kirkham and N Creutzfeldt, 'Reform of the Administrative Justice System: A Plea for Change and a Research Agenda' (UKAJI, 2019) https://ukaji.org/2019/09/16/reform-of-the-administrative-justice-system-a-plea-for-change-and-a-research-agenda/.

[91] ibid 3.

[92] ibid 4.

[93] https://ajc-justice.co.uk.

[94] www.gov.uk/government/groups/administrative-justice-advisory-group.

This work aims to build bridges between institutions of the administrative justice system that help people with similar problems to be able to resolve them more efficiently. Currently, two pilots are running, one between the LGSCO and the Special Educational Needs and Disability (SEND) tribunal and the other between the Housing Ombudsman and the Property Chamber, who have co-designed a partnership programme. These are ongoing (as of October 2021) and have a huge potential to increase access for users of the administrative justice system as well as saving cost and time – also for those working in ombuds and tribunals. The partnership represented an important stepping stone in creating the conditions for major administrative justice reform.[95]

The familiarisation idea was born out of an initiative in 2010 when an informal conversation between the judge of the newly created first-tier charity tribunal and the charities commissioner resulted in a memorandum of understanding (MOU). They agreed to divide the appeals between the two organisations – procedural and customer services complaints would fall under the charity commissioners remit, whereas substantial areas to be remedied would fall to the charity tribunal. The MOU set out how and when they would direct the public towards the pathway best suited to their needs, the order of priority, the need for a liaison officer, the requirement of regular meetings, the exchange of decisions and the sharing of their annual reports.[96] Although the model is no longer in operation due to structural changes, it is a useful starting point for further discussions.

A workshop hosted by the AJC (Ombuds and Tribunals Working Party in October 2019) offered, for the first time, an opportunity for ombuds and tribunal judges to sit around a table and engage with each other's work. Part of the discussion resulted in firming up the two pilots.

The LGSCO and the SEND tribunal are collaborating on a pilot concerning the overlap in jurisdiction of the special educational needs and disability. The LGSCO currently upholds nine out of ten cases put before it. It was recognised that the public experience of both tribunals and ombuds was a frustrating and fragmented one, and that the ombudsman was only able to provide partial remedies owing to legislative restrictions. Although local authorities are working under considerable pressure, appeal rights are routinely compromised and unsustainable decisions are made. Both organisations welcome a fresh approach to create a more coherent administrative justice framework. Ultimately, however, legislative change is required to sweep the barriers away. This does not need to be contentious; instead, it could enhance both organisations and allow them to work in parallel. The pilot is underway, though it has currently been halted due to the COVID-19 pandemic.

The Housing Ombudsman and the Property Chamber have started conversations and are planning their pilot. The Housing Ombudsman has seen a rapid increase in

[95] N Creutzfeldt and R Kirkham, 'Understanding How and When Change Occurs in the Administrative Justice System: The Ombudsman/Tribunal Partnership Developments in England' (2020) 42 *Journal of Social Welfare and Family Law* 253.

[96] A copy of this is on file with the author.

demand for its services over recent years, showing an obvious appetite for redress through the scheme. Signposting between schemes was not straightforward, as this is a rapidly changing sector and there are a number of alternative redress schemes available (including more than one ombudsman dealing with housing). It is a complex environment for leaseholders, with a number of complaints falling outside of the Housing Ombudsman and Property Chamber's jurisdiction. There is a desperate need to signpost early on in the process and the initiative to work together with tribunals is highly welcome. This opens up a wider question about the logistics of different jurisdictions working together – a joint portal might be a solution. The President of the First-Tier Property Chamber does not anticipate the need for legislative reform, but will have a conversation with the HMCTS reform team to discuss design options. This pilot started, with meetings in late 2019, but is now at a standstill due to the current pandemic. Both pilots, and others, will resume as soon as it is safe to do so.[97]

A note of caution: whilst it is important for processes to work for the people who use them, it is problematic to make this value the only executive benchmark. Other factors need to be taken into consideration. For example, it could be argued that having fragmented administrative justice organisations creates a 'network effect' that makes genuine abuse of power less likely or more difficult to hide. We need to be mindful of what might be lost (if anything) if we try to simplify procedures for users.

These pilots demonstrate willingness and initiative from those in charge of the institutions to drive change and embrace a new approach to access to justice for their users. These developments are tied up, however, not only with the current COVID-19 pandemic, but also with the digitalisation of justice. The procedures of ombuds, unlike those of tribunals, are by default online, and in some cases have an option to talk to a person over the phone. Documents are shared electronically and communication is through email. Most tribunals are paper-based, and participants appear in person for a hearing. Despite these differences in procedures, as mentioned above, the jurisdictions of some ombuds and tribunals overlap. This means that if a system of interoperability is set up, and people can be directed to the best institution for them to approach, time, cost and frustration would be saved. In light of the digitalisation agenda, and the halt that the pandemic has put on the ombuds/tribunals partnership from developing, I propose a theoretical lens through which to inform the design and evaluation of the partnership as well as the digital agenda.

IV. Digital Legal Consciousness: A New Research Agenda

In this section, I offer a framework to think about wider notions of justice and how digitalisation meets those demands. How do people who use digital services

[97] This project is currently underway: https://www.nuffieldfoundation.org/project/delivering-administrative-justice-after-the-pandemic.

and those who administer them understand the role of the law? What can we learn about access to justice, open justice and the rule of law? How does the digitalisation of procedures and places influence what we think about the law? Is technology a facilitator or disrupter of our legal consciousness?

Our legal consciousness is how we think about the law and our encounters with legal institutions, and it is capable of change. Building on legal consciousness research, I propose here a framework through which users of a (digital) justice system can be better understood and, at the same time, suggest how designers of such systems can use this framework to create systems of justice that users will perceive as being fair and just.

A. Legal Consciousness

Research into legal consciousness allows us to discover different images of legality, attitudes towards law and specific context-related narratives.[98] Although we all have our own legal consciousness, it does not exist in an individual vacuum but is constantly renegotiated and constructed by our surroundings. The social construction of legality by society away from the formal sites of law in everyday life *constitutes* the rule of law in an important sense.[99] To study legal consciousness is to study the background assumptions about legality that structure and inform routine thoughts and actions.[100] These are arguably altered by the use of technology to seek justice in the modern state.

Legal consciousness is produced and revealed in what people *do* as well as what they *say*.[101] Cowan studied why people do and do not challenge welfare decisions by illustrating the formation of legal consciousness.[102] He bases his analysis on the interaction perspective,[103] which states that legal consciousness is situated within

[98] M Hertogh, 'A "European" Conception of Legal Consciousness: Rediscovering Eugen Ehrlich' (2004) 31 *Journal of Legal Studies* 455; S Silbey, 'After Legal Consciousness' (2005) 1 *Annual Review of Law and Social Science* 32; SE Merry, *Getting Justice and Getting Even: Legal Consciousness among Working-Class Americans* (University of Chicago Press, 1990); A Sarat, '"... The Law Is All Over:" Power, Resistance, and the Legal Consciousness of the Welfare Poor' (1990) 2 *Yale Journal of Law & The Humanities* 343; D Engel, 'How Does Law Matter in the Constitution of Legal Consciousness?' in B Garth and A Sarat (eds), *How Does Law Matter?* (Northwestern University Press, 1998); N Mezey, 'Out of the Ordinary: Law, Power, Culture and the Commonplace' (2001) 26 *Law & Social Inquiry* 145; D Cowan, 'Legal Consciousness: Some Observations' (2004) 67 *MLR* 928.

[99] P Ewick and S Silby, *The Common Place of Law: Stories from Everyday Life* (University of Chicago Press, 1998).

[100] S Halliday and B Morgan, 'I Fought the Law and the Law Won? Legal Consciousness and the Critical Imagination' (2013) 66 *Current Legal Problems* 1; P Ewick and S Silbey, *The Common Place of Law: Stories from Everyday Life* (University of Chicago Press, 1998); A Sarat and T Kearns (eds), *Law in Everyday Life* (University of Michigan Press, 1995).

[101] Ewick and Silby (n 98) 46.

[102] Cowan (n 96).

[103] D Cowan and S Halliday with R Hunter, *The Appeal of Internal Review: Law, Administrative Justice and the (Non)emergence of Disputes* (Hart Publishing, 2003) chs 5–6.

the interactions between, in his example, the welfare applicant and the bureaucrat. In other words, it is used as a tool to explore the citizen–bureaucracy relationship. Cowan argues that this relationship influences applicants' ideas about the nature of the process and the value of challenging decisions: 'interactions between applicant and bureaucracy provided the lens through which the applicant understood the decision on their application'.[104] Legal consciousness is produced by the signals imparted during the interaction as they contribute to the production of a set of immutable rules.[105] The studied interactions are face-to-face interactions, the text used in decision letters (the quality differs, and some can easily be misread) and making sense of the decisions. Cowan finds that these three areas point to how law is seen and produced through the interactions with bureaucracy.

Based on these findings, we can assume that a process can have a tremendous influence on how we construct our legal consciousness. How can this be translated into the ombuds and tribunals pilots?

The tribunals and ombuds are promoted as a system that is accessible for all, helping ordinary people with their grievances. The public aspirations of the tribunal system in the UK are framed as providing 'easily accessible, speedy, informal and inexpensive' justice for all.[106] However, Busby and McDermont[107] found that the system can be experienced as legalistic, lengthy and intimidating. Interestingly, these are similar qualities to those I found in my study of users of ombuds systems describing their expectations and experiences with the ombuds process.[108] Overall, the legal consciousness tradition has stressed the complexity of perceptions of legality within which people often attack localised deficiencies of law and the inequalities it produces while retaining respect for the legitimacy of law as a whole.[109] What happens if this is transferred into the online delivery of justice through technology?

The social construction of legality as a common currency will influence how we make sense of everyday interactions, as well as when we seek out dispute resolution. In a large empirical study of ombuds, I found that 'people's expectations [towards ombuds] are based on their existing expectations of the legal system'. In my data, I observed a shift in expectations about the process and its effect on perceptions of ombuds.[110] Expectations change throughout the complaint journey. As people are unsure of what to expect, their expectations are closely entwined with the outcome they receive.[111] Why does this matter? Research into legal consciousness can tell

[104] ibid 942.

[105] ibid 950.

[106] Donovan Commission, *The Royal Commission on Trade Unions and Employers' Associations Report* (Cmnd 3623, 1968) 157.

[107] N Busby and M McDermont, 'Workers, Marginalised Voices and the Employment Tribunal System: Some Preliminary Findings' (2012) 41 *Industrial Law Journal* 166.

[108] Creutzfeldt, 'What Do We Expect of Ombudsmen? (n 72).

[109] E Kirk and N Busby, 'Led Up the Tribunal Path? Employment Disputes, Legal Consciousness and Trust in the Protection of Law' (2017) 7(7) *Oñati Socio-legal Series* 1.

[110] Creutzfeldt, 'What Do We Expect of Ombudsmen? (n 72).

[111] N Creutzfeldt and B Bradford, 'Dispute Resolution Outside of Courts: Procedural Justice and Decision Acceptance among Users of Ombuds Services in the UK' (2016) 50 *Law and Society Review* 985.

us something about the set of preconceptions people who use the justice system have and what influences them. Users of ombuds, for example, have no clear set of expectations of this quasi-judicial system. I argued elsewhere that people who deal with an ombuds are influencedby the sociocultural environment of the legal culture[112] to which they are accustomed. This culture is one that shapes beliefs about the justice system, the trust we place in law. Legal consciousness was used to bring additional nuances to understanding the nature of engagement of users and non-users in a study of tribunals.[113]

In sum, legal consciousness research can inform a better construction of a user experience through a complaints process. Research shows that our legal consciousness can be influenced throughout a process when engaging with the justice system. It can help those who administer and design procedures to be mindful of their execution. Ideally, benchmarks need to be placed throughout the process to make sure that the person experiencing it has the opportunity to ask questions and to clarify the outcome.

If we know that people will engage with a justice system guided, among other things, by their legal consciousness, how can that help in the ombuds/tribunals partnership and in the move to digitalisation? The ombuds/tribunals partnership is attempting to improve the existing system by making it easier for the user to be directed between the two bodies. This involved the staff of both bodies designing programmes of interoperability and shared training. This can be developed and implemented in a digital space. How do people experience this digital space? This question opens up an important new research agenda.

B. Digital Legal Consciousness

I will set out here a research agenda for thinking about legal consciousness in the digital space. Part of this is to think about digital consciousness. We embed a lot of our daily lives and routines in a digital space. We bank online, we date online, we order food online, for example. This has produced a digital consciousness that we have learned to navigate and trust. We use our digital consciousness as a basis for accessing a digital legal space. How can we trust this space and how does this space do our existing legal consciousness justice? This, I propose, is a new research agenda: how do we translate our existing legal consciousness into the digital space? How does our digital consciousness interact with (and/or produce) the digital legal consciousness? What makes us trust a digital justice space?

The shift of the justice system into the digital space brings with it a mix of expectations: expectations from those who design the system that it works and

[112] Building on Freidman's definition of legal culture as 'the values and attitudes which bind the system together, and which determined the place of the legal system in the culture of the society as a whole': LM Friedman, 'Legal Culture and Social Development' (1969) 4 *Law & Society Review* 29, 34.

[113] Kirk and Busby (n 107).

expectations from those who use them that it works. The system *working* means different things here; for those who design it (tech people and legal minds), the technology has to work and be user friendly, and must deliver justice. For those who use the system, it has to be easily accessible, easy to manoeuvre and easy to understand. The challenge here lies in ensuring that the online process carries the same weight as a judgment coming from a court, for example. To think about how law works in society is to understand that it does not exist in a vacuum. It is a social phenomenon that exists in a time and place, and its use raises questions about policy, philosophy and political theory.[114] A change in how law functions in society is rarely due to a textual change, but rather a change of social configuration as a result of changes and shifts in society at large.[115]

This justice space I am talking about is the created space in which we can resolve disputes online, either through a local, national mechanism or through a global one (like eBay and Amazon). We need to think about how we engage in this space, what we expect from it and how this differs from our expectations towards the justice system we hold dear now. Can we translate our legal consciousness, which forms throughout our lives and provides us with a sense of what law is and how it operates, into the digital space?

I suggest in the last chapter of my book[116] on ombuds and alternative dispute resolution that theoretical and empirical dimensions of the complex new digital justice space have to be explored through interdisciplinary approaches and methodological pluralism. New patterns of digital legal consciousness are emerging. These patterns can be context specific, or specific to a legal culture or a shared one. Data needs to be collected to be able to develop claims about an emerging digital legal consciousness.[117]

[114] L Friedman, 'Is There a Modern Legal Culture?' (1994) 7 *Ratio Juris* 117, 118; J Oyrehagan Sunde, K Skodvin and S Koch, *Comparing Legal Cultures* (Fagbokforlaget, 2017).

[115] Oyrehagan Sunde et al (n 112) 2.

[116] Creutzfeldt, *Ombudsmen and ADR* (n 9).

[117] N Creutzfeldt, 'Towards a digital legal consciousness?' *European Journal of Law and Technology* December 2021 (available at: https://ejlt.org/index.php/ejlt).

8

Complaint Handling Effectiveness: What Can We Learn from Industry-Based Ombudsmen Schemes?

JOHN McMILLAN

I. Introduction

The large number of ombudsman offices that exist both globally and within nations enables valuable comparative analysis of their performance and strengths. This opportunity has been seized by individual offices and ombudsman associations, and in academic symposia. Learning from the experience of others doubtless underpins the vitality, adaptation and adoption of the ombudsman model in new settings.[1] A recurring – and negative – theme in early comparative analysis was between industry-based ombudsman schemes and parliamentary (or public sector) ombudsman offices. A dominant view at the time was that the ombudsman title should be applied only to bodies that were independent of government, had been established by legislation and had a jurisdiction focused on public sector maladministration. That view held sway in the International Ombudsman Institute, which initially denied membership to industry ombudsman schemes.[2]

The justifications that were given for differentiating between parliamentary and industry ombudsman schemes were not confined to their formal legal and structural differences. It was also said, for example, that industry-based schemes

[1] A recent Australian example is the recommendation of the Australian Competition & Consumer Commission that an independent ombudsman scheme be established to resolve consumer complaints and disputes with digital platform providers such as Google and Facebook: Australian Competition and Consumer Commission, *Digital Platforms Inquiry: Final Report* (2019) recommendation 23.

[2] The IOI has since broadened its membership basis but retains a distinction between voting members who meet the traditional criteria and other members who support IOI principles: www.theioi.org, 'IOI Membership'. Note also that s 28A of the New Zealand Ombudsman Act 1975 effectively preserves the use of the term 'Ombudsman' for public sector oversight bodies. The nature and scope of that power is examined in *Financial Services Complaints Ltd v Chief Parliamentary Ombudsman* [2021] NZHC 307.

were not truly independent as they were funded by industry participants and were typically governed by a board that would include industry representatives. Another line of disapproval was that industry schemes focused almost exclusively on resolution of individual consumer complaints and did not have a broader public policy or accountability role. Those factors retain relevance in evaluating individual offices, but they no longer overshadow a broader evaluation of the strengths and weaknesses of different ombudsman models. There is no longer a clear-cut distinction between industry and parliamentary schemes: some parliamentary offices also have an industry jurisdiction;[3] and some industry schemes are established and regulated by statute.[4]

Nor is there a clear-cut distinction between the dispute resolution roles of industry and parliamentary schemes: a common feature is that both schemes handle complaints from consumers/citizens who claim to be financially disadvantaged through online interactions with government and private sector service providers in high-volume decision-making areas that utilise automated decision-making based on rules that can be inaccessible or fast-changing. Commonly, too, ombudsman staff – including the ombudsman – have worked in both parliamentary and industry schemes.[5] Not surprisingly, parliamentary and industry ombudsman schemes now band together in professional associations to explain ombudsman craft, promote best practice complaint handling and facilitate networking. Examples are the Australian and New Zealand Ombudsman Association[6] and the former British and Irish Ombudsman Association, now called the Ombudsman Association.

This chapter builds on those trends by sketching the growth of the main three industry-based ombudsman schemes in Australia,[7] then highlighting some worthy features of the schemes. This dimension of ombudsman developments has received comparatively less academic attention than parliamentary ombudsman features. The analysis focuses on features of the industry ombudsman schemes that differentiate them from parliamentary ombudsman offices but warrant consideration as generic or desirable ombudsman features.

[3] For example, the Commonwealth Ombudsman in Australia is also the Postal Industry Ombudsman, the Overseas Students Ombudsman, the Private Health Insurance Ombudsman and the VET Student Loans Ombudsman: Ombudsman Act 1976 (Cth) Parts IIB, IIC, IID, IIE.

[4] For example, the Australian Financial Complaints Authority is established pursuant to the Corporations Act 2001 (Cth), s 1050, and must meet mandatory requirements and comply with general considerations set out in the Act, ss 1051, 1051A.

[5] For example, Mr Colin Neave was the Banking and Financial Services Ombudsman, and later the Commonwealth Ombudsman. Ms Deirdre O'Donnell was the Western Australian Ombudsman, and later the Telecommunications Industry Ombudsman.

[6] ANZOA was established by industry ombudsman offices following their exclusion from other networks, and – notwithstanding the all-encompassing title of the organisation – did not initially invite parliamentary ombudsmen offices to join. Unity and friendship now flourish!

[7] Two other examples of stand-alone schemes with private sector jurisdiction are the Transport Ombudsman Victoria and the Health Ombudsman Queensland.

II. Development of Industry-Based Ombudsman Schemes in Australia[8]

A. Background

Commencing in 1989, Australia has seen the growth of a large number of industry-based ombudsman schemes in fields such as banking, finance, insurance, superannuation, telecommunications, transport and utility services (electricity, gas, water). Some of the schemes operate nationally, and some operate within individual States. The prime impetus for the industry schemes was similar to that for parliamentary ombudsman offices. New and flexible dispute resolution mechanisms were required to address the growing power imbalance between service providers and recipients. This was all the more urgent because of the rising volume and complexity of service transactions.

In other respects, the impetus for industry ombudsman schemes could differ from that for parliamentary offices. The latter were usually established following a law reform review,[9] and sometimes through a government/parliamentary initiative that encountered open questioning or subtle resistance from the public sector agencies that would fall within its jurisdiction. The impetus for industry ombudsman schemes sometimes came from consumer groups. This gained some support from major industry players who could see the need for new dispute resolution mechanisms. Government regulatory agencies also pushed for reforms that would augment their own regulatory role. Those pressures were reflected in the design and role of industry-based schemes. The rhetoric stressed the need for mechanisms that could effectively resolve consumer disputes about products and services and enforce the financial rights of consumers. Jurisprudentially, the schemes were cast as mechanisms for customer/alternative dispute resolution. This was initially captured in the titles of some schemes that were described at the time as centres for handling enquiries and complaints and resolving disputes.

[8] I acknowledge the considerable assistance of a paper by two former industry ombudsmen – C Neave and J Pinnock, 'Setting the Scene: Industry-Based Customer Dispute Resolution Schemes' (paper presented to the National Alternative Dispute Resolution Advisory Council Conference, Sydney, 4–5 September 2003) – and the Wikipedia entries for some of the ombudsman schemes. See also S Smith (ed), *In the Consumer Interest: A Selected History of Consumer Affairs in Australia 1945–2000* (Society of Consumer Affairs, 2000). In *Telecommunications Industry Ombudsman Ltd v Commissioner of State Revenue* [2017] VSC 286, the Supreme Court (relying on Professor Stuhmcke's expert evidence) surveyed the history of industry ombudsman schemes and the TIO (in the context of a ruling that the TIO scheme was established for a 'charitable purpose' as understood in a payroll taxation law).

[9] For example, the Commonwealth Ombudsman was established based on the recommendations of the Commonwealth Administrative Review Committee (Report, 1971) and the Committee on Administrative Discretions (Interim Report, 1973). The Commonwealth Ombudsman was only one part of the wider reforms to administrative review processes that followed those reports. The other reforms included creation of a tribunal with wide jurisdiction to review administrative decisions (the Administrative Appeal Tribunal), a statutory process for judicial review and freedom of information legislation: see R Creyke and J McMillan (eds), *The Kerr Vision of Australian Administrative Law – At the Twenty-Five Year Mark* (CIPL, ANU, 1998).

The focus on the resolution of individual complaints was accompanied by a recognition that schemes could also play a broader systemic improvement and regulatory compliance role. This dimension was built into the complaint-handling and funding models, which envisaged that a complaint could be escalated and charged a higher fee to a scheme member if the complaint raised broader and unresolved issues. Schemes commonly included a referral mechanism for serious matters to be brought to the attention of government regulatory agencies. The inclusion of industry, consumer and other representatives in the scheme council or board also preordained that a perspective broader than individual complaint resolution would be adopted by the scheme. As industry-based schemes developed, it became more common to align them with the ombudsman movement and to bestow that title on a scheme. This is illustrated in the main Australian industry-based schemes that will now be described.

B. Banking, Finance and Insurance Schemes

The first industry-based scheme to be established in Australia was the Australian Banking Industry Ombudsman, established in 1989.[10] It has been transformed three times subsequently – as the Banking and Financial Services Ombudsman in 2003, the Financial Ombudsman Service (FOS) in 2008 and the Australian Financial Complaints Authority (AFCA) in 2018 (headed by a Chief Ombudsman).[11] Those changes in the form and description of this ombudsman scheme responded to a growing diversity in services offered by financial service providers and the crossover of different financial products. For example, the creation of FOS in 2008 was the result of a merger of the banking ombudsman with two other bodies – the Financial Industry Complaints Service and the Insurance Ombudsman Service. Two other schemes joined the following year – the Credit Union Dispute Resolution Centre and the Insurance Brokers Disputes Limited. A further broadening occurred in 2018, when AFCA replaced FOS, the Credit and Investments Ombudsman and the Superannuation Complaints Tribunal. AFCA is now a single ombudsman service for all financial complaints.

The growth in size, membership and workload of this ombudsman scheme also paints a picture.[12] The banking ombudsman commenced with 24 member banks; by 2016, FOS had over 5500 member organisations; and by March 2021,

[10] A similar scheme had been set up two years earlier in the UK.

[11] It is notable that the AFCA was one of the few regulatory bodies that emerged unscathed from a recent royal commission into financial services. The report of that commission made scathing findings about banks and official regulators, but pointedly made no suggestions for reform to the AFCA: K Hayne, *Royal Commission into Misconduct into the Banking, Superannuation and Financial Services Industry – Final Report, Volume 1* (AGPS, 2019) 482. That finding meant that the Royal Commission did not provide a detailed study of the AFCA.

[12] The figures and details in the following discussion are principally taken from information on the websites of the industry ombudsman schemes.

AFCA had over 40,000 members. Complaint numbers grew steadily, to the point that FOS received 34,095 complaint matters in 2015–16. There has been a threefold growth in complaint matters received by AFCA, which recorded more than 153,000 matters in its first two years of operation. The AFCA outcomes for complainants are significant. In the first two years, 72 per cent of complaints were resolved either by agreement with or a decision in favour of the complainant; compensation or rewards totalling $477.4M were awarded; and 508 matters were progressed to a systemic investigation. The scale of AFCA operations is reflected in its staffing, of approximately 780 employees in March 2021. The decision-makers comprise the Chief Ombudsman, 32 other ombudsman, 17 adjudicators and numerous part-time panel members.

C. Telecommunications Schemes

The Telecommunications Industry Ombudsman (TIO) – the first such scheme internationally – was established as a national scheme in 1993. The dual impetus was the privatisation of the Australian government telecommunications provider (it was formerly within the jurisdiction of the Commonwealth Ombudsman) and the emergence of new private sector telecommunications providers. The legislation regulating the industry requires service providers to enter into the TIO scheme.[13]

The workload of the TIO has expanded and varied over time in line with the increase in the number of telephone, mobile phone and Internet service providers, and diversification in the services they provide (such as bundled services and hardware). Complaints about Internet services were the largest proportion (36 per cent) of the 127,151 complaints received in the 2019–20 reporting year. The TIO also logged 318,797 contacts that year, the investigation of 32 systemic matters and the referral of 25 matters to the government regulator, the Australian Communications Media Authority (ACMA). The number of members of the TIO scheme was 1390 in June 2020. A proposal was floated in a government consultation paper in 2018 to replace the TIO with a new external dispute resolution body.[14] The proposal was not implemented.

D. Energy, Water and Electricity Schemes

The first utilities ombudsman scheme in Australia – and, indeed, globally – commenced in the State of Victoria in 1996. It was titled the Electricity Industry Ombudsman (Victoria). The creation of the scheme accompanied the privatisation of the government electricity provider and the market entry of new providers.

[13] Telecommunications (Consumer Protection and Service Standards) Act 1999 (Cth) Part 6.

[14] Consumer Safeguards Review, *Report to the Minister for Communication and the Arts, Part A: Complaints Handling and Consumer Redress* (September 2018).

The initiative to establish the scheme came from industry, but amidst strong government and consumer pressure for a scheme tailored to the restructured electricity industry. A similar restructuring of the gas and water supplies led to those industries joining the scheme, in 1999 and 2001 respectively. The scheme was retitled the Energy and Water Ombudsman (Victoria) (EWOV). An accompanying subsequent development was the enactment of legislation making it a licensing condition that the service provider join an approved customer dispute resolution scheme.[15] There were 516 members of the EWOV scheme in June 2020. The number of complaints received that year was 23,786 (a decrease from over 36,000 complaints in 2016).

A similar trend has occurred in other States, where utilities ombudsman schemes have been established on the EWOV model in response to government-initiated industry restructuring. Over time, those offices have been enlarged and rebadged, and participation in the scheme is a licence condition for service providers. The Energy and Water Ombudsman NSW was established in 1998; the Energy Ombudsman Tasmania in 1998 (an office hosted by the Tasmanian Ombudsman); the Energy and Water Ombudsman South Australia in 2000; the Energy Ombudsman Queensland in 2007; and the Energy and Water Ombudsman Western Australia in 2013 (an office hosted by the WA Ombudsman).

III. Noteworthy Features of Industry-Based Ombudsman Schemes

Not all industry schemes are the same, and a combined discussion of noteworthy features carries the risk of generalisation. There are nevertheless common themes that reflect the similar evolution of the large industry-based schemes over the past three decades.

Many of the following examples relate to AFCA. It is the largest scheme, and both the oldest and newest as a scheme that has evolved and been enlarged through the merger of numerous other schemes.

A. Legal Framework for Industry-Based Ombudsman Schemes

A defining characteristic of the classic ombudsman is that it is an office created by statute. This is regarded as a hallmark of an ombudsman's security and independence, and differentiates the office from complaint bodies created administratively

[15] Electricity Industry Act 2000 (Vic), s 28; Gas Industry Act 2001 (Vic), s 36.

by government agencies or industry bodies. Some of the forerunners of the current industry ombudsman schemes were set up by industry councils either through the agreement of industry participants or by incorporation of a complaints-handling body. Over time, as government has become more reliant on industry schemes as a co-regulatory mechanism, legislation has been enacted to embed the schemes in industry practice.

A well-developed example of this trend is the legislative basis for AFCA. The Corporations Act provides that the minister administering the Act may authorise an external dispute resolution scheme that, once established, 'is known as the AFCA scheme and the operator is known as AFCA'.[16] At any time there can only be one scheme in force. AFCA is separately incorporated under corporations law. The minister may authorise a scheme only if satisfied that the scheme meets 'mandatory requirements' set out in the Corporations Act.[17] The requirements are extensive and include that: the scheme permits membership to all entities required to join such a scheme; the scheme is funded by members; complainants are not charged a fee; an independent assessor for the scheme is appointed; independent reviews of the scheme's operation and procedures are conducted; the managing board will include an equal number of industry and consumer representatives and an independent chair; the complaints mechanism must be accessible; complaints must be resolved in a way that is fair, efficient, timely and independent; complaint determinations are binding upon members; and material changes to the scheme rules must be approved by the government regulator (the Australian Securities and Investments Commission (ASIC)).

In authorising a scheme, the minister may also take 'general considerations' into account.[18] These are the six principles – the CDR Benchmarks – that (as explained below) have been the national benchmarks for industry-based customer dispute resolution schemes since 1997: accessibility, independence, fairness, accountability, efficiency and effectiveness of the scheme. Legislative requirements of a comparable though different kind apply to the other major industry ombudsman schemes. Telecommunications legislation provides that a carriage service provider of telephone, mobile or Internet services must enter into a scheme 'to be known as the Telecommunications Industry Ombudsman scheme'; it is to be operated by an incorporated body of the same name.[19] The Minister may determine standards for the TIO scheme, having regard to the six principles in the CDR Benchmarks. Other provisions in the telecommunications statute require an independent review of the TIO scheme at least every five years, and for the government regulator – ACMA – to make rules and regulations on membership of the scheme.[20]

[16] Corporations Act 2001 (Cth), s 1050(1).
[17] Corporations Act 2001 (Cth), s 1051.
[18] Corporations Act 2001 (Cth), s 1050(2).
[19] Telecommunications (Consumer Protection and Service Standards) Act 1999 (Cth), s 128.
[20] Telecommunications (Consumer Protection and Service Standards) Act 1999 (Cth) ss 129–33A.

Legislation in the States that have an energy ombudsman scheme anticipate that government will approve such a scheme and that retailers will join the scheme.[21] Though there are variations from one statute to another, the laws specify essential criteria for a scheme, including accessibility for consumers and scheme independence of retailers. Another feature of the state legislation is that it is enacted in furtherance of an obligation imposed upon States that have adopted the National Energy Retail Law to establish a two-tiered dispute resolution framework: retailers are required to provide for internal resolution of small customer complaints and to join an energy ombudsman scheme.[22] This framework has also been badged as the National Energy Customer Framework by the market regulator, the Australian Energy Market Commission.

B. CDR Benchmarks

An overarching feature of the rules framework for industry-based ombudsman schemes is the Benchmarks for Industry-Based Customer Dispute Resolution (CDR Benchmarks). These were developed jointly by government and industry ombudsman schemes and were released in 1997 by the Commonwealth government. They were reissued in 2015 by the Commonwealth Minister for Small Business, accompanied by a supplementary guide, *Key Practices for Industry-Based Customer Dispute Resolution* (Key Practices).[23] The benchmarks are important in many ways. They promote national consistency and minimum standards for dispute resolution, both in internal complaint resolution and by external industry ombudsman schemes. They have been carried through into the statutory criteria that are applied by government in accrediting industry ombudsman schemes.

The elaboration of the CDR Benchmarks in the Key Practices amplifies their value. Compliance with the benchmark standards has become the central focus of the periodic reviews that are a required procedure for industry-based ombudsman schemes. Of particular importance is that the benchmarks require a scheme to operate independently of scheme members – which lends weight to the schemes being badged with the ombudsman title. The benchmarks contain the following six 'underlying principles':[24]

> *1. Accessibility*
> The scheme makes itself readily available to customers by promoting knowledge of its existence, being easy to use, and having no cost barriers.

[21] For example, in Victoria the Electricity Industry Act 2000 (Vic), s 28 and the Gas Industry Act 2001 (Vic), s 36; and in NSW the Electricity Supply Act 1995 (NSW), s 96B and the Gas Supply Act 1996 (NSW), s 33G.

[22] Part 4 of the National Energy Retail Law, which is a schedule to the National Energy Retail Law (South Australia) Act 2011 (SA).

[23] The CDR Benchmarks and Key Practices are published on the website of The Treasury, www.treasury.gov.au.

[24] The CDR Benchmarks as reissued in 2015 also include a brief description of 'purpose' following each 'underlying principle'. These underlying principles can be usefully contrasted with five principles

2. Independence
The decision-making process and administration of the scheme are independent from scheme members.

3. Fairness
The scheme produces decisions which are fair and seen to be fair by observing the principles of procedural fairness, by making decisions on the information before it, and by having specific criteria upon which its decisions are based.

4. Accountability
The scheme publicly accounts for its operations by publishing its determinations and information about complaints and highlighting any systemic industry problems.

5. Efficiency
The scheme operates efficiently by keeping track of complaints, ensuring complaints are dealt with by the appropriate process or forum and regularly reviewing its performance.

6. Effectiveness
The scheme is effective by having appropriate and comprehensive terms of reference and periodic independent reviews of its performance.

The Key Practices spell out the practical steps that schemes can take to implement each of the underlying principles. This additional guidance is provided, as explained in the minister's foreword to the Key Practices as the CDR Benchmarks were widely adopted and regarded as 'immutable' standards for industry-based dispute resolution. Further elaboration was therefore appropriate. There is a close parallel between the Key Practices and the Australian standard on complaints management.[25] An example of how a key practice elaborates an underlying principle is the guidance provided on the principle of 'accessibility': the scheme and its members must make customers aware of the scheme; access to the scheme must be free of charge and available through various formal and informal modes; people must be assisted to complain; complaints must be resolved in a non-adversarial manner and through alternative dispute options; and legal action (for example, debt recovery) should be suspended while a complaint is under investigation.

The guidance given on the principle of 'independence' is also illustrative: a scheme must have an 'overseeing entity' (such as a board or council) that has an independent chair and consumer and industry participants; the overseeing entity must 'oversee the independence of the office's operation'; the head decision-maker of the scheme (for example, ombudsman) is to be appointed for a fixed term by

that Kirkham and Gill suggest should guide reform of parliamentary ombudsman offices, which are that those ombudsman should: have a bolder role within the administrative justice system; benefit from a presumption that their jurisdiction applies to all public services; possess a broad toolkit of powers; be subject to a duty to report on their engagement with citizens and delivery of administrative justice; and be subject to a range of accountability mechanisms. See R Kirkham and C Gill, 'Five Principles for a New Public Services Ombudsman' in R Kirkham and C Gill (eds), *A Manifesto for Ombudsman Reform* (Palgrave Macmillan, 2020). These principles appear designed to encourage institutional improvement, while the CDR Benchmarks discussed in the text are arguably more focused towards ensuring compliance with minimum standards.

[25] Australian Standards, *Guidelines for Complaint Management in Organisations* (AS/NZS 10002, 2014).

the overseeing entity; the scheme is to select its own staff; conflicts of interest concerns are to be managed in a transparent manner; the scheme is to have sufficient funding to manage its caseload; and there should be wide consultation about any proposed change to the jurisdiction or terms of reference of the scheme.

Notable points in the other four CDR Benchmarks are: procedural fairness shall be observed in dispute resolution; there shall be detailed reporting on the operations of the scheme; special procedures will be adopted for dealing with systemic industry problems and bringing them to the attention of government regulators; participating organisations shall develop well-publicised internal dispute resolution mechanisms; and the operation of the scheme shall be reviewed regularly by an independent party who consults with stakeholders.

C. Scheme Constitution, Rules, Guidelines and Codes

The rules framework for industry ombudsman schemes includes several other public documents, of which four will be noted: the constitution of the corporation, complaint resolution rules, operational guidelines and industry codes. The following discussion looks principally at the AFCA documents.

(i) Constitution

AFCA is a not-for-profit company that is incorporated under the Corporations Act 2001 (Cth). As such, it has a constitution that outlines how it is constituted, its objects, membership, assets, board governance, meetings, rule-making and reporting.

(ii) Rules

AFCA's Complaint Resolution Scheme Rules are made by the Board of AFCA and are approved by ASIC. They explain the complaint resolution process – for example, the underlying principles for complaint resolution, eligible complaints, decision-makers, information gathering by AFCA, notifications to parties, procedural fairness procedures, confidentiality, remedies, effect of determinations, treatment of systemic issues and complaints about AFCA service.

(iii) Guidelines

The Operational Guidelines to the Rules, also made by AFCA, are an explanatory guide to the Scheme Rules. For example, as to the rule stating that 'AFCA may assist Complainants to submit a complaint', the Operational Guidelines explain the types of assistance that can be provided.

The Rules and Operational Guidelines are both outward and inward facing. They explain to complainants and financial firms how matters will be handled, and also guide AFCA staff so as to ensure internal regularity and consistency in complaint resolution. This links directly to the CDR Benchmarks, which require that complaint resolution be fair, accountable, efficient, effective and transparent. Importantly, too, the Rules and Operational Guidelines have been regularly updated, on average twice a year.

(iv) Codes

Industry codes of practice are an important element of the regulatory framework. They are generally devised within industries and are voluntarily adopted individually by members of the industry. Codes underpin industry self-regulation, though government often plays a direct role in their development and operation. ASIC, for example, can approve a code by legislative instrument,[26] and identify provisions of the code that will be legally enforceable – 'as a signal to consumers that this is a code they can have confidence in [and] to raise standards and to complement the legislative requirements'.[27]

AFCA has a strong focus on industry compliance with the codes, both in its complaint resolution and in its general oversight. AFCA's website gives prominence to five banking and insurance codes that financial firms commit to observe – for example, on specific topics such as loans and account management, in customer liaison and complaint resolution, and through observing principles such as transparency and accountability. In complaint resolution, AFCA has regard to whether the code standards have been observed, and it may grant a remedy (such as compensation) in the event of a breach. AFCA also undertakes compliance monitoring through Code Compliance Committees that operate separately for each code. The committees undertake general monitoring of industry compliance and provide advice and guidance to financial firms.

A similar rules framework applies in the other industry ombudsman schemes, but with immaterial textual differences. For example, the TIO complaint-handling rules are titled 'Terms of Reference'; they include explanatory text and are accompanied by other guides on 'Complaint Handling Procedures' and 'Systemic Issue Guidelines'. The equivalent procedural guideline in EWON and EWOV is called the 'Charter'.

D. Scheme Governance and Stakeholder Liaison

A conventional governance structure for industry ombudsman schemes is a corporate board and a lead ombudsman who is also the Chief Executive Officer

[26] Corporations Act 2001 (Cth), s 1101A.
[27] ASIC Regulatory Guide 183, 'Approval of Financial Services Sector Codes of Conduct', paras RG 183.3–4.

(CEO). There may also be a stakeholder liaison council or network, and formal arrangements with government regulatory and policy agencies for direction, reporting and liaison. This governance model is principally tailored to three considerations – complying with corporation law requirements, guaranteeing the functional independence of a scheme and ensuring the scheme is responsive to industry and consumer interests. This is illustrated in the AFCA arrangements.

The AFCA Board of Directors, established by the AFCA Constitution, is responsible for overall corporate governance, including making the Scheme Rules, strategic and policy direction, financial management, appointment of the ombudsman and commissioning independent reviews. The Board comprises an independent chair and an equal number (between three and five) of industry directors and consumer directors. The inaugural chair and some directors were appointed by the responsible minister; all subsequent appointments are made by the Board.[28] The term of appointment is up to three years (with the option of reappointment).

The inaugural AFCA chair was the Hon Helen Coonan, a former Australian government cabinet minister, lawyer and chair of several corporations and advisory bodies. The Board has a diverse membership which positions it well to uphold the independence of the scheme, to monitor compliance with the CDR Benchmarks and to oversee scheme governance and management.

The Chief Ombudsman is the lead decision-maker and CEO of the scheme. The Chief Ombudsman is appointed for a fixed term and on conditions set by the Board. The Board does not have an explicit power to remove the Chief Ombudsman; the Constitution provides only that a vacancy arises in the usual circumstances of bankruptcy, unsound mind or undeclared conflict of interest.

The relationship between the Chief Ombudsman and the Board will undoubtedly bear on the operation of the scheme. There can be a risk of untoward Board domination or intrusion into the Chief Ombudsman's role. On the other hand, the Chief Ombudsman's ongoing answerability to the Board is likely to both steady and invigorate the execution of the Chief Ombudsman's role. Overall, industry, consumer and government respect for the scheme can be enhanced when there is a constructive working relationship between the Chief Ombudsman and the Board. A similar governance structure of a board and ombudsman exists in the other industry ombudsman schemes. Equally, the chairs of the other schemes are people respected for independence in fields such as politics, law and community service.[29] There are other minor variations. For example, the TIO scheme has a Board Nominations Committee to make recommendations on filling board vacancies. The EWON scheme has a Consultative Council that meets at least twice a

[28] The appointment process is outlined in AFCA's 'Nominations and Remuneration Committee Charter'.

[29] The TIO Board Chair is the Hon Michael Lavarch, former Commonwealth Attorney-General. The EWON Board Chair is Mr Tony Crawford, former chief executive of a national law firm. The EWOV Board Chair is Mr Paul Sheehan, former test cricketer and college headmaster.

year with members and consumer representatives. The number and qualification of board members also differ among the schemes.

Another important governance element is the relationship between the schemes and government regulatory and policy agencies. Each of the statutes under which the schemes are established nominates a government entity as a person or body who can approve the scheme, issue directions or set standards. Those entities are – for AFCA, the minister and ASIC;[30] for the TIO, the minister and ACMA;[31] for EWON, the minister;[32] and for EWOV, the Essential Services Commission.[33]

The most explicit framework, applying to AFCA, provides that ASIC may (by legislative instrument) issue regulatory requirements relating to any of the mandatory requirements or general considerations applying to AFCA.[34] Other powers conferred on ASIC are: to approve changes to the AFCA scheme; to issue enforceable directions to AFCA relating to the value of claims that may be made under the AFCA scheme; and to issue directions to ensure adequate financing of the scheme and compliance with regulatory requirements.[35] AFCA also has a statutory obligation to provide details of regulatory breaches of which it is aware to ASIC, the Australian Prudential Regulatory Authority and the Commissioner of Taxation.[36]

Regulatory guidance on each of those matters and how ASIC performs its oversight role, is spelt out in ASIC Regulatory Guide 267, *Oversight of AFCA*. This 55-page guide spells out the principles and values that AFCA is expected to observe, the identification and handling of systemic issues, referral of serious matters to regulatory bodies, the self-reporting requirements applying to financial firms, public reporting of complaint data, promotion of the AFCA scheme, accessibility for complainants, litigation test case procedures and arranging independent reviews of the AFCA scheme. Regulatory requirements are also issued by ASIC from time to time on specific matters, such as the rules to be applied by AFCA in handling matters impacted by the COVID-19 pandemic.[37]

Formal liaison arrangements are also in place for other industry ombudsman schemes. For example, the TIO has adopted and published memoranda of understanding with ACMA and the Australian Consumer and Competition Commission (ACCC). Like the ASIC regulatory guides, these memoranda facilitate information sharing about systemic issues and complaint trends. A requirement of the National Energy Retail Law is that energy ombudsman schemes will 'identify and advise on systemic issues as a means of preventing complaints and disputes'.[38] Memoranda

[30] Corporations Act 2001 (Cth) ss 1050(1), 1051(5).

[31] Telecommunications (Consumer Protection and Services Standards) Act 1989 (Cth), s 128(9), (11).

[32] Electricity Supply Act 1995 (NSW), s 96B(1). The NSW Act also acknowledges the role of the Australian Energy Market Commission, which is a national energy market regulator.

[33] Electricity Industry Act 2000 (Vic), s 28(1).

[34] Corporations Act 2001 (Cth), s 1052A.

[35] Corporations Act 2001 (Cth) ss 1052B, 1052BA, 1052D.

[36] Corporations Act 2001 (Cth), s 1052E.

[37] AFCA Scheme Authorisation 2018 (Cth), cl 11.

[38] National Energy Retail Law (South Australia) Act 2011 (SA), s 84(1)(d).

of understanding are also in place between, for example, EWOV and the Victorian Essential Services Commission, the Australian Energy Market Commission and the ACCC. At a more informal level, there is regular contact between the industry ombudsman schemes and the government regulators and policy agencies. The schemes are regularly consulted by government on consumer and market issues and on policy development generally. This work is supported by research sections within the industry ombudsman schemes.

E. Complaint-Handling Framework

Each industry ombudsman scheme has, as noted above, published a guide to the complaint resolution process, variously called the Rules (AFCA), Terms of Reference (TIO) or Charter (EWON and EWOV). Those guides have an accustomed ombudsman tone that describes the principles to be applied in dispute resolution and the process for receiving complaints, resolving them, gathering information, exercising investigation powers, making determinations and handling service complaints about the scheme.

A few features of the industry ombudsman scheme framework are particularly notable, using AFCA once again as the main case study. First, an important differentiating feature of industry ombudsman schemes (as spelt out in their procedural guides) is the power to make determinations that are typically binding on members, though not on complainants. The remedies may include an award of financial compensation, waiver or variation of a debt, refunding a charge, honouring a claim or varying a financial contract. AFCA can award quite high compensation amounts – for insurance claims to a ceiling of $1.085 million, for credit facilities to a ceiling of $5425 million and for non-financial loss to a ceiling of $54,000. The TIO can make a binding determination to a ceiling of $50,000 and a recommendation to a ceiling of $100,000.

Secondly, the industry ombudsman complaint handling Rules or Terms of Reference are published as a discrete document that is formally endorsed by the scheme board and that comprehensively sets out the complaint resolution procedure. The guides are both informative and prescriptive. They deal with matters that go to the heart of ombudsman methodology and technique – how procedural fairness will be met, alternative dispute resolution options, formal dispute resolution stages, timelines for each stage, decision-makers, identification of systemic issues, and referral of misconduct and systemic problems to regulators. The complaint procedures are tied to the CDR Benchmarks. As such, they lay down standards for internal and external appraisal of scheme performance. This ensures a degree of procedural consistency among industry ombudsman schemes, and fortifies their capacity to learn from each other and to lift overall performance.

Thirdly, there is a high degree of transparency in complaint resolution, in several ways. The AFCA Rules explain that if a matter cannot be resolved by informal methods such as negotiation or conciliation, a preliminary assessment may be provided in writing to the parties, setting out the tentative findings and recommendation to resolve the complaint. The parties may accept that assessment or request that the matter proceed to a Determination. The submissions of the parties are shared with each other, subject to confidentiality considerations.

A Determination can be made by a designated AFCA decision-maker (ombudsman, adjudicator or panel). A Determination must be in writing and supported by reasons. Determinations are ordinarily published on the AFCA website without identifying the parties. In 2020, AFCA published 4054 determinations and withheld only eight on confidentiality grounds. A keyword search facility is available on the website. Another website resource is a list (and links) of all court decisions relating to AFCA and predecessor schemes. This provides a handy and accessible guide to legal precedents.[39] A comparable resource on the TIO website is the TIO 'Systemic Investigation Reports' (six reports in 2019–20). Examples of issues dealt with in those reports were the impact of COVID-19 on phone and Internet complaints, misleading telemarketing, consumer debt, family violence and the causes of small business complaints.

Fourthly, the AFCA scheme includes the appointment of an Independent Assessor, who can receive complaints from any party about AFCA's standard of service in resolving complaints (but not about the merits of a Determination). The current Assessor is a member of the Victorian Bar.

The Assessor's role is confined to making recommendations, which may include payment of non-financial compensation for the loss or inconvenience suffered by a party. The Assessor received 183 complaints in 2020, and all recommendations were accepted by AFCA.

Fifthly, a standard requirement applying to industry ombudsman schemes is that an independent public review of the scheme shall be undertaken periodically – usually every five years, although an initial review of AFCA was required after two years. The reviewer is to consult widely with interested parties, such as scheme participants, board members, complainants and government, consumer and industry bodies. The report of the review is published and formally submitted both to government and to the scheme board.

An approach commonly adopted in the independent reviews has been to focus on scheme compliance with some or all of the CDR Benchmarks. Particular attention is usually given to how a scheme discharges its core function of resolving complaints and whether recommendations from previous independent reviews have been implemented. The review also provides a horizon-scanning opportunity to gauge if the scheme is well positioned to respond to matters such as technological change, government cultural expectations and royal commission or inquiry findings.

[39] For a thorough analysis of this dimension of ombudsman work, see A Stuhmcke, 'Ombudsman Litigation: The Relationship between the Australian Ombudsman and the Courts' in G Weeks and M Groves (eds), *Administrative Redress In and Out of the Courts* (Federation Press, 2019).

IV. Learning from Industry Ombudsman Schemes

Industry-based ombudsman schemes have many strengths. These include:

- a clear and accessible rules framework that explains how the scheme is established and how it functions and resolves disputes;
- a governance structure that enables diverse stakeholder views to be fed into the scheme at all levels, accompanied by reporting back to stakeholders;
- measures to ensure that industry members must participate in the scheme;
- measures to ensure the scheme operates independently of the direct control or influence of members or other stakeholders;
- a complaint-handling system of principles and procedures that ensures complaints are handled efficiently and effectively, and that a suitable remedy can be provided;
- a funding model that enables the scheme to adapt to membership size and caseload fluctuations;
- practices that ensure transparency in dispute resolution;
- a clear definition of the procedures that separately apply to complaint resolution, identification of systemic issues and reporting of serious matters to government regulators; and
- periodic independent reviews of scheme performance and compliance with complaint-handling benchmarks.

How relevant are those features to parliamentary ombudsman schemes?

There are points of both similarity and difference between industry and parliamentary schemes. They share, on the one hand, the same common objective of providing an independent mechanism that is available to consumers to seek redress against large entities in the public and private sector. There is the same shared commitment to ensure those entities are responsive and accountable. In a nutshell, there is a common commitment to the principles of ombudsmanship – independence, impartiality, accessibility, effectiveness and fairness.

There are differences nevertheless in the cultural setting and working environment for industry and parliamentary ombudsman schemes. Industry schemes are strongly focused on consumer protection ideals. Parliamentary offices give special attention to upholding the rule of law and ensuring government accountability. In a practical sense, the issues the schemes deal with can vary markedly: different considerations are in play when, for example, a parliamentary scheme investigates unlawful government detention or coercion, as against an industry scheme investigating predatory commercial practices.

Each ombudsman scheme necessarily develops a model and approach that is attuned to its own jurisdiction and cultural setting. It is also open to each ombudsman, appointed as an independent officer for a fixed term, to bring their own perspective and objectives to the role. There is an acceptance nonetheless that schemes can benefit from drawing on best practice from other schemes. With that in mind, the following broad observations are made about worthy features of industry ombudsman schemes that may warrant closer attention by parliamentary ombudsman offices. These observations are made against the backdrop of the observation of the Productivity Commission in its 2014 report to government on Access to Justice that 'Submissions to this inquiry consistently saw industry ombudsmen as relatively better performers than government schemes … and their design features seem to contribute to this'.[40] A similar opinion is expressed in an academic analysis of industry ombudsmen, that 'an increasing consumerism has driven consumer ombudsmen to be more transparent and responsive to consumers', leading to 'innovations and performance outcomes [that] are seen to be responding to consumers' wishes'.[41]

A. Setting Out the Complaint Framework

The industry schemes helpfully and systematically set out, in one or two documents, the rules and principles to be followed and applied in scheme management and dispute resolution. It is not always as easy to find such a clear and accessible statement applying to parliamentary offices. Issues that are not always teased out in a structured and methodical fashion include the way that systemic issues are identified and handled, the principles of maladministration being applied by the ombudsman or the remedies that may be used in dispute resolution.

The failure to spell matters out in a clear and discrete form may have the consequence that some valuable powers or options are underutilised. Two examples from offices that I have worked in are that the Commonwealth Ombudsman's power to refer disputed legal issues to the Administrative Appeals Tribunal for an advisory opinion has been used only once in over 40 years;[42] and the NSW Ombudsman's power to make a special report to the Parliament calling on a minister to explain why a recommendation was not accepted has only been used once.[43]

[40] Productivity Commission, *Access to Justice Arrangements* (Report No 72, 2014) ch 9, 337, 339.

[41] C Hodges, 'The Private Sector Ombudsman' in M Hertogh and R Kirkham (eds), *Research Handbook on the Ombudsman* (Edward Elgar, 2018) 68–69.

[42] Ombudsman Act 1976 (Cth), ss 10A, 11. The exercise of that power was examined in *Re Reference under Section 11 of the Ombudsman Act 1976 for an Advisory Opinion; Ex parte Director-General of Social Services* (1979) 2 ALD 86. That decision of the Administrative Appeal Tribunal has acquired particular authority in Australian law because it was made by Justice Gerard Brennan, who later became Chief Justice of the High Court of Australia.

[43] The inquiry was convened under Ombudsman Act 1974 (NSW), s 27. My work in the inquiry was published as NSW Ombudsman, *Operation Prospect: Second Report on Developments* (2017). That report and its wider circumstances are discussed in M Aronson, 'Ombudsmen and Crimes Busters: Ships Passing in the Night' in Weeks and Groves (n 39).

B. Transparent Dispute Resolution

An orderly and comprehensive published framework for dispute resolution can also promote transparency by prompting an ombudsman office to distil its experience and insights in a range of publications (such as case decisions, reports, guides and fact sheets). This provides both a precedent base for the office and guidance for stakeholders.

Here, again, the industry ombudsman websites are notable for the range of publications that are available and kept up to date. These publications not only record the work of the office, but also provide guidance to industry, consumers and regulators on insights that can be drawn from the complaint-handling experience of the scheme and the ombudsman's expectations of industry members. Notably, industry ombudsmen schemes have been at the forefront in targeting a broader audience by developing formats such as webinars to convey the scheme's insights and expectations.

C. Service Delivery Complaints

Another perennial challenge facing parliamentary offices that has not been handled as well as it could be is the issue of complaints about the service provided by the office. A comparison can be drawn with the AFCA arrangement for an Independent Assessor to handle service complaints about the scheme.

For parliamentary ombudsman, there is usually no formal external mechanism (apart from judicial review) to review how complaints are handled by the office. A common explanation is that a review is unnecessary as the office can only make recommendations arising from an investigation. The practice generally adopted by ombudsman offices is to establish an internal procedure for handling service complaints, and to reassure applicants that a service complaint will be handled by an officer who was not earlier involved in handling the matter.

The main exception is Victoria, where a Victorian Inspectorate was established in 2011 to monitor Victorian integrity agencies, including the Ombudsman.[44] The Inspectorate can receive complaints from the public. This is similar to the practice of appointing an independent or parliamentary inspector to provide oversight of the work of an anti-corruption or integrity commission, and to deal with complaints about misconduct and abuse of power.[45] This mechanism is partly a response to the classic rhetorical question, *quis custodiet* – who guards the guardians?

[44] Victorian Inspectorate Act 2011 (Vic).
[45] For example, Independent Commission Against Corruption Act 1988 (NSW), Part 5A.

D. Advisory/Consultative Council

A central governance element in industry ombudsman schemes is a board, comprising industry and consumer representatives and an independent chair. This meets corporations law requirements, but also keeps the scheme attuned to stakeholder interests and expectations. The sector that perhaps benefits most from this arrangement is the consumer sector that may otherwise lack a regular forum or channel through which its representatives can collaborate and clarify systemic complaint issues with the ombudsman.

Parliamentary ombudsman offices interact regularly with parliamentarians, government agencies, community representatives and professional organisations (as well as complainants). Would the offices benefit from a more formal consultative arrangement, such as an advisory committee? Two Commonwealth precedents are the Privacy Advisory Committee and the Information Advisory Committee, which were established as part of the revamp of Australian information access and privacy laws.[46] The membership of both is to include members from inside and outside government.

My experience, having chaired both committees, is that they can play a valuable role in several ways. Meetings require the office to report on its activities to an alert and knowledgeable external group of people. The regular meeting schedule facilitates active discussion (and reflection) on office performance from one meeting to the next and whether targets are being met. Important issues can be highlighted that may have been sidelined in the office. The members of the committees can also play a broader liaison role in government, industry and community circles. That said, both committees languished after government failed to renew or make fresh appointments during a tumultuous period when government planned (but did not follow through on) a restructuring of the information and privacy scheme. Nevertheless, the option of formally establishing a broadly based consultative forum attached to a government oversight agency has merit and should not be overlooked. Certainly, the industry ombudsman schemes provide a good example of such an arrangement being vibrant and ongoing.

E. Periodic Review

The periodic independent reviews of industry ombudsman schemes have played an important role in their evolution and adaptation.[47] The anticipation of a

[46] Privacy Act 1988 (Cth), s 82; Australian Information Commissioner Act 2010 (Cth), s 27.

[47] This aspect of these ombudsman schemes mirrors the approach taken by those Australian jurisdictions which have adopted a statutory bill or charter of rights, which typically require periodic reviews of those statutes. See, eg Charter of Human Rights and Responsibilities Act 2006 (Vic), ss 44–45; Human Rights Act 2019 (Qld), ss 95–96 (requiring reviews of the relevant Act to be conducted four and eight years after its commencement).

forthcoming review by an independent reviewer whose report will be published can be a powerful stimulant for the board and leadership of the scheme to maintain a steady focus on compliance with the CDR Benchmarks. The review reports can also be a valuable resource for government regulatory agencies that have a broader responsibility to ensure overall industry integrity and consumer awareness.

Parliamentary ombudsman offices routinely conduct internal reviews of their systems and performance, engage consultants to assist in this process and restructure in response to government and social trends. The annual reporting process and consultation with parliamentary oversight committees[48] are also stimuli for organisational improvement. The only statutory requirement for a periodic review of an Australian parliamentary ombudsman office is in Queensland, where a strategic review is to occur at least every seven years.[49]

Parliamentary ombudsman, both in Australia and internationally, sometimes question the option of a regular external review. The reviews can be time-consuming and distracting, there may be an unbalanced focus in the review on specific complainant gripes, the reviewer may not fully grasp the complexity and subtlety of the balancing exercise the ombudsman's office faces in handling thousands of complaints that are diverse in character and the recommendations from the review may go nowhere if they require a legislative or budgetary response by government. Against that must be weighed the opportunity an independent reviewer has to consult stakeholders who may not otherwise be motivated or comfortable enough to express their views. An independent review also plays a practical role in encouraging the ombudsman's office to keep an eye on matters that may arise in a forthcoming review. The review can also provide a positive opportunity for the office to highlight difficulties that might otherwise sink in the annual reporting process. In short, 'reviews are intended to provide assurance on an ongoing basis that the institutions are performing to a high standard'.[50]

Periodic independent reviews are nowadays a common requirement applying to stand-alone statutory schemes.[51] The widespread adoption of this mechanism attests to a belief in its value. Parliamentary ombudsman offices were established before this mechanism became conventional. It may be time to update the ombudsman framework.

[48] For example, in NSW, the Parliamentary Committee on the Ombudsman, the Law Enforcement Conduct Commission and the Crime Commission, established by the Ombudsman Act 1974 (NSW), s 31A.

[49] Ombudsman Act 2001 (Qld), s 83. For the most recent review, see S Webb, *Strategic Review of the Office of the Queensland Ombudsman* (January 2018).

[50] P Wilkins, 'Parliaments and Their Watchdogs: The Role of Periodic Statutory Reviews' (paper presented to the Australian Study of Parliament Group 2017 Annual Conference).

[51] Two examples from my own experience are *Review of the Narcotic Drugs Act 1967: Final Report* (report to the Federal Minister for Health, July 2019) and *Review of the My Health Records Legislation: Final Report* (report to the Federal Minister for Health, December 2020).

V. Conclusion

Industry and parliamentary ombudsman schemes both have strong recognition and respect across government, industry and the community.[52] Their complaint-handling and dispute-resolving roles are similar and well understood. Mutual respect and cooperation among offices has grown. Joint endeavours are common, through combined ombudsman associations and in activities such as training, seminars and outreach activities. Sharing of resources and insights is regular. There are nevertheless underlying differences between industry and parliamentary ombudsman schemes at various points – how they are established, their governance structure, the type of complaints they deal with and how they measure their success. Those differences need to be understood in evaluating ombudsman ideals and achievements. Equally, however, the differences provide a rich setting in which individual offices can reassess their practices and objectives. Evolution, adaptation and remodelling have been hallmarks of the ombudsman story internationally.[53]

[52] For example, see Productivity Commission (n 40) ch 9.

[53] J McMillan, 'Future Directions for Ombudsman Offices – Four Trends, Two Reflections' (2014) 77 *AIAL Forum* 10.

9

Decentred Regulation of the Ombudsman Sector: UK Style

RICHARD KIRKHAM

I. Introduction

Through a study of the UK, this chapter explores how the ombudsman sector is regulated. Its starting premise is that the role of the ombudsman as a core accountability institution is not fixed and is best viewed as contestable.[1] This contestation gives rise to a number of predictable pressure points on the institution. To manage and offset these pressures and to retain the confidence of the various stakeholders that it seeks to influence, the sector benefits from operating in a robust regulatory structure. Without the evidence and support base that such a structure provides, an ombudsman will be in a weaker position to influence periodic shifts in political perspective on the wider administrative justice landscape, including those which could directly alter its own function and roles.

The core claim of this chapter is that, in the UK at least, the last 10–20 years has seen a profound shift in the way regulation and accountability of the ombudsman sector is carried out. Formerly, for the provision of assurance ombudsman schemes were reliant on top-down approaches, in particular through legislative oversight and a series of legally supported standards built into an office's institutional design, such as on independence and procedural fairness.[2] But there are strong reputational incentives for ombuds to move beyond these formal solutions and to innovate to secure reputation. In the UK, this bottom-up drive to enhance its accountability has been a feature of the ombudsman sector in recent years. The end result is a highly decentred system of regulation in which the formal state methods of oversight of the sector only partly explain how assurance is secured.

[1] For a good summary of this contestation, see C Harlow and R Rawlings, *Law and Administration*, 4th edn (Cambridge University Press, 2021) 561–81.

[2] See, eg Ombudsman Association, *Rules of Association*, sch 1; Ombudsman Association, *Membership Application/Re-validation Check List: Ombudsman Member* www.ombudsmanassociation.org/the-ombudsman-association.php.

This chapter argues that there are strong practical and theoretical reasons to defend this approach, but there are also risks and limits, some of which are highlighted by the UK experience.

In analysing the phenomenon of decentred regulation in the ombudsman sector, this chapter starts by identifying the basic reputational and accountability problem that the sector is obliged to address. It then charts the approach that has evolved in the UK towards this challenge and anticipates some of the likely pressure points on any regulatory regime involving watchdogs, and which are likely to be relevant to ombuds around the world. The chapter concludes with some considerations of the institutional solutions that can be adopted to reduce further the likelihood of future problems and to address current stress points.

II. The Ombudsman Sector as a Regulatory Problem

In this chapter, the oversight of the ombudsman sector is considered as a regulatory problem, one which is shared by a range of public watchdogs. A common challenge for watchdogs is securing accountability,[3] as well as maintaining relevance and quality in the face of shifting social needs and political pressures.[4] In exploring this combined challenge, there is benefit to be derived from moving beyond standard ombudsman scholarship and drawing on ideas contained in the literature on regulation,[5] public administration[6] and organisations.[7]

Watchdogs are 'auxiliary precautions',[8] specialised bodies designed to promote a range of socially accepted 'constitutional' expectations of public office and 'to outwit and outflank'[9] the potential for the holders of public power to abuse that power. In the ombudsman context, this aspiration is captured by the broad goal of administrative justice. Powerful normative arguments can be made for such unelected forms of accountability.[10] In particular, the watchdog solution

[3] M Lodge and L Stirton, 'Accountability in the Regulatory State' in R Baldwin, M Cave, R Martin and M Lodge (eds), *The Oxford Handbook of Regulation* (Oxford University Press, 2010).

[4] M Busuioc and M Lodge, 'The Reputational Basis of Public Accountability' (2016) 29 *Governance* 247.

[5] There is a vast literature on regulation that this chapter only begins to tap into. See generally Baldwin et al (n 3); I Ayres and J Braithwaite, *Responsive Regulation: Transcending the Deregulation Debate* (Oxford University Press, 1992).

[6] See, eg Busuioc and Lodge (n 4); M McCubbins, R Noll and B Weingast, 'Structure and Process, Politics and Policy: Administrative Arrangement and the Political Control of Agencies' (1989) 75 *Virginia Law Review* 431; M Power, *The Audit Society: Rituals of Verification* (Oxford University Press, 1997).

[7] See, eg M Suchman, 'Managing Legitimacy: Strategic and Institutional Approaches' (1995) 20 *Academy of Management Review* 571.

[8] J Madison, 'Federalist No 51' in I Kramnick (ed), *J Madison, A Hamilton, and J Jay, The Federalist Papers* (Penguin, 1987).

[9] J Waldron, 'Political Theory: An Inaugural Lecture' (2013) 21 *Journal of Political Philosophy* 1, 1.

[10] E Rubin, 'The Myth of Accountability' (2005) 103 *Michigan Law Review* 2073.

can 'lock in' a public commitment to predetermined expectations (eg of good administration) and thereby encourage trust in public and private bureaucracy.[11] Along these lines, the ombudsman sector can be understood as a key cog in the construction of a public 'trust network' around the delivery of both public and consumer services,[12] and even as a promoter of democratic dialogue.[13] In doing so, ombuds operate primarily, although not exclusively, through the provision of a more sympathetic and proportional dispute resolution service than the courts, one which potentially offers therapeutic benefits for the aggrieved and important lessons to administration.[14]

However laudable their goals, though, all watchdogs occupy an uncertain place in the constitutional order in terms of both role and status, and are vulnerable to shifts in democratic sentiment. Just as the twentieth-century growth of the unelected watchdog sector came about in part through the perceived limitations of traditional command and control structures of political accountability,[15] so popular confidence in unelected watchdogs can wane in the face of critical narratives.[16] Watchdogs can be viewed as undemocratic, bureaucratic and out of touch with public demands and experiences, stifling of innovation, and generally ineffective and inefficient. Such concerns may not be well founded, but they can be taken advantage of by governments looking to reduce external scrutiny and such concerns can become embedded in the perception of the citizens whose interests are supposed to be promoted by watchdogs. This latent, and sometimes realized, tendency gives rise to a demand, and a need, for watchdogs to account for their delivery of functions and adherence to appropriate standards. In particular, to garner loyalty, the sector needs to avoid being seen as designed primarily to conceal disagreement about the quality of public services or broader social and political values.[17]

The need for accountability of watchdogs raises the familiar question of 'Who guards the guardians?'[18] To manage the demand for accountability, in the classical Westminster model of the constitution, public power is ordinarily called to account through the political process. Of the main devices for achieving political accountability of the unelected state, one – the use of executive rewards and punishments – is highly limited in the context of watchdogs, given the importance attached to their need for independence and autonomy.

[11] McCubbins et al (n 6).

[12] D Vitale, 'A Trust Network Model for Social Rights Fulfilment' (2018) 38 *OJLS* 706.

[13] M Doyle and N O'Brien, *Reimagining Administrative Justice: Human Rights in Small Places* (Palgrave Macmillan, 2019).

[14] C Dieson, 'The Justice Obsession Syndrome' (2008) 30 *Thomas Jefferson Law Review* 487, 500–05.

[15] R Stewart, 'Reformation of American Administrative Law' (1974–75) 88 *Harvard Law Review* 1667.

[16] Busuioc and Lodge (n 4).

[17] A Koo, 'The Role of the English Courts in Alternative Dispute Resolution' (2018) 38 Legal Studies 666, 676.

[18] M Shapiro, 'Who Guards the Guardians? Judicial Control of Administration' (University of Georgia Press, 1988).

Hence, formally, the main emphasis for securing *political* control of watchdogs is through the imposition of reporting duties and oversight by the legislature, not the executive.[19] Yet the literature in the fields of regulation and public administration has long cast doubt on the capacity of the legislature to secure sufficient accountability of a range of unelected regulatory and watchdog institutions. A first common limitation to political oversight is the privatisation of large chunks of what might formerly have been considered public work, a phenomenon which has led to much of the watchdog sector operating in the private realm and not actively overseen by the legislature.[20] A second limitation is the expanded influence of self-regulation and the internationalisation of standards, a process which has led to the legislature often operating a secondary role when it comes to scrutiny of watchdogs.[21] A further limitation is the complexity and variety of accountability tasks that need to be performed in the modern state, and doubts as to the ability of the political branch to deliver the scale of scrutiny that is required.[22]

Over time, these limitations have led to the accountability of watchdogs becoming reliant on an additional and highly fragmented and decentred range of overlapping opportunities for scrutiny.[23] This chapter uses a study of the UK to argue that this account of fragmentation accurately mirrors what has occurred in the ombudsman sector. It then further uses insights from the regulatory literature to provide guidance on the circumstances within which watchdogs are more or less likely to be successful in achieving their stated goals.

III. Decentred Regulation and the UK Ombudsman Sector

A. Context

In the UK, governments of different political persuasions have, over the last 50 years, encouraged the growth of complaint handling through methods outside the courts and tribunals. Today, the ombudsman sector alone collectively receives over half a million complaints per annum about public and private service providers. This policy has been developed in response to a perceived increased demand for greater access to both civil and administrative justice,[24] coupled with a lack

[19] Lodge and Stirton (n 3) 352.

[20] ibid.

[21] J Black, 'Constructing and Contesting Legitimacy and Accountability in Polycentric Regulatory Regimes' (2008) 2 *Regulation & Governance* 137.

[22] Power (n 6).

[23] J Black, 'Decentring Regulation: Understanding the Role of Regulation and Self-regulation in a "Post-regulatory World"' (2001) 54 *Current Legal Problems* 103.

[24] R Kirkham, 'A 2020 Vision for the Ombudsman Sector' (2016) 38 *Journal of Social Welfare and Family Law* 103.

of capacity to deliver justice through the judicial system alone. These underlying drivers continue to dominate public policy discourse and look set to continue.[25] Even with the rise of online dispute resolution[26] and the digitisation agenda,[27] it is unlikely that this current reliance on ombuds will recede any time soon given their embedded position within multiple sectors.[28]

At a public policy level, therefore, a trade-off has been made which has resulted in access to formal justice in the courts being heavily rationed, and alternative forms of free 'efficient and mass processing' informal forms of justice, as delivered through the complaint-handling model of dispute resolution, being readily facilitated by the government. Notably, a generic feature of this process in the UK is that the resultant complaints branch has grown up in a reactive fashion to bespoke problems in the administrative and civil justice system. The end product is a diverse interrelated network of ombudsman and other complaint-handling bodies, with, for instance, at least 19 statutory and non-statutory schemes in operation that are potentially open to judicial review.[29]

As the sector grew, little legislative attention was given to constructing a formal system of ongoing oversight. Despite the occasional government sponsored review,[30] and the calls of several ombuds and the Ombudsman Association (OA) for a more holistic approach, the sector has generally developed in response to events and with minimal regard to any overarching design principles or its place in the justice system. Most likely, many of those responsible for implementing these new justice solutions were barely aware of the need for structured regulation,[31] so when later opportunities to regulate the sector have come around they have not been taken up with any real commitment. For instance, when obligations under EU law provided an opportunity to regulate the consumer ombudsman sector,[32] the choice was made to distribute regulatory responsibilities across a series of pre-existent sector-specific market regulators,[33] rather than establishing one 'super-regulator'

[25] For a discussion of this balance between the courts and alternative dispute resolution, see C Hodges, *Delivering Dispute Resolution: A Holistic Review of Models in England and Wales* (Hart Publishing, 2019).

[26] ibid ch 7, 250.

[27] J Tomlinson, *Justice in the Digital State: Assessing the Next Revolution in Administrative Justice* (Bristol University Press, 2018).

[28] For a recent discussion of this policy trend away from the courts, see Hodges (n 25), in particular chs 6 and 9.

[29] For details, see R Kirkham, 'The Ombudsman, Accountability and the Courts' (Nuffield Foundation, 2021) www.sheffield.ac.uk/law/research/centres-and-institutes/procedural-fairness-accountability-and-ombudsman.

[30] See, eg Cabinet Office, *Review of the Public Sector Ombudsmen in England* (2000); R Gordon, *Better to Serve the Public: Proposals to Restructure, Reform, Renew and Reinvigorate Public Services Ombudsmen* (Stationery Office, 2014).

[31] For an analysis of the ad hoc fashion in how design in the administrative justice system is ordinarily carried out, see V Bondy and A Le Sueur, *Designing Redress: A Study about Grievances against Public Bodies* (Public Law Project, 2012).

[32] EU Directive on Consumer ADR, 2013/11/EU.

[33] The Alternative Dispute Resolution (ADR) for Consumer Disputes (Competent Authorities and Information) Regulations 2015 (as amended by the Alternative Dispute Resolution for Consumer Disputes (Amendment) Regulations 2015).

for alternative dispute resolution (ADR).[34] In adopting a light-touch regulatory approach, the government simultaneously encouraged competition in ADR provision in the expectation that this would drive up standards.[35] Through this approach, the end result has been the imposition of minimal regulatory standards only, largely focused on reporting requirements and easy-to-measure performance standards.

This history has left four overlapping forms of control operating over the sector: institutional design coupled with political oversight, self-regulation, legal control and ground-level innovation.

B. Institutional Design and Political Oversight

The ombudsman sector in the UK has its foundation in the so-called classical ombudsman model.[36] Within this model, to guarantee the legitimacy of the office, reliance is placed on the institutional safeguards of independence and autonomy built into the ombudsman design, features which are often confirmed in statute. Additionally, a measure of formal political external oversight of the ombudsman sector is provided for through scrutiny by the legislature to call to account an office's operational performance. In the UK, all schemes report their performance annually, although by no means all directly to Parliament. Five schemes in the UK[37] are regularly required to give evidence to the legislature. A sixth, the Local Government and Social Care Ombudsman, has intermittently been required to give evidence to Parliament.[38] Other schemes can be called before Parliament, but such events are rare.[39]

Evidence sessions before Parliament can be the forum for challenging lines of inquiry on the performance of ombuds. However, ordinarily the process is centred on the duty of the ombudsman to report, and this can drive the focus of scrutiny that takes place. Overall, the intensity of the process is variable and its impact unreliable. Not all sessions lead to a select committee report; they are ordinarily

[34] R Kirkham, 'The Consumer Ombudsman Model and the ADR Directive: Lessons from the UK' in P Cortes (ed), *The New Regulatory Framework for Consumer Dispute Resolution* (Oxford University Press, 2016).

[35] For a review of the divergence in the Consumer ADR sector, see C Gill, N Creutzfeldt, J Williams, S O'Neill and N Vivian, *Confusion, Gaps and Overlaps: A Consumer Perspective on the Current Alternative Dispute Resolution System for Disputes Between Consumers and Businesses* (Citizens Advice, 2017).

[36] S Carl, 'The History and Evolution of the Ombudsman Model' in M Hertogh and R Kirkham (eds), *Research Handbook on the Ombudsman* (Edward Elgar, 2018).

[37] The Parliamentary Ombudsman, Health Service Ombudsman, Northern Ireland Public Services Ombudsman, Scottish Public Services Ombudsman and Public Services Ombudsman for Wales.

[38] See, eg Housing Communities and Local Government Committee, *Work of Local Government & Social Care Ombudsman Reviewed* (March 2019).

[39] For example, in February 2019, the Service Complaints Ombudsman gave evidence to the Defence Committee: Defence Committee, *Fairness without Fear: The work of the Service Complaints Ombudsman* (HC 2017–19, 1889).

one-off events, and are not necessarily accompanied by any extensive supporting research or follow-up report. In terms of rigour, the process may also be compromised by the ombudsman's status as a junior co-regulator of public authority activity, in which role it often works alongside the very same select committee that scrutinises its work.

C. Self-regulation and the Internationalisation of Standards

In the absence of regular formal external oversight, another regulatory solution is for bodies of like-minded professionals to establish and maintain their own system of self-regulation. Through such an approach, professional peer control is used to establish and dictate the process of setting standards in the sector, and to ensure compliance through the means of controlling entry into the profession and periodic oversight, including a complaint process against practitioners.[40]

Some elements of a shift towards self-regulation can be observed in the ombudsman sector, with the most active and consistent forms of standard-setting being non-governmental and voluntary. In the UK, the OA acts as a professional coordinating body, bringing together the different schemes operating in the sector.[41] Even without statutory backing, the OA is well positioned to provide assurance to consumers and citizens as to the standards delivered by different schemes. The OA membership criteria also help homogenise an international standard for the institution, by effectively integrating the criteria lain down by the International Ombudsman Institute[42] and the Council of Europe Venice Principles.[43]

Despite its potential, though, the OA is currently at best a weak form of self-regulation, as it has multiple purposes and operates more as a vehicle for the evolution and dissemination of best practice than as a regulator. Over time, the ambition of the OA has increased. For instance, by way of guidance, it has in recent years put in place a Service Standards Framework[44] and a Caseworker Competency Framework[45] for its members. Neither framework is enforceable, however. To the extent that the OA possesses a control power, it is through its capacity to consider

[40] This is a point pursued by Stuhmcke in her work: see A Stuhmcke, 'Ombuds Can, Ombuds Can't, Ombuds Should, Ombuds Shan't: A Call to Improve Evaluation of the Ombudsman Institution' in Hertogh and Kirkham (n 36).

[41] Formed in 1993, the OA was formerly called the British and Irish Ombudsman Association and has a wider brief than the UK. For more details, see www.ombudsmanassociation.org/the-ombudsman-association.php.

[42] International Ombudsman Institute, 'Bye-Laws' (2012) www.theioi.org/ioi-news/current-news/by-laws-available-online.

[43] Council of Europe, *Principles on the Protection and Promotion of the Ombudsman Institution*, CDL-AD(2019)005-e.

[44] Ombudsman Association, 'Service Standard Framework' www.ombudsmanassociation.org/sites/default/files/2021-01/Service%20Standards%20Framework.pdf.

[45] Ombudsman Association, 'Caseworker Competency Framework' www.ombudsmanassociation.org/best-practice-and-publications/oa-caseworker-competency-framework.

membership applications and periodically revalidate them. The process is not without impact,[46] and to carry the title 'ombudsman' an organisation must be a member of the OA.[47] Moreover, the criteria for membership of OA are in many organisational respects more onerous than the domestic legal criteria required for an ombudsman, as embedded in the statutory or non-statutory constitutions of UK ombudsman schemes.

Nevertheless, none of these domestic or international measures detail any expectation of ongoing regulation or periodic evaluation of the sector.[48]

D. The Supervisory Role of the Courts

In the UK, over a 30-year period, the judiciary has developed a strong influence over the ombudsman sector. The main driver for judicial oversight comes from complainants, and sometimes bodies under investigation, challenging the decision-making of an ombudsman. In the UK, an ombudsman decision can be challenged in judicial review and in some instances statutory appeal. In total, there have been almost 300 reported cases in which decisions of ombudsman-like institutions have been considered in a full hearing.[49] The courts can also exercise influence over the ombudsman sector through several other forms of legal proceeding, such as those claims/appeals brought against an ombudsman which refer to general legal duties under contract or employment law, equality legislation,[50] data protection laws[51] or the Freedom of Information Act.

Despite the relatively small number of cases brought against an ombudsman, the courts act as one of the main independent guardians of the standards applied by ombuds,[52] establishing a heavily rationed but occasionally significant supervisory role over the sector.[53] This role is performed through the delivery of three main functions.[54] First, a measure of individual redress is provided. Albeit for the vast majority of complainants redress through the courts is an unrealistic option, a small handful of ombudsman decisions are quashed. Second, and more significantly, the courts offer institutional support for the authority of the

[46] For instance, in 2017, the Retail Ombudsman lost the right to use the title of 'Ombudsman'. Details of this event are sparse on the OA website, but it has been charted by H Dewdney and M Williamson, 'More Ombudsman Ombishambles' (18 February 2018) 13–14 https://ceoemail.com/oo2final.pdf.

[47] Companies House, Guidance, Annex A, 51–52.

[48] See Stuhmcke (n 40).

[49] Over half of these cases have been brought against the Pensions Ombudsman: Kirkham (n 29) [2.27].

[50] See, eg *Blamires v Local Government Ombudsman* Case No 3SP00071, Leeds County Court, 21 June 2017.

[51] See, eg *Morley v The Ministry of Defence and others* [2019] NIMaster 1.

[52] R Kirkham and A Stuhmcke, 'The Common Law Theory and Practice of the Ombudsman/Judiciary Relationship' (2020) 49 Common Law World Review 56.

[53] R Kirkham and E O'Loughlin, 'Judicial Review and Ombuds: A Systematic Analysis' [2020] *PL* 680.

[54] For the full evidence of this claim, see Kirkham (n 29).

ombudsman process. They do this in providing a mechanism through which the legitimacy of the ombudsman system is formally upheld and by assisting in managing persistent complainants towards closure. Third, the courts interrogate and probe the integrity and robustness of the legal framework around the ombudsman sector. Occasionally, this work encourages the development of higher standards in decision-making. Additionally, the courts can provide support for the ombudsman sector by clarifying the institutional relationships between an ombudsman and other organisations, and the responsibilities owed towards an ombudsman.

E. Ground-Level Innovation

All of the above processes are relatively standard regulatory methods. However, taken together, despite evidence of much good practice, the regularity and intensity of independent oversight of the sector through the methods of political, self-regulatory and judicial control is variable and sometimes infrequent. This shortfall leaves an important space for additional forms of oversight to operate within, albeit a space with no clearly defined mandate.

In many respects, the most dynamic aspect of ombudsman regulation in recent years has come from ombuds themselves. Placed under pressure by a number of developments, including peer pressure created by an expanded ombudsman community, most schemes have sought to innovate and introduce new measures in a bid to defend and enhance their reputation. For instance, many schemes now publish online almost all of their decisions.[55] Internal systems for dealing with complaints and reviewing decisions are now routinely publicised and reported on.[56] Peer review and externally appointed reviews are now common features of the sector,[57] and most schemes have introduced forms of corporate governance which invite external scrutiny of their work on a more regular basis than the legislature. Such innovations are not required by legislation, yet have quickly become engrained features of the ombudsman process.

F. Decentred Regulation as the Dominant Solution

To summarise, as a direct consequence of the relative lack of governmental interest in the sector, the legal and regulatory framework in which ombuds operate has become highly decentred, with new solutions being created over time to resolve

[55] For a good example, see www.lgo.org.uk/decisions.

[56] See, eg SPSO, *Annual Report and Accounts 2019–20* www.spso.org.uk/news-and-media/annual-report-and-accounts-2019-20-published.

[57] For a recent example, see P Tyndall, C Mitchel and C Gill, *Value for Money Study: Report of the Independent Peer Review of the Parliamentary and Health Service Ombudsman* (2018) www.ombudsman.org.uk/sites/default/files/Value_for_Money_report_final.pdf.

problems as they have arisen.[58] Thus, the original formal design of ombuds in the UK has over time been supplemented by a self-regulatory approach, coupled with a combination of informal bottom-up initiatives and the judiciary's adoption of a supervisory role over the sector. These later developments have been used to fill in gaps and uncertainties in the wider legal framework and nudge ombuds towards operating higher standards of decision-making and transparency.[59] This outcome is in effect a design choice, in that governments past and present have eschewed the option of setting up a bespoke body to oversee the sector, and generally intervene only on a reactive basis or for reasons of budgetary control. The question that needs to be explored is whether the resultant solution is sufficient and, if it is not, to where we might look for potential solutions.

IV. The Challenge of Regulation in the Ombudsman Sector

In search of possible clues as to the adequacy of the current decentred regulatory regime, this section borrows insights from the fields of regulation and public administration that help provide guidance on the likely circumstances within which watchdogs are more or less likely to be successful in achieving their stated goals. Here, three generic identified challenges of the watchdog world are used to shape the analysis of the ombudsman sector's decentred regulatory regime.[60] First, being unelected, watchdogs need to construct and maintain strong legitimacy claims that persuade stakeholders of their continued value, and these claims will occasionally be contested. Second, watchdogs are required to operate in a complex institutional environment in which the bodies they investigate and the accountability agents they are required to work alongside will ordinarily have more resources and stronger legitimacy claims. Third, to retain reputational authority, watchdogs need to demonstrate and communicate their effectiveness in delivering on their legitimacy claims.

A. Constructing Legitimacy Claims

(i) The Risks of Fitting in and Complacency

Much has been written on the normative question of what an ombudsman should do, but arguably a more important practical question is how an institution comes to be regarded as legitimate by its stakeholders.[61] The concept of legitimacy is a reference to the degree of support a body enjoys for its work and the level of

[58] Black (n 23).
[59] Kirkham and O'Loughlin (n 53).
[60] Black (n 21) 144.
[61] ibid 144.

influence and power leverage it can exert on other bodies and individuals.[62] Not being grounded in either majoritarian or judicial reasoning, watchdogs enjoy legitimacy only to the extent that they can 'engender and maintain the belief that they are the most appropriate ones for the functions assigned to them'.[63] The multiple ways in which that confidence can be lost needs to be anticipated and protected against. Without legitimacy, the ability of unelected agents to exert meaningful influence falls away.

Like many watchdogs, a particular challenge an ombudsman faces is that the office is required to influence a range of politically protected bodies that are more economically and constitutionally powerful than itself. This inequality in power between 'accountor' and 'accountee' is a typical regulatory problem, which raises the risk that in order to yield some influence, an ombudsman is required to make concessions in the degree to which it delivers its legal mandate, and even becomes partially captured by the bureaucratic environment that it is embedded within.[64] In turn, this power imbalance may lead to an ombudsman adhering to a set of values that are insufficiently critical, and generally too deferential to the organisations that it oversees.

This concern of excessive deference is made more plausible by the informality that is built into the ombudsman method and by the relative lack of transparency in its process when compared to judicial processes of dispute resolution. Thus, there is a risk that in focusing on the values of speed, efficiency and keeping stakeholders happy, ombudsman offices might lose sight of deeper conceptions of justice and the more dynamic contributions that the office can deliver.[65] An alternative risk is that the office could become viewed more as a procedure for managing complainant expectations through and out of the system rather than a strong justice institution.[66]

One recent study has concluded that, over time, in its attempts to deliver its core goals, the office has come to operate as a 'managerial ombudsman'.[67] By this model, the ombudsman is best understood as 'a nested institution, operating within and constrained by its wider institutional context and influenced by and reflecting broader patterns of change in public administration and the wider justice system'.[68] That the ombudsman is influenced by its environment is not by itself problematic. Instead, the underlying issue is the compatibility of adopting a managerial approach closely attuned to the values of the bodies that it oversees

[62] D Beetham, *The Legitimation of Power* (Macmillan, 1991).

[63] G Majone, 'The European Commission: The Limits of Centralization and the Perils of Parliamentarization' (2002) 15 *Governance* 375, 389.

[64] On regulatory capture and how to defend against it, see I Ayres and J Braithwaite, 'Tripartism: Regulatory Capture and Empowerment' (1991) 16 *Law and Social Inquiry* 435.

[65] See, eg Doyle and O'Brien (n 13).

[66] S Gilad, 'Accountability or Expectations Management? The Role of the Ombudsman in Financial Regulation' (2008) 30 *Law and Policy* 227.

[67] C Gill, T Mullen and N Vivian, 'The Managerial Ombudsman' (2020) 83 *MLR* 797.

[68] ibid 828.

with the core purposes of the ombudsman. Writing specifically about the public sector, Gill et al conclude:

> The danger with adopting [managerial values] is that the ombudsman loses its ability to maintain an independent critique of public institutions, which are themselves dominated by a managerial ethos. A managerial ombudsman, overseeing a managerial public administration may serve merely as a tool for maintaining the current administrative orthodoxy rather than as a means of challenging it.[69]

A particular concern, therefore, is that, as efficient and earnest as the complaint system may be, in decision-making it may also become too focused on adopting uncritically prevalent bureaucratic standards as defined by the overseen sector itself. This concern matches the cynicism as to the value of the ombudsman sector that exists amongst some of its current and former users,[70] which identifies a lack of critical edge in ombudsman performance. Capturing this cynicism, Hockey described in a recent article some ombuds as operating as 'closed-circuit complaint systems'. By this description, Hockey is describing a system which is 'designed to adjudicate on whether an organization … has complied with [its] own rules and procedures for handling complaints'.[71]

Thus, a form of 'confirmation bias' might set in within an ombudsman's decision-making structure, which limits its capacity to reflect upon the appropriateness of the standards that it is applying.[72] This risk is particularly problematic when dealing with complainants poorly equipped to resist and push the boundaries of the dominant norms. Over time, therefore, ombuds may become too tolerant of low public service standards, and unless professional/bureaucratic standards are carefully calibrated, cynicism and fatalism towards ombudsman decision-making may be an equally likely response of complainants,[73] together with a sense of 'sham justice'.[74]

(ii) The Solutions: Conforming, Manipulating and Informing

To retain the long-term confidence of stakeholders with the goals of the office, the decision-making structure of the ombudsman needs to be capable of marrying the standards of justice applied to the reasonable expectations of both users and service providers. To manage this challenge, the literature on organisations

[69] ibid 827.

[70] See, eg the evidence submitted by LGO Watch and Public Service Ombudsman Watchers, which talks of the '15 Pillars of Injustice', in Communities and Local Government Committee, *The Work of the Local Government Ombudsman* (HC 2012–13, 431-II) Ev w17–24.

[71] D Hockey, 'The Ombudsman Complaint System; a Lack of Transparency and Impartiality' (2021) 21 *Public Organization Review* 33.

[72] D Kahneman, *Thinking, Fast and Slow* (Allen Lane, 2011).

[73] See C Gill and N Creutzfeldt, 'The "Ombuds Watchers": Collective Dissent and Legal Protest amongst Users of Public Services Ombuds' (2018) 27 *Social and Legal Studies* 367.

[74] Joe Tomlinson has argued that 'sham justice' exists where institutions are perceived to promise a level of justice that the institution is not equipped to deliver, see J Tomlinson, 'The Gap between Promise and Performance: Strong, Weak, Modest and Sham Systems of Administrative Justice' (*Admin Law Blog*, 2017).

identifies a number of plausible strategies.[75] A decentred regulatory approach facilitates the use of these diverse strategies because it is based on the input of multiple regulators and thereby creates multiple dialogue channels through which alternative perspectives on the values promoted by the ombudsman can be heard, tested and verified. These different routes can be used to allow more contestation of the values being applied in the sector, trigger institutional learning by ombuds and thereby buttress an institution's legitimacy claim while reducing the likelihood of regulatory capture.[76]

Along these lines, various solutions can observed within the UK ombudsman sector. One obvious organisational strategy to enhance legitimacy is to conform overtly to external standards in order to demonstrate adherence to publicly acceptable expectations of operational activity.[77] Here, the supervisory role of the courts, whilst inconvenient on occasion, has value to the ombudsman sector in providing for regular verification of an ombudsman's work and its adherence to rule-of-law standards. In particular, through judicial review, the procedural fairness of the ombudsman method has been regularly confirmed by the courts.[78] By this approach, therefore, the value of the ombudsman in promoting justice can be piggybacked onto a more well-established value system with a higher profile.

Up to a point, regular attendance at Parliament can also be viewed as a conforming strategy. Ongoing external political oversight, whether by the executive or Parliament, brings a different perspective on the expectations of office to that imposed by the law, one which offers a viewpoint on the efficacy of various performance standards in the sector. Sometimes such intervention has made a difference to the policy of an ombudsman.[79]

A second organisational strategy, also commonly applied by ombuds, is to manipulate the landscape in which it operates by setting new sector standards which go beyond the law and prevalent formal expectations, in order to demonstrate a proactive commitment to doing things better.[80] Here, the input of the OA is the most significant example of the ombudsman sector building up a set of more robust sector-wide standards to enhance its legitimacy claim.[81] However, given the OA's relatively low public profile, this manipulation strategy is likely to have limited impact on the wider public in the ombudsman context. Likewise,

[75] Suchman (n 7) 586.

[76] Ayres and Braithwaite (n 5) 440.

[77] ibid 587.

[78] See, eg *Maxwell v The Office of the Independent Adjudicator for Higher Education* [2011] EWCA Civ 1236.

[79] See, eg Pressure from a Parliamentary Select Committee led to Baroness R Fritchie, *Review of the Health Service Ombudsman's Approach to Complaints that NHS Failure Led to Avoidable Death* (2013) and a subsequent decision of the ombudsman to accept more complaints for investigation. Parliamentary and Health Service Ombudsman, *My Expectations for Raising Concerns and Complaints* (2014) www.ombudsman.org.uk/publications/my-expectations-raising-concerns-and-complaints.

[80] Suchman (n 7) 589.

[81] See, eg Ombudsman Association (n 2).

appeal to international standards such as those introduced in the Council of Europe Venice Principles, which are modelled on existing sector-developed standards, are unlikely to be sufficient to secure confidence amongst all stakeholders. As has been noted in the broader organisational literature: 'Managers must guard against becoming so enamored with their own legitimating myths that they lose sight of external developments that might bring those myths into question.'[82]

Given the risks of complacency and negative perceptions of the office, a watchdog is wise to go further than relying on processes and standards to defend its model. A watchdog, therefore, needs also to move beyond *conforming* and *manipulating* strategies, to devise the means to *inform* itself more frequently of external perspectives on its operation, so as to foresee emerging challenges and reflect more critically on its existing methods.[83] With such advance warning, a watchdog can alter its goals and processes to realign itself in accordance with evolving sectoral expectations. Along these lines, a number of techniques have emerged in the UK ombudsman sector.

First, outreach attempts are now integrated into many schemes, through the establishment of stakeholder-specific advisory groups. By such processes, opportunities for voice and participation amongst a range of stakeholders can be encouraged and ombuds more regularly challenged to defend the value choices made, and often in a more direct fashion than through available political routes.[84]

Another technique is to protect the reputation of organisations by 'policing internal operations more closely'.[85] In this respect, the standard-setting of the OA is of assistance in building in a toolkit for quality control, but the 'policing' metaphor is more notable in the manner in which many schemes have added to their corporate governance structure a formal 'board' to oversee the work of the office on a more regular basis than can be achieved by the legislature. The corporate model has value in that it invites external critical friends to sit on the 'board' and, depending on its remit, can both advise and potentially scrutinise the work of the ombudsman. This solution is common in the private sector and is mimicked on an informal basis by several public sector schemes. It was also included as a formal part of the design for the now defunct proposal for a new Whitehall-based public services ombudsman in 2016.[86]

Another option by which to enhance external inputs is to encourage peer-based best practice reviews. By this approach, the sector itself is beginning to pre-empt the need for external review by embedding a practice of evaluation of

[82] Suchman (n 7) 595.
[83] ibid 594.
[84] Ayres and Braithwaite (n 5) 484–91.
[85] Suchman (n 7) 595.
[86] B Thompson, 'The Challenges of Independence, Accountability and Governance in the Ombudsman Sector' in R Kirkham and C Gill (eds), *A Manifesto for Ombudsman Reform* (Palgrave MacMillan, 2020).

the office through review by a peer in the profession.[87] Several such reviews have already occurred,[88] and the need for a periodic peer review could eventually be included within the criteria of the membership of the OA.[89]

A similar method, and one that has also been deployed regularly in the UK ombudsman sector, is to establish ad hoc 'independent' reviews in response to crises. The value of independent reviews is centred on their capacity to bring new perspectives to bear, and more information and authority, in order to resolve a particular problem. Although causality is difficult to establish, there are several well-documented instances where the process of independent review has played a role in the adaptation of policy and structure within ombudsman schemes. Although the independent review is commissioned by the ombudsman scheme itself, some of the most noticeable examples have involved the government or the legislature requiring some form of external or quasi-independent review to take place.[90]

The full rigour and independence of such reviews is challengeable and will in any event be limited by their terms of reference. Nevertheless, as a minimum, what such reviews can evidence is a process by which significant organisational change is either proposed or acknowledged as necessary by an authority external to the ombudsman scheme itself. In terms of publicly acknowledging a problem, generating new ideas or oiling the wheels of change, the input of such reviews should not be underestimated and will have more force still where they are followed up by the legislature.[91]

B. Managing Accountability Relationships

(i) Risks of Stagnation and Poor Fits

As already noted, watchdogs are required to work through multiple accountability relationships that are 'dialectical' in nature.[92] In other words, in terms of both resources and access to political power, often both investigated bodies and partner accountability agents will be stronger organisations than the watchdog. The nature of the relationships that result can cause challenges.

[87] For a review of the powerful role that such self-regulatory initiatives could play, see Stuhmcke (n 40).

[88] See, eg Tyndall et al (n 57).

[89] International Ombudsman Institute, *Guide to Peer Reviews* (2020) Best Practice Paper Issue 4, www.theioi.org/ioi-news/current-news/best-practice-paper-on-peer-review.

[90] R Thomas, J Martin and R Kirkham, 'Independent External Evaluation' (January 2013); Communities and Local Government Committee, *Further Review of the Local Government Ombudsman* (HC 2013–14, 866); Communities and Local Government Committee, *The Work of the Local Government Ombudsman* (HC 2012–13, 431).

[91] For instance, following (and alongside) a parliamentary review and two independent reviews of the office, the Local Government Ombudsman underwent significant restructuring which was acknowledged in a later parliamentary review: Communities and Local Government Committee, *Further Review of the Local Government Ombudsman* (HC 2013–14, 866).

[92] Black (n 21) 140.

One challenge is that investigated bodies will have powerful cognitive reasons to obstruct or reject the watchdog's work. Given the residual incentives for public bodies to cheat on their commitments, a dominant solution is to integrate into a watchdog's design offsetting institutional safeguards to equip them better to exert the moral suasion necessary to secure results. With these design features in place, the office can be demonstrably heralded as expert, independent, rigorous and fair in its work.

This focus on a protected institutional model is ordinarily considered vital to a watchdog's success, but it carries with it a source of potential weakness if the original design that is implemented proves to be flawed in some respect or simply becomes outdated. Potentially, the restrictions imposed by the original legal design might lead to stagnation or underperformance if the watchdog lacks the capacity to adapt itself to the needs of the present or to respond quickly enough to events.

In the UK, this risk has been realised for several schemes, with arguments for legislative reform being a feature of ombudsman discourse for at least 20 years. There has been widespread acceptance across a broad spectrum of stakeholder opinion of the need for the office to expand its armoury to enable it to become a more dynamic accountability institution.[93] Despite such apparent consensus, successive governments have failed to move on reform either because it has not been a legislative priority or because of deeper objections to the creation of a more powerful ombudsman model. The end result is that, in order to fend off criticisms of the institution, affected ombuds are required to focus on finding workaround patch solutions instead.[94]

Another challenge that flows from a watchdog's dialectic power relationship with public authority is that the work of a single accountability agent is more powerful if it can be interlinked with the oversight effects of other branches of the constitution. In effect, in order to get around power imbalances, watchdogs need to be involved in a series of co-regulatory partnerships, deployed to bolster mutual efforts to achieve administrative justice or accountability of public power. The legislature in particular can be expected to have a mutual interest in using the intelligence of an ombudsman to inform its scrutiny of the executive, and in return to assist the ombudsman in withstanding moments of tension. The courts, too, stand to benefit from the reduced pressures on them where ombuds operate as effective alternative providers of justice.

However, the effectiveness of such partnerships cannot be assumed as the partners will have alternative interests, and a counter-concern is the cluttered network that is created. As the regulatory state has grown over the last century,

[93] Public Administration Select Committee, *Time for a People's Ombudsman Service* (HC 2013–14, 655).

[94] N Creutzfeldt and R Kirkham, 'Understanding How and When Change Occurs in the Administrative Justice System: The Ombudsman/Tribunal Partnership as a Catalyst for Reform?' (2020) 42 *Journal of Social Welfare and Family Law* 253.

a familiar set of criticisms of unelected accountability revolve around the dangers of over-auditing and redundancy, particularly insofar as an extended accountability network can be inefficient, ineffective and cause confusion.[95] This apparent negative outcome need not necessarily be the case,[96] but it cannot be taken for granted that an ombudsman is situated appropriately within the wider architecture of the administrative justice system.

(ii) Solutions: The Importance of Catalysts for Change and Maintaining Partnerships

To address the risks of stagnation, ombuds need to have access to realistic and effective means of addressing problems with its institutional design. In this respect, again the more diverse regulatory model that has evolved in the UK has assisted in compensating for the apparent stasis at the political level, this time by providing potential alternative opportunities for driving change. More than in other countries, the UK ombudsman sector has been impacted by the intervention of the courts, who have come to act as a potential catalytic point for change and in doing so have alleviated some of the problems that can be created by outdated legislation. By accident more than design, judicial intervention has occasionally triggered recalibration and institutional learning within the sector. Numerous examples exist of ombuds altering their approach to complaint handling as a result of judicial decisions, with the process particularly useful in forcing occasional revaluation of the procedural fairness dimension of the ombudsman's work.[97]

The power of judicial intervention illustrates that even within the decentred regulatory system of the sector, the state retains an essential role. But if the aim is to address the risks of stagnation, the courts can only be one part of the solution, as not all cases are appropriate for judicial consideration of the standards applied by the ombudsman and in any event such cases occur by chance. Therefore, there also needs to be a capacity for legislative intervention, as it is often only the legislature that can bring about the changes necessary to address the underlying problems that cause stagnation.

To achieve legislative change, other catalysts may be required. One option that has yet to be explored in the UK in full is formalising the process of independent review so that it actively buys the legislature into the process. At present, the power of political reviews is reduced by their tendency to be reactive and infrequent. In the political realm, it is ordinarily only in response to a crisis that the ombudsman sector is subject to serious scrutiny as to the standards of organisational performance, and decision-making, that it is delivering.

[95] T Schillemans, 'Redundant Accountability: The Joint Impact of Horizontal and Vertical Accountability on Autonomous Agencies' (2010) 34 *Public Administration Quarterly* 300, 330.
[96] C Scott, 'Accountability in the Regulatory State' (2000) 27 *Journal of Law and Society* 38.
[97] See Kirkham and O'Loughlin (n 53) 693–94.

Thus, a further option to avoid stagnation is to enshrine in legislation a requirement for mandatory statutory periodic review (eg once every seven years).[98] Periodic review is only embedded in one of the statutory schemes operating in the UK (and this review process is not independent),[99] and is not a requirement of either the ADR accreditation scheme or membership of the OA. To maximise the perception of independence and actively to engage ongoing scrutiny, such periodic reviews should directly involve, and report to, the legislature.[100]

At the risk of the watchdog becoming isolated or ill-fitting in the wider administrative justice system, the UK system has no top-down formal process for overseeing or organising the administrative justice system. This leaves the relevant institutions themselves to isolate and support areas of mutual benefit. In the ombudsman sector, part of the attraction behind the arguments in favour of constructing more powerful ombudsman models with powers of own-initiative investigation is that it brings the ombudsman more actively into the accountability network, and makes the office more obviously useful to the parliamentary branch.[101] Likewise, in the UK there are currently ongoing discussions between the tribunal and ombudsman sectors, primarily driven by a desire to enhance the mutual capacity of the two sectors to deliver shared goals in the promotion of administrative justice.[102]

A final example of a partnership dynamic developing in the ombudsman sector is in the impact of the courts, through judicial review, in strengthening the expectation that public authorities respect the findings of the ombudsman sector. In three cases,[103] judicial decisions have required public bodies to respond more fully and appropriately to reports of the ombudsman office rather than allow the executive to dictate their response. In each case, this precipitated a process that led eventually to systemic redress for a large body of citizens.

C. Securing and Communicating Reputational Authority

(i) Disengagement of Stakeholders

A final set of risks for a watchdog is simply one of effectiveness, and a concern that stakeholders, particularly citizens, become unconvinced that the office

[98] See, eg the Ombudsman Act 2001 (Qld), s 21.
[99] Local Government Act 1974 (UK), s 23(12).
[100] See Stuhmcke (n 40) 425–26.
[101] On own-initiative powers, see Gill et al (n 67).
[102] See Creutzfeldt and Kirkham (n 94) 10.
[103] R (Bradley) v Secretary of State for Work and Pensions and Parliamentary Commissioner for Administration [2007] EWHC 242 (Admin); R (Equitable Members Action Group) v HM Treasury [2009] EWHC 2495 (Admin); R (Gallagher & Anor) v Basildon District Council [2010] EWHC 2824 (Admin); R (Nestwood Homes Developments Ltd) v South Holland District Council [2014] EWHC 863 (Admin).

succeeds in delivering its goals. For ombuds, a key line of criticism focuses on their ability to deliver quality justice. Here, there are a series of long-standing concerns with the growth of all forms of ADR, such as its potential to encourage negotiated settlements disadvantageous to the weaker party, or that the intrinsic public value of justice systems might be undermined if too much onus is placed on 'the consumerization of civil justice'.[104] A broader concern is that the overuse of ADR might obstruct the development of judicial precedent over large areas of civil justice.[105]

The social value that users place on ombuds is evidenced in part, and imperfectly, by expressions of discontent when expectations are not met. Periodic concerns as to the quality of service provided by ombuds has long been a feature of parliamentary reviews.[106] The Internet age, however, has mobilised the organisation of the user perspective, and provided a highly transparent and accessible platform through which to express 'voice' in a semi-organised and strategic manner. This capacity has encouraged the growth of a user-driven phenomenon, sometimes labelled 'ombuds watchers',[107] through which disillusionment with the ombudsman model of justice is expressed in group activities. This movement has been characterised as a form of 'dissenting collectivism',[108] with the goals of ombuds watchers several, including the provision of a support structure for aggrieved users of public services, advice in pursuing complaints, lobbying and campaigning for reform.[109]

Despite their potentially unrepresentative nature, ombuds watchers illustrate the potential for declining confidence amongst users. From the reputational perspective of the ombudsman,[110] such groups are also difficult to ignore, and in the UK have achieved some successes in raising debate in Parliament[111] and on occasion the support of longer standing consumer support organisations.[112] From an organisational perspective, persistent complainants are also extremely costly. One study into agencies of accountability in Australia found that persistent

[104] Lord Neuberger, 'Equity, ADR, Arbitration and the Law: Different Dimensions of Justice' (Keating Lecture, Lincoln's Inn, 2010) [14].

[105] OM Fiss, 'Against Settlement' (1984) 93 *Yale Law Journal* 1073; H Genn, 'What Is Civil Justice For? Reform, ADR, and Access to Justice' (2012) 24 *Yale Journal of Law and the Humanities* 397.

[106] See, eg Communities and Local Government Committee, *The Work of the Local Government Ombudsman* (HC 2012–13, 431).

[107] For a broader discussion, see Gill and Creutzfeldt (n 73).

[108] S Halliday and B Morgan, 'I Fought the Law and the Law Won?' Legal Consciousness and the Critical Imagination' (2013) 66 *Current Legal Problems* 1.

[109] See, eg https://phsothetruestory.com/.

[110] Black (n 21).

[111] See, eg the reference to work of the 'Local Government Ombudsman Watch' in the proceedings of the Select Committee on Communities and Local Government, eg *The Work of the Local Government Ombudsman* (HC 2012–13, 431) ch 3.

[112] See Patients Association, Letter to the Secretary of State for Health (December 2014) www.patients-association.org.uk/press-release/letter-secretary-state-regarding-phso.

complainants made up less than one per cent of the overall workload, 'but consumes between 15% and 30% of all resources'.[113]

(ii) Strategies for Managing Ongoing Discontent

The wider literature on watchdogs highlights that it is in the interest of watchdogs to be proactive in demonstrating a strong legitimacy claim. This entails a need for organisations to manage 'the communicative structures in which legitimacy claims and accountability relationships are articulated and constituted'.[114] Some of the means by which ombuds achieve this goal have already been mentioned, such as their reliance on the strategy of demonstrating their conformity to legal and professional standards, and adjusting those standards to reveal a commitment to raising standards.

Notably, though, in the UK ombudsman sector, ombuds have added new processes to communicate more visibly the methods they use to protect the propriety of the ombudsman method and subject themselves to scrutiny. For instance, a particular burden that the sector faces is in managing complaints towards closure, with significant numbers of complainants reluctant to accept ombudsman determinations. To address this, as a matter of routine complainants in most schemes are now provided with an opportunity to complain about the quality of ombudsman service, with some schemes adding to this process an extra layer of independent oversight.[115] There remains more disagreement around the need for the ombudsman decision itself to be reviewed internally, but here, too, several schemes have developed transparent formal processes of decision review.[116] This is not just about satisfying complainants, as it also creates a useful management tool, is potentially beneficial for institutional learning within the ombudsman office and provides staff with an added incentive to firm up decisions before they are published. Being an internal process, there will be a limit to which the perception of fairness can be enhanced by decision review, but the reports provided by different ombudsman schemes show that a good number do lead to decisions being reopened.[117]

A second common strategy to enhance the communication of their legitimacy is for ombuds to disseminate more information and increase the transparency of their operations.[118] The goal here is to tackle some of the standard criticisms of the sector, such as: the competence of decision-makers; an excessive reliance

[113] P Mullen and G Lester, 'Vexatious Litigants and Unusually Persistent Complainants and Petitioners: From Querulous Paranoia to Querulous Behaviour' (2006) 24 *Behavioral Sciences and the Law* 333, 335.

[114] Black (n 21) 144.

[115] See, eg Financial Ombudsman Service, *The Independent Assessor's Annual Report 2019/20* www.financial-ombudsman.org.uk/files/288906/IA-annual-report-2020.pdf.

[116] See, eg Housing Ombudsman, 'Requesting a Review of Our Decision' (2020) www.housing-ombudsman.org.uk/wp-content/uploads/2020/12/Requesting-A-Review-of-Our-Decision.pdf.

[117] See, eg SPSO (n 56).

[118] Suchman (n 7) 578–79.

on paper-based decision-making; institutional bias towards service providers; the general opaque nature of decision-making; and the absence of a detailed definition of the standards applied.[119] Such allegations are difficult to refute, but in partial response the practice of a number of schemes has been to publish online all reports and decision statements.[120] Publication policies provide a means to improve the institution's claim to providing justice in two specific regards: through (i) detailing the reasoning and good administration standards being applied in decision-making and (ii) providing a public defence of the quality and procedural fairness of ombudsman decision-making. Publication policies have a further value in the disciplining effect that the exercise places on ombudsman offices to evidence the quality of their reasoning,[121] and also offer potential in terms of evidencing towards a wider body of stakeholders the consistency in which the office applies standards of administrative fault.

A final strategy worth noting here is the adoption by some private sector schemes of a 'Standards Board'. A Standards Board is made up of a cross-section of interested parties in the issues raised in ombudsman complaints, eg representatives of users of services, providers and regulators. Its role is not to reconsider ombudsman decisions, but to offer feedback on a sample.[122] As with the proposals on publishing decisions and integrating decision reviews, the goal is twofold: first, to provide increased assurance that fair and correct decisions are being made; and second, to integrate a forum in which the standards being applied within an ombudsman are being challenged and tested from external perspectives.

V. Some Concluding Regulatory Lessons for the Ombudsman Sector

This chapter has mapped how regulation is carried out in the modern ombudsman sector. It has identified that in the UK there has been a large shift towards decentred regulation, by which oversight is dependent on a variety of localised solutions.[123] This regulatory framework has probably been stumbled on by default more than chosen,[124] but in the UK context at least it represents the most likely future for the ombudsman sector. In this final section, the potential for decentred regulation securing a consistent set of standards across the full diversity of the sector is considered alongside its most significant shortcomings.

[119] See, eg Communities and Local Government Committee (n 70) Ev w17-24.

[120] See, eg www.lgo.org.uk/decisions.

[121] Draft Public Services Ombudsman Bill, sch 1, para 7 partly addresses this point, but is insufficient as currently written.

[122] See, eg Dispute Resolution Ombudsman, www.disputeresolutionombudsman.org/team/board.

[123] Black (n 23).

[124] A point made by Sarah Nason, Ann Sherlock, Huw Pritchard and Helen Taylor, *Public Administration and a Just Wales* (Nuffield Foundation, 2020) 1. More generally, see Bondy and Le Sueur (n 31).

From the government perspective, in terms of establishing effective control over ombudsman performance, there are advantages to the decentred solution, not least that it largely passes on the burden of organising regulation to a variety of other actors that can be expected to call the ombudsman to account. This solution can work because the sector cuts across different systems (political, business, legal), each with a strong interest in the output of ombuds, making it likely that there will be 'regulation in many rooms'[125] even without the intervention of governmental control. In addition, being relatively weak institutions, ombuds have a strong reputational incentive to retain legitimacy in the eyes of their key stakeholders in order to retain the authority of their profession. This incentive means that ombuds themselves will be constantly pushed to innovate in order to find ways to satisfy their users, a pattern of behaviour that matches what has occurred in the UK over a number of years.

A further benefit of the decentred approach is that it matches the natural complexity of the sector. Although the sector has a uniform purpose, its growth has been ad hoc, with delivery fragmented across multiple different institutions, each set up with subtly different powers and purposes. In this context, a uniformly imposed regulatory model would risk becoming unduly inflexible.

Whilst allowing for necessary flexibility and adaptation, an aspiration of most professions is to achieve some uniformity of standards for reasons of reputational gain in the 'brand'. In the right context, decentred regulation is capable of delivering gradual homogenisation. The patterns of behaviour that foster homogenisation have been identified in the literature on organisational change,[126] some of which mirror those found in the ombudsman sector.

To begin with, a key context in which homogenisation of standards is most likely to occur is where 'the organizations in a field transact with agencies of the state'.[127] A key explanation for this trend is the resource reliance of much of the sector on the government. This reliance may encourage separate schemes to be highly attuned to consistent messaging from that single source of power.

The background interest of the state in the role of the ombuds also creates a useful latent potential for a uniform set of standards being coercively enforced. As this case study of the UK ombudsman sector has shown, although local actors are largely trusted to deliver appropriate outcomes and performance standards, within decentred regulation rarely used hierarchical systems remain in place to coerce organisations into behaving in prescribed ways if necessary. This account describes well the periodic input of Parliament in the ombudsman sector, and

[125] Black (n 23) 108, citing L Nader and C Nader, 'A Wide Angle on Regulation: An Anthropological Perspective' in R Noll (ed), *Regulatory Policy and the Social Sciences* (University of California Press, 1985).

[126] P DiMaggio and W Powell, 'The Iron Cage Revisited: Institutional Isomorphism and Collective Rationality in Organizational Fields' (1983) 48 *American Sociological Review* 147.

[127] ibid 155. This idea was also explored by S Halliday, 'The Governance of Compliance with Public Law' [2013] *PL* 312.

also the ongoing supervisory judicial role. The judicial input may be sporadic and random in nature, but it does operate as a source of considerable pressure that exerts influence, and can be called upon if necessary to enforce homogeneous legal standards.

A third force for homogenisation of standards is the existence of strong cultural similarities between the different organisations in that field. In particular, when organisations are poorly understood and vulnerable or in search of cultural legitimacy, there is a tendency for them to model their operations on sister organisations.[128] As a result, ideas that are generated by one organisation are then copied elsewhere.[129] An example of this tendency in the ombudsman sector was the decision of the Financial Ombudsman Service to publish all of its decisions online. This practice has subsequently been adopted by several other schemes and is now pushed as best practice in the sector.

Finally, and linked, homogenisation is assisted by the collective efforts of members of an occupation to define the conditions and methods of their work.[130] The drift towards the professionalisation of values and the herding of those values is a strong feature of the ombudsman sector. The OA was first formed in 1993. Membership of this association has demanded adherence to certain set standards and today various sub-groups of the OA add detail to specific aspects of the ombudsman's work. This is a sector-specific approach which is supported by a wider international community.

The experience of the UK ombudsman sector, therefore, provides a positive story of how decentred regulation can be an effective strategy for enhancing quality and pursuing consistent standards. However, it is a decentred system that remains built around a powerful and necessary legal framework of formal institutionalism. It is because ombuds are constructed to be inherently rule-bound bureaucratic organisations that promote the rule of law[131] that Parliament, and in particular the courts, are able to exert significant influence on the development of standards in the ombudsman sector even when their interventions are intermittent. This firm base allows for professional networks to operate effectively as co-regulators. In the ombudsman sector, these networks are particularly strong and well organised, and act as 'engines' to diffuse and imbue new legal standards and to react to and anticipate nudges from both the courts and Parliament.[132]

Notwithstanding the merits and potential of a decentred regulatory approach, however, it also contains inbuilt weak points. In particular, if the profession itself becomes the main monitor and standard-setter and if external oversight is too

[128] J March and J Olsen, *Ambiguity and Choice in Organizations* (Universitetsforlaget, 1976).
[129] DiMaggio and Powell (n 126) refer to this as 'mimetic' behaviour.
[130] ibid 152.
[131] J McMillan, 'Ombudsman and the Rule of Law' (2005) 44 *AIAL Forum* 1.
[132] Halliday (n 127) 320–21.

rare, then complacency and a mismatch between the ombudsman standards and public expectations become real risks. To address this challenge, processes need to be embedded that expose an office to regular, and diversified, alternative perspectives. This is a process that should be broadened out to engage partner administrative justice institutions, and above all Parliament, in a periodic willingness to rethink the joint solutions that have been devised to deliver justice and call public power to account.

10

Reform of a National Ombudsman Scheme – A Journey

ROB BEHRENS

This chapter is concerned with reforming a large, national, ombudsman institution in a modern state. It poses no grand theory of effective change management since ombudsman schemes are extraordinarily diverse in terms of size, mandate and purpose, and are shaped by a myriad of political cultures. There is no golden ombudsman age to refer to, only the application of the lessons of lived experience, of 'Praxis',[1] and of the need for ombudsman leaders to engage, listen and act on the views of citizens, service users and stakeholders both inside and outside the organisation. This must be done in a way which seeks to generate public trust.

Establishing and maintaining trust is a perennial challenge for public bodies in the modern state. This is particularly the case for ombudsman schemes, which most often have no coercive power and rely on moral force or authority. There are at least four key elements to public trust.[2] One concerns the perceived honesty and independence of a professional group and the ability of professionals to make public interest decisions untrammelled by vested interest or narrow party-political interest. Secondly, even if independence is manifest, no profession is trusted unless it exhibits a core competence in serving the public. Thirdly, there is continuing public support for 'the development of a strong internal culture fostering standards and openness as means for improving professional integrity and increasing confidence in public institutions'.[3] A fourth key element is the manifestation of 'active trust' and trustworthy behaviour by professions and oversight bodies alike. This is necessary in both personal and corporate behaviour, not least in ombudsman offices, where the ombudsman often personifies the scheme. People must be treated with dignity, respect and fair dealing to draw on citizens' propensity to

[1] Q Hoare and G Nowell Smith (eds), *Selections from the Prison Notebooks of Antonio Gramsci* (Lawrence & Wishart, 1971) 321–472.

[2] R Behrens, *Public Trust and the Ombudsman: The Case of the OIA* (March 2015) 10th Anniversary Series, Paper 1.

[3] Committee on Standards in Public Life, *Survey of Public Attitudes towards Conduct in Public Life 2012* (2013) 6.

trust, even where their disclosures to researchers suggest they do not or might not. Following Baroness O'Neill, 'The evidence suggests that we still constantly place trust in many of the institutions and professions we profess not to trust'.[4]

This chapter explains how the UK Parliamentary and Health Service Ombudsman (PHSO, the Ombudsman) has addressed this challenge. Steps taken included: a new strategic plan tied to a revised vision, values and behaviours; the reform of the operating model, including a clinical advice review and more flexible approaches to case resolution; enhanced professional development for case handlers; significant transparency and outreach initiatives, including the publication of case summaries; the introduction of annual meetings and Radio Ombudsman; new complaints standards for frontline complaint handlers in the National Health Service (NHS); and a new quality programme to monitor and promote the effectiveness of PHSO casework, alongside the structured feedback taken quarterly from a significant cross-section of service users. These initiatives are broadly related to the values of honesty, independence and reciprocal trust, the development of competence and the fostering of a transparent, internal culture. This suggests that success in reforming an ombudsman office is intimately related to the establishment of trust or its re-establishment where trust has been lost.

My journey as PHSO in the UK began in 2017, when engagement with citizens and service users had reached the point of being seen as problematic. The general context is a well-documented decline of citizen deference, an associated growth in assertiveness, the rise of the 'relational' state, where citizens are seen as collaborative partners, and the 'burning platform' of public trust.[5] PHSO was judged to be in crisis,[6] and in need of a renaissance or restorative journey to address a cluster of serious challenges, circulating around the restoration of competence and trust.

PHSO is an independent, Crown appointment, reporting to Parliament, not ministers. The Office of the PHSO began life as a classic, national ombudsman service in 1967, in the wake of some fairly deferential analysis about the importance of not breaking the link between citizens and Members of Parliament.[7] What emerged was a limited scheme, requiring complainants to go to the Ombudsman through their MP and focusing on a small number of serious and complex cases.[8] The role of Health Service Commissioner (HSC) was created in 1973 via the NHS Reorganisation Act. However, only non-clinical (ie administrative) complaints about the NHS were allowable. An Act of 1993 consolidated the Health Service

[4] O O'Neill, *A Question of Trust: The BBC Reith Lectures* (Cambridge University Press, 2002) 13.

[5] R Behrens, 'Ombudsman Values – A Guide to Practice' in M Hertogh and R Kirkham (eds), *Research Handbook on the Ombudsman* (Edward Elgar, 2018) 461–63.

[6] P Tyndall, C Mitchell and C Gill, *Value for Money Study: Report of the Independent Peer Review of the Parliamentary and Health Service Ombudsman* (November 2018) www.ombudsman.org.uk/sites/default/files/Value_for_Money_report_final.pdf.

[7] Behrens (n 5) 457–60.

[8] ibid 458.

Commissioner's powers, and further legislation in 1996 saw clinical judgement (and general practitioners) come under the HSC's jurisdiction. The disjunction between, on the one hand, the radical change in citizen expectations about the State and its services, and on the other the relative conservatism in legislative provision for the Ombudsman since 1967, noted in this paragraph and the one immediately below, constitutes a significant tension in this narrative.

The cautious founding remit and the incremental organisational development compromised effective relations with citizens from the start. Beyond the integration of the roles of Parliamentary Commissioner and the Health Service Commissioner, there was a marked absence of holistic thinking, and this led to the creation of a succession of separate schemes for local government, pensions, policing, prisons, housing and higher education. Such incremental action complicated the pathway for citizen complainants, something already compromised by the creation, *ab initio*, of an 'MP filter' to PHSO, ruling out – to this day – the possibility of direct approach to the Ombudsman if complaining about a UK government department or its agencies.

By 2017, PHSO, one of the largest national ombudsman schemes in the world, had 450 staff in London and Manchester, was in receipt of 120,000 inquiries and 30,000 complaints, and conducted approximately 3000 full investigations each year. The Office was beset with multiple problems. These included: significant ministerial criticism over its lack of sensitivity in dealing with cases involving child deaths; confusion about its core function; a massive 24 per cent budget cut to be delivered over three years; the resignation of its two senior leaders in 2016–17; poor staff morale; and Brexit causing delay over ombudsman reform. All of this combined to produce a loss of trust across a wide range of stakeholders, including complainants.

As incoming Ombudsman, I had had plenty of time to think through how to address the cumulative problems – the appointment process took six months, and there was then a three-month interlude before taking up post. I brought from my past a small number of abiding convictions. One was that competence and transparency lie at the heart of public trust.[9] Another was that while there are many leadership styles available, organisations in crisis benefit particularly well from inclusive leadership, where action is based on intense listening and conversation or exchange. In this situation, leaders should not claim to be infallible, but should hold themselves accountable for failures as well as success. The third conviction was about the value of learning from and exchanging with ombudsman colleagues around the world about values, strategies and good practice. As the only candidate with ombudsman experience on a short-list of five, this unremarkable commonplace became something of a mantra. Solidarity and comradeship with ombudsman colleagues were not only a key to personal well-being (especially in the pandemic to come), but also the gateway to rich comparative learning and an appreciation of the commonality of challenges in a broad and diverse profession.

[9] Behrens (n 2).

All of this required medium-term planning, as well as a concern about today and tomorrow. It also required a committed, skilled and resilient leadership team, including non-executives as well as executives. Here, I was fortunate to join up with two exemplary leaders, already in place. One was Amanda Campbell (later Amroliwala), the newly arrived Chief Executive, and the other was Elisabeth Davies, the senior non-executive board member. In every sense it was a team effort, needing the patience associated with the understanding that a journey of uncertain length was being undertaken which would require focus, flexibility and stout companions. In the words of Lewis Carroll's *Hunting of the Snark* (1874),

> For England expects – I forbear to proceed:
> 'Tis a maxim tremendous, but trite:
> And you'd best be unpacking the things that you need
> To rig yourselves out for the fight.[10]

I. The Inheritance

Previous holders of the office of Parliamentary and Health Service Ombudsman in the UK, Ann Abraham (2002–12) and Dame Julie Mellor (2012–17), had engaged in much strategic thinking about the extent to which, on grounds of public value and limited resource, a national ombudsman service could or should investigate the preponderance of cases brought to it. In this sense, they were seeking to address, in their different ways, the structural flaw in the founding legislation which had put the emphasis on the limited role of the Ombudsman, making it supplementary and emphatically deferential to Parliament in handling complaints. In the words of the Preface to the portentous Whyatt Report by Justice in 1961, which first articulated the idea of a British ombudsman, the proposed scheme was 'a real Charter for the little man' in dealing with bureaucratic injustice, something 'the man of substance … near to the establishment' could deal with.[11] What resulted was what the Treasury called 'a specific and limited scheme' designed to 'confine the Ombudsman's caseload to the minimum conceivable'.[12] This intention was carried out for many years. Between 1967 and 2000, in no single year did the Office issue more than 374 statutory reports or decisions, and in a number of years it issued far fewer.[13]

[10] L Carroll, *The Hunting of the Snark: An Agony in Eight Fits* (1876) www.literaturepage.com/read/huntingofthesnark-11.html.

[11] Lord Shawcross, *The Citizen and the Administration: The Redress of Grievances* (Stevens & Sons, 1961) xiii.

[12] R Gregory and P Giddings, *The Ombudsman, the Citizen and Parliament: A History of the Office of the Parliamentary Commissioner for Administration and Health Service Commissioners* (Politicos, 2002) 77–81.

[13] ibid Appendix D, 448.

In April 2005, following public consultation, Ann Abraham set up a new inclusive operating model that ensured that most new complaints be accepted as an investigation. Yet this did not last long. In the wake of concerns about inconsistency and internal quality control, the Ombudsman introduced a more restrictive mechanism, via an 'assessment' process, which went live in April 2007. This was done alongside organisational reform, including the introduction of a delegation scheme called 'Organising for the Future'.[14] The term 'no worthwhile outcome' became a specific case closure code for PHSO when this assessment process was introduced. Under this practice, many cases were closed with the explanation that PHSO did not see a worthwhile outcome to investigating. The term was aimed at encapsulating a consideration of proportionate use of public funds and whether an investigation would be in the public interest. However, it became a toxic term for many complainants, who saw it as PHSO making a value judgement on what were very serious and important issues that individuals had been pursuing for a long time. As such, many complainants raised their dissatisfaction with their MPs.[15]

Following criticism from the Parliamentary Select Committee,[16] staff were advised to stop referring to 'no worthwhile outcome' in their assessment decisions. Yet it was not entirely removed as a reason for case closure until Baroness Fritchie was invited by Dame Julie Mellor to review PHSO's approach to investigating potentially avoidable deaths in 2012. In her report, Baroness Fritchie concluded that PHSO's use of no worthwhile outcome 'could be experienced as unsympathetic, particularly in sensitive cases …'[17]

Dame Julie Mellor reintroduced a more expansive approach in late 2012 under her five-year strategy, 'Delivering More Impact for More People'. In Strategic Aim 2, PHSO committed to help more people by investigating more complaints and to provide an excellent service for customers. This included using different ways to investigate and resolve different types of complaint and setting high standards for the service provided.[18] PHSO had investigated 421 individual complaints in 2011–12, but pledged to investigate thousands of complaints by 2018.[19] In line with the Fritchie recommendations, all potentially avoidable death cases were to be accepted unless there was an exceptional reason not to do so.[20]

[14] Office of the Parliamentary and Health Service Ombudsman, *Resource Accounts 2006–07* (The Stationery Office, 2007, HC 839) https://assets.publishing.service.gov.uk/government/uploads/system/uploads/attachment_data/file/250657/0839.pdf.

[15] A Medlock, 'The Climate of Change: A History of PHSO's Service Design' (unpublished, 2016).

[16] PHSO, 'Review of the Health Service Ombudsman's Approach to Complaints that NHS Service Failure Led to Avoidable Death' www.ombudsman.org.uk/sites/default/files/Review_of_the_Health_Service_Ombudsman%E2%80%99s_approach_to_complaints_that_NHS_service_failure_led_to_avoidable_death.pdf.

[17] ibid.

[18] PHSO, 'Our Strategic Plan 2013–2018', 8 www.ombudsman.org.uk/sites/default/files/Strategic_plan_2013-18_final.pdf.

[19] ibid 11.

[20] PHSO (n 16).

However, Fritchie had also referred to long-standing service issues, describing a competent but remote and empathy-light service that took too long to resolve issues that had dogged PHSO for decades. The Health Minister, Jeremy Hunt, severely and publicly criticised the Ombudsman for insensitive case handling in two landmark cases, each involving avoidable child deaths in the NHS. In the case of three-year-old Sam Morrish, who had died from undiagnosed sepsis, the Health Minister criticised the Ombudsman for treating bereaved relatives with a lack of compassion and sensitivity, demanding she be more 'humane' in dealing with families who had lost loved ones because of NHS errors.[21] And in the case of Joshua Titcombe, a baby who died in hospital at seven days old, he implored the Ombudsman to 'have a heart for grieving families'.[22] In the same case, Dr Bill Kirkup's independent *Report of the Morecambe Bay Investigation* expressed concern at the failure of the Ombudsman to conduct an early investigation into the case in 2009, when she had an opportunity to report on systemic failings at the hospital trust by examining Joshua Titcombe's death.[23]

Criticism of the handling in these cases was supplemented by two critical reports from the Patients Association, in 2014 and 2015.[24] To add to the sense of dysfunctionality, PHSO's accounts were qualified by the National Audit Office on two counts in the financial year 2014–15.[25] It was unsurprising that, around this time, scores in the confidential annual staff surveys reached a low ebb. Only 23 per cent of staff thought the PHSO leadership team had a clear vision of future direction, and only 49 per cent understood the aims and objectives of the Office.[26] Collectively, all of this constituted 'an unprecedented and sustained level of criticism of an independent public body dealing with the higher levels of the NHS complaints process'.[27]

These were grievous reputational blows, and they lingered. The Ombudsman's response was to engage in extensive research to develop a Service Charter.[28]

[21] L Donnolly, 'Jeremy Hunt Rebukes Health Watchdog over Three-Year-Old Sam's Death' *The Telegraph* (28 June 2014) www.telegraph.co.uk/news/health/news/10933028/Jeremy-Hunt-rebukes-health-watchdog-over-three-year-old-Sams-death.html.

[22] SK Templeton, 'Watchdog Told to Have a Heart for Grieving Parents' *The Times* (6 September 2015) www.thetimes.co.uk/article/watchdog-told-to-have-a-heart-for-grieving-parents-s022rjqr77n.

[23] B Kirkup, *The Report of the Morecambe Bay Investigation* (March 2015) 10.

[24] Patients Association, 'Parliamentary and Health Service Ombudsman: The "Peoples" Ombudsman – How It Failed Us' (November 2014) https://minhalexander.files.wordpress.com/2017/05/phso-the-peoples-ombudsman-how-it-failed-us-final4.pdf; Patients Association, 'PHSO – Labyrinth of Bureaucracy' (March 2015) www.dropbox.com/s/6vnx65ndjme1c76/PHSO-Labyrinth-of-Bureaucracy-Follow-Up-to-the-Patient-Association-PHSO-report.pdf?.

[25] PHSO, *Annual Report and Accounts 2014–15* (HC 570, 9 November 2015) file:///C:/Users/960769/Downloads/UK_PHSO_Annual%20Report_2014_2015_EN.pdf.

[26] PHSO, 'Employee Survey' www.ombudsman.org.uk/sites/default/files/PHSO_staff_survey_2016_presentation_final.pdf.

[27] L Donaldson, 'Clinical Advice Review Commissioned by the Parliamentary and Health Service Ombudsman, Report of the Independent Adviser to the Review' (PHSO, December 2018) 12.

[28] PHSO, 'Creating a Service Charter for the Parliamentary and Health Service Ombudsman' (February 2016) www.ombudsman.org.uk/sites/default/files/Creating_a_Service_Charter_for_the_Ombudsman_report_by_OPM.pdf.

The Charter became operational in July 2016, with specific commitments related to 'Giving you the information you need', 'Following an open and fair process' and 'Giving you a good service'.[29] It was backed up with two important initiatives. The first was the introduction of independent measurement of complainant views of performance, measured and published on a quarterly basis.[30] The second was the development of an operating model to concretise the Service Charter commitments in PHSO case-handling processes.[31]

What was the underlying cause of the unprecedented criticism and dissatisfaction expressed through this period? The answer to that question was critical in navigating the journey ahead. In this writer's view, the causes were structural, not interpersonal, and they return us to the tension between the needs generated by citizens served by a modern state and the limited capacity of a national ombudsman service hampered by an outdated mandate and therefore 'stuck in time'.[32] Three elements stand out. First, despite significant changes to the nature of the modern state under Thatcherism and Blairism in terms of privatisation and the interconnection between public and private provision, the core mandate of PHSO remained largely unaltered from the limited scheme created in 1967. Secondly, even where incremental reform was undertaken, including the bringing together of complaints about central government and public bodies with complaints about the NHS, this was done in an uncritical fashion. For example, until 2009, the NHS complaints procedure used to operate on three levels. The first was at the frontline service level. The second was at the level of the Healthcare Commission, the NHS regulator. The third level was the Ombudsman. But the abolition of the Healthcare Commission and its replacement by the Care Quality Commission prompted the government to merge the second and third levels under the jurisdiction of the PHSO. As Sir Liam Donaldson, former Chief Medical Officer in England, has pointed out, in its last full year of complaints operation, the Healthcare Commission received nearly 8000 requests for review, employed 150 staff to deal with complaints and spent £9.6 million on this aspect of its service.[33] Any ombudsman service would have found this additional workload to be challenging, but with no change of mandate and with the bereavement and trauma associated with large numbers of serious health complaints now transferred to PHSO, the service inevitably came under intense pressure. Third, and related, in the light of the widespread decline in public trust in the activities of the modern state, the ingredients of public trust – independence, competence, transparency and engagement featuring mutual trust – were insufficiently addressed by an ombudsman service under considerable strain.

[29] PHSO, 'Our Service Charter' (July 2016) www.ombudsman.org.uk/sites/default/files/page/FINAL_PHSO_service_charter.pdf.

[30] PHSO, 'Performance against Our Service Charter' www.ombudsman.org.uk/service-charter.

[31] PHSO, 'PHSO Service Model' www.ombudsman.org.uk/sites/default/files/Service_model_flowchart_20160409.pdf.

[32] Public Administration Committee (2014) https://publications.parliament.uk/pa/cm201314/cmselect/cmpubadm/655/65506.htm.

[33] www.ombudsman.org.uk/sites/default/files/PHSO_Clinical_Advice_Review_Report_of_Independent_Adviser.pdf.

II. The Journey

Shortly after taking up post, I agreed to do a long and impromptu question and answer session at the annual All-Staff Conference for more than 400 colleagues in Manchester. Colleagues had seen recordings of my pre-appointment scrutiny hearing before a joint meeting of the Select Committee on Public Administration and Constitutional Affairs and the Health Committee,[34] and were curious. They were exhausted by the storms the organisation had been through, puzzled by what the organisation wanted to achieve, desperate for professional development and policy guidance to enable them to do a challenging job, and very interested in a conversation about the way forward. At the same time, they were frankly sceptical about the organisation's ability to deliver meaningful change.

This was the beginning of a journey of unknown length. All the clear indications were, however, that the journey would be brief. The Select Committee pointed out that, in the light of the government's commitment to ombudsman reform,

> [w]hile the Ombudsman is appointed by the Queen for a non-renewable fixed term of no longer than seven years, we expect that, in this case, the appointment of the Ombudsman will cover the period until the draft Public Service Ombudsman Bill is enacted, and a new Ombudsman is appointed.[35]

There was an element here of the refrain in the Groucho Marx song 'Hello. I Must Be Going' from the film *Animal Crackers*! What was required was a disposition focused on the development of a medium-term reform strategy, but always alert to the strong possibility that ombudsman legislative reform would curtail the journey to make way for an inaugural Public Service Ombudsman. As the government's wider preoccupations of withdrawal from the European Union and then dealing with the COVID-19 pandemic took their toll of parliamentary focus and time, the chances of ombudsman legislative reform 'softly and suddenly vanished away'.[36] As this is written, the journey is now more than four years long.

III. Engagement and Adjustment

Inclusive leadership is a natural ally of engagement with colleagues and stakeholders. It is neither charismatic nor hierarchical. It majors on exchange inherent in conversation and requires leaders at all levels of the organisation. It is transformational and values-led, and is rooted in teamwork. Inclusive leadership is

[34] Oral evidence, R Behrens, 18 January 2017, http://data.parliament.uk/writtenevidence/committeeevidence.svc/evidencedocument/public-administration-and-constitutional-affairs-committee/preappointment-hearing-parliamentary-and-health-service-ombudsman/oral/45499.html.

[35] Appointment of the Parliamentary and Health Service Ombudsman Fifth Report of the Health Committee of Session 2016–17 Eighth Report of the Public Administration and Constitutional Affairs Committee of Session 2016–17, HC 810, 19 January 2017, paras 4, 5.

[36] Carroll (n 10).

not a soft option. It recognises that conflict is endemic and a sign of organisational good health if addressed transparently. It also recognises that leaders look externally, not just internally, and that while leaders always listen, they do not always follow.[37] Where leaders wish to rise above pious moralising and make a difference, they first have to engage with their own colleagues and co-workers, to convince them that the journey is understandable, worthwhile and navigable. In that sense, then, the first point of call was (and is) to engage and to adjust internally, emphasising that trust is reciprocal.

Figure 1 New Strategic Plan 2018–21

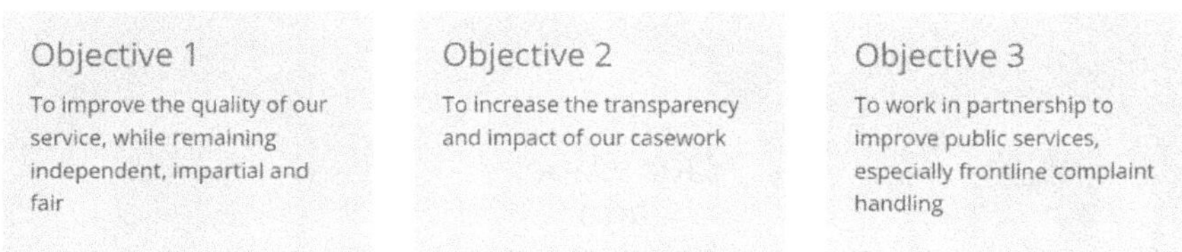

During 2017, the Ombudsman and the Chief Executive gathered all staff in a series of small-group meetings to discuss PHSO's vision and values, and the strategic plan for the future. It emerged that few colleagues could name the core values of the organisation. However, there was strong endorsement for independence and impartiality, and a keen interest in organisational defence of caseworkers making difficult decisions in the face of obfuscation from bodies in jurisdiction. In terms of vision and strategy, colleagues wished for greater clarity on whether case resolution was at the heart of PHSO's focus, notwithstanding the importance of pressing for policy change. And in performing challenging jobs, colleagues again reiterated that without continuous professional training and development, the potential for delivering robust decisions would be fatally compromised.

Having secured preliminary consent for the direction of travel, winning back external trust necessitated public consultation with external stakeholders on a new three-year strategic plan.[38] This confirmed a public appetite for a return to ombudsman essentials, involving an improved quality of service, while remaining independent, impartial and fair, increasing the transparency and impact of PHSO casework, and working in partnership to improve public services, especially frontline complaint handling. The feedback was that admirable and necessary meta-planning to create a new, joined-up public service ombudsman scheme had deflected the organisation from the bread-and-butter issues of individual case resolution and overemphasised the relative importance of the aim of policy improvement over case handling. In trying to create a modern public service

[37] *The Art of the Ombudsman: Leadership through International Crisis* (Parliamentary and Health Service Ombudsman and the International Ombudsman Institute, May 2021) file:///C:/Users/960769/AppData/Local/Temp/UK_PHSO_Survey%20Repror_Art%20of%20OM_EN.pdf.

[38] PHSO, 'Our Strategy 2018–2021' www.ombudsman.org.uk/sites/default/files/page/Our%20strategy%202018-2021.pdf.

Figure 2 Reinventing our values

ombudsman located in the modern state, and to draw on the analogy I had used in the parliamentary pre-appointment hearing, where I described the job as 'playing the piano and moving it upstairs at the same time', there had been too much location planning and not enough piano playing.

IV. Improving Service Quality – Changes to the Service Model, Focus on Professional Development and More Flexible Approaches to Resolution, and Commissioning Clinical Advice

Much of the Service Charter set out how, in following an open and fair process, PHSO would listen, explain how case handling would be undertaken and how decisions and recommendations would be reached. Evidence would then be shared and the Office could then 'discuss with you what we are seeing'. However, the prevailing culture was one of gathering information, analysis and decision, rather than face-to-face engagement. The justification was necessary 'efficiency' or 'proportionality'. This was particularly important because the numbers of investigations were being substantially increased without any expansion to the casework team.

In addition, before my arrival in 2017, PHSO began an organisational restructure to address weaknesses in service delivery and, additionally, to reduce spending brought about by a significant cut in resources of 24 per cent over three years required by the Comprehensive Spending Review. This included moving the majority of operations from London to Manchester, where property rental is considerably less expensive. Relocation involved the departure of experienced caseworkers unwilling or unable to move north and the recruitment and induction of over 100 new caseworkers.

As part of this restructure, the Office introduced a revised operating model which ensured that a single caseworker completed both the 'Assessment' (Step 2) and 'investigation' (Step 3) stages of a complaint. This removed a time-consuming 'handover' phase between different caseworkers at these two stages. It also aimed to improve complainants' experience by ensuring they had a single point of contact throughout the handling of their complaint.

However, until fairly recently, the long-standing debate about the relative merits of adjudication and mediation, which has been a feature of practitioners in (for example) the international ombudsman world of higher education, was not participated in by PHSO.[39] The culture had given insufficient emphasis to exploring alternatives to the typically British ombudsman approach to case resolution, which is the use of investigation to make decisions. As a result, PHSO had insufficiently resourced the core professional development of its caseworking staff in a way which had undermined both confidence and morale. The organisation felt too constrained by the legislation and believed its power to intervene required it to conduct a formal investigation. Under the new strategic plan, a less risk-adverse and more modern approach enabled PHSO to do a range of things that had not been tried before. PHSO began researching how to pilot and evaluate mediation and other early resolution methods, principally by learning from the work of others across the ombudsman community.[40]

A new early dispute resolution (EDR) pilot was launched in 2019. Following accredited, professional training, the EDR team began to use mediation techniques to resolve complaints without the need for an investigation. This involves bringing complainants and the organisations they complain about together, by teleconference,

[39] R Behrens, *Being an Ombudsman in Higher Education: A Comparative Study* (ENOHE, 2017).

[40] PHSO, *Annual Report and Accounts 2018–2019* (HC 2198, 22 July 2019) 12, www.ombudsman.org.uk/sites/default/files/PHSO_Annual_Report_and_Accounts_2018-2019.pdf.

video conference or in person, and facilitating a resolution-focused conversation between the two. To date, there have been high levels of satisfaction from the small numbers of both complainants and organisations who have agreed to a mediated approach. EDR assisted by involving parties in resolving disputes without putting them through the more time-consuming process of an investigation where this was not necessary. It enables resolution of more cases earlier in the process:

> Prior to the meeting I felt that the complaint was quite minor and was unsure as to why it hadn't been resolved previously and had got to this stage but I think [when] it was spoken about between us we could then see each other's point of view. I felt the process was dealt with … professionally by the Ombudsman and they kept independent throughout, and I felt supported through the process. I would happily support trying this process again if required.[41]

Training and development are not panaceas for lack of structural coherence, but they are prerequisites for adding value where vision, values and strategy are clear and aligned. In late 2017, a new Casework Development Programme was researched and launched to make sure caseworkers had the skills and knowledge necessary to provide a consistently high-quality service. The training was developed using a combination of an in-house learning and development team, seconded caseworkers and commissioned external consultancy.

Figure 3 Professional skills programme

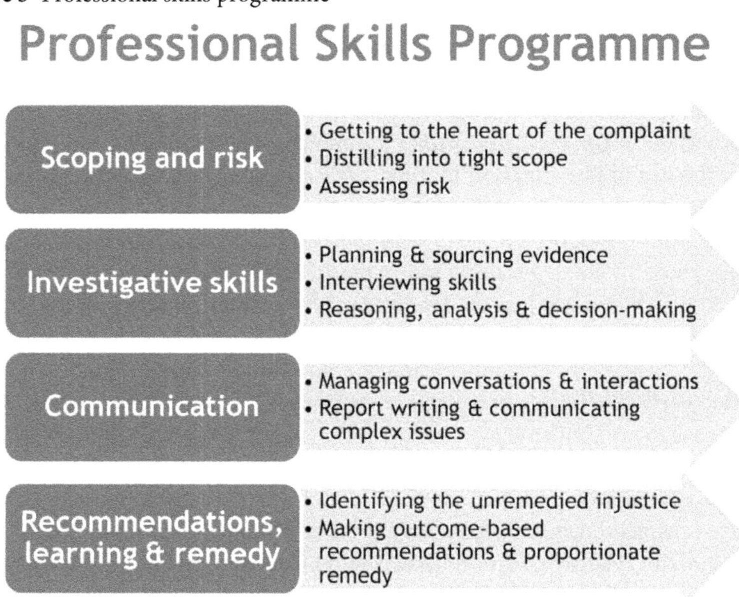

[41] PHSO, *Annual Report and Accounts 2019–2020* (HC 444, 20 July 2020) www.ombudsman.org.uk/sites/default/files/The%20Ombudsman%E2%80%99s%20Annual%20Report%20and%20Accounts%202019-2020_Website.pdf.

It had a number of elements. First was the development of role-ready training, a five-day modular induction course about legal powers, how to gather and balance evidence and investigative techniques. Professional skills came next. A modular programme was developed to enhance professional skills and ensure consistency in how casework staff approach the different stages of the investigative process. Modules were created dealing with scoping and risk, investigative skills, communication, and recommendations and remedies. Third, alongside this, a development programme was created providing skills to deal with vicarious trauma, and equality, diversity and inclusion. There were also workshops for non-caseworkers on the demands of the casework process, for managers in approaching human resources issues, and a new interactive leadership workshop for line managers to encourage good practice. Training was also delivered on how to effectively mentor staff to prepare managers and those in influencing roles for the revised mentoring scheme.

Fourth, alongside these initiatives, the Accreditation of Senior Caseworkers was launched, with three modules on communication, assessment and scoping, investigations (planning, evidence-gathering and analysis) and recommendations and remedies. Graduates of this programme are awarded the Advanced Certificate in Professional (Ombudsman) Practice.[42]

Figure 4 Developmental programme

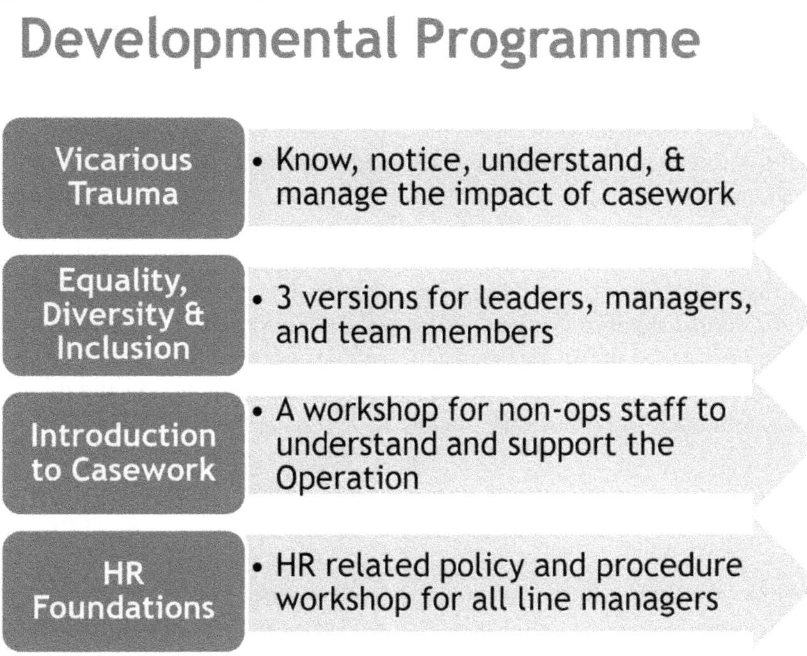

[42] PHSO, *Annual Report and Accounts 2017–2018* (HC 1388, 18 July 2018) www.ombudsman.org.uk/sites/default/files/PHSO_Annual_Report_and_Accounts_2017_2018.pdf.

Figure 5 Accreditation of senior caseworkers

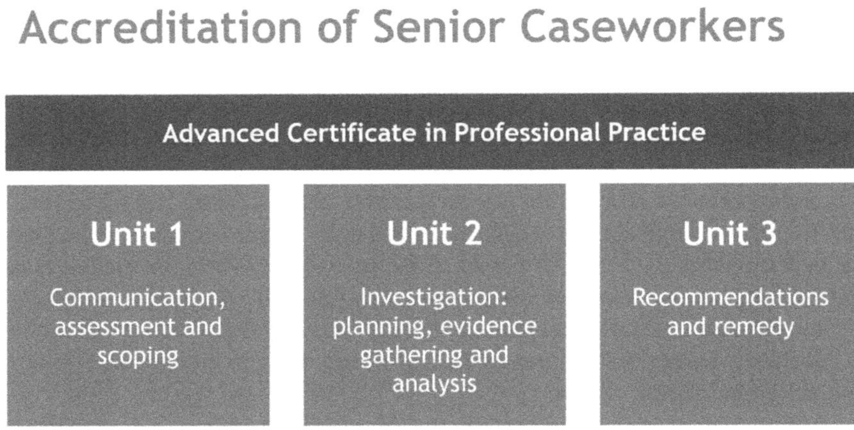

Through a professional qualifications and further education sponsorship scheme, funding was offered to several members of staff to complete professional qualifications relevant to their roles and careers. Staff also attended a range of mandatory and induction courses, on such subjects as data protection and health and safety. In addition, every colleague had access to online learning resources from how-to guides and videos to podcasts, self-assessment questionnaires and articles to support their professional and personal development via our new i-learn platform.[43]

More recently, the Learning and Development Team supported the development of a Training Academy for new caseworkers. The Academy offers corporate induction and mandatory e-learning modules, as well as classroom training. After initial training, new caseworkers are assigned to work for a dedicated Academy operations manager to provide high levels of support and guidance. They remain in this environment for a number of months, before moving on to work in operational casework teams.[44] In three years, beginning in 2017–18, staff undertook more than 6000 days of formal learning – close to five days per person each year. This constituted significant enhancement of the Office's training and development offer, and addressed the oft-repeated concern that case handlers were being asked to undertake challenging tasks without the underpinning induction and development associated with professional practice.

V. Clinical Advice Review

One area of activity which was not considered sufficiently before 2017 was the commissioning and use of clinical advice in investigating health complaints. As

[43] ibid 38–39.
[44] PHSO, *Annual Report and Accounts 2019–2020* (n 41) 15.

incoming Ombudsman, this seemed like a significant omission, given the preponderance of health cases in PHSO's complaints portfolio and given the centrality of clinical advice to at least half of all the health decisions made.

The Clinical Advice Review started in autumn 2018. Its immediate context was the creation of a new Ombudsman's Clinical Standard to give greater clarity and predictability to what benchmark case handlers would use in considering the appropriateness of care and treatment. Clinicians who were complained about were now asked explicitly to disclose what guidance, policies and standards they followed in making decisions about care and treatment.[45] This followed a legal challenge dating back to a case in 2012.[46]

The Review was led by non-executive director Sir Alex Allan, with Sir Liam Donaldson, former Chief Medical Officer in England, acting as the independent adviser. Donaldson found structural weaknesses in the existing methods of commissioning and using clinical advice. Some of this had evolved from what he regarded as a 'beyond anachronistic' clinical judgement paradigm. This was drawn from legislation enshrined in PHSO culture, and overly focused on a view of maladministration rooted in individual clinical decision-making rather than service organisation and delivery.[47] Donaldson had a strong view that complaints were 'very procedurally driven'. However, a necessary 'in the round' understanding could not be achieved without clinical expertise and without a systems perspective. This holistic approach was not, in Donaldson's judgement, part of PHSO processes and needed to be.[48]

The Review Report was published in March 2019, and its recommendations were clustered into five main themes: greater integration of clinical advisers into the casework process; better communication with those involved in a complaint, especially with complainants about the process and detail of commissioning advice; more balance in presenting evidence to ensure that appropriate weight is given to the opinions of patients and complainants on clinical events; applying a wider range of appropriate investigatory methods to counteract the cultural bias in which there is focus on the possible culpability of individual clinicians; and the appointment of a Medical Director to oversee the development of the new arrangements.[49]

PHSO has recognised the operational and cultural significance of these recommendations and taken most of them forward. They demonstrate that

[45] PHSO, 'The Ombudsman's Clinical Standard' www.ombudsman.org.uk/sites/default/files/0434_Clinical_Standards_Final.pdf.

[46] *Miller v The Health Service Commissioner for England* [2018] EWCA Civ 14, www.bailii.org/ew/cases/EWCA/Civ/2018/144.html.

[47] Donaldson (n 27) 6.

[48] ibid 9, 16.

[49] PHSO, 'Clinical Advice Review Final Report' www.ombudsman.org.uk/sites/default/files/Final_Report_Clinical_Advice_Review.pdf; PHSO, 'Our Response to the Clinical Advice Review Final Report' www.ombudsman.org.uk/sites/default/files/Our_Response_to_the_Clinical_Advice_Review.pdf.

whatever the value of creating a joined-up public service ombudsman scheme may be, there will always need to be specificity in dealing with discrete areas of public policy complaints like health. It is inconceivable for case handlers to make judgements about the exercise of clinical judgement without having access to separate and independent clinical advice, and the way this is done is a powerful contributor to perceptions of trust and the integrity of the process. This makes the investigation of health complaints different to investigations about government departments.

The ambition is to increase the quality and frequency of exchanges between clinical advisers and case handlers without losing the essence of an independent ombudsman decision. In 2019–20, a successful pilot was run in which senior caseworkers shared their provisional views on cases with clinical advisers to ensure that their advice was being reflected accurately in these reports. This has been implemented across all senior casework teams. The Office also commenced multidisciplinary meetings as recommended by the Review. These are an opportunity for colleagues with expertise in different fields (complex cases may require more than one clinical adviser) to come together to discuss cases with case handlers and test thinking early on and before provisional views are sent out.

Together, these changes integrate clinical advisers more effectively into the system. There has also been improved communication with complainants, with the publication of new information to help complainants understand the role of clinical advice from the outset of an investigation and an Office-wide project to improve report-writing skills. A pilot has also taken place to share clinical advice with complainants in advance of the dissemination of provisional views. Here, the outcome has been mixed. Not all complainants wish to see the relevant clinical advice, and those that do, despite reassurances to the contrary, can tend to assume that the upcoming decision will be clinician, not ombudsman, led.[50] This is why it is a fundamental requirement of any modern ombudsman service to be able to demonstrate that it balances evidence between complainant and body in jurisdiction, and (especially in health cases) that it considers all relevant evidence and relevant experience, not just written evidence.

As far as balancing evidence is concerned, new guidance was issued for caseworkers to ensure that all oral relevant evidence is gathered and considered, not just written evidence.[51] This means taking full account of both the complainants' and the organisation's evidence even where the evidence might be personal experience and not written down. Associated training is to follow. Donaldson also suggested that existing investigative approaches need to be reviewed to ensure serious enough consideration is given to holistic, organisational and cross-care

[50] PHSO, *Annual Report and Accounts 2019–2020* (n 41).

[51] PHSO, 'Balancing Evidence Guidance' (7 May 2020) www.ombudsman.org.uk/publications/balancing-evidence-guidance.

provider dynamics in assessing standards of care and service delivery. A project has begun to benchmark PHSO investigatory processes with comparator organisations to create a 'systems' team to pilot 'holistic' investigations with appropriate training. Necessary re-engineering of PHSO investigative procedures will follow.

VI. Engagement with Citizens and Service Users – Transparency and Outreach Work

The importance of transparency as a stimulus to professional integrity and increasing confidence in public institutions has been a key theme of the Reports of the Committee on Standards in Public Life,[52] which established openness as one of its seven principles.[53] As a former Secretary to that Committee, and a proponent of the use of transparency as a vehicle in the promotion of public trust,[54] this writer had no hesitation in placing transparency at the heart of PHSO's strategic plan for 2018–21. The building of public trust has an unmistakeable impact on operational effectiveness and reform. First, there is an emphatic pledge to publish more casework and casework statistics online. This would enable complainants, the public and bodies in jurisdiction to have a greater understanding and confidence in the role of the Ombudsman. This is particularly important where comparative research suggests that a key challenge for all ombudsman services is a lack of public understanding of what ombudsman schemes do.[55] Secondly, there was a pledge to develop the impact of PHSO insight reports, which are laid before Parliament for consideration by select committees, so that lessons from casework and systemic reviews can contribute to raising standards in public services.[56] And thirdly, a decisive aim was set out to open up PHSO as an organisation by holding annual open meetings, introducing a regular podcast, called Radio Ombudsman, and launching the Annual Ombudsman Lecture. Demystification is a key role of accountability institutions in the modern state.

Progress on developing greater transparency has been considerable, with progress in beginning to publish most senior casework decisions from spring 2021. In working towards this, increasing numbers of case summaries are now published regularly online.[57] These have included: detailed accounts of individuals failed by the Home Office in the Windrush scandal; a vulnerable adult

[52] N Martin and I Taylor, 'Survey of Public Attitudes towards Conduct in Public Life 2012' www.researchgate.net/publication/274379514_Survey_of_public_attitudes_towards_conduct_in_public_life_2012.

[53] Committee on Standards in Public Life, 'The Seven Principles of Public Life' (31 May 1995) www.gov.uk/government/publications/the-7-principles-of-public-life/the-7-principles-of-public-life-2.

[54] Behrens (n 2).

[55] Behrens (n 37).

[56] PHSO, 'Our Strategy 2018–2021' (n 38).

[57] https://decisions.ombudsman.org.uk/.

murdered by a patient on probation and under the supervision of a privately owned community rehabilitation company; the avoidable death of a six-month-old baby after multiple opportunities to diagnose and treat were missed; and parents who were instructed by their hospital trust to change their own child's tracheotomy tube in emergencies.

The publication of quarterly health statistics reports included data on the complaints investigated and summaries of cases investigated. The Office also published its first annual casework report in March 2020.[58] The report provided an in-depth annual review of parliamentary and health casework, and was shared with key stakeholders. New templates for publishing decisions were developed, and writing skills training was introduced. Workshops were also held with complainants, advocacy groups and bodies in jurisdiction to understand how they would want to use decisions when they are published.[59]

As far as systemic insight reports are concerned, even without the power of own-initiative investigation, PHSO placed significant material in the parliamentary and public domain. Landmark reports were produced on the weaknesses of mental health provision across the health service,[60] how NHS eating disorder services are failing patients,[61] the poor treatment of whistleblowers in the Health Service,[62] systemic failures in the care of young people in mental health hospitals,[63] the need for radical reform of complaint handling in frontline bodies across the health service and government departments,[64] and weaknesses in the operation of continuing healthcare.[65]

Three concrete ways of demonstrating transparency were the introduction of annual open meetings, the creation of Radio Ombudsman and the introduction of the Annual Ombudsman Lecture in partnership with leading universities.

[58] PHSO, *The Ombudsman Casework Report 2019* (HC 63, 3 March 2020) www.ombudsman.org.uk/publications/ombudsmans-casework-report-2019-0.

[59] PHSO, *Annual Report and Accounts 2019–2020* (n 41).

[60] PHSO, *Maintaining Momentum: Driving Improvements in Mental Health Care* (HC 906, 19 March 2018) www.ombudsman.org.uk/sites/default/files/page/Maintaining%20momentum-driving%20improvements%20in%20mental%20health%20care-%20Report-Final-Web-Accessible.pdf.

[61] PHSO, *Ignoring the Alarms: How NHS Eating Disorders Are Failing Patients* (HC 634, 6 December 2017) www.ombudsman.org.uk/sites/default/files/page/ACCESSIBILE%20PDF%20-%20Anorexia%20Report.pdf.

[62] PHSO, *Blowing the Whistle: An Investigation into the Care Quality Commission's Regulation of the Fit and Proper Persons Requirement* (HC 1815, 13 December 2018) www.ombudsman.org.uk/sites/default/files/page/0463_FPPR_Report_Accessible.pdf; 'Report by the Parliamentary and Health Service Ombudsman into a complaint made by Dr L' www.ombudsman.org.uk/sites/default/files/2019-07/PHSO%20FPPR%20Final%20Report%20-%2017%20July%202019_0.pdf.

[63] PHSO, *Missed Opportunities: What Lessons Can Be Learned from Failings at the North Essex Partnership University NHS Foundation Trust* (HC 2260, 11 June 2019) www.ombudsman.org.uk/sites/default/files/page/Missed_opportunities_What_lessons_can_be_learned_from_failings_at_the_North_Essex_Partnership_University_NHS_Foundation_1.pdf.

[64] PHSO, *Making Complaints Count: Supporting Complaints Handling in the NHS and UK Government Departments* (HC 390, 15 July 2020) www.ombudsman.org.uk/publications/making-complaints-count-supporting-complaints-handling-nhs-and-uk-government.

[65] PHSO, *Continuing Healthcare: Getting It Right First Time* (HC 872, 3 November 2020) https://www.ombudsman.org.uk/sites/default/files/Continuing_Healthcare_Getting_it_right_first_time.pdf.

Some of these initiatives have been impaired as a result of remote working and lockdown associated with the COVID-19 pandemic. The introduction of an annual open meeting has allowed service users, stakeholders and members of the public to listen to and question directly – through attendance or live streaming – the Ombudsman about performance over the course of the year. It also provides a platform for counterparts and stakeholders – once including the then Chair of PHSO's Parliamentary Oversight Committee, Sir Bernard Jenkin – to contextualise and comment on the work of the ombudsman institution more broadly.[66]

Radio Ombudsman has had (at the time of writing) 23 public episodes since autumn 2017, and has included interviews with complainants, regulators, leaders of advocacy groups, the former President of the UK Supreme Court and ombuds colleagues from around the world. A smaller number of episodes with PHSO colleagues have been recorded during the COVID-19 pandemic to promote cross-Office communication during challenging times. The aim of the published episodes was to explore the challenges of service delivery from a number of different perspectives, and to debate how to generate trust and improve what is looked for in resolving cases. Scott Morrish, for example, spoke frankly of his experience of the weaknesses of ombudsman investigations in the light of his five-year engagement with PHSO following the death of his three-year-old son, Sam, from a treatable condition in 2010:

> Trust has eroded so heavily in many aspects of government and authority that it is not enough now just to assure people that you're trustworthy. You actually have to demonstrate that you're trustworthy; and actually you can't do that by resorting to a process that is designed behind closed doors, that's monitored behind closed doors, that is basically beyond any form of scrutiny.
>
> Obviously, when you've watched your son die, and you know there are questions that are unanswered, it's nigh-on impossible for you – or any anybody else – to convince me that the questions that I think need answering are irrelevant. 'Process' can't address those things … you've got people, and process, and purpose. If the purpose of the Ombudsman is purely to reach a robust adjudication, that takes you down one process route. If the purpose is also to hold the systems accountable for improvement, beyond simply arriving at a judgement as to whether a complaint is valid or invalid, you have to go further, and that needs a different methodology.
>
> Now, at the moment, the Ombudsman's processes are so rigid and so inflexible that it's very hard for them to go back. It's not an iterative process, it is very much a linear process, or at least that's how it seems: 'We're going to tick this box, tick this box, tick this box, and now we've got a robust, defensible set of findings, so we're going to leave it there.' That isn't how families live.[67]

[66] PHSO, 'Meet the Ombudsman: Annual Open Meeting 2018' (22 May 2018) www.ombudsman.org.uk/open-meeting-2018; PHSO, 'Meet the Ombudsman: Annual Open Meeting 2019' (2 October 2019) www.ombudsman.org.uk/news-and-blog/events/meet-ombudsman-annual-open-meeting-2019.

[67] PHSO, 'Transcript of Radio Ombudsman #7: How Can the NHS and the PHSO Get Better at Learning from Mistakes?' www.ombudsman.org.uk/news-and-blog/podcast/transcript-radio-ombudsman-1-how-can-nhs-and-phso-get-better-learning-mistakes.

From another perspective, Claire Murdoch, NHS England's National Director for Mental Health, spoke movingly of her reaction to PHSO's publication *Ignoring the Alarms: How NHS Eating Disorder Services Are Failing Patients*:[68]

> I think the first thing to say is that, particularly with the anorexia report that you're talking about here, I've been impressed with the report. I thought it was fair. It's painful reading. These are the sorts of things that I, and probably other professionals who care passionately, feel hurt by – but not hurt in a wounded way, hurt because we probably recognise it as a really searing, independent insight to things we must fix, things we must address, things we must do better.[69]

The Annual Ombudsman Lecture has taken place twice at the London School of Economics, and one is scheduled at Manchester University. The Inaugural Lecture was subsequently published in *The Research Handbook on the Ombudsman.*[70]

Engagement with experts by experience like Scott Morrish, James Titcombe and William Powell has had a cathartic effect on PHSO colleagues. They have opened up what Michael Oakeshott called 'a conversation' with the possibilities of communication, listening and learning without a proposition to be defended or conclusions sought.[71] The engagement with Claire Murdoch and other service providers is equally important. It demonstrates for those without direct experience that service delivery is complex and challenging, and – in the health service – informed by a humanity and integrity which should not be overlooked. All of this helps to negate what Marc Hertogh has called 'the alienating experience' of ombudsman communication, which can, routinely, be arcane and legalistic. Engagement on Radio Ombudsman can add to the 'radiating effects' an ombudsman can bring to the wider population by explaining government process and its impact in accessible language.[72]

VII. Reaching Out

After 2017, PHSO once again became a full and welcomed member of the UK and international ombudsman community, participating wholeheartedly in the meetings of the International Ombudsman Institute (IOI) in Brussels, Barcelona, Belfast, Edinburgh and Nicosia. PHSO co-hosted a seminar on Ombudsman Peer

[68] PHSO, *Ignoring the Alarms: How NHS Eating Disorder Services Are Failing Patients* (HC 634, 6 December 2017) www.ombudsman.org.uk/sites/default/files/page/ACCESSIBILE%20PDF%20-%20Anorexia%20Report.pdf.

[69] PHSO, 'Transcript of Radio Ombudsman #7: Driving Improvements in Mental Health Care' www.ombudsman.org.uk/news-and-blog/podcast/transcript-radio-ombudsman-7-driving-improvements-mental-health-care.

[70] Hertogh and Kirkham (n 5) 457–73.

[71] M Oakeshott, *Rationalism in Politics and Other Essays* (London, University Paperbacks, 1967) 197–247 ('The Voice of Poetry in the Conversation of Mankind').

[72] M Hertogh, 'Why the Ombudsman Does Not Promote Public Trust in Government: Lessons from the Low Countries' (2013) 35 *Journal of Social Welfare and Family Law* 245, 249–55.

Review with the IOI in London, led the development of IOI guidance[73] on the subject, and led the peer review of the Sindic de Greuges, the Ombudsman of Catalonia, in Barcelona.[74]

All this cooperation brought home the rich tapestry of diverse ombudsman practice around the world and the central importance of the work of the Venice Commission of the Council of Europe in producing *Principles on the Protection and Promotion of the Ombudsman Institution* (the Venice Principles) in 2019. These are a recognised set of 25 shared principles to steer good ombudsman practice in upholding the independence and effectiveness of ombudsman offices throughout Europe.[75] The Venice Principles were unanimously endorsed by the United Nations General Assembly in December 2020.[76] Both international practice and the benchmarks of the Venice Principles are essential context for reforming any national ombudsman scheme. National and international exchange are not a 'fancy franchise', or sinister obeisance to transnational non-governmental organisations. Rather, they are a remedy to the bunkerism that had followed extensive criticism of PHSO before 2017, and a source of vibrant ideas and comparative thinking.

Alongside exchanges with other national and international ombudsman schemes, in the years 2018–20, PHSO staff held outreach meetings with 191 UK agencies, advocacy groups and other stakeholders. The purpose of the visits was to learn about the bodies under jurisdiction and the challenges they face, to meet service users and to promote effective working relationships with those on the frontline of complaint handling.[77]

By way of context and more specifically, PHSO pledged in its 2018–21 strategic plan to emulate the practice of sister organisations (the Scottish Public Services Ombudsman and the Independent Adjudicator for Higher Education in England and Wales) in developing a complaint standards framework for bodies in jurisdiction. *Making Complaints Count: Supporting Complaints Handling in the NHS and UK Government Departments*[78] was two years in the making and was laid before Parliament in July 2020. Its publication marked the launch of a public consultation[79] about the need for agreed complaints standards within the NHS and, eventually, more widely. The research undertaken showed a very

[73] R Behrens, 'Peer Review of the Office of the Catalonian Ombudsman' (26 June 2020) www.theioi.org/ioi-news/current-news/best-practice-paper-on-peer-review.

[74] Peer Review of the Sindic de Greuges de Catalunya (April 20200 www.ombudsman.org.uk/sites/default/files/2020-06/Peer%20review_SGC_Abril_2020.pdf.

[75] Venice Commission of the Council of Europe, *Principles on the Protection and Promotion of the Ombudsman Institution* (3 May 2019) Opinion No. 897 / 2017, www.venice.coe.int/webforms/documents/default.aspx?pdffile=CDL-AD(2019)005-e.

[76] IOI, 'United Nations Recognises Importance of Independent Ombudsman' www.theioi.org/ioi-news/current-news/united-nations-recognises-importance-of-independent-ombudsman.

[77] PHSO, *Annual Report and Accounts 2018–2019* (n 40); PHSO, *Annual Report and Accounts 2019–2020* (n 41).

[78] PHSO, *Making Complaints Count* (n 64).

[79] The survey can be found at https://phso.researchfeedback.net/s.asp?k=158013209525.

broad consensus that the complaints system in the NHS (ie frontline complaints handling) needs reform, investment and strengthening. There are three core weaknesses. First, there is no single vision for how staff are expected to handle and resolve complaints. Too many organisations provide their own view on 'good practice' and staff are left confused as to which one to follow, often leading to variable experiences for those who complain. Secondly, staff do not get consistent access to complaint-handling training to support them in what is a complex role, which should be recognised as a professional skill. When staff do get training, the quality and consistency of what is covered is variable. Thirdly, public bodies too often see complaints negatively, not as a learning tool that can be used to improve their service. This often leaves complaints staff feeling that they are not valued or supported by senior leaders in their organisation and that they lack the resources to carry out their role effectively.[80]

Despite the COVID pandemic, which severely limited the number of face-to-face meetings and visits to bodies in jurisdiction, research in advance of the public consultation was interactive and focused on service users and stakeholders. Interviews were conducted with senior staff and frontline complaint handlers in the NHS and government departments, and with patient advice liaison services, GP practice managers and medical defence organisations. Advice and advocacy organisations were also interviewed to capture their views of the impact of frontline complaint handling on the complainants they represented and what factors contribute to negative experiences. These interviews took place between May and December 2019. The emphasis was emphatically inclusive, with extensive engagement and support from the public, advocacy groups, regulators and stakeholders.[81]

The resulting Complaint Standards were launched at the end of March 2021, with pilots planned throughout England. The Standards aim to make sure that: senior leaders of health services promote a learning and improvement culture in their organisation, investing in their staff so that they can learn from complaints and make improvements; organisations train staff to seek feedback from service users, and ensure people can provide feedback easily, with issues resolved in an open and responsive way; staff are trained to carry out a detailed look into complaints that is thorough, empathetic, objective, evidenced-based and supportive of those who make a complaint and staff who are subject to a complaint; and staff provide clear and accountable decisions based on the facts, and are empowered to put things right when mistakes are identified.[82] Having learned from the pilot phase and met the concerns of stakeholders, the Standards will be incorporated into PHSO decision-making.

[80] PHSO, *Making Complaints Count* (n 64).

[81] PHSO, 'Report on Complaint Standards Consultation' 24 March 2021, www.ombudsman.org.uk/publications/report-complaint-standards-consultation.

[82] PHSO, 'NHS Complaint Standards: Summary of Expectations' (Pilot Spring 2021) https://www.ombudsman.org.uk/sites/default/files/NHS_Complaint_Standards_Summary_of_expectations_Spring_2021_A.pdf.

VIII. Towards a New Quality Standard

The focus on service delivery had conceptual as well as practical dimensions. In terms of conceptual development, as already stated, one precious element of inheritance was the Service Charter of 2016, containing commitments which were regularly tested against independently tested opinions of PHSO's service users. To have this data, consisting of the opinions of 4000 service users annually, was, in comparative terms, impressive, given that very few other public service ombudsman schemes either had a Service Charter or were able to test it regularly against service user opinion.

Nevertheless, the organisation set about bolstering the utility of the data by supplementing it with systematic parallel scores for the opinions of bodies in jurisdiction who had been complained against. In addition, encouraged by the Select Committee on Public Administration and Constitutional Affairs (PACAC) in successive annual scrutinies, greater focus was given in the surveys on whether or not service users had experienced PHSO as an 'impartial' service notwithstanding the outcome of the complaint. The testing of user opinion already interrogated whether 'We listen carefully to complainants and the organisations we investigate and we make impartial and fair decisions based on relevant evidence'.[83] An independent research company carried out focus groups and a number of in-depth interviews on this issue with complainants who had recently used PHSO service.[84] The research concluded that PHSO should combine the feedback already received from complainants and organisations on a number of key Charter commitments that directly relate to impartiality and fairness. This combined total would provide a single, well-rounded score on whether PHSO demonstrated it acted impartially. These conclusions have now been accepted and adopted.[85]

These developments were not individual initiatives, but part of a wider attempt to construct a quality strategy which informs a balanced scorecard approach to effectiveness and efficiency. The key variables measured are Timeliness, Resource Planning (productivity), Service Charter Scores and Quality. How to measure these variables, particularly Quality, has been for ombudsman officers around the world, and in the words of one of the current editors of this volume, 'a riddle,

[83] PHSO, 'Our Vision and Values', www.ombudsman.org.uk/about-us/who-we-are/our-vision-and-values.

[84] PHSO, 'Complainant Feedback: Charter Commitment 10' (March 2020) www.ombudsman.org.uk/sites/default/files/ORS_Summary_Report_on_Impartiality_March_2020.pdf.

[85] PHSO, 'Research into Fairness and Impartiality' www.ombudsman.org.uk/about-us/corporate-information/how-we-are-performing/performance-against-our-service-charter/research-fairness-and-impartiality. In future, PHSO will combine the scores on the following commitments: '5. We will listen to you to make sure we understand your complaint; 8. We will gather all the information we need, including from you and the organisation you have complained about before we make our decision; 9. We will share facts with you, and discuss with you what we are seeing; 11. We will explain our decision and recommendations, and how we reached them.'

wrapped in a mystery inside an enigma'.[86] In an attempt to unwrap this enigma, PHSO invested heavily in a quality programme, developed by a new PHSO Quality Team and overseen by a Quality Committee of PHSO's oversight board.

There are a number of features to this programme. First is the research and adoption of Quality Standards to benchmark casework. These standards replace the former reliance on the measurement of process assurance, where the integrity of the process rather than the quality of a decision was measured. Secondly, in addition to casework manager assessment of individual cases before dissemination, there is now quality assurance of the work of casework and operations managers by the Quality Team. This is supplemented with the participation of the Deputy Ombudsman and Chair of the Quality Committee. The outcome of this assurance is a RAG rating of how Quality Standards have been applied in individual cases, and feedback, coaching and training for casework managers and caseworkers in light of the outcome of the assurance. The use of the Quality Standards is designed to ensure that: equal account is taken of the views of complainants and organisations investigated; that evidence has been evaluated rigorously to make an impartial decision; that legal and clinical advice, where sought, has been appropriately applied; and that clear rationales are given for decisions made. All of this is culturally important in terms of persistent suggestions of an over-reliance on process. The outcome of the application of the Quality Standards will be published on a quarterly basis starting in late 2021. The initiative adds normative assessment of work produced to supplement the strongly felt and expressed assessments already derived from user views of how their complaints are handled.[87]

IX. Accountability

After 2017, the renaissance of PHSO was overseen in the annual scrutiny by the Public Administration and Constitutional Affairs Committee of the House of Commons:

> The Ombudsman is independent of the Government, the NHS and Parliament. The postholder is accountable to Parliament, through the Public Administration and Constitutional Affairs Committee (PACAC), for the overall performance of the PHSO and for its use of resources. This has traditionally been through an annual evidence session based on the PHSO annual report and accounts. PACAC does not inquire into individual cases. However, the Ombudsman can lay reports before Parliament, often to highlight cases that he decides raise issues of wider concern, which the Committee

[86] A Stuhmcke, IOI Conference Wellington, 2012 – quote attributed to Justice Michael Kirby file:///C:/Users/RB%20Media%20PC/Downloads/Wellington%20Conference_27.%20Working%20Session%20F_Anita%20Stuhmcke%20Paper%20(8).pdf.

[87] J Bradshaw, 'A Taxonomy of Social Need' in G McLachlan (ed), *Problems and Progress in Medical Care*, 7th series (Oxford University Press, 1972).

(or another select committee) may then scrutinise. An example published during 2017/18 was Ignoring the Alarms: How NHS eating disorder services are failing patients, that was laid before Parliament on 8 December 2017.[88]

While small amounts of myopic, error-prone and voluble armchair speculation on social media, mostly from former complainants, chastised PHSO for its alleged lack of accountability and use of benchmarks from 'transnational non-governmental organisations',[89] the lived experience of being Ombudsman and Accounting Officer was somewhat different. PHSO accounts must be signed off by the Comptroller and Auditor-General at the National Audit Office (NAO), and two qualifications in the 2014–15 accounts unleashed unremitting oversight by NAO and its senior representative sitting permanently on the PHSO Audit Committee.

Of course, the Select Committee scrutiny did not address the outcome of individual cases, but the questioning was often adversarial and always well informed and intense. There was agreement with the Select Committee that a small number of long-standing, unresolved cases – the most serious of which involved the circumstances surrounding the death of Robbie Powell 30 years ago – that were no longer within the remit of PHSO would benefit from independent reviews sponsored by relevant government departments.[90] The government explained that it was considering possible approaches before determining the next steps. Nothing has subsequently appeared.[91]

Additionally, and at the invitation of the Select Committee, PHSO submitted itself to a groundbreaking Ombudsman Peer Review in 2018. This was led by Peter Tyndall, Ombudsman for Ireland and at the time President of the IOI. Following a review of all relevant documents, a two-day visit to the PHSO's Manchester office and unrestricted access to and private meetings with staff, the report concluded:

> In recent years, the Parliamentary and Health Service Ombudsman (PHSO) has faced organisational crisis. Issues affecting its previous leadership also resulted in a loss of trust in the PHSO. To use a medical metaphor familiar from the Ombudsman's casework, this report concludes that, under its current leadership, the organisation is

[88] PHSO, *Annual Scrutiny 2017/18: Towards a Modern and Effective Ombudsman Service* (HC 1855, 19 March 2019) para 4, https://publications.parliament.uk/pa/cm201719/cmselect/cmpubadm/1855/1855.pdf.

[89] B Newsome, 'Healthcare Needs an Ombudsman' *The Critic* (8 August 2020) https://thecritic.co.uk/healthcare-needs-an-ombudsman/.

[90] 'We agree that the PHSO is not the correct body to carry out inquiries into historic cases. However, there remains a need for them to be addressed, both in the interests of the families involved and in ensuring that any safety lessons that can still be learnt are. We therefore endorse and repeat our predecessor Committee's recommendation; that the Department of Health and Social Care should develop a proportionate, time limited, mechanism to independently investigate and address those cases where legitimate questions or grievances remain': PHSO, *Annual Scrutiny 2016–17* (HC 492, 17 April 2018) https://publications.parliament.uk/pa/cm201719/cmselect/cmpubadm/492/492.pdf.

[91] House of Commons Public Administration and Constitutional Affairs Committee PHSO, *Annual Scrutiny 2016–17: Government Special Report of Session 2017–19* Ordered by the House of Commons to be printed 24 July 2018, Appendix 1. https://publications.parliament.uk/pa/cm201719/cmselect/cmpubadm/1479/1479.pdf.

> moving out of 'critical care' and into 'recovery'. Overall, from facing a set of severe challenges, the organisation is on its way to becoming an efficient and effective modern ombudsman service, which provides significant value for its stakeholders … The PHSO's current senior leadership team is a significant strength of the organisation. The panel were impressed by the strong direction provided by senior leaders and the bold steps they had taken as part of their transformation programme. This included the development of a clear strategy and a holistic, cross-organisational approach to improving the structures and processes needed to deliver on that strategy. In the context of significant pressures and historical problems, the panel considered that the PHSO was now laying strong foundations for the future efficiency and effectiveness of the organisation. The panel was confident that, if current progress was maintained, the PHSO's transformation programme would be successfully implemented.[92]

There were, however, some areas that the panel considered could be improved. These included: the need to retain specialist and expert knowledge in the context of moving to a generalist casework model; the inefficiency caused by the (then) current case management system and the need to ensure that the IT strategy was sufficiently forward looking; and the current level of manager-sign off on decisions, which was likely to prove inefficient in the longer term and would need to be revised once the organisation stabilised.[93]

The panel also noted that in terms of remit and jurisdiction, PHSO was operating within statutory constraints that limited its potential to deliver greater value in the future. Ombudsman reform in this area had already been debated significantly, but should include: removal of the MP filter; development of a more integrated jurisdiction (to create one public service ombudsman); a more flexible statutory scheme for casework and reporting; own-initiative powers of investigation; and a Complaints Standards Authority function.[94] A key point here is that the reform and effective operation of even an independent public body is not wholly dependent on those who run the organisation, but depends upon the provision of an effective mandate from government and Parliament.

Members of the Peer Review Panel were called before the PACAC Select Committee, which endorsed its conclusions.

> Based on the evidence they presented we accept the Peer Review Panel's conclusion that the PHSO is 'moving out of critical care and into recovery', and that it is 'on its way to becoming an efficient and effective modern ombudsman service, which provides significant value for its stakeholders'.[95]

PHSO addressed the areas for improvement, invested heavily in IT infrastructure, launched a new casework management system and created new specialist teams dealing with continuing healthcare and with parliamentary complaints.

[92] Tyndall et al (n 6).
[93] ibid para 10.4.
[94] ibid.
[95] PHSO *Annual Scrutiny 2017/18* (n 88).

X. Discussion

Ultimately, the salient questions about the UK's ombudsman 'system' after 2017 are 'Did anything get better and for whom?', 'How did the scheme manage through the COVID-19 pandemic?' and 'What remains to be done?' The danger of projects of this kind is that the practitioner ombudsman insists that she or he is 'right about everything'[96] and covers reality with a rosy glow. A very small but vocal minority of disaffected complainants used social media to argue that nothing changed after 2017, that PHSO remained 'unaccountable' and 'corrupt' and that its staff had 'trousered public money', displayed misconduct in public office, and lied and dissembled. No reputable public body has countenanced these allegations.

There is valuable literature about the importance of empathising with, listening to and respecting complainants,[97] some of whom have had their anger fuelled by bereavement and grief. But this does not remove the genuine dilemma of whether or not to cease exchanges with abusive complainants at some point in order to protect the integrity and security of the colleagues who work with and for the Ombudsman. All cases are different, and have to be judged individually and in the context of well-advertised organisational policy. However, in the words of Thuli Madonsella, exemplary Public Protector in South Africa, 'Being treated badly is not an excuse for behaving badly'.[98] The appropriate organisational behaviour, as set out by Chris Gill and Carolyn Hirst, contemplates the ultimate use of decisive action of the kind adopted by PHSO:

> We also recognise that the actions of complainants who are angry, demanding or persistent may result in behaviour towards our staff which is, or is experienced as being, unacceptable. We will, therefore, apply the relevant organisational policies and procedures … to protect staff who are complained about from unacceptable behaviour such as unreasonable persistence, threats or offensive behaviour including discrimination.[99]

There is no substance to the suggestion that nothing has changed, but that is not to be confused with a claim that PHSO, in one great leap forward, became an exemplary ombudsman service. It didn't, though the journey towards that goal took significant steps, notwithstanding the unprecedented disruptions of the COVID-19 pandemic, which took PHSO down a road 'less travelled'.[100]

[96] L Kolakowski, *Is God Happy? Selected Essays* (London, Penguin Classics, 2012) 115–40 ('My Correct Views on Everything: A Rejoinder to EP Thompson').

[97] See, eg C Gill and C Hirst, *Being Complained About: Good Practice Principles and Guidelines* (Hirstworks, 2019) https://eprints.gla.ac.uk/222770/7/222770.pdf.

[98] Thuli Madonsella, Twitter, 15 November 2017. See T Gqubule, *No Longer Whispering to Power: The Story of Thuli Madonsela* (Jonathan Ball Publishers, 2017) for an account of how Madonsela spoke 'truth unto power' and challenged corrupt practices during Jacob Zuma's presidency.

[99] Gill and Hirst (n 97) 5.

[100] This well known phrase is taken from R Frost, *The Road not Taken* (1916) www.poetryfoundation.org/poems/44272/the-road-not-taken.

On the positive side, staff morale recovered as they bought into the challenge of engaging with complainants. In 2019, 85 per cent of colleagues understood the aims and objectives of PHSO, compared to 49 per cent in 2016.[101] The 'Engagement Index' (commitment to and appreciation of the organisation) stood at 65 per cent, compared to 52 per cent in 2016.[102] Significantly, this improvement was maintained during the pandemic lockdown. In a confidential survey conducted in October 2020, the clear understanding of PHSO's objectives remained at 85 per cent. The staff 'Engagement Index' rose again to 66 per cent, 82 per cent of colleagues believed that the Ombudsman and CEO had 'a clear vision' for the future of PHSO (compared to 77 per cent in 2019) and 87 per cent of staff believed that the Ombudsman and CEO were sufficiently visible. The acceleration of professional development opportunities, including policy and skills development in effective communication, empathetic approaches, conflict resolution and investigation, was warmly welcomed. In 2020, 55 per cent of staff reported that this activity would help them develop their career, whether at PHSO or elsewhere.

The insistence that PHSO become a learning organisation with a more open and democratic culture in which mistakes were issues for corporate learning not individual blame constituted something of a cultural transformation. Here, the publication of a report into the poor handling of a case involving an avoidable death was reviewed from the perspective of learning from mistakes.[103] James Titcombe, no stranger to the inadequacies of ombudsman complaint handling and now a member of the recently constituted Expert Advisory Panel, wrote:

> Today's report is a candid account of how PHSO got a number of these aspects significantly wrong, and the consequences this had on the family involved … As is too often the case, it is only because of the extraordinary efforts of the complainant to persevere through a sometimes very challenging and complex complaints process that serious failures were eventually identified … Today's report details several changes that have been made by PHSO in recent years. These measures include: new processes to ensure consistent allocation of caseworkers; a new casework management system; a training and accreditation framework for caseworkers; improved data governance; communications training for staff; updated policies and guidance on how evidence from organisations and complainants should be equally considered. I am pleased to learn that the Ombudsman is currently piloting a new approach that gives complainants the opportunity to see clinical advice and have a meaningful discussion about it with their caseworker.[104]

[101] www.ombudsman.org.uk/sites/default/files/PHSO_Staff_survey_2019.pdf.

[102] ibid.

[103] PHSO, 'Report of a Review into PHSO's Handling of Mr Nic Hart's Case from August 2014 to December 2017' (9 January 2020) www.ombudsman.org.uk/publications/report-review-phsos-handling-mr-nic-harts-case-august-2014-december-2017.

[104] J Titcombe, 'Learning from Mistakes: An Open and Honest Review of Failings in Handling a Serious Complaint' (9 January 2020) www.ombudsman.org.uk/news-and-blog/blog/learning-mistakes-open-and-honest-review-failings-handling-serious-complaint.

Most key performance indicators have been met in terms of the timing of case closures, the central elements of the strategic plan being implemented and stakeholder relationships being significantly repaired. What have been slower to change are the scores relating to complainant experience at PHSO. These essentially flatlined after 2017. The balanced judgement of the Patients Association – once a severe critic of PHSO – is worth noting:

> PHSO's performance certainly doesn't seem to have deteriorated, which is arguably quite impressive of itself given the extent of the organisational change it has undergone during this period. Its own Service Charter data shows a mix of modest improvement, overall flatlining and slight deterioration, depending on the measure in question. Those where there has been progress outnumber those where things have got worse. But, just as there has been no drastic decline in PHSO's performance, there has not been a step-change improvement either. As PHSO's changes start to be more widely felt, we would hope to see clear evidence that patients' and complainants' experiences of the services are indeed improving as a result.[105]

The PACAC Select Committee was in broad agreement. The Committee would be 'particularly interested in the PHSO's changes to its commissioning and handling of clinical advice, and whether these changes improve feedback from those who use the Ombudsman'.[106]

In terms of ombudsman engagement with complainants, a connected structural issue concerned the remit of PHSO and its governing legislation. In a coruscating foreword to *A Manifesto for Ombudsman Reform*, Jim Martin, former Scottish Public Services Ombudsman, wrote that

> Politicians, academics, and it must also be said practitioners … have whiled away the 2000s tinkering with the old, broken system while any serious consideration of a new Ombudsman model and new ways of working were rarely considered … Grey sky thinking has bedevilled the debate.[107]

This is emphatically true, and in the face of existential state crises over Brexit and the COVID-19 pandemic, immediate prospects for wholesale ombudsman reform have disappeared. The case for an ombudsman service needing fundamental reform has been articulated on very many occasions,[108] none more clearly than by the Public Administration Select Committee. For example, in its 2014 report, *Time for a People's Ombudsman Service*, it said:

> The restrictive legislation governing the Parliamentary and Health Service Ombudsman (PHSO) means it is unable to meet the standard set by Scotland, Wales, Northern

[105] Patient's Association (26 May 2020) www.patients-association.org.uk/Blog/phso-the-facts-and-evidence.

[106] PACAC (3 July 2020) https://publications.parliament.uk/pa/cm5801/cmselect/cmpubadm/117/11703.htm.

[107] R Kirkham and C Gill (eds), *A Manifesto for Ombudsman Reform* (Palgrave Macmillan, 2020).

[108] National Audit Office, *Citizen Redress; What Citizens Can Do if Things Go Wrong in the Public Services* (HC 2004–05, 21); Law Commission, *Public Services Ombudsmen* (Law Com No 329, 2011); R Gordon, *Better to Serve the Public: Proposals to Restructure, Reform, Renew and Reinvigorate Public Service Ombudsmen* (Cabinet Office, 2014).

Figure 6 Service charter scores: 2016–20

Giving you the information you need	Annual scores			
Commitment	**2016-17**	**2017-18**	**2018-19**	**2019-20**
1. We will explain our role and what we can and cannot do	79%	78%	79%	79%
2. We will explain how we handle complaints and what information we need from you	81%	79%	80%	79%
3. We will direct you to someone who can help with your complaint if we are unable to, where possible	68%	85%	78%	72%
4. We will keep you regularly updated on our progress with your complaint	74%	75%	81%	79%
Overall section score	**76%**	**80%**	**79%**	**77%**

Following a fair and open process	Annual scores			
Commitment	**2016-17**	**2017-18**	**2018-19**	**2019-20**
5. We will listen to you to make sure we understand your complaint	68%	70%	73%	72%
6. We will explain the specific concerns we will be looking into	81%	84%	88%	87%
7. We will explain how we will do our work	73%	71%	77%	77%
8. We will gather all the information we need, including from you and the organisation you have complained about, before we make our decision	43%	45%	48%	51%
9. We will share facts with you, and discuss with you what we are seeing	65%	62%	68%	70%
10. We will evaluate the information we've gathered and make an impartial decision on your complaint	-	-	-	-
11. We will explain our decision and recommendations, and how we reached them	59%	58%	53%	47%
Overall section score	**65%***	**65%***	**68%***	**67%**

Following a fair and open process	Annual scores			
Commitment	**2016-17**	**2017-18**	**2018-19**	**2019-20**
12. We will treat you with courtesy and respect	89%	88%	90%	89%
13. We will give you a final decision on your complaint as soon as we can	55%	53%	53%	50%
14. We will make sure our service is easily accessible to you and give you support and help if you need it	61%	61%	67%	65%
Overall section score	**69%**	**67%**	**70%**	**68%**

* this score has been amended to ensure comparable scoring methodologies are used throughout

Ireland and elsewhere. An ineffective instrument of democratic accountability cannot remedy failures in public service delivery. PHSO is impeded by out-of-date legislation so it fails to meet the expectations of today's citizens. It is, as Scotland's Public Service Ombudsman put it, in danger of being 'stuck in time'. The UK needs new legislation. The Ombudsman should be seen as a People's Ombudsman service as well as Parliament's Ombudsman.[109]

[109] House of Commons Public Administration Select Committee (PASC), *Time for a People's Ombudsman Service* (HC 2013–14, 655) para 45, https://publications.parliament.uk/pa/cm201314/cmselect/cmpubadm/655/655.pdf.

Reform would address a number of key blocks on engagement with citizens. These included 'the iniquitous restriction on citizens' direct and open access to PHSO, known as the "MP filter"', which 'must be abolished, as is already the case in respect of NHS complaints'. The Ombudsman should have 'own-initiative' powers to investigate areas of concern without having first to receive a complaint. There should be 'the creation of a single public services ombudsman for England' and it should be 'a distinctive ombudsman service for UK non-devolved matters'. And Parliament should strengthen the accountability of PHSO, so that departmental select committees could make greater use of the intelligence gathered by the PHSO to hold government to account.[110]

What emerged from this persistent and evidence-based policy engagement was the doomed Draft Public Service Ombudsman Bill of December 2016.[111] In the wake of a veto by a single senior cabinet minister,[112] this Bill was shorn of the radical proposal to give the Ombudsman 'own-initiative' powers, crucial for addressing the concerns of hard-to-reach vulnerable and disadvantaged groups. In any event, the Draft Bill went nowhere in the face of the Referendum on whether the UK should leave the European Union and the subsequent anguish over withdrawal.

While PHSO and, indeed, the wider Public Service Ombudsman Group of the Ombudsman Association returned again and again to the imperative of ombudsman reform, this did not distract practitioners from the daily toil of seeking better engagement within existing arrangements. We worked hard to escape the political climate of very cautious incrementalism on crucial aspects of administrative justice questions. We did this through engagement with academics, international counterparts, the Venice Principles and interested stakeholders. Some of us were also spurred on by a drive towards a more professional operation in which (ultimately) an ombudsman would be seen as part of a profession.

The engagement with ombudsman academics was rich and meaningful. Conversations took place through (for example) the Ombudsman Association and the Administrative Justice Council. Academics rose to the practitioner challenge that the 2016 reform proposal failed not only because of the legislative logjam caused by Brexit, but by the lack of hard evidence to support the need for reform. What began as a roundtable on legislative reform in 2019 developed into a stimulating book of readings edited by Richard Kirkham and Chris Gill, *A Manifesto for Ombudsman Reform*.[113] In this, Chris Gill wrote powerful chapters on the value of own-initiative and Complaint Standards Authority powers. Nick O'Brien set out what he called a 'demos prudential future' for the ombudsman institution resting on 'a democratic suite of preferences: for democratic participation, for community engagement with the practice of human rights principles

[110] ibid.

[111] Draft Public Service Ombudsman Bill, presented to Parliament by the Parliamentary Secretary, Cabinet Office by Command of Her Majesty December 2016.

[112] Personal information.

[113] Kirkham and Gill (n 106).

and for deliberative decision-making'.[114] O'Brien pointed out there were 'already elements' of PHSO practice that 'presage a demos prudential future':

> Some of those elements are acknowledged in [the Peer Review] Value for Money: the development of outreach work through initiatives such as Radio Ombudsman; the increased transparency of outcomes and communication more generally; the purposeful publication of special thematic reports on issues such as mental health, sepsis and the treatment of eating disorders ...[115]

Naomi Creutzfeld, who has written on the cultural dimension of managing user expectations across national borders,[116] wrote with clarity about the challenges of procedural fairness, managing complainant expectations and the importance of looking to the interest of ombudsman staff as well as service users when 'things go wrong'.[117]

Reaching outside the UK, PHSO entered into a partnership with the IOI, assisted by Glasgow University, to conduct a survey of national ombudsman schemes and associated leadership challenges. With 53 returns from 38 countries across the world, the four biggest challenges were perceived to be: the public's lack of knowledge and understanding of the ombudsman's role; a lack of appropriate resources; disruption from national or international crises; and meeting expectations of complainants and service users.[118] Each of these four challenges is directly relevant to ombudsman experience in the UK, and has a link to engagement with service users. Three emerging themes are worth noting. First, the survey brought home the pioneering work being undertaken in Europe – in the Netherlands, Catalonia and Greece, for example – to use outreach work to connect with communities that might not ordinarily complain. Secondly, the importance of the disruption of national or international crises has been emphasised by the COVID-19 pandemic, which has spread across the world. All national ombudsman schemes were, of course, affected by the development of the pandemic.

This was particularly the case for PHSO, since the majority of complaints handled derive from complaints about the NHS. When the NHS went into crisis management mode, PHSO, like most public services in the UK, moved to remote working. Contingency planning for exceptional circumstances had been triggered by the close proximity of PHSO offices to the Manchester Arena, which was bombed in May 2017. As a result, the move to remote working at the beginning of 2020 and the necessary IT support were approached in good order. In response to the emergency measures taken by hospitals to deal with the COVID-19 emergency,

[114] N O'Brien, 'The Public Services Ombud and the Claims of Democracy' in Kirkham and Gill (n 106) 50–51.

[115] ibid 51.

[116] N Creutzfeld, *Ombudsmen and ADR: A Comparative Study of Informal Justice in Europe* (Palgrave Macmillan, 2018).

[117] N Creutzfeldt, 'Managing Complaints: Focusing on Users and Non-users of the System' in Kirkham and Gill (n 106) 109–25.

[118] Behrens (n 37).

Figure 7 Leadership challenges facing ombudsman offices

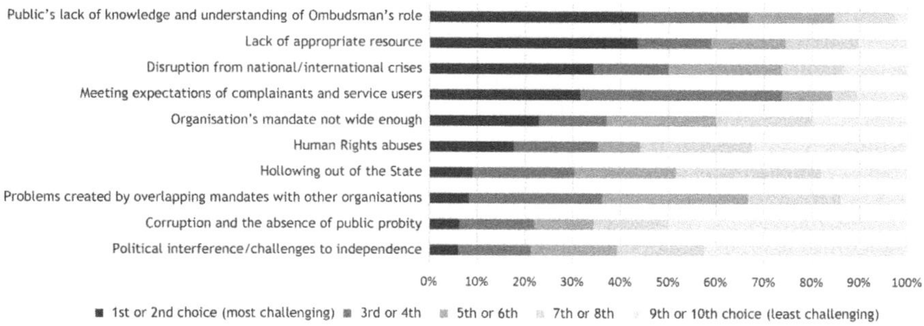

PHSO paused investigations into health service complaints between the end of March and the beginning of July 2020. The telephone inquiry lines were kept open throughout and complainants were advised of the pause either by telephone or email (according to their choice). While this situation delayed case resolution and ruled out direct personal contact at either the home of the complainant or PHSO offices, the response was overwhelmingly understanding.

The duration of the pandemic had a significant impact on PHSO operations. Case handling continued to be impaired even after the resumption of health investigations in July 2020. While morale was maintained, remote working and hospitals in crisis continued to limit the capacity of bodies in jurisdiction to participate in investigations in timely fashion. This, combined with emerging childcare needs, stress and sickness associated with prolonged lockdown, diminished productivity and led to a growth in unallocated complaints at the beginning of 2021. As a result, PHSO was forced into prioritising more serious complaints and managing user expectations in the handling of an unavoidable backlog.

Thirdly, the survey brings home again a point made by the independent peer review of PHSO in 2018 – that PHSO is an outlier in terms of its European national ombudsman counterparts, not only in terms of its outdated governing legislation, but also in its focus on health service complaints:

> Internationally, healthcare is an unusual jurisdiction for a public services ombudsman, as a result of many countries having mixed (rather than public) systems of healthcare provision or because specialist remedies are provided for complaints in the health context. The healthcare jurisdiction is also distinctive in the sense that it allows for the review of substantive clinical judgment, whereas UK public ombudsman offices are generally restricted to looking at matters of maladministration or service failure.[119]

Beyond health service complaints and looking at complaints about government departments, PHSO's ambition to engage more directly with citizens is hampered by the MP filter, which requires complainants to go to their MP before bringing complaints to the Ombudsman. This undoubtedly had an effect on the relatively

[119] Tyndall et al (n 6) 10.

small numbers of complaints about the Windrush scandal and the 'hostile environment' applied by the Home Office to British citizens of Caribbean origin suspected of not having 'leave to remain' in the UK.[120] And any ombudsman reform legislation will need to consider carefully Sir Liam Donaldson's expressed concerns about two aspects of the health remit: that the removal of a second-tier handling mechanism of health complaints in 2009 and passing them to PHSO overloaded the Ombudsman's capacity.

Of course, an ombudsman's life without specific goals and aims is unthinkable. One of the lessons of recent PHSO history is that however good strategic thinking and planning has been, it serves no good purpose unless it is implemented effectively.[121] Another is that however hard trust is to establish, it is even harder to re-establish it after it has broken down. Nevertheless, in accounting for the progress of PHSO reform and revival since 2017, there is room for reflecting on unanticipated developments which charted 'the road less travelled'.

One was the insistence, throughout the job competition in 2016 and early 2017, that whoever was appointed as Ombudsman would be the last of 10 PHSO officers and that the role required a short 'caretaker' function to oversee the transition into the planned-for Public Services Ombudsman. More important, no colleague in the IOI, or anywhere else, anticipated the COVID-19 pandemic or its profound impact on ombudsman operations. The COVID pandemic placed a premium on staff morale in working remotely, on the imagination of ombudsman schemes continuing to reach out to citizens and service users without meeting them in person, on the role ombudsman offices would play in the essential learning exercises required following the pandemic,[122] and on what Peter Tyndall has called the necessary 'visible leadership' of ombudsman colleagues.

What sustained this ombudsman was three things. First, the zeal, solidarity, support and comradeship of colleagues within PHSO, around the UK and throughout the world through dark times. Second was the abiding conviction that whatever the institutional structure of the national ombudsman office, a key ingredient of effective transformation must be the steps towards turning the ombudsman office into the summit of a profession, not a gift to the 'Great and the Good'.[123] The revitalisation of training and development and the introduction of accreditation for caseworkers were early but necessary steps along that path.

Finally, the personal engagement with patients and complainants and service users in myriad settings across the country – in small villages, the House of Commons,

[120] A Gentleman, *The Windrush Betrayal: Exposing the Hostile Environment* (Guardian Faber, 2019)

[121] Only 11% of staff subscribed to the view that 'Changes here are well managed' in 2016. D Ivey, 'Employee Survey: Presentation of Results to Staff, November 2016' (PHSO, November 2016) www.ombudsman.org.uk/sites/default/files/PHSO_staff_survey_2016_presentation_final.pdf.

[122] Behrens, Letter to the Chancellor, 19 May 2020, www.ombudsman.org.uk/sites/default/files/Rob%20Behrens%20to%20Michael%20Gove%20Duchy%20of%20Lancaster%20re%20covid%20lessons%20learnt.pdf.

[123] Behrens (n 39).

hospital trusts, Millbank Tower, rural Durham – brought home the integrity of the overwhelming majority of people who need the ombudsman service, the privilege of serving and the huge job that remains. By way of illustration, I conclude with the following exchange in a Mental Health Hospital in Sussex, early one morning:

> Patient: Are you a lawyer?
>
> Ombudsman: No. Why do you think that I am?
>
> Patient: No one comes here at 8am in the morning in a suit and tie unless they are a lawyer.
>
> Ombudsman. Actually, I am the Ombudsman.
>
> Patient: What the hell is that?

There is much to be done.

11

Ombudsman and Counter-democracy: Gas Quakes in the Netherlands and the Democratic Role of the National Ombudsman

MARC HERTOGH

I. Introduction[1]

On a quiet Wednesday morning on 22 May 2019 at around 5:45 am, the small Dutch village of Westerwijtwerd was hit by a major earthquake.[2] The quake had a magnitude of 3.4 on the Richter scale and was felt by many people across the province of Groningen, in the northeast corner of the Netherlands. Like most previous tremors, this quake was caused by gas production in the area.[3] Groningen has one of the world's largest natural gas fields. For many years, this has been one the major building blocks of the Dutch economy. The Groningen gas field is owned by a joint venture of Royal Dutch Shell and Exxon Mobil called NAM (Nederlandse Aardolie Maatschappij). Decisions about gas extraction are made between NAM and EBN (Energie Beheer Nederland), a state-owned company. The Dutch government is financially involved in gas extraction via EBN. The annual income from domestic use and export of gas to the national budget is around €5.7 billion.[4]

[1] Unless indicated otherwise, all quotations from newspapers, ombudsman reports and other sources were translated from Dutch into English by the author.

[2] S Osborne, 'Groningen Earthquake: Dutch Province Hit by Tremor Blamed on Decades of Gas Extraction' *The Independent* (22 May 2019) www.independent.co.uk/news/world/europe/groningen-earthquake-today-netherlands-gas-extraction-fracking-a8924846.html.

[3] P Buis, 'Dutch Houses Shiver Amid Gas-Field Quakes' *Wall Street Journal* (27 March 2013) www.wsj.com/articles/SB10001424127887323501004578386622459462656.

[4] G Perlaviciute, L Steg, EJ Hoekstra and L Vrieling, 'Perceived Risks, Emotions, and Policy Preferences: A Longitudinal Survey among the Local Population on Gas Quakes in the Netherlands' (2017) 29 *Energy Research & Social Science* 1.

Since 1991, the process of gas extraction has triggered almost 1400 seismic events. More recently, their magnitude and frequency have been increasing.[5] Although these earthquakes have not yet caused any casualties; they have damaged many houses and other buildings.

Thousands of people have filed property-damage claims against NAM. The gas firm does not contest that its activity is the cause of the quakes, and says it will compensate owners for all property damage. However, even after several years, most residents have still not received their money. This has left many of them angry and confused. As one observer has noted, 'most people are not afraid that their roof will collapse. [But] they're mostly frustrated because they don't know how to get on with their lives.'[6] There is also a general feeling that the government is not really interested in their problems and does not do enough to help them. As a result, public trust in public authorities is low. Or, as one resident puts it: 'I no longer believe in help from the government; money is clearly more important than the well-being of the people of Groningen.'[7]

What role can ombudsmen play in cases like these? Most ombudsman studies focus on the ombudsman's role as a complaint handler. In these studies, the institution is primarily conceived as an important tool for individual dispute resolution. Yet, in addition to this 'legalistic' role, the ombudsman also has an important 'democratic' role. Ever since the development of the institution in Sweden and Denmark, the position of the classical ombudsman has been closely connected with Parliament, and one of the aims of the institution is to strengthen electoral democracy. According to the French historian and philosopher Pierre Rosanvallon, however, this conventional approach to democracy is too narrow. In his view, for democratic systems to be stable (especially with the erosion of citizens' confidence in political leaders and public institutions), there also need to be powers of 'oversight' as a credible way of organising mistrust. He calls this *counter-democracy*.[8] This is not the opposite of democracy, but rather a form of democracy that complements the usual electoral-representative system. According to Rosanvallon, the ombudsman is one of the powers of oversight which can help citizens hold the executive accountable between elections.

This chapter will explore the 'counter-democratic' role of the (public sector) ombudsman. To analyse this in greater detail, I will use an empirical case study which focuses on the role of the Dutch National Ombudsman in the aftermath of the gas field earthquakes in the Netherlands. First, I will briefly discuss the

[5] A Raval, 'Dutch Residents Lose Patience after Years of Tremors. Calls to Halt Groningen Gas Production as Frequency and Magnitude of Quakes Increase' *Financial Times* (15 February 2018) www.ft.com/content/ab953430-10a6-11e8-940e-08320fc2a277.

[6] M Middel, 'Rutte op bezoek in Groningse sloopwijk: "We zijn in een hel terechtgekomen"' *NRC* (11 March 2020) www.nrc.nl/nieuws/2020/03/11/rutte-op-bezoek-in-gronings-sloopdorp-we-zijn-in-een-hel-terechtgekomen-a3993476.

[7] Gronings Perspectief, *De maatschappelijke impact van de beving van Westerwijtwerd* (2019) 37.

[8] P Rosanvallon, *Counter-Democracy: Politics in an Age of Distrust* (Cambridge University Press, 2008).

democratic role of the ombudsman and I will introduce Rosanvallon's concept of 'counter-democracy' (section II). Next, I will focus on the case of the gas field earthquakes (section III), then I will describe the prominent role of the National Ombudsman (section IV). Based on these findings, I will then discuss some of the stronger and weaker points of the 'counter-democratic' role of the ombudsman (section V). I will conclude the chapter with an assessment of what this Dutch story tells us about the ombudsman in the modern state (section VI).

II. Ombudsman and Democracy

It is common to focus on the ombudsman as a 'legal' institution and to emphasise its role in individual complaint handling and dispute resolution. However, this perspective tends to overlook the fact that the ombudsman is also (or, some would say, primarily) a 'democratic' institution. Kirchheiner, for example, writes about the ombudsman debate in the Netherlands:

> When the installment of the National Ombudsman was discussed in the Netherlands … there was a tendency to consider the institute as an additional form of legal protection (in addition to already existing legal remedies). In principle this is incorrect, because that's not the essence of the institute … In my view, the ombudsman institute should be understood in the context of democratic values …[9]

Similarly, speaking about the situation in the UK and in other countries, O'Brien argues that 'the ombud can be seen to form part of a model of social ordering that owes more to the democratic tradition of ancient Greece than the juristic model of ancient Rome'.[10] Following this argument, this section will discuss two different views on the ombudsman as a democratic institution. Traditionally, the ombudsman is primarily aimed at strengthening the electoral democracy. However, the ombudsman can also play an important role in a counter-democracy.

A. Electoral Democracy

Although the history of the institution is much older, an important foundation of the modern ombudsman lies in the introduction of the Danish 'Folketingets Ombudsmand' in 1954. This is often considered a prime example of the 'classical' ombudsman model. This type of ombudsman is appointed by Parliament and has several 'soft' powers of investigation, recommendation and reporting. The ombudsman is charged with the double function of improving the legal rights of

[9] HH Kirchheiner, *De Nationale ombudsman in democratisch perspectief* (Koninklijke Vermande, 1984) 10.

[10] N O'Brien, 'Ombudsmen and Public Authorities: A Modest Proposal' in M Hertogh and R Kirkham (eds), *Research Handbook on the Ombudsman* (Edward Elgar Publishing, 2018) 47.

the individual and strengthening the parliamentary rule.[11] The primary goal of the ombudsman is to support the work of Parliament, through the handling of individual complaints and by monitoring the relationship between the citizen and the state. The Danish model sits at the base of the proliferation of the ombudsman idea around the globe. This is illustrated by, for example, the instalment of the ombudsman in New Zealand (1962), the Norwegian Parliamentary Ombudsman (1963) and the Parliamentary and Health Service Ombudsman in the UK (1967). The strong parliamentary connection of the British office is also reflected in its famous 'MP filter', whereby all complaints must be referred to the ombudsman by a Member of Parliament.

B. Counter-democracy[12]

The 'classical' ombudsman operates within the boundaries of the formal, representative democracy. Rosanvallon believes, however, that conventional definitions of democracy, which are restricted to the electoral process, are too narrow. In his view, a more adequate account would include 'the various ways in which the people are able to check or hold to account their representatives or the government, irrespective of the electoral process'.[13] Rosanvallon describes contemporary society as a 'society of distrust'.[14] In reaction to this situation, he argues that – historically speaking – democracies have developed in two directions. First, a variety of measures have been developed to improve the quality of 'electoral democracy'. At the same time, however, a series of institutional social counter-powers has also evolved 'in order *to compensate for the erosion of confidence, and to do so by organizing distrust*'.[15] He refers to these organised forms of distrust as 'counter-democracy':

> By 'counter-democracy' I mean not the opposite of democracy but rather a form of democracy that reinforces the usual electoral democracy as a kind of buttress, a democracy of indirect powers disseminated throughout society – in other words a durable democracy of distrust, which complements the episodic democracy of the usual electoral-representative system.[16]

According to Rosanvallon, there are three generic mechanisms whereby citizens can hold their rulers accountable between elections: oversight, prevention and judgment. The first mechanism of 'oversight' refers to the various means whereby

[11] S Carl, 'The History and Evolution of the Ombudsman Model' in Hertogh and Kirkham (n 10) 20.

[12] The term 'counter-democracy' may be too radical for some readers. A more accurate term might be 'alter-democracy' or 'extra-democracy' (because it is not the *opposite* of democracy, but rather a form of democracy that *complements* the usual electoral democracy). However, in this chapter, I will use Rosanvallon's original terminology.

[13] G Stedman Jones, 'Foreword' in Rosanvallon (n 8) xi.

[14] Rosanvallon (n 8) 11.

[15] ibid 4.

[16] ibid 8.

citizens are able to monitor and publicise the behaviour of elected and appointed rulers (the people as watchdog); the second mechanism of 'prevention' refers to their capacity to mobilise resistance to specific policies (the people as veto players); and the third mechanism of 'judgment' refers to the situation in which individuals or social groups use courts to bring delinquent politicians to judgment (the people as judge).[17]

In Rosanvallon's work, the power of oversight takes three forms: vigilance, denunciation and evaluation. 'Vigilance' means permanent monitoring of the actions of government; 'denunciation' exposes the wrongdoings of politicians; and 'evaluation' utilises expert analysis to review and critique government policies.[18] These powers of oversight can be exercised by different actors. These 'overseers' can be vigilant citizens and (online) social movements, but they may also include independent authorities. Rosanvallon argues that bureaucracies and representative governments have a 'structural tendency toward dysfunctionality'.[19] Therefore, 'monitoring agencies are useful precisely because they remedy this structural deficit'.[20] According to Rosanvallon, these external monitoring authorities include ombudsmen, 'who help citizens bring their individual problems and needs to the attention of otherwise rigid and inaccessible bureaucratic systems'.[21] In the rest of the chapter I will focus on this 'counter-democratic' role of the ombudsman.

III. Gas Quakes in the Netherlands: A Disaster in Slow Motion[22]

Thus far, the position of the ombudsman in a system of 'counter-democracy' has only been discussed in brief and abstract terms.[23] But how does the ombudsman use his 'counter-democratic' instruments in everyday practice? To answer this, I will focus on the role of the Dutch National Ombudsman in the aftermath of the gas field earthquakes in the Netherlands. First, this section will discuss the background of the gas quakes. In the next section, I will explore the active role of the National Ombudsman.

[17] P Rosanvallon, *Democratic Legitimacy: Impartiality, Reflexivity, Proximity* (Oxford University Press, 2011) 7; see also PC Schmitter, 'A Discussion of Counter-democracy: Politics in an Age of Distrust' (2010) 8 *Perspectives on Politics* 887.

[18] See also C Ansell, 'Review: Counter-democracy: Politics in an Age of Distrust' (2011) 89 *Public Administration* 698.

[19] Rosanvallon (n 8) 73.

[20] ibid.

[21] ibid 71.

[22] This part of the case study is primarily based on media reports and on a secondary analysis of previous studies.

[23] O'Brien (n 10) 47; M de Langen, E Govers and R van Zutphen, 'Effectiveness and Independence of the Ombudsman's Own-Motion Investigations: A Practitioner's Perspective from the Netherlands' in Hertogh and Kirkham (n 10) 391.

A. Earthquakes Caused by Gas Production

The earthquake in the village of Westerwijtwerd was caused by the extraction of natural gas from the surrounding flatlands of Groningen, the northernmost province in the Netherlands. Since it was discovered in 1959, the Groningen gas field has been one of Europe's richest sources of gas. For more than half a century, Groningen gas has heated most homes in the Netherlands, powered factories and helped pay for the Dutch welfare state. However, these benefits have now been outweighed by the side effects of gas production. Decades of extraction have reduced pressure on the gas-bearing rocks below the surface, causing them to contract. This has led to more than a thousand tremors since the mid-1980s. In recent years, their frequency and magnitude have been increasing. Since 1986, about 100 tremors have been of a magnitude of 2.0 or more on the Richter scale and there have been three more serious quakes of a magnitude of 3.4 or higher, with a maximum strength of 3.6 (the Huizinge earthquake in 2012).[24] Although the earthquakes are small by international standards, the flatness of the Groningen area means buildings are unable to withstand even light tremors.[25] As a result, thousands of homes and buildings have been damaged and real estate prices have dropped dramatically.[26] According to a recent study, 410,000 residents of the province of Groningen are exposed to induced earthquakes: they live in a postcode area where damage has been recognised by the oil company responsible. Some 170,000 people (adults and children) have experienced damage to their property and more than 68,000 adults' homes have been damaged multiple times. If you include children, the number affected is approximately 85,000.[27] Nicole, one of the local residents, talks about her experiences in a newspaper interview. At her home in the village of Appingedam, she points to sagging external walls and cracked ceilings: 'In 10 years it went from a good house to a ruin.'[28] Heavy beams buttress her house, inside and out, and it is scheduled to be torn down.

B. Bureaucratic Claim Procedures

Thousands of residents have filed claims for compensation. However, many of them complain about the bureaucratic and often lengthy claim procedures.

[24] S Reed, 'Earthquakes Are Jolting the Netherlands. Gas Drilling Is to Blame' *New York Times* (24 October 2019) www.nytimes.com/2019/10/24/business/energy-environment/netherlands-gas-earthquakes.html.

[25] Raval (n 5).

[26] P Boelhouwer and H van der Heijden, 'The Effect of Earthquakes on the Housing Market and the Quality of Life in the Province of Groningen, the Netherlands' (2018) 33 *Journal of Housing and the Built Environment* 429.

[27] Gronings Perspectief, 'Summary of the Final Report' (2018) www.groningsperspectief.nl/wp-content/uploads/2018/02/Summary-of-results.pdf.

[28] Reed (n 24).

Until 2018, NAM was responsible for assessing and paying for repairs. More recently, this role has been taken over by government agencies that assess damages and bill the joint venture. However, this has not prevented growing frustration over repairs and compensation. In 2019, a local newspaper documented the bureaucratic experiences of 101 homeowners in a book called *Ik wacht*, or *I'm Waiting*.[29] A reviewer summarised the book as 'Kafka in Groningen'. Recent figures show that 850 people have been waiting for compensation for over two years.[30] Many residents also say that the energy companies and the government have ignored or deflected their complaints. One observer summarises their feelings as follows: 'People want a concrete solution for their homes. Instead, they are given new rules and constantly changing promises.'[31]

A recent psychological study shows that many people feel angry and powerless.[32] Another study estimates that some 10,000 adults in the Groningen area suffer from stress-related health problems. Many people blame their stress on bureaucracy and conflicts concerning damage procedures.[33] Monique, a local resident, explains in an interview that some people still hope for better housing while others are in a permanent state of shock: 'Their lives feel like the earthquakes, a bit shaky.'[34]

Yvonne, who is the project leader of a local public health service organisation, describes the situation as follows: 'We use the guidelines for disasters, because this is a disaster in slow motion.'[35]

C. Distrust of Authorities

Local residents feel abandoned by the national government.[36] The most affected villages are less than three hours by train from The Hague (the seat of the Dutch government) and other big cities like Amsterdam and Rotterdam, but by Dutch standards this region is far from the country's political and economic heartland. As local resident Jeannette, whose house needs major repairs, notes: 'Nobody in The Hague realized what was going on for a long time. I suppose it is because we are in the north and not in the Amsterdam–Rotterdam area.'[37]

[29] Dagblad van het Noorden (ed), *Ik wacht: 101 verhalen uit het aardbevingsgebied* (Uitgeverij Balans, 2019).

[30] M Miskovic, 'Meer dan 850 mensen wachten al langer dan twee jaar op vergoeding bevingsschade' *RTV Noord* (31 March 2020) www.rtvnoord.nl/nieuws/220717/Meer-dan-850-mensen-wachten-al-langer-dan-twee-jaar-op-vergoeding-bevingsschade.

[31] I van der Linde, 'Ramp in Slow Motion: "Doe iets!"' *De Groene Amsterdammer* (4 December 2019) www.groene.nl/artikel/doe-iets.

[32] Perlaviciute et al (n 4).

[33] Gronings Perspectief (n 27).

[34] Reed (n 24).

[35] van der Linde (n 31).

[36] Gronings Perspectief (n 27).

[37] Reed (n 24).

A social psychologist, who is involved in a long-term study on the effects of the gas quakes, puts it like this: 'Normally in a democracy, citizens are looked after. However, most people in Groningen feel that this is no longer the case.'[38]

Against this background, distrust of authorities is high. For example, Mr Warink, who is a local resident who has been involved in several compensation procedures, argues that his frustrations are shared by many others: 'Politicians have lost the trust of the people here.' 'Now, they won't believe anything they say.'[39]

According to a public health official, this could result in a lasting lack of confidence in authorities: 'People develop distrust towards everything that has been promised. Children share in this distrust and anger. They are brought up with the notion that you can't trust the government.'[40]

As will be demonstrated in the next section, the Dutch National Ombudsman has played an important role in the aftermath of the gas field earthquakes.

IV. The Role of the National Ombudsman[41]

The National Ombudsman of the Netherlands (the Ombudsman) is an independent and impartial institution, which assesses complaints from citizens about all aspects of public administration, defends the interests of the citizen and monitors the quality of public services in the Netherlands.[42] The Ombudsman is appointed by the House of Representatives for a period of six years, and his legal status and responsibilities are established by the Dutch Constitution (Article 78a) and the Dutch Ombudsman Act (Wet Nationale ombudsman), which was passed in 1981. In essence, the Ombudsman is empowered to scrutinise the manner in which public authorities fulfil their statutory responsibilities. An investigation may be instigated at the Ombudsman's own initiative or further to a complaint from a member of the public. The Ombudsman is concerned with virtually every area of public administration, from government ministries and their executive agencies (such as the Tax and Customs Administration) to the bodies that administer social benefits, the police, water boards, provinces and municipalities. In practice, most cases are solved by a quick 'intervention'. The Ombudsman will contact the public administration concerned and will encourage the authority to contact the complainant directly in order to arrive at an outcome which is acceptable to all

[38] Van der Linde (n 31).

[39] S Montlake, 'Why Holland Aims to Leave $80 Billion in The Ground' *Christian Science Monitor* (22 November 2019) www.scribd.com/article/436409826/Why-Holland-Aims-To-Leave-80-Billion-In-The-Ground.

[40] Van der Linde (n 31).

[41] This part of the case study is based on an analysis of media reports and ombudsman publications.

[42] For a brief summary of the position of the National Ombudsman of the Netherlands, see www.nationaleombudsman.nl/international/the-institution.

concerned. In more complex cases, the Ombudsman can also decide to investigate a complaint in more detail. His findings are published online and in a written report.

As will be argued below, the Ombudsman has used his investigatory powers creatively to play a flexible and undogmatic role in the aftermath of the gas field earthquakes. This section will discuss three examples: (i) the publication of an unsolicited critical report on the way in which the Dutch authorities have handled complaints and claim procedures; (ii) the organisation of regular working visits to the most affected areas in the north of the Netherlands; and (iii) the publication of two open letters of concern.

A. Bureaucratic Spaghetti

Firstly, the Ombudsman has used the investigation of an individual complaint to publish a critical review about the way that the Dutch authorities have dealt with the aftermath of the gas field earthquakes. In 2016, the Ombudsman handled a complaint from 'Mrs De Vries', who lives in one of the villages close to the Groningen gas field.[43] In the light of the recent tremors and the growing uncertainty, Mrs De Vries decided that she wanted to move to another part of the country. However, she was unable to sell her house (even after she lowered the asking price). In response to her request, a local government agency offered to buy her house, but Mrs De Vries did not agree with their offer. After this, the local authority refused to answer any of her questions. The same happened when Mrs De Vries took her case to the Ministry of Economic Affairs and to the office of the 'National Coordinator' for gas quakes. After five months, she received a brief formal reaction from this office saying they it is not qualified to deal with her complaint. The Ombudsman decided that this amounted to a case of maladministration and that the Minister of Economic Affairs (who is responsible for the National Coordinator) has acted improperly.

However, the Ombudsman did not just publish his decision in this individual case, but took the opportunity to comment on the situation in Groningen in more general terms as well. In the final report, with the telling title 'Bureaucratic Spaghetti?', the Ombudsman added an extra section, in which he was very critical about the passive position of the government and the resulting bureaucracy. Moreover, he was worried that this will further undermine public trust:

> The level of confidence in the government has diminished among many people in Groningen. This is not only true for Mrs. De Vries. The National ombudsman is concerned about this. … The lack of trust appears to be related to the unwillingness to acknowledge the relation between gas production, earthquakes and the damage

[43] Nationale ombudsman, *Rapport – Bestuurlijke spaghetti? Een onderzoek naar de wijze van klachtafhandeling door het ministerie van Economische Zaken* (18 April 2016) 2016/35, www.nationaleombudsman.nl/system/files/rapport/20160035%20.pdf

> to homes as well as the unwillingness of the state to accept responsibility and take adequate steps … The present uncertainty – related to claims procedures, responsibilities, privacy-concerns and complaint-handling – may be characterized as a situation of 'bureaucratic spaghetti'.[44]

B. Ombudsman on Tour

Secondly, the Ombudsman has made several visits to the villages that are most hit by the earthquakes. In 2019, he and 15 of his staff members made a visit to the province of Groningen. To meet as many people as possible, they set up a number of 'pop-up living rooms' in shopping centres (complete with a carpet, a sofa and an old-fashioned floor lamp to create a cosy atmosphere) and held several working visits with local governments and other organisations. According to the Ombudsman, it is not hard to find a common thread in all their conversations: 'The government doesn't keep its promises, they don't listen, or someone's questions are left unanswered.'[45]

In the same year, the Ombudsman also held a special 'surgery' in some of the most affected villages. He explained the purpose of these meetings to the local residents as follows: 'I've come here to listen.'[46]

He reported his findings in several interviews for local and national newspapers. One of the main themes in these interviews was the lack of progress that had been made in compensating people for their damaged homes. Moreover, he related his latest findings to the report on 'Bureaucratic Spaghetti' (see above), which he had published three years earlier:

> Over the years, this spaghetti has increased rather than diminished … What has happened in the past three years? Only a few small things. It is quite staggering. Everybody agrees with what I've been saying. But meanwhile, I don't see anything happening.[47]

A second theme in these local conversations was that many people felt that they were treated with suspicion. When they reported damages, the authorities first wanted to make sure that they were not fraudsters who were trying to profit from the special circumstances. The Ombudsman strongly condemned this approach: 'Put your trust in these people. Take a risk in doing the right thing for the right people and don't focus on fraudsters.'[48]

In a number of subsequent visits to Groningen, the Ombudsman kept track of the progress that was being made in compensating people for their damages

[44] ibid 2.

[45] M Middel, 'Groningers doen verhaal tegen de ombudsman: "Dat lucht op"' *NRC* (17 April 2019) www.nrc.nl/nieuws/2019/04/17/het-lucht-op-mijn-verhaal-te-doen-a3957178.

[46] Van der Linde (n 31).

[47] ibid.

[48] ibid.

and in the rebuilding of their homes. He repeatedly aired his concerns about the long delays in newspaper interviews: 'I've talked to so many people who are disappointed, all of whom have been wondering what will happen to their homes for the past four years.'[49]

Moreover, he urged the national authorities to take action: 'Don't wait any longer, but begin. That's the only way you can slowly win back people's trust.'[50]

The Ombudsman also criticised the strong focus on complex legal procedures for the compensation of damages. He called for a more pragmatic approach instead:

> This legal balderdash about a single crack should finally be over.[51]
>
> Send all the lawyers home! Be fair to people and tell them: this is going to take a while. People want to be in charge themselves. Now it's all about systems in which people have to fit in.[52]

Finally, in his reports about these local visits, the Ombudsman pledged his strong commitment to the region: 'I won't let go of Groningen. That's the promise I made on Friday. I will be back soon.'[53]

C. Letters of Concern

Thirdly, the Ombudsman has written several open letters to the national and local authorities in which he has formulated his concerns about the way in which they deal with the aftermath of the earthquakes. For example, in 2017 the Ombudsman sent an open letter to the then newly installed national government with the following heading:

> To the new Cabinet:
>
> A foundation with cracks. Stop building on distrust and take the people from Groningen serious![54]

[49] 'Ombudsman was "nog nooit zo somber" over versteviging Groningse huizen' *NOS Nieuws* (8 February 2020) https://nos.nl/artikel/2322093-ombudsman-was-nog-nooit-zo-somber-over-versteviging-groningse-huizen.html.

[50] G van Hofslot, 'Begin gewoon met de versterking in Groningen. Het geld, de plannen en de mensen zijn er' *Dagblad van het Noorden* (8 February 2020) www.dvhn.nl/groningen/Nationale-Ombudsman-Begin-gewoon-met-de-versterking-in-Groningen-Het-geld-de-plannen-en-de-mensen-zijn-er-25329349.html.

[51] Nationale ombudsman, 'Stop juridisch geneuzel over enkele scheur' *Hart van Nederland* (24 May 2019) www.hartvannederland.nl/nieuws/2019/nationale-ombudsman-stop-juridisch-geneuzel-over-enkele-scheur/.

[52] Van der Linde (n 31).

[53] Nationale ombudsman (n 51).

[54] Nationale ombudsman, 'Oproep Nationale ombudsman en Kinderombudsman aan nieuw kabinet over Groningen' (6 April 2017) www.nationaleombudsman.nl/system/files/bijlage/Oproep%20Nationale%20ombudsman%20en%20Kinderombudsman%20aan%20nieuw%20kabinet%20over%20Groningen.pdf.

In the letter, the Ombudsman explained that over the past years he had made several visits to the province of Groningen to talk to residents and local officials. Moreover, he referred to his previous critical report (see above). On his website, the Ombudsman explained the motivation for his appeal to the new government as follows:

> Citizens count on a trustworthy government. We stand at the beginning of new opportunities with a new Cabinet which is about to start. We have to learn from previous years and draw lessons from this. There can be no more bureaucratic spaghetti. The government is there for its citizens and not the other way around. People from Groningen deserve a government that says: 'Yes, we will stand by you' …[55]

The Ombudsman argued that the new government needs to take the following six steps: (1) restore trust; (2) take responsibility; (3) put the security of residents first; (4) provide generous payment of damages; (5) promote transparency; and (6) work on bespoke solutions.

In 2019, the Ombudsman wrote a second 'letter of concern' addressed to local officials and several government ministers.[56] The letter was published one day before the start of a top-level administrative meeting. In an interview with a local news site, the Ombudsman justified this initiative as follows: 'Because of all the pressure on ministers and administrators, things are moving. That's the reason for my letter; with it I want to increase the pressure further.'[57]

In the letter, the Ombudsman explained that he had been following the case of the gas field earthquakes for several years and that he had seen the big impact on people up close. He argued that this crisis calls for a different approach. In his view, the 'vulnerable relation between citizens and the state is increasingly under pressure'.[58] Therefore, it is important that these people's problems are finally recognized; that claims procedures will be based on 'high trust'; that local residents will remain involved, with adequate room for their voice and participation; and that all levels of government will act together to restore public trust. The Ombudsman concluded his open letter as follows: 'I hope that today you will be able to work together to take steps that are in the best interest of the people of Groningen and that the perspective of the local residents will take center stage.'[59]

[55] www.nationaleombudsman.nl/nieuws/2017/een-fundament-met-scheuren-stop-met-bouwen-op-wantrouwen-en-neem-groningers-serieus.

[56] Nationale ombudsman, 'Minister en Groninger bestuurders, zet vandaag nog stappen in het belang van de Groningers' (5 juni 2019) www.nationaleombudsman.nl/nieuws/2019/nationale-ombudsman-ministers-en-groninger-bestuurders-zet-vandaag-nog-stappen-in-het

[57] Nationale ombudsman, 'Geef vertrouwen aan Groningers' *RTV Noord* (5 June 2019) www.rtvnoord.nl/nieuws/209364/Nationale-Ombudsman-schrijft-zorgenbrief-Geef-vertrouwen-aan-Groningers.

[58] Nationale ombudsman (n 56).

[59] ibid.

V. Discussion: Does the Ombudsman Reinforce Democracy?

Based on the case of the gas field earthquakes, what are some of the stronger and weaker points of the 'counter-democratic' role of the ombudsman? And how does Rosanvallon's theory compare to practice? In this section, I will focus on the situation in the Netherlands. More comparative and empirical research is needed to see if these findings may be also be generalised to other public sector ombudsmen.

A. Ombudsman and Oversight

In Rosanvallon's view, the system of 'counter-democracy' is based on three mechanisms whereby citizens can hold their rulers accountable: oversight, prevention and judgment. In the case of the gas field earthquakes, the role of the Ombudsman primarily reflects the function of oversight.[60]

The most important dimension of the 'oversight' role of the Ombudsman is *vigilance*, understood as the 'permanent close scrutiny of the actions of government'.[61] Part of this function is 'to sound the alarm and protest, especially in times of crisis or conflict'.[62] Moreover, vigilance 'helps to define the political arena and establish government priorities'.[63] In the case of the gas field earthquakes, the National Ombudsman uses his reports, his local visits and his letters of concern to monitor and criticise the way in which the Dutch government has handled thousands of damage claims. Through strategic timing (for example, the day before a top-level administrative meeting) and by publishing press releases on the institute's website, the Ombudsman also successfully generates a lot of media attention for his actions. All these elements combined have put the case of the gas field earthquakes firmly on the political agenda. Although it is difficult to establish a direct causal link with the work of the Ombudsman, this is perhaps best illustrated by the fact that the Dutch House of Representatives has recently announced a parliamentary inquiry into the gas production in Groningen.

A second important dimension of the 'oversight' role of the Ombudsman in the aftermath of the gas field earthquakes is *denunciation*. According to Rosanvallon, denunciation in this sense means 'to make known, to expose, to unveil, to reveal' certain wrongdoings of politicians.[64] Although originally aimed at revealing

[60] The Dutch case also illustrates how the Ombudsman can operate as part of what Ackerman has called the 'integrity branch' of government. See B Ackerman, 'The New Separation of Powers' (2000) 113 *Harvard Law Review* 633.

[61] Rosanvallon (n 8) 33.

[62] ibid 39.

[63] ibid 40.

[64] ibid 42.

scandals or cases of corruption, the target of denunciation is now simply any 'action or behavior that is dubious but legal',[65] aimed at 'what society considers "abnormal" or unjust'.[66] A clear illustration of denunciation is the way in which the Ombudsman has revealed how the administrative damage claims procedure has turned into 'bureaucratic spaghetti'. In his reports, the Ombudsman has also unveiled how the handling of property-damage claims is focused too much on potential fraudsters and he has exposed the limits of a strictly legal approach.

A third, but less prominent, dimension of the 'oversight' role of the Ombudsman is *evaluation*. Evaluation involves 'carefully researched, technically sophisticated, often quantified judgment of specific actions or more general policies'.[67] The goal of evaluation is to use specific expertise to improve the quality and efficiency of governmental management. We see some elements of this dimension when the Ombudsman refers in his reports and press releases to specific (external) studies on, for example, the social, economic or health effects of the gas field earthquakes.[68]

Next to 'oversight', Rosanvallon's other two 'counter-democratic' mechanisms seem less important in the everyday operations of the Ombudsman. With regard to 'prevention' (the capacity to mobilise resistance against certain policies), there have been several street demonstrations and other types of protests.[69] Also, under public pressure, the Dutch government has decided that the natural gas extraction from the Groningen gas field will be completely terminated in 2022.[70] However, it is not clear to what extent any of these developments are directly related to the Ombudsman. The fact that his decisions are legally non-binding prevents him from blocking new policies. For the same reason, the Ombudsman is less suited to initiate a process of 'judgment' (aimed at bringing delinquent politicians to court).

B. Does the Ombudsman Strengthen Electoral Democracy?

Rosanvallon's central argument is that the system of counter-democracy ultimately 'reinforces the usual electoral democracy as a kind of buttress'.[71] However, some critics have argued that 'Rosanvallon's book often seems to stop short of

[65] ibid 51.

[66] ibid 52.

[67] ibid 52.

[68] See, eg Boelhouwer and van der Heijden (n 26); Gronings Perspectief (n 27); Onderzoeksraad voor Veiligheid, *Aardbevingsrisico's in Groningen. Onderzoek naar de rol van veiligheid van burgers in de besluitvorming over de gaswinning (1959–2014)* (Onderzoeksraad voor Veiligheid, 2015).

[69] J Pieters, 'Thousands March against Gas Extraction in Groningen' *NL Times* (8 February 2017) https://nltimes.nl/2017/02/08/thousands-march-gas-extraction-groningen.

[70] Dutch Cabinet, 'Termination of Natural Gas Extraction in Groningen' (29 April 2018) www.government.nl/latest/news/2018/03/29/dutch-cabinet-termination-of-natural-gas-extraction-in-groningen.

[71] Rosanvallon (n 8) 8.

examining the actual effects of increased oversight'.[72] Based on the case of the gas field earthquakes, how does the Dutch National Ombudsman support (electoral) democracy? For example, what is his role in promoting democratic values, fighting inequality and restoring public trust in government?

One important aspect of the Ombudsman's counter-democratic role is that he approaches the aftermath of the gas field earthquakes not as a legalistic problem, but as a democratic one.

The primary aim of his interventions is not that each individual gets the right amount of compensation (although this remains important). Instead, he focuses on monitoring and improving the relationship between state and citizen. In his reports, during his local visits and in his letters of concern he repeatedly emphasised the importance of democratic values, such as transparency, participation, a trustworthy government and taking citizens seriously. This echoes the ideas of several early ombudsman scholars, who saw the distinctive value of the ombudsman 'to impart more humanity … into the behavior of the administration … pushing the modern administration beyond mere justice, towards the recognition of a duty of active kindness'.[73] Likewise, Kirchheiner wrote about the the Justitieombudsman (JO) in Sweden: 'The JO institution should be seen principally within a context of democratic values, where the personal responsibility of the official towards the citizen is of primary importance.'[74]

Especially interesting in the context of the gas field earthquakes is that Kirchheiner drew a connection between these democratic values and feelings of security:

> As long as the official … in his contact with the citizen, is not fully aware of his responsibility towards the individual, the danger remains that the individual's *feelings of security* will be adversely affected by an official who, for example, exceeds his authority or acts arbitrarily, incorrectly, or tardily. The feelings of security, based on the freedom of thought, include not only feelings of security in the narrow sense of the word, but also feelings of safety, humanity, and human dignity. The individual's feelings of security are a *conditio sine qua non* for a sound democracy.[75]

Some commentators have criticised Rosanvallon's positive approach to counter-democracy for ignoring the issue of inequality because 'Access to its mechanisms of oversight, prevention, and judgment is unevenly distributed throughout the society'.[76] The institution of the ombudsman is also vulnerable to this criticism. In relation to the Dutch National Ombudsman (and most other public sector

[72] Ansell (n 18) 706.

[73] A Shonfield, *Modern Capitalism: The Changing Balance of Public and Private Power* (Oxford University Press, 1965) 427. See also M Doyle and N O'Brien, *Reimagining Administrative Justice. Human Rights in Small Places* (Palgrave Macmillan, 2020) 13–30.

[74] HH Kirchheiner, 'The Ideological Foundation of the Ombudsman Institution' in GE Caiden (ed), *International Handbook of the Ombudsman: Evolution and Present Function* (Greenwood Press, 1983) 23.

[75] Kirchheiner (n 74) 23 (emphasis in original).

[76] Schmitter (n 17) 889.

ombudsmen), previous studies have identified the so called 'Matthew effect'.[77] This means that the very people that the ombudsman is in part designed to impact and assist, namely the disadvantaged and least networked sections of our communities, are the least likely to access an ombudsman. In the aftermath of the gas field earthquakes, however, the Dutch National Ombudsman has adopted a new approach. Rather than passively waiting for people to file a formal complaint, he has actively reached out to the people in Groningen himself. They can now directly approach the Ombudsman during his frequent visits to the area or share their concerns in one of the 'pop-up living rooms' at their local town square. In this way, the Ombudsman gives voice to the earthquake victims in Groningen. Many people who felt that they were ignored by the (national) authorities are now able to share their experiences with the Ombudsman. By including their stories in his reports, letters of concern and press releases, their concerns have also gained a more prominent position on the political agenda. This new approach has reduced the inequality and inaccessibility of the Ombudsman (at least for the people in Groningen). However, it remains to be seen if this new approach will be able eliminate the 'Matthew effect' completely.

Rosanvallon chose as the central point of departure for his study 'the erosion of citizens' confidence in political leaders and institutions'.[78] In his view, the various powers of counter-democracy have evolved 'to compensate for the erosion of confidence, and to do so by organizing distrust'.[79] In the case of the gas field earthquakes, the Ombudsman has repeatedly emphasised that the level of confidence in the government has diminished among the people in Groningen. For example, in his report on bureaucratic spaghetti, he argued that the lack of trust is related to the unwillingness of the Dutch authorities to acknowledge the relation between gas production and the damage to homes and to the unwillingness of the state to accept responsibility. Likewise, in one of his open letters to the Dutch government, he urged them to restore trust. In this way, the Ombudsman uses his powers of 'oversight' to organise distrust. However, the long-term effects of this remain unclear. Considering the results from previous research,[80] it seems unlikely that the actions of the Ombudsman will lead to a full restoration of public trust in Groningen and elsewhere.

[77] See B Hubeau, 'The Profile of Complainants: How to Overcome the "Matthew Effect"?' in Hertogh and Kirkham (n 10) (and the literature cited therein).

[78] Rosanvallon (n 8) 1.

[79] ibid 4.

[80] S van Roosbroek and S van de Walle, 'The Relationship between Ombudsman, Government, and Citizens: A Survey Analysis' (2008) 34 *Negotiation Journal* 287; M Hertogh, 'Why the Ombudsman Does Not Promote Public Trust in Government: Lessons from the Low Countries' (2013) 35 *Journal of Social Welfare and Family Law* 245.

VI. Conclusion

What role does the ombudsman play in the modern state? It is common to regard the ombudsman as a form of dispute resolution whose primary task is the adjudication of individual disputes. However, the findings from the case study on the aftermath of the gas field earthquakes suggest that it may be time to reimagine the position of the ombudsman. In addition to his traditional 'legalistic' role, the ombudsman can also play an important 'democratic' role. Seen through the lens of jurisprudence, the ombudsman should focus on individual grievances. However, seen from a perspective of 'demosprudence', the ombudsman should also look at 'the underlying relational deficit that gave rise to the grievance' and work on 'building bridges between citizen and state'.[81] In the Netherlands, the National Ombudsman operates as an active mechanism of 'oversight'. By focusing on 'vigilance' and 'denunciation' (and to a lesser extent on 'evaluation'), the Ombudsman has constantly monitored and criticised the Dutch government, and has exposed important shortcomings in the lengthy and bureaucratic process of damage claims. Moreover, he has used his powers of oversight to promote important democratic values and he has put the stories of people whose houses were damaged by the earthquakes firmly on the political agenda. In this way, the Ombudsman makes an important contribution to a system of 'counter-democracy', which complements and reinforces the usual electoral democracy. However, it is less obvious that the Ombudsman is equally accessible for all members of society and it remains to be seen if his actions will be able to restore public trust in government in Groningen and elsewhere.

The story of the Groningen gas field earthquakes also illustrates that the two systems of counter-democracy and electoral democracy are strongly interconnected. Ombudsman and Parliament are not competitors; rather, they are mutually dependent and keep each in other balance. On the one hand, electoral democracy cannot ignore counter-democracy. The interventions by the Dutch National Ombudsman play an important role in the political debate. On the other hand, counter-democracy cannot completely ignore electoral democracy either. No matter how effective the Ombudsman is in criticising government ministers and Members of Parliament for the way in which they have handled the aftermath of the gas field earthquakes, for any real legal or financial reforms he ultimately depends on their support.

[81] Doyle and O'Brien (n 73) 85.

12

Towards Therapeutic Complaints Resolution

JANE WILLIAMS, CHRIS GILL AND CAROLYN HIRST

I. Introduction

The structure of this chapter is as follows. It starts by considering the role of UK public service ombuds and the extent and nature of problems with UK internal public service complaint systems. We then highlight research undertaken with public services employees, which illustrates the potentially dysfunctional impact that complaint systems can have on them and describe how we subsequently developed guidelines to help reduce these harms. Our research, which included learning from implementing the guidelines, has led us to consider the need for change in the design of complaint-handling systems, so that the act and process of complaining is more therapeutic and does not impact negatively on any complaint system actors.[1]

We move on to consider therapeutic jurisprudence and its application to complaint systems, and then explore the extent to which the current redress designer role of public services ombuds in the UK supports more therapeutic approaches. The chapter concludes by arguing that in the context of UK public services, where ongoing relationships are at the heart of many citizen–state interactions, ombuds play a key role as therapeutic actors in designing, encouraging and modelling an ethic of care for the well-being of everyone affected by complaint systems.

[1] C Gill, M Sapouna, C Hirst and J Williams, 'Dysfunctional Accountability in Complaint Systems: The Effects of Complaints on Public Service Employees' [2019] *PL* 644.

II. The Ombud in the Modern State: 'An Architect of Governance'

The evolution of ombud schemes has been described elsewhere,[2] not least in *A Manifesto for Ombudsman Reform*[3] and in the contributions made by others in the current volume. Gill et al have identified a significant development in the role and practice of ombuds in the UK, arguing that the New Public Management practices that have transformed public administration in the last 30 years have also led to a more 'managerial' approach to ombuds' work.[4] There has long been a debate in ombudsman circles as to the best, or the best balance, of roles for an ombud.[5] For example, past debates have revolved around whether ombuds should concentrate resources on complaint handling (firefighting); conducting more in-depth investigations on the causes of systemic complaints and using these findings to focus efforts on remedying repeated maladministration (fire-watching); or being proactive and intervening even before complaints are received so as to prevent them occurring in the first place (fire prevention).[6]

A number of UK public service ombuds (UKPSOs) now have a redress designer role, with responsibility for the design of public service complaint systems. Following a critical review of complaint handling in Scotland,[7] the Scottish Public Services Ombudsman (SPSO) was the first to be given the role of simplifying complaints procedures.[8] The SPSO Complaints Standards Authority (CSA) subsequently developed standardised Model Complaints Handling Procedures for bodies within jurisdiction (BwJ).[9] The CSA model has been replicated in Northern Ireland, although at the time of writing the relevant provisions have yet to be brought into force.[10] The Public Service Ombudsman (Wales) Act 2019 also grants these powers to the Public Services Ombudsman for Wales (PSOW). The Parliamentary and Health Service Ombudsman (PHSO) has called for

[2] See, eg M Hertogh and R Kirkham, 'The Ombudsman and Administrative Justice: From Promise to Performance' in M Hertogh and R Kirkham (eds), *Research Handbook on the Ombudsman* (Edward Elgar, 2018) 1–16; R Kirkham, 'The Ombudsman, Tribunals and Administrative Justice Section: A 2020 Vision for the Ombudsman Sector' (2016) 38 *Journal of Social Welfare and Family Law* 103; D Wakem, 'The Changing Role of the Ombudsman' (2015) 63 *Administration* 15.

[3] R Kirkham and C Gill (eds) *A Manifesto for Ombudsman Reform* (Palgrave Macmillan, 2020).

[4] C Gill, T Mullen and N Vivian, 'The Managerial Ombudsman' (2020) 83 *MLR* 797.

[5] See, eg C Harlow, 'Ombudsmen: "Hunting Lions" or "Swatting Flies"' in Hertogh and Kirkham (n 2) 73–90; C Gill, 'The Evolving Role of the Ombudsman: A Conceptual and Constitutional Analysis of the 'Scottish Solution' to Administrative Justice' [2014] *PL* 662.

[6] R Snell, 'Australian Ombudsman – A Continual Work in Progress' in M Groves and HP Lee (eds), *Australian Administrative Law* (Cambridge University Press, 2007).

[7] L Crerar, *Independent Review of Regulation, Audit, Inspection, and Complaint Handling* (Scottish Government 2007).

[8] Design authority powers were translated into legislative provisions through s 119 of the Public Services Reform Act Scotland 2010, which amended the Scottish Public Services Ombudsman Act 2002.

[9] www.spso.org.uk/the-model-complaints-handling-procedures.

[10] Public Services Ombudsman (Northern Ireland) Act 2016, ss 34–42.

similar CSA powers,[11] and is currently (again at time of writing) consulting on a non-statutory Complaint Standards Framework for the English National Health Service.[12]

This design role can be related to the ombud's role in relation to good governance[13] and the concept of 'value-added ombudsmanry',[14] which elevates ombuds from having the basic mandate of providing redress to being an 'architect of better governance'. It also reflects a general tendency towards the adoption of a more systemic and preventative approach, with a modern emphasis among UK ombud schemes on managerial and design activities. In the context of this chapter, the move towards redress design presents an opportunity to (i) address problems in the current complaint systems at first tier (section III below) and (ii) do so in ways that foreground a change in paradigm from complaint-handling approaches being adversarial, consumerist and managerial to ones that are more relational, consensual and therapeutic (see section V below).

One of the implications of ombuds adopting a designer role is that they have a much greater influence on redress than before, leading to an opportunity to bring about more positive change in complaint systems and public administration in order to address the systemic and widespread problems of first-tier complaint handling.

However, we will also argue that the credibility of UK ombuds as designers of more therapeutic redress systems also depends on ombuds' own practices setting the tone for what is good practice elsewhere. If ombud processes themselves are anti-therapeutic, then we cannot expect the complaint systems, which they sit at the apex of, to be therapeutic. As architects of governance, the ombuds are not simply authorities that can issue statutory/non-statutory guidance and monitor its compliance, but they are also role models.

III. Problems with Internal Complaint-Handling Systems in the UK

A. The Confusing and Complex Complaints Landscape in the UK

Current systems for public service complaint handling in the UK are based on the Citizen's Charter model.[15] Charter reforms were derived from managerial

[11] PHSO, *Making Complaints Count: Supporting Complaints Handling in the NHS and UK Government Departments* (2020) 51 www.ombudsman.org.uk/publications/making-complaints-count-supporting-complaints-handling-nhs-and-uk-government.

[12] www.ombudsman.org.uk/csf.

[13] British and Irish Ombudsman Association, *Guide to Principles of Good Governance* (BIOA, 2009). The British and Irish Ombudsman Association is now called the Ombudsman Association.

[14] G Paquet, 'The Judgment of Wider Courts: Ombuds as Producers of Governance' (2009) 20 www.gouvernance.ca/publications/09-06.pdf.

[15] Gill et al (n 1).

values associated with New Public Management and led to growth in accountability mechanisms.[16] This resulted in public service complaints systems providing a means by which service providers can be held to account for breaches of service standards. Internal complaint systems in the UK have mainly been a means of satisfying unhappy customers and providing management information to improve services.[17] Allsop and Jones refer to this as the managerial complaint-handling model, emphasising internal resolution, consumer satisfaction and service improvement.[18]

The public service complaint-handling landscape in the UK has been subject to significant criticism, being described as confusing, complex, costly and not serving the interests of complainants.[19] These views highlight the continuing complexity of the current redress landscape and the need for complaint systems to be more integrated, easier to navigate, addressing gaps and more consistent in complaint handling across ombuds and other complaint bodies. Data shows that UK citizens are much less likely to complain about public services than the private sector, with the main reason (52 per cent) for not complaining being that they did not think it would make any difference.[20] A Citizens Advice report stated that this meant that as many as 15 million people may not have followed up their poor experience with a formal complaint.[21] In addition, if citizens do complain, they are less likely to be satisfied than comparators in the private sector.[22] There have

[16] J Clarke, J Newman and M McDermont, 'Delivering Choice and Administering Justice: Contested Logics of Public Services' in M Adler (ed), *Administrative Justice in Context* (Hart Publishing, 2010) 25–46.

[17] P Birkinshaw, 'Grievances, Remedies and the State – Revisited and Reappraised' in Adler (n 16).

[18] J Allsop and K Jones, 'Withering the Citizen, Managing the Consumer: Complaints in Healthcare Settings' (2008) 7 *Social Policy and Society* 233.

[19] L Crerar, *Independent Review of Regulation, Audit, Inspection, and Complaint Handling* (Scottish Government, 2007); Citizens Advice, 'Learning from Mistakes' (2016) www.citizensadvice.org.uk/Global/CitizensAdvice/Public%20services%20publications/Learning-from-mistakes.pdf; P Dunleavy, S Bastow, J Tinkler, S Goldchluk and E Towers, 'Joining up Citizen Redress in UK Central Government' in Adler (n 16); National Audit Office, *Public Service Markets: Putting Things Right When They Go Wrong* (NAO, 2015) www.nao.org.uk/wp-content/uploads/2015/06/Putting-things-right.pdf; Public Administration Select Committee, *More Complaints Please!* (House of Commons, 2014) www.publications.parliament.uk/pa/cm201314/cmselect/cmpubadm/229/229.pdf HC229; UK Government, *Transforming Public Services: Complaints, Redress, and Tribunals* (2004); Which?, 'Make Complaints Count' (March 2015) www.staticwhich.co.uk/documents/pdf/make-complaints-count-report---march-2015-397971.pdf.

[20] Citizens Advice (n 19) 3 and 15.

[21] ibid 10.

[22] NAO (n 19) 8; K Slater and G Higginson, *Understanding Consumer Experiences of Complaint Handling* (Citizens Advice, 2016) 50 www.citizensadvice.org.uk/Global/CitizensAdvice/Consumer%20publications/Understanding%20consumer%20experiences%20of%20complaint%20handling_DJS%20report%20final_June2016%20(2)%20(1).pdf. For a summary of the management literature on this subject, see T Sourdin, J Carlson, M Watts, C Armstrong and T Carlyle-Ford, 'Return on Investment of Effective Complaints Management: Public Sector Organisations' (SOCAP, 2020) www.socap.org.au/public/98/files/Documents/Research/ROI%20Report-Public%20Organisations%20-%20June%202020.pdf.

been several high-profile public inquiries which have highlighted the failure of complaint handling, particularly in the health service,[23] but in other sectors too.[24] In 2020, the PHSO noted that 'what complaints staff tell me about their role and experience often provides a raw picture of a complaints system that is in urgent need of reform and investment' and that this situation was likely to worsen as a result of the impact of the COVID-19 pandemic on public services.[25]

As described earlier, simplification, standardisation and efficiency in order to address some of these problems have been the top priorities of the CSA approach in Scotland and the other devolved administrations, as part of their 'architect of governance' approach. The PHSO, who is seeking similar powers, has pointed to the positive experience in Scotland, where the SPSO has been able to reduce complexity by introducing a unified framework for complaints across the sector.[26] However, despite the introduction of a common complaints standard, recent research from Citizens Advice Scotland suggests that knowledge on how to contact public services in Scotland with a complaint is still 'quite poor'.[27] Research in general on the effectiveness of the CSA approach is limited, and it is noted that the development of these standards has been undertaken without any significant empirical work being available to inform it in order to show whether what people do not like about first-tier complaint handling is being addressed by the standards.

In terms of complaints about ombud schemes themselves, while satisfaction levels with ombuds are higher than public services,[28] they are still lower than satisfaction levels found in private sector schemes.[29] There is also evidence that, for a small minority of ombud users, significant levels of dissatisfaction are experienced with the ombud process.[30] While these 'ombuds watchers' may be in a minority, they are a persistent and vocal critical voice, with users left angry, wishing they had not bothered and feeling like the whole system is corrupt.[31]

[23] A Clwyd and P Hart, *A Review of the NHS Complaints System: Putting Patients Back in the Picture* (The Stationery Office, 2013); B Kirkup, *The Report of the Morecambe Bay Investigation* (The Stationery Office, 2015); Francis R, *Report of the Mid Staffordshire NHS Foundation Trust Public Inquiry* (The Stationery Office, 2013).

[24] Crerar (n 7); Public Administration Select Committee, *More Complaints Please!* (London, House of Commons, 2014) www.publications.parliament.uk/pa/cm201314/cmselect/cmpubadm/229/229.pdf.

[25] PHSO (n 11) 6.

[26] ibid 50.

[27] Citizens Advice Scotland, 'Holding Public Services to Account in Scotland Open Government Partnership: Report on work by Citizens Advice Scotland' (CAS, 2020) 16 www.cas.org.uk/system/files/publications/holding_public_services_to_account_in_scotland-_citizens_advice_scotland_research_report_1.pdf.

[28] NAO (n 19).

[29] N Creutzfeldt, 'Trusting the Middle-Man: Impact and Legitimacy of Ombudsmen in Europe' (ESCR, 2015) 20 http://westminsterresearch.wmin.ac.uk/17179/1/ombuds_project_report_NC.pdf.

[30] C Gill and N Creutzfeldt, 'The "Ombuds Watchers": Collective Dissent and Legal Protest among Users of Public Services Ombuds' (2017) 27 *Social & Legal Studies* 367; Patients Association, *PHSO: A Labyrinth of Bureaucracy* (2015).

[31] See, eg D Reynolds, *What's the Point of the Ombudsman?* (PHSO The Facts, 2020).

B. The Effects of Complaints on Staff: The Missing Dimension

There are three dimensions to complaint handling – providing redress for the complainant, using complaints to improve services and ensuring that staff members recover effectively from being complained about.[32] While the first two dimensions have been considered within UK complaint systems, Johnson and Michel note that the third dimension, which they term 'employee recovery', has been largely ignored in complaint systems.[33] In particular, we have found that little is known about the impact on complaint handlers.

Empirical studies on the impact of complaints on staff have largely been limited to the healthcare sector. Wu published an editorial in the *British Medical Journal* in which he said that 'although patients are the first and obvious victims of medical mistakes, doctors are wounded by the same errors: they are the second victims'.[34] Ullstrom et al found that professionals may be affected in two ways after an adverse event: first, by the incident itself, and second, by the manner in which the incident is handled.[35] Other studies suggest that receiving a complaint is associated with feelings of anxiety, depression and reduced job satisfaction, with the impact varying from moderate to severe.[36] There is also evidence that complaints can lead to defensive practices, such as offering a more limited service and practising by the rules.[37]

Complaints also have the potential to damage relationships, reducing both trust and a sense of goodwill towards patients.[38] As seen from the health sector research, complaint systems, processes and approaches can be traumatic for the person complained about. An event is thought to produce a traumatic response when the stress resulting from that event overwhelms the individual's psychological ability to cope.[39] Complaints can also impact negatively on those complaining

[32] R Johnson and S Michel, 'Three Outcomes of Service Recovery: Customer Recovery, Process Recovery and Employee Recovery' (2008) 28 *International Journal of Operations & Production Management* 79.

[33] ibid.

[34] A Wu, 'Medical Error: The Second Victim' (2000) 320 *British Medical Journal* 726 www.ncbi.nlm.nih.gov/pmc/articles/PMC1117748/.

[35] S Ullstrom, A Sachs, J Hansson, J Øvretveit and M Brommels, 'Suffering in Silence: A Qualitative Study of Second Victims of Adverse Events' (2014) 23 *BMJ Quality & Safety* 325 http://qualitysafety.bmj.com/content/qhc/23/4/325.full.pdf.

[36] T Bourne, L Wynants and M Peters, 'The Impact of Complaints Procedures on the Welfare, Health and Clinical Practise of 7,926 Doctors in the UK: A Cross-Sectional Survey' (2015) 4 *BMJ Open* 1 http://bmjopen.bmj.com/content/bmjopen/5/1/e006687.full.pdf; J Bruers, B van Dam, R Gorter and M Eijkman, 'The Impact of a Formal Complaint on Dutch Dentists' Professional Practice: A Survey Study' (2015) 16 *BMC Oral Health* 104.

[37] A Jain and J Ogden, 'General Practitioners' Experiences of Patients' Complaints: Qualitative Study' (1999) 318 *British Medical Journal* 1596. For a recent ombuds report highlighting defensive practices, see PHSO (n 11).

[38] W Cunningham, 'The Immediate and Long-Term Impact on New Zealand Doctors Who Receive Patient Complaints' (2004) 117 *The New Zealand Medical Journal* 1198.

[39] S Straussner and A Calnan, 'Trauma through the Life Cycle: A Review of Current Literature' (2014) 42 *Clinical Social Work Journal* 323.

(and could re-traumatise), and we consider that there is likely to be ongoing chronic stress/trauma for those who are constantly working with complaint and conflict.

IV. Case Study: Being Complained About

A. Research on the Impact of Being Complained About

Health sector research relating to being complained about has reported negative effects on both staff well-being and functionality. However, impact has been under-researched in other public services. We began to address this gap in our 2017 study, which examined the effects of being complained about in two Scottish public services. We chose local authority planning departments and housing associations because they represented contrasting areas of public service provision across the following dimensions: types of service users, the nature of the relationship, statutory function and context, and public/independent sector service provision. They also had relatively high levels of complaints to the SPSO.[40]

Our research project used a mixed methods sequential design.[41] An online survey – sent to all local authority and housing association chief executives in Scotland (with a cover letter from the SPSO encouraging participation) – aimed to obtain a quantitative sense of the nature and types of effects experienced in each sector.[42] The survey received 132 responses. This was followed by in-depth qualitative telephone interviews with 16 staff members who volunteered when completing the survey. Descriptive statistics were used to analyse the online survey. Interviews were analysed using thematic analysis.[43]

Most survey respondents reported that being subject to a complaint affected their work practice (71 per cent) and their well-being (67 per cent).[44] A significant minority (15 per cent) had been affected 'a great deal'. Sixty-one per cent of respondents considered that being complained about made them more wary when dealing with certain service users: 29 per cent felt more distrustful, with 26 per cent starting to see service users as a risk. Fifty-seven per cent worried

[40] SPSO, *Cases Received by Sector* (2017) www.spso.org.uk/sites/spso/files/communications_material/statistics/201617/ReceivedbySubjectandAuthority2016-17.pdf.

[41] J Creswell and V Plano Clark, *Designing and Conducting Mixed Methods Research* (Sage, 2011).

[42] There were 141 survey responses, with nine excluded due to missing/incorrect data, resulting in a sample of 132 respondents. Of these, 64.4% (n = 85) were from housing associations and 35.6% (n = 47) were from planning departments.

[43] V Braun, and V Clarke, 'Using Thematic Analysis in Psychology' (2006) 3 *Qualitative Research in Psychology* 77.

[44] Figures cited here are rounded to the nearest whole number and percentages relate to the proportion of respondents answering the particular question (rather than the proportion of survey participants as a whole).

about receiving other complaints in the future. There were positive and negative views on how the complaint affected their work:

- 48 per cent now tried to communicate better with service users;
- 40 per cent felt more secure as a result of good complaint handling by the organisation;
- 27 per cent were now less sure about their work practice; and
- 22 per cent saw the complaint as a wake-up call and opportunity to do things differently.

Most respondents (57 per cent) felt well supported by their organisations during the complaint process, although 22 per cent did not. The support found most useful in helping respondents through the complaint included:

- line manager support (41 per cent);
- support from colleagues (20 per cent);
- being involved in the complaint handling (19 per cent); and
- support from friends and family (15 per cent).

In terms of the qualitative data, most respondents reported some positive effects on their practice. This included improved communication, becoming more sensitive to service user needs and being better equipped to meet them. However, negative emotional effects resulting from being complained about were common. Planning interviewees quotes are referred to as P1, P2, etc and housing interviewees as H1, H2, etc. Interviewees reported feeling upset, hurt, angry, anxious and attacked: 'I was quite shocked, and a bit hurt by it … And then I just felt a bit angry' (P8). For a minority, the experience was traumatic: 'It was dreadful, it was one of the worst things that's happened to me as an employee' (P5). The experience was described as dislocating and undermining interviewees' confidence in their work practice: 'I thought … did I mess up, basically? So it does make you question your own judgement' (P3).

A strong theme amongst planning interviewees was that effects were particularly severe where complaints were perceived as an attack on professionalism: 'So when someone's obviously questioning your professional territory, it does concern you' (P3). The strong professional identity amongst planners was seen as raising the stakes when complaints were made. There were frequent references to the perceived motivation of complainants when describing negative effects. This was more prevalent among housing staff, whose view was that their organisation used a 'customer is always right' approach: 'I got told obviously that I had upset the [complainant] and because that's how the [complainant] felt, the complaint had to be upheld' (H1).

A range of issues were raised about the complaint process. Most staff wanted to have their say: 'I think the thing that worked the best was when we actually had to sit down, in a discussion … There was opportunity to give my side of the story' (H5).

Being kept informed was important, but some interviewees felt that '[I was] not necessarily fully aware about what's going on' (P3). Similar to research where consumers emphasise the importance of receiving an explanation,[45] good explanations were key for helping staff accept decisions, especially if they were adverse. Several interviewees mentioned difficulties arising from colleagues being involved in investigating complaints: 'The complaint was as much to do with [manager's] attitude towards me as [the complaint itself]' (P5). Interviewees focused less on the need for additional support and more on ensuring a fair complaint process. A number said that avoiding blame allocation and making the focus of complaints about organisational improvement was important.

While exploratory in nature, our study suggested that, as in the healthcare sector, complaints can have a significant effect on the well-being and work practices of staff working in public services. Context appeared to be a significant influence on the prevalence and types of effects resulting from being complained about, so we expected complaints to have different effects in different areas of public service delivery. We found that effects on staff were not wholly negative, and for most are likely to be mixed, which presents a more variegated picture than that suggested in the traditionally dichotomous discussion of accountability systems. Importantly, our findings included that the design and operation of complaints procedures appeared to be significant factors in helping to explain the likelihood of negative effects resulting from a complaint.

B. Being Complained About – Good Practice Principles and Guidelines

The research findings described above led to the development of the Being Complained About Good Practice Principles and Guidelines (the Guidelines). The Guidelines drew on both our research findings and from learning related to human factors and the use of the 'Just Culture' approach.[46] The Guidelines aim to mitigate the negative impact of complaints through the application of clear processes which both involve and support the person complained about. The SPSO was involved in developing the Guidelines from the start. Feedback on early drafts was sought and received from the Law Society of Scotland and the Scottish Legal Complaints Commission. The draft Guidelines were circulated by the Ombudsman Association to members, with 12 ombud organisations responding with positive and constructive comments.

[45] See, eg Slater and Higginson (n 22) 53; J Williams, C Gill, N Creutzfeldt and N Vivian, 'Participation as a Framework for Analysing Consumers' Experiences of Alternative Dispute Resolution (ADR)' (2020) 47 *Journal of Law and Society* 271.

[46] NHS Improvement, 'A Just Culture Guide' (NHS, 2018) www.england.nhs.uk/wp-content/uploads/2021/02/NHS_0932_JC_Poster_A3.pdf; for general information on Just Culture, including the guide, see www.england.nhs.uk/patient-safety/a-just-culture-guide/#about-our-guide.

The finalised version of the Guidelines[47] was launched in February 2019, with content organised under the following headings:

1. Introduction
2. Guideline Principles
3. Expected Behaviours
4. Immediate Action Following Notification of a Complaint
5. Complaint Resolution Discussions
6. Complaint Investigation and Decision
7. Review of a Complaint Decision
8. Complaints and Professional Conduct
9. Action Relating to a Complaint
   Appendix One – Action Relating to a Complaint

The underlying ethos of the Guidelines is that both the complainants and the staff complained about have a right to be heard, understood and respected. The Guideline principles are fairness, transparency, confidentiality and efficiency – which also reflect the principles promoted by the Ombudsman Association in relation to good complaint handling.[48] The Guidelines are available as a free resource for organisations to choose to adopt and use. They are not prescriptive and can be adapted by an organisation to suit their existing complaint-handling policy, processes, terminology and approaches.

Funding was subsequently received from the University of Glasgow's ESRC Impact Acceleration Account to implement the Guidelines and to test and refine the findings and insights from their implementation. Work included a pilot case study on the impact of implementing the Guidelines in a public service organisation – Castle Rock Edinvar Housing Association (CRE), which employs around 215 staff. A survey of CRE staff before the introduction of the Guidelines found that of those who had been subject to a complaint (35 staff member responses), 37 per cent reported their work practice being affected a great deal, while 57 per cent were affected to some extent. Seventeen per cent worried a great deal about being complained and 66 per cent worried about this to some extent. In relation to the complaints process design, a number of potential issues were identified:

- 49 per cent of respondents disagreed that they had been involved in deciding how the complaint would be dealt with;
- 40 per cent said that the potential consequences of complaint processes were not clear;
- 40 per cent had not been told the outcome at the same time as the complainant;
- 34 per cent had not been told immediately about a complaint;

[47] www.gla.ac.uk/schools/law/research/groups/lawreform/beingcomplainedabout/.
[48] BIOA, 'Guide to Principles of Good Complaint Handling' (2007) www.ombudsmanassociation.org/sites/default/files/2021-03/BIOAGoodComplaintHandling.pdf.

- 31 per cent were not provided with support;
- 23 per cent thought the process was not fair to staff;
- 23 per cent had not been involved in the learning process;
- 17 per cent disagreeing that the process was transparent; and
- 17 per cent did not have the opportunity to comment on the complaint.

Thirteen staff members, who had been named/involved in complaints where a staff member had been complained about, were interviewed to understand their experiences in more depth. Potential barriers to improvements for those complained about were identified and the Guidelines were adapted to suit the CRE context. Amendments included: involving Human Resources at an earlier stage in the process; requiring investigating managers to provide feedback to the line manager of the person complained about on recommendations and next steps; and removing references to professional conduct and instead referring to investigations normally being suspended where criminal conduct is alleged/police investigation is ongoing.

The amended guidance was adopted as a CRE policy and circulated to all staff. Feedback on the implementation process was obtained from nine of the staff members interviewed earlier. Seven considered that the new guidance had changed their practice. However, organisational barriers (such as lack of central ownership of complaints and a propensity not to deal with issues requiring resolution) remained problematic for some. In the light of this learning, CRE intends to:

- include dealing with complaints in all job descriptions;
- define required conflict behaviours – in particular for frontline roles – and recruit in relation to these;
- consider induction/initial training needed, as well as ongoing training/development; and
- produce a summary document about what a manager needs to do when a staff member is complained about, together with a version for staff members.

This case study added to the knowledge about the impact on those complained about. Insights also include that:

- organisations need to do more than just introduce the Guidelines to overcome barriers and implement more supportive approaches to staff. Other issues (workload, lack of training, lack of role clarity) also have the potential to result in negative effects for staff handling complaints and those complained about; and
- the way in which an organisation deals with challenge and dispute internally can also affect how staff members view and deal with external complaints. The successful implementation of change to minimise the impact of complaints on staff requires a more holistic review of both internal and external complaints processes and practices.

V. Towards Therapeutic Complaint Resolution

A. What Can We Learn from Therapeutic Jurisprudence?

Our findings that existing complaint systems were not producing optimal outcomes for those complained about led us to consider whether complaint systems should adopt a less harmful/more therapeutic approach for all and the potential significance of therapeutic jurisprudence for ombuds in relation to: (i) their design role and (ii) more generally in terms of improving their own complaint-handling practices.

Therapeutic jurisprudence (TJ) describes a field of inquiry, developed by Wexler and Winick,[49] which has been defined by the International Society for Therapeutic Jurisprudence as 'an interdisciplinary field of philosophy and practice that examines the therapeutic and anti-therapeutic properties of laws and public policies, legal and dispute resolution systems, and legal institutions'.[50]

Wexler[51] used a wine bottle metaphor to explain therapeutic jurisprudence: the bottle represents structures, while the wine represents specific contextual practices. The focus of TJ literature is on the effects that rules, procedures and roles within legal and dispute resolution systems have on the people who come into contact with those systems[52] and which inevitably give rise to unintended consequences, which may be either beneficial (therapeutic) or harmful (anti-therapeutic). It draws attention to the effects of systems and seeks to build up an empirical body of knowledge about these in order to maximise the likelihood of therapeutic outcomes.[53]

The TJ literature does not advocate that therapeutic values should trump other values, such as due process or accountability. Instead, it argues for a consideration of the therapeutic effects of systems to the extent that such consideration is compatible with other values.[54] This has been referred to as using therapeutic practices within the interstitial spaces left open around legally shaped rules, procedures and roles.[55] For example, Campling[56] made the case for intelligent

[49] D Wexler and B Winick, *Essays in Therapeutic Jurisprudence* (Academic Press, 1991).

[50] https://intltj.com/about/therapeutic-jurisprudence/.

[51] D Wexler, 'Guiding Court Conversation along Pathways Conductive to Rehabilitation: Integrating Procedural Justice and Therapeutic Jurisprudence' (2016) 1 *International Journal of Therapeutic Jurisprudence* 367.

[52] M Herzog-Evans, 'Release and Supervision: Relationships and Support from Classic and Holistic Attorneys' (2016) 1 *International Journal of Therapeutic Jurisprudence* 23.

[53] P Spencer, 'From Alternative to the New Normal: Therapeutic Jurisprudence in the Mainstream' (2014) 39 *Alternative Law Journal* 222.

[54] A Campbell, 'A Case Study for Applying Therapeutic Jurisprudence to Policymaking: Assembling a Policy Toolbox to Achieve a Trauma-Informed Early Care and Learning System' (2019) 63 *International Journal of Law and Psychiatry* 45.

[55] Wexler and Winick (n 49).

[56] P Campling, 'Reforming the Culture of Healthcare: The Case for Intelligent Kindness' (2015) 39 *British Journal of Psychology Bulletin* 1.

kindness in reforming the healthcare culture and DiFonzo et al[57] used forgiveness theory to investigate the effects of organisational apology and restitution on eliciting forgiveness of a transgressing organisation after a transactional psychological contract breach. Forgiveness theory proposes that victims are more likely to forgive offenders when victims' positive offender-oriented emotions replace negative ones. It has been shown that emotion replacement is at the heart of the moral repair process and that apology and restitution bring about the emotional changes necessary for moral repair to occur.[58]

TJ can be considered as a subset of legal psychology: the scientific study of mind and behaviour as it affects or is affected by the law. Randall and Haskell[59] considered trauma-informed approaches to law and restorative justice. They make the point that the law regularly encounters and deals with people, both as victims and offenders, whose lives have been shaped and harmed by traumatic events. They also advance the general argument that more effective, fair, intelligent and just legal responses must work from a perspective which is trauma informed. It is our belief that this also applies to complaint handling, particularly in the public sector. TJ has yet to be deployed in the complaint-handling context, despite there being considerable potential to do so: there is significant congruence here with effects identified in the literature on healthcare complaints, which indicates that the TJ framework is likely to be of value in this context.

The value of applying the TJ framework to complaint handling – and, in doing so, introducing the concept of 'therapeutic complaint resolution' (TCR) – is that it provides a more sophisticated framework and language within which to discuss the positive and negative effects of accountability in public sector complaint systems. Using therapeutic jurisprudence as a lens through which to study complaint systems also calls attention to the real-world effects of dispute resolution systems, and seeks to complement existing values – such as due process or accountability – with a new emphasis on the lived experiences of actors in these systems. Indeed, Jones and Kawalec argue that therapeutic jurisprudence validates concerns about emotional well-being and draws attention to important issues that tend to be ignored in the traditional legal and bureaucratic emphasis on neutrality, impersonality and rationality.[60]

It is recognised that a limitation of TJ is that therapeutic practices tend to be context sensitive and not necessarily applicable across the board. So, in moving

[57] N DiFonzo, A Alongi and P Wiele, 'Apology, Restitution, and Forgiveness after Psychological Contract Breach' (2020) 161 *Journal of Business Ethics* 53.

[58] M Walker, *Moral Repair: Reconstructing Moral Relations after Wrongdoing* (Cambridge University Press, 2006); N Cugueró-escofet, M Fortin and M Canela, 'Righting the Wrong for Third Parties: How Monetary Compensation, Procedure Changes and Apologies Can Restore Justice for Observers of Injustice' (2014) 122 *Journal of Business Ethics* 253.

[59] M Randall and L Haskell, 'Trauma-Informed Approaches to Law: Why Restorative Justice Must Understand Trauma and Psychological Coping' (2013) 36 *Dalhousie Law Journal* 501.

[60] E Jones and A Kawalec, 'Dissolving the Stiff Upper Lip: Opportunities and Challenges for the Mainstreaming of Therapeutic Jurisprudence in the United Kingdom' (2018) 63 *International Journal of Law and Psychiatry* 76.

towards a focus on public service complaints and not seeking replicability to other disputing contexts, TCR is in some ways more limited, but also has more potential for theorising in this area. It is also considered that the field of disputation has spawned a range of theories and models that could be integrated into TCR. Generally, these theories and models have not been concerned centrally with well-being. However, to the extent that they enhance processes and outcomes, we might expect them to have a role in enhancing well-being.

B. The Role of Ombuds in Encouraging Therapeutic Approaches to Complaint Handling

In light of the key roles of UKPSOs, first as the designer and architect of public service complaint systems and second as a role model in setting the tone for good practice elsewhere, what evidence is there that UKPSOs currently display and support a therapeutic approach to complaint handing?

The TJ literature highlights the importance of dispute processes which allow active participation, solution-focused approaches, systems providing parties with a voice in proceedings and decisions being taken in a manner that feels fair to the parties.[61] These aspects are likely to be equally relevant to both complainants and those who are complained about. There are, therefore, many aspects of UKPSO practices which lend themselves well to TCR practices, including their relative informality, an emphasis on righting individual injustice, an inquisitorial approach to investigating complaints and an emphasis on organisational learning and addressing systemic issues. In their design role, UKPSO guidance for BwJ on effective complaint-handling practice emphasises the importance of accessibility, fairness, dealing with complaints promptly and the need for effective communication, being proportionate and investigating appropriately.[62] The SPSO updated their Model Complaint Handling Procedures in January 2020 to take account of the Guidelines, and the updated procedure now includes references to supporting staff.[63]

[61] P O'Byrne, 'Therapeutic Jurisprudence and the Sentencing of Family Offenders: Does the Sentencing "Bottle" in Victoria Need to Change?' (2016) 1 *International Journal of Therapeutic Jurisprudence* 147.

[62] In addition to SPSO's Model Complaint Handling Standards, another good example of ombuds and patients' organisations collaborating on guidance is LGO/Healthwatch/PHSO, My Expectations for Raising Concerns and Complaints: Vision Report (2015) www.ombudsman.org.uk/sites/default/files/Report_My_expectations_for_raising_concerns_and_complaints.pdf. See also Local Government and Social Care Ombudsman, *Effective Complaint Handling for Local Authorities* (2020) www.lgo.org.uk/information-centre/news/2020/oct/new-complaints-handling-guide-offers-advice-to-local-authorities; PHSO, 'Principles of Good Administration' (2009) www.ombudsman.org.uk/about-us/our-principles/principles-good-administration; PHSO, 'Principles of Good Complaint Handling' (2009) www.ombudsman.org.uk/sites/default/files/page/0188-Principles-of-Good-Complaint-Handling-bookletweb.pdf.

[63] See, eg paras 33, 48, 62 and 68 of the SPSO's 'Local Authority Model Complaints Handling Procedure' (2020) www.spso.org.uk/sites/spso/files/csa/LAMCHPPart3.pdf.

However, anti-therapeutic effects still continue to exist in the public services complaints landscape. In terms of the investigation process, research examining the effects of coronial investigation processes on professional actors finds that anti-therapeutic effects can be produced by various aspects of investigation procedures, including: delays, lack of communication, unclear decisions, lack of ability to comment on decisions and lack of emotional sensitivity.[64] We also know from our research that both complainants and those complained about can be harmed by delays, lack of communication, unclear decisions, the lack of ability to comment on decisions and a lack of emotional sensitivity. The 2020 PHSO review of complaint handling in the health service in England and in central government bodies also highlighted delays and poor communication as common themes.[65] Hogg et al found that the common focuses of patient complaints in the UK and other high-income countries are poor staff attitudes, behaviour and communication.[66]

A recent review of clinical advice in health complaints at the PHSO highlighted a number of aspects of complaint handling by the PHSO which potentially combine to act in a non-therapeutic manner.[67] The independent expert report commissioned by this review criticised the PHSO for being too procedurally driven and at times failing to take sufficient account of the 'rich and important insights' from complainants.[68] The final review report highlighted how families and patients felt that their views were not given proper weight and how they felt 'disbelieved by default'.[69] Recent qualitative research on impartiality for the PHSO highlights the perception by some complainants that there is a 'mismatch' between the complainants on the one hand and the organisation being complained about, and that insufficient account was taken of the human impact of the experience.[70] The research also highlighted the requirement for open communication and the need to treat complainants with compassion, empathy and understanding.[71]

[64] I Freckelton, 'Therapeutic Jurisprudence Misunderstood and Misrepresented: The Price and Risks of Influence' (2007) 30 *Thomas Jefferson Law Review* 30.

[65] PHSO, *Making Complaints Count: Supporting Complaints Handling in the NHS and UK Government Departments* (HC 390, 15 July 2020) https://www.ombudsman.org.uk/sites/default/files/%28HC%20390%29%20-%20Making%20Complaints%20Count-%20Supporting%20complaints%20handling%20in%20the%20NHS%20and%20UK%20Government%20Departments.pdf.

[66] R Hogg, J Hanley and P Smith P, 'Learning Lessons from the Analysis of Patient Complaints Relating to Staff Attitudes, Behaviour and Communication, Using the Concept of Emotional Labour' (2018) 27 *Journal of Clinical Nursing* 004.

[67] PHSO, *Clinical Advice Review Final Report* (2019) www.ombudsman.org.uk/sites/default/files/Final_Report_Clinical_Advice_Review.pdf.

[68] L Donaldson, *Report of the Independent Adviser to the Clinical Advice Review Commissioned by the Parliamentary and Health Service Ombudsman* (2018) 13 www.ombudsman.org.uk/sites/default/files/PHSO_Clinical_Advice_Review_Report_of_Independent_Adviser.pdf.

[69] PHSO, *Making Complaints Count* (n 65) 7.

[70] Parliamentary and Health Service Ombudsman (PHSO) *Complainant Feedback: Charter Commitment 10 Summary Report of Findings Opinion Research Services* (2020) www.ombudsman.org.uk/sites/default/files/ORS_Summary_Report_on_Impartiality_March_2020.pdf.

[71] ibid paras 1.23, 1.25 and 1.26.

In Scotland, a small, qualitative review of 12 complaint files in relation to GPs, health boards and the SPSO highlighted how there was little account of feelings, only facts, and that 'in the majority of responses there is no apparent understanding of the distress experienced by the complainant'.[72] In 2019, the PHSO pledged to change the culture of the organisation to be more attuned to the patient and family experience.[73] The Patients Association[74] recently noted that there had been improvements in how PHSO communicates and keeps patients updated (although it also noted that there had been a reduction in satisfaction with the PHSO explaining its decisions).

One of the drivers for complaining in relation to public services is said to be the desire to ensure that it does not happen again or to someone else.[75] In Australia, Spigelman, a former Chief Justice of New South Wales, has commented on how ongoing relationships are at the heart of citizen–state interactions.[76] The rebuilding of these relationships in the context of public services therefore has potential for significant therapeutic benefits. Ensuring that learning happens in practice is thought to be very challenging. The PSOW has highlighted how, 'despite numerous reports' outlining cultural weaknesses in public sector complaint handling, including defensiveness and a blame culture, these cultural issues continue and can mean that the user does not receive a fair, just and timely outcome to their complaint.[77]

The PHSO has also highlighted the existence of a defensive culture in relation to English health and UK government disputes. Learning from complaints does not always happen. Despite the fact that the Local Government and Social Care Ombudsman has previously reported twice on education, health and care plans, its recent focus report continues to highlight an uphold rate of 87 per cent compared to an overall average of 58 per cent.[78] In his review of existing research, Gill concluded it is difficult to draw any conclusions on how effective ombuds are

[72] CAS (n 27) 18.

[73] PHSO, 'Our Response to the Clinical Advice Review' (2019) 19 www.ombudsman.org.uk/sites/default/files/Our_Response_to_the_Clinical_Advice_Review.pdf.

[74] Patients Association, 'Position Statement: PHSO' (2020) www.patients-association.org.uk/Handlers/Download.ashx?IDMF=6592b5d6-ca60-49f0-9f1d-a6f739d28614.

[75] M Bismark, T Brennan, R Paterson R, P Davis and D Studdert, 'Relationship between Complaints and Quality of Care in New Zealand: A Descriptive Analysis of Complainants and Non-complainants Following Adverse Events' (2006) 15 *Quality and Safety in Health Care* 17; Citizens Advice (n 19); R Friele and E Sluijs, 'Patient Expectations of Fair Complaint Handling in Hospitals: Empirical Data' (2006) 6 *BMC Health Services Research* 106.

[76] JJ Spigelman, 'Foundations of Administrative Law: Toward General Principles of Institutional Law' (1999) 58 *Australian Journal of Public Administration* 3.

[77] Public Services Ombudsman for Wales, 'Ending Groundhog Day Lessons from Poor Complaint Handling' (WPSO, 2018) 10 www.ombudsman.wales/wp-content/uploads/2018/03/Ending-Groundhog-Day-Lessons-in-Poor-Complaint-Handling.pdf.

[78] Local Government and Social Care Ombudsman, 'Not Going to Plan? – Education, Health and Care Plans Two Years on. Focus Report: Learning Lessons from Complaints' (LGSCO, 2019) 1 www.lgo.org.uk/information-centre/news/2019/oct/a-system-in-crisis-ombudsman-complaints-about-special-educational-needs-at-alarming-level.

at encouraging organisational learning as there is no significant evidence base to draw on.[79]

In practice, uphold rates vary significantly. For example, in 2019/2020, uphold rates varied from 20 per cent (PSOW) to 72 per cent (Office of the Northern Ireland Ombudsman).[80] The terminology of uphold/not uphold in itself has potential to operate in an anti-therapeutic manner: first, in driving win/lose behaviours, and second, because a simple uphold/not upheld fails to capture the complexity of decision-making in the public sector. Annual reports from the Housing Ombudsman and the PSOW appear to have moved away from that language. Creutzfeldt's research suggests that citizens' experiences of uphold and not uphold may not correspond with the way that schemes classify it.[81] Donaldson's review into the nature of clinical advice by the PHSO also highlighted the unhelpful nature of a system that requires ombudsman to either 'uphold' or not a complaint which fails to convey the 'nuanced nature' of many judgements on whether a health complaint is justified or not.[82] In the context of consumer alternative dispute resolution schemes, Williams et al found that dissatisfaction centred around the lack of effective participation by the parties in shaping outcomes, which led to strong feelings that schemes were 'placating' or 'isolating' them and failing to effectively engage with them.[83] It is noted that the SPSO is encouraging a resolution approach to complaints, with its 2020 Good Practice Guidance saying that the outcome of a complaint can now be resolved, upheld, partially upheld or not upheld.[84]

A significant gap in the literature is that we simply do not know enough about the impact complaint processes have on individual complaint handlers within the public service organisations or at ombuds themselves. The research that does exist is limited to the impact of querulous and unreasonable conduct

[79] C Gill, 'What Can Government Agencies Learn from the Ombudsman?' in Hertogh and Kirkham, *Research Handbook on the Ombudsman* (n 2) 298–318.

[80] Public Services Ombudsman for Wales, *Annual Report 2019/2020* (2020) 6, www.ombudsman.wales/wp-content/uploads/2020/07/PSOW-Annual-Report-and-Accounts-2019-20.pdf; NIPSO, *Ombudsman's Report 2019–2020* (2020) 22, https://nipso.org.uk/site/wp-content/uploads/2020/11/Ombudsmans-Report-2019-20.pdf.

[81] In Creutzfeldt's research, the outcome was in favour or partial favour of the complainant in 19.7% of cases in the public sector compared to 60.8% in the private sector: Creutzfeldt (n 29) 32. The PHSO annual report at the time indicated an uphold rate in full or part of 37%: ibid 15. The uphold rate for the LGO was not included in its annual report that year. All decisions are however published. See Creutzfeldt (n 29) 20; PHSO, *Annual Report and Accounts 2014/2015* (2015) 15, www.ombudsman.org.uk/sites/default/files/2016-10/Annual%20Report%202014-15_0.pdf; LGO, *Annual Report 2014/15* (2015) www.lgo.org.uk/information-centre/about-us/our-performance/lgo-annual-reports.

[82] Donaldson (n 68) 23. A recent Healthwatch report also argued that this distinction is unhelpful since upholding a complaint can drive defensive behaviours and a blame culture while not upholding a complaint can result in missed opportunities for learning: Healthwatch, 'Shifting the Mindset: A Closer Look at NHS Complaints' (2020) 11 www.healthwatch.co.uk/sites/healthwatch.co.uk/files/20191126%20-%20Shifting%20the%20mindset%20-%20NHS%20complaints%20.pdf.

[83] Williams et al (n 45).

[84] SPSO, 'Good Practice Guidance: Alternative Complaint Resolution Approaches' (2020) www.spso.org.uk/sites/spso/files/csa/Alternative%20Complaint%20Resolution%20Approaches.pdf.

on complaint handlers.[85] While this research is important and had a significant impact on practice, this emphasis on inappropriate and potentially dysfunctional behaviour fails to address the wider potentially anti-therapeutic elements of complaint handling, as it tends to treat the symptoms rather than the cause of these behaviours. A recent report on complaint handling in the public sector in Australia highlighted the often-challenging work of complaint handling and the need to recruit staff with the right skills, including excellent communication skills, empathy, evidence-based investigation skills and peer support.[86] It is noted that a recent research study with complaint handlers in the financial sector highlighted the active role that group support and dialogue plays in supporting individual complaint handlers' fair decision-making.[87]

C. Suggestions for Enhancing Therapeutic Complaint Handling Practices

Returning to Wexler's metaphor,[88] a pragmatic response to our research findings would be for ombuds to move towards the approach of 'new wine in an old bottle'. While not changing the current design paradigm, they could introduce or enhance practices which have been found to be more therapeutic and so make complaint handling less traumatic for all – in effect, to retain the adversarial character of complaint systems, but with attempts to soften their edges. However, it is acknowledged that the 'bottle' or structure within which complaint handling takes places may impose limits on these more therapeutic practices.

Relevant to our proposals here for the incremental reform of complaint systems are that observations from participants in our original and case study research concentrated in the main on procedural fairness and communication. This included being given an opportunity to respond to a complaint and state one's case, being heard and being provided with information and updates throughout the complaints process. Such recognition could be complemented

[85] New South Wales Ombudsman, *Managing Unreasonable Complainant Conduct Practice Manual*, 1st edn (NSWO, 2009); G Lester, B Wilson, L Griffin and P Mullen, 'Unusually Persistent Complainants' (2004) 184 *British Journal of Psychiatry* 352; P Mullen and G Lester, 'Vexatious Litigants and Unusually Persistent Complainants and Petitioners: From Querulous Paranoia to Querulous Behaviour' (2006) 24 *Behavioural Sciences and the Law* 333; G Skilling, M Øfstegaard, S Brodie and L Thomson, 'Unusually Persistent Complainants against the Police in Scotland' (2012) www.sipr.ac.uk/Plugin/Publications/assets/files/PCCS_querulous_complainers.pdf; G Skilling, 'Querulous Complainants' (2017) www.spso.org.uk/sites/spso/files/csa/Querulous%20Complainants%20WEB.pdf.

[86] Sourdin et al (n 22).

[87] J Williams, C Gill and G McBurnie, '"It's the Most Ethical Job I Have Ever Had": Complaint Handling and Fair Decision-Making' [2020] *International Journal of Business Governance and Ethics*, DOI: 10.1504/IJBGE.2021.10035729.

[88] Wexler (n 51).

by a range of emotionally intelligent and empathetic communication practices.[89] Other aspects involved better support for all and a stronger learning focus. It is known that where procedures are perceived to be fair and the outcomes of complaint resolution are seen as more legitimate, the well-being of system actors will be enhanced (see, eg Lind and Tyler[90] and Thibault and Walker,[91] and the significant body of academic work derived therefrom). For staff, the benefits of such a system might include the development of more positive and trusting relationships with service users, enhanced well-being at work, and a more human and sensitive means through which issues of public concern can be aired. In this respect, what staff and complainants want from therapeutic justice is the same.

These suggestions fit well with countering the anti-therapeutic practices identified by Freckelton in his exploration of the experiences in coronial investigation processes.[92] There are also therapeutic effects where dispute resolution processes allow active participation and a solution-focused approach, providing parties with a voice in proceedings and allowing decisions to be taken in a manner that feels fair to the parties.[93] Doyle and O'Brien[94] consider the role of an ombud as a storyteller, helping to restore trust by using narrative interpretation, so that reports also interpret and convey what an ombud sees and hears, and in doing this acts as a 'bridge-builder' between the citizen and the state.

These shifts in communication and procedural fairness in complaint handling are fairly uncontroversial and, in fact, conform to aspects of good practice already recognised in the complaint-handling literature. Indeed, suggestions about enhanced procedural fairness and interpersonal treatment fit strongly with prescriptions for improving satisfaction levels among complainants.[95] The novelty of these suggested approaches lies in applying them to staff as well as to complainants, with implications for ombuds here relating to their own staff recruitment, required competencies and training.

Our view is that there is much that ombuds can learn from being more trauma aware in their own work – and from using this awareness to better design

[89] M King, 'Restorative Justice, Therapeutic Jurisprudence and the Rise of Emotionally Intelligent Justice' (2008) 32 *Melbourne University Law Review* 1096. For a discussion of the importance of exchanging perspectives, engaging in dialogue and the need for judges to establish some kind of relationship with the parties in the Dutch administrative courts, see A Verbung and B Shueler, 'Procedural Justice in Dutch Administrative Court Proceedings' (2014) 10 *Utrecht Law Review* 56. All of these elements resonate with a therapeutic complaint resolution approach.

[90] E Lind and T Tyler, *The Social Psychology of Procedural Justice* (Plenum Press, 1988).

[91] J Thibault and L Walker, *Procedural Justice: A Psychological Analysis* (Lawrence Erlbaum, 1975).

[92] I Freckelton, 'Death Investigation, the Coroner and Therapeutic Jurisprudence' (2007) 15 *Journal of Law and Medicine* 242.

[93] O'Byrne (n 61).

[94] M Doyle and N O'Brien, *Reimagining Administrative Justice: Human Rights in Small Places* (Springer Nature, 2019).

[95] C Orsingher, S Valentini and M de Angelis, 'A Meta-analysis of Satisfaction with Complaint Handling in Services' (2010) 38 *Journal of the Academy of Marketing Science* 169; K Van den Bos, L Van der Velden and E Lind, 'On the Role of Perceived Procedural Justice in Citizens' Reactions to Government Decisions and the Handling of Conflicts' (2014) 10 Utrecht Law Review 1.

complaint systems and approaches relating to both internal and external conflict. Trauma-informed practice was developed in the USA in the early 2000s.[96] Menschner and Maul's[97] trauma-informed model of care is now widely used in human services. Trauma-informed care has also been introduced in the UK in the criminal justice system, the homelessness sector, schools, and children and family services. This has resulted in a positive shift to providing a trauma-informed approach – moving from thinking 'What is wrong with you?' to considering 'What happened to you?'[98] Ombuds could both promote a greater awareness of trauma-informed practice and model these approaches in their own ways of working. In the service recovery literature, Hibbert et al point out that 'dysfunctional' behaviour, particularly in the case of vulnerable consumers, can relate to consumers genuinely trying to cope with factors beyond their control.[99] Their work highlights how the organisations can drive dysfunctional behaviour and how vulnerable consumers in particular may be acting unintentionally as they lack clarity over the rules and how they are supposed to act or simply do not have the resources to comply with those expectations.

We know that there may be increased costs in terms of time, effort and complexity resulting from greater engagement of employees and enhanced communication. In particular, offering enhanced procedural protections – such as formal rights to reply or automatic rights to discuss a complaint – could slow complaint processes down, leading to increased administrative costs and dissatisfaction among complainants.

D. Towards a Model of Therapeutic Complaint Resolution?

As we have also argued elsewhere,[100] a longer-term approach to creating a more therapeutic complaints system would be to reform the bottle itself. To the extent that it is possible, the therapeutic effects relating to complaint handling could be maximised in this TCR model and anti-therapeutic effects minimised. It is envisaged that ombuds could use their statutory CSA powers/non-statutory influence on design/redesigning positive therapeutic effects into complaint handling systems. Our view is that the application of therapeutic jurisprudence is likely to be broadly similar in its effect for complainants and the person complained about, whose experiences of the current complaints systems can be equally negative.

[96] E Alessi and S Kahn, 'Using Psychodynamic Interventions to Engage in Trauma-Informed Practice' (2019) 33 *Journal of Social Work Practice* 27.

[97] C Menschner, and A Maul, *Key Ingredients for Successful Trauma-Informed Care Implementation* (Center for Health Care Strategies, 2016).

[98] A Sweeney, B Filson, A Kennedy, L Collinson and S Gillard, 'A Paradigm Shift: Relationships in Trauma-Informed Mental Health Services' (2018) 24 *BJPsych Advances* 319.

[99] S Hibbert, M Piacentini and M Hogg, 'Service Recovery following Dysfunctional Consumer Participation' (2012) 11 *Journal of Consumer Behaviour* 329.

[100] Gill (n 1).

A key therapeutic change is for ombuds and complaint handlers to become more aware of their potential role as 'therapeutic actors'[101] and to approach both complainants and those complained about with an 'ethic of care' for their well-being. There is also merit in moving away from assigning a 'rightness' and a 'wrongness' in complaint outcomes (which can lead to feelings of winning or losing) and moving towards an outcome of resolution. Relational rights would be substantive in this approach, with compassion becoming a central component of complaint-handling procedures.[102] We know that complainants often have ongoing relationships with their public service providers and that conflicts can be deeply rooted and enduring, going beyond just satisfying interests and involving needs which are non-negotiable (to do with identity, justice, self-esteem, respect and fairness). There is value in having a therapeutic approach which also serves to repair harm and restore relationships. An approach which recognises the value of reconciliation similar to the approach taken by the Reconciliation Commission of South Africa may be particularly relevant for the long-standing complex disputes dating back many years. Currently legislation limits the abilities of ombuds to adopt such practices.

This therapeutic approach could draw on human-centred design (HCD) principles for putting the user's voice at the centre of the dispute system design process and, in doing so, to counter much of the asymmetrical and systemic power which can permeate public service complaint systems.[103] Miller points out that 'users' are not a homogeneous group and that the type of justice a system user is seeking will be integral to shaping the design process, as will their unique needs and behaviours. She also questions whether HCD is appropriate for all types of dispute system design. A design-centred approach should also ensure that the voice of BwJ are also taken into account since they will bear the responsibility of ensuring that these systems work in practice. In recent years, UKPSOs have engaged in significant outreach work with BwJ and the introduction of model complaint-handling procedures have been widely consulted upon. More research evaluating the impact of these standards for complainants, staff and BwJ could, however, usefully be undertaken to provide an empirical base for future work.

A TCR model could also move away from the concept of public services being 'goods to be delivered' to seeing them more as relationships to be nurtured and sustained. It would emphasise co-production and delivery, with common interests so that all parties have a stake in and a responsibility for services. This model would also shift perceptions of the citizen as a selfish actor with narrow

[101] O'Byrne (n 61).

[102] J Herring, *Caring and the Law* (Bloomsbury, 2013); J Herring, 'Compassion, Ethics of Care and Legal Rights' (2017) 13 *International Journal of Law in Context* 158.

[103] A Miller, 'What Human-Centered Design Can Tell Us about the State of Dispute Systems Design' (MA thesis, University of Victoria, 2019) http://dspace.library.uvic.ca/bitstream/handle/1828/10882/Miller_Alyson_MADR_2019.pdf?sequence=1&isAllowed=y.

consumer interests[104] towards a broader notion of co-production and delivery, with complaining being active participation in public governance.[105]

Concepts from the therapeutic jurisprudence literature such as mediation, which are solution-focused and oriented towards positive future outcomes,[106] could be used to shift complaint handling towards this non-adversarial paradigm. The TCR model could also draw on insights relating to the importance of participation as both a process value and in shaping outcomes in consumer experiences of alternative dispute resolution.[107]

However, it is recognised that this TCR model requires a significant reconceptualisation of the relationship between citizens and the administration and, on that basis alone, it could be rejected as unrealistic. There are also practical objections to applying this approach – for example, in areas of complaints involving fundamental rights where mediation may not be appropriate, or where the issues being complained about are transactional and a more discursive process for resolving concerns would be disproportionate. More fundamentally, the approach could be seen as undermining the accountability function of complaint systems by moving them away from objectively evaluating whether standards have been delivered to a more nebulous and subjective process of deliberation.

To conclude, we propose that empirical enquiries into TCR be developed further with reference to a set of hypotheses derived from the disputing literature. The ultimate aim will be to address the current shortfalls of TJ by developing theoretically sound propositions with regard to therapeutic practices, developed and refined in the context of empirical enquiry. More research is needed to better understand the effects (good and bad) of ombud design processes on the well-being and emotions of system actors: complainants, those complained about and complaint handlers. There is the potential to build up a significant body of empirical knowledge that can shape future complaint-handling practice and be used as evidence to inform the role of ombuds as 'architects of governance'.

[104] B Brewer, 'Citizen or Customer? Complaints Handling in the Public Sector' (2007) 73 *International Review of Administrative Sciences*, 549.
[105] N O'Brien, 'Administrative Justice in the Wake of I, Daniel Blake' (2018) 1 *The Political Quarterly* 82.
[106] King (n 89).
[107] Williams et al (n 45).

13

High Official at Street Level: A Multi-method Study on the Consultation Days of the Austrian Ombudspersons

JULIA DAHLVIK, AXEL POHN-WEIDINGER AND MARTINA KOLLEGGER

I. Introduction

Public ombuds institutions, by monitoring the functioning of administrations, can play a vital role in ensuring decent bureaucratic processes, administrative justice and adherence to the rule of law. The key pillar of an ombud's work is made up of citizens' complaints. Citizens who have experienced maladministration can typically address ombuds institutions in different ways (in 40 per cent of all European ombuds institutions, however, citizens are obliged to submit their complaint in written form).[1] To ensure facilitated access to justice through the ombuds, institutions can take different measures. One such measure is the personal encounter, as offered by the Austrian Ombudsman Board (Volksanwaltschaft, AOB), which regularly holds consultation days throughout the country. Similar activities can or could be found in numerous other countries: in their comparative study in the 1990s, for example, Kempf and Mille reached the conclusion that out-of-town consultation days constitute a common practice of ombudspersons.[2] They found that 68 per cent of the included 48 ombudspersons offer (out-of-town) consultation days, promoting a low-threshold access to their services. However, we know little about these encounters between citizens and ombudspersons. How do they play out? What are both parties' motives, practices and experiences?

[1] G Kucsko-Stadlmayer, *European Ombudsman-Institutions: A Comparative Legal Analysis Regarding the Multifaceted Realisation of an Idea* (Springer, 2008).

[2] U Kempf and M Mille, 'Rolle undFunktion des Ombudsmannes – Zur Personalisierten Parlamentarischen Verwaltungskontrolle in 48 Staaten' (1992) 23 *Zeitschrift Für Parlamentsfragen* 29.

Scholars have mainly studied the public ombuds with regard to various legal aspects.[3] Additionally, some literature exists on organisational dimensions, for instance, investigating complaint-handling practices[4] or expectation management,[5] or concerning the variety of goals of ombuds institutions.[6] Another strand of research has produced knowledge on users' sociodemographic profiles,[7] their expectations[8] and acceptance of decisions,[9] as well as users' 'normative profiles'.[10] These studies typically investigate the extent to which ombuds institutions provide easy access to legal support for the entire population, but also how the legal knowledge of ombuds users differs from that of the overall population.

On the other hand, there is a long tradition of research on face-to-face encounters between citizens and public officials within bureaucracies.[11] These encounters are often studied from the perspective of 'street-level bureaucracy', a term coined by Lipsky, who presented the first paper on the topic in 1969. 'Street-level bureaucrats … are those men and women who, in their face-to-face encounters with citizens "represent" government to the people.'[12] Typically based on ethnographic data, recent research in this area has studied, for instance, how citizens or applicants and public professionals negotiate the

[3] G Roy and PJ Giddings. 'The Ombudsman Institution: Growth and Development' in PJ Giddings (ed), *Righting Wrongs: The Ombudsman in Six Continents* (IOS Press, 2000); LC Reif, *The Ombudsman, Good Governance, and the International Human Rights System* (Martinus Nijhoff, 2004); M Hertogh and R Kirkham (eds), *Research Handbook on the Ombudsman* (Edward Elgar, 2018).

[4] J Dahlvik and A Pohn-Weidinger, 'Administering Access to the Ombudsperson. A Case Study on the Austrian Ombudsman Board' in Hertogh and Kirkham,*Research Handbook on the Ombudsman*(n 3).

[5] S Gilad, 'Juggling Conflicting Demands: The Case of the UK Financial Ombudsman Service' (2009) 19 *Journal of Public Administration Research and Theory* 661.

[6] PY Baudot and A Revillard, 'Le médiateur de la république: périmètre et autonomisation d'une institution' (2011) 139 *Revue française d'administration publique* 339.

[7] S Van Roosbroek and S Van de Walle, 'The Relationship between Ombudsman, Government, and Citizens: A Survey Analysis' (2008) 24 *Negotiation Journal* 287. B Hubeau. 'The Profile of Complainants: How to Overcome the 'Matthew Effect'?' in Hertogh and Kirkham, *Research Handbook on the Ombudsman* (n 3).

[8] N Creutzfeldt, 'What Do We Expect from an Ombudsman? Narratives of Everyday Engagement with the Informal Justice System in Germany and the UK' (2016) 12 *International Journal of Law in Context* 437.

[9] N Creutzfeldt and B Bradford, 'Dispute Resolution Outside of Courts: Procedural Justice and Decision Acceptance among Users of Ombuds Services in the UK' (2016) 50 *Law & Society Review* 985.

[10] M Hertogh, 'Why the Ombudsman Does Not Promote Public Trust in Government: Lessons from the Low Countries' (2013) 35 *Journal of Social Welfare and Family Law* 245.

[11] JM Prottas, *People-Processing: The Street-Level Bureaucrat in Public Service Bureaucracies* (Lexington Books, 1979); CT Goodsell, *The Public Encounter: Where State and Citizen Meet* (Indiana University Press, 1981); M Lipsky, *Street-Level Bureaucracy: Dilemmas of the Individual in Public Service* (Russell Sage Foundation, 2010); KPR Bartels, *Communicative Capacity: Public Encounters in Participatory Theory and Practice* (Policy Press, 2015); V Dubois, *The Bureaucrat and the Poor: Encounters in French Welfare Offices* (Routledge, 2016).

[12] M Lipsky, 'Toward a Theory of Street-Level Bureaucracy' (paper presented at the American Political Science Association Conference, 1969).

meaning of law and thus influence street-level decision-making in the individual case[13] or how frontline employees create resources to cope with tensions.[14]

In the fields of access to justice and, more concretely, legal advice and ombuds work, however, face-to-face interaction is rarely studied. Some scholars have compared the effects of telephone or online services to personal encounters in the context of advice centres. The findings suggest that the shift away from face-to-face consultation has important effects on accessibility and content:[15] demographic characteristics as well as the types of problems addressed in telephone advice are significantly different according to the type of service. In addition, Smith and Paterson conclude that digital delivery cannot replace face-to-face services. 'Put starkly, clients will be lost if consulting rooms are closed and people are expected to use the phone or the internet.'[16]

Although we therefore know that offers such as personal consultation can play an important role, they are rarely the focus of ombuds research. In this chapter, we aim to fill the identified research gaps by exploring the role of ombuds consultation days from the point of view of users and professionals. Empirically, this chapter is based upon a case study on the Austrian Ombudsman Board, in which we apply a multi-method approach that allows us to study face-to-face encounters between ombudspersons and citizens from multiple angles. The chapter ask the following questions: what are users' and ombudspersons' motivations and experiences regarding the consultation days? How do ombudspersons' and users' practices shape the encounter? What are the effects of the consultation days, for both professionals and users?

The chapter starts with a short presentation of our case and our methodological approach. After that, we briefly review the organisational rationale behind the consultation day in order to study the extent to which the aims of this measure are realised. We discuss our findings concerning the socio-demographic factors for consultation day usage, followed by a consideration of other factors why citizens make use of the public encounter, including their conceptions of the law and previous experiences with public administration. In the next section, we explore the involved actors' different practices and strategies through the analysis of two short sequences of interactions we have observed. Following this, we discuss the articulation of the actors' expectations and their confrontation with possibilities of realisation as key functions of the consultation day. Finally, we briefly sum up the experiences made by complainants during the public encounter.

[13] LEF Johannessen, 'Negotiated Discretion: Redressing the Neglect of Negotiation in "Street-Level Bureaucracy"' (2019) 42 *Symbolic Interaction*, 513; J Dahlvik, *Inside Asylum Bureaucracy: Organizing Refugee Status Determination in Austria* (Springer, 2018).

[14] A Schneider, B Bullinger and J Brandl, 'Resourcing under Tensions: How Frontline Employees Create Resources to Balance Paradoxical Tensions' (2021) 42 *Organization Studies* 1291.

[15] NJ Balmer, M Smith, C Denvir and A Patel (2012) 'Just a Phone Call Away: Is Telephone Advice Enough?' (2012) 34 *Journal of Social Welfare and Family Law* 63.

[16] R Smith and A Paterson, 'Face to Face Legal Services and Their Alternatives: Global Lessons from the Digital Revolution' (2014) 83 https://strathprints.strath.ac.uk/56496/1/Smith_Paterson_CPLS_Face_to_face_legal_services_and_their_alternatives.pdf.

A. Case Study and Methods

The AOB was established in July 1977 as one of the supreme bodies of the Republic of Austria. It monitors all authorities, administrative bodies and departments of the state, the provinces and the local government authorities in the entire federal territory.[17] From its beginning, the AOB's key task has been to investigate complaints from citizens and to assess whether the administration is acting within the law and complies with general administrative principles. The complaint may involve inactivity of the authority, a legal opinion that does not comply with the respective laws or an act of gross negligence. The AOB consists of three members, elected by the Austrian Parliament (National Council) for a term of six years, each in charge of one area of responsibility comprising several subjects. In 2018, the AOB received more than 16,000 complaints.[18] Currently, the AOB has around 90 employees; around half of them are legal experts handling the cases.

The fact that the AOB provides consultation days with the ombudspersons personally make this outreach measure rather special.[19] The three ombudspersons offer these face-to-face encounters on a regular basis in different district authorities throughout the nine Austrian provinces.[20] The consultation day allows citizens to both meet the ombudsperson in person and file a complaint orally. Key points of the complaint are recorded by members of the legal staff. In theory, the complainant does not have to be able to read and write to file a complaint. Thus, the consultation day can be viewed both as a symbol and as a practical means to secure for citizens a low-threshold access to their right of administrative control.

This ambition to provide easy, unbureaucratic access to justice appears in almost every AOB annual report since 1977. As early as in the AOB's second report to the Parliament, the aim to provide easy access to justice was explicitly stated: 'In order to guarantee equal opportunities for all citizens to submit their (legal) matters irrespective of their residence, the ombudspersons hold consultation days in all federal states of Austria.'[21] Even if the consultation day itself has no legal foundation, the measure has become an integral part of the AOB's organisational culture and institutional design.

[17] The two provinces Tyrol and Vorarlberg have their own provincial ombudspersons (*Landesvolksanwältin*) responsible for cases concerning the administration of the respective province (not for federal issues).

[18] Volksanwaltschaft, *Bericht der Volksanwaltschaft an den Nationalrat und an den Bundesrat 2018* (Volksanwaltschaft, 2019).

[19] In addition, the AOB features another unique outreach measure, a weekly broadcast in public TV, which, however, cannot be explored within the scope of this chapter. Both outreach measures are discussed in J Dahlvik, A Pohn-Weidinger and M Kollegger, 'Access to Administrative Justice and the Role of Outreach Measures: Empirical Findings on the Austrian Ombudsman Board' [2021] *International Journal of Law in Context* 1 (online first) https://doi.org/10.1017/S1744552321000501.

[20] On average, the AOB holds 230 consultation days per year (own calculation based on analysis of annual reports).

[21] Volksanwaltschaft, *Zweiter Bericht der Volksanwaltschaft an den Nationalrat* (Österreichische Staatsdruckerei, 1979) 7.

Our case study is built on a multi-method approach, combining multiple perspectives, including qualitative and quantitative approaches, to get an in-depth understanding of the consultations days as an outreach measure of the AOB. The findings discussed in this chapter are part of a larger study; our analysis here is built on annual reports of the AOB, qualitative interviews with staff members and ombuds users, a survey amongst users, and participant observation of the encounter between complainants and the ombudsperson. The different data sets provide different kinds of information which, when integrated, paint a vivid picture of the consultation day as an institution. The approach followed in the analysis of the different sets of data can be called 'crystallisation'. Richardson, who introduced this concept, points out that 'the central imaginary is the crystal, which combines symmetry and substance with an infinite variety of shapes, substances, transmutations, multidimensionalities and angles of approach'.[22] This approach to analysis takes into account the complementarity of different research methods and aims at comprehensiveness rather than internal validity.[23]

In order to explore the historical development of the number of consultation days and the overall number of individual contacts held since the foundation of the ombuds institution, we analysed the AOB's annual reports to the National Council from 1979 to 2017. Subsequently, we conducted qualitative semi-structured interviews with 32 staff members (caseworkers and administrative staff)and ombudspersons (including seven former ombudspersons and staff) between 2017 and 2019 to gain an understanding of the rationale behind this specific outreach measure from an organisational perspective. In the same time period, semi-structured interviews were conducted with 27 complainants, allowing us to gain insights on consultation day users' motives, expectations and experiences. The interviews were analysed through coding and categorising following the Grounded Theory approach.[24]

Additional data was produced through a survey among citizens, carried out on paper and online in May and June 2018. In sum, 8274 users of the AOB were contacted and 1914 replies were returned (23 per cent response rate). The data was analysed by means of frequencies and correlations; in this chapter, we focus on the results regarding users' expectations and experiences regarding the consultation day.

An additional set of data is based on our participatory observation of consultation days. We participated in 23 consultation days throughout six Austrian provinces. This data allows us to identify ombudspersons' and complainants' strategies and practices in the interaction, which, in turn, provide hints on the function

[22] L Richardson, 'Writing: A Method of Inquiry' in NK Denzin and YS Lincoln (eds), *Handbook of Qualitative Research* (Sage Publications, 2000) 934.

[23] N Mays and C Pope, 'Qualitative Research in Health Care. Assessing Quality in Qualitative Research' (2000) 320 (7226) *British Medical Journal* 50.

[24] BG Glaser and AL Strauss, *The discovery of grounded theory : strategies for qualitative research* (de Gruyter, 1967).

of these encounters. The observation protocols were analysed through coding and categorising following the Grounded Theory approach.[25]

II. The Ombuds Consultation Day: Intentions and Usage

Data from the AOB's annual reports to the National Council between 1979 and 2017 show that, on average, the AOB has held 228 consultation days per year since its foundation (Table 1). The aim to approach citizens is also emphasised in a current brochure, which states the motto of the current office holders: 'We are not waiting for complaints within the walls of our institution, but we are actively approaching citizens, thus facilitating the access to our institution.'[26] Table 1 shows that while the overall number of individual contacts within the actual consultations with the ombuds has been declining over time – with strong variations in between – the number of consultation days has been relatively stable. This stability indicates the importance of the consultation day as an element of the institutional design of the AOB that has proven useful. Over the time span of 39 years, the AOB has counselled 69,511 citizens at 8951 consultation days.

A. The Organisational Rationale and its Realisation

Concerning the uses and effects of the consultation day from the perspective of the AOB as an organisation, our interviews with ombuds staff reveal three major

Table 1 Number of consultation days and visits (1979–2017)

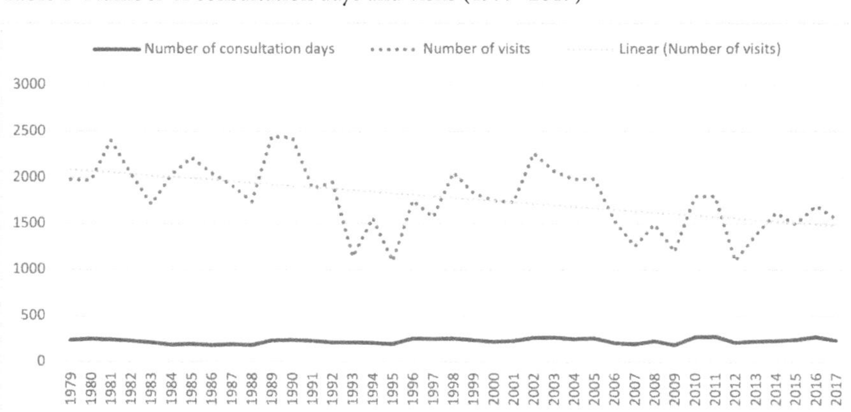

Source: Own calculations based on the AOB's annual reports to the National Council from 1979 to 2017.

[25] ibid.

[26] Upcoming dates for consultation days throughout the country can be retrieved from the ombuds' homepage.

topics. First, staff believe that the consultation day should offer low-threshold access for any population, including older persons – the largest user group – and vulnerable social groups. One caseworker stressed that these population groups are not necessarily comfortable with online forms and email, and pointed out that there are also people who are unable to write down their complaint. 'And that's the point of this house [the AOB], there needs to be low-threshold access … Therefore, these local consultation days are still very, very important'.

Our qualitative interviews with complainants showed that in fact a motive for delivering complaints orally lies in the fact that a considerable number of citizens favour personal contact over electronic correspondence. Being asked whether it was important to him to talk to the AOB personally, one complainant said, 'Well, I never would have written to them. I preferred a one-to-one conversation' (citizen K). The high number of citizens who prefer personal contact may also be related to the fact that a large proportion of AOB users belong to birth cohorts preceding the age of digitalisation. Nonetheless, there are also complainants who, despite their advanced age, preferred to contact the AOB by email, as exemplified by one elderly complainant: 'I wrote to them. Well, I do everything online' (citizen M).

Another interviewed caseworker highlighted that 'independent from whether and to what degree one can help them, often it's just important … to have a place where one can go and complain' (caseworker G). Touching upon the issue of vulnerable groups, she pointed out that she regularly holds consultation days in prisons, where she thinks that it is even more important than for many other groups 'because they don't have that easy access'.

A second element of the staff's discourse is that people should have the possibility to meet the ombudsperson (who they often know from TV) in person. The employees all agreed that the complainants should have the opportunity to talk to the ombudsperson directly: 'that in itself has a very great value. And they [the citizens] also want that. They don't want to see me but they want to talk to the boss' (caseworker H). Behind these statements we see the idea of a human institution and a personalised relation as opposed to the anonymous bureaucratic institutions the AOB controls. Another official highlights that 'nothing [is] worse than when the AOB is just that abstract thing from Vienna' (caseworker M). In fact, as our survey shows, the large majority of consultation day users do find it important to speak to the ombudsperson personally: 92 per cent of the consultation day users answered that it was important to them to submit their problem personally, and 88 per cent of the complainants said that it was important to them to meet the ombudsperson, not a member of the legal staff.

A third theme is that the consultation day is important for the institution itself 'because they [the interactions] seriously mirror the population's opinions and worries' (administrative staff P). Another interviewee thinks it is important that the ombudspersons are in direct contact with the complainants because otherwise they will often only sign the answer letters without being involved in the case. Another staff member mentioned an additional aspect of the consultation day that is relevant for the institution and clerks' everyday work (rather than for the complainant): 'I think it's good to get into contact with the people, not only always to see the paper, but the actual people … Of course, it's something different when one has a face to the file' (caseworker B). In this perspective, the public encounter is thus not only potentially useful for the citizens, but can also help the institution and its employees do a better job.

Having outlined the key aspects why the consultation day is relevant from the ombuds' perspective, we will now show whether the mentioned aim of providing low-threshold access can be met through that measure. Following this, we will consider the factors that influence who uses the AOB's consultation day.

B. Socio-demographic Factors for Consultation Day Usage

The survey among the users of the AOB included several questions regarding usage of the consultation day; the answers enabled us to sociologically characterise the citizens who visit the consultation day and thus how easily accessible the consultation day is for citizens.

The results of our survey reveal that higher percentages of permanently unemployable citizens (38 per cent) and pensioners (30 per cent) tend to approach the AOB than employed (22 per cent) or unemployed citizens (23 per cent). We also found that self-employed persons have higher consultation rates than employed persons. In part, this might be explained by self-employed persons being more experienced at dealing and negotiating with public authorities, and thus show a preference for personally approaching the AOB through the consultation day. At the same time, the business hours of the consultation day – during the day – requires citizens to be flexible in their time management, which seems easier for pensioners and self-employed citizens. Moreover, dealing with the legal aspects of their own business and the need for self-administration might encourage self-employed citizens to seek legal advice when they confront a problem in their dealings with bureaucracy.

Regarding the complainants' inclination to visit the consultation day, there was no statistically significant difference with respect to the variables of gender, marital status and citizenship. Furthermore, there were no significant differences between citizens' occupational positions (low, middle, high qualification), nor between blue and white collar workers and civil servants. Concerning the age of the complainants, however, a positive correlation between increasing age and consultation day use is observable (see higher rates of pensioners mentioned above).

In addition, citizens with compulsory or vocational education tend to visit the consultation day more frequently (32 per cent) than citizens with higher education (high school and university) (23 per cent). This result is noteworthy since the proportion of less-educated citizens is significantly under-represented among the overall population of complainants (including users and non-users of the consultation day). This finding indicates that the consultation day indeed constitutes an effective means to promote a low-threshold access to the ombuds institution. This finding also underpins previous studies, which have shown that lower-educated citizens show a preference for seeking personal contact with administrative bodies. Lower-educated complainants have no other possibility than to approach the ombuds through the consultation day if their lack of writing skills and comprehension of legal matters as well as legal jargon is preventing them from engaging in a written discourse.[27]

C. Other Usage Factors: Conceptions of the Law and Experiences with Public Administration

To understand the wider implications of consultation day usage, we explored ombuds users' conceptions of the law and their general experiences with public administration, following Hertogh's work on 'normative profiles' of ombuds users.[28] We found that citizens' attitudes towards public administration and law play a relevant role in attending a consultation day. Our survey shows that especially those citizens who have had negative or very negative experiences with public authorities show a tendency to approach the AOB personally, via the consultation day. Moreover, we find a significant relationship between usage of the consultation day and the degree of trust citizens set in public authorities and the legal system: citizens who state that they have 'no trust' in public authorities tend to use consultation days more frequently than citizens who have 'a lot of trust'. The results follow the same logic as far as citizens' trust in the legal system is concerned.

Our interpretation of these results is that complainants with low trust and prior negative experiences have high hopes in the personal encounter and believe that the probability to gain attention increases through personal contact. An explanation for this lies in the assumption that reduced trust in public authorities goes hand in hand with mistrust in public authorities' primary means of communication – the written discourse. Because of this, those complainants prefer direct, personal contact with the AOB. Another explanation could be that in the course of their encounters with public authorities, many complainants have noticed that public officials are equipped with considerable discretionary powers.[29] Thus, they assume that because of their personal appearance at the consultation day, the ombudsperson would be more inclined to employ her discretionary powers in their favour. This was also expressed in our qualitative

[27] V Dubois, *The Bureaucrat and the Poor: Encounters in French Welfare Offices* (Routledge, 2016).
[28] See n 11.
[29] SB Collins, 'The Space in the Rules: Bureaucratic Discretion in the Administration of Ontario Works' (2016) 15 *Social Policy and Society* 221; LEF Johannessen (n 13).

interviews with complainants. We discovered that one of the main reasons for approaching the AOB through a consultation day is that personal contact is being viewed as a possible means to warrant immediate intervention.[30] Through their physical presence, some complainants aim to induce a sense of urgency and spur the AOB into action. Thus, some complainants attend consultation days repeatedly. Being asked whether she embraced the opportunity to submit her concern at the consultation day, one of the complainants declared, 'I went to the consultation day three times, because I felt so hopeless' (citizen F). Our survey shows that 28 per cent of the consultation day users went to more than one consultation day. An explanation for this may lay in citizens' positive experiences with preceding consultation days, or it can be viewed as a method to increase the pressure on the ombudspersons or to spur the AOB into action.

In a similar line, regarding complainants' legal consciousness, our study reveals significant differences between consultation day users and non-users. We tested legal consciousness by asking citizens to what extent they agree with four conceptions of law which were inspired by the four forms of legal consciousness described by Ewick and Silbey[31] and by Fritsvold.[32] In comparison to citizens who do not make use of the consultation day, consultation day users more often conceptualise the law as an unpredictable and arbitrary exercise of power against the interests of individuals. In this view, the law is seen as the epitome of an unjust social system, which has to be opposed by a collective of self-organised citizens. This insight points to the circumstance that those citizens who view the law as a coercive apparatus that is out of their range of influence tend to set their hopes rather into a personal dialogue with the ombudsperson than into a written complaint. In other words, the consultation day is most frequently used by citizens who conceptualise the ombudspersons as personalised 'public watchdogs', who side with the governed subject and aim to eradicate societal injustice.

Furthermore, we tested whether citizens' overall expectations towards the AOB influence their decision to attend a consultation day or not. We found that citizens who expect 'an apology', 'to be treated respectfully and with dignity' and 'to call the authority to account' are more inclined to use the consultation day than citizens who attribute less importance to these concerns. This means that especially those citizens who ascribe moral responsibility to the AOB, for example the restoration

[30] Citizens' perception that the ombudspersons have a certain amount of power is not least promoted by the ombudspersons' enthusiastic performance in the weekly broadcast on public television, *Bürgeranwalt* (citizens' lawyer). People tend to assume that the ombudspersons will process their concerns as enthusiastically as the cases broadcasted on television.

[31] P Ewick and SS Silbey, *The Common Place of Law: Stories from Everyday Life* (University of Chicago Press, 1998).

[32] E Fritsvold, 'Under the Law: Legal Consciousness and Radical Environmental Activism' (2009) 34 *Law & Social Inquiry* 799. See also A Pohn-Weidinger and J Dahlvik, 'Can We Import the Concept of Legal Consciousness? On the Relation between Legal Consciousness and Legal Culture in Susan Silbey's Work' in G Mouralis, A Kretschmann and U Zeigermann (eds), *Laypersons in Law. Social Science Perspectives on Non-professionals* (Routledge, forthcoming).

of human dignity, neutralising insults or punishing guilty parties, tend to make use of the public encounter. This finding corresponds to our results concerning complainants' legal consciousness and attitudes towards public officials and the law. Distrust against public authorities, conceptualising law as a means to subject citizens and the conviction that this injustice has to be opposed by a collective of self-organised citizens are frequently based on negative experiences with administrative bodies. In order to compensate for these bad experiences, this group of complainants calls on the AOB through a direct encounter. In other words, the stronger the case is tied to negative personal experiences and the stronger the moral dimension of the complaint is, the more citizens tend to reach out for a personal encounter with the ombudsperson.

To better understand complainants' motives for addressing the AOB, we also asked them about their aims. Interestingly, complainants with a rather neutral stance towards the question 'how important was it for you to find a solution to your problem' ('rather important'/'rather unimportant') are less inclined to attend a consultation day than complainants who stated that finding a solution to their problem is 'very important' or 'completely unimportant'. In other words: personal contact with the ombudspersons is sought by those groups of complainants who either have a pressing personal problem or are personally only marginally involved but are highly engaged in their commitment to helping fellow citizens. Complainants who state that solving their problem is 'completely unimportant' to them frequently only aim to highlight deficits in the public administration or to make the AOB aware of a 'specific case', or they simply want to be 'well-advised'.

Since we now have a better picture not only of the rationale behind the consultation day but also of the typical user, in the following section we will present two examples of how the interaction between citizen, ombudsperson and ombuds staff plays out during the consultation. We will see how citizens present themselves and their problems, and how the ombuds staff deals with them in the face-to-face encounter.

III. How Citizens and Ombuds Staff Use the Public Encounter

In this section, we first explore the consultation day on the basis of our participant observation. The aim is to identify the involved actors' different practices and strategies through the analysis of two short sequences of observed interactions with two different ombudspersons, thereby gaining hints on the function of these public encounters.[33] Following this, we discuss the articulation of expectations

[33] For the purpose of this chapter, the observation protocols have been somewhat shortened to the main course of the conversation. The analysis focuses on the interaction rather than on the issues brought up by the complainants since this would go beyond the scope of this chapter.

and their confrontation with possibilities of realisation as key functions of the consultation day.

A. Issues and Practices in the Face-to-Face Encounter

The first example of a consultation takes place in the AOB headquarters in Vienna in the ombudsperson's office. The ombudsperson is a woman, who is not a lawyer but has a pedagogical background and was an active politician before joining the AOB. The complainant is a woman in her early 30s; her words and actions suggest that she has high educational status and legal knowledge. Whereas her age makes her an untypical case, she is a good example of that fact that better educated persons turn to the AOB more often (even if we have shown above that the consultation day mitigates this effect). The problem she presents to the ombuds concerns a planned construction.

(i) Shortened Protocol of Observed Consultation 1

The woman explains that a hotel is scheduled to be built in a municipality that is located at a lake [called Laketown here]. She complains that this is against the legal designation of the concerned pieces of land; in addition, she sees the construction plans as an eyesore in the landscape. She explains that there has already been a similar case in this area. She then complains that she has no possibilities to do anything against this unjust practice. The dialogue develops as follows:

> *Complainant (C)*: The environmental lawyer told me that I don't have party status … This is not the first case in Laketown. It's always the same people with the same trick. We are not talking about a random area – it's directly by the lake.
>
> *Ombudswoman (O)*: We can't give anyone a moral lecture or request a justification by the mayor. If it's decided, it's decided. The municipal supervision should take care of such things.
>
> *C:* You can't do anything?
>
> *O:* No, neither when the issue is pending, nor when it's closed. I really don't have an idea what we could do here. You would have to file a complaint with the authority.
>
> *C:* They [the authority] just say, 'It's in process,' but they actually don't do anything.
>
> *O:* Normally, the authority has to react and to make a statement. I'm thinking whether we could make an ex officio inquiry.
>
> *Legal caseworker (L):* You have to inform the authority about the incorrect use of the land.
>
> *The caseworker explains the legal procedure.*
>
> *C:* I understand the legal framework and also your position but can we put up with that?
>
> *L:* It's not against the legal designation of the land, it's a usage problem.
>
> *O:* You have to file a written complaint and then [we could maybe do something] … We need it in cold print.

C: Maybe media attention could help.

O: Yes, that will probably be more effective.

O and L discuss the issue and reach the conclusion that the authority has discretionary powers in the concerned case.

O: Please do something, when the authority doesn't react.

C: I would have thought that the AOB could do something.

L: We can't put the authority under general suspicion; we need concrete information, a written complaint, and so on.

L looks at her watch and the list of registered complainants for today's consultations.

O: It's on you now; choose which path you want to follow.

C: Isn't that infidelity and abuse of office?

O: When the municipality squanders money … you need to break political majorities. Go to the meeting of the municipal council!

L: You have to make a political claim in this issue.

C: The municipality is heavily indebted.

L: We can only do something when the authority has acted wrongly.

O: We can ask the authority if and what they have done in this regard.

The observed sequence is helpful for understanding certain key issues and practices that are present in many other consultation day interactions; as our data shows, some of the observed practices are independent of the ombudsperson, while others seem to be related to the ombudsperson.

We see that the complainant has legal knowledge, which allows her to be persistent; she not only brings into the discussion construction against legal designation of land and disfigurement of the landscape, but also tries to make the AOB act by considering whether it is possible to talk about infidelity and abuse of office in the present case. It seems evident that she is proceeding strategically to reach her goal. The young woman does not present a personal problem that she wants the AOB to solve, but expresses that she is fighting for the common good, for the preservation of the landscape and against political trickery and misspending of public money. Like many other complainants, she had expected that the AOB would be willing and able to help, and is disappointed when she is informed that this is not the case.

A practice that is present in most consultations, and typically shared between the ombudsperson and the caseworker, is to explain to the complainant the limits of the AOB's competence. This is often used to explain why the AOB cannot become active in the case at hand. In the present observation, we see that the ombudswoman and the caseworker try to convince the complainant that the AOB cannot get involved in the issue because there is no evidence of maladministration. However, we have often observed at consultations some uncertainty regarding the AOB's possibilities of action. The present sequence shows that the ombudsperson and the caseworker discuss the case brought forward by the woman, deliberating the AOB's possibilities. Whereas the ombudswoman briefly mentions the possibility of initiating an ex officio investigation, this idea is not taken up by the caseworker, who possibly does not see much use in such action. It is also typical that the ombudsperson is more willing than the caseworker to help the complainant; while, for the ombudsperson, it is important that she and the institution have a good reputation for being helpful and committed, the caseworker rather tries to save themself work by immediately dismissing unpromising cases. Concerning the solution of the case, they urge the complainant to make the next step herself. Although in the beginning the ombudswoman says that she cannot request a justification from the mayor concerned, eventually she concedes that the AOB can make an inquiry to the authority about any actions taken in this regard.

The division of the different roles played in the interaction also becomes visible in another aspect: the fact that the ombudswoman is not a lawyer might be the reason why the caseworker here takes the role of explaining the details of the legal procedure in this case to the complainant. This way, the caseworker tries to convince the complainant that the AOB cannot become active. Instead, both the complainant and the ombudswoman stress that non-legal ways – namely, media and politics – might be effective means to act against the unjust practices observed by the complainant.

Another key topic of all consultations, related to the AOB's possibilities of action, is the importance of written documents. In almost any conversation, the ombudsperson and the caseworker stress that they can only take action when they have the relevant documents. 'We need it in cold print,' the ombudswoman says in the observed observation.

An additional topic that was already mentioned in the survey and in our interviews, and which is also visible in the observation, is that the consultation days are always characterised by a certain time pressure. In the discussed sequence, the caseworker compares the current time on her watch with the schedule to see whether they are still in time. Every complainant is allocated a time slot of approximately 15 minutes. Complainants are often aware that they need to explain their problems within a short time – and ideally in an ordered and structured manner. Time management can be difficult and stressful when complainants have complex stories to tell, as we show in the following example.

The second example consultation takes place in one of the Austrian provinces in the premises of a district authority. The ombudsperson is a man, a lawyer who was an active politician before joining the AOB. The complainant is a woman in her late 30s; her educational background is unclear. The problem concerns the health of the complainant's daughter.

(ii) Shortened Protocol of Observed Consultation 2

The woman explains that she is here because of her 15-year-old daughter, who has a complex medical history. The current problem is that the daughter's urinary bladder has not functioned since a surgery five months ago. According to the doctor, the problem cannot be due to the surgery. The conversation develops as follows:

Ombudsman (O): When was that? What's the current state?

Complainant (C): I don't know where to go. Everywhere they dismiss us because she's under 18. I'm desperate. How can I help my child?

The complainant provides the requested details and then explains her daughter's long medical history.

O: What do you expect from the AOB? Where should we help? The surgery was the problem?

C: I want a neutral expert report that has nothing to do with the hospital.

O: Have you been to the patient's ombuds? What does the health insurance fund say? Do you get support from there?

C (starting to cry): Every doctor says something different. We have an appointment only in November! I don't want to miss anything [until then].

O: Well, I can't control the doctor's schedule.

C: I understand that.

O: If the health insurance fund causes problems, we can make contact with the patients' ombuds when we have the diagnostic findings. Everywhere you go, tell them that we have spoken personally so that they get frightened. And it's important that you keep records of everything. Now, it's important that you get an independent expert report. We're waiting for you to send us the findings. Let's hope [] the best!

After the complainant has left, the caseworker checks the schedule and mentions that they are 15 minutes in default. With regard to the present case, the ombudsman comments to me and the caseworker, 'We're also in charge of those things; we're the last instance. I thought to myself, "Let her talk," she needed to get if off her chest.'

This interaction is different from the first example in several ways, but similar to many other consultations. In this sequence, the complainant is overwhelmed by her situation and stresses the complexity of the case. It was striking to see in many consultations that persons who address the ombuds often have a several-years-long history of intricate, partly connected problems in their lives. Complainants then often have difficulties in telling their story in a structured way in a short time, but also in identifying and focusing on the key problem for which they need the ombuds' support. In the present interaction, we see that the ombudsman tries to find out the complainant's expectations vis-à-vis the AOB; this is one strategy to further the search for a solution within a limited amount of time. In other ombudspersons' consultations (not included in this chapter), we have seen another strategy, namely to focus on the identification of the (key) problem, rather than on the person's expectations.

Another aspect overtly present in this interaction are emotions: the complainant is desperate and cries. The woman wants to help her child, but does not know how. Throughout our observation, we have found that this is particularly the case when social and welfare issues are concerned, such as youth welfare, unemployment or health. In this regard, after the woman has left, the ombudsman highlights an important but informal function of the ombuds institution, namely to serve as an 'agony aunt'. The relevance of the emotional aspects of the public encounter should not be underrated; the personal contact with the ombuds is often seen as a means of emotional support. This became particularly obvious in our qualitative interviews with complainants. Besides her outspoken preference to speak face to face, one complainant said, 'It was important, emotionally; to sit in front of people who want to devote themselves to the problem, or at least listen to it' (citizen H). Those citizens who display a certain degree of tension and suffering in particular appreciate the attention that, in the ideal case, is devoted to them at the consultation day. Besides legal advice, they seek benevolence and compassion.

Other than that, we can see that the AOB, while unable to make legally binding decisions, has other important powers which can be used by the complainant: the ombudsman tells the woman to use their personal meeting as a lever when interacting with various authorities. The latter will thereby be reminded that there is a watchdog who will scrutinise their actions.

Nonetheless, there are also commonalities between the two example consultations, in particular the importance of documents – the AOB can only become active when it has the diagnostic findings – and the clarification of the AOB's competence – the AOB cannot intervene in the doctor's schedule. Also, the time pressure under which the consultation takes place is evident since the caseworker mentions that they are 15 minutes behind schedule.

With respect to time management at the consultation day, the complainants' opinions were fairly heterogeneous in our survey. Being asked whether they had enough time to explain their complaint, 44 per cent of complainants 'fully agreed' and 22 per cent agreed. The other third of complainants stated that there was not enough time to outline their complaint. Our observations have repeatedly shown that complainants typically make an effort to explain their problem in an intelligible and concise manner since they want to make the best of the time dedicated to them and avoid rejection. For many complainants, however, this seems to pose a severe challenge. In our qualitative interviews, some complainants stated that the ombudsperson devoted plenty of time to them, 'I was inside for at least one hour – there was nothing left to say. We really discussed everything' (citizen K), while others complained that 'there was hardly time for me – I could have elaborated on it much more, provide detailed explanations' (citizen H2).

Considering the importance citizens ascribe to the consultation day, it is not surprising that more than 80 per cent of the complainants 'strongly agreed' when asked if they had prepared themselves for the consultation day. Only 7 per cent stated that they did not (or almost not) prepare themselves. This self-assessment is also in accordance with our observations during the consultation days. A large number of complainants bring along well-organised documents – not only official documents, but all kinds of 'evidence', such as photographs, handwritten records or own calculations.

B. The Management of Complainants' Expectations

The two example observations illustrate the importance of the face-to-face encounter due to its multiple functions, despite certain limitations such as the time frame. For the complainant, the functions include the possibility of an authentic, personal presentation of the problem, to clarify things and ask questions, to find help and sometimes simply to load off emotions and to talk to someone. For the ombudsperson and staff, on the other hand, the functions of the consultation day include representation in the sense of being there for the citizen, but also learning about people's problems and, above all, the possibility to inform the complainant about the AOB's competences and its limitations. When we take a close look at these interactions, we can learn much about individuals' expectations towards the AOB and how the ombuds deals with these expectations. Articulating expectations and confronting them with their possibilities of realisation are thus key functions of the consultation day.

In this regard, the complainants' sayings and doings in the two observed sequences highlight several issues that we found also in our survey and in the interviews with staff and complainants, as discussed above. Most importantly, it becomes visible how expectations towards the AOB are expressed implicitly as well as explicitly; at the same time, the encounter is a place where personal life experiences and frustrations are aired. The examples also show that both complainants set high hopes into the direct interaction with the ombudspersons. It seems that they expect that, due to their personal appearance at the consultation day, the ombudspersons will be more inclined to employ their discretionary powers in their favour. These findings correlate well with the results of our survey on consultation day users' expectations. The complainant in the first observation seems to be an example of a person who believes that the law as it is executed by the concerned authority in this case needs to be opposed by a collective of self-organised citizens, with the ombuds' support; with this attitude towards the law, the woman belongs to a larger group of consultation day users, as we have seen from our survey. Like many other complainants, she ascribes a certain moral responsibility to the AOB. In contrast, in the second example, the emotional support provided by the ombudsperson seems to play a key role – this function of the consultation day was also highlighted in interviews with staff.

Considering the sayings and doings of the ombudsperson and staff in both observed sequences, it becomes clear how complainants' expectations are managed.[34] With respect to the ombudspersons and the caseworkers, our observations of the consultation days revealed different approaches to the management of expectations. Because the encounters are set within a tight time frame, ombudspersons and caseworkers have to decide quickly whether a case is 'worth' further investigation. The central questions the ombuds are concerned

[34] S Gilad, 'Accountability or Expectations Management? The Role of the Ombudsman in Financial Regulation' (2008) 30 *Law and Policy* 227.

with are: is the AOB allowed to initiate legal proceedings? Is the audit endowed with good prospects?

In an interview, a caseworker emphasised the importance of avoiding empty promises: complainants need to understand 'how far we can go, what we have to do, what we must do, what we can do'. Especially at the consultation day, one has to 'watch out sensitively' in order to avoid casting a negative light on the AOB by making promises which ultimately cannot be kept (caseworker L). The interviewee explained that newcomers are 'inoculated' with this code of conduct in internal courses.

In some cases, the observer gets the impression that the ombudsperson is only taking on a certain case for in-depth scrutiny in order to avoid disappointing the complainant and maintaining a positive image. The members of the legal staff, in contrast, tend to make citizens aware of the probable forlornness of reviewing their cases if the latter do indeed seem in vain. However, irrespective of the outcome of citizens' complaints, the moment they put forward their complaint is a moment of particular importance, since this is the opportunity to spur the AOB into action. In many cases, the AOB is their last resort.

While complainants often hope for an immediate solution, both sequences are also examples of the fact that the consultation frequently ends as an open situation, that is, the AOB is waiting for the complainant to make the next step (eg contact the authority concerned or send certain documents) or a caseworker will take a look at existing documents at a later stage after the consultation day to decide if and what can be done. These two strategies allow the ombudsperson to keep her face and to make a committed impression, even if the caseworker later on has to inform the complainant that nothing can be done in her case. In some cases, however, where it is clear that the AOB definitely cannot intervene, complainants are informed about that on the spot.

There might be a link between citizens' disappointment in the case that the AOB will not intervene and the fact that, as our survey shows, in sharp contrast to complainants who did not use the consultation day option, there is a decrease in trust with respect to both the public administration and the legal system among consultation day users. Citizens who did not use the consultation day stated more frequently that their contact with the AOB has contributed to neither an increase nor a decrease in their trust in the public administration and the rule of law.

In our study, we also asked the complainants about their experiences with the consultation day. Above, we discussed how users experienced the limited time that was dedicated to them. Overall, our qualitative interviews with complainants paint a heterogeneous picture with regard to these experiences. With respect to general framework conditions, such as their reception by the ombudsperson and the legal staff in the office, citizens' answers ranged from 'excellent' and 'comfortable' to 'very uncomfortable'. As already mentioned, we were able to observe different practices and approaches among the three ombudspersons during the consultation days. While there may be various factors shaping users' experiences – including their expectations, their personality, etc – the behaviour of ombudspersons and staff definitely also influences their experiences. With respect to the ombudspersons' approachability and treatment of complainants, for instance, statements range from 'she listened to me carefully' (citizen F) to 'I found it difficult to talk to her' (citizen D). We found similar results regarding complainants' experiences with ombudspersons' ethical consciousness: when asked how the ombudsperson responded to his complaint, one citizen said, 'He laughed at me and went away' (citizen M), while another citizen emphasised that after discussing his request, 'we talked from human to human' (citizen P). Citizens also observed that ombudspersons display different levels of professional behaviour when it comes to the review of their files. While one citizen stated, 'she really reviewed everything, even the photographs' (citizen P), another citizen, who even visited the same ombudsperson, explained, 'the edited folder, maps, photographs, nothing was reviewed' (citizen D). When asked about their overall impression of the consultation day, complainants' responses also illustrated the broad range of experiences, from 'I was positively surprised' (citizen H) to 'rather a negative experience' (citizen S).

IV. Conclusion

The objective of this chapter was to address a gap in socio-legal ombuds research concerning the public encounter between citizens and ombudspersons. While existing studies typically focus either on the individuals or on the institution, we find it necessary to investigate the place where both parties meet and interact. To date, there is little knowledge on both users' and ombuds' motivations and experiences regarding the public encounter. This chapter addressed exactly these issues; moreover, we were interested in ombudspersons' and users' practices during these street-level encounters.

Through our multi-method empirical study on the consultation days of the Austrian Ombudsman Board, we were able to shed light on a number of different aspects from various perspectives, with the result of a comprehensive picture of this outreach measure. We found that the intention to provide low-threshold access to the institution can be partly fulfilled through the consultation day, since lower educated people have slightly higher usage rates concerning these encounters. As far as users' age is concerned, however, there is a strong bias towards the elderly. In our survey and interviews, we found a variety of factors that influence who addresses the AOB through the personal encounter; these include not only socio-demographic factors, but also citizens' legal consciousness and their previous experiences with public administration. How far-reaching connections to individuals' legal consciousness and attitudes towards the state are is illustrated by the fact that more citizens who do not trust public authorities and the legal system tend to use the consultation day than do those who do trust these institutions.

Moreover, both complainants' general expectations towards the AOB and how important it is for them to find a solution to their problem influence their decision to attend a consultation day. At a time when public service administrations are tending to dematerialise their procedures and reduce face-to-face interactions with their users, assuming that e-mail, FAQ pages and at best a telephone call will suffice, it seems important to underline how important in terms of access to administrative justice face-to-face interactions are to citizens with fewer socio-economic resources and who tend to have lost trust in the public institutions.

Through the analysis of observed interactions between ombudspersons and complainants, we were also able to study key issues, as well as both parties' practices and strategies in the face-to-face encounter. It became clear not only how different complaints and their presentation can be, but also that time pressure is an important characteristic of this setting. The two examples were particularly instructive for understanding the multiple functions of these personal consultations. The setting offers complainants an open 'stage' that can be used for numerous purposes: to apply for help in an urgent matter, to gain information and/or to unload their (negative) emotions. The ombudsperson, in contrast, represent the ombuds office through direct contact with the citizen, and explains the ways in which the AOB may help. Overall, the expression of citizens' expectations concerning their case and the extent to which they can be met are key functions of the consultation day. Finally, we found that users' experiences during the public encounter were very heterogeneous.

In conclusion, it seems vital to conduct further empirical research on the encounters between citizens and ombuds institutions, especially since the ombuds is often the last resort. Socio-legal scholars have for too long ignored these crucial interactions where citizens hope to restore their trust in the public administration and the rule of law. We believe that comparative approaches that include public ombuds institutions in different national contexts will provide useful insights to promote theory building in this field.

14

Reimagining the Classical Ombud: Disability Rights, Democracy and Demosprudence

NICK O'BRIEN

I. Introduction: Human Rights and a Crisis of Identity

The place of the classical ombud in the common law world is, in its modern form, the product of the post-war 'social democratic moment', albeit with strongly libertarian inflection. As such, it represents an attempt to humanise the apparatus of the welfare state and to tame its potentially alienating bureaucracy. It is to that extent an aspect of the administrative justice fabric. Yet its remit of maladministration rather than unlawfulness and its mandate of influence rather than sanction distinguish it from the role played by the judiciary. In normative aspiration and practical technique based on investigation, report and recommendation, the classical ombud carves for itself an extrajudicial niche in the constitutional architecture.

That extrajudicial niche reflects a set of priorities that stand in contrast to those of an administrative law perspective shaped by classical liberalism.[1] First, law is displaced from its autonomous pedestal and instead conceived as just one aspect of political discourse. Secondly, public administration emerges not as a necessary evil, but as a positive social good. Thirdly, the ambition of law and regulation is not merely the prevention of bad practice on the part of the state, but the encouragement and facilitation of good practice, with due recognition that courts and rules are not necessarily the best way of achieving such outcomes. Finally, the object of the exercise is not the protection of individual libertarian rights as an end in themselves, but instead the fostering of the common good, and in the case of the ombud the 'humanisation' of state bureaucracy.[2]

[1] M Loughlin, *Sword and Scales: An Examination of the Relationship between Law and Politics* (Hart Publishing, 2000); A Tomkins, 'In Defence of the Political Constitution' (2002) 22 *OJLS* 157; M Loughlin, *Public Law and Political Theory* (Clarendon Press, 1992) 105–33.

[2] M Loughlin, 'The Functionalist Style in Public Law' (2005) 55 *University of Toronto Law Journal* 361.

Especially since the political convulsions of 1989, the ombud institution has, however, been seduced by a style of liberal-legalistic governance that in fact has much in common with classical liberalism and that places individual libertarian rights and the rule of law narrowly conceived at its centre. As a result, the ombud has been drawn into the international human rights framework, evolving into new distinctive forms that have attracted description as 'human rights ombudsman', 'equality ombudsman', 'hybrid classical–human rights ombudsman' and 'thematic ombudsman'. Some national and subnational ombuds have as a result found themselves designated by the United Nations as 'national human rights institutions' and 'national preventive mechanisms', or by the European Union as 'national equality bodies'.[3]

This separatist movement of human rights and equality ombuds within the modern state has exposed the classical ombud to a crisis of identity. Perched uncomfortably between adherence to its traditional remit of maladministration and the embrace of an apparently all-consuming human rights mission, to which it has 'more limited exposure' than its human rights siblings, the classical ombud remains in search of a role.[4]

The preferred resolution of this crisis has entailed, sometimes covertly, often timidly, the absorption of human rights vigilance (including in respect of equal treatment and non-discrimination) within the classical 'maladministration' remit. As a result, international civil rights norms become, albeit indirectly, an unavoidable aspect of good administration; classical ombuds emerge as part of the national human rights *structures* in a liberal democracy (even if not technically national human rights *institutions*); and the classical ombud is seen as well placed to 'bring human rights back home' (in the sense of helping infuse the daily encounters of citizen and state with human rights values and a human rights vision).[5] As the International Ombudsman Institution has emphasised, 'The Ombudsman is a promoter of human rights and good administration', and the failure of a public authority to take account of human rights is an aspect of maladministration.[6]

This preferred resolution has to some extent proved successful, enabling classical ombuds to accommodate human rights discourse without becoming fully fledged 'human rights ombuds', and even when 'human rights' has not been their native language. The reception of human rights as part of governance in the modern liberal-democratic state is irresistible. To excise human rights entirely

[3] LC Reif, 'Ombudsman Institutions and Article 33(2) of the United Nations Convention on the Rights of Persons with Disabilities' (2014) 65 *University of New Brunswick Law Journal* 213.

[4] ibid 238.

[5] S Halliday and P Schmidt (eds), *Human Rights Brought Home: Socio-legal Perspectives on Human Rights in the National Context* (Hart Publishing, 2004).

[6] International Ombudsman Institute, *Developing and Reforming Ombudsman Institutions* (2017) 7–8.

from the evolving remit of the classical ombud would be to impoverish its contribution and undermine its credibility.

Yet there persists a nagging sense of dislocation, an enduring awkwardness of fit. This chapter aims to discover a resolution to the human-rights identity crisis afflicting the classical ombud by means that go beyond the orthodox rapprochement yet fall short of the wholesale conversion of classical ombuds to dedicated human rights ombuds. It argues that the classical ombud does indeed have an important human rights role. To realise that distinctive role in practice, the classical ombud must engage in a process of reimagining, not just of its own function, but of human rights also.

The route proposed for that exercise of imagination lies in part with disability rights, and in particular with the UN Convention on the Rights of Persons with Disabilities, which opened for signature in 2007. Through a consideration of the way in which the emergence of disability rights since 1990, some decades after the establishment of most classical ombuds, has transformed contemporary understanding of substantive human rights (including equality rights) and their implementation, the chapter will seek to reimagine the values that the classical ombud is entrusted to promote and the methods it should deploy to realise those values in its work.

The proposed route also entails, however, the recovery of a style of legal thought that is an alternative to that of classical liberalism. Contemporary 'demosprudence' reasserts the emphases of a communitarian alternative. The move from a jurisprudential to a 'demosprudential' framework, like the move away from classical liberalism, entails the prioritisation of democratic politics over a narrowly conceived notion of the rule of law, and looks beyond the courts to the political community for the interpretation and realisation of legal principle.[7] The demosprudential accent is on ensuring that when 'the state meets the street' the encounter is shaped by ethical concern for the common good and for principle as an instrument of democracy. Disability rights yield an essential resource for enabling the classical ombud's effective participation in that democratic, and demosprudential, project. It is not so much that the classical ombud should in some way add 'disability rights' to its remit, or indeed acquire new powers that stretch beyond its standard repertoire of investigation, decision, report and recommendation, but rather that in heeding the urgency of disability rights it should rediscover its inherent and already-present possibilities.

[7] L Guinier and G Torres, 'Changing the Wind: Notes towards a Demosprudence of Law and Social Movements' (2014) 123 *Yale Law Journal* 2742; U Baxi, 'Demosprudence versus Jursipdrudence: The Indian Judicial Experience in the Context of Comparative Constitutional Studies' (2014) 14 *Macquarie Law Journal* 3; B Ray, 'Demosprudence in Comparative Perspective' (2011) 47 *Stanford Journal of International Law* 11.

II. Misleading Emphases: Legalism, Libertarianism and Litigation

There are three initial emphases within the international human rights framework that, although posing potential obstacles to this demosprudential reimagining of the classical ombud, invite preliminary consideration: the emphasis on human rights as a set of essentially legal rules; the emphasis on human rights as primarily about civil and political rights; and the emphasis on individual litigation in court as the typical way of giving force to such entitlements.

All three emphases create the misleading impression that the classical ombud is necessarily excluded from serious engagement with human rights, either because its introduction predated by some margin the apotheosis of human rights that occurred in particular after 1989 or because its conventional maladministration remit appears to be of a quite different order from, and largely impervious to, human rights as commonly understood: the classical ombud has no remit to make legal findings by establishing the breach of legal rules; for the most part, the work of the classical ombud in humanising the state bureaucracy will be concerned with 'social' entitlement, such as access to healthcare, social care, transport, housing and education, rather than with the violation of civil rights, such as the right to vote, the right to free assembly or the right to freedom of speech; and if the resolution of individual disputes by legally enforceable decision is the dominant mode of engagement with human rights, the classical ombud's lack of enforcement powers is a fatal blow. Each of these emphases is, however, susceptible to significant revision.

A. Legalism

The first emphasis invokes 'human rights' as primarily a 'legal concept' and so the property first and foremost of lawyers and judges, with little scope for the deployment of human rights norms by those who are not expressly charged with the exercise of legal or judicial functions. It is, of course, true that there is a 'legal' aspect to human rights and that they appear in legal instruments that make them look like ordinary laws. However, human rights law, unlike most other law, is more 'mission statement' than a series of detailed rules, and human rights language more an 'Esperanto of the virtuous' than the technical jargon of a professional caste.[8] As a result, human rights are normative in the way that principles, not rules, are normative.

[8] C Gearty, *Can Human Rights Survive?* (Cambridge University Press, 2005) 44; C Gearty, 'Against Judicial Enforcement' in C Gearty and V Mantouvalou (eds), *Debating Social Rights* (Hart Publishing, 2012).

Principles, unlike legal rules, are not binary in the sense that they simply are or are not violated. Instead, principles can be satisfied to varying degrees and so be subject to 'progressive realisation'. Indeterminacy and vagueness may count against the credibility of norms that identify as rules, but less so against those that identify as principles. Furthermore, the vagueness of principles can be obviated by testing them against a prior set of 'background principles', such as effectiveness, participation, accountability and equality.[9]

The aim of this principled rather than legalistic approach is to recognise human rights as 'permeating the political culture more generally, influencing decision-making in a proactive sense, and guiding behaviour, rather than only as a response to complaints that they have been violated'.[10] Some, like the British Institute of Human Rights, have tried to distil the essence of human rights and their mission into a few key principles, captured in the acronym FREDA – fairness, respect, equality, dignity and autonomy. The project of identifying such basic principles points to the realisation that there is nothing inherently 'legalistic' about the way in which human rights represent a set of serviceable norms. Even the human rights judgments of the domestic or transnational courts, such as the European Court of Human Rights in Strasbourg, are often more like philosophical reflections than detailed legal arguments, accessible to a non-legal audience without any special technical knowledge. The actual practice of human rights, even in a judicial setting, therefore yields the overarching aim of human rights as 'the pursuit of human dignity, or some equivalent type of meta-principle, whereby each human person, qua human person, is seen to possess an intrinsic worth that should be respected'.[11]

B. Libertarian Civil Rights

Secondly, there is an emphasis within evolved human rights discourse on 'civil rights' as an expression of a 'negative' concept of liberty – freedom from state intrusion in respect of things like freedom of speech, freedom of movement, freedom of assembly and freedom from unreasonable restraint – that associates rights protection and promotion primarily with matters of criminal justice, privacy and security, and thereby marginalises the positive duties of the state to procure the common good. In common law jurisdictions, like the UK, 'social rights have been detached from the human rights/civil liberties mainstream for decades', to the extent that 'human rights are usually understood as denoting

[9] S Fredman, *Human Rights Transformed* (Oxford University Press, 2008) 65–91.

[10] ibid 90.

[11] C McCrudden, 'Human Rights Theory and Comparative International Law Scholarship' in A Lawson and L Waddington (eds), *The UN Convention on the Rights of Persons with Disabilities in Practice: A Comparative Analysis of the Role of Courts* (Oxford University Press, 2018) 605.

civil and political entitlements and having little if anything to do with socio-economic concerns'.[12] As a former UN Rapporteur on the Right to Access to Health put it in 2017, in the UK the 'human rights system' is 'rigged', in that it 'privileges civil and political rights and neglects social rights'.[13]

Such rigging serves to reinforce the view that human rights fall outside the day-to-day work of most classical ombuds, who rarely find themselves involved in matters of war and peace, or even crime and punishment. Yet among the most active human rights ombuds are those in Latin America, whose protection and promotion of social rights in particular has been noted by academic researchers.[14] Some practitioners, especially within the classical ombud world, may be apprehensive about the 'aspirational' and indeterminate quality of social rights, preferring instead the reduction of rights to 'enforceable legal standards'.[15] Yet in many parts of the world, the human rights ombud has been identified as the type of national human rights institution that deals 'more than others with economic, social and cultural rights' and has 'long experience in tackling economic and social issues relating to the public sector'.[16]

C. Litigation

Thirdly, and finally, there is an emphasis on a human rights model that recognises dispute resolution for individual 'victims', and litigation followed by an enforceable judicial finding, as the only legitimate response to human rights grievances. In the light of the classic tripartite constitutional separation of powers between legislature, judiciary and executive, more complex 'polycentric' disputes about the allocation of public funds are considered matters for the legislature, not the judiciary. Social rights are in turn assigned paradigmatic status as examples of such non-justiciable entitlements. As a result, social rights are perceived as second-order entitlements, their normative value diminished by their lack of legal enforceability by individual

[12] C O'Cinneide, 'The European Social Charter and the UK: Why it Matters' (2018) 29 *King's Law Journal* 275, 276.

[13] P Hunt, *Social Rights Are Human Rights but the UK System is Rigged* (Centre for Welfare Reform, 2017) 7.

[14] E Moreno, 'The Contribution of the Ombudsman to Human Rights in Latin America, 1982–2011' (2016) 98 *University of Miami Law Review* 112, 117.

[15] J McMillan, 'The Ombudsman's Role in Human Rights Protection – An Australian Perspective' (paper presented at the 11th Asian OA Conference, Bangkok, November 2009).

[16] G De Beco, 'The Role of National Human Rights Institutions in the Promotion and Protection of Economic, Social and Cultural Rights: Historical, Theoretical and Critical Perspectives' in E Brems, G De Beco and W Vandehole (eds), *National Human Rights Institutions, and Economic, Social and Cultural Rights* (Intersentia, 2013) 22. *cf* T Pegram, 'Accountability in Hostile Times: The Case of the Peruvian Human Rights Ombudsman 1996–2001' (2008) 40 *Journal of Latin American Studies* 51; T Pegram, 'The Bolivian Human Rights Ombudsman and Economic, Social and Cultural Rights' in Brems et al (ibid) 57; E Peruzzotti, 'The Societalization of Horizontal Accountability: Rights Advocacy and the Defesnor del Pueblo de la Nacion in Argentina' in R Goodman and T Pegram (eds), *Human Rights, State Compliance and Social Change Assessing National Human Rights Institutions* (Cambridge University Press, 2012) 243.

litigants. What is perceived to be at stake in social rights adjudication is instead the discretion to allocate and prioritise public resources. To that extent, social rights are judged unenforceable by the courts and amenable instead to political deliberation, a matter in essence for the legislature, whether national, regional or local, and not for the judiciary, or quasi-judicial agencies judged to operate according to similarly fatal constraints. As a result, in most liberal democracies, the courts have been denied an explicit role in social rights adjudication (a notable exception being South Africa) or consigned to the marginal consideration of 'directive principles' for the allocation of social rights entitlement (eg in Ireland and India).

Alternative means of giving force to such entitlements have nevertheless emerged, without loss of democratic legitimacy and often with features that would not be strangers to classical ombud practice. In Europe, for example, while the civil rights of individuals contained in the European Convention can be adjudicated upon in the court in Strasbourg, the Social Charter, without a forum for 'legal enforcement' of that sort, is instead entrusted to the oversight of a Committee of the Council of Europe, which discharges that obligation for the most part by receiving and investigating complaints from civil society, by conducting its own investigations and then making recommendations to the state in question.

These three emphases and the apparent obstacle they pose to the task of reimagining do not therefore withstand preliminary scrutiny. Human rights need not be seen as primarily 'legal' norms; they need not be seen to concern exclusively civil rights entitlements, in a way that marginalises the classical ombud's remit and typical coverage; and they need not be seen exclusively as matters either for the courts (civil rights) or the legislature (social rights), with no legitimate means for giving force short of enforcement.

III. Disability Equality and the UN Convention on the Rights of Persons with Disabilities

A. The 'New Paradigm' of Disability Rights: Progressive Equality, Civil Society and Agency Network

The advance of disability rights since the Americans with Disabilities Act 1990, and in particular the UN Convention on the Rights of Persons with Disabilities (CRPD), offers an essential resource for challenging more robustly these misplaced emphases. Central to that challenge is a new paradigm of equality law that rebalances 'positive' social rights priorities with the more familiar 'negative' civil rights entitlements. Three particular features of the CRPD are especially significant.[17]

[17] S Fredman, 'Disability Equality: A Challenge to the Existing Anti-discrimination Paradigm' in A Lawson and C Gooding (eds), *Disability Rights in Europe: From Theory to Practice* (Hart Publishing, 2005).

First, there is the strength of its central vision and dominant values, which are 'ethical' not legal, about social change and practice rather than the application of rules. Secondly, instead of a libertarian and negative concept of liberty, the approach taken entails a positive and egalitarian concept of liberty, concerned not with the deprivation of liberty in institutional settings, but with the practical emancipation of the person in a community setting and the deployment of institutions, when necessary, to realise that aim. Thirdly, and finally, the approach is resolutely communitarian rather than individualistic, with an emphasis on the mobilisation of a network of agencies, with due recognition of the social self, embedded in a web of family and communal ties, and with the full participation of disabled people themselves and of civil society.

The CRPD opened for signature in March 2007, having been adopted by the UN in December 2006. Legal commentators, and indeed the UN Committee with responsibility for oversight of the CRPD, have since then promulgated what they describe as a 'progressive' or 'human rights' model of equality.[18] Such a model aims to transcend not just the symmetrical model of formal equality, but also the later model of substantive equality, by prioritising redistribution, recognition, participation and accommodation. In practice, this approach entails, instead of the pursuit of a 'level playing field' or even materially similar 'outcomes', the more ambitious objectives of reversing disadvantage, promoting dignity and worth as central values, changing oppressive social structures, and facilitating full and active social participation.

General Comment 6 is also explicit in prescribing a method and style of realisation that goes beyond individual enforcement: where inequality is 'systemic', individual compensation is not enough, but should instead give way to 'forward-looking, non-pecuniary remedies'.[19] To achieve such remedy and so advance 'human rights equality', those agencies with oversight must have the discretion to commence investigation by way of their 'own initiative' with what the General Comment refers to as an '*actio popularis*', and to pursue a diverse range of interventions to change culture and perception.[20]

Disability equality, in its progressive or human rights form, is to that extent driven by values that arise from a particular conception of the dignity of the human person: 'The CRPD relates to the concept of human dignity more than any other human rights treaty. Respect for the human dignity of disabled persons is the purpose.'[21] Moreover, 'Human rights law as moral law and as ideology is not only

[18] Committee on the Rights of Persons with Disabilities, 'General Comment No 6 (2018) on Equality and Non-discrimination' (adopted at the 19th session, 14 February–9 March 2018); T Degener, 'A New Human Rights Model of Disability' in V Della Fina et al (eds), *The United Nations Convention on the Rights of Persons with Disabilities* (Springer, 2017) 41; S Fredman, J Kuosmanen and M Campbell, 'Transformative Equality: Making the Sustainable Development Goals Work for Women' (2016) 30 *Ethics and International Affairs* 177.

[19] Committee on the Rights of Persons with Disabilities (n 18) C 22.

[20] ibid G 53.

[21] Degener (n 18) 48.

a reflection of political conflict among states, or a reflection of global and domestic power relations; it is also a tool for social transformation.'[22]

Like all human rights treaties, the CRPD 'announces … a worldview' and invites a 'process of change'. That process of change, once it has been 'embedded in the national architecture of power', is expected to 'carry the social model of disability rights to the heart of power'.[23] The 'core idea' of the CRPD is that 'humans cannot be reduced to an essence, that we are who we are because of our interactions in community'.[24] Its central values, far from reinforcing neoliberal values of efficiency, competition and individual choice, are instead

> interdependence, shared not atomised personhood, and a vision of the community as framing individuation, consistent with the Aristotelian view that the best freedom is the right to belong, to be seen to belong and to be valued as part of something beyond the self.[25]

In addition to advancing a progressive conception of equality, the CRPD proposes a determinedly communitarian approach to the realisation of its substantive provisions. Article 33 offers a template for realisation that goes beyond conventional approaches by judicial and indeed quasi-judicial agencies.[26] Each state party is required by Article 33(2) to 'maintain, strengthen, designate or establish' a 'framework' to promote, protect and monitor implementation. Included within such a framework must be at least one 'independent mechanism'. In establishing the framework, regard must be had to the UN's Paris Principles, such as the importance of independence and effectiveness, which must shape the establishment of National Human Rights Institutions.[27] Importantly, Article 33(3) requires that civil society, and in particular disabled people and their organisations, be involved and participate fully in the domestic process for realising the entitlements contained in the CRPD. An Optional Protocol to the CRPD additionally provides a mechanism for individuals, and importantly for groups, to communicate alleged violations of the Convention to the overseeing UN Committee, which can investigate and make recommendations to which the relevant state party must respond.

[22] ibid 51.

[23] G Quinn, 'Foreword' in G de Beco (ed), *Article 33 of the UN Convention on the Rights of Persons with Disabilities: National Structures for the Implementation and Monitoring of the Convention* (Martinus Nijhoff, 2013) vii.

[24] G Quinn and A Arstein-Kerslake, 'Restoring the "Human" in "Human Rights": Personhood and Doctrinal Innovation in the UN Disability Convention' in C Gearty (ed), *The Cambridge Companion to Human Rights Law* (Cambridge University Press, 2012) 54.

[25] ibid 40.

[26] For Art 33 more generally, see M Raley, 'Article 33 of the Convention on the Rights of Persons with Disabilities: Broader Implications for Human Rights Law' (2016) 39 *Dublin University Law Journal* 157.

[27] G de Beco and R Murray, *Commentary on the Paris Principles on National Human Rights Institutions* (Cambridge University Press, 2014).

B. The CRPD and the Courts

The CRPD reinforces the need for a recalibration of any residual emphasis on legalism, libertarianism and litigation in ways which are salient to the practices of the classical ombud. Emphasis on principles not legal rules, equality and social rights not individual and libertarian civil rights, and responses to grievance other than litigation and individual dispute resolution draws renewed attention to the ombud institution, in both its human rights and classical manifestations.

That renewed attention is especially justified in part by the distinctive, and quite limited, role played so far by national courts, at both first instance and appellate level, in 'domesticating' the CRPD. Comparative research published in 2018 reinforces the suspicion that the CRPD, like most other treaty and international legal instruments, is essentially seen as 'programmatic' and therefore not easily given direct effect by domestic courts around the world. Instead, more typical has been 'indirect interpretative effect', including through the development of the common law, the 'bolstering' of existing interpretations of domestic law and the advancement of more 'progressive' interpretations. The authority of the CRPD in practice is to that extent 'moral' rather than 'legal', 'expressive' rather than imperative.[28] As Anna Lawson has remarked, its most powerful impact lies in its 'juris-generative potential' and in its sharing of a new 'normative universe', realising a fundamental 'belief change regarding persons with disabilities by better informing societies about [them], particularly by promoting a social model understanding of disability and an awareness of the importance of human rights responses'.[29] The true value of the CRPD can to that extent be said to lie, as already noted, in its construction and dissemination of 'meta-principle' in the concepts of equality, autonomy and especially dignity. As Christopher McCrudden has observed, and not just in relation to the CRPD and the UN Convention on the Elimination of All Forms of Discrimination against Women, dignity is 'the concept that above all others is most commonly found in all international human rights instruments and, increasingly, in judicial practice and appears to be upheld as fundamental to human rights, as a whole'.[30]

In addition to reflections on normative content, the 2018 research has prompted observation about the quality of judicial response to human rights claims and in particular to their provisional, revisable and dialogic quality. Human rights adjudication emerges as

> an enterprise in which the judge is not only engaging with the dispute in hand, attempting to arrive at a justified and reasoned judgment, but also doing so in a context in which the nature of the judge's resolution of the question is provisional.[31]

[28] H Smith and M Stein, 'Mexico' in Lawson and Waddington (n 11) 314; A Geisinger and M A Stein, 'A Theory of Expressive International Law' (2007) 60 *Vanderbilt Law Review* 77.

[29] A Lawson, 'Uses of the Convention on the Rights of Persons with Disabilities in Domestic Courts' in Lawson and Waddington (n 11) 569.

[30] C McCrudden, 'Human Rights Theory and Comparative International Law Scholarship' in Lawson and Waddington (n 11) 605.

[31] ibid 607.

The 'provisional and (politically) temporary' quality of human rights adjudication encourages not only critical reflection, but also 'dialogic and dialectic processes' that 'embrace sustained and reflexive contestation, pluralism, judicial institutions and social activism'.[32]

IV. CRPD and the Human Rights Ombuds: 'Lawyer' or 'Activist'?

The provisional, dialogic and reflexive quality of CRPD adjudication by the courts invites comparable engagement with the CRPD by the ombud, an institution whose extralegal ethos, mandate of influence rather than sanction, and proximity to public concerns and the public interest should, notwithstanding the perceived limitations of its legislative foundation, make it even more readily receptive than the courts to the CRPD's vision, values and practices.

Published assessment of ombud engagement with the CRPD in fact presents a mixed picture. It is one in which encouraging response to the progressive character of the CRPD is accompanied by regressive tendencies that reflect the frequently conservative character of the ombud institution in practice and its inclination to seek refuge within the often fragile scaffolding afforded by its explicit legislative mandate and behind the perceived certainties of enforceable legal entitlement and civil rights provision.

A. Legal Alignment

As Linda Reif has shown, human rights ombuds in particular have in several jurisdictions been identified as national framework mechanisms under Article 33 CRPD.[33] Human rights ombuds in, for example, Spain, Portugal, Argentina, Poland and Hungary have deployed a variety of techniques in discharging the three functional requirements of an Article 33 institution: protection; promotion; and monitoring. The task of protection has typically been discharged by the technique of investigation, either in response to individual complaints or through the use of own-initiative powers of investigation, even in the absence of an individual complaint. A number of these investigations have concerned social rights entitlement, for example, on the resourcing of education (Spain, Poland), social services (Spain) and transport facilities (Argentina) for disabled people. This investigative activity, although often explicitly linked to particular protections under specific articles of the CRPD, is nevertheless the sort of activity that is

[32] ibid 608.
[33] Reif (n 3).

typically available to the classical ombud and in fact forms the largest part of the classical ombud's staple fare. Similarly, promotional practices by way of awareness raising and research are in principle activities that a well-resourced classical ombud is able to undertake, albeit perhaps without the urgency and focus that are entailed by a dedicated human rights or, more specifically, CRPD role.

The most distinctive practices of the human rights ombuds in their protection and monitoring of the CRPD, and which stand in contrast to the techniques deployed by classical ombuds, result for the most part in their explicit alignment with the 'law'. That alignment is apparent especially in direct or practical support for court action based on the CRPD; in the testing of domestic legislation against CRPD requirements; in the scrutiny of existing legal entitlement; in advice on treaty ratification; and in explicit promotion of law reform. For example, in Poland, the Ombudsman has initiated court action on issues such as the age of consent to psychiatric treatment and on pension entitlement, and in Hungary on the compatibility of domestic laws with treaty obligations. Monitoring work, frequently combining CRPD with Optional Protocol to the Convention against Torture (OPCAT) functions, has typically involved the inspection of mental health facilities (eg Spain, Poland).[34] In the discharge of these law-aligned and inspection activities, the human rights ombud strays well beyond the typical remit of the classical ombud, and in ways that are framed explicitly by legal considerations, negative libertarian entitlements and an enforceability or compliance approach. The classical ombud, by contrast, with its mandate of influence, has traditionally been quarantined from the exercise of precisely such a mandate of legally aligned sanction, even when its remit has been one of promoting humane and ethical administration.

B. Competing Mentalities

The accommodation and exercise of such law-aligned practices by human rights ombuds are not without some tension with an alternative tradition of community engagement and extralegal ethos. The competing mentalities at play within a human rights or equality ombud charged with the task of promoting, protecting and monitoring the entitlements of disabled people can be gauged from empirical research on the Swedish Discrimination (or Equality) Ombudsman (the Diskriminerings Ombudsmannen). The Swedish Discrimination Ombudsman is a thematic ombud, with EU national equality body status, which in 2009 brought together separate institutions for gender, disability, ethnicity and sexual orientation, with additional coverage for transgender issues, religion or other belief and age.[35]

[34] ibid passim.
[35] Diskriminerings Ombudsmannen, *About the Equality Ombudsman* (Tabergs tryckeri, 2009).

Especially revealing is the Ombudsman's (and its Disability Ombudsman predecessor's) engagement with civil society, and in particular with disabled people's organisations.[36] Between 1994 and 2006, social democratic parties held power in Sweden and collaboration with non-governmental organisations (NGOs) was encouraged. Between 2006 and 2014, a centre-right liberal coalition came into office and encouraged the Discrimination Ombudsman to distance itself from NGOs in order to reinforce the agency's independence from the mobilisation of civil society. At the same time, disability policy underwent reform, whereby anti-discrimination laws gave disabled individuals the chance to litigate to protect their individual entitlements rather than promote the public good. This was, in other words, an instance of that Eurolegalism that witnessed the withdrawal of the state from welfare protection, instead transferring a new role of rights protection to litigation by individual 'consumers', with the Discrimination Ombudsman complicit in that task.[37]

From 2009 onwards, the new integrated Ombudsman's main challenge was to ensure that the anti-discrimination legislation and the law on parental leave were followed. The range of powers included investigating (but not determining) individual complaints, providing information on anti-discrimination rights and on how to assert them, representing individuals in court, providing information on how to promote rights and prevent discrimination, and delivering education on protection against discrimination. In addition, the Ombudsman had the task of supervising 'active measures' – in other words, the overall performance on equality issues of schools, universities and employers – in particular by reviewing gender equality plans and equal treatment plans.[38]

By contrast, between 1994 and 2009, despite the legal power to bring cases, the separate Disability Ombudsman had exercised a largely conciliatory role in cooperation with civil society and disabled people's organisations, making very little use of its litigation powers.[39] The advent of the new integrated Discrimination Ombudsman in 2009 therefore heralded a new commitment to legal enforcement, with collaboration with civil society limited increasingly to individual cases and with the emphasis on individual protection. The new approach was not deemed to be a success. In 2011, the Swedish government forced the resignation of the first Discrimination Ombudsman, Katri Linna, and in 2012 the Swedish National Audit Office reported that 'The overall picture is that the Discrimination Ombudsman has put substantial resources into handling discrimination cases received from

[36] A Lejeune, 'Legal Mobilization within the Bureaucracy: Disability Rights and the Implementation of Antidiscrimination Law in Sweden' (2017) 39 *Law and Policy* 237.

[37] ibid 252–53; A Orford, 'Europe Reconstructed' (2012) 75 *MLR* 275, 286.

[38] Diskriminerings Ombudsmannen (n 35).

[39] R Banakar, 'When Do Rights Matter? A Case Study of the Right to Equal Treatment in Sweden' in P Schmidt and S Halliday (eds), *Human Rights Brought Home: Socio-legal Perspectives on Human Rights in the National Context* (Hart Publishing, 2004) 165, 171–78; Lejeune (n 36).

individuals. This has affected the Discrimination Ombudsman's ability proactively to combat discrimination and oversee active measures.'[40]

As a result, the Discrimination Ombudsman underwent significant organisational change after 2011: instead of investigating all complaints, the Ombudsman now selected the cases most likely to produce new case law before the labour court, and at the same time put more resources into raising awareness of disability rights among employers and workers, and into using the law to force employers to adopt employee training programmes and diversity plans, to create new management structures, or to change recruitment processes as a means of fostering increased organisational compliance with the law. Such changes of approach and prioritisation of resources were, it is important to note, achieved within the existing legislative structure of the Ombudsman's remit and as a result of a strategic response to political pressures rather than to law reform as such.

Revealingly, empirical research among the Ombudsman's staff indicates that those who had come from disability NGOs believed they needed to work with disability rights organisations to acquire knowledge about daily experience of disabled workers and about the barriers they faced. Those with a human rights law background considered that legal enforcement was their sole concern and were dismissive of partnership with disability organisations. As one employee remarked:

> I was recruited as a litigation officer. I'm now organizing training. The main change, and the main problem I face right now is that I'm supposed to work with non-profit organisations and I've never done that before. I'm a lawyer, I'm used to litigation, not being an activist.[41]

That comment, and the dichotomy it discloses between being a 'lawyer' and being an 'activist', is fundamental to the choices available to an ombud in the construction of her identity, even where the legislative scaffolding may appear constraining. Despite the tendency for human rights and equality ombuds to align with 'the law' and adopt court-centred and legalistic strategies, the spirit of the CRPD, as identified above, is at odds with such an approach. In other words, it begins to become clear that once disability rights are admitted within the purview of the ombud, strict legal alignment is scarcely an option. Full identification of the ombud with a self-consciously activist role no doubt fails to sit comfortably with the finely calibrated quasi-judicial role that the classical ombud has frequently constructed for itself, whilst nevertheless indicating some of the qualities that the CRPD requires of any agency set on promoting and protecting disability rights as part of a broader equality function. As already suggested, and as will be argued further below, invocation of a demosprudential perspective opens up the possibility of identifying the classical ombud with neither legal alignment nor overt activism, but with a distinctive function whose bilingual facility bridges the divide between state and street, frontline bureaucracy and citizen engagement.

[40] Cited in Lejeune (n 36) 250.
[41] Lejeune (n 36) 250.

V. The Classical Ombud and Disability Rights

A. Core Functions and Legal Norms

The question arises of what role emerges for the classical ombud in protecting, promoting or monitoring the rights of disabled people, within a range of practices consistent with the spirit of the CRPD, even in the absence of an explicit human rights or equality mandate. The answer can in part be found in the practices of classical ombuds, who, through the discharge of their 'core functions' (investigation, recommendation, report), have addressed disability rights issues.

As Linda Reif has observed, classical ombuds also rely on law for the most part when considering disability issues, 'predominantly on domestic law' but also 'occasionally' on international human rights law, such as the CRPD.[42] For example, in Ireland and the UK, in the Canadian states of British Columbia, Quebec and Ontario, and in Australian states such as New South Wales, Reif finds examples of classical ombuds investigating, either by way of response to individual complaint or through the use of own-initiative powers, issues such as the refusal of mobility allowances to older people (Ireland); the quality of healthcare services for disabled people (UK); education, home and community support (British Columbia, Quebec); services for young adults with developmental difficulties, mental health services for children, waiting lists for disability support payments and the use of restraint in places of detention (Ontario); and the general standard of public services for disabled people (New South Wales).[43] As Reif points out, in some of these investigations there is explicit reference to the CRPD as a way of framing the norms against which the activity of a public authority is being judged. More often, there will be reliance on domestic legal norms.[44]

B. Keeping to the Narrow Ledge

The tendency of classical ombuds, notwithstanding their extralegal and principled remit, to operate 'in the shadow of the law' and to seek refuge in the certainty of rules combines with an aspiration towards legalistic neutrality in such a way as to restrain the deployment of techniques that might engage civil society and agency networks more ambitiously. The result is a tendency to cling to the narrow ledge of established practice.

The danger of such reliance upon conventional pre-CRPD practice can be illustrated by reference to one distinctive aspect of the classical ombud's remit in Ireland and the way in which it has been discharged. Unusually for a

[42] Reif (n 3) 238.
[43] ibid 238–41.
[44] ibid 238.

classical ombud, the Irish Ombudsman has express authority under the Disability Act 2005 to examine complaints about access to public buildings, services, information, heritage sites and sectoral plans. The indications are that this power has scarcely been used: in 2017 and 2018, for example, there were just two complaints made, and in 2018 both were discontinued because they were made 'prematurely' (ie before being considered by the body complained of). The Ombudsman remarked that disabled people and the advice sector needed relevant information and should be made aware of their ability to take complaints to the Ombudsman. To that end, the Ombudsman published a five-page fact sheet.[45]

This specific disability rights power is additional to the general classical ombud power, which, as noted above, has on occasion been used by the Irish Ombudsman to investigate matters that relate particularly to disabled people. In recent years (2017 and 2018), the individual cases highlighted by the Ombudsman in annual reports have included examples relating to payment for higher specification hearing aids, delay in treating a woman with diabetes, backdating of the Disability Allowance and the payment of allowances for children with intellectual impairment (Annual Report 2017); as many as 67 complaints about the Disabled Drivers Medical Board of Appeal; and a thematic report on nursing homes, which included consideration of the availability of support to enable people to live in their own homes (Annual Report 2018).[46]

Moreover, the Ombudsman's wider commitment to disability rights was reinforced by the publication of a letter to the Irish Cabinet in January 2020 highlighting two transport issues that have a negative impact on disabled people: the delay of over six years in the government's replacement of the Mobility Allowance and Motorised Transport Grant scheme, which was closed in 2013 following a report by the Ombudsman identifying a breach of the Equal Status Act 2000; and the very narrow eligibility criteria for obtaining tax relief under the Disabled Drivers and Disabled Passengers scheme.[47] In addition, the Ombudsman drew attention in the Annual Report 2018 to the steps that it had taken to become compliant with the public sector equality and human rights duty contained in the Irish Human Rights and Equality Commission Act 2014.[48] In the context of emphasising the adoption of a 'positive approach to implementing this duty', the Ombudsman pointed to the establishment of an internal working group, a committee and a series of workshops.[49]

[45] Ombudsman, *Improving Public Services (Annual Report 2017)* www.ombudsman.ie./publications/annual-reports/annual-report-2017-1/; Ombudsman, *Delivering Outcomes (Annual Report 2018)* www.ombudsman.ie/publications/annual-reports/Ombudsman-AR-2018-ENG-Final-for-Web.pdf.

[46] ibid.

[47] Ombudsman, Letter to the Cabinet (9 January 2020) www.ombudsman.ie.news/ombudsman-highlights-disa/.

[48] Ombudsman, *Delivering Outcomes* (n 45).

[49] ibid.

A number of provisional observations follow from the Ombudsman's approach, each in turn exemplifying a tendency to stick closely to the narrow ledge of established classical ombud practice, with considerations of 'neutrality', 'boundary' and individual agency largely prevailing. First, for the most part, the Ombudsman's disability rights interventions have been closely aligned to domestic law and the efficient operation of existing welfare schemes rather than the more expansive range of principles disclosed by the CRPD. It is perhaps significant that Ireland, although it signed the CRPD in March 2007, did not ratify it until March 2018, becoming the last EU country to do so. Yet, as noted above, reference has been made to the CRPD by the Ombudsman in individual cases, suggesting that it was an available resource even before formal ratification and its limited invocation was not merely the result of any statutory inhibition. Furthermore, it is widely expected that the CRPD should be indicative of human rights norms, even for states that have not yet ratified it.[50]

Secondly, the stand-alone power to consider complaints under the Disability Act 2005 appears to have been singularly ineffective, quite simply because individual complainants have failed to come forward. It is very unlikely that this paucity of individual complaints indicates that disability rights are already comprehensively realised in Ireland. Although the Ombudsman has indicated the importance of raising awareness among disabled people and their advisers, the apparent lack of success in that regard suggests that a less individualistic approach, supported by the more effective insertion of the Ombudsman in the broader disability and accountability network of agencies and by the use of own-initiative powers, in collaboration with civil society, might yield more positive results.

Thirdly, the positive equality and human rights duty represents a fundamental shift in equality law, transferring the burden of compliance from the individual to institutions. Whilst it is important that an ombud institution should recognise the implications for its own internal management, even more important is the use of the duty to inform expectations about the performance of public authorities, even when the Ombudsman is not the body with 'legal enforcement' powers. It is not clear that the Ombudsman has yet operationalised the duty so that it becomes part of the normative framework against which bodies within jurisdiction are evaluated. To invoke the duty in a way that is consistent with the ethos of the CRPD is not to suggest that the Ombudsman should usurp the function of other national human rights and equality institutions or indeed hold itself out as the primary locus of legal enforcement. On the contrary, such invocation should instead mesh with the established mandate of the classical ombud to humanise public administration and to give force to legal principle in a way that serves the common good, albeit with the additional weight and reach afforded by the CRPD.

[50] L Waddington, 'The Domestication of the Convention on the Rights of Persons with Disabilities: Domestic Legal Status of the CRPD and Relevance for Court Judgments' in L Waddington and A Lawson (eds), *The UN CRPD in Practice* (Oxford University Press, 2018) 538.

C. Broadening the Conversation, 'Making Rights Real'

To gauge more clearly the positive difference envisaged by the CRPD and by the 'paradigm shift' it entails, including for classical ombud practice, it is instructive to turn to an example of the part played by a classical ombud as a single agency within a multi-institutional framework under Article 33. Examples of classical ombuds being deployed in this way are relatively rare, but include Denmark, Luxembourg, Senegal and Greece. Most salient, however, is the work of the New Zealand Parliamentary Ombudsman.

The New Zealand Ombudsman was the first to be established in a British Commonwealth common law country, just ahead of the UK, in 1962.[51] Following New Zealand's ratification of the CRPD on 25 September 2008, the Ombudsman, together with the Human Rights Commission and the Convention Coalition (a group of seven disabled-people's organisations), was designated as part of the national Independent Monitoring Mechanism (IMM) under Article 33 of the CRPD, with shared responsibilities to protect, promote and monitor the rights it contains. The Ombudsman's role as part of the IMM remains that of receiving and, where appropriate, investigating complaints about the administrative conduct of state sector agencies. That function is discharged by reference to the overriding normative test of whether the agency has acted 'reasonably and fairly'. As a result of the CRPD, the relevant assessment includes 'looking at whether the agency has taken principles of the Convention into account'. As the Ombudsman makes clear, there should not be any expectation that every complaint will be investigated, but only those where an investigation is 'necessary'. Additionally, the Ombudsman can use the residual power to initiate investigations without receiving a complaint if an issue of concern has been identified that 'needs to be addressed'.[52]

As Linda Reif reported in 2014, the New Zealand Ombudsman has conducted investigations on home modification reimbursement policies, examination policies and procedures for disabled students, reasonable accommodation of healthcare for disabled prisoners, and difficulties faced by disabled people when communicating with government agencies. In addition, as an OPCAT national prevention mechanism, the Ombudsman monitors and inspects facilities where disabled people may be confined: reports have, for example, been issued on psychiatric and intellectual disability units, and have led to changes in practice.[53] More recently, in February 2019, the Ombudsman announced two investigations, undertaken at his own initiative, into the Ministry of Health's services for people with intellectual disabilities. The particular focus of the investigations is the delay in the availability of beds, leading in some cases to people

[51] LB Hill, *The Model Ombudsman: Institutionalising New Zealand's Democratic Experiment* (Princeton University Press, 1976).

[52] https://www.ombudsman.parliament.nz/what-we-can-help/fair-treatment-disabled-people.

[53] Reif (n 3) 240.

being detained unnecessarily in prison or other unsuitable places because there is nowhere else for them to go; and the quality of data collected relating to the deaths of intellectually disabled people in forensic and residential care. Although the Ombudsman has not opened a general public consultation, there have been site visits and face-to-face interviews with people in secure facilities and their families, as well as with officials and medical professionals. An opportunity was also provided for anyone to raise concerns about their individual circumstances with the Ombudsman.[54]

The approach taken by the current Ombudsman, Judge Peter Boshier, reflects the values of the CRPD. As he has explained, in investigations and communications, it is his practice to make explicit reference to relevant articles in the CRPD and to request evidence to show that the CRPD is being taken into account and adhered to by particular agencies. He has also been active in informing disabled people of their entitlements under the CRPD and its usefulness in individual advocacy, encouraging them to refer to the CRPD in their dealings with public authorities and asking them to show how they take the CRPD into account. In recognition of the social model of disability, he also makes it clear that his job is to 'ask what society has or has not done which is obstructing people with disabilities from the full enjoyment of their rights – not how their physical or mental impairment has affected the enjoyment of their rights'.[55] The CRPD also provides the abiding rationale for the investigation of complaints, namely, that there is frequently a gap between disability policy on paper and the reality of people's lives:

> It is therefore necessary to compare policies and reports with information received directly from persons with disabilities sharing their experiences and views. This is why complaints … are important, and ultimately provide persons in the disability community with an avenue for their concerns to be considered, and possibly investigated.[56]

The coordinated work of the Ombudsman with the other agencies which form part of the IMM is conducted within a broad programme entitled 'Making Disability Rights Real'. This entails the active solicitation of views on progress from disabled people and forms the centrepiece of the four-year report to the UN. The invitation to the public at large, and to disabled people in particular, is to 'join the conversation', including by attending one of the public consultations organised by the IMM so it can hear 'community thoughts and experiences' about the implementation of the CRPD.[57]

[54] https://www.ombudsman.parliament.nz/resources/making-disability-rights-real-2014-2019-0.

[55] P Boshier, untitled speech delivered to the Blind Citizens' Annual Conference, Wellington, 8 October 2016.

[56] ibid.

[57] NZ Ombudsman, *Making Disability Rights Real 2014–2019* https://www.ombudsman.parliament.nz/resources/making-disability-rights-real-2014-2019-0.

The work of the Ombudsman in contributing directly to the implementation function of the IMM can be gauged from an investigation completed in June 2016 into inclusive education, one of the priorities identified as part of the first Making Disability Rights Real initiative.[58] The purpose of the report was to focus on the current implementation of Article 24 CRPD on the right to inclusive education, especially when the New Zealand government had announced a major review and reform of the Education Act 1989. Part of the report comprised a 'snapshot' of complaints data from both the Human Rights Commission and the Office of the Ombudsman. Taking account of the four key principles promoted by the UN Committee as central to an inclusive education framework (namely, availability, accessibility, acceptability and adaptability), the Ombudsman was able to provide narrative reports on 11 complaints in the years 2013–15 relating to students with special educational needs. During the same period, the Human Rights Commission received approximately 120 complaints about disability discrimination at school, including a significant proportion (roughly 30 per cent) to do with suspension and exclusions. The numbers are therefore quite modest, especially in respect of the Ombudsman's work. Nevertheless, the data elicited from the combined intelligence reflected perceived 'shortcomings' in the provision of inclusive education in New Zealand, namely, the failure of the legislative framework to incorporate inclusive education or reasonable accommodation principles; the ineffectiveness of National Education Goals; and a general failure to address bullying of disabled students. The IMM was on that basis able to recommend legislative reform, collaboration across sectors, enhanced data collection and revision of the national Disability Strategy and Action Plan.[59]

It is notable that even in the context of an IMM under the CRPD, a classical ombud is only one of many players, its role constrained by habitual reliance on individual complaints, albeit supplemented by own-initiative investigation. Moreover, some of the issues identified reflect libertarian concerns reinforced by OPCAT responsibilities that focus on deprivation of liberty within restricted environments. Realignment of domestic law with international prescription also features prominently. Nevertheless, the ombud's access to real-life experiences in combination with the collaborative operation of the IMM enables practices that are an important counterbalance to legal, libertarian and litigation values.

First, the norms used to shape expectations of public authorities are derived not just from the legal content of the CRPD, but from the broader aspiration to achieve an 'in-depth transformation of education systems, not only in legislation and policy, but also in the mechanisms for funding, administration design, delivery and monitoring of education', and thereby enable all students to learn in inclusive environments.[60] Secondly, there is a strong and self-conscious emphasis

[58] NZ Ombudsman, *The Right to an Inclusive Education (Implementation Report)* (June 2016) https://www.ombudsman.parliament.nz.

[59] ibid.

[60] ibid 6.

on using individual complaints not as an end, but as indicators of broader public concern, especially as informed by the contribution of intelligence from disabled people themselves, thereby contributing to broad systemic change. Thirdly, the IMM framework entails that the classical ombud does not operate in isolation but is necessarily part of a network of institutions that collectively dovetail in their work to bring about meaningful change. Given the broad and permissive legislative framework of the classical ombud, and the large measure of discretion such legislation typically leaves to the ombud in devising and operationalising strategic priorities, the CRPD in these various ways provides an invaluable resource for constructing such priorities in a manner that is consistent with, and indeed represents the concrete realisation of, the ombud's overarching and humanising mission, reimagined for twenty-first-century impact. In short, the example of the New Zealand Ombudsman reinforces the argument that for classical ombud practice to be true to its established humanising ambitions and cognisant of disability rights, and indeed egalitarian values more generally, it needs to incorporate a shift of emphasis from individual to community, from legal (and other) rules as norms to broader principle, and from isolated organisational culture to work within wider institutional networks. Those shifts are the central aspects of a broader reimagining of the classical ombud as facilitator of alternative conversations, regulatory networks and democratic participation.

VI. Conclusion: Demosprudence and the Democratic Ombud

In conclusion, the reimagining called for entails a move from a jurisprudential to a 'demosprudential' framework, from a close alignment to law and its enforcement to a heightened democratic sensibility. 'Demosprudence' seeks to broaden the reach of legal discourse and embed its interpretation and development, not so much in the courts as in the democratic polity at large. To that extent, it is egalitarian and communitarian, not libertarian and individualistic. It is also a means of making the response to citizen grievance more democratic, with ambitions that embrace social and cultural change rather than legal compliance. Its preoccupations are more to do with the ability of social movements and mobilised communities to make, interpret and change expectations (including expectations created by the law), and far less to do with legal precedent, law enforcement and adversarial process as a means of establishing legal 'truth' or advancing the rule of law, narrowly conceived.[61]

[61] L Guinier and G Torres, 'Changing the Wind: Notes towards a Demosprudence of Law and Social Movements' (2014) 123 *Yale Law Journal* 2742; U Baxi, 'Demosprudence versus Jursipdrudence: The Indian Judicial Experience in the Context of Comparative Constitutional Studies' (2014) 14 *Macquarie Law Journal* 3; B Ray, 'Demosprudence in Comparative Perspective' (2011) 47 *Stanford Journal of International Law* 11.

Yet, despite its egalitarian provenance, demosprudence recognises the privileged function of certain 'role-literate participants' in democratising response to citizen grievance. An example of these role-literate participants might be the dissenting judge, who articulates minority perspectives that nevertheless resonate and percolate over time, becoming focal points for alternative conversations. In the light of the CRPD and its revision of human rights and 'enforcement', the classical ombud can be acknowledged as another credible role-literate participant, one whose mastery of principles as norms, of communitarian engagement and of facilitation of networked vigilance enables her to 'ground and frame the discourse', to enable civic participation and create bridges between sectional interests.[62] In such a capacity, the ombud is a bridging institution, an enabler and coordinator of productive conversations, across boundaries and across interest-bargaining positions.

It is increasingly clear that many human rights ombuds, not least in Latin America, already occupy such a role, even to the extent of attracting characterisation as 'policy entrepreneurs'.[63] Indeed, the designation of such ombuds as 'People's Defender' or 'Defensoria del Pueblo' invites subscription to a demosprudential ethos of this sort. Yet an inclination to seek refuge in alignment with the law is, as demonstrated above, often irresistible, even for human rights ombuds. The obstacles to a classical ombud adopting an alternative demosprudential identity are, on the face of it, even more considerable. It has been argued in this chapter, however, that once disability rights enter the governance arena, such reimagining becomes inevitable even for the classical ombud. Furthermore, wholesale conversion to the human rights ombud model need not be the inevitable destination of such reimagining.

This chapter has drawn attention to various unfortunate emphases both in the construction of contemporary human rights discourse and of modern ombud practice: a preference for legalism, which privileges rules over principle; for libertarianism, which privileges the individual victim of negative state encroachment on civil rights over the common good and social and relational entitlement; and for individual litigation and allied forms of reactive dispute resolution over proactive and goal-driven strategic intervention. These emphases are brought into sharp relief by the expectations of the CRPD version of human rights and the new paradigm of disability rights. It has been suggested that the antidote lies in the prioritisation instead of principles as norms as an antidote to legalism; of a progressive egalitarianism as an antidote to libertarianism; and of community and civic society as an antidote to individualism in the form of litigation and dispute resolution.

[62] Guinier and Torres (n 61).

[63] CA Barco, 'The Transposition of the Ombudsman Model to the Human Rights Model Domain: Its Role as a Policy Entrepreneur' in M Hertogh and R Kirkham (eds), *Research Handbook on the Ombudsman* (Edward Elgar, 2018) 188.

It is the concluding contention of this chapter that the classical ombud, whatever the pretensions of the human rights ombud, is well placed to defeat the encroaching pathologies identified. To do so, it must accommodate the reimagining entailed by the new paradigm of disability rights and of the CRPD, not just in the specific protection and promotion of disability rights, but as a template for its practice more generally. That paradigm relieves individual 'victims' from the burden of 'enforcing' human rights norms and frees individual 'perpetrators' from resorting to personal regimes of self-improvement. By emphasising the priority of principles, community and network over rules, over individualism and over boundary-observing but isolated accountability agencies, the CRPD prescribes a set of antidotes that lie within the grasp of the classical ombud, without conversion to the very different ethos of the human rights ombud. Indeed, it has been suggested that human rights ombuds are themselves sometimes liable to the unfortunate emphases identified. The classical ombud, armed with own-initiative investigation powers, an ability to engage actively with a range of civil society partners and a willingness to form part of a network of accountability agencies, is well placed to deploy its traditional function of investigation, report and recommendation in such a way that the institutions with which it is in conversation can themselves develop practices that are, in the context of the new post-CRPD human rights ethos, virtuous and pragmatic. In discharging its mandate in this way, the classical ombud remains true to a democratic, indeed demosprudential, style of legal thought that, transcending classical liberalism and its twentieth-century reinvention, grounds its origins, informs its heritage and holds out promise for its enduring legacy.

15

A Guardian Illuminated: The Role of New Zealand's Parliamentary Ombudsman in the Health and Disability System

RON PATERSON

New Zealand's 'health watchdog',[1] the Health and Disability Commissioner (HDC), is firmly embedded in the country's health and disability system, with the Commissioner's complaint rulings widely reported in the media and used to educate health practitioners and healthcare organisations about their obligations to respect patients' rights, communicate effectively and provide good quality care. The impact of the HDC legislation and decisions is well described in academic literature.[2]

Less well known is the oversight role of New Zealand's Parliamentary Ombudsman in the health and disability system. This chapter examines three areas in which the Ombudsman plays a significant but under-reported role: protecting *access* to healthcare and disability services; promoting *transparency* in the health and disability system (in relation to patient safety, healthcare quality and practitioner complaint history); and watching the watchdog, to ensure the *fairness* of HDC complaint decisions.

[1] Media commentators routinely refer to HDC as New Zealand's health watchdog.

[2] See, eg P Skegg, 'A Fortunate Experiment? New Zealand's Experience with a Legislated Code of Patients' Rights' (2011) 19 *Medical Law Review* 235, concluding that 'New Zealand's experience with a legislated Code of Rights warrants its characterisation as a fortunate experiment'. See also A Merry and M Seddon, 'Quality Improvement in Healthcare in New Zealand. Part 2: Are Our Patients Safe – and What Are We Doing About It?' (2006) 119 (No 1238) *New Zealand Medical Journal* 1, 2, commending HDC for facilitating 'a world-leading focus on addressing aspects of the system … rather than only seeking individual scapegoats when things go wrong'.

I. Origins and Evolution of Ombudsman in New Zealand[3]

New Zealand was the first common law country to follow the Scandinavian example and create a Parliamentary Ombudsman, with enactment of the Parliamentary Commissioner (Ombudsman) Act 1962, the predecessor of the current Ombudsmen Act 1975. The jurisdiction of the Ombudsman was initially limited to central government departments and organisations, but in 1968 was extended to cover education boards and health boards.[4] The Ombudsman was given a major additional function under the Official Information Act 1982 (OIA): to investigate and review complaints about decisions made by ministers and central government agencies about requests for information – effectively acting as a freedom of information commissioner. An important distinction is that whereas the Ombudsman's powers at the conclusion of an Ombudsmen Act investigation are recommendatory only,[5] a ruling that information should not have been withheld and should be released is legally binding on the minister or relevant agency.[6]

In 2007, the Ombudsman was designated a National Preventive Mechanism under the Crimes of Torture Act 1989, which gives effect to New Zealand's obligations under the Optional Protocol to the Convention against Torture and other Cruel, Inhuman or Degrading Treatment or Punishment (OPCAT). In its OPCAT role, the Ombudsman monitors the treatment of residents in places of detention, including mental health, intellectual disability and dementia facilities, and makes recommendations to improve the treatment and care of residents.[7]

Much of the work of the Ombudsman is invisible. The Office of the Ombudsman publishes annual reports and reports on inspection of places of detention, and brief case notes (and occasionally a full decision or 'opinion') following investigations of complaints about the reasonableness or lawfulness of public agency decisions, or into refusals to provide official information upon request. For an institution said to bring 'the lamp of scrutiny to otherwise dark places, even over the resistance of those who would draw the blinds',[8] the inner workings of the Ombudsman's office remain somewhat mysterious to the agencies and complainants who deal with it.

Journalists covering the health and disability sector become familiar with the Official Information Act and may complain to the Ombudsman if stonewalled

[3] For a comprehensive critique of the role of the Ombudsmen in New Zealand, see G Palmer, 'Constitutional Reflections on Fifty Years of the Ombudsmen in New Zealand' (2013) 25 *Victoria University of Wellington Law Review* 780.

[4] By the Parliamentary Commissioner (Ombudsman) Amendment Act 1968 (NZ).

[5] Ombudsmen Act 1975 (NZ), s 22(3).

[6] Official Information Act 1982 (NZ), s 32. A 'public duty' to release the information comes into effect at the expiry of 20 working days from communication of the Ombudsman's recommendation, unless a countervailing Order in Council is issued by the Governor-General.

[7] Space precludes an assessment of this aspect of the New Zealand Ombudsman's work in this chapter.

[8] *Re Ombudsman Act* (1970) 72 WWR 176, 192–93 (Alta SC, per Milvain CJ).

by the health bureaucracy, and specialist public lawyers may seek recourse to the Ombudsman as an alternative to the expensive remedy of judicial review in the High Court. Yet few people working in the health and disability system, let alone patients and the public in New Zealand, are aware of the Ombudsman's review powers, which touch on important issues of access, transparency and the fairness of the complaint system.

The relative invisibility of the health and disability work of the New Zealand Ombudsman stands in contrast to the prominence of such work in many international Ombudsmen offices, notably the Parliamentary and Health Service Ombudsman (PHSO) in the UK,[9] which publishes influential reports based on the insights from investigating complaints about a problem area in the NHS.[10] The Scottish Public Services Ombudsman also makes impactful recommendations following investigations of health-related complaints.[11]

The Australian states and territories, and New Zealand, have created specialist health complaint entities, which effectively function as health ombudsmen.[12] Writing of the Australasian entities and the PHSO, Healy and Walton note:[13]

> The health ombudsmen warrant attention as a unique regulator within the health sector in that their core statutory mandate is to respond directly to the grievances of citizens/consumers. Health ombudsmen are important because health sectors generally have been slow to respond to patient concerns about their treatment, despite the right to complain being a key principle in public administration and in market economies.

The New Zealand Ombudsman is empowered to initiate 'own-motion' investigations.[14] An Ombudsman-initiated investigation is usually prompted by serious or systemic issues, where the Ombudsman thinks that intervention has

[9] In relation to health service complaints, the Ombudsman is technically the Health Service Commissioner for England, with jurisdiction over complaints about the NHS in England, derived from the Health Service Commissioners Act 1993 (UK). The Health Service Ombudsman jurisdiction is described in M Seneviratne, *Ombudsmen: Public Services and Administrative Justice* (Butterworths, 2002) ch 5.

[10] Examples of PHSO NHS insight reports include PHSO, *Care and Compassion? Report of the Health Service Ombudsman on Ten Investigations into NHS Care of Older People* (February 2011); PHSO, *Time to Act: Severe Sepsis – Rapid Diagnosis and Treatment Saves Lives* (September 2013). An independent review of the PHSO noted that the sepsis report 'helped to get the issues onto the agenda and catalysed new approaches to diagnosis and treatment. The PHSO has worked with regulators, professional bodies, and public bodies to bring about change in this area … [showing] the clear value the PHSO can add – bringing the insights from complaints to the fore of public discussions': P Tyndall, C Mitchell and C Gill, 'Value for Money Study: Report of the Independent Peer Review of the Parliamentary and Health Services Ombudsman' (2018) 26.

[11] See G McBurnie, 'Understanding the Response from Bodies in Jurisdiction to Ombudsman Investigations – a New Conceptual Model', ch 4 in this volume.

[12] See R Paterson and J Manning, 'Complaint Resolution, Quality Improvement and Public Protection: The Diverse Roles of Australasian Health Complaints Entities' in I Freckelton and K Peterson (eds), *Tensions and Traumas in Health Law* (Federation Press, 2017) 671.

[13] J Healy and M Walton, 'Health Ombudsmen in Polycentric Regulatory Fields: England, New Zealand and Australia' (2016) 75 *Australian Journal of Public Administration* 492, 493.

[14] Ombudsmen Act 1975 (NZ), s 13(3).

the potential to result in wider administrative improvement. The equivalent power has been invoked by ombudsmen internationally to launch major inquiries, for example into the quality of residential aged care in British Columbia.[15]

The own-motion power has rarely been used by the New Zealand Ombudsman in relation to the public health and disability system. Two examples of Ombudsman own-motion investigations into publicly funded health and disability services are an inquiry into health services in prisons[16] and another into the Ministry of Health's collection, use and reporting of information about the deaths of people with intellectual disabilities receiving residential support.[17] No doubt the Ombudsman has understandably preferred to let the specialist Health and Disability Commissioner exercise its statutory power to commence an 'own-initiative' investigation into systemic issues in the provision of health and disability services.[18] In recent years, the Ombudsman's most visible health and disability system work has been in its periodic reports of inspections of mental health inpatient units, under the OPCAT jurisdiction.[19]

The success of New Zealand's 'health ombudsman' – the Health and Disability Commissioner – may have contributed to a perception that the Parliamentary Ombudsman's residual role is not particularly noteworthy. In this chapter, I aim to correct that misapprehension and shed some light on the oversight role of the Ombudsman in the health and disability system. I draw on published opinions, case notes and reports, and my own experience as Health and Disability Commissioner (2000–10) and Ombudsman (2013–16). I argue that the Ombudsman is an important guardian, whose protective powers deserve to be better known.

II. Protecting Access to Healthcare and Disability Services[20]

A general right of access to publicly funded healthcare and disability services is not specified in statute or common law in New Zealand. No such right is

[15] BC Ombudsperson, *The Best of Care: Getting it Right for Seniors in British Columbia (Part 1)* (December 2009) Public Report No 46; BC Ombudsperson, *The Best of Care: Getting it Right for Seniors in British Columbia (Part 2)* (February 2012) Public Report No 47. For an analysis of the work of classic ombuds institutions on seniors' issues in 19 jurisdictions (the UK, Ireland, and most Canadian provinces/territories and Australian states/territories), see L Reif, 'Ombuds Institutions: Non-judicial Mechanisms for the Protection and Promotion of the Rights of Older Persons', ch 16 in this volume.

[16] Chief Ombudsman Elwood and Ombudsman Wakem, *Investigation of the Department of Corrections in Relation to the Provision, Access and Availability of Prisoner Health Services* (2012).

[17] Chief Ombudsman Boshier, *Off the Record: An Investigation into the Ministry of Health's Collection, Use and Reporting of Information about the Deaths of People with Intellectual Disabilities* (July 2020).

[18] In practice, HDC's own-initiative power has seldom been used, perhaps reflecting the resource constraints of an agency facing an increasing volume of complaints.

[19] See, eg Chief Ombudsman Boshier, *Report of an Unannounced Follow Up Inspection of Wards 34, 35 and 36, Waikato Hospital, under the Crimes of Torture Act 1989* (March 2020).

[20] This section draws heavily on R Paterson, 'Access to Health Care' in P Skegg and R Paterson (eds), *Health Law in New Zealand* (Thomson Reuters, 2015) 67.

articulated in the New Zealand Public Health and Disability Act 2000 or in the New Zealand Bill of Rights Act 1990. The legislative framework for the health and disability system stipulates as a purpose, 'to facilitate access to … appropriate, effective, and timely health services … and disability support services',[21] but that is subject to what is 'reasonably achievable within the funding available',[22] and is combined with a population health purpose of 'the improvement, promotion, and protection' of the health of New Zealanders.[23] Legislation also envisages prioritisation of health and disability services.[24] The need to ration care and services is thus implicitly, if not explicitly, recognised by statute.

New Zealand's Code of Health and Disability Services Consumers' Rights[25] affirms rights (including to adequate information and an appropriate standard of care) enjoyed by patients and disability services consumers who receive healthcare or disability services, but does not provide a right of access in the first place. For patients, the Code rights are rights *in* healthcare, not rights *to* healthcare. However, some of the Code rights have been interpreted to support rights to fair and effective district health board systems for handling patient referrals, and to information about the availability of and waiting times for publicly funded healthcare, and thus touch on access issues.[26]

In limited circumstances, legislation gives an individual the right to be provided with publicly funded treatment or healthcare. Examples include patients subject to compulsory mental health treatment;[27] persons subject to compulsory care for intellectual disability;[28] prisoners;[29] persons detained under public health legislation;[30] individuals in need of emergency treatment;[31] and vulnerable adults, in the care of a hospital or other healthcare facility, who are unable to provide themselves with the necessaries.[32]

[21] New Zealand Public Health and Disability Act 2000 (NZ), s 3(1)(d).

[22] New Zealand Public Health and Disability Act 2000 (NZ), s 3(2).

[23] New Zealand Public Health and Disability Act 2000 (NZ), s 3(1)(a)(i).

[24] In light of the advisory role of the National Health Committee, pursuant to the New Zealand Public Health and Disability Act 2000 (NZ), s 13(1).

[25] Enacted as a Schedule to the Health and Disability Commissioner (Code of Health and Disability Services Consumers' Rights) Regulations 1996 (NZ), and referred to hereafter as the Code or the Code of Rights.

[26] See Paterson (n 20) 67, para 3.9.

[27] Mental Health (Compulsory Assessment and Treatment) Act 1992 (NZ), s 66.

[28] Intellectual Disability (Compulsory Care and Rehabilitation) Act 2003 (NZ), s 51.

[29] Corrections Act 2004 (NZ), s 75.

[30] In situations where the Health Act 1956 authorises compulsory detention and treatment (eg ss 92ZA(1)(a), (f) and 126), a duty to provide such treatment can reasonably be inferred: Paterson (n 20) 74.

[31] Doctors who are able to provide necessary healthcare to someone in an emergency are subject to a professional and ethical requirement to provide such care. The Medical Council affirms a doctor's duty to assist in a medical emergency, stating: 'A doctor is at risk of being professionally or criminally responsible if he or she fails to render prompt and appropriate medical care to any person (whether the patient is a current patient or not), in a medical emergency.' Medical Council of New Zealand, 'A Doctor's Duty to Help in a Medical Emergency' (2006) para 4.

[32] Crimes Act 1961 (NZ), s 151.

Judicial review proceedings by individual patients seeking to challenge a refusal to fund a medicine or procedure, or a denial of access to healthcare, are rare in New Zealand. This no doubt reflects access to justice considerations[33] and the difficult hurdles to be overcome before a court will intervene. Traditionally, New Zealand courts, like their Anglo-Australian counterparts, have shown a high degree of deference to the policy decisions of health-funding agencies and the clinical priority decisions of individual doctors. An exceptional case, in which individual patients succeeded in judicial review proceedings, is *Walsh v Pharmac*, concerning funding of the breast cancer medication Herceptin.[34]

An alternative but little-known remedy is to seek review of a funding policy or denial of access to publicly funded healthcare by the Ombudsman. In response to a complaint or 'of his own motion', the Ombudsman may 'investigate any decision or recommendation made, or any act done or omitted … relating to a matter of administration … affecting any person … in [a] personal capacity' by a range of scheduled organisations (including the Ministry of Health, district health boards and Pharmac[35]) or by 'any officer, employee, or member' of such an agency.[36]

The purpose of the Office of the Ombudsman is to provide simple, inexpensive and direct redress for citizens adversely affected by the conduct of administration.[37] Although there is discretion for the Ombudsman to refuse to investigate a matter if 'under the law … there is an adequate remedy … to which it would have been reasonable for the complainant to resort',[38] the expense of litigation means that complainants cannot reasonably be expected to bring judicial review proceedings. The availability of judicial review is not treated as a bar to an Ombudsman investigation.[39] New Zealand's 'no fault' accident compensation scheme covers treatment injuries and bars medical negligence claims for compensatory damages,[40] so the possibility of an aggrieved patient bringing such a claim is not a consideration

[33] Including the cost of bringing such a claim and the lack of knowledge, at a time of a personal or family health crisis, of the reasons for a decision and how to challenge it.

[34] *Walsh v Pharmaceutical Management Agency* [2010] NZAR 101. This High Court decision turned on a narrow but important point of procedural fairness, namely whether the funder had undertaken adequate consultation on its new policy to fund a high-cost medicine, Herceptin, for nine weeks for women with a particular subtype of breast cancer. For a detailed critique of the decision and its socio-political context, see J Manning, 'The Herceptin Interception: New Zealand's Pharmac and the Herceptin Funding Issue' [2011] *New Zealand Law Review* 663.

[35] Pharmac is a Crown entity, the Pharmaceutical Funding Agency, created under the New Zealand Public Health and Disability Act 2000, Part 4. It determines which medicines and pharmaceutical products are publicly funded in New Zealand.

[36] Ombudsmen Act 1975 (NZ), s 13(1).

[37] S Elias, 'Life Beyond Legality', speech to the Australian and New Zealand Ombudsman Association (May 2013).

[38] Ombudsmen Act 1975 (NZ), s 17(1)(a).

[39] Nor does the possibility of judicial review proceedings fall within the bar on an Ombudsman investigation in circumstances where the complainant has a statutory right to apply to a court for a review 'on the merits of the case' (Ombudsmen Act 1975 (NZ), s 13(7)(a)).

[40] Accident Compensation Act 2001 (NZ), ss 20, 317.

for the Ombudsman. However, complainants are expected to have raised their concerns with the relevant agency before making a complaint to the Ombudsman.[41]

On completion of an investigation or inquiry, the Ombudsman may form an opinion that the relevant decision

> (a) appears to have been contrary to law; or (b) was unreasonable, unjust, oppressive or improperly discriminatory, or was in accordance with a rule of law or a [statutory] provision … or a practice[42] that is or may be unreasonable, unjust, oppressive, or improperly discriminatory; or (c) was based wholly or partly on a mistake of fact or law; or (d) was wrong.[43]

In the event of the exercise of a discretionary power for an improper purpose or taking into account irrelevant considerations, or the failure to give reasons for the exercise of a discretionary power, the Ombudsman may make findings to that effect.[44] The Ombudsman is required to report his opinion to the parties, and 'may make such recommendations as he thinks fit' to remedy the situation.[45]

These are significant powers, which could potentially be used to challenge a rationing decision.[46] In practice, like the courts on judicial review, successive Ombudsmen have generally taken a cautious approach and restricted their review to the lawfulness and procedural fairness of the challenged decision, notwithstanding the statutory power to review the reasonableness of a decision.

A rare example of a case where a New Zealand Ombudsman intervened in a health-rationing decision turned on the procedural unfairness of a regional health-funding authority's reversal of its original decision to fund a costly surgical procedure for an individual patient.[47] Days before a scheduled operation, the authority had revoked an earlier approval of funding of gender reassignment surgery for the complainant, a transsexual. The Ombudsman accepted that the health authority was entitled to reclassify gender reassignment surgery as a cosmetic procedure that was not funded. The issue was whether it was

[41] If the complainant has not first raised the issue with the agency complained about, an Ombudsman may exercise the s 17(1)(a) discretion to refuse to investigate the complaint on the basis that 'it appears to him that under … existing administrative practice there is an adequate remedy … to which it would have been reasonable for the complainant to resort'.

[42] A 'practice' may include a policy followed by an agency.

[43] Ombudsmen Act 1975 (NZ), s 22(1).

[44] Ombudsmen Act 1975 (NZ), s 22(2).

[45] Ombudsmen Act 1975 (NZ), s 22(3).

[46] To underpin such a challenge, a complainant may seek to gather information about a district health board's prioritisation decisions by making an information request to the board (Official Information Act 1982 (NZ), s 12). A refusal by a board to make such 'official information' available can be reviewed by the Ombudsman in response to a complaint (OIA, ss 28(1), 28(3)). If, following investigation, the refusal is found to have been unjustified, the Ombudsman may recommend release of the information (OIA, s 30(1)). An individual may also request a written statement of the reasons for a decision or recommendation affecting that person in his or her personal capacity (OIA, s 23(1)(c)), and may complain to the Ombudsman about an agency's refusal to provide such a statement.

[47] Chief Ombudsman Elwood opinion, case no W40303, *13th Compendium of Case Notes of the Ombudsmen* (Office of the Ombudsman, 2003) 25.

administratively unfair to reverse the earlier approval. The complainant had been given no indication of the proposed policy change, nor an opportunity to be heard on a decision that clearly affected her adversely. It was held to be unreasonable for the health authority not to honour its earlier undertaking. The Ombudsman recommended that, subject to a satisfactory clinical assessment, the authority fund gender reassignment surgery as originally approved, together with all associated costs. The recommendation was duly implemented.

The creation of a legitimate expectation of funding was also the basis of the Ombudsman's intervention in another case. The Ombudsman found it unreasonable for the Ministry of Health to reduce funded family care to 40 hours per week, where a father (caring for his adult son with an intellectual disability) had been told by the disability support service that 59 hours per week of funded family care had been awarded.[48]

In a case where Pharmac had declined to approve exceptional circumstances funding for an expensive medicine to treat a patient's rare metabolic disorder,[49] the Ombudsman closely scrutinised the lawfulness and reasonableness of Pharmac's relevant policy and noted:[50]

> [T]he Ombudsmen are not restricted to examining only the merits of a decision taken by the agency complained of. The Ombudsmen can also examine the law or policy under which that decision was taken and comment on its reasonableness or otherwise … [however] this jurisdiction must be exercised with discretion.

Although the Ombudsman did not express an opinion on the merits of the case or on the appropriateness of the relevant policy, he made detailed comments about desirable modifications to the policy and informally recommended that Pharmac allow the complainant to make further submissions seeking short-term trial funding of the medicine. The Ombudsman also expressed doubt as to the lawfulness of Pharmac's interpretation of the residual power for district health boards to fund medicines not listed on the Pharmaceutical Schedule. The case is a strong indication of the potential scope of Ombudsman review in relation to health-rationing decisions.[51]

In another case, the Ombudsman found a disability-funding policy to be unreasonable.[52] The Ministry of Health had refused to reimburse the $8100 cost of housing modifications – undertaken to allow the complainant's disabled husband to live at home – in accordance with a policy that required prior

[48] Ombudsman Donnelly case note, case no 419489 (October 2016).

[49] The patient was one of eight adults in New Zealand known to be suffering from Pompe disease.

[50] Ombudsman McGee opinion, case no 343665 (July 2013) paras 107–08.

[51] In another decision, the Ombudsman concluded that Pharmac had acted not unreasonably in funding Opdivo ahead of Keytruda (medications for treatment of melanoma), taking account of its statutory objective of obtaining the best health outcomes within available funding: Ombudsman Donnelly case note, case no 428401 (December 2017).

[52] Ombudsman McGee case note, case no 177449 (October 2010, published December 2017).

approval. The modifications were necessary and not excessive, but the complainant had arranged them without prior approval, despite knowing that approval was required in order to be eligible for funding. Her husband's discharge from hospital had been imminent and she was concerned the approval process would not be completed in time for her to have the work done.

It was noted that the 'jurisdiction as Ombudsman extends to whether a decision has been made in accordance with a policy that is itself unreasonable'.[53] The Ombudsman referred to the prior legislative history, including an earlier statutory entitlement to support; criticised the legislative basis of the new policy as 'unspecific … and therefore unreasonable as standing on its own. It does not confer or define entitlements to … support even though there [had] been an expectation or assumption [of such support] since at least 1975'; and found the policy of discretionary retrospective funding to be unreasonable as it 'unduly prefers the convenience of the administration over recognition of need'.[54] The Ombudsman recommended review of the policy and consideration of a payment of the claimed amount to the complainant if her application would have met the relevant criteria for funding had it not been made retrospectively. This case illustrates the ability of the Ombudsman to review the merits or fairness of a funding policy under the head of 'reasonableness'.

The application of New Zealand's reciprocal health agreement with Australia, made under the Health Benefits (Reciprocity with Australia) Act 1999, was held to be unreasonable in a case where an Australian resident received treatment at a New Zealand public hospital for high blood pressure, having been without his usual medication for several days, and was later invoiced. The Ombudsman found it was unreasonable to deny the complainant's application for public funding simply because there was no clinical record that treatment was immediately necessary.[55]

Complaints alleging a failure by a district health board to consult with affected parties and the public are also sometimes the subject of complaint to the Ombudsman. In one case, the Ombudsman criticised the failure to consult on an extension of a publicly funded abortion service into Southland. The case is unusual since most challenges to service reconfiguration involve the closure, rather than the extension, of a service. The complainants claimed that lack of consultation had deprived them of the opportunity to put the case for other health services to be funded, to improve access in Southland. The Ombudsman noted that

> where a decision-maker such as a district health board knows that a funding or access decision … is likely to be controversial and to arouse strong views within the community, it is good administrative practice to allow community participation in the decision-making process.[56]

[53] ibid para 26.
[54] ibid para 43.
[55] Ombudsman Donnelly case note, case no 458017 (March 2018).
[56] Ombudsman Paterson case note, case no 338469 (August 2013). *cf* the statement of Gendall J on the duty of Pharmac to consult, in *Walsh v Pharmaceutical Management Agency* [2010] NZAR 101, [189].

III. Promoting Transparency in the Health and Disability System

The need for greater transparency in the health and disability system has been a common refrain in New Zealand and internationally this century. Yet in practice, public agencies often hide health decision-making processes and related information from public scrutiny. The reality is at odds with the legislative framework for freedom of information, and the frequent rhetoric about transparency and accountability.

The responses of public health authorities during the COVID-19 pandemic has been a refreshing exception, with uncharacteristic openness from ministers and health officials in fronting the news media every day, to update the community on the latest information and the state of pandemic planning. A National Ethics Advisory Committee 2007 report, *Getting Through Together: Ethical Values for a Pandemic*, highlights why open decision-making is important:[57]

> Decision-making processes that are open and transparent may help to show that decision-making has been done well. Where the reasons for decisions are not apparent, trust in decision-makers may be undermined. Informing people of the reasons on which decisions are based may also promote compliance with difficult measures such as quarantine and restricted social interaction.

This rationale is consistent with the aims of the OIA. The purposes of the Act include 'to increase progressively the availability of official information to the people of New Zealand' and the overriding principle is that information should be publicly available 'unless there is good reason for withholding it'.[58]

Unfortunately, many health agencies have mastered the art of delay and obfuscation when responding to requests for information. A request for information held by an agency, followed by an OIA complaint to the Ombudsman in the event of refusal to supply the requested information, is an effective way to bring information to light.[59] Media exposure of problems in the health system are often the result of a journalist's OIA request, initial denial by an agency, involvement of the Ombudsman following a complaint by the journalist and eventual release of information, such as a critical external review or internal communications about a sensitive new programme.[60]

[57] National Ethics Advisory Committee, *Getting Through Together: Ethical Values for a Pandemic* (NEAC, 2007) 27.

[58] Official Information Act 1982 (NZ), ss 4(a), 5.

[59] See R Paterson, *The Good Doctor: What Patients Want* (Auckland University Press, 2012) 121, where I argued that one way to improve patient care is to lift the veil of secrecy and provide better information for patients and the public, and noted that 'investigative journalists have on occasion invoked freedom of information legislation to great effect, to compel disclosure of health data in the public interest'.

[60] Recent examples include N Jones, 'Heart Problems: Scathing Review Exposed Serious Flaws at Cardiac Unit' *New Zealand Herald* (13 April 2021) A1, A3; P Bagshaw, P Goodman and B Cox, 'Official Information Act Investigation of the Ministry of Health's Process to Assess the Southern District

Decisions of the Ombudsman following investigation of refusals to provide health-related information have paved the way for greater transparency in relation to patient safety, healthcare quality and the complaint history of a practitioner or healthcare organisation. In the discussion below, I focus on the impact of Ombudsman OIA rulings relating to (i) serious adverse event information, (ii) surgical complications and mortality data and (iii) complaint history – topics that matter to patients, clinicians and the public. I also note Ombudsmen Act decisions highlighting the need for (iv) transparency in decision-making processes.

A. Serious Adverse Event Information

In 2007, the *Dominion Post* newspaper requested 'serious and sentinel event' reports[61] held by the Capital & Coast District Health Board (DHB), under the OIA. Such reports may flag patient safety problems in a hospital. The Ombudsman ruled that the reports should be released with redactions to protect privacy and confidentiality interests.[62] Public interest considerations favoured the release of some information to promote the accountability of the DHB and to assure the public that identified deficiencies were being remedied. The Ombudsman considered that information illustrating what happened and what corrective measures were taken in each case should be released. The DHB subsequently released the reports, with redactions.

In the aftermath of the Capital & Coast case, the Quality Improvement Committee[63] coordinated the national release of sentinel event information for all DHBs in 2008. The careful release of data and explanatory material avoided the risk that sensationalist media reports and statistically unsound league tables would undermine public confidence. Over the past decade, the release of annual 'Learning from Adverse Events' reports from the Health Quality and Safety Commission has become routine, consistent with an open culture of reporting and learning from mistakes. 'Open disclosure' has become part of the way the health system does things, although there remains significant variation in the policy and practice of individual DHBs.[64]

Serious adverse event information may be legally protected as a 'protected quality assurance activity' (PQAA). Like many countries, New Zealand has passed

Health Board's Readiness to Join the National Bowel Screening Programme in 2018' (2021) 134 *New Zealand Medical Journal* 99.

[61] Reports on serious adverse events involving unanticipated patient death or serious injury.

[62] Ombudsman Wakem case note, case no W55001 (November 2007).

[63] The Quality Improvement Committee (full name, the National Health Epidemiology and Quality Assurance Committee) was a ministerial advisory committee appointed in 2007 and replaced in 2010 by the Health Quality and Safety Commission, created under the New Zealand Public Health and Disability Act 2000, s 59A.

[64] S McLennan and J Moore, 'New Zealand District Health Boards' Open Disclosure Policies: A Qualitative Review' (2019) 16 *Journal of Bioethical Inquiry* 35.

legislation to protect from disclosure approved activities 'undertaken to improve the practices or competence of 1 or more health practitioners by assessing the health services performed by those practitioners'.[65] The protection conferred means that clinicians can review their work with a view to improvement, in the knowledge that any information generated cannot be disclosed to a third party or in a judicial proceeding or investigation. In return for the statutory privilege accorded to PQAAs, persons responsible for the activity are required to file annual reports with the Minister of Health about actions taken, recommendations and improvements from such activities – a form of accountability to ensure that improvements are actually being made.[66]

Following a refusal of a request to the Minister of Health to release PQAA annual reports for 2007–11, a journalist complained to the Ombudsman. The claimed grounds for refusal were that release of the reports could lead to the identification of individuals and deter health practitioners from undertaking quality assurance activities in the future. The Ombudsman noted the strong public interest considerations favouring disclosure of the annual reports, including the need for greater openness and transparency regarding the outcomes of quality assurance processes and the accountability of health practitioners and organisations. The Minister of Health accepted that PQAA annual reports should be released under the OIA, subject to redactions to protect individual privacy,[67] and that in future the reports would be proactively released on the Ministry of Health website.[68] The case is a further example of the use of the OIA to release official information in the interests of patient safety.[69]

B. Surgical Complications and Mortality Data

Health sector agencies hold a lot of healthcare quality information that should be in the public domain. In 2014, *New Zealand Herald* journalist Martin Johnston requested, from Southern, Auckland, Waikato, Capital & Coast and Canterbury DHBs, their volume data for cardiothoracic and neurosurgery, and complications and mortality data for such surgery, by individual surgeon. The request was denied and Johnston complained to the Ombudsman under the OIA.[70]

[65] Health Practitioners Competence Assurance Act 2003 (NZ), s 53.

[66] Health Practitioners Competence Assurance Act 2003 (NZ), s 58.

[67] Health Practitioners Competence Assurance Act 2003 (NZ), s 60(1) permits to disclosure of non-identifying information from protected quality assurance activities.

[68] *Report of the Ombudsman for the Year Ended 30 June 2014* (2014) 37.

[69] The outcome is consistent with a prediction in Paterson (n 59) 122.

[70] Johnston followed a line of investigative journalists overseas who invoked freedom of information legislation to compel disclosure of health data. The newspaper *Newsday* used this tactic successfully in New York State in 1990 to obtain and publish surgeon-specific cardiac mortality data. *The Guardian* newspaper used freedom of information laws to obtain and publish similar data about cardiac surgeons in the northwest of England in 2005. In both cases, the public interest in disclosure was seen to override any privacy concerns – even though the information enabled comparisons of individual doctors.

Johnston's OIA complaint spurred a lot of discussion among health sector leaders, fearful of damage to public confidence from unreliable league tables. The Medical Council sought to raise the level of debate, publishing a discussion paper on 'Better Data – The Benefits to the Profession and the Public'.[71] The Ministry of Health and the Health Quality and Safety Commission (HQSC) held workshops for key stakeholders and health consumer representatives.[72] The HQSC ultimately published a paper on the transparency of information related to healthcare interventions.[73]

The case required a careful balancing of the potential for damage from the release of raw data with the benefits of requiring limited disclosure. The countervailing interests are summarised in the Ombudsman's decision. On the one hand:[74]

> Releasing individual surgeons' outcomes data in its current state would do more harm than good given the current state of information in the New Zealand health sector. Public reporting of data that is misleading, incomplete or otherwise of poor quality could erode public confidence in the health system, undermine teamwork and result in surgeons seeking to avoid complex procedures.

On the other hand:[75]

> There is a public interest in the availability of information about the outcomes of health care interventions, including surgery. Aside from the general public interest in transparency, such information is important for:
>
> a. patient autonomy and choice – information about a particular service, practitioner, or treatment can assist patients making decisions about their health care;
> b. accountability – the generation and supply of information to the public is a means by which health care organisations and practitioners can be held accountable for the services they provide; and
> c. quality improvement – there is good evidence that collecting, analysing and publishing risk-adjusted data on key indicators leads to improvements in quality.

The Ombudsman concluded that the DHBs were required to release data about the numbers and types of procedures performed by individual surgeons,[76] but not complications, readmission and mortality data at individual surgeon level, since the public interest did not outweigh individual privacy.

Noting that 'New Zealand lags behind other comparable healthcare systems in disclosure of performance and outcomes information',[77] the Ombudsman recommended progressive release of further information over a five-year period – that

[71] Medical Council of New Zealand, 'Better Data – the Benefits to the Profession and the Public' (2015).

[72] As Ombudsman, I attended the workshops and meetings with HQSC leaders.

[73] HQSC, 'Position Paper on the Transparency of Information Related to Health Care Interventions' (2016).

[74] Ombudsman Paterson opinion, 'Request for Surgical Complications Data', case nos 402136, 402138, 402140, 402142, 402144 (June 2016) 2–3.

[75] ibid 25.

[76] This was consistent with an earlier Ombudsman Paterson opinion, 'Request for Information Concerning a General Surgeon', case no 371760 (November 2014).

[77] Ombudsman opinion, 'Request for Surgical Complications Data' (n 74) 3.

the Ministry of Health and HQSC provide publicly available, annual updates, from June 2017, on progress towards publication of meaningful quality of care measures across specialties by June 2021, specifically:[78]

> the selection, development and public reporting of quality of care measures (including outcomes data) that:
>
> - are meaningful to consumers
> - are meaningful to the clinicians who provide their care
> - are meaningfully attributable to the clinicians or service providing that care, and
> - increase the availability of information to the people of New Zealand.

In response to the decision, the Ministry and HQSC developed a rationale and strategy for public reporting to be effective in New Zealand: 'Guiding Principles: Towards the Publication of Clinical Performance and Outcome Data'.[79] Since 2016, HQSC has published four annual updates on 'increasing transparency in New Zealand health care', with specific programmes relating to ischaemic heart disease, orthopaedics and cancer services, and a dashboard on health system quality bringing together 70 indicators of quality across 20 DHBs in one dashboard.[80]

Commentators have described the Ombudsman's OIA ruling in favourable terms:[81] 'we are lucky enough to have been challenged on our approaches to the public reporting of outcomes data from our health services at a time when international evidence is growing'.

C. Complaint History

Over time, most health practitioners and healthcare organisations will be the subject of a complaint. Some may be 'frequent fliers' who receive a disproportionate share of complaints. In the New Zealand health sector, complaint history information is held by employers (such as DHBs), health regulators (such as the Medical Council and the Nursing Council) and the Health and Disability Commissioner (HDC), the independent agency charged with assessing and investigating complaints about healthcare and disability service providers.

[78] ibid 27–28.

[79] C Shuker, G Bohm, R Hamblin, A Simpson, D St George, I Stolarek, J Wilson and AF Merry, 'Progress in Public Reporting in New Zealand since the Ombudsman's Ruling, and an Invitation' (2017) 130 *New Zealand Medical Journal* 11, Figure 1.

[80] For the most recent update, see HQSC, 'Fourth Annual Update on Increasing Transparency in Aotearoa New Zealand Health Care' (September 2020).

[81] Shuker et al (n 79) 17.

Unlike other countries, such as Australia and the UK, New Zealand health regulators, or 'responsible authorities', are not covered by the OIA and routinely refuse requests from journalists for details of a registered health practitioner's complaint history. However, amendments to the Health Practitioners Competence Assurance Act in 2019 point to Parliament wanting greater transparency about regulatory performance, with regular, independent reviews of how effectively and efficiently a responsible authority is performing its functions, and publication of recommendations and actions taken.[82] Each responsible authority is required to publish a 'naming policy', intended to:[83]

> a) enhance public confidence in the health professions for which the authority is responsible and their disciplinary procedures by providing transparency about their decision-making processes; (b) ensure that health practitioners whose conduct has not met expected standards may be named where it is in the public interest to do so; and (c) improve the safety and quality of health care.

HDC is an entity covered by the OIA. In 2008, HDC developed a naming policy that indicates when HDC will proactively name or publish identifying information about a health practitioner, healthcare organisation or other provider found in breach of the Code of Rights.[84] In practice, very few individual practitioners have been named by application of the policy.[85]

Against this backdrop, complaints to the Ombudsman following unsuccessful OIA requests to DHBs and HDC (entities covered by the OIA) are an avenue for journalists and interested members of the public to seek to find out whether a practitioner is a 'frequent flier' with a track record of multiple complaints. The adjudication of such complaints involves balancing the privacy interests of an individual practitioner against the public interest in such information, for reasons of safety, choice and accountability.

Judge Cartwright, in her *Report of the Cervical Cancer Inquiry*, the landmark New Zealand inquiry that led to the creation of HDC, highlighted the public interest in the availability of information about practitioners:[86]

> The vast majority [of patients] want information, a chance to take part in a treatment decision, the opportunity to decline inclusion in a trial, and the right to *ensure that a negligent, rude or incompetent doctor's reputation is known* so that other patients can choose alternative health care (emphasis added).

[82] Health Practitioners Competence Assurance Act 2003 (NZ), s 122A.

[83] Health Practitioners Competence Assurance Act 2003 (NZ), s 157B(2).

[84] For the current version of the policy, see Health and Disability Commissioner, 'Naming Providers in Public HDC Reports' (2019) www.hdc.org.nz/media/5387/naming-providers-in-public-hdc-reports.pdf.

[85] See R Paterson, 'Assessment and Investigation of Complaints' in Skegg and Paterson (n 20) ch 9, 920–21.

[86] S Cartwright, *Report of the Committee of Inquiry into Allegations into the Treatment of Cervical Cancer at National Women's Hospital and into Other Related Matters* (Government Printer, 1988) 172.

Research based on access to complaint data held by Australian health complaint entities found that 3 per cent of doctors accounted for 49 per cent of complaints,[87] and prompted this author's observation:[88]

> [A]bove a certain threshold (eg, three or more complaints within 3 years) commissions and medical boards should make the number and nature of multiple complaints against an individual doctor a matter of public record – a move consistent with public expectations of greater transparency of health information and with freedom of information laws.

The application of the OIA to a request for disclosure of a health practitioner's complaint history with HDC was considered by the Ombudsman in a test case in 2013.[89] The Ombudsman developed general principles as a guide for future cases where requests are made under the OIA to HDC for a health practitioner's complaint history and for use, by analogy, by DHBs responding to similar OIA requests.[90]

The Ombudsman noted:[91]

> There is no single public interest consideration in relation to OIA requests about the complaint history of a health practitioner. A range of public interests need to be taken into account, including:
>
> a. transparency about complaints and concerns about health practitioners;
> b. the safety and quality of health care and the competence of health practitioners;
> c. fairness to practitioners who may suffer reputational damage where complaints are made public (especially where the complaint has not been investigated and may not even have been notified to the practitioner); and
> d. accountability for the performance of HDC (as the public watchdog agency responsible for assessing and investigating complaints about health practitioners) and DHBs (in monitoring the quality of health and disability services).

The Ombudsman rejected a submission that the public interest in disclosure should be 'discounted simply because of the assumed proper oversight of HDC and regulatory bodies such as the Medical Council', noting:[92]

> There is a significant public interest in the public being able to access information about:
>
> a. complaints made to a statutory agency such as HDC, given its high profile and statutory role in assessing and investigating complaints against health practitioners; and
> b. the outcome of HDC's handling of a complaint.

[87] M Bismark, MJ Spittal, LC Gurrin, M Ward and DM Studdert, 'Identification of Doctors at Risk of Recurrent Complaints: A National Study of Healthcare Complaints in Australia' (2013) 22 *Quality and Safety in Health Care* 532.

[88] R Paterson, 'Not So Random: Patient Complaints and "Frequent Flier" Doctor' (2013) 22 *Quality and Safety in Health Care* 525, 527.

[89] Ombudsman Paterson opinion, 'Request for Health Practitioner Complaint History with HDC', case no 355627 (June 2016).

[90] ibid para 29 and Appendix 1.

[91] ibid para 25.

[92] ibid para 27.

In a similar vein, in another case the Ombudsman considered that there was a public interest in release, under the OIA, of the identity of DHBs in six-monthly reports from HDC on the rate of complaints per 100,000 patient discharges in each DHB. Concerns about potential damage to public confidence based on unreliable data could be overcome by the provision of appropriate caveats and contextual information when releasing the information.[93]

D. Transparency of Decision-Making Processes

Although reference to the public interest in transparency appears most often in Ombudsman decisions under the OIA, lack of transparency may be a relevant factor in reviews of the reasonableness of administrative action, under the Ombudsmen Act. An example is a case about the reasonableness of decisions made by Pharmac in relation to public funding of melanoma medications. Although, on the facts, Pharmac had provided an adequate level of transparency, the Ombudsman noted:[94]

> It was vitally important that the New Zealand public are provided with adequate information and that commercial considerations do not override transparency. Although Pharmac's negotiating position would be prejudiced if detailed commercial information was released, and Pharmac's processes are often complicated, it should be as open as possible about the progress of funding applications, particularly in cases of high public interest. Pharmac has an important role that impacts on health options for the New Zealand public. It must keep New Zealanders adequately informed to promote transparency, accountability and public confidence in decision-making.

Another example of Ombudsman review for lack of transparency relates to HDC. The duty to provide reasons was cited in an Ombudsman review of a decision by the Commissioner to take no further action on a complaint made by a family member of a deceased patient. The Ombudsman determined that HDC had acted unreasonably by failing to give adequate reasons for its decision, and noted:[95]

> It is crucial to the proper exercise of HDC's statutory discretion that adequate reasons are provided for a decision. This is recognised by section 38(4) of the Act, which states that where the Commissioner decides to take no action, the Commissioner must inform the complainant and the health care provider of the decision and the reasons for it. The common law duty to act fairly also requires a decision-maker in a role such as

[93] Ombudsman Paterson case note, case no 406561 (January 2016). HDC now publishes such reports with identifying information – see, eg, 'Complaints to the Health and Disability Commissioner Involving District Health Boards: Report and Analysis for the Period 1 January to 30 June 2019' (2019) 3 www.hdc.org.nz/media/5347/complaints-to-hdc-involving-dhbs-jan-jun-2019.pdf.

[94] Donnelly (n 51) para 27.

[95] Ombudsman Paterson unpublished opinion, case no 392450 (June 2016). The case is discussed in J Manning, '"Fair, Simple, Speedy and Efficient"? Barriers to Access to Justice in the Health and Disability Commissioner's Complaints Process in New Zealand' [2018] *New Zealand Law Review* 611, 629–32.

> the Commissioner's to provide reasons for the exercise of a statutory discretion. Those reasons should be sufficiently cogent to enable the parties to understand how the decision was arrived at.

Even where the empowering statute does not specify a duty on a decision-maker to give reasons, there is a strong argument that transparency and fairness to affected persons means that reasons should be provided. Where a statute specifies mandatory relevant considerations for a decision-maker in the exercise of discretion, a failure to provide reasons may render the decision vulnerable to review for lack of fairness.[96]

IV. 'Watching the Watchdog' to Ensure the Fairness of HDC Complaint Decisions

One reason for the relative invisibility of the New Zealand Ombudsman's role in the health and disability system is the prominence of the 'health watchdog', the HDC. Established in 1994, with broad jurisdiction over complaints about the provision of healthcare or disability services, including complaints about registered health practitioners,[97] the HDC is a 'one-stop shop' for complainants (consumers, families and third parties) who allege a breach of the Code of Rights and do not wish to seek, or are unable to achieve, resolution direct with the provider.

The purpose of the HDC complaint system is 'to facilitate the fair, simple, speedy, and efficient resolution of complaints'.[98] The Commissioner is given wide discretion in the handling of complaints and, subject to the provisions of the Act, 'may regulate his or her procedure in such manner as he or she thinks fit'.[99] The HDC Act makes no provision for dissatisfied complainants or providers to seek a review or appeal of the Commissioner's decision.

In this context, the Ombudsman has played an important but largely invisible role in 'watching the watchdog' to ensure that HDC's processes and decisions are fair, investigating complaints of unreasonableness made under the Ombudsmen Act and of unjustified withholding of information under the OIA – HDC being an entity covered by both statutes and subject to Ombudsman review.

[96] An example is the discretion given to the Commissioner (under the HDC Act, s 45(2)(f)) to refer providers found in breach of the Code to the Director of Proceedings to consider further proceedings. In exercising this discretion, the Commissioner must have regard to specified mandatory relevant factors (HDC Act, ss 44(2), 44(3)). Yet HDC decisions, even in cases of significant breaches of the Code, seldom spell out the factors considered by the Commissioner in a decision whether or not to refer. Such an omission may provide fertile ground for Ombudsman review.

[97] The responsible authority for each health profession required to refer all patient complaints to HDC under the Health Practitioners Competence Assurance Act 2003 (NZ), s 64.

[98] HDC Act 1994, s 6.

[99] HDC Act 1994, s 59(4).

A. Procedural Fairness

The Ombudsman has confirmed that under the OIA providers are entitled to see a summary of the complaint made against them, in light of the 'high public interest in adherence to the principles of natural justice and fairness', even when the complaint is not to be investigated.[100] During the complaint assessment or investigation by HDC, the Commissioner may decline to provide information while it is still being gathered,[101] but the Ombudsman has confirmed that, once the file is closed, parties are entitled to see relevant documentation (subject to privacy protections).[102]

The Commissioner's initial practice was not to disclose the identity of clinical advisors who provide HDC with expert advice on complaints during the assessment or investigation of the complaint. Following the intervention of the Ombudsman, the Commissioner decided to disclose the names of advisors in decisions, noting:[103] 'While I am not convinced that I am legally required to provide the name of the expert, I feel it will strengthen my reports by adding transparency and accountability to the process.'

Delays in HDC processes are a frequent source of complaint from complainants and providers. The Ombudsman has confirmed that long delays in the assessment of a complaint, leaving parties in limbo and causing stress and uncertainty, are unreasonable.[104] Conversely, the Ombudsman has sometimes intervened to ensure that, in its haste to complete an investigation, HDC has not given a provider an unreasonably short time to respond to a provisional opinion – a useful sanction where a Commissioner unduly focused on speed and efficiency, and deluged with a backlog of open files, may be tempted to set short time frames for response at the expense of fairness.

Recognising the volume of complaints handled by HDC, and the discretion given to HDC to regulate its procedure, the Ombudsman has noted that it is 'strictly for [the Commissioner] to determine whether the opportunity to be heard involves a face to face meeting'.[105] In the vast majority of complaints about HDC, the Ombudsman undertakes some enquiries (which may prompt HDC to

[100] Ombudsman McGee case note, case no 178237 (August 2010). In practice, the Commissioner almost invariably sends the provider a copy of the full complaint and seeks a response.

[101] Subject to the need to ensure procedural fairness by giving parties the opportunity to comment on relevant information, in particular in a provisional decision. See the discussion in s (iii) below re fairness in the assessment of a complaint.

[102] Personal knowledge of the Ombudsman's interpretation of the application of the OIA to complaints of refusal to provide access to HDC file information.

[103] R Paterson, 'Naming Advisors: Pros and Cons' *New Zealand GP* (31 May 2001).

[104] Chief Ombudsman Boshier opinion, case nos 466864, 482749, 486627 (December 2020). HDC took three years nine months, one year nine months and three years three months, respectively, to complete its 'preliminary assessment' of the complaints. Under the HDC Act, s 33(2), the Commissioner must 'promptly notify [the parties] of the Commissioner's assessment'.

[105] Chief Ombudsman Elwood letter to Commissioner Paterson re case no 00HDC05372 (17 April 2003). In practice, few parties to HDC investigation are interviewed face to face.

reconsider a matter) but declines to initiate an investigation. In 2019/2020, there were 61 requests to the Ombudsman for review of an HDC decision, but only three resulted in an Ombudsman investigation.[106]

However, the Ombudsman has signalled a willingness to scrutinise HDC's exercise of discretion in the handling of complaints, in the face of vocal concerns from complainants and providers. To provide some context, it is necessary to explain the two stages of preliminary assessment and investigation of a complaint under the HDC Act, and the Commissioner's handling options, having assessed a complaint. In a significant amendment to the original statute, by the Health and Disability Commissioner Amendment Act 2003, Parliament gave HDC additional complaint-handling options, notably the power to take 'no further action' on a complaint when, having undertaken a preliminary assessment of the matter, the Commissioner 'considers that, having regard to all the circumstances of the case, any action or further action is unnecessary or inappropriate'.[107]

The result, over time, has been that HDC has taken 'no further action' on over one-third of all complaints, and undertaken a formal investigation in only around 5 per cent of complaints.[108] This has led Joanna Manning, a leading academic commentator, to raise access-to-justice concerns.[109] In serious cases, complainants are being denied a formal investigation ruling from New Zealand's health watchdog, and the possibility of bringing a claim before the Human Rights Review Tribunal, a precondition of which is an HDC investigation and finding that a provider breached the Code.[110] Similar concerns from dissatisfied complainants have led to a petition to the Health Select Committee of Parliament seeking that the HDC Act be amended to give complainants and respondents the right to appeal decisions made by the Commissioner, citing:[111]

> [A] striking pattern for over nearly two decades and by more than one Commissioner of making decisions to take No Further Action (NFA) on sometimes serious complaints with serious outcomes, of not undertaking formal investigations of serious complaints despite complainants' requests, and of reaching decisions that 'no breach' of the Code has occurred, despite expert advice that there has been 'significant departure' from acceptable standards of care by the provider concerned and from which complainants are unable to appeal.

A right of appeal may not be necessary if dissatisfied parties are aware of the ability to complain to the Ombudsman, and if the Ombudsman is willing to take a

[106] Letter from Office of the Ombudsman to Dr G Ashton re request for information about complaints against HDC (15 April 2020).

[107] Health and Disability Commissioner Act 1994 (NZ), s 38(1).

[108] Data from *Annual Report for the Year Ended 30 June 2020* (HDC, 2020) 17. The remainder of complaints to HDC are referred to another agency, sent to an HDC health and disability consumer advocate to resolve, withdrawn or declined as outside of jurisdiction.

[109] Manning (n 95).

[110] Health and Disability Commissioner Act 1994 (NZ), s 51.

[111] 'Petition of Renate Schutte: A Right to Appeal Decisions Made by the Health and Disability Commissioner', presented to the Health Committee, New Zealand Parliament, 22 June 2020.

more interventionist stance in cases where HDC has clearly acted unreasonably. There are signs of successive Ombudsmen responding to recurrent concerns about: (i) the reasonableness of HDC conducting what is, in effect, an investigation, during a prolonged preliminary assessment of a complaint; (ii) the reasonableness of a decision not to investigate a complaint; and (iii) the fairness of HDC's process during the assessment of a complaint. These three types of case are considered below.

(i) An Investigation in All but Name

In a case where HDC had written to the complainant stating that 'I do not consider that further investigation by this Office is necessary', the Ombudsman noted that it was inaccurate and potentially confusing to describe the assessment process as an investigation;[112] an investigation requires notification to the parties of the Commissioner's intention to investigate a matter.[113] The matter is not simply one of linguistics. The HDC Act specifies protections during an investigation,[114] and conducting a 'mini-investigation' during the assessment phase risks denying the parties these safeguards, such as the right to respond to proposed adverse comment and to contest what is, in all but name, a Commissioner's opinion on whether the provider's conduct breached the Code. And, as noted above, only an investigation and breach finding enables an aggrieved person to bring a claim before the Human Rights Review Tribunal (HRRT).

In an important ruling, the Ombudsman noted:[115]

> The preliminary assessment's purpose is to make a prompt initial determination about how the complaint should be handled. The Commissioner has a specific and prescribed statutory function of investigation. I do not see how the preliminary assessment could have been intended as vehicle for extensive information gathering, nor as a means by which to determine, through a detailed and sustained level of analysis, the standard and appropriateness of care provided to a healthcare consumer …

If assessment of the complaint requires 'extensive information gathering and/ or obtaining in-depth expert advice' (actions which are 'typically the hallmarks of an investigation'),[116] HDC should initiate a formal investigation.[117] The Ombudsman deprecated HDC's apparent approach that 'initiating an investigation is a detrimental punitive action against a provider that should generally be

[112] Chief Ombudsman Wakem opinion, case no 310944 (October 2013).
[113] Health and Disability Commissioner Act 1994 (NZ), s 41.
[114] See the HDC Act, ss 41(b)(ii) and 67.
[115] Boshier (n 104) para 97. The HDC was found to have acted unreasonably in the prolonged assessment of all three cases, and asked to apologise to the complainants.
[116] ibid para 102.
[117] By notice to the parties, under s 41(1) of the HDC Act.

avoided unless serious malpractice is identified'.[118] If there appear to have been more than 'mild' departures from an appropriate standard of care, an investigation should be undertaken. The upshot will be that HDC investigates a higher proportion of complaints, inevitably leading to more breach opinions and potentially more HRRT claims.

(ii) An Unreasonable Decision Not to Investigate

In addition to a prolonged assessment being an unreasonable way to handle a complaint, the conclusion of such a process by a decision to take 'no further action' may in itself be unreasonable, particularly where the evidence gathered indicates at least moderate lapses of care and the complainant seeks the vindication of a breach ruling and the consequent right of access to the HRRT. The HDC Act is silent on the factors to be weighed by the Commissioner in deciding to launch an investigation, apart from the requirement that 'any action of a … provider is, or appears to the Commissioner to be, in breach of the Code'.[119] Surprisingly, there is no indication in the statute that investigation should be the preferred option whenever the allegations are serious.[120] A Commissioner exercising the section 38(1) discretion[121] to take no further action might consider that, 'having regard to all the circumstances of the case', an investigation is 'unnecessary' because care deficiencies have been identified and remedied, and an apology offered to the complainant, or 'inappropriate' because nothing further (apart from a formal breach finding) is likely to be achieved.

It is not the role of the Ombudsman to second-guess the decisions of HDC about what complaint resolution avenue is most suitable for the particular case. But it is important that discretion is exercised in a principled and consistent way. In a powerful assertion of its oversight role in 'watching the watchdog', the Ombudsman recommended that HDC develop a 'clearly defined and transparent' policy on the factors to be considered when deciding to take no further action, and when to instigate an investigation, with 'comprehensive guidelines for staff and decision-makers'.[122] Curiously, the Ombudsman did not specify that HDC should publish the guidelines on its website, but fairness and transparency support such a requirement. Parties need to be able to understand the basis on which a decision has been made and to seek a review if the decision appears unreasonable.[123]

[118] Boshier (n 104) para 137.
[119] Health and Disability Commissioner Act 1994 (NZ), s 40(1).
[120] R Paterson, 'Assessment and Investigation of Complaints' in Skegg and Paterson (n 20) ch 29, 910.
[121] Health and Disability Commissioner Act 1994 (NZ), s 38(1).
[122] Boshier (n 104) paras 152, 156. In two cases, the Ombudsman considered it unreasonable for HDC to take no further action and not investigate; the Ombudsman recommended that HDC reconsider both cases.
[123] See discussion above in s IIID re transparency of decision-making processes.

(iii) Fairness in the Assessment of a Complaint

There is no requirement in the HDC Act that the Commissioner give parties an opportunity to comment on a proposed 'no further action' decision after preliminary assessment of a complaint. However, the High Court has noted that 'the first requirement is that the resolution of complaints be fair'.[124] In *Meek v Health and Disability Commissioner*, Clifford J stated:

> The Commissioner should not go too far when he 'triages' complaints ... The greater the extent of the Commissioner's inquiry into the circumstances of the complaint as part of a preliminary assessment, in my view the more likely it will be that the resulting factual context may result in the rules of fairness and natural justice giving rise to an obligation to consult the complainant before making that preliminary assessment.[125]

A similar approach, that HDC must act fairly in assessing a complaint, is evident in Ombudsman decisions. In one case, the Ombudsman recognised that during the assessment phase the complainant should be provided with a reasonable opportunity to comment on relevant information (such as expert advice or further information from a provider) considered by the Commissioner in reaching a decision, and be given an opportunity to comment on a preliminary decision to take no further action.[126]

B. Merits Review

The above cases are examples of Ombudsman intervention on the basis of procedural fairness. Ombudsmen seldom express an opinion on the merits of an HDC decision. Ombudsman opinions typically open with a self-denying ordinance: that he or she will not review the substance of the administrative decision complained about. Yet the Ombudsman is legally able to do precisely that. As noted by former Chief Justice Elias, citing Dworkin's analogy of 'the hole in the doughnut'[127] into which the courts will not intrude in reviewing the lawfulness of executive decision-making, the Ombudsman can 'go into the hole in the doughnut'.[128] The plain words of section 22(1)(b) of the Ombudsmen Act (is the Ombudsman 'of the opinion that the decision ... was unreasonable'?) do not suggest the limited scope of review for irrationality, nor even the judicial 'rainbow of review', whereby New Zealand courts have more intensely scrutinised executive decisions where human or fundamental rights are affected.[129]

[124] *Meek v HDC* [2016] NZHC 1205, [62].
[125] ibid [64].
[126] Wakem (n 112) para 35.
[127] R Dworkin, *Taking Rights Seriously* (Harvard University Press, 1978) 31.
[128] Elias (n 37) 6.
[129] See, eg the statement of Blanchard J that, in cases 'involving human rights', 'a less restricted approach' might be taken to unreasonableness review (*Pharmaceutical Management Agency Ltd v Roussel Uclaf Australia Pty Ltd* [1998] NZAR 58, 66 (Court of Appeal). See, generally M Taggart, 'Proportionality, Deference, Wednesbury' [2008] *New Zealand Law Review* 423.

In practice, Ombudsmen avoid merits review and focus on review of the legality of a challenged decision (does it appear 'to have been contrary to law',[130] for example by being *ultra vires*, taking into account irrelevant considerations, or by the fettering of discretion by adherence to a rigid policy?) or on issues of procedural fairness, as discussed above. There is little evidence of the Ombudsman delving into HDC's assessment of matters of clinical judgement – in contrast to the health service complaints work of the PHSO in the UK, where the empowering statute specifically permits the Ombudsman (as Health Service Commissioner) to look into the 'merits of a decision to the extent that it was taken in consequence of the exercise of clinical judgment'.[131]

A more interventionist approach is evident in one New Zealand case, where the Ombudsman reviewed the reasonableness of an HDC opinion that a dentist had failed to comply with professional standards. The Ombudsman scrutinised the expert evidence on which the Commissioner had relied and concluded that it was 'gold standard' (reflecting dentistry as taught at the School of Dentistry rather than as practised) and that it was unreasonable to find a breach of right 4(2) of the Code.[132] However, in a later case, the Ombudsman declined to intervene in a contest of experts on the question of the appropriateness of a general practitioner's cardiac care, noting that 'with regard to what is "established practice", … I cannot interfere with your decision on that matter'.[133]

Over the 25 years during which HDC has been assessing and investigating complaints of alleged breaches of the Code of Rights, successive Ombudsmen have declined to look at the merits of a complaint when contacted by a party unhappy about an HDC decision. A justification for this 'hands off' approach is given by David McGee,[134] who suggests that it is impracticable and possibly illegitimate for the Ombudsman to substitute his or her view for a specialist review agency's view of the merits of the case.[135] McGee argues that 'Ombudsman

[130] Ombudsmen Act 1975 (NZ), s 22(1)(a).

[131] Health Service Commissioners Act 1993 (UK), s 3(1). The clinical judgement basis for jurisdiction was added by the Health Service Commissioners (Amendment) Act 1996 (UK). It has been trenchantly criticised by a leading international patient safety expert: 'No modern authority on health service quality would accept this clinical judgement paradigm as the basis for investigation a complaint about poor quality or unsafe care. It is beyond anachronistic': L Donaldson, *Clinical Advice Review Commissioned by the Parliamentary and Health Service Ombudsman: Report of the Independent Adviser to the Review* (PHSO, 2018) 6. For discussion of implementation of the Clinical Advice Review by the PHSO, see R Behrens, 'Reform of a National Ombudsman Scheme – A Journey', ch 10 in this volume.

[132] Chief Ombudsman Elwood opinion, case W40440 (2001). Right 4(2) of the Code states: 'Every consumer has the right to have services provided that comply with legal, professional, ethical, and other relevant standards.'

[133] Elwood (n 105).

[134] Dr McGee was a New Zealand Parliamentary Ombudsman from 2007 to 2013, and was responsible for handling complaints about HDC.

[135] D McGee, 'Review of Reviewers' (paper presented at the 25th Australasian and Pacific Ombudsman Regional Conference, Canberra, March 2010). See also P Giddings, 'The United Kingdom Health Services Commissioner Schemes' in R Gregory and P Giddings (eds), *Righting Wrongs: The Ombudsman in Six Continents* (IOS Press, 2000) 149, where the author notes that the Ombudsman's 'procedures of political and administrative accountability may not seem so apposite' to matters of clinical judgement.

review is a generalist review, not a specialist review', and that when reviewing the decisions of specialist reviewers, 'the Ombudsman's function falls back onto making a judgment of the fairness and effectiveness of the process followed by the decision-maker'.[136]

A similar approach is evident from the courts on judicial review. In one case, the High Court considered that the tenor of the HDC legislation indicates that 'hard'-look judicial review is not appropriate:[137] 'Parliament has entrusted the Commissioner with his particular qualifications, with expressing opinion on what will often be complex medical issues. No doubt, as he exhibited in this case, he will often wish to obtain independent expert medical advice.' And on informed consent issues:[138] 'a judgment as to what a patient would expect is something the Commissioner is well if not uniquely qualified to express'.

There is a risk that in venturing to express an opinion on resolution of a complex, contested allegation of medical negligence, the Ombudsman may appear naïve, as in the following statement:[139]

> I have some concern with the overall impact of your approach of basically moving from one view of the complaint to an opposite view, apparently after the development of a somewhat adversarial environment generated by the complainant's concerns and actions.

This comment suggests a failure by the Ombudsman to appreciate the highly contested nature of some health complaints and that fairness may require the Commissioner to revise a provisional opinion.

A further risk is that, in reviewing HDC's adjudication of what are effectively medical negligence claims[140] – which in New Zealand cannot form the basis of a civil claim for compensatory damages, under the country's no-fault accident compensation scheme[141] – the Ombudsman may fail to apply a clear and consistent standard of review of alleged service failures in areas involving the exercise of clinical judgement. The Ombudsman could then face judicial review.[142] The perils are well illustrated in the damning judgment of the Court of Appeal (England and Wales) in the *Miller* case:[143]

> The standard chosen by the ombudsman is beguilingly simple but incoherent. It cannot provide clarity or consistency of application to the facts of different cases. There is no

[136] ibid 4.

[137] *Stubbs v Health and Disability Commissioner* [2010] NZHC 415, [52].

[138] ibid [53].

[139] Elwood (n 105).

[140] The majority of complaints to HDC raise concerns about the appropriateness of care, which usually fall to be determined by the Commissioner's assessment of whether, in terms of right 4(1) of the Code, health or disability services have been provided 'with reasonable care and skill'.

[141] Accident Compensation Act 2001 (NZ), s 317.

[142] Notwithstanding the protection of the privative clause in s 25 of the Ombudsmen Act 1975 (NZ).

[143] *Miller v The Health Service Commissioner for England* [2018] EWCA Civ 144, [82]. The *Miller* judgment offers salutary lessons for New Zealand's Health and Disability Commissioner, which in several respects operates in a similar way to the Health Service Commissioner for England.

> yardstick of reasonable or responsible practice but rather a counsel of perfection that can be arbitrary. It runs the risk of being a lottery dependent on the professional opinion of the advisor that is chosen. It is unreasonable and irrational and accordingly, unlawful.

Yet, in a context where judicial review or review by the Ombudsman are the only avenues open to a party who believes an HDC decision is substantively wrong or unjust, it is arguable that closer scrutiny of the Commissioner's opinion may be justified – particularly in cases where an opinion seems plainly unreasonable. The Commissioner is required to fulfil specified criteria for appointment, including expertise and experience in the health and disability system and the needs of consumers.[144] But, given that the Commissioner is a lay person without clinical qualifications,[145] who relies on expert clinical advice, should the Ombudsman (or a High Court judge on judicial review) give undue deference to HDC opinions on the merits of a complaint, particularly in relation to contentious issues of diagnosis or treatment where expert advice is available for scrutiny? Naturally, over time, the Commissioner becomes experienced in assessing advice from clinical experts and forming a view on the reasonableness of care. But he or she is not infallible, and another independent reviewer, whose staff have not been caught up in handling the file – and the crossfire of an aggrieved complainant and an indignant provider – may bring a fresh perspective to the evidence.[146]

On balance, there is much to be said for McGee's view that the Ombudsman should exercise restraint before questioning the judgement of a specialist review agency like HDC on the merits of a case. As noted in a 2016 case, 'evaluating expert advice involves an exercise of HDC's judgment which an Ombudsman should not lightly interfere with, unless the outcome appears to be capricious'.[147]

[144] Health and Disability Commissioner Act 1994 (NZ), s 10(1).

[145] That has been the case for the first four Health and Disability Commissioners, including the author.

[146] For a striking example of two High Court judges forming their own view on the reasonableness of a cardiologist's treatment, albeit in the context of an appeal in relation to an accident compensation claim of 'medical error', see *Ambros v Accident Compensation Corporation* (High Court, Auckland, CIV 2004-404-3261, 21 March 2005), Harrison J and Heath J. The judges interrogated the evidence of four medical experts and reached a different conclusion (ie that the treatment was unreasonable) to the experts, HDC, the Accident Compensation Corporation and a District Court judge.

[147] Paterson (n 95).

16

Ombuds Institutions: Non-judicial Mechanisms for the Protection and Promotion of the Rights of Older Persons

LINDA C REIF

I. Introduction

Older persons are not always seen as rights holders in the modern state.[1] While international and domestic human rights laws apply to seniors, the norms often do not address explicitly the particular challenges that they face. However, as populations are ageing, the international human rights system is starting to respond through treaty and soft law. This is described as a shift towards a rights-based approach to ageing.[2]

Older persons also need to have access to remedial mechanisms to enforce their human rights and the other laws that can protect them. Beyond the courts, state-based non-judicial mechanisms can also increase senior citizens' access to justice. These mechanisms include ombuds institutions. Ombuds institutions include national human rights ombuds institutions – also classified as national

I am extremely grateful to Barrett Smith-Ackerl and Megan Ferguson for their excellent research assistance.

[1] See, eg Australia Royal Commission into Aged Care Quality and Safety, *Neglect*, 3 vols (Interim Report 31, October 2019) 216, 241 agedcare.royalcommission.gov.au/ (international disabilities rights law applied to young people in aged care facilities but only general references to rights to mobility, autonomy, dignity and legal capacity for seniors); Australian Law Reform Commission, *Elder Abuse – A National Legal Response* (Final Report, ALRC Report 131, May 2017) paras 1.18, 2.78–2.99 www.alrc.gov.au/wp-content/uploads/2019/08/elder_abuse_131_final_report_31_may_2017.pdf (application of UN Principles for Older Persons which is not framed in human rights terms, use of a 'human rights-based framework'). The terms 'older persons', 'older adults', 'seniors' and 'the elderly' will be used interchangeably in this chapter.

[2] European Union Agency for Fundamental Rights, *Shifting Perceptions: Towards a Rights-Based Approach to Ageing* (2018) 5 (*Shifting Perceptions*).

human rights institutions (NHRIs) – subnational human rights ombuds institutions and classic-based ombuds at all levels of governance.[3]

This chapter scrutinises critically the protection and promotion of the human rights of older persons by national human rights ombuds institutions, subnational human rights ombuds and classic-based ombuds institutions. To set the scene, it discusses the challenges faced by seniors that can lead to violations of their human rights and explores how the human rights of seniors often intersect with the human rights of women, persons with disabilities and individuals who are confined involuntarily, in particular geriatric prisoners and residents of closed senior care facilities. It also describes the developing international law on the rights of older persons. To assess ombuds work in relation to seniors and their rights, this chapter surveys a selection of classic and human rights ombuds institutions from North America, Europe, Australasia and Latin America, representing most of the regions with the largest shares of older adults in the population.[4] It demonstrates that these ombuds institutions differ both in their prioritisation of older persons who are impacted negatively by the conduct of public and private actors and in their application of international and domestic human rights norms to support their investigations and other work involving seniors.

While many classic-based and human rights ombuds address public and private sector failures affecting seniors, only a smaller subset place a high priority on older persons and their rights. I argue that more classic-based and human rights ombuds institutions need to pay greater attention to the human rights of seniors, rely more on the international and constitutional human rights of older persons in their work, apply all of their functions to protect and promote the rights of seniors and reform their institutional operating practices to mainstream seniors' rights. Doing so can assist in improving older adults' access to justice. The terrible impact of the COVID-19 pandemic on vulnerable seniors has galvanised some ombuds institutions to action through use of their own-motion investigations and inspections of closed facilities to try to improve the treatment of seniors. However, this attention needs to be maintained and expanded permanently since public and private sector neglect and marginalisation of seniors has long predated the pandemic and can be expected to continue into the future as populations age and public budgets are constricted.

[3] LC Reif, *Ombuds Institutions, Good Governance and the International Human Rights System*, 2nd rev edn (Brill Nijhoff, 2020).

[4] United Nations, Department of Economic and Social Affairs (UNDESA), Population Division, *World Population Ageing 2019*, UN Doc ST/ESA/SER.A/444 (2020) 5–7. The surveys in this chapter were conducted using desk-based research in spring 2020, and the choices of regions and specific ombuds institutions were based on the availability of English or Spanish language reports on the ombuds institutions' websites.

II. Typology of Ombuds Institutions

Independent public sector ombuds institutions can protect and promote the rights of older persons. This chapter scrutinises the work of national and subnational human rights ombuds institutions and classic-based ombuds institutions.[5]

National human rights ombuds institutions are one type of NHRI.[6] They are predominant in Europe and Latin America, and scattered through other regions.[7] By 2019, they constituted about 64 per cent of all national ombuds institutions.[8] In addition to powers of complaints-based and own-motion investigations, national human rights ombuds institutions usually have additional powers, such as community mediation and bringing or intervening in constitutional court and other court actions.[9] Many also have an array of human rights promotion responsibilities, such as advice to government, making law reform proposals, education, training, research and raising public awareness. Some institutions also have partial or full jurisdiction over the private sector as well as the public sector. Their state's international human rights obligations are often internalised in domestic law, and ombuds institutions are typically directed to apply these international obligations and/or constitutional rights.[10] Human right ombuds usually have a legality assessment standard but some also have broader extralegal assessment standards.

NHRIs should comply with the UN Paris Principles, as interpreted by the General Observations of the Global Alliance of National Human Rights Institutions (GANHRI).[11] These are soft law standards for the legal architecture, operating practices and budgets of NHRIs. National human rights ombuds comprise over 40 per cent of GANHRI's accredited NHRIs.[12] NHRIs must be independent, have jurisdiction to protect and promote all human rights, have a spectrum of human rights promotion responsibilities and receive adequate financial and human resources. GANHRI recommends that NHRIs should have full jurisdiction over the public and private sectors.[13]

I also classify as human rights ombuds national ombuds institutions that have been given one or more additional human rights mandates pursuant to treaty law obligations.[14] The Optional Protocol to the UN Convention against Torture

[5] Thematic ombuds are excluded. See Reif (n 3) 70–80.
[6] ibid 161–68. See also human rights commissions/institutes.
[7] ibid 19.
[8] ibid 20, app I.
[9] ibid 228–44. A few human rights ombuds have public inquiry powers.
[10] ibid 258–60, 262–68.
[11] ibid 156–61, 168–88; Principles Relating to the Status of National Institutions, UN GA Res 48/134, UN Doc A/RES/48/134 (20 December 1993) Annex (Paris Principles); for GANHRI General Observations: www.ganhri.org/accreditation. GANHRI has a working group on ageing.
[12] Reif (n 3) 166–67 (a total of 115 NHRIs).
[13] ibid 185–86.
[14] ibid 5.

and Other Cruel, Inhuman or Degrading Treatment or Punishment (OPCAT) requires states to establish National Preventive Mechanisms (NPMs) to visit facilities where persons are involuntarily confined and make recommendations to the state on preventing torture and other ill treatment.[15] These facilities include prisons, healthcare facilities and dementia units. Article 33(2) of the UN Convention on the Rights of Persons with Disabilities (CRPD) obligates states to establish framework mechanisms to protect, promote and monitor the implementation of the CRPD.[16] EU directives require Member States to establish national equality bodies (NEBs) to implement the non-discrimination obligations in the directives.[17] Numerous human rights ombuds institutions in Europe have been designated as OPCAT NPMs, included in Article 33(2) CRPD mechanisms, and operate as EU NEBs.[18] Some Latin American human rights ombuds have OPCAT NPM and/or Article 33(2) CRPD obligations, New Zealand's Ombudsman exercises both mandates and Australia has recently given its Commonwealth Ombudsman OPCAT NPM duties.[19]

Subnational human rights ombuds institutions are located in a number of countries, such as Spain, Russia, Argentina and Australia, where several states have human rights mandates.[20] They have similar responsibilities to their national counterparts, but they are not NHRIs since their jurisdiction only covers a portion of the state's territory.[21]

By 2019, the remaining 36 per cent of national ombuds were classic or classic-based institutions, without express human rights mandates.[22] They are scattered throughout the world, primarily in the North American, Caribbean, African and Asia-Pacific regions.[23] More are found at subnational levels of governance, including in Canada, Australia and the UK. In addition to complaints-based and own-motion investigation powers, classic-based ombuds often enjoy additional powers, ranging from compliance audits to good governance promotion, and, while most have traditional soft powers of recommendation, some can resort to stronger means, including a few with coercive remedial powers.[24]

An increasing amount of classic-based ombuds work raises human rights issues, and such ombuds sometimes apply international and domestic human

[15] ibid 336–40; Optional Protocol to the Convention against Torture and Other Cruel, Inhuman or Degrading Treatment or Punishment, UN GA Res 57/199 (18 December 2002), 2375 UNTS 237, (2003) 42 ILM 26 (in force 22 June 2006, 90 contracting parties on 4 June 2020) (OPCAT).

[16] Reif (n 3) 357–65; Convention on the Rights of Persons with Disabilities, UN GA Res 61/106, Annex I, UN Doc A/RES/61/106 (in force 3 May 2008, 181 contracting parties on 4 June 2020) (CRPD).

[17] Reif (n 3) 404–06.

[18] ibid 342–43, 366–67, 405.

[19] ibid 343, 353–57, 367–70, 717–18.

[20] ibid 19, 714–18. See Victoria (full mandate) and Western Australia (WA) (OPCAT NPM member).

[21] ibid 162–63.

[22] ibid 20, app I. Classic-based ombuds have additional mandates beyond fighting maladministration.

[23] ibid 13–14.

[24] ibid 228–44. Ombuds with coercive remedial powers located mainly in Africa and Asia-Pacific.

rights norms in their reports and other activities. Classic-based ombuds apply domestic law through their legality assessment standard, including the direct application of internalised international human rights law obligations and constitutional rights, and use unimplemented obligations to interpret domestic law.[25] Many classic-based ombuds also have broader extralegal assessment standards that enable them to apply non-internalised international human rights obligations and nonbinding soft law in determining what is proper or wrong conduct.[26] Indeed, classic-based ombuds in common law jurisdictions such as Canadian provinces, Australian states and Northern Ireland sometimes ignore their legal system's formal legal barriers to the reception of international human rights norms and apply the norms directly in their work.[27]

The legal framework and operating practices of ombuds institutions provide the foundation for the recognition, protection and promotion of the rights of older persons in ombuds work in the modern state. In order to put their statutory functions and operating practices to best use, ombuds institutions need to be aware of the global ageing phenomenon, the challenges faced by older persons, the violations of their rights and the developing body of international human rights law for older persons.

III. Older Persons and the Global Ageing Phenomenon

At what point in life does an adult become an older person? Countries and organisations use different age minimums. The most common entry points are 60 or 65 years of age, although some UN bodies take a contextual approach.[28]

According to the UN:

> Population ageing is a global phenomenon. Virtually every country in the world is experiencing growth in both the size and the proportion of older persons in the population … Globally, the share of the population aged 65 years or over increased from 6 per cent in 1990 to 9 per cent in 2019. That proportion is projected to rise further to 16 per cent in 2050.[29]

Population ageing rates are highest in East and South-East Asia, Latin America and the Caribbean.[30] The largest numbers of seniors are found in East and South-East

[25] ibid 260–64.

[26] ibid 265–69.

[27] ibid 269–77, 281–84.

[28] See eg *World Population Ageing 2019* (n 4) 5 (UNDESA, 65 years): International Labour Organization, *What about Seniors? A Quick Analysis of the Situation of Older Persons in the Labour Market*, ILO STAT no 1 (May 2018) ('older persons' are aged 55 years or more, while 'seniors' are aged 65 years or more); Amnesty International, *'Fleeing my Whole Life': Older People's Experience of Conflict and Displacement in Myanmar* (17 June 2019) 4 (*Fleeing my Whole Life*) (UN High Commissioner for Human Rights contextual approach).

[29] *World Population Ageing 2019* (n 4) 2.

[30] ibid.

Asia, Europe, Australia, New Zealand and North America; these regions also have the highest share of seniors in the population, and this share is projected to remain steady to 2050.[31] Women form a majority of older persons.[32] Globally, women live five years longer than men on average, and the gender gap is most pronounced for persons aged 80 or more years.[33] The number of persons in this latter age category is increasing rapidly – estimates are that it will increase by almost 300 per cent in the 2019–50 period to a total of 426 million persons.[34]

IV. Challenges Faced by Older Persons and Violations of their Human Rights

Seniors face challenges that may come with the onset of old age or because of their ageist treatment at the hands of others. Ageism is the 'negative social construct of a particular age group'.[35] Ageist treatment of older persons is based on negative stereotypes – that they are burdensome, less capable and weak – and ageism ignores the diversity of seniors and the many contributions they make in the public and private spheres.[36] Ageism partly plays out in microaggressions against older persons or their marginalisation, but it also results in behaviour that violates their human rights.

Employers and other actors engage in age discrimination against seniors. Explicit or implicit age discrimination can be seen in the ethical guidelines that use age as a triage criterion in access to healthcare for coronavirus victims.[37] Seniors often experience intersectional discrimination whereby their additional identities – such as being female, disabled, indigenous or a racial minority – compound the degree and impact of the age discrimination.[38]

Some older persons face increased health problems and they can experience discrimination in and barriers to accessing health services.[39] They may live with disabilities, which may be long-standing or are those physical and cognitive disabilities that can develop during the ageing process.[40] In fact, on a global basis,

[31] ibid 5–7.

[32] E Dugarova, *Ageing, Older Persons and the 2030 Agenda for Sustainable Development* (United Nations Development Programme, 2017) 8–9.

[33] ibid 2 (only 63 men for every 100 women).

[34] ibid 5.

[35] *Shifting Perceptions* (n 2) 7.

[36] ibid 5–7; Dugarova (n 32) 11–13.

[37] S Michalowski, 'The Use of Age as a Triage Criterion' in C Ferstman and A Fagan (eds), *Covid-19, Law and Human Rights: Essex Dialogues* (School of Law and Human Rights Centre, University of Essex, 1 July 2020) 93–100.

[38] See, eg AN Davis, 'Intersectionality and International Law: Recognizing Complex Identities on the Global Stage' (2015) 28 *Harvard Human Rights Journal* 205.

[39] *Shifting Perceptions* (n 2) 10–11; UNDESA, 'Health and Well-Being in Older Age' www.un.org/esa/socdev/ageing/documents/BriefingPaperHealthandWellbeing.pdf.

[40] *Shifting Perceptions* (n 2) 12–13.

'older persons represent the majority of the overall population of persons with disabilities'.[41] In turn, these disabilities affect seniors' autonomy, legal capacity, the ability to live independently and vulnerability to abuse.[42] Elder abuse manifests in neglect and psychological, financial, physical and sexual abuse in the home and in care institutions.[43] Older people suffer uniquely from the consequences of armed conflict and displacement, and they are overlooked in humanitarian aid operations.[44] Some older persons live in poverty with insufficient social services and pensions.[45]

A number of older persons in high-income countries live in public or private assisted-living and long-term care residences. There may be inadequate numbers of facilities to meet the needs of seniors and they may provide substandard care.[46] Some seniors in long-term care, especially those with dementia, are restricted physically or pharmacologically.[47] The COVID-19 pandemic uncovered systemic neglect, underfunding, understaffing and poor health and care standards in many facilities in Europe, North America and Australia, with their residents comprising a large percentage of the total number of persons who succumbed to the virus.[48] The pandemic also made seniors vulnerable to discrimination in access to life-saving therapies, severe social isolation and loss of home care and employment.[49]

Geriatric prisoners form an often increasing percentage of the population of correctional facilities in high-income countries.[50] They have complex needs concerning their health, disabilities and difficulties in coping with physical facilities designed for younger inmates.[51] For example, in Canada, elderly prisoners

[41] UN General Assembly, 'Rights of Persons with Disabilities: Report of the Special Rapporteur on the Rights of Persons with Disabilities', UN Doc A/74/186 (17 July 2019) 4 (2019 Special Rapporteur Report).

[42] ibid 9–16.

[43] Y Yon et al, 'Elder Abuse Prevalence in Community Settings: A Systematic Review and Meta-Analysis' (2017) 5 *Lancet Global Health* 147, 152–54; *Shifting Perceptions* (n 2) 11.

[44] *Fleeing my Whole Life* (n 28) 47; Dugarova (n 32) 15.

[45] *Shifting Perceptions* (n 2) 11; Dugarova (n 32) 14–15.

[46] eg S Sinha and M Nicin, 'A Wake-Up Call on Long-Term Care' *The Globe and Mail* (26 May 2020) A13 (Canada); *Neglect* (n 1).

[47] *Neglect* (n 1) 193–216.

[48] See, eg UN, *Policy Brief: The Impact of COVID-19 on Older Persons* (May 2020); C Perkel, 'Ford Vows to Take Action after Military Report on Five Ontario Long-Term Care Homes', *The Globe and Mail* (26 May 2020); Council of Europe Commissioner for Human Rights, 'Lessons to Be Drawn from the Ravages of the COVID-19 Pandemic in Long-Term Care Facilities' (Strasbourg, 20 May 2020); Australia Royal Commission into Aged Care Quality and Safety, *Aged Care and COVID-19: A Special Report* (1 October 2020) agedcare.royalcommission.gov.au/sites/default/files/2020-12/aged-care-and-covid-19-a-special-report.pdf.

[49] FRA, *Coronavirus Pandemic in the EU – Fundamental Rights Implications: With a Focus on Older People*, Bulletin #3 (1 May–31 May 2020) 11–12, 38–39; *Policy Brief: The Impact of COVID-19 on Older Persons* (n 48); AGE Platform Europe, *COVID-19 and Human Rights Concerns for Older Persons* (Brussels, 18 May 2020); Human Rights Watch, 'Rights Risks to Older People in COVID-19 Response: Combat Ageism; Ensure Access to Health Care, Services' (7 April 2020).

[50] See eg R Bedard, L Metzger and B Williams, 'Ageing Prisoners: An Introduction to Geriatric Health-Care Challenges in Correctional Facilities' (2016) 98 *International Review of the Red Cross* 917.

[51] ibid. See also A Khechumyan, *Imprisonment of the Elderly and Death in Custody* (Routledge, 2018).

comprise 25 per cent of the inmates in federal institutions; they do not have adequate health or palliative care, they are bullied by younger inmates and the authorities do little to assist in their rehabilitation.[52] The pandemic exacerbated the health risks faced by geriatric prisoners.

Gender issues and women's rights violations are exacerbated by the high percentage of women in the seniors' population, including intersectional discrimination. Older women are susceptible to gender- and age-based violence, including intimate partner violence, abuse in care settings and harm resulting from cultural prejudices.[53] They have higher rates of disability, including dementia, probably because of their longer life spans.[54] Older women with disabilities experience proportionally higher rates of poverty, violence and institutionalisation.[55] Older women experience higher rates of poverty than older men across the world, often as a consequence of their unequal access to education, paid work or good employment throughout their lives.[56] This is compounded by additional gender-based discrimination that excludes them from pensions and social security benefits, gives them lower pensions and benefits compared to men and prohibits them from inheriting assets or controlling their own finances.[57] Older women were 'more likely to be exposed to COVID-19 because they form the majority among older people needing care, social care staff and informal carers'.[58]

V. Developing International Law on the Human Rights of Older Persons

The challenges faced by seniors demonstrate that their human rights are being infringed, implicating their civil, political, economic, social and cultural rights. The coronavirus response has exacerbated their plight, affecting their rights to life, health and freedom from discrimination.[59] Ombuds institutions need to

[52] Correctional Investigator of Canada and Canadian Human Rights Commission, *Aging and Dying in Prison: An Investigation into the Experiences of Older Individuals in Federal Custody* (28 February 2019); J Ling, 'Canada's Elder-Care Crisis Grinds Away in Our Jails, Too', *The Globe and Mail* (1 June 2020) A11.

[53] UNDESA, *Neglect, Abuse and Violence Against Older Women*, UN Doc ST/ESA/351 (2013); C Martin, D Rodríguez-Pinzón and B Brown, *Human Rights of Older People: Universal and Regional Legal Perspectives* (Springer, 2015) 28–32.

[54] *Shifting Perceptions* (n 2) 12–13.

[55] 2019 Special Rapporteur Report (n 41) 6.

[56] Dugarova (n 32) 9.

[57] ibid (women also often provide most of the unpaid care for their spouses); International Labour Organization, *World Social Protection Report 2017–19: Universal Social Protection to Achieve the Sustainable Development Goals* (International Labour Office, 2017) 78, 85; *Shifting Perceptions* (n 2) 11–12.

[58] AGE Platform Europe (n 49) 6.

[59] FRA (n 49) 11, 38–39.

familiarise themselves with the relevant UN and regional human rights treaty obligations of their state and other international instruments that apply to older adults, as well as the different methods by which these international norms can be applied in ombuds investigations and other work involving seniors.[60]

A. UN International Instruments

Older adults enjoy the general protections of human rights treaties such as the International Covenant on Civil and Political Rights (ICCPR) and the International Covenant on Economic, Social and Cultural Rights (ICESCR).[61] For example, the ICCPR includes the right to life and prohibits discrimination, torture and other ill treatment. The ICESCR includes rights to health, work, social security and an adequate standard of living.[62]

As noted above, several thematic UN human rights treaties intersect with and protect some human rights of seniors. The CRPD protects the rights of all persons with disabilities, including seniors. For example, Article 6 recognises that women with disabilities experience intersectional discrimination and the CRPD treaty committee (CtRPD) has stated that older women with disabilities must enjoy all of the CRPD's protections, including freedom from violence, intersectional discrimination and negative stereotyping by public and private actors.[63] The CRPD also has more general age-sensitive obligations, such as on access to justice, combating stereotyping, health services, violence prevention and access to social protection and poverty reduction programmes.[64] The OPCAT NPM visits to closed institutions should always monitor older persons confined in closed institutions to protect them from being subjected to torture or other ill treatment. This includes

[60] For methods of application of international human rights law by human rights and classic ombuds, see text accompanying nn 10, 25–27.

[61] International Covenant on Civil and Political Rights, (1966) 999 UNTS 171 (in force 23 March 1976, 173 parties by 4 June 2020) (ICCPR); International Covenant on Economic, Social and Cultural Rights, 993 UNTS 3, (1967) 6 ILM 360 (in force 3 January 1976, 170 parties by 4 June 2020) (ICESCR).

[62] eg UN Committee on Economic, Social and Cultural Rights (CtESCR), General Comment No 6: The Economic, Social and Cultural Rights of Older Persons (24 November 1995); General Comment No 20, UN Doc E/C.12/GC/20 (2 July 2009) para 29 (ICESCR, Art 2(2), eg discrimination in finding work, accessing training and access to pensions); General Comment No 23 (2016) on the Right to Just and Favourable Conditions of Work (Art 7 of the ICESCR), UN Doc E/C.12/GC/23 (27 April 2016) para 47(b); General Comment No 21, UN Doc E/C.12/GC/21 (21 December 2009) paras 28–29 (ICESCR, Art 15(1)(a), eg improving seniors' cultural rights and access to cultural resources and institutions). See also CtESCR, *Trujillo Calero v Ecuador*, Views, UN Doc E/C.12/63/D/10/2015 (14 November 2018) (rights to social security and nondiscrimination, denial of retirement pension for older woman).

[63] CRPD; CtRPD, General Comment No 3 (2016) on Women and Girls with Disabilities, UN Doc CRPD/C/GC/3 (25 November 2016).

[64] CRPD, Arts 8, 13, 16, 25(b), 28(b). But see P Harpur, 'Old Age Is Not Just Impairment: The CRPD and the Need for a Convention on Older Persons' (2016) 37 *University of Pennsylvania Journal of International Law* 1027, 1049–58 (seniors' rights treaty needed given gaps in CRPD).

seniors with cognitive impairments in closed elder-care facilities and geriatric prisoners and detainees.[65]

The UN Convention on the Elimination of All Forms of Discrimination against Women (CEDAW) contains women's civil, political, economic, social and cultural rights.[66] Its treaty committee (CtEDAW) issued General Recommendation No 27 on the rights of older women in 2010.[67] General Recommendation No 27 connects state obligations in CEDAW to aspects of ageing and identifies intersectional discrimination that women experience as they age. It includes state obligations concerning women's education, work and pension benefits, health, housing/social benefits, economic empowerment, marriage, property and inheritance rights, and eliminating gender-based violence.

The UN has not yet drafted a thematic treaty on the rights of older persons. It is discussing the possibility in the Open-ended Working Group on Ageing, but states have mixed views on the desirability of a treaty.[68] There are some nonbinding instruments on older persons, but only the more recent take a human rights approach.[69] An earlier instrument is the UN Principles for Older Persons, which calls for seniors to have independence in economic and social terms, lives of dignity and security, access to health and other care services, and fair treatment.[70] Its only explicit reference to human rights for seniors applies when they reside in health or care facilities.[71]

B. Regional Human Rights Treaties

The Inter-American human rights system created a bespoke treaty, the Inter-American Convention on Protecting the Human Rights of Older Persons (ICOP), which applies in most cases to persons aged 60 or older.[72] The ICOP is

[65] eg L Grenfell, 'Aged Care, Detention and OPCAT' (2019) 25 *Australian Journal of Human Rights* 248. OPCAT NPM jurisdiction extends to private facilities, Reif (n 3) 337.

[66] Convention on the Elimination of all Forms of Discrimination against Women, (1979) 1249 UNTS 13 (in force 3 September 1981, 189 parties by 4 June 2020) (CEDAW).

[67] CtEDAW, General Comment No 27 on Older Women and Protection of their Human Rights, UN Doc CEDAW/C/GC/27 (16 December 2010).

[68] A Herro, 'Advocating a UN Convention on the Rights of Older Persons in the United Kingdom: The Case for a Radical Flank' (2019) 11 *Journal of Human Rights Practice* 132,133; A Herro, 'The Human Rights of Older Persons: The Politics and Substance of the UN Open-Ended Working Group on Ageing' (2017) 23 *Australian Journal of Human Rights* 90; L Poffé, 'Towards a New United Nations Human Rights Convention for Older Persons?' (2015) 15 *Human Rights Law Review* 591. For an early argument in favour of a treaty, see K Tang, 'Taking Older People's Rights Seriously: The Role of International Law' (2008) 20 *Journal of Aging and Social Policy* 99.

[69] eg Human Rights Council resolutions on the human rights of older persons; Madrid International Plan of Action on Ageing (endorsed by General Assembly in 2002); Proclamation on Ageing, UN GA Res 47/5 (16 October 1992); Vienna International Plan of Action on Ageing (1982), endorsed in UN GA Res 37/51. See also UN Independent Expert on the enjoyment of all human rights by older persons.

[70] United Nations Principles for Older Persons, GA Res 46/91 (1991) Annex.

[71] ibid para 14.

[72] Inter-American Convention on Protecting the Human Rights of Older Persons, A-70 (2016) 55 ILM 985 (in force 11 January 2017, 7 parties by 4 June 2020, including Costa Rica), Art 2 (ICOP). ICOP also applies when domestic legislation provides a minimum age that is lesser or greater up to 65 years.

designed to promote, protect and ensure the rights of seniors based on principles that include: equality and non-discrimination; the dignity, independence, proactivity and autonomy of older persons; their physical, economic and social security; their participation, integration and full and effective inclusion in society; differentiated treatment for the effective enjoyment of their rights; their well-being and care; and gender equality.[73] It requires states parties to protect the rights of older persons in both the public and private spheres. ICOP-protected rights include those to equality and non-discrimination, life and dignity, independence and autonomy, participation and community integration, freedom from violence, free and informed consent on health matters, social security, work, health, property, housing, accessibility and personal mobility, and access to justice.[74] There are also dedicated rights of seniors who are receiving long-term care.[75]

The American Convention on Human Rights and other regional human rights treaties, such as the San Salvador Protocol, as interpreted by the Inter-American Commission on Human Rights and Inter-American Court of Human Rights, can also protect the rights of seniors.[76] Further, persons and NGOs can launch petitions to the Inter-American Commission complaining that an ICOP state has violated the treaty and those states may submit to the jurisdiction of the Inter-American Court with respect to the interpretation or application of the ICOP.[77]

In Europe, EU Member States are bound by treaty law and secondary legislation that protect against age-based discrimination.[78] The EU Charter of Fundamental Rights (Charter) was given binding effect by the Treaty on European Union.[79] Article 21(1) of the Charter prohibits discrimination, including on the basis of age, and Article 25 enshrines some rights for seniors: 'The Union recognises and respects the rights of the elderly to lead a life of dignity and independence and to participate in social and cultural life.'[80] Article 34(1) of the Charter gives older adults rights to social security benefits and social services. However, the Charter has limited applicability: it binds EU institutions and other bodies, and EU Member States when they are implementing EU law in their domestic systems.[81]

[73] ibid Arts 1, 3.

[74] ibid Arts 5–9, 13, 17–21, 23–24, 26, 31.

[75] ibid Art 12.

[76] American Convention on Human Rights (1969) OAS TS No 36 (adopted 22 November 1969, in force 18 July 1978, 24 contracting parties on 4 June 2020) (ACHR); Additional Protocol to the American Convention on Human Rights in the Area of Economic, Social and Cultural Rights, OAS TS No 69 (in force 16 November 1999, 16 contracting parties on 4 June 2020) Art 17 (right to special protection in old age); Martin et al (n 53) 218–19, 221–24. See eg *Poblete Vilches et al v Chile* (2018) Inter-Am Ct HR (Ser C) No 349 (rights of older person in health-related matter to health, life, personal integrity, dignity and access to information).

[77] ICOP, Art 36.

[78] Treaty on European Union, Art 6(1) and Treaty on the Functioning of the European Union, Arts 10, 19 [2012] OJ C326/13; *Shifting Perceptions* (n 2) 15–20 (Employment Equality Directive prohibits age discrimination in the employment context and EU Court of Justice jurisprudence holds that nondiscrimination on the grounds of age is a general principle of EU law).

[79] Charter of Fundamental Rights of the European Union [2012] OJ C326/02.

[80] ibid.

[81] ibid Art 51.

The Council of Europe oversees the European Convention on Human Rights (ECHR) and its protocols, and the European Court of Human Rights (ECtHR) interprets and applies the treaties.[82] While the treaties do not refer explicitly to the rights of older persons, ECtHR judgments have addressed their human rights either directly or indirectly.[83]

The African Charter on Human and Peoples' Rights states that 'The aged and the disabled shall … have the right to special measures of protection in keeping with their physical or moral needs'.[84] The African Union adopted a Protocol to the African Charter on the Rights of Older Persons, but it has not yet entered into force.[85]

C. The Right of Access to Justice

Australian research indicates that seniors, compared to other population subsets, are less likely to seek assistance in resolving their legal issues, experience the highest barriers in accessing justice and receive the 'least optimal outcomes' when they do try to seek justice.[86] Access to justice can be classified as a human right, and this includes the right of older persons to access to justice.

The right to an effective remedy before a domestic tribunal for rights violations is contained in a number of international instruments.[87] A few treaties contain or have been interpreted to contain the right of access to justice. The CRPD gives disabled persons the right of access to justice on an equal basis with others, 'including through the provision of procedural and age-appropriate accommodations, in order to facilitate their effective role as direct and indirect participants … in all legal proceedings'.[88] Article 31 of the ICOP enshrines the right of seniors to access to justice.[89] It places primary importance on the right to a judicial hearing, but it

[82] European Convention for the Protection of Human Rights and Fundamental Freedoms (adopted 4 November 1950, in force 3 September 1953, 47 states parties) (ECHR) as amended, with substantive human rights in Protocols 1, 4, 6, 7, 12 and 13; ECHR, www.echr.coe.int/Pages/home.aspx?p=basictexts&c. There are also COE subject-specific human rights treaties and the social charter system.

[83] European Court of Human Rights Press Unit, *Elderly People and the European Convention on Human Rights* (February 2019); Strasbourg Observers, 'Age and Gender Discrimination: Laudable Anti-Stereotyping Reasoning in Carvalho Pinto v Portugal' (28 September 2017); M De Pauw, 'Interpreting the European Convention on Human Rights in Light of Emerging Human Rights Issues: An Older Person's Perspective' (2014) 8 *Human Rights & International Legal Discourse* 235.

[84] African Charter on Human and Peoples' Rights (1982) 21 ILM 58, Art 18(4).

[85] Protocol to the African Charter on Human and Peoples' Rights on the Rights of Older Persons in Africa (adopted 31 January 2016); 2019 Special Rapporteur Report (n 41); DM Chirwa, 'Guarding the Guardians: A Critical Appraisal of the Protocol to the African Charter on the Rights of Older Persons in Africa' (2019) 19 *Human Rights Law Review* 53.

[86] S Sage-Jacobson, 'Access to Justice for Older People in Australia' (2015) 33 *Law in Context: A Socio-Legal Journal* 142, 151, 159.

[87] eg Universal Declaration of Human Rights, UN GA Res 217A(III), UN Doc A/810 (1948), Art 8 (UDHR); ECHR, Art 13; ACHR, Art 25.

[88] CRPD, Art 13.

[89] ICOP, Art 31.

also requires states to create and strengthen public policies and programmes to promote alternative dispute settlement mechanisms.[90] It does not mention NHRIs or other ombuds. CtEDAW General Recommendation No 33 defines women's access to justice liberally to include nonjudicial state bodies such as NHRIs and other types of ombuds institutions.[91]

National human rights ombuds as NHRIs and other types of ombuds institutions with the appropriate structures and operating practices serve as mechanisms to enhance the access to justice not only of older women, but of all seniors through their complaints-based and own-motion investigations, litigation powers and other responsibilities.[92]

VI. Classic Ombuds Institutions: Protecting and Promoting the Rights of Older Persons

This section surveys the work of classic ombuds institutions on seniors' issues in 19 jurisdictions: the UK, Ireland, and most Canadian provinces/territories and Australian states/territories.[93] Almost none gather statistics on the age demographics of their complainants, so it is difficult to uncover the number of older persons who lodge complaints or whether they encounter barriers in making complaints.[94]

Ombuds institutions can highlight their prioritisation of older persons' needs through operating practices such as website accessibility options (eg large print), seniors sections and online information brochures. They can also create separate sections or chapters in their annual reports devoted to investigations and other work for seniors. Just over one-half of the classic ombuds surveyed provided website accessibility options.[95] About one-third also had sections on their website or online brochures devoted to seniors' issues.[96] A few indicated they engaged in

[90] ibid Arts 3(n), 31.

[91] UN CtEDAW, General Recommendation No 35 on Women's Access to Justice, UN Doc CEDAW/C/GC/33 (3 August 2015) paras 59–60.

[92] Reif (n 3) 41–42, 278–84, 760–62; MS Ameermia and P Mhodi, 'The Role of the SAHRC in Facilitating Access to Justice through Litigation' (2020) 21(1) *ESR Review* 11. See, eg ombuds assistance in Austria, discussed above in ch 13.

[93] Research focused on their websites, four most recent annual reports and all own-motion reports. Ombuds in New Brunswick and Northwest Territories excluded due to absence of online annual reports.

[94] Exceptions are the UK Parliamentary and Health Services Ombudsman (PHSO), *The Ombudsman's Annual Report and Accounts 2018–2019* 43 (38% of complainants between 55 and 74 years old, 5% aged 75 or older, although methodology may undercount the numbers) and Scotland Ombudsman in the pre-2011 period.

[95] Ombuds in British Columbia (BC), Newfoundland and Labrador (NL), Ontario, New South Wales (NSW), Queensland, Tasmania, UK-PHSO, Northern Ireland (NI), Scotland and Wales.

[96] Ombuds in Nova Scotia (NS) (website section and brochure), NL (brochure), Quebec (subsections and useful tips), Northern Territory (section), NI (leaflet), Wales (fact sheet) and Ireland (fact sheet, guidelines, model complaints re: private nursing homes). The BC Ombudsperson had a website section on seniors in past years. Web pages, brochures etc on disabilities will include seniors with disabilities, eg ombuds in NSW.

outreach visits to seniors.[97] Some had added COVID-19 updates. A handful of these explicitly mentioned seniors and relevant investigations.[98] Only a few classic ombuds had discrete sections in their annual reports on investigations and other work concerning problems experienced by older persons.[99]

Classic ombuds devote most of their efforts to investigating complaints lodged by members of the public and many also engage in a relatively small number of own-motion (or 'systemic') investigations and other work such as law reform submissions to government. An analysis of the work of the 19 ombuds found that while most undertake some work addressing the concerns of older persons, ombuds in British Columbia (BC), Quebec and the UK are the most active, based on their remits (such as a wide jurisdiction over the healthcare sector) and/or their institutional prioritisation of seniors.

Overall, the treatment of seniors in elder-care facilities most commonly forms the basis of complaints and own-motion investigations. Substandard administrative oversight of these facilities has long been in the sights of classic ombuds. Complaints include: staff shortages that affect quality of care, fee increases when the resident fails to pay income tax, waiting list problems, double-charging by private facilities, and conflicts between families and facility staff, culminating in curtailment of visits by non-resident spouses who complain about the treatment of their spouse or ejection of residents due to the alleged behaviour of their visiting relatives.[100] Lax standards and violation of the tenancy rights of seniors in private residential care homes are major sources of complaints for Quebec's Public Protector.[101]

The poor conditions in and treatment of residents in elder-care facilities have produced a number of own-motion or public interest reports. For example, in Canada, the BC Ombudsperson issued two extensive Best of Care reports that detailed the conditions and rights of seniors in residential care.[102] The reports address issues such as improving access to information about residential care, the legal ambiguity surrounding the rights of seniors in such facilities, establishing and enforcing quality of care standards, improving staff qualifications and training, complaints procedures and facility closures. Among its numerous

[97] Ombuds in Alberta, Nova Scotia and Queensland.

[98] Ombuds in BC, Ontario, Quebec, NSW and Ireland.

[99] Ombuds in BC, NS (often combined with youth issues), Quebec (under health and social services) and Ireland (focus on nursing homes). Sections on disabilities also include seniors with disabilities, eg ombuds in NSW.

[100] eg Québec Ombudsman, *2018–2019 Annual Report* 95–96; Québec Ombudsman, *2017–2018 Annual Report* 72–73; BC Ombudsperson, *2017/2018 Annual Report* 47; Nova Scotia Ombudsman, *2016–2017 Annual Report* 23; Ontario Ombudsman, *2015–2016 Annual Report* 51; Ireland Ombudsman, *Annual Report 2019: Making Complaints Drive Improvements* 14.

[101] eg Québec Ombudsman, *2018–2019 Annual Report* 72; Québec Ombudsman, *2017–2018 Annual Report* 74–75; Québec Ombudsman, *Private Seniors Residences: More than Just Rental Businesses*, Summary (2016).

[102] BC Ombudsperson, *The Best of Care: Getting It Right for Seniors in British Columbia (Part 1)*, Public Report No 46 (December 2009); BC Ombudsperson, *The Best of Care: Getting It Right for Seniors in British Columbia (Part 2)*, Public Report No 47 (February 2012).

recommendations, the Ombudsperson proposed a bill of rights embedded in law for all seniors in residential care, which led to the passage of legislation containing a bill of rights for residents of public and private care facilities.[103]

Ireland's Ombudsman issued reports on the right to nursing home care and on subsidies to patients in private nursing homes.[104] The nursing home care report responded to numerous complaints that seniors could not get placements through their health boards and resorting to private homes had placed severe financial burdens on them and their families. It relied on domestic law to hold that the state had violated its long-standing legal obligations to provide nursing home care for all persons who need it.[105]

The COVID-19 pandemic exacerbated the chronic poor conditions in long-term care residences. In 2020, after the Canadian military had to assist in providing care in these facilities, Quebec's Public Protector launched a major own-motion investigation into the response of the public authorities to the pandemic in public and private seniors' residences.[106] The investigation aims to identify improvements needed, based on the deficiencies known before the pandemic and uncovered during the crisis, and recommend how to improve responses to future pandemics or crises.[107] The Ontario Ombudsman also began an own-motion investigation into the provincial government's standards for and oversight of long-term care homes after the military uncovered egregious pandemic conditions.[108]

Other common problems for seniors investigated by classic ombuds are healthcare, palliative care, home care services, income assistance, disability benefits and other social services, pensions, difficulties in completing government-mandated paperwork, and the accessibility of public transportation and parking. Gender issues rarely arise explicitly in complaints, an exception being the UK's changes to women's state pension age and problematic handling of their complaints.[109] However, elder-care issues and income

[103] *The Best of Care (Part 1)* (n 102) 29–30, 51–54. The Residents' Bill of Rights includes rights to a care plan, protection and promotion of their health, safety and dignity, participation in their own care, freedom of expression, transparency and accountability. The BC Ombudsperson also monitored the implementation of the reports' recommendations until 2019, eg *Systemic Investigation Update – The Best of Care: Getting It Right Getting It Right for Seniors in British Columbia (Part 2)* (February 2019) 4 (68 of 176 recommendations implemented).

[104] eg Ireland Ombudsman, *Who Cares? An Investigation into the Right to Nursing Home Care in Ireland* (November 2010); Ireland Ombudsman, *Nursing Home Subventions: An Investigation by the Ombudsman of Complaints Regarding Payment of Nursing Home Subventions by the Health Boards* (January 2001).

[105] *Who Cares?* (n 104) 49–67, 123–35.

[106] Perkel (n 48) (more than 80% of COVID-19 deaths in Quebec were in long-term care facilities); Le Protecteur du Citoyen, 'The COVID-19 Crisis and Seniors' Residences: The Québec Ombudsman Will Investigate', Press Release (26 May 2020).

[107] Le Protecteur du Citoyen (n 106).

[108] Ontario Ombudsman, 'Ontario Ombudsman to Investigate Government's Oversight of Long-Term Care Homes During Pandemic', Press Release (5 June 2020).

[109] UK PHSO, *The Ombudsman's Annual Report and Accounts 2018–2019* 29 (investigation paused pending outcome of judicial review).

assistance cases arguably have gender elements to them, given women's longer average life expectancies and more limited economic resources. Ombuds also assist disabled seniors and geriatric prisoners either explicitly or through their investigations on problematic treatment of the larger subpopulations.[110] At the same time, ombuds assistance can also combat intersectional discrimination in these areas.

When overseeing health sector administration, some classic ombuds also have jurisdiction over the quality of medical treatment. For example, UK PHSO reports are extremely critical of NHS care of older persons and palliative care.[111] The Northern Ireland Public Services Ombudsman (NIPSO) takes a human rights approach to its work, involving application of core human rights norms and the UK's international human rights law obligations – typically ECHR provisions implemented domestically by the Human Rights Act.[112] The NIPSO issued several public interest investigation reports in 2020 on the substandard medical care and oversight of elderly women in hospital.[113] The NIPSO relied on general human rights principles or the ECHR in most of these reports. In particular, in an investigation finding that a hospital failed to ensure the participation of the patient's family in the issuance of a do-not-resuscitate order, the NIPSO decided that the hospital trust violated Article 8 of the ECHR, ie the right of the patient and her family members to a private and family life.[114]

Few of the classic ombuds supported their findings and recommendations with international or domestic human rights norms. As noted above, the NIPSO applies the UK's international human rights obligations and basic human rights principles. The Public Services Ombudsman (PSO) for Wales has also started to apply the NIPSO's human rights approach. In 2019–20, the PSO found that in over 10 cases the administrative authorities had 'failed to consider or safeguard the human rights of service users'.[115] Some of them addressed seniors' concerns.

[110] See, eg Northern Territory Ombudsman, *Women in Prison II – Alice Springs Women's Correctional Facility*, 2 vols (May 2017); NSW Ombudsman, *Annual Report 2017–2018* 67–68, 108, 116, 130–35 (persons with disabilities); NSW Ombudsman, *Abuse and Neglect of Vulnerable Adults in NSW – the Need for Action* (2 November 2018) (includes elder abuse). See also NSW Ombudsman, *Submission to the Australian Law Reform Commission's Inquiry on Protecting the Rights of Older Australians from Abuse* (August 2016).

[111] UK PHSO, *Breaking Down the Barriers: Older People and Complaints about Health Care* (2015) (seniors are most frequent users of health services but among least likely to complain); UK PHSO, *Dying without Dignity: Investigations by the Parliamentary and Health Service Ombudsman into Complaints about End of Life Care* (2014); UK PHSO, *Care and Compassion? Report of the Health Service Ombudsman on Ten Investigations into NHS Care of Older People* (14 February 2011) (some cases evidencing total failure to provide basic care).

[112] Reif (n 3) 269–71; UK, Human Rights Act, 1998, c 42. FREDA principles comprise fairness, respect, equality, dignity and autonomy.

[113] eg NIPSO, *Investigation of a Complaint Against the Western Health and Social Care Trust* (2020) NIPSO Ref: 16990 (*Western*); NIPSO, *Investigation of a Complaint Against the South Eastern Health and Social Care Trust* (2020) NIPSO Ref: 14634, 58 (participation principle).

[114] *Western* (n 113) 7, 45 (also violated participation principle).

[115] Public Services Ombudsman for Wales, *Equality and Human Rights Casebook 2019–20*, 5.

They included an investigation into the conduct of hospital staff who trimmed the beard and facial hair of an elderly Sikh patient with dementia contrary to his religious beliefs, with his family taking the view that this conduct resulted in his rapid decline and death.[116] The PSO found that the patient had not consented to this and the hospital's conduct engaged the patient's human rights in the ECHR, specifically the prohibition of degrading treatment and the rights to respect for his private/family life and manifest his religion. The PSO's recommendations to the health board included cultural and human rights training for staff members. Also, the PSO found that the ECHR rights of an elderly female patient under ECHR rights to private and family life were 'likely to have been compromised' based on failure to respect her dignity at the end of her life when she was unnecessarily shuttled between hospitals and died on a trolley.[117]

Some ombuds reports addressing wider problems, which encompass those experienced by seniors, rely on international human rights instruments (eg CRPD, the Convention against Torture and UN guidelines on prisoners' rights) or domestic constitutional human rights (eg Canadian Charter of Rights and Freedoms).[118]

VII. Human Rights Ombuds Institutions: Protecting and Promoting the Rights of Older Persons

This section surveys the work of human rights ombuds institutions in 13 jurisdictions, in Europe, Australasia and Latin America.[119]

[116] ibid 6, 16–17.

[117] ibid 6, 10–11. See also engagement of ECHR, Art 8 in cases where a county council insufficiently considered the needs of a woman with dementia when assisting with finding an alternative placement for her and where a health board failed to engage in proper transfer planning for end-of-life care, ibid 11–12, 14.

[118] eg *Abuse and Neglect of Vulnerable Adults in NSW* (n 110) 30, citing CRPD; *Women in Prison II* (n 110) vol 1, 32–39 and vol, 2 84–96, citing UN Convention Against Torture and Other Cruel, Inhuman or Degrading Treatment or Punishment, 1465 UN TS 85 (in force 26 June 1987, 169 parties at 4 June 2020); UN Standard Minimum Rules for the Treatment of Prisoners, UN GA Res 70/175 Annex, UN Doc A/RES/70/175 (17 December 2015) (Nelson Mandela Rules); UN Rules for the Treatment of Women Prisoners and Non-custodial Measures for Women Offenders, UN GA Res 65/229, UN Doc A/RES/65/229 (21 December 2010) (Bangkok Rules); BC Ombudsperson, *Committed to Change: Protecting the Rights of Involuntary Patients under the Mental Health Act* (March 2019) Special Report No 42, 9, 12, 19–20, citing Canadian Charter of Rights and Freedoms, Part I of the Constitution Act, 1982, being Schedule B to the Canada Act 1982 (UK), 1982, c 11 (includes seniors with Alzheimer disease).

[119] Ombuds/NHRIs in Sweden, Finland, Estonia, Poland, Armenia, Netherlands, Portugal, Spain, New Zealand (NZ), Australia-Commonwealth, Australia-WA, Australia-Victoria and Costa Rica. Ombuds in Finland, Portugal, Spain, Estonia, Poland, Armenia and Costa Rica are GANHRI-accredited NHRIs. Research focused on their websites, four most recent annual reports and all own-motion reports.

All of the human rights ombuds provided website accessibility options.[120] However, only a few had website sections or information dedicated to seniors, including coronavirus information linked to older persons.[121] Almost one-half had separate sections in their annual reports on the rights of seniors.[122] The Parliamentary Ombudsman (PO), which together with the Human Rights Centre (HRC) and Delegation comprises Finland's NHRI, prioritises the rights of older persons by dedicating a legal adviser to the area.[123] Similar to classic ombuds, few collect statistics on the age demographics of complainants.[124]

Conditions in elder-care residential facilities are frequently addressed in complaints-based and own-motion investigations. Issues include insufficient numbers of beds, restrictions on visits by family, insufficient staff numbers, the overuse of physical and other restraints without consent, lack of privacy during hygiene procedures, poor nutrition and hygiene, and the closure of facilities.[125] The pandemic has also focused NHRI attention on the risks to the elderly, especially those in care homes.[126] The Netherlands National Ombudsman (NO) is a human rights ombuds based on its children's rights ombuds function.[127] The NO has investigated barriers to accessing formal care faced by persons with dementia and their informal carers, including reduction in home care services while waiting for residential care.[128]

[120] Ombuds/NHRIs in Sweden, Finland, Netherlands, Portugal, Spain, Estonia, Poland, Armenia, NZ, Australia-Commonwealth, Australia-WA, Australia-Victoria and Costa Rica.

[121] Ombuds/NHRIs in Finland, Portugal, Spain, Poland and NZ (OPCAT NPM function) had website sections, ombuds in Poland, Armenia and Costa Rica provided brochures and other information, and Portugal had a dedicated phone line for seniors. Six had online coronavirus/seniors' information and the Costa Rica NHRI provided this information in its annual report.

[122] Ombuds in Finland, Portugal, Spain, Estonia, Armenia, Costa Rica (equality and nondiscrimination section).

[123] Parliamentary Ombudsman of Finland, *Summary of the Annual Report 2018* 11 (Finland *2018 Annual Report*). The Costa Rica NHRI legislation calls for an internal unit on the protection of seniors, but it is not in place, Reif (n 3) 553–54.

[124] Ombuds in Costa Rica and Portugal provided statistics.

[125] eg Finland *2018 Annual Report* (n 123) 12; Swedish Parliamentary Ombudsman, *Annual Report 2018/19: Summary in English* 74 (family visit restrictions constitute violation of spouse's ECHR right to family life); Spain Defensor del Pueblo, *Executive Summary 2019 Annual Report* 5–6 (Spain *2019 Report*); Spain Defensor del Pueblo, *Atención a personas mayors. Centros residenciales: Separata del Informe annual* (2020); Spain Defensor del Pueblo, *Residencias publicas y privadas de la tercera edad* (2010); Estonia Chancellor of Justice, *Chancellor's Year in Review: 2017–2018* 'Dignified Ageing'; Estonia Chancellor of Justice, *2016–2017 Overview of the Chancellor of Justice Activities* 31–33, 37–38 (Estonia *2016–2017 Report*); Armenia Human Rights Defender, *2017 Annual Report* 48–49; Victorian Ombudsman, *Investigation into Department of Health oversight of Mentone Gardens, a Supported Residential Service* (2015).

[126] Costa Rica Defensoría de los Habitantes, *Informe Annual de Labores 2019–2020* 3 (Costa Rica *2019–2020 Report*).

[127] Reif (n 3) 425–31 (informally applies international human rights obligations under its general mandate).

[128] Netherlands Ombudsman, Ombudsman for Children and Ombudsman for Veterans, *Organise Oversight! Annual Report 2019* 25–26 (*Organise Oversight!*); Netherlands Ombudsman, *Safeguard Care* (2018); Netherlands National Ombudsman, *Everyone Must Be Able to Participate: Annual Report 2018* 16 (Netherlands *2018 Report*).

The healthcare problems faced by seniors are often investigated. These include long waiting times to see specialist physicians, obtain diagnostic imaging and undergo surgery; lack of potable water; and deficiencies in geriatric services and health law protections for seniors.[129]

Age discrimination investigations involving older persons include forced retirement of police officers, unequal treatment in amateur sporting events and refusal to issue credit cards to seniors.[130] Poland's Commissioner for Human Rights (CHR) fights unequal treatment of seniors using the constitution's equality rights and anti-discrimination provisions.[131]

Economic issues include problems with retirement pensions, old-age benefits and other social and financial supports.[132] Spain's Defensoría del Pueblo (Defender of the People institution) has cited the constitutional and international cultural rights of older persons whose public pensions were reduced or halted after they continued to engage in creative work after retirement.[133] Poland's CHR receives numerous complaints about state retirement pensions that are too low and differential sizes of women's pensions.[134] The Netherlands NO found that the poverty and high cost of living in the Dutch Caribbean territories negatively impacted seniors who are given substandard state pensions and live in extreme poverty.[135] The NO concluded that 'an effective poverty reduction policy for this group should be pursued as a priority'.[136] Portugal's Provider of Justice (PJ) has monitored the demolition of slums to ensure that the elderly inhabitants were rehoused in appropriate accommodations.[137]

Human rights ombuds have responded to the difficulties experienced by seniors in accessing the digital world, including government requirements to file tax documents online and deficient landline telephone services.[138] They have investigated

[129] Spain Defensor del Pueblo, *La atención sociosanitaria en España: Perspectiva gerentologica y otros aspectos conexos* (2000); Costa Rica *2019–2020 Report* (n 126) 40–41, 45–47, 51–53.

[130] Estonia Chancellor of Justice, *Chancellor's Year in Review: 2018–2019* 'Social Security'; Estonia Chancellor of Justice, *Chancellor's Year in Review: 2017–2018* 'Equal Treatment'; Estonia *2016–2017 Report* (n 125) 42.

[131] Poland Commissioner for Human Rights (CHR), *Human Rights in Poland in 2018: Summary of the Ombudsman's Report* 54–55 (Poland *2018 Report*).

[132] Spain *2019 Report* (n 125) 16–17; Portuguese Ombudsman NHRI, *Report to the Parliament 2016* 46 (Portugal *2016 Report*); Costa Rica *2019–2020 Report* (n 126) 40; Victorian Ombudsman, *Investigation into the Financial Support Provided to Kinship Carers* (2017) (insufficient financial support for kinship carers, usually older females).

[133] Spain Defensor del Pueblo, *Executive Summary 2016 Annual Report* 105–06 (Spain *2016 Report*), citing Spain Constitution, Art 20(1)(b), ICESCR, UDHR.

[134] Poland *2018 Report* (n 131) 28.

[135] *Organise Oversight!* (n 128) 47–49 (jurisdiction over Bonaire, Saba and Sint Eustatius); National Ombudsman, *Focus on the Elderly in the Caribbean Netherlands* (no date).

[136] *Organise Oversight!* (n 128) 48.

[137] Portugal *2016 Report* (n 132) 110.

[138] Spain *2019 Report* (n 125) 15–16; Spain *2016 Report* (n 133) 129; Costa Rica *2019–2020 Report* (n 126) 40.

inadequate administrative responses to deceitful consumer practices targeting the elderly.[139] Another category of complaints involves accessibility, such as subpar facility design, inadequate bus services for spouses to visit their partners in care homes and unjust enforcement of parking fines for elderly disabled drivers.[140]

Human rights ombuds often engage in work to protect and promote women's rights, but the rights of older women are rarely explicitly canvassed. Victoria's Ombudsman has highlighted the shortcoming in healthcare and assistance for older female prisoners.[141] Portugal's PJ has emphasised that older women are especially vulnerable to domestic violence, and Poland's CHR has called for increased funding for NGOs supporting older female victims of gender-based violence.[142] More generally, Costa Rica's NHRI addresses violence against seniors and the CHR deals with domestic violence against older persons with disabilities.[143]

Human rights ombuds who are OPCAT NPMs visit places where persons are deprived of their liberty and make recommendations on avoiding or ending torture and other ill treatment. The covered facilities include residential care facilities for older persons, including dementia units. NPM visits to elder-care facilities have uncovered deaths due to medical malpractice, poor nutrition and hygiene, overuse of physical restraints, inadequate healthcare and lack of privacy.[144] The New Zealand Ombudsman is a member of the OPCAT NPM. Its jurisdiction was extended in 2018 to cover private elder-care facilities, including dementia units.[145] After the COVID-19 pandemic started, the Ombudsman undertook inspections to assess how elder-care facilities were responding.[146] The Ombudsman issued a Statement of Principles for these facilities on complying with New Zealand's international human rights obligations during the pandemic, including upholding the obligation to prohibit torture and other ill treatment, providing special

[139] Spain Defensor del Pueblo, *Executive Summary 2018 Annual Report* 9 (Spain *2018 Report*); Poland *2018 Report* (n 131) 37.

[140] Spain *2018 Report* (n 139) 4; Victorian Ombudsman, *Annual Report 2018* 60.

[141] Victorian Ombudsman, *Implementing OPCAT in Victoria: Report and Inspection of the Dame Phyllis Frost Centre* (2017) 74, 94–95.

[142] Portugal Provedor de Justiça, *Contribution of the Portuguese Ombudsman to the List of Issues in Relation to the Fifth Periodic Report of Portugal on the International Covenant on Civil and Political Rights* (February 2020) 4; Portuguese Ombudsman NHRI, *Report to the Parliament 2015* 75; Poland Commissioner for Human Rights, *Summary of the Report on the Activity of the Commissioner for Human Rights in 2016* 87–88.

[143] Costa Rica Defensoría de los Habitantes, *Informe Annual de Labores 2018–2019* 31–38; Poland Commissioner for Human Rights, *Summary of the Report on the Activity of the Commissioner for Human Rights in 2017* 75 (Poland *2017 Report*).

[144] Spain Defensor del Pueblo, *MNP 2016: Annual Report 2016* 161; Spain Defensor del Pueblo, *NPM 2015 Spain's National Preventive Mechanism against Torture* 71–77 (advocates for domestic law reform to comply with CRPD); Finland *2018 Annual Report* (n 123) 102–10, 127, 141.

[145] Reif (n 3) 353–57. While most NPMs were already NHRIs before their designation, a few classic-based ombuds were transformed into human rights ombuds when they were given NPM status in New Zealand, Denmark, Iceland and Luxembourg, Reif (n 3) 341.

[146] New Zealand Ombudsman, 'Parliament's Independent Watchdog to Inspect Secure Aged Care Facilities', Media Release (15 April 2020).

attention to seniors' healthcare needs, limiting restrictive measures in accordance with human rights standards and providing quarantined persons with daily meaningful human contact.[147] Human rights ombuds/NPMs have also uncovered unsatisfactory conditions and healthcare for geriatric prisoners, detainees and patients in psychiatric institutions.[148]

Some human rights ombuds have been designated as or included in their country's CRPD Article 33(2) framework to protect, promote and monitor disability rights and oversee CRPD implementation.[149] This work should include the rights of seniors with disabilities. The New Zealand Ombudsman is included in the national framework. It provides disability rights protection through complaints-based and own-motion investigations, and some promotional work through information initiatives.[150] Finland's NHRI comprises the Article 33(2) framework: the PO inspects elder-care dementia units and the HRC promotes the rights of persons with disabilities.[151] Human rights ombuds without this formal mandate can still protect the rights of disabled seniors.[152]

Some ombuds in EU countries are NEBs that fight discrimination covering grounds that include gender and occasionally even age.[153] This mandate can extend to cover discrimination in the private sector. For example, the CHR is Poland's NEB and its age discrimination cases have included an earlier retirement age for female judges and accessibility problems for the elderly in public housing.[154]

Other human rights protection cases may implicitly include the elderly, including the rights of persons with disabilities and geriatric prisoners, and the difficulties faced by persons lacking computer skills.[155]

Some NHRIs also promote the human rights of seniors. For example, since 2019, Finland's PO and HRC have engaged in systemic work to promote and monitor the rights of older persons after Parliament gave the NHRI additional funding

[147] New Zealand Ombudsman, *Statement of Principles* (April 2020).

[148] Swedish Parliamentary Ombudsman, *National Preventive Mechanism – NPM Report from the OPCAT Unit 2011–2014* 44 (inadequate attention to precarious health of elderly female prisoner); Poland *2017 Report* (n 143) 24 (take needs of elderly into account in execution of their detention and prison sentences); Armenia Human Rights Defender, *The Activity of Human Rights Defender of Republic of Armenia in 2016 as National Preventive Mechanism* 50; Armenia Human Rights Defender, *Ad Hoc Public Report on Safeguarding the Right to Health of Persons Deprived of Liberty in Penitentiary Institutions* (2017) 5–10 (citing international and domestic rights to health); New Zealand Ombudsman, *Investigation of the Department of Corrections in Relation to the Provision, Access and Availability of Prisoner Health Services* (2012) 107–11.

[149] eg ombuds in Finland, Estonia, Poland, NZ and Costa Rica.

[150] Reif (n 3) 367–70.

[151] Finland *2018 Annual Report* (n 123) 17, 50–71.

[152] eg Victorian Ombudsman, *Investigation into State Trustees* (2019) (State Trustees' mismanagement of seniors' finances and failure to take Victoria's Charter of Human Rights and Responsibilities and CRPD into account).

[153] Reif (n 3) 404–06.

[154] Poland Commissioner for Human Rights, *Report on the Activities of the Commissioner for Human Rights in the Area of Equal Treatment in 2017* 39, 53–54.

[155] eg Netherlands *2018 Report* (n 128) 17 (digitalisation problems).

for this purpose. Its work includes research and public-awareness raising.[156] The PO also makes law reform proposals to improve the rights of seniors.[157] Costa Rica's NHRI issued a brochure on the rights of older persons and the corresponding obligations of the authorities.[158] Poland's CHR advocates for a comprehensive national strategy for the elderly and greater support for the proposed UN treaty on the rights of older persons.[159]

All of the human rights ombuds in the survey address the human rights of older persons. But some prioritise this area more compared to others, such as the NHRIs in Finland, Portugal, Spain, Estonia, Poland and Costa Rica.[160] The investigatory and other work of human rights ombuds target the same core issues addressed by classic-based ombuds: conditions in elder-care facilities, healthcare, physical and online accessibility, and economic and social services matters. Human rights ombuds, however, pay more attention to age-based discrimination. Human rights ombuds that are OPCAT NPMs have an additional weapon to tackle ill treatment of confined seniors, especially when their country has explicitly extended this mandate to private sector elder-care facilities. The survey found that some human rights ombuds occasionally expressly rely on international and domestic human rights obligations that protect seniors to support their findings. These include references to UN and European human rights instruments and domestic constitutional rights, and span civil, political, economic, social and cultural rights. However, in many cases, the institutions only refer to fundamental or human rights in the abstract.

Human rights ombuds also address the rights of older persons indirectly through the attention they give to the rights of women, persons with disabilities and those who are involuntarily confined. Seniors with disabilities and geriatric prisoners are occasionally highlighted, but the rights of older women are rarely discussed explicitly. This needs to change, given that a material percentage of seniors are female.

VIII. Conclusion: Improving Protection and Promotion of the Human Rights of Older Persons

This review of the work of classic-based and human rights ombuds institutions in the modern state demonstrates that the poor treatment of older persons by public

[156] Finland Human Rights Centre, *Annual Report 2019* 19–22; Finland Human Rights Centre, *Annual Report 2018* 4, 26.

[157] Finland *2018 Annual Report* (n 123) 13; Parliamentary Ombudsman of Finland, *Summary of the Annual Report 2017* 28.

[158] Costa Rica Defensoría de los Habitantes, *Derechos de las personas adultas mayors* (no date).

[159] Poland *2017 Report* (n 143) 16.

[160] Those ombuds whose human rights mandates are limited to OPCAT NPM and/or CRPD, Art 33(2) duties are more limited in their abilities to do so, ie the ombuds in NZ and Australia (Commonwealth and WA). The Australia-Commonwealth Ombudsman is the NPM Coordinator and Commonwealth NPM, but Australian NPMs do not yet have jurisdiction over aged-care facilities, Reif (n 3) 709, 717–18.

and private sector bodies is addressed by ombuds institutions to differing degrees. Some have worked in this area for years, while others have placed it higher on their agenda more recently. Both types of ombuds institutions handle the same core issues: conditions surrounding long-term care, healthcare, home care, accessibility, and economic and social services issues. The human rights of seniors are rarely recognised by classic-based ombuds. In comparison, while human rights ombuds refer to seniors' human rights more often than their classic-based counterparts, surprisingly, specific international and constitutional norms are not cited frequently by the human rights ombuds institutions surveyed. Further, some classic-based and human rights ombuds do not appear to prioritise older persons and their rights, although the COVID-19 pandemic may change this to some extent. The paucity of statistics on the numbers of older complainants makes it difficult to assess whether seniors (or their representatives) make complaints at a level reflective of their population size, whether there are barriers to seniors' accessing ombuds justice and, if so, the nature of those barriers.

In conclusion, both types of ombuds can institute operating practices that can enhance ombuds justice for older persons, especially by adopting best practices. A higher priority must be placed on older persons in ombuds investigations and their other work.[161] The human rights of older persons also need to be understood and applied in relevant cases. Even classic-based ombuds can apply seniors' human rights through a variety of methods, including the human rights approach developed in Northern Ireland.[162] Accordingly, ombuds staff must be trained in international and domestic human rights laws and their relevance to seniors. Further, the rights and needs of seniors must be mainstreamed throughout the work of the institution and, if possible, staff should be dedicated to the area. Ombuds also need to increase their awareness of intersectional discrimination issues impacting seniors. In particular, the gender-based rights of older women must be given more attention.

Since it appears that there are barriers faced by some seniors in making complaints to ombuds institutions, ombuds institutions need to be more proactive in exercising their own-initiative functions to help the elderly. Egregious or systemic harm suffered by seniors should be addressed more often in ombuds own-motion investigations and other own-initiative work. As Finland's PO states: 'Because the elderly or their family members only rarely file complaints, the Ombudsman's power to carry out inspections and investigate … either based on them or for other reasons on the Ombudsman's own-initiative is essential.'[163] In addition, human rights ombuds litigation powers should be used more often

[161] This is occasionally a statutory requirement, eg Portugal PJ is instructed to prioritise own-motion investigations to protect vulnerable populations including seniors, Reif (n 3) 408.

[162] See text accompanying nn 112–14.

[163] Finland *2018 Annual Report* (n 123) 13 (inspections power covers closed institutions).

to enhance the constitutional and other legal rights of seniors.[164] Human rights ombuds also need to increase their promotion of the rights of older persons, given that seniors are often marginalised or overlooked in contemporary society. Research, education, public-awareness raising, training of public officials, advice to government and law reform proposals on improving the rights of older adults are all very important.

Human rights ombuds designated as OPCAT NPMs must have jurisdiction over seniors in closed facilities, extending to private for-profit elder-care facilities, other facilities housing seniors with disabilities and asylum holding centres. NPM staff should include persons with expertise in geriatrics and geriatric medicine, or the NPM should commission experts in these areas.[165] Similarly, those ombuds in Article 33(2) CRPD frameworks should pay greater attention to seniors with disabilities.

More ombuds need to collect and disaggregate data on seniors (and their representatives) as complainants. Barriers faced by seniors to accessing ombuds justice need to be identified and dismantled. For example, older persons are less likely to be digitally connected, so more traditional forms of communication are needed for seniors, such as telephone, TV, radio, and hard copy reports and brochures.[166] Ombuds staff should undertake regular outreach visits to and inspection of elder-care facilities. Seniors should become more visible in ombuds reports, including case examples and using sections dedicated to older persons. Their needs should be more visible on the institution's website, including a separate and accessible web page.

Finally, ombuds institutions must also look inwards. In addition to accessible facilities, websites and other means of communications, they need age diversity among their staff, and they should provide statistics on this in the annual report.[167] Regional offices and local outreach initiatives are also important to get closer to older persons and their representatives.

[164] eg IOI, 'Latvia: Ombudsman's Office Informs about Work in the Field of Fight against Poverty' (18 June 2020) IV (Constitutional Court action argued that state's low minimum old-age pension base unconstitutional).

[165] eg Finland *2018 Annual Report* (n 123) 14.

[166] UN *Policy Brief: The Impact of COVID-19 on Older Persons* (n 48). See Portugal PJ phone line for seniors (n 121).

[167] eg Netherlands *2018 Report* (n 128) 56 (12.5% of staff were aged 60 and over).

INDEX

www.ingramcontent.com/pod-product-compliance
Ingram Content Group UK Ltd.
Pitfield, Milton Keynes, MK11 3LW, UK
UKHW020231290926
15470UKWH00002B/468

9 781509 943241